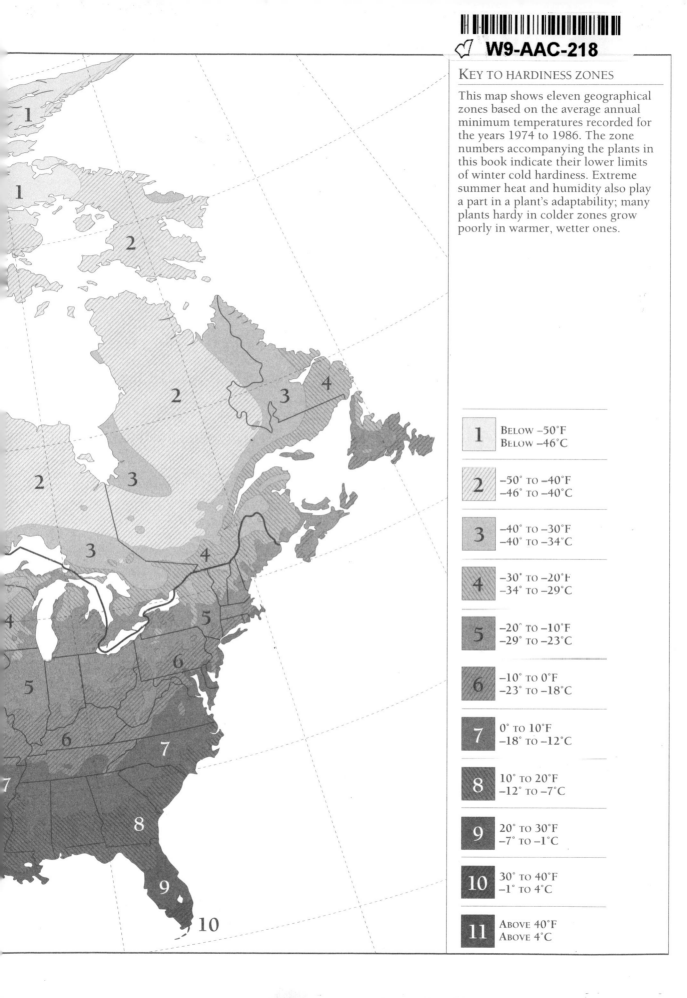

KEY TO HARDINESS ZONES

This map shows eleven geographical zones based on the average annual minimum temperatures recorded for the years 1974 to 1986. The zone numbers accompanying the plants in this book indicate their lower limits of winter cold hardiness. Extreme summer heat and humidity also play a part in a plant's adaptability; many plants hardy in colder zones grow poorly in warmer, wetter ones.

Zone	Temperature
1	BELOW –50°F / BELOW –46°C
2	–50° TO –40°F / –46° TO –40°C
3	–40° TO –30°F / –40° TO –34°C
4	–30° TO –20°F / –34° TO –29°C
5	–20° TO –10°F / –29° TO –23°C
6	–10° TO 0°F / –23° TO –18°C
7	0° TO 10°F / –18° TO –12°C
8	10° TO 20°F / –12° TO –7°C
9	20° TO 30°F / –7° TO –1°C
10	30° TO 40°F / –1° TO 4°C
11	ABOVE 40°F / ABOVE 4°C

PRUNING
&TRAINING

PRUNING
& TRAINING

CHRISTOPHER BRICKELL
— DAVID JOYCE —

www.dk.com

PROJECT EDITOR LOUISE ABBOTT
PROJECT ART EDITOR STEPHEN JOSLAND

US CONSULTANT PAUL W. MEYER
US EDITORS MARY SUTHERLAND, RAY ROGERS
EDITOR MARTHA SWIFT

DTP DESIGNER CHRIS CLARK

MANAGING EDITOR FRANCIS RITTER
MANAGING ART EDITOR DEREK COOMBES

PHOTOGRAPHY PETER ANDERSON

ILLUSTRATIONS KAREN COCHRANE
ADDITIONAL ARTWORK SARAH YOUNG,
JOHN HUTCHINSON

PRODUCTION RUTH CHARLTON,
HILARY STEPHENS

National Library of Canada Cataloguing in
Publication
Brickell Christopher
    Pruning & training / Christoper Brickell and
David Joyce.
    Includes index.
    ISBN 1-55363-017-3
    1. Pruning. 2. Plants – Training. 3. Pruning –
Pictorial works. 4. Plants – Training – Pictorial
works. I. Joyce, David. II. Title. III. Title: Pruning
and training.
SB125.B75 2003   635.9'1542   C2002-905768-X

Color reproduction by Colourscan, Singapore
Printed and bound in Slovakia by Neografia

03 04 05/3 2 1

CONTENTS

INTRODUCTION

ORNAMENTAL TREES

TREE FRUITS

ORNAMENTAL SHRUBS

SOFT FRUITS

CLIMBING PLANTS

ROSES

HOW TO USE THIS BOOK

This book begins with an explanation of how plants grow, how gardeners take advantage of various growth habits by pruning and training to achieve different effects, and how pruning tools are used. The chapters that follow are arranged by plant type, and each chapter starts with information specific to the plant type in question: the types and forms within the plant group, basic and specialized pruning and training techniques, the needs of newly planted and established specimens, and renovative treatment. Beyond these sections, each chapter describes in detail the pruning requirements of many species on a plant-by-plant basis. In the cases of ornamental trees, ornamental shrubs, and climbing plants, the plants are organized by botanical name into alphabetical dictionaries. The plants in the chapters on tree fruits, soft fruits, and roses, however, are grouped according to their pruning and training needs in order to avoid needless repetition. Roses, for example, are grown in four general forms, and are therefore grouped as modern bush roses, standard roses, shrub roses, and climbing roses, rather than alphabetically. Feature pages and sections on special plant groups or techniques also appear throughout the book.

BASIC TECHNIQUES

Each chapter has a detailed introduction, describing the basic techniques needed to maintain the plant group – for example, ornamental shrubs – covered by that chapter. Initial training of plants, pruning of established plants, and renovation are discussed, then demonstrated in the plant-by-plant section that follows. Subjects covered in the chapter introduction also include types and forms, showing the diversity within the plant group

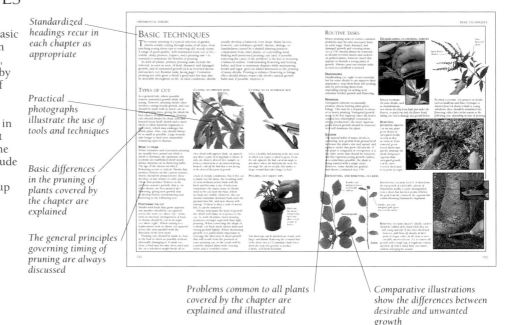

Standardized headings recur in each chapter as appropriate

Practical photographs illustrate the use of tools and techniques

Basic differences in the pruning of plants covered by the chapter are explained

The general principles governing timing of pruning are always discussed

Problems common to all plants covered by the chapter are explained and illustrated

Comparative illustrations show the differences between desirable and unwanted growth

SPECIAL TECHNIQUES

Particular ways of training and pruning the various plant groups for special effects are discussed in each chapter. They include cutting trees and shrubs back for special stem and foliage effects (pollarding and coppicing); pleaching trees; wall training; training shrubs and climbers on certain stems as standards; topiary; hedges; and pinch-pruning subshrubs such as fuchsia and coleus. The many imaginative ways of growing climbing plants and climbing roses include pergola-training, swags, and growing through host plants. These special techniques are explained and illustrated with many clear photographs, step-by-step artworks, and illustrations of finished results.

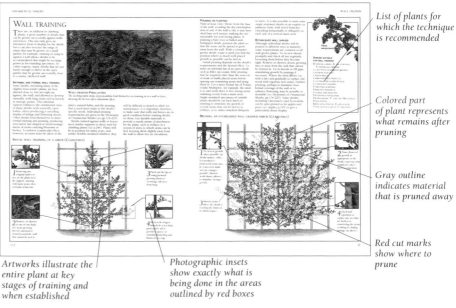

List of plants for which the technique is recommended

Colored part of plant represents what remains after pruning

Gray outline indicates material that is pruned away

Red cut marks show where to prune

Artworks illustrate the entire plant at key stages of training and when established

Photographic insets show exactly what is being done in the areas outlined by red boxes

PLANT DICTIONARIES

The chapters on ornamental trees, ornamental shrubs, and climbing plants each include an alphabetical plant-by-plant dictionary. The dictionary entries are of varying lengths for different genera, depending on the size of the genus and the complexity of its pruning and training needs. Within each genus, any species, hybrids, or cultivars with atypical pruning or training requirements are individually discussed. Illustrations include portraits showing the habit or some ornamental feature; step-by-step photographic sequences showing the plant being pruned or trained; and artworks that demonstrate extensions or variations of basic techniques given in that chapter's introduction. Cross-references are given when a technique is covered elsewhere.

Plants are ordered according to their botanical names, and synonyms and many common names are also given. The chapters on ornamental trees and shrubs include silhouettes showing the size and shape of selected species at maturity. Species or cultivars not discussed in detail are briefly listed, and each spread also carries a list of further genera, with concise training and pruning instructions for each.

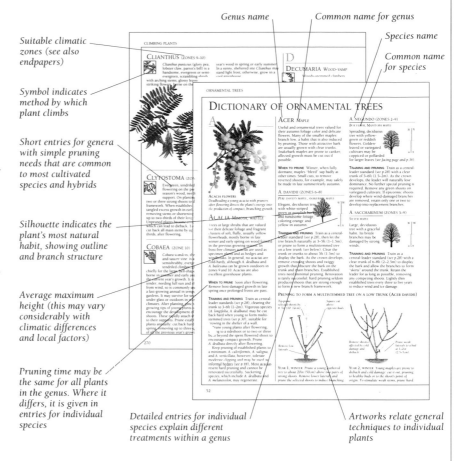

Genus name

Common name for genus

Species name

Common name for species

Suitable climatic zones (see also endpapers)

Symbol indicates method by which plant climbs

Short entries for genera with simple pruning needs that are common to most cultivated species and hybrids

Silhouette indicates the plant's most natural habit, showing outline and branch structure

Average maximum height (this may vary considerably with climatic differences and local factors)

Pruning time may be the same for all plants in the genus. Where it differs, it is given in entries for individual species

Detailed entries for individual species explain different treatments within a genus

Artworks relate general techniques to individual plants

PLANT-BY-PLANT GROUPS

The plants in the chapters on tree fruits, soft fruits, and roses are organized into groups to which many identical basic techniques can be applied. These chapters begin with general information on basic procedures, routine tasks, and common problems, followed by information specific to each type of plant in the group. Within the chapters on tree fruits and soft fruits, the hardy fruits are arranged in widely recognized groupings, such as pome fruits, stone fruits, cane fruits, and bush fruits. The tender fruits, because of their diversity, are listed alphabetically according to their botanical name, as are nuts. Roses are grouped according to their growth habit. Other plant groups, where general techniques can be applied to all members, are given their own feature pages; these include conifers, palms, bamboos, and grasses.

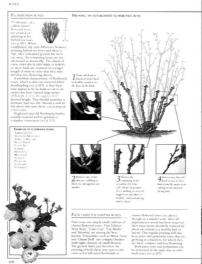

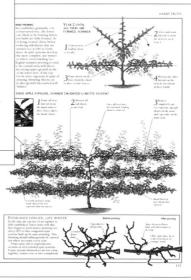

ROSES

Photographic insets illuminate artworks showing the specific pruning requirements of different types of bush, standard, shrub, and climbing rose. Typical cultivars are named for each type, to aid identification.

FRUIT

Within the sections on individual fruits (such as apples or peaches), general information on the fruit in question is followed by specific information about popularly grown forms, such as bushes and fans. Both the formative training and established pruning of the form are explained and illustrated.

INTRODUCTION

Understanding how plants grow and appreciating their individual needs and responses to pruning makes it easier to choose the correct pruning and training techniques for each

At the simplest level, the purpose of pruning and training is to make sure that plants are as healthy and vigorous as possible, free of structural weakness, and at the least risk of being infected by disease. The effects of expert pruning, however, go beyond this straightforward aim. With additional knowledge of how pruning and training influences the way in which plants grow and perform, the gardener can not only improve their natural appearance but also enhance ornamental features such as flowers and foliage, increase crops, and create striking plant features and combinations. Understanding the principles of how and why plants respond to pruning is the key to realizing their potential.

"How do you prune it?" is one of the most commonly asked questions about plants. There is often more than one correct answer, because many can be grown and pruned in different ways to produce different effects. While pruning is often a complex subject, for many plants pruning can be kept very simple, since they require little more than the removal of dead, diseased, or damaged wood to keep them in good health.

There are special considerations that will influence the type and degree of the pruning that you undertake. Some people prefer immaculate, formal gardens in which each plant is neatly and symmetrically shaped, while others prefer to allow natural, sometimes unexpected growth

habits to develop. In some situations, pruning to restrict size may be important – to increase the range of plants that can be grown in a limited space, or under glass, for example.

In most cases, however, the aim is simply to ensure a healthy, soundly structured, and pleasingly shaped plant. Remember that sound early training lays firm foundations for a fine mature specimen, and that, at any stage in its life, pruning causes some stress to a plant, so it should never be done without good reason. If you choose the right plant for the right situation and desired effect, much unnecessary corrective pruning can be avoided.

MOP-HEAD FUCHSIA
Many small ornamental plants lend themselves to novel training and pruning methods. The technique of pinch-pruning can be used to produce brilliant flowering displays.

STANDARD SHRUB
Border planting plans can be transformed by imaginative training; this Buddleja alternifolia, naturally an untidy, spreading shrub, becomes a striking focal point trained as a standard.

HOW PLANTS GROW

For plants to grow, they must have food, water, light, and a suitable climate. Plants have adapted to a vast range of habitats, and their needs regarding climate (*see facing page, below*) are correspondingly diverse. However, provided that individual needs are met, most plants grow in a similar way.

Plants have the ability to modify the structure and function of their cells throughout their lives. Thus, not only can they reproduce sexually, they are also able, given the right conditions, to regenerate as entire plants from, for example, a small section of stem, root, or leaf separated from the parent plant.

This vital ability is exploited by gardeners every time a plant is propagated. The most active site of cellular activity is at soft, green shoot tips, where hormones are manufactured that stimulate and control the plant's growth. Extension growth is made principally from just below the topmost (apical) bud – the growing point or "leader." The apical bud imposes what is called "apical dominance," whereby the hormones move down the stem and inhibit the growth of the side buds ("lateral" buds). These buds will break into growth to form branches only when the growing tip has grown away

strongly. If the apical bud is damaged, a single sideshoot may grow up strongly and reimpose apical dominance, but in some cases, two or more growing tips share apical dominance and form dual or multiple leaders (*see p.26*).

The second area of intense cellular activity is in the cambium layer, which surrounds the plant stem just beneath the tough, outer skin, or bark. It is this area of activity that enables plants to be grafted; if genetically compatible, the cambium tissue of two stems fuses when pressed closely together. The growth at the cambium layer increases the stem girth. Not only does the stem thicken, it also becomes sturdier as specialized strengthening tissue develops. In woody plants, this process is known as lignification ("becoming woody"). The buildup of strong, woody stems is stimulated by stem movement, such as that caused by flexing in the wind. This is why low stakes are preferable during a tree's early years – they allow stem flexing, and this helps to produce strong trunks (*see Staking, p.23*).

HOW PLANT GROWTH ADAPTS
The main objective of a plant is to grow to maturity, then reproduce, usually by means of setting seed. Some plants fulfill this function quickly, and then die – the plants we call "annuals" and "biennials." Woody and herbaceous perennial plants

PARTS OF A PLANT

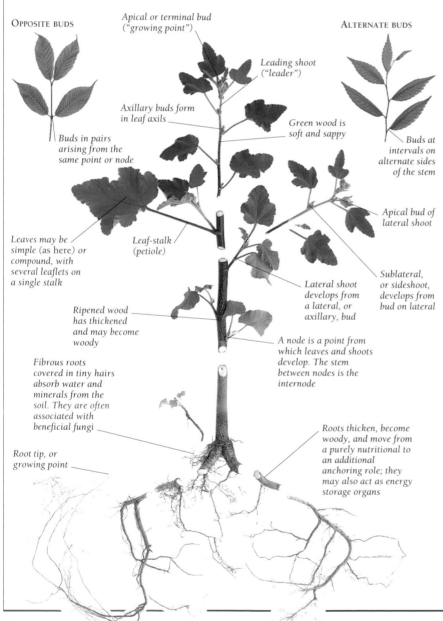

OPPOSITE BUDS

Buds in pairs arising from the same point or node

Leaves may be simple (as here) or compound, with several leaflets on a single stalk

Ripened wood has thickened and may become woody

Fibrous roots covered in tiny hairs absorb water and minerals from the soil. They are often associated with beneficial fungi

Root tip, or growing point

Apical or terminal bud ("growing point")

Leading shoot ("leader")

Axillary buds form in leaf axils

Green wood is soft and sappy

Leaf-stalk (petiole)

ALTERNATE BUDS

Buds at intervals on alternate sides of the stem

Apical bud of lateral shoot

Sublateral, or sideshoot, develops from bud on lateral

Lateral shoot develops from a lateral, or axillary, bud

A node is a point from which leaves and shoots develop. The stem between nodes is the internode

Roots thicken, become woody, and move from a purely nutritional to an additional anchoring role; they may also act as energy storage organs

CROSS-SECTION THROUGH A PLANT STEM

Tough, outer skin, or bark, minimizes water loss from the stem surface and protects the soft tissue within

In the cambium layer, cells divide and diversify to create vascular bundles of transporting tissues and increase stem girth

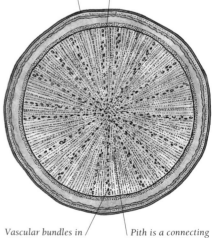

Vascular bundles in stem tissue carry water, nutrients, sugars, and growth hormones up and down the stem

Pith is a connecting matrix for other tissues. It dies, is lignified, and forms the heartwood

"Stag-headed" dieback

Oaks protect the main body of the tree by isolating entire branches suffering from dieback with "natural barriers." The dead wood will be shed without harming the tree.

Stem dieback

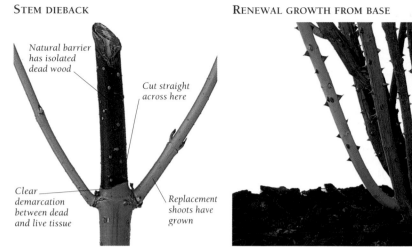

Natural barrier has isolated dead wood

Cut straight across here

Clear demarcation between dead and live tissue

Replacement shoots have grown

A stub left by incorrect pruning has died back to the next active buds, which, protected by the barrier the plant has formed to halt the dieback, have produced healthy shoots.

Renewal growth from base

Continual renewal growth from the base of the plant acts as insurance for this rose, in case any of its main stems are damaged, become diseased, or simply die of old age.

take longer to reach maturity, but then gain the advantage of being able to repeat the reproductive process many times. These plants must develop tissue that is cold- and weather-resistant in order to survive from year to year. Trees and shrubs produce hard, woody tissue that resists winter cold. In harsher climates, the soft top growth of some shrubs may be killed by cold, but the plant is still able to regenerate, producing new shoots from buds on its woody base that will grow and flower in a single season. Deciduous plants also shed their most vulnerable parts, the leaves, and become dormant in winter. Many plants, such as roses (*see above right*), combine these strategies.

Plants adapt in many other ways to their environment. They grow toward sunlight and develop a branched habit to expose the maximum leaf area to the sun and optimize photosynthesis (*see p.15*), and extend their roots to maximize anchorage and exploit the soil for moisture and nutrients. They can adapt their growth to adverse conditions, for example, by developing shorter, stubbier growth on the side of the plant buffeted by a prevailing wind (producing distorted "wind-pruned" crowns).

ADAPTATIONS TO DAMAGE AND DISEASE
Plants are often able to limit the spread of disease, which usually attacks the vulnerable, soft upper growth. By the actions of certain chemicals, they form a "natural barrier" across the stem, isolating the diseased portion from the main body of the plant. When the barrier is complete, the isolated portion dies, becomes dry and brittle, and eventually is shed. This defense mechanism is best observed – and understood – in trees, but can be seen in many woody plants. These plants respond to wounding by transporting protective chemicals to the site of the wound to create a natural barrier, which isolates the damaged tissue and defends the body of the tree from colonization by wood-rotting organisms.

Over time, the tree reinforces this barrier by forming an air- and watertight seal over the wound. This process originates in the cambium layer, where cells divide rapidly to form scar or callus tissue, which extends from the edges inward over (continued on p.12)

THE INFLUENCE OF CLIMATE

Climatic influence on plant growth is profound and is not limited simply by the range of average seasonal temperatures. Climate also influences length of growing season, the way plants flower and mature, and if and when they become dormant.

GLOSSARY OF CLIMATIC TERMS
CONTINENTAL Found at the center of large land masses: has clearly defined seasons, with hot summers, when growth is rapid, matures well, and becomes more able to withstand the cold winters. Rainfall all year, often highest in summer.
MARITIME A climate warmed by the nearby presence of a sea mass, which evens out seasonal temperature fluctuations. Wood may not mature well in summer and be less cold hardy; mild springs induce early growth, susceptible to late frost.
MEDITERRANEAN Has hot, dry summers, with most rain falling during the mild,

almost frost-free, winters. Mediterranean plants dislike wet, cold winters.
MICROCLIMATE Describes local conditions found in a specific site. A "frost-pocket" is a localized, relatively cold microclimate. Artificial microclimates include sunny walls; plants benefit from reflected heat and light, which helps to mature wood and increase hardiness and flowering potential.
SUBTROPICAL Highest temperatures in summer, with a definite cool season in which plants may become dormant. May have seasonal or evenly distributed rain.
TEMPERATE Climates with a relatively narrow range of temperatures, having warm summers and cool winters (warm temperate) or cooler summers and cold winters (cool temperate), linked by intermediate spring and autumn conditions. Rainfall occurs year-round.
TROPICAL Has high temperatures year-round; may have high rainfall, seasonally or throughout the year. Growth may be

continuous without a distinct dormant season. Arid tropics have low rainfall; plants grow immediately after seasonal rains, which can be unreliable.

PLANT HARDINESS
Generally speaking, hardiness refers to the ability of a plant to withstand minimum winter temperatures. In this book, it is designated by USDA hardiness zone ranges. Temperatures indicated by these numbers appear on the endpaper map. Although useful as an indicator of a plant's dependability in a given area, a hardiness zone range should not be considered as absolute. Many factors, including soil type and fertility, soil moisture and drainage, humidity, and exposure determine a plant's growth and reaction to its environment. Note: Many plants are frost-tender when young but fully hardy when mature; this also applies to mature and immature wood.

(continued from p.11) several years to close the wound. The more damage there is to the cambium tissue – by a torn wound or a rough cut – the slower this process will be. The use of wound paints interferes with this process and is no longer recommended (see also p.22).

The intervention of the gardener can help a plant recover from damage or disease. It is always best to remove dead wood; it may be colonized by harmful organisms becoming a source of infection. However, if a plant has already formed a natural barrier between live and dead wood, never cut below it, or the plant will have to expend energy needlessly by forming either scar tissue or another barrier farther down the stem.

In some situations, pruning cuts must be made back into live, healthy wood. Diseases like canker (see near right) spread so rapidly that the plant has no time to build defense barriers, and may die unless the affected portion is swiftly "amputated." Where a plant is damaged, a clean cut beyond all damage will heal far more quickly than the rough wound.

Never make a larger cut than is necessary. The term "target pruning" describes the process of making the smallest, cleanest wounds possible, at points where the plant's own defense mechanisms are most active. When removing woody branchlets or branches, even if they are completely dead, do not cut into the main branch or trunk or even flush with it, or you will stress the plant's defenses and cause structural weakness by allowing in wood-rotting organisms. The point at which a branch forks from a main stem develops

LIFE-THREATENING DISEASE AND DAMAGE

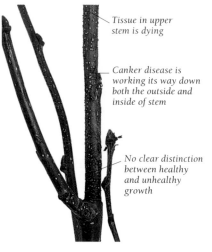

Tissue in upper stem is dying

Canker disease is working its way down both the outside and inside of stem

No clear distinction between healthy and unhealthy growth

DISEASED WOOD *Canker spreads rapidly, and affected growth must be cut well back to where both the surface and interior of the stem are completely healthy and clean.*

SPLIT-BRANCH CROTCH *Wind has split this narrow-angled branch away from the trunk, causing serious damage. The branch should never have been allowed to develop.*

structurally in a complex way (see below). As it thickens, cylinders of strengthening tissue form a seamless "sleeve" from the main stem along the "arm" that is the shoot. At the junction, a thickened, reinforcing "branch collar" forms that takes the strain caused by branch's increasing weight and by wind. The branch collar is also the most active site of the tree's natural defenses. Always cut just beyond it (see below).

Some wounds are so large and jagged that they never seal completely and remain vulnerable to infection. If the plant has several stems, the damaged

one may be cut out at the base. If the damage has occurred at a large branch crotch on a single-trunked tree, neither plant nor gardener may be able to remedy it, and professional advice should be sought; it may be necessary to remove the tree. Such damage often occurs because branches make too narrow a crotch angle with the main stem. Removing shoots likely to develop into such branches is the best way to minimize the risk of later damage. The preventative aspect of correct pruning and training is just as important as its corrective role later in a plant's life.

CROSS-SECTION THROUGH A BRANCH CROTCH

The position of the branch collar and bark ridge indicates where to make the least harmful cut. Make the cut on the branch just beyond the branch collar, at an equal and opposite angle to that made by the bark ridge on the main stem.

FROST DAMAGE

TARGET PRUNING
A small, clean cut beyond the branch collar closes up (occludes) rapidly and keeps the plant's natural defense barriers intact.

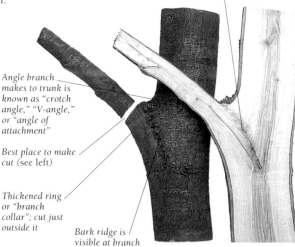

Branch crease, where internal structures of branch and trunk merge, is visible externally as the "bark ridge"; never cut into it

Angle branch makes to trunk is known as "crotch angle," "V-angle," or "angle of attachment"

Best place to make cut (see left)

Thickened ring or "branch collar"; cut just outside it

Bark ridge is visible at branch crotch, or fork

It is correct to prune frost damage back into completely healthy wood, cutting to a bud, but not when more cold is likely; the cut will expose buds previously sheltered by the (albeit damaged) upper stem and foliage, and further frosts may also damage them.

PRINCIPLES OF PRUNING AND TRAINING

The foundations of good gardening lie in good cultural practice (*see p.15*), ensuring that plants' basic needs for food, water, and light are met. The foundations of good pruning lie in two primary principles. The first should be always to assess the whole plant before making any cuts, and the second is never to cut without good reason. There are, however, many good reasons for pruning.

The most important and the most routine pruning tasks are the removal of any dead, diseased, and damaged tissue. Prompt action helps plants remain healthy, and appropriate pruning cuts improve their chances of recovery from damage and disease (*see facing page*). Additional pruning and training will be used for a host of other good reasons: to produce safe, structurally sound specimens; to create pleasing shapes that best display plants' ornamental qualities; to stimulate vigorous growth and encourage other desirable habits (for example, dense, bushy growth in hedging plants); and to enhance flowering and fruiting.

The key fact underlying the techniques used for all of these objectives is that when material is removed from a plant, either through natural causes or by a pruning cut, the plant will usually respond by making new growth elsewhere. Gardeners can prune to induce growth where and when it is wanted, and vary the direction, quantity, and vigor of this growth as desired.

BREAKING APICAL DOMINANCE
When a stem is broken or cut and the sap flow is stopped, the apical dominance of the terminal bud is also broken. Shoots then sprout from buds immediately below the wound and from lower down on the stem, sometimes on portions of stem or trunk where no buds were visible. These latent or dormant buds remain concealed beneath the bark until stimulated into growth.

Because apical dominance is strongly associated with vertical growth, it may also be broken by pulling a vertical shoot down and tying it in horizontally. This reduces the sap flow so that the terminal bud loses much of its dominance. A number of sideshoots then develop simultaneously from buds along the stem; all will grow upward with similar vigor and are much more likely to flower and fruit. This technique is ideal for climbing and other long, flexible-stemmed plants, and for cordon or espaliered fruit trees, to increase flowering and fruiting displays and crop yields. (*Continued on p.14.*)

BREAKING APICAL DOMINANCE BY CUTTING THROUGH A STEM

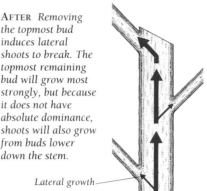

BEFORE *With the terminal bud intact and maintaining apical dominance, vigor is primarily directed into further upward growth. Lateral buds on the stem may be slow to develop into shoots.*

Upward growth

AFTER *Removing the topmost bud induces lateral shoots to break. The topmost remaining bud will grow most strongly, but because it does not have absolute dominance, shoots will also grow from buds lower down the stem.*

Lateral growth

PINCH-PRUNING (COLEUS)
Using finger and thumb to "nip out" the main terminal bud of this cutting and those of its lateral shoots results in dense, bushy growth, rather than a single vertical stem.

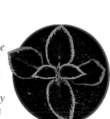

Before: single stem grown from cutting

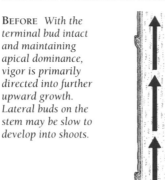

After: growth when shoot tips have been regularly pinched out

CUTTING BACK TO OLDER WOOD
Suitable plants can be cut back to areas where no buds are visible. Dormant buds, clustered at the base of the plant, are stimulated by hard pruning to "break" through the bark that conceals them, resulting in a mass of shoots.

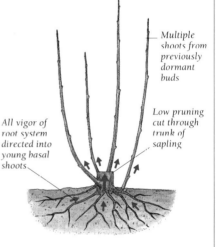

Multiple shoots from previously dormant buds

Low pruning cut through trunk of sapling

All vigor of root system directed into young basal shoots

HORIZONTAL TRAINING (ROSE)

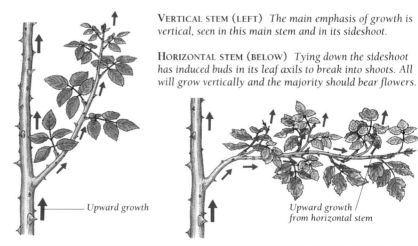

VERTICAL STEM (LEFT) *The main emphasis of growth is vertical, seen in this main stem and in its sideshoot.*

HORIZONTAL STEM (BELOW) *Tying down the sideshoot has induced buds in its leaf axils to break into shoots. All will grow vertically and the majority should bear flowers.*

Upward growth

Upward growth from horizontal stem

HOW PLANTS ARE GROUPED

In botanical classification the grouping of most importance to gardeners is the "genus," which includes a variable number of "species." Species may be interbred to create "hybrids," indicated by the prefix "x." Within a species there may be natural variants (for example, with a different flower color), and cultivated varieties, or "cultivars," maintained to perpetuate a distinctive quality. Thus *Lonicera* is a genus, while *Lonicera japonica* and *L. nitida* are species (*see below*); *L. × heckrottii* is a hybrid. *L. nitida* 'Baggesen's Gold' is a cultivar, selected for its golden leaves.

Plants are grouped in genera according to shared characteristics such as flower form and petal number, whereas pruning and training needs depend on growth habit and flowering season, so the requirements of species within a genus may vary considerably.

SAME GENUS, DIFFERENT HABIT

LONICERA NITIDA "BAGGESEN'S GOLD' *This evergreen, dense shrub species has branched, rigid stems and small glossy leaves, and is often used as a hedge.*

LONICERA JAPONICA *This is typical of the climbing species we know as honeysuckles, with long, slender, twining stems and a profusion of flowers.*

INFLUENCING VIGOR OF REGROWTH

Restricting shoot growth by pruning stimulates the production of new growth elsewhere on the plant. In general, the harder the pruning, the more vigorous the regrowth will be – provided that the individual plant is healthy and tolerant of hard pruning. Conversely, pruning lightly, or not at all, results in limited regrowth. So if, for example, the growth of a shrub becomes unbalanced, prune the weakest side back hard, and either leave the other side alone, or trim it back very lightly to shape.

Pruning hard will not necessarily limit a plant's size – quite the reverse – unless it is regularly repeated, as with such special techniques as coppicing. For many shrubs and trees, repeated hard pruning to restrict size merely weakens the plant. It is always best to choose a plant that fits the available space, rather than having to cut it back continually.

TIMING OF PRUNING

The timing of pruning is critical and is directly related to the age and type of flowering wood. Late summer- and autumn-flowering shrubs, for example, flower on the current season's growth and are pruned in spring to encourage vigorous shoots that will flower later in the same year. Spring and early summer-flowering shrubs flower on the previous season's growth and are pruned after flowering, to permit new wood to grow and ripen, then bloom in the following year. In some cases, flowers are borne on

SAME GENUS, DIFFERENT TRAINING

FREESTANDING BUDDLEJA *Many buddlejas can be cut back hard each year, producing tall, vigorous, arching stems that may grow to 6ft (2m) and flower in a single season.*

spurs arising from a framework of old wood; the spur wood is pruned back to the framework at the appropriate season, depending on flowering time. With some plants, other factors must also be taken into account; plants that "bleed" when cut, for example, should not be pruned in spring, when the pressure of rising sap will cause profuse bleeding. If evergreens are pruned too early in spring or too late in summer, they produce soft new growth that may be damaged by frost or cold wind.

SAME SPECIES (SYRINGA MEYERI), DIFFERENT TRAINING

NEAR-NATURAL FORM (ABOVE) Syringa meyeri *naturally forms a neat, bushy shrub covered with growth to the ground.*

TRAINED FORM (LEFT) *Special training as a standard results in a quite different effect.*

WALL-TRAINED BUDDLEJA *Species that require only moderate pruning can, because much growth is retained each year, be wall-trained as a permanent feature.*

PRUNING TO DIRECT GROWTH

Pruning to direct growth may be as simple as cutting to a bud that faces in the desired direction. It is usually combined with training shoots in the required direction, either to form a framework or to replace branches or fill in gaps in a framework that is already established.

PRUNING FOR SPECIAL EFFECTS

Plants may be pruned to produce a number of special effects, such as topiary (*see p.48*), or by using special techniques such as coppicing or pollarding (*see p.36*), which can produce brilliant winter stems or larger, more colorful leaves, or perpetuate a display of attractive juvenile foliage, as with many *Eucalyptus*. With more complex pruning and training, some plants that make attractive natural specimens can be trained in controlled forms such as standards. Formal wall training of a tree or shrub displays flowers to great effect, although it may take many years and require annual maintenance.

Many plants respond well to a variety of pruning techniques, but it is vital to be sure that they will respond in the desired way. Do not assume that all plants in the same genus respond in the same way to pruning – they often do, but they may vary widely in the way that they grow, and thus in their pruning and training needs. *Clematis viticella*, for example, is cut back almost to the base every year in spring, while *C. alpina* needs minimal pruning. Plants within a genus may also differ in their tolerance of pruning, and so while one is stimulated by hard pruning, another may respond with poor growth and no flowers, and may even die of shock.

CARE AND CULTIVATION

While removal of dead, diseased, and damaged wood is always positively beneficial to the plant, other types of pruning inevitably remove material that actively provides the plant with its source of energy. The process by which a plant manufactures energy, photosynthesis (*see right*), takes place in its leaves. Green chlorophyll traps the energy of sunlight and uses it to convert water and carbon dioxide into a food source that takes the form of sugars and carbohydrates. Oxygen is a by-product that is released into the atmosphere.

The more contrived the garden effect annual cutting down to a framework, for example – the more you deprive the plant of useful foliage. Stimulating more abundant flowering or fruiting also makes considerable demands on the plant's energy. In general, the more material you remove, and the more frequently you do it, the greater will be the plant's needs for nutrients. If a plant is to remain in good health and be stimulated rather than stressed by pruning, it is essential to provide the plant with sufficient nutrients and water to fuel and sustain its new growth. The plant needs a complete fertilizer that contains a balanced formulation of nutrients, including nitrogen, phosphates, and potassium, along with essential trace elements.

FEEDING AND MULCHING

Apply a balanced fertilizer at the manufacturer's recommended rate in spring. Use only recommended quantities; too much will scorch or burn, or otherwise damage, the plants. If repeated applications are required, in cool climates feed until no later than midsummer, since soft growth produced late in the year will be more vulnerable to damage by frost.

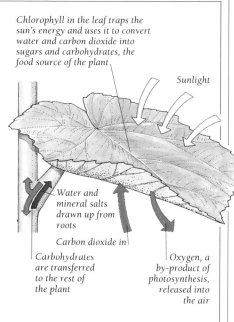

Chlorophyll in the leaf traps the sun's energy and uses it to convert water and carbon dioxide into sugars and carbohydrates, the food source of the plant

Sunlight

Water and mineral salts drawn up from roots

Carbon dioxide in

Carbohydrates are transferred to the rest of the plant

Oxygen, a by-product of photosynthesis, released into the air

PHOTOSYNTHESIS

The leaf is the primary site of photosynthesis; stomata (pores) on the underside open and close to control the exchange of gases.

Apply a mulch after fertilizing onto moist soil in spring (*see below right*). Avoid the immediate area around the base of the plant. Mulching regulates soil temperatures, conserves soil moisture, and, by blanketing the ground, helps to control weeds that will compete with the ornamental plants for water and nutrients. To be effective, a mulch needs to cover the entire area beneath the leaf canopy. Where specimen shrubs or trees are grown in lawns or rough grass, it is essential to keep an area at least 3ft (1m) in diameter free of grass and weeds during the establishment period.

MULCHING
Apply a mulch 3–4in (7.5–10cm) deep after fertilizing in spring, avoiding the immediate trunk or stem base.

FEEDING
Apply a balanced fertilizer onto moist soil in spring. Spread it evenly over the root zone and rake it in lightly.

TOOLS AND EQUIPMENT

It is well worth investing in the best garden equipment you can afford. The ideal is to have an appropriate tool on hand for every task. You will achieve the best result by using the correct tool. This is particularly important with cutting tools. Using pruners to cut overly thick stems can damage both plant and tool, as well as making the job uncomfortable and, over time, tiring.

Make sure before you buy that you find the tools comfortable to use; feel their weight and check that they fit into your hand well, are easy to grip, and can be used without strain.

CUTTING TOOLS

Pruners are the most useful of cutting tools and can be used for all soft growth and on woody stems of up to ½in (1cm) in diameter. Do not try to exceed their capabilities; use a pair of loppers to cut through thicker branches.

Many people do not realize that there is a "right way up" for each cut when using pruners. The thinner blade (the upper blade, when holding the pruners normally) should always be nearer the bud or stem junction to which you are cutting. To achieve this, it is often necessary to turn your hand so that your palm is facing downward (*compare above right and below*).

Never cut wire with the blades of pruners; it will damage them. There is sometimes a wire-cutting notch that can be used on the outer edge of the blades.

A saw has several uses: cutting thick, woody growth; cutting away stubs from the bases of roses; and thinning old, knobby spur systems. Choose a special pruning saw designed for garden use;

THE "WRONG" AND "RIGHT" WAY TO CUT WITH PRUNERS

INCORRECT USE *When pruners are held normally (thin blade up), this lateral (above left) cannot be cut off correctly; the thick blade is nearer the trunk and thus determines the cut's position. The cut is made too far from the main stem (above right), leaving a stub that may die back.*

CORRECT USE *By turning the pruners over, the thin blade is nearer the trunk, and the cut can be made precisely where it is required.*

household saws clog up quickly when cutting green wood. Double-edged saws often damage nearby growth, and amateur gardeners rarely need to, and in most cases should not, tackle jobs large enough to require a bow saw.

Always have a garden or pruning knife on hand for smoothing cuts and nipping out soft growth. Do not use it to cut string; it will blunt the blade.

Shears can be used on plants such as lavender and heather that need regular clipping, and for hedges and topiary. Wavy-edged shears trap shoots as they are cut so that they are not pushed out with the scissor action of the blades; they are useful for precise topiary work. Other pruning tools include long-handled tree pruners, which often have saw or fruit-picking attachments. They can be used on trees and climbing

plants to which access by ladder is impossible. It is, however, difficult to make precisely positioned cuts. A half-moon lawn edger can be used to chop at the edges of thicket-forming plants; chopping through and removing the roots when cutting out peripheral stems restricts their spread far more effectively than pruning above ground. A sharp-edged spade can be used to do the same job.

TOOL MAINTENANCE

Always clean and dry tools thoroughly after use, particularly those with cutting blades. A final wipe with an oily rag will keep blades rust-free and in good condition. If you have been pruning out diseased plant material, disinfect tools before moving on to prune other growth, or before putting them away.

USING CUTTING TOOLS CORRECTLY

USING PRUNERS CORRECTLY *A sharp pair of pruners will cut quickly and easily through small, woody stems of no more than (approximately) the thickness of a pencil.*

USING PRUNERS INCORRECTLY *Tugging and wrestling to cut this thick stem is tearing and bruising plant tissue and also blunting the pruner blades.*

USING LOPPERS CORRECTLY *A stem whose girth will fit entirely within the bite of the loppers is easy to cut. The long handles exert extra leverage, so little effort is required.*

FRUIT LADDER
This useful ladder has a prop, or "back leg."
Its tapering top can reach well into the tree.
It is ideal for pruning branched-head trees
with no trunk against which to prop a ladder.

Dip them in a diluted disinfectant
recommended for garden use and dry
carefully. Always keep cutting blades
sharp. This is not only important for
making clean cuts; working with
inefficient tools is frustrating and
makes gardening a chore rather than
a pleasure. Working with shears that
need sharpening, oiling, or tightening
is particularly irksome.

DISPOSAL OF PRUNED MATERIAL
Soft prunings can be composted, but
woody material takes too long to break
down unless you have access to a garden
shredder. Never compost or shred
diseased plant material. Although the
heat within a compost heap can kill

certain pathogens, there is no guarantee
that all will be destroyed. Dispose of it
as waste.

SAFETY
Accidents are rare when the right tool
for the job is used correctly, provided
that you do not attempt tasks that are
beyond your capabilities. Tree-felling
and the removal of large branches must
always be carried out by professionals
(*see* Major tree surgery, *p.35*).
    Ideally, you should never use a ladder
when alone. Do not overstretch to
reach growth while up a ladder, and be
very careful when stepping off a ladder
onto a tree.
    Remember that stems that you are
pushing or pulling in order to tie in or
cut more conveniently can spring back,
especially when cut. In addition to
gardening gloves, plastic goggles are
recommended when working with
thorny stems at head height.
    Some plants exude sap when cut, with
irritant effects ranging from a mild rash
to dizziness and vomiting. The hairs on
certain plant stems can also be irritants.
Sumacs, euphorbias, and fremonto-
dendrons are particularly notorious for
their harmful effects.

TETANUS
The tetanus bacterium is carried in soil,
and enters through breaks in the skin.
It is sensible and highly advisable for
gardeners to have regular tetanus shots.
Children are inoculated automatically
as part of their vaccination schedule,
whereas adult boosters last for 10 years.
If you cut yourself in the garden or
greenhouse and have not been
inoculated or cannot remember when
your last inoculation was, see a doctor
or go to the emergency room.

POWER TOOLS
Power tools are invaluable for some
pruning tasks, provided that they are
used with strict attention to safety.
A nylon-line trimmer can be used
to prune back large expanses
of some groundcover
shrubs, such as
Hypericum calycinum.
Many types of hedge
trimmers are available:
in general, small, light,
single-edged,
double-action
models with
narrowly spaced
teeth are the best
for controlled
clipping and
shaping. Electric
trimmers, rather than
gas-driven ones, are lighter
and more convenient to use. For any
trimmer that is powered with an
electrical cord, use a plug or adapter
with a circuit breaker or ground fault
circuit interrupter (GFCI) to protect
you if you should inadvertently cut
through the cord. Never trim wet
plants, or in wet weather.
    Protective goggles are essential
when trimming with power tools, and
earplugs or ear protectors are also
recommended. If using a trimmer for
the first time, get a demonstration of
its correct and safe use.
    Chainsaws are potentially very
hazardous. No one should use one
without suitable training, and no
reputable business will rent one to
you if you are inexperienced in its
use. Correct use gives good results
and helps prevent accidents.

Ear protectors

Goggles

USING LOPPERS INCORRECTLY *A stem that*
is too wide for the blades strains the loppers;
it is unlikely that the branch can be cut
cleanly with a single cutting action.

USING A PRUNING SAW *A small, curved*
pruning saw is ideal for cutting thick wood
and stubs, and can be used without damaging
other growth in confined or awkward places.

USING A KNIFE *On cuts big or small, rough*
edges should be smoothed with a knife. Use a
garden knife or a special pruning knife, which
has a curved blade for a more controlled cut.

ORNAMENTAL TREES

A tree can be the most striking single feature in a garden.
Careful training and pruning to ensure an attractive form and a sound
branch structure will be amply repaid over many years

In most gardens, trees are the element of greatest structural importance. Their potential size and longevity demand that careful thought must be given, before planting, to the choice of species and the forms in which they are to be grown.

A wide range of trees is available to suit most growing conditions, and this will include a good selection of small trees that can be accommodated in today's relatively small yards. The techniques of grafting, pruning, and training all have roles in making the most of trees of ornamental value.

The characteristic growth pattern of a tree in the wild – its natural form or "habit" – may be affected by many factors, among them disease, damage, drought, or the proximity of other plants. These can result in trees of unusual appearance that, although often attractive in the wild, are undesirable for the garden or street. In these contexts a tree needs not only to be pleasing to the eye, but also to have a sturdy, well-balanced branch structure that will ensure a long and healthy life.

Formative training in a tree's early years is essential, either to make the best of a natural habit or to produce one of a number of trained "forms." Most trees need very little pruning and training once they are established, but the future of a mature tree is often determined by the way it is trained when young. All is not necessarily lost when a tree has been neglected. Many trees can be successfully rejuvenated by skillful renovation. This may call for the use of power equipment and the removal of large branches. These operations, along with tree felling, are so potentially dangerous that they should be undertaken only by professional arborists.

POLLARDED CATALPA
Many trees are suitable for pollarding, which produces a tree with a compact, bushy crown on a clear trunk. The technique is best initiated from the start, but can sometimes be used to transform a tree that has been disfigured by damage.

WELL-SHAPED NYSSA SYLVATICA
Almost all trees benefit from training to enhance their habit of growth; a beautifully formed tree makes a lasting contribution to the landscape.

TREE FORMS

A well-grown tree is trained when young into one of several broad categories of tree forms. In many cases, training will have been aimed simply at producing a well-shaped example of a natural habit. Some tree forms are, however, produced and maintained solely through pruning and training methods. In the nursery industry, standardized descriptions are used, often not only of the tree's form but also of its measurements, to help buyers make their choice. In addition, a tree should never be purchased without its eventual size and spread being known, or it may outgrow its situation, entailing tree surgery or even removal.

As trees mature and develop, some of the rigid form distinction created in the nursery may be lost. Unless the tree's safety is threatened, this is rarely a problem requiring action; the tree will be no less pleasing for an informal habit of growth. Some of the more strictly trained and manipulated forms, however – particularly those involving grafting – require careful control to ensure that the ornamental effect is not lost. Conversely, it is often possible to modify the form and development of a bought tree – clearing a trunk of lower branches to turn it into a standard, for example – if a different effect is desired.

BRANCHED-HEAD STANDARD
These have a single, clear trunk that divides and branches to form an open-centered crown. A common natural form (for example, of chestnut trees), it can also be produced at the formative stage, either by top-grafting (as for some *Prunus*) or by cutting back a young tree's main stem (*see* p.29) to stimulate branching at a given height.

HALF-STANDARD
Growers use several terms to describe young standard trees of varying heights and proportions. A "half-standard" should have a clear trunk of 30–40in (75–125cm) and a small crown. The form is often lost with age; some trees can be pruned to retain the proportions of a half-standard, such as *Laurus nobilis* (bay).

FEATHERED TREE
The natural form of most young trees, with trunks clothed in lateral branches almost to ground level. Though many shed their lower branches as they develop naturally into standards, a number retain this form into maturity with minimal training (*see* p.27) – for example, many conifers.

CENTRAL-LEADER STANDARD
The tall, strong trunk of these trees persists all the way through the crown, terminating in a distinct leading shoot. This is a very common form in nature – for example, *Quercus rubra* and *Corylus colurna*. It can also be produced (*see* p.28) by gradually removing the lower branches from a young feathered tree to leave a clear trunk of about 5–6ft (1.5–2m).

FASTIGIATE TREE
These narrow, columnar trees have light, upswept branches, usually from top to bottom, from central trunks that often fork narrowly into two or more stems some way into the crown. It is a wholly natural growth habit that cannot be created through pruning and needs little pruning to maintain. Many conifers grow in this way, as does *Populus nigra* var. *italica* (Lombardy poplar), and *Acer rubrum* 'Columnare'.

BUSH

Some trees – for example, medlars – develop naturally in a bush form, with a rounded head of branches on a very short trunk. However, bush trees are more commonly produced by fruit growers, using pruning and training to form bearing trees that are not too tall, and therefore easy to harvest.

MULTISTEMMED TREE

These trees resemble very large shrubs, with several distinct main stems, or trunks, emerging at the base or from a short stem. These may be slender, upright and clear of branches, as with many birches, or clothed with branches to form a dense thicket. The form may be created by pruning (*see* p.30).

WEEPING STANDARD

A weeping standard (*see* p.28) is often formed by top-grafting a weeping cultivar onto a stock plant with a clear stem. The branches weep either straight down from a central point or, like *Fraxinus excelsior* 'Pendula' (weeping ash), cascade outward to form a mushroom-shaped head.

BASIC TECHNIQUES

Trees are trained and pruned chiefly to keep them vigorous, healthy and, by forming a strong, well-balanced branch framework, stable. Pruning can also influence shape and size, and enhance features such as bark or flowers.

Pruning and training are most important in the early years, laying the foundations of a well-shaped mature tree. Once a tree is established, pruning is more often than not confined to the removal of dead, diseased, damaged, or wayward growth, directing energy into maintaining a strong, shapely specimen.

The younger a tree is when pruned, the more active the healing process, and the younger the growth that is cut, the faster the wounds close. Prune shoots, where necessary, before they become woody, and twigs before they develop into branches.

As with all plants, hard pruning stimulates a more vigorous response than light pruning. Unless using special techniques such as pollarding and coppicing (see p.36), pruning hard in order to restrict a tree's size is counter-productive, so choose trees that will

not outgrow the space available. The removal of large branches, due to damage, disease, or neglect, should always be a last resort. Never remove healthy branches at random in an attempt to improve or alter a mature tree's form. It is risky for the amateur "surgeon," and the tree itself may be left not only disfigured but also vulnerable to disease and possibly dangerously unstable. Major pruning that needs to be done from a ladder, or involves the removal of large limbs, should always be undertaken by professional arborists.

MAKING CUTS

Every cut, large or small, should be cleanly made so that plant tissue is not torn or bruised. Slanting cuts are usually preferable, since rain cannot collect on the surface as with a horizontal cut; trapped moisture encourages fungal rots. Cuts should ideally be made either close to a bud, at a fork on a branch, or just beyond a branch collar – the slight swelling just before it joins its main branch or the trunk (see also p.12).

WHEN TO PRUNE
The time at which a tree is pruned is important. It is usually best carried out at the same time as wood is shed in nature. In winter, snow, ice, and wind break off dead wood and weak branches on trees that are fully dormant. The wounds close swiftly once strong growth begins in the spring.

However, most trees tolerate moderate pruning to correct localized problems at any time. Key exceptions are trees that "bleed" sap profusely from pruning wounds, such as birches and walnuts, which normally should never be pruned when the sap is, or is about to start, rising (from mid- to late winter to midsummer) and trees that are susceptible to disease at certain times of the year. The Dictionary of Ornamental Trees (pp.52–91) gives timings for pruning individual trees.

CUTTING TO A BUD
Select a healthy, strong bud pointing in a direction that will give the new shoot room to develop, without crossing or crowding other growth so that stagnant air (which encourages disease) builds up in the center of the tree. This is normally an outward-facing bud. On trees with opposite buds, the bud facing inward can be rubbed off to encourage outward growth of the remaining bud. Never make a cut half-way between buds or branches. It will (continued on p.22)

CUTTING TO AN ALTERNATE BUD

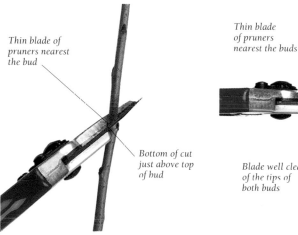

Thin blade of pruners nearest the bud

Bottom of cut just above top of bud

Make a slanting cut at a point about ¼in (5mm) above the bud. The gentle slope will allow moisture to roll off the cut surface, discouraging the development of disease.

CUTTING TO OPPOSITE BUDS

Thin blade of pruners nearest the buds

Blade well clear of the tips of both buds

Cut squarely across the shoot above a healthy pair of buds, as close as you can without grazing and damaging the buds. A pair of healthy shoots should then develop.

EFFECT OF CLEAN AND ROUGH CUTS ON THE HEALING PROCESS

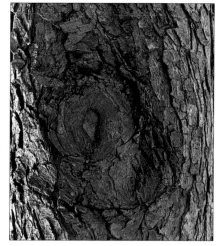

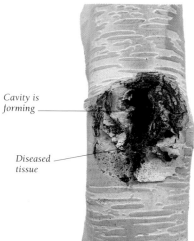

Cavity is forming

Diseased tissue

CLEAN CUT *A clean cut encourages protective new wood – callus or scar tissue – to form most rapidly. The visible cut surface gradually shrinks and is finally "occluded."*

ROUGH CUT *Fungal spores that cause fast-spreading rots can easily invade torn and jagged tissue. This infected wound on the trunk may endanger the whole tree.*

(*continued from p.21*) leave a stub that, without active buds, will wither and die. The normal healing process may be disrupted, allowing disease to penetrate.

Sometimes a cut must be made at a point where there are no visible buds – for example, when coppicing a tree (*see p.36*). The pruning cut should stimulate a dormant bud: cut away any stub left when the newer shoot appears.

MAKING LARGER CUTS

Large pruning cuts, which may take many years to close, are potential entry points for disease. It is important to make cuts that close with maximum speed. If the cut is smooth and made in the correct position, the callus, or scar tissue, grows uninterruptedly from around the edge of the wound to its center, sealing it and preventing the entry of harmful organisms. Once the process is under way, do not further trim wound edges, since this may disrupt the production of callus tissue.

If a sawn surface is rough, it should immediately be smoothed, especially around the edge. A curved pruning knife is the best tool, though professionals often use a chisel. Care must be taken not to enlarge the wound. Gouging into a main branch or trunk may interrupt sap flow and kill tissue.

CUTTING OFF BRANCHES

The general practice in the past was to remove larger branches with a "flush" cut, right up against the stem. It is now recognized that the branch collar – the ring of slight swelling at its base (*see also p.12*) – should be left intact. This means making a very gently angled cut, slightly away from the main branch or trunk but without leaving a distinct stub. If the branch collar is difficult to find, start the cut on the top of the branch ½–1in (2–3cm) away from the crotch, then cut downward at a slight outward angle. Use a pointed bow saw to remove large branches as its narrow blade minimizes friction. A pruning saw (*see p.16*) is adequate for small branches.

WOUND PAINTS

Wound paints used to be widely applied to cuts to provide an artificial barrier against infection while they closed, but recent research has shown that they do not assist the callusing process much – and some may even hinder it. Exposed tissues are never sterile before the treatment is applied; moreover, some micro-organisms are dormant in healthy wood and develop only when the tissue just under the bark is damaged, either by improper pruning or storm or cold damage. In these cases, therefore, harmful organisms will effectively be sealed in behind the paint. At present,

CUTTING OFF A BRANCH

Trees recover most rapidly from large cuts if these are smooth and do not damage the branch collar. If the branch is large, remove the bulk of it first (always in small, manageable sections), to minimize the weight of what will fall last. Then support, or first make an undercut on, what remains to be cut away, because if it falls under its own weight before the final downward cut is completed, it may tear the bark and damage the tree.

1 Reduce the weight of the branch to control the final cut. Some 12in (30cm) away from the trunk, saw a quarter of the way into the branch from the underside. This partial cut stops the bark from tearing down the trunk if the branch accidentally breaks.

3 If the remaining stub is still heavy or awkward to support securely, make another undercut 2–3in (5–8cm) from the trunk. Then make the final cut following the line of the branch collar from top to bottom (see Cutting to the branch collar, top of page).

no paint has proved totally impermeable to air and water – the two principal carriers of plant diseases. The fungicidal properties of wound paints are also of dubious benefit; copper naphthenate, for example, prevents the plant's "natural barrier" against disease (*see p.11*) from forming. Wound paints may also kill nonharmful organisms such as sugar

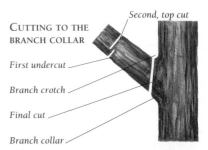

CUTTING TO THE BRANCH COLLAR

Second, top cut

First undercut

Branch crotch

Final cut

Branch collar

2 Cut squarely down from the top of the branch about 2in (5cm) beyond the undercut (farther away from the trunk) until the branch falls away. The undercut ensures that you do not need to try to support the weight of the branch, provided the area beneath is clear.

FINISHED CUT *The final cut downward must be completely smooth; if an undercut was first made, ensure that the final cut is either closer to the trunk or meets the undercut exactly. Smooth any rough edges with a pruning knife, without enlarging the wound.*

fungi, which can inhibit wood rot. While fruit growers with large orchards where disease could spread rapidly may be reluctant to give up their use, wound paints are now considered unnecessary and even inadvisable. Future research in the area of biological control may perhaps provide new paints for which there is a role in the garden.

STAKING

A newly planted tree may need temporary support. The aim of staking should be to steady the tree during establishment. The method used depends on the planting site and the type and size of the tree. While trees used to be staked rigidly, research now shows that a little free movement helps to strengthen the trunk. Low stakes and looser ties that allow the tree to flex in the wind are now recommended, except in special cases. Two low stakes, with flexible bands between them and the tree (*bottom left*) are ideal. When planting a bare-rooted tree, insert the stake into the hole first, then spread the roots carefully around it; never drive a stake through a dense root system or force roots around the stake. Position the stake on the side of the prevailing wind. Stakes should be treated with a preservative and driven at least 24in (60cm) into the ground. Ties should hold the plant loosely. Even with short stakes, it helps to position the ties as low down as possible. Always use padding or a spacer so that ties do not rub directly against the bark: abrasions may affect the future health of the tree. Ties must be checked and adjusted as the tree's girth expands. Ties that are not loosened as the tree grows will cut into the bark and stop food and water from reaching the branches. Remove the stakes as soon as possible after the tree is stabilized, usually after one growing season.

LOW STAKE

A stake that is less than one-third of the tree's height enables the tree to flex and its stem to increase in thickness and strength. Using a spacer keeps the stake clear of the trunk, so that its roughly sawn top does not chafe and damage the young tree's tender bark.

ANGLED STAKE

A short, angled stake can be placed clear of a containerized tree's root ball and inserted into the ground after planting. Lean the stake at 45° into the prevailing wind. Use a belt tie in a figure eight, or padding, to stop the stake from chafing the bark.

TALL STAKE

A tall stake does not allow the trunk to build up strength. However, tall stakes (preferably one on each side) are occasionally useful: for trees that are top-grafted or have heavy, pendulous branches; in very exposed sites; or if a new leading shoot needs to be trained in.

TWO STAKES

A pair of short stakes, driven into the bottom of the planting hole on either side of the root ball, can be used for all trees, but especially for those bought as containerized or root-balled specimens. Flexible ties allow the trunk to flex and strengthen in the wind.

GUY-WIRES

If planting a large tree, support it with guy-wires until its roots have grown sufficiently (usually in about two growing seasons) to stabilize the weight of the crown. Take strong wire through low, sturdy forks in the crown. Lengths of hosepipe threaded onto the wire will stop it from cutting into the tree. Use angled pegs fitted with wire turnbuckles so you can make sure that the trunk is trained vertically. Mark small pegs clearly so they are not a hazard to people or machinery. Guy-wires are also useful for multistemmed trees with several angled trunks.

INITIAL TRAINING

The chances of a tree developing a sturdy, well-balanced framework and being long-lived are greatly enhanced if it gets a good start. The requirements of all trees in the first and second growing seasons (a period often referred to as the "nursery" stage) are much the same. More specific training into the various tree forms (see pp.27–30) does not normally begin until the second winter.

Gardeners often buy young trees pretrained (see facing page) but it is possible to start with a tree you have propagated yourself, a young sucker uprooted from around an existing tree (provided it has not been grafted), or a bought tree that has not yet been trained (these may only be available from a specialty grower and will possibly have to be purchased by mail order). Very young trees consisting only of unbranched, upright stems are known as "maiden whips," or simply "whips." When a good complement of laterals has developed (usually after two growing seasons, although growth is occasionally very vigorous in the first year) they are referred to as "feathered" whips.

When selecting trees and considering how they are to be trained, think carefully about your requirements and the limitations of your site. Make sure that the tree you have in mind is suitable for training into the form you would ideally like (and vice versa). Always ascertain its maximum height and spread, and whether special pruning to restrict size, using such techniques as pollarding, is an option. The Dictionary of Ornamental Trees (pp.52–91) provides detailed information for individual trees.

If the tree is not to be planted in its final site from the start, use a small patch of ground as a "nursery bed" to care for young plants together.

RAISING YOUNG TREES

Plants raised from seed, root cuttings, or softwood cuttings will usually grow, initially, as a single, upright shoot with a terminal bud. A hardwood cutting generally produces its new leading growth from the uppermost side bud: if a multistemmed tree is required, lower buds on the cutting are allowed to grow, but if only one trunk is required, the lower buds are rubbed out.

Many tree cultivars are produced by grafting: joining the scion – the selected cultivar (in the form of a bud or buds, or a length of stem) – to a rootstock from a compatible plant. The point at which the two tissues are fused (the graft union) is usually visible as a slight swelling, near the base of the trunk on "bottom-

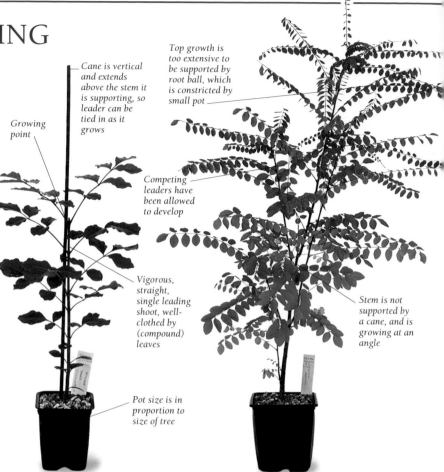

Cane is vertical and extends above the stem it is supporting, so leader can be tied in as it grows

Growing point

Top growth is too extensive to be supported by root ball, which is constricted by small pot

Competing leaders have been allowed to develop

Vigorous, straight, single leading shoot, well-clothed by (compound) leaves

Stem is not supported by a cane, and is growing at an angle

Pot size is in proportion to size of tree

WELL-TRAINED YOUNG TREE
At the end of its first growing season, this ash seedling is upright, vigorous, and healthy. Its pot is large enough to accommodate, without constriction, a root system capable of supporting the top growth.

NEGLECTED YOUNG TREE
Lack of care in the first two years results in a young tree that already stands little chance of becoming a well-shaped mature specimen. Without remedial action, this honey locust will grow to be badly shaped and lopsided.

grafted" trees. "Top-grafting" – joining the scion at the top of a clear trunk grown from the rootstock – is mainly used to produce weeping standards. These are rarely sold until they are several years old, and have special pruning and training needs (see p.28). While bottom-grafting is a technique that can be practiced by the amateur, top-grafting is rarely feasible except for the professional grower. Trees that you have bottom-grafted yourself will need to be trained and pruned using the same techniques followed in the nursery industry.

A tree produced by bud-grafting will grow away from the graft point as a single shoot. Any growth from the stock plant, either from the stem below the graft point or from the roots, must be removed completely as seen.

Where a short section of the scion's stem is grafted on to the stock plant, it is the topmost side bud that will produce the new leading shoot, (continued p.26)

Shoot from terminal bud will grow to extend leader, continuing the main stem

Side buds will develop into lateral shoots unless rubbed off

Graft union, still covered with protective tape

Any growth from below graft will be of stock plant and must be removed

YOUNG GRAFTED TREE
A recently grafted tree can be lightly staked, not only to keep the leading shoot growing straight, but also to protect it from stress and breakage at the graft point.

BUYING YOUNG TREES

Purchased trees may suffer more problems than those propagated and trained in the garden. Actual physical defects are rare where growers take pride in their good reputation, although shoots may have been removed for propagation, spoiling the form. There may, however, be "hidden" tissue damage, perhaps caused by roots drying out, insufficient hardening off or acclimatization, or stress during transportation. If you can, select and collect young trees personally so that you can assess nursery conditions and look trees over for potential problems. Transport them carefully: many trees are killed between nursery and yard. Containerized trees quickly desiccate or scorch if left to stand in hot sun or on hot asphalt or concrete. A tree transported on an open truck or roof rack, with its foliage buffeted in the wind, suffers considerable stress.

SELECTING PARTLY TRAINED TREES

There is an obvious, time-saving advantage in purchasing three- or four-year-old trees, but there are disadvantages too. Most problems are caused by root-to-shoot imbalance – top growth that is far too large for the root ball to sustain once the intensive nursery feeding and watering has stopped. The spread of a container-grown tree should not be more than three or four times the width of the container. Laterals that are overlong compared with the rest should be pruned to a single bud.

A common problem is that the tree has been made to look almost too attractive to the prospective buyer – perhaps it has been allowed to flower or fruit when energy would have been better spent on growth, or fertilized too heavily to stimulate lush green shoots that will not survive cold. Small, sturdy trees that have been "grown hard" nearly always make the best mature specimens.

ROOT PRUNING ON PLANTING

Bare-rooted trees are particularly vulnerable to damage during lifting and transporting. As soon as they are exposed to the air, the fine feeder roots begin to dry out and die. To minimize the area of cut surface, cleanly cut away roots with abrasions and ragged, broken ends. Prune mis-shapen or lopsided roots so that there is a good spread emanating from the stem. Shape the planting hole to accommodate long roots; do not wind roots in a hole that is too small. Generally, container-grown or root-balled trees should not have their roots pruned when transplanting. Roots that are tightly packed will be very slow to penetrate the surrounding soil, so where roots are constricted, tease them out. Cut back only those roots that have been damaged or those that are wrapping around the outside of the root ball – for example, by growing through the bottom of the container.

TRANSPLANT SHOCK

Young plants thrive in nurseries, grown close together. When their environment suddenly changes – to isolation and exposure to strong winds, hot sun, and severe cold – their growth rate may be set back. Some trees are resilient; others, no matter how carefully they are moved, suffer considerable postplanting shock. The older the tree when moved, the more serious the problem. Also, trees can lose up to 90 percent of their roots during transplanting.

The second most common reason why newly planted trees fail to "grow away" well is that their top growth is too large for their root system: the roots, struggling to sustain the overlarge tree, cannot absorb the extra nutrients and moisture necessary to make new growth. If the problem continues into the second growing season, lightly thin crowded interior branches but do not cut back the tips. It is important to maintain the buds that produce root stimulating hormones. Mulch the tree and keep well watered, and fertilize *lightly* with a slow release fertilizer.

SELECTING TREES FOR PURCHASE

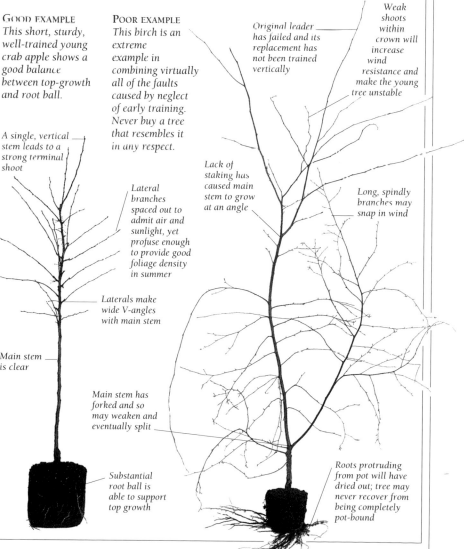

GOOD EXAMPLE
This short, sturdy, well-trained young crab apple shows a good balance between top-growth and root ball.

A single, vertical stem leads to a strong terminal shoot

Main stem is clear

POOR EXAMPLE
This birch is an extreme example in combining virtually all of the faults caused by neglect of early training. Never buy a tree that resembles it in any respect.

Lateral branches spaced out to admit air and sunlight, yet profuse enough to provide good foliage density in summer

Laterals make wide V-angles with main stem

Main stem has forked and so may weaken and eventually split

Substantial root ball is able to support top growth

Original leader has failed and its replacement has not been trained vertically

Weak shoots within crown will increase wind resistance and make the young tree unstable

Lack of staking has caused main stem to grow at an angle

Long, spindly branches may snap in wind

Roots protruding from pot will have dried out; tree may never recover from being completely pot-bound (*continued from p.24*) just as on a cutting, so if a single stem is required, buds below this point should be rubbed out. Remove growth from the stock plant as for a budded tree.

FIRST-YEAR TRAINING
During the first growing season, leaves and sometimes small shoots will appear along the length of the main stem. Do not remove these unless they become damaged or diseased; the tree needs every leaf possible to manufacture food for further growth.

During the following winter, a strong, healthy young tree should not need much pruning, but at this stage any weak or wayward-growing shoots may be cut out. If the leading shoot is growing poorly, replace it by cutting it back to a strong bud or young shoot, if a suitable one has developed; this should then develop into a vigorous shoot to train vertically as a new leader during the next growing season.

Do not stake unless the tree is weak and unstable. If staking is necessary, stake loosely, so the tree can move in the wind, thereby building strength. Take care not to damage roots with stakes. Any laterals that compete with the leader should be removed.

COMPETING LEADERS
A vigorous lateral that threatens the dominance of the leader must be shortened or removed. If the leading shoot of a tree with opposite buds has been damaged and a pair of dual leaders has grown, select only one (*see below right*). If neither is suitable, cut lower down the stem to a pair of buds, rubbing out one of the new shoots that develop.

SECOND-YEAR TRAINING
As the young tree develops strong laterals along its main stem or stems, remove only growth that is dead, diseased, or damaged, or any competing leaders. It is essential to maintain strong main or leading shoots that will form either the single, central trunk, or the several trunks of a multistemmed tree. If competing leaders are not dealt with, there are likely to be problems arising from crossing branches and an unsound framework.

BROKEN LEADER
If the leader is "lost" – it dies back, is damaged by cold, or is broken – prune it back to the nearest sound, strong lateral that can be trained vertically to take its place. If there are as yet no laterals, prune to a healthy bud and then train the resulting shoot. On a tree with opposite buds, remove the weaker shoot or one of the pair of buds in order to direct all energy into the new leader.

COMPETING LEADER
On this young tree, competing leaders have been neglected and now form an upright cluster at the tree's apex. Further training into a structurally sound and well-shaped form will be impossible unless a single leader is selected and the rest removed. With a pair of sharp pruners, cut out any competing leaders.

This strong, upright shoot is best candidate to become new leader

These vigorous low shoots also threaten leader's dominance; cut them back by one-third to half of their length

Remove all competing leaders close to tree's main stem without tearing bark, leaving a ragged wound, or damaging selected leader

SELECTING A LEADER
Where competing leaders have been allowed to develop, the topmost shoot may now not necessarily be the best choice as the new leader. Here, the lower shoot has grown stronger and straighter.

BROKEN LEADER
Cut a damaged leader back to a strong, healthy shoot that is growing almost vertically. Attach a stake to extend the original support until the new leader is growing strongly. If there is no suitable shoot, cut back to a strong bud and tie the new growth to the stake as it develops.

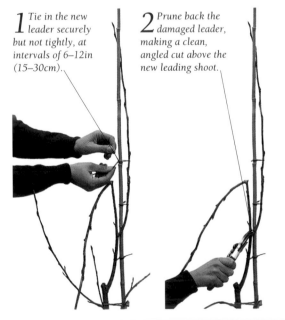

1 *Tie in the new leader securely but not tightly, at intervals of 6–12in (15–30cm).*

2 *Prune back the damaged leader, making a clean, angled cut above the new leading shoot.*

DUAL LEADERS
On trees with opposite buds, the loss of the leader will, if the tree is neglected, result in a pair of new leaders. Here, although the shoot on the left is stronger, the other will be easier to train in the line of the original main stem.

FORM TRAINING

If not already in their final site, two-year-old trees can be planted out and form training can continue *in situ* without further disturbance to the root system. They can be pruned and trained into a variety of tree forms. Some trees are only suited to one way of growing, while with others there is more choice. Evergreen trees (*see below*) are usually trained as feathered trees, with a single stem clothed with laterals to ground level. There is more scope for training deciduous trees in the various ways shown on the following pages, although in many cases the soundest structure is simply a well-shaped version of the habit the tree would naturally adopt. The Dictionary of Ornamental Trees (*pp.52–91*) gives advice on suitable forms for individual trees.

FEATHERED TREE

This is the easiest tree form to produce. All that is necessary is to remove dead, diseased, or damaged wood, together with any laterals that cross another shoot or form too narrow an angle of attachment with the main stem. Where the crotch angle is narrow, the junction is potentially weak; heavy branches may break from the trunk at this point. Take care that a prevailing wind, shade, or competition from other plants do not cause lopsided growth: it is better to remedy the cause than correct the effects.

TRAINING A FEATHERED TREE

Aim to maintain a straight main stem and remove any laterals that are not well spaced and positioned to ensure a balanced, well-shaped tree. If laterals grow more vigorously on one side, tip-prune the branches on the weaker side to stimulate their growth.

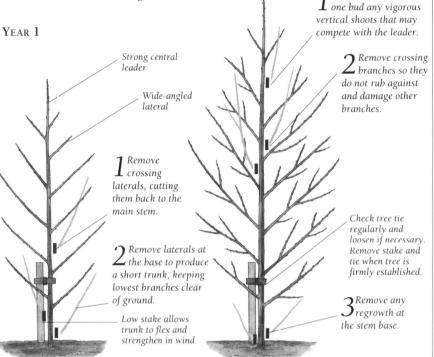

YEAR 1

Strong central leader

Wide-angled lateral

1 Remove crossing laterals, cutting them back to the main stem.

2 Remove laterals at the base to produce a short trunk, keeping lowest branches clear of ground.

Low stake allows trunk to flex and strengthen in wind

YEARS 2 AND 3

1 Prune out or cut to one bud any vigorous vertical shoots that may compete with the leader.

2 Remove crossing branches so they do not rub against and damage other branches.

Check tree tie regularly and loosen if necessary. Remove stake and tie when tree is firmly established.

3 Remove any regrowth at the stem base.

SHAPING A YOUNG EVERGREEN

Cut out competing leader to main stem

Shorten lanky branches that spoil symmetry of tree

Stake leader in an exposed site

Remove badly placed lateral branches

Thin dense bushy growth to allow air into center of plant

EVERGREEN TREES

The crowns of broadleaved evergreen trees, as opposed to conifers (*for which see p.40*), are heavy with foliage even in winter and offer a great deal of resistance to strong winds. It is not advisable, therefore, to grow the majority of evergreen trees with tall clear trunks as the weight of snow or the force of gales could snap the trunk, particularly of grafted specimens. Most evergreens are, therefore, best treated as feathered trees (*see above*) with a strong central leader. The majority naturally form a compact, conical shape. If the leader is lost, a new one must be trained in, and any competing leaders should be removed (*see facing page*). If a long leader has grown and laterals are not developing, as occurs with some hollies, shorten by half the section that is bare of branches. Pinching out the tips of sideshoots also encourages a dense habit from an early age, desirable for evergreens intended to become hedges or topiary.

Bushiness is desirable only for certain evergreens. An open framework of branches suits some large-leaved species, such as the evergreen magnolias. This may entail thinning growth, targeting first any shoots that are unhealthy, weak, or poorly placed. Prune growth when young, since large wounds on evergreens are slow to heal, particularly in tropical climates. Evergreens should in general be pruned from late summer to before midwinter, which avoids the profuse bleeding of sap to which many are prone in spring; despite retaining their foliage, evergreens have a dormant and growing season just like deciduous trees.

STANDARD TREES

Standard trees have a length of clear trunk, surmounted by a crown through which the leader persists (a central-leader standard) or that divides into several main branches (a branched-head standard). Many standards develop naturally, their lower branches dying off and being shed as upper laterals develop and cut off the light (a process known as "shading out"). However, in order to produce or enhance the effect of a clear trunk, lower branches can be pruned from feathered trees. This should be done gradually and early in a tree's life to reduce the size of the pruning scars.

Although the crowns of central-leader and branched-head standards develop in different ways, their trunks are cleared in the same way, gradually over several years. Stripping the trunk of all laterals all at once will cause dormant buds low down on the stem to produce further growth and inhibit top growth. In some cases, removal of all foliage from a stem hitherto shaded by leaves may lead to sun scorch or frost cracks. Another reason for removing laterals in stages is that their foliage helps provide the tree with energy, enabling the main stem or stems to grow thick and strong. The laterals temporarily retained are often described as "stem builders."

CENTRAL-LEADER STANDARD

For a central-leader standard, pruning and training is directed into maintaining a main stem that extends through the crown. The principal danger is that the leader will be lost, either through damage or because another vigorous shoot overtakes it. However, both problems can be rectified (see Broken leader and Competing leader, p.26). A long, sturdy stake lashed to the tree's main stake can be used to support a new leader and ensure vertical growth.

BRANCHED-HEAD STANDARD

Branched-head standards do occur naturally (for example, many oaks) but the habit may take years to develop, the leader gradually losing apical dominance (see p.10) to a number of strong lower framework branches.

However, pruning is commonly used to form a branched head on trees that would otherwise grow to a central leader to a considerable height. As the tree may naturally tend to revert to up-ward growth, a branched-head standard can sometimes only be maintained by pruning, although this becomes less necessary or possible with old trees. A well-trained young tree, with problems promptly dealt with, will not need much attention in maturity; a neglected one may eventually require major surgery.

CENTRAL-LEADER STANDARD

As a guide to clearing the trunk in stages, each year divide the length of the tree's main stem from the ground to the topmost lateral into approximate thirds.

YEAR 1, WINTER

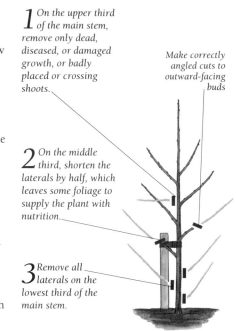

1 *On the upper third of the main stem, remove only dead, diseased, or damaged growth, or badly placed or crossing shoots.*

Make correctly angled cuts to outward-facing buds

2 *On the middle third, shorten the laterals by half, which leaves some foliage to supply the plant with nutrition.*

3 *Remove all laterals on the lowest third of the main stem.*

WEEPING STANDARDS

There are two forms of weeping standard: natural and grafted. If naturally weeping, the habit is vertical (provided the tree is well staked), then arching at a height that varies with the tree. Do not cut away any branches growing upward: they will eventually arch over, raising the height of the tree and producing the characteristic and attractive tiered effect.

In other cases, a prostrate cultivar is grafted onto the clear stem of a stock plant. Because the branches all grow away in the same horizontal plane they can become congested, and side-shoots crossing the center at awkward angles should be removed early on. On most top-grafted trees, upward growth will spoil the weeping form and should be removed.

Shoots growing on the clear stem should always be removed. As trees mature, shorten branches nearing the ground to a bud or sideshoot.

Staking is often required for some years after the head develops. A tall, strong stake may be needed as the head of a weeping tree often develops rapidly and may prove too heavy to be supported by the trunk until this has increased considerably in girth.

YOUNG WEEPING STANDARD

Keep the trunk clear of lateral growth, particularly on top-grafted trees, ideally by pinching off the entire shoot while the growth is still soft. The more mushroom-shaped (cascading as opposed to weeping) the crown, the more likely it is that growth will become congested. Suppressed growth will die, and should be regularly removed to prevent a buildup of debris.

TOP-GRAFTING

A short length of stem may be grafted onto the clear stem of the stock plant; shoots then develop from its several buds, as here. The alternative is budding: two or even three buds may be inserted to ensure that the standard will have a balanced head, important for the stability as well as the look of the tree.

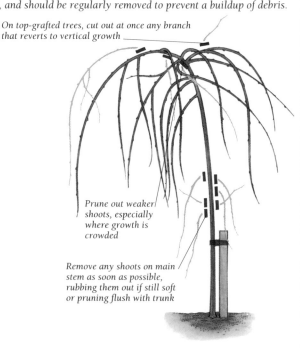

On top-grafted trees, cut out at once any branch that reverts to vertical growth

Prune out weaker shoots, especially where growth is crowded

Remove any shoots on main stem as soon as possible, rubbing them out if still soft or pruning flush with trunk

YEARS 2 AND 3, WINTER

1 On the upper third of the tree, remove any badly positioned or crossing shoots.

2 Shorten all laterals on the middle third of the trunk by two-thirds of their length.

3 Remove the lowest laterals, shortened in the previous year.

Loosen tie as tree's girth increases. Remove tie and stake once tree is firmly established

YEAR 4, WINTER

1 Remove all lateral growth on the desired length of clear stem.

2 As the crown of branches develops, remove crossing shoots to avoid congestion.

BRANCHED-HEAD STANDARD

In the first two or three years, train as for a central-leader standard, above. When three or four strong laterals have developed above the desired height of clear trunk, the leader can be pruned to form the branched head. The selected laterals will become the framework branches of the crown.

YEAR 3 OR 4, WINTER

1 Remove the leading shoot, cutting to just above the uppermost of three or four strong laterals that will form the crown's framework branches.

2 Shorten laterals on the upper half of the desired length of trunk, leaving a portion of each for another year to act as a "stem-builder."

3 Remove crossing and strongly upward-growing sublaterals.

Check and loosen tie if necessary

4 Remove all growth on the lower half of the trunk.

YEAR 4 OR 5, WINTER

1 Cut out any leading shoot or upward-growing branch that threatens to dominate the crown.

2 Shorten growth to balance the shape, cutting where possible to outward-facing buds or shoots to encourage an open-centered crown.

3 Cut out any crossing or crowded branches.

Remove tie and stake once tree is firmly established

4 Clear one or two whorls of laterals from the trunk. There may be some regrowth stimulated by the pruning cuts made above: rub or cut shoots off as they emerge.

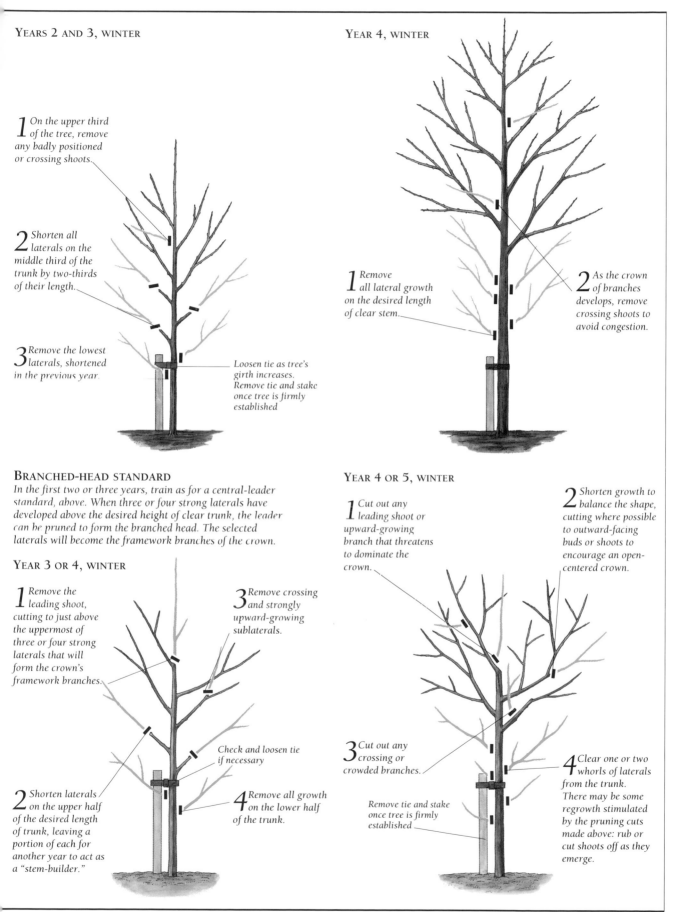

MULTISTEMMED TREE

This form occurs naturally in trees that sucker – produce shoots from the base – or branch very low down, although pruning can enhance this effect by controlling the number and spacing of the trunks. A similar effect can be achieved by planting several single-stemmed trees close together. The multistemmed form can also be created by cutting a tree back hard (*see below*) so that several new stems develop. The cut stimulates low dormant buds, which should shoot strongly the following year. Only certain species (*see pp.52–91*) respond well to this treatment. Never apply it to grafted cultivars.

The several trunks of multistemmed trees can either be left clothed with lateral branches, giving a thicketlike appearance, or cleared to show off attractive – perhaps silvery, coppery, or textured – bark. The latter option is more popular in a garden context, and for best effect the number of main stems should be restricted by selecting the required number of strong, well-spaced shoots early in the tree's life and cutting out any weak or surplus shoots. Clear the stems of lower branches as for a central-leader standard (*see p.28*).

Trees that have a naturally suckering habit may produce more shoots from the base as they mature. This growth must be removed to maintain the desired number of stems unless a replacement for a damaged or diseased trunk is needed. Conversely, new basal stems

CORKSCREW TREES

Certain cultivars of hazel and willow produce twisted twigs and stems. They are usually multistemmed, with main branches springing from a short trunk. Let them develop naturally, removing only dead, diseased, damaged, or crossing growth. Once the tree is established, light pruning to restrict size, accentuate its form, or to thin growth can be carried out without spoiling the natural habit. These trees tend to become congested and thinning reduces stress on the twisted, load-bearing branches. A small crack on a healthy stem will heal quickly, but the branch will have been weakened and, ideally, should be removed.

Corkscrew hazels and willows are usually ungrafted and tolerate complete renovation; they can be cut to the ground in winter. The extensive root system will sucker freely as a result: select only the best of the new stems (or only one if a single trunk is desired), and prune out weak or badly placed ones.

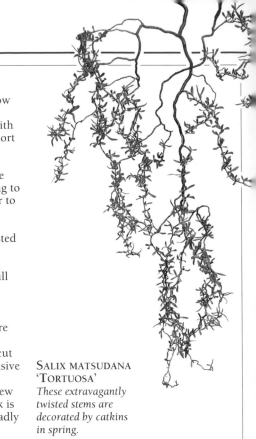

SALIX MATSUDANA 'TORTUOSA'
These extravagantly twisted stems are decorated by catkins in spring.

growing from regularly cut back, or coppiced, trees (*see p.36*) tend to become sparser as the years go by.

Inward-growing branches on a multistemmed tree may need to be thinned to avoid congestion and to maintain the ornamental appearance of the group of trunks. If too much growth is removed,

however, one or more stems may be left isolated and may then splay out from the group, possibly breaking. If this happens it may be necessary to cut isolated stems to the base since they will spoil the ornamental effect. Well-spaced young shoots from the base can then develop as replacements.

PRODUCING A MULTISTEMMED FORM FROM A SINGLE-STEMMED TREE

YEAR 1, WINTER

Cut the main stem of a two-year-old tree straight across at the desired height – at lowest, as here, 3in (8cm) from the ground. Trim the wound so there are no rough edges.

YEAR 2, WINTER

Select three or four strong, well-spaced shoots, preferably of equal vigor to encourage even development. Remove all other shoots, cutting them back to the base.

YEAR 3, WINTER

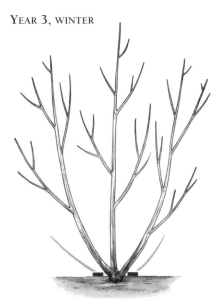

Let laterals develop, removing only the lowest if clear stems are desired. Remove any new suckers. These cuts in turn may stimulate basal regrowth; remove in subsequent years.

PRUNING ESTABLISHED TREES

Although established trees do not need the regular pruning required by many shrubs and climbers, all benefit from regular checks and routine maintenance throughout their lives, no matter how natural their manner of growth. Some, such as trees with variegated foliage and top-grafted weeping standards, need extra attention. The safest pruning times for non-essential pruning are given in the Dictionary of Ornamental Trees (pp.52–91). However, it is always safer to correct the problems outlined on these pages as soon as they are seen; check large, older trees, which are not pruned frequently, in midwinter and late summer for defects that should be corrected.

DEAD AND DISEASED WOOD

All plants have natural defense mechanisms that must be taken into account when cutting away dead and diseased wood. Once diseased, tree tissue never becomes healthy again; instead, the tree forms a natural, chemical barrier (*see also p.11*) between diseased and healthy wood. In most cases, provided the disease is not too widespread, the diseased part is walled off and isolated from the remaining healthy part.

The presence of unshed dead wood, host to fungal rots as it decays, poses a health hazard to the tree. Cutting the dead portion out completely – that is, cutting back into live wood – will force the tree to waste energy healing a wound where an efficient barrier already existed. Cut dead wood out, therefore, just above the line (usually quite distinct) between live and dead wood.

If an entire main branch seems dead right up to the trunk or large limb, cut it

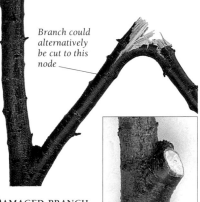

DAMAGED BRANCH
Remove the branch
(inset) *or, if replacement growth at this point is greatly desired (see over), cut straight across below all damage to a node, if visible. If shoots do not develop in the following growing season, remove the stub.*

off just as you would a healthy branch (*see p.22*). Do not attempt to cut out dead wood from the live trunk or limb, or you will create a break in the barrier between dead and live wood through which disease can spread back into the whole tree.

If disease is still active, however, there will be no clear demarcation between dead and live wood. Therefore, when cutting off diseased wood, it is essential to cut well below the signs of infection and inspect the cut surface carefully – if disease or discoloration is still visible, more wood must be cut away.

STAG-HEADED TREES

Old trees often become "stag-headed," with gaunt, dead branches sticking out of the top of the crown. The cause is

EFFECTS OF LEAVING A STUB THAT DIES
If new shoots do not develop from a stub, it dies and may become diseased. This bracket fungus indicates serious rotting. Prune back to clean wood. If the cut surface still shows rot at the crotch or main trunk, the tree cannot be saved.

usually deep-seated disruption to surrounding land: possibly adjacent building development, soil compaction, or changes in the local water table. Trees can survive for many years in this condition; however, if you find them unsightly, have their condition assessed by a professional arborist.

TORN BRANCHES AND BARK

Branches that are partially broken, for example, by lightning damage, the weight of snow, or the action of vandals or grazing animals, rarely mend if tied back in position. It is usually better to cut them out or shorten them to a suitable replacement shoot below the damage. Bark that has been knocked or torn off a tree is unlikely to reunite with the cambium layer. (Continued p.32:)

TORN BARK ON THE TRUNK OF A TREE

DAMAGE AT THE BRANCH COLLAR *This injury often results from vandalism. The only course is to remove the branch, and trim and smooth the wound with a pruning knife. Keep the area of cut surface as small as possible.*

ABRADED BARK *Incorrect staking and tying is a major cause of bark scrapes. Here the tie has been pushed up, and over time has chafed the bark and pulled the tree over. Reposition the tie correctly and smooth any rough edges.*

EFFECTS OF TORN BARK *This badly damaged ginkgo is not thriving. The new shoot that has developed below the damaged area shows that the passage of food and growth-inducing substances up the trunk is barred by the wound. In addition, the orange markings show that disease has taken hold. There is little that can be done for this tree.*

(*Continued from p.31.*) The wound is best opened and allowed to dry out, after you have pared any rough edges with a knife. Major damage to bark at the base of a tree is a serious problem that could affect the tree's safety. It is therefore important to avoid causing damage with garden machinery.

EPICORMIC SHOOTS

Epicormic shoots are those produced from dormant buds, often completely invisible under bark until stimulated into life. This stimulus may be a pruning cut: many trees have a tendency to produce fast-growing epicormic shoots – known as "water" shoots – around the site of pruning wounds. These must be rubbed out as they emerge, or they will proliferate and divert energy from the rest of the tree. On some species, strong shoots may be kept – to replace a broken branch, for example – provided that others are removed (*see right*). On other trees, this type of growth is so succulent that it will never become strong enough to make a safe new branch. These trees are identified in the Dictionary of Ornamental Trees (*pp.52–91*).

SUCKERS

Trees such as *Populus tremula* (aspen) naturally develop shoots, or suckers, from their root systems, while some species, such as *P. nigra* (black poplar), produce them only when a root is damaged. Suckers do not harm a tree, though they may be unsightly. The easiest way to control them is to grow the tree on a lawn, where the suckers will be regularly sheared off by mowing. Otherwise, suckers must be cut off at the point of origin, paring away the surrounding tissue to remove dormant buds nearby. Simply digging or pulling suckers up will stimulate these buds into

THINNING REGROWTH FROM A LOPPED BRANCH

Last shoot will be shortened to this bud

All surplus and wayward shoots have been removed. Rub out any subsequent regrowth from these pruning sites

BEFORE *This damaged branch has been lopped, initially giving a clumsy appearance. However, many strong new shoots have now appeared, from which, by careful selection, balanced regrowth can be developed.*

AFTER *A strong shoot has been selected at each of the four "compass points," to give each plenty of room. Cut them back by at least half, varying lengths so that sideshoots will not develop in an unnatural "mophead."*

growth. Never use herbicide on suckers, as it will be taken up by the tree's roots.

The rootstocks of grafted trees (particularly some *Prunus*) also tend to shoot from below the ground. Suckers from below a graft point must always be removed at the point of origin, as above, as swiftly as possible. If they are left, the stock plant, often more vigorous than the grafted tree, will take over from it.

Take care when planting naturally suckering species since suckers may spread beyond the boundaries of your property. *Ailanthus* (tree of heaven) and *Robinia* (locust) are notorious "fence-leapers," the former so much so that its cultivation is prohibited in certain parts of the world.

REVERSION

Many trees have variegated cultivars, with splashes or edgings of gold or silver on their leaves. These cultivars are vegetatively propagated from sports – naturally occurring mutations – of the original, green-leaved tree, and just as the tree mutated to produce this effect, so it may partially revert back to plain foliage. Any shoots with green foliage on a variegated form should be cut out immediately. The same problem may arise with cultivars that have been developed for their unusual "cut" or feathery leaves; shoots bearing leaves of the plainer, "normal" shape should also be removed. When a tall tree reaches maturity, removing reverted shoots is easier said than done, but while they are not harmful to the tree, they will rise to dominance if left.

PROPPING AND BRACING

Extra-long and picturesque branches or reclining trees may need to be propped or braced to stop them from breaking. Forked posts made of wood, stone, or specially designed metal supports are suitable, but do not use wrought ironwork, which may cut into the branch. With all supports, it is advisable to place some padding between the crutch and the branch, so that slight movement does not result in chafing of the branch. Burlap or old carpet are both suitable materials.

The support needs to take the weight of the branch without forcing it upward, which will create other stresses at the point where it joins the trunk.

Commonly grown trees that sometimes

GROWTH FROM ADVENTITIOUS BUDS

SUCKERS AND EPICORMIC SHOOTS *This willow tends not only to produce occasional shoots on its clear trunk but also sends up suckers from underground. Both types of growth should be removed as soon as seen.*

"WATER" SHOOTS *A pruning cut may stimulate dormant (sometimes called "latent") buds into life. Shoots that develop where they are not wanted must be rubbed out or cut off as soon as possible.*

REVERTED SHOOTS

On variegated or fancy-leaved cultivars, remove at their point of origin entire shoots that have reverted to plain foliage as soon as they are seen.

WITCH'S BROOM

Clusters of twiggy growth such as this are harmless, but may be removed if found unsightly. Remove the branch at its point of origin, or shorten it to a replacement shoot below the affected area.

require propping are *Cedrus libani* (cedar of Lebanon), *Cercis siliquastrum* (Judas tree), *Morus* (mulberries), and *Catalpa bignonioides* (Indian bean tree).

CAVITIES AND HOLLOW TRUNKS

Tree cavities, usually in the trunk, are caused by damaged or old tissue decaying and eventually rotting away. They rarely cause problems in an otherwise healthy tree, and should never be cleaned out, enlarged, drained, or plugged with any artificial material such as concrete. Research has now shown that water filling a cavity actually reduces harmful fungal activity.

A tree trunk that is split by lightning must immediately be inspected by a professional arborist. However, old hollow or even split trunks are not necessarily unsafe, especially if they are short and broad. A hollow trunk of live wood can be very strong, protected from disease by a natural barrier (*see p.11*) between live tissue and the rotting heart-wood. A large tree should be inspected by a professional for health and safety: if its branches are unsafe, it may still be salvageable by pollarding or thinning (*see p.36*).

WITCHES' BROOMS

Trees can develop dense clusters of stunted twigs and foliage on their branches. These witches' brooms, as they are known, are the result of attack by certain fungi, insects, or mites. They do not harm the rest of the tree, so they can safely be left. If they are unsightly, as they often are on hackberries, the entire branch may be cut back below the affected area at a suitable point, such as a junction with a main branch.

ROOT-PRUNING ESTABLISHED TREES

Many trees make excellent container plants. The reduction in vigor that results from restricting the size of the root system, either in pots or with barriers, enables many tender species to be grown under glass. Container-growing is often combined with hard pruning (*see Coppicing and pollarding, p.36*) to further restrict the tree's size. Most trees dislike being pot-bound, and will occasionally require root pruning, as for a container-grown shrub (for step-by-step illustrations, *see p.154*).

Root pruning by digging and making spade cuts into the ground around an established tree is sometimes recommended to restrict growth, particularly for fruit trees (for step-by-step illustrations, *see p.101*). It is vital to use the correct method, and cut the roots well away from the trunk, or the tree's stability may be affected.

CRUTCHES FOR LOW BRANCHES
Prop low branches if they add to a tree's picturesque appeal. A crutch of old wood or driftwood gives a natural effect.

FELLING A SMALL TREE

Never fell a large tree yourself (*see overleaf*). This work is best left in the hands of a professional arborist. Small trees, however, may need removing simply because they are no longer wanted, or because they have grown up as suckers or seedlings in a neglected garden. Cut the trunk about 3ft (1m) from the ground, so that the stump can be used to lever the roots out of the ground. If you need professional help, and providing the site is accessible, winching with chains or stump grinding are options for removing the stump. If it must be left, cut it flush with the ground. Seek professional advice about chemical stump killers.

1 From the side on which you want the tree to fall, make a downward cut one-third of the way through the trunk, using a sharp bow saw.

2 Make a horizontal cut below the first cut until they meet. Then take away the small wedge of wood between the two cuts. This should ensure that, with the final cut, the tree falls in the right direction.

3 From the opposite side of the tree, about 1½in (4cm) above the base of the wedge cut, saw horizontally until the wood splits downward and the tree topples over.

RENOVATION

There are many situations in which more extensive tree pruning than that outlined on the previous pages will be necessary – to renovate a neglected tree, or one that has grown lopsided or become unsafe; to bring an overgrown tree back under control; or to fell an unwanted or unsound tree. Much tree renovation work is potentially dangerous. Major tree surgery (*see facing page*) and the felling of large trees should never be undertaken by the amateur gardener. Even for minor renovation, assessment by a professional arborist is often advisable.

SAFETY MEASURES

The specialized tools and equipment designed for tree surgery should never be used by untrained personnel. Chainsaws are particularly dangerous: amateurs must never use them from within the crown of a tree, or attempt, when standing on the ground, to cut a branch that is above waist height.

Felling trees with trunks more than 6in (15cm) in diameter, or lopping main branches and lowering them safely to the ground, are arduous tasks that should not be undertaken by anyone not accustomed to strenuous physical exercise. Sawing, lifting, and guiding long lengths of wood may strain rarely used muscles, particularly if the body twists to work in awkward positions.

If at all possible, work from the ground. A ladder propped up in a tree is likely to be unstable. The higher the ladder is climbed, the more branches will lean away as they take the weight: stepping off the ladder into the tree may make a branch spring back alarmingly. If you are climbing even part-way into a tree, always wear a hard hat with a chin-strap and safety glasses. Never work when bark is wet and slippery. Never work alone, and make sure your companion remains on the ground. Clear the area of garden furniture, equipment, and other tools before you begin, and keep children and pets away.

LEGAL PRECAUTIONS

Before any work is done, check whether the tree is legally protected; if so, permission from the appropriate organization may be necessary for felling or even the removal of branches. Check whether the work you intend could threaten overhead wires or underground pipes or cables: if so, you must bring in a trained professional to do the job and inform the relevant authority.

The most bitter disputes between neighbors often result from misunder-standings over boundaries. It is both

CORRECTING UNEVEN GROWTH ON A SMALL TREE

YEAR 1 *Do not be tempted to cut the stronger side back too hard. Instead, tip-prune its branch leaders, which will result in limited regrowth, and prune the growth on the weaker side hard, stimulating a vigorous response that will balance the tree's form.*

YEAR 2 AND AFTER *Strong new shoots should have developed on the weaker side. In this and subsequent winters, remove only those that cross other shoots, or that will spoil the symmetry of the crown as it develops. Patience is needed while the tree regrows.*

courteous and wise to advise neighbors of your intentions if your tree borders their property, and may be legally necessary if you wish to prune a tree in a neighbor's yard that encroaches on your property.

MINOR RENOVATION OF SMALL TREES

A tree may have its growth stunted on one side through suppression by a neighboring tree or structure. If the factor causing the lopsided growth – suppression by a neighboring larger tree, or shade cast by an outbuilding, wall, or fence – is to remain, there is no point in remedial pruning. However, if it is removed, it is possible to prune correctively over several years to restore a more even shape (*see above*).

Neglect may cause any number of minor problems to accumulate – dead, diseased, and damaged wood, crossing or obstructing branches, overcrowding, wayward shoots, or new growth obscuring a previously clear trunk. If branches have become very low and spreading, they must be removed or propped (*see p.32*), since they may be placing considerable strain on the trunk. If the trunk splits, air, water, and decay fungi may gain entry: a hollow trunk may develop, or the tree may die.

In the first year of renovation of a small tree, remove all unhealthy and

dead wood, suckers, and crossing branches that are damaging bark by rubbing. This will improve its general overall condition. In the second and, if necessary, the third year, reduce overcrowding (some of which will have been caused by regrowth from the previous year's cuts), and remove or shorten other branches as necessary to enhance the shape. Remove only one or two entire branches in any one year, cutting them out in sections to reduce the risk of tearing the bark.

TIMING AND AFTERCARE

It is best to tackle any renovation work during the dormant season, with certain exceptions (*see pp.52–91*); with deciduous trees, the form will be seen more clearly, and work be made much easier, in the absence of foliage.

After minor renovation, apply a top-dressing of balanced, slow release fertilizer according to the instructions. In some cases, an old tree may not have been fertilized for a long time – if at all – so don't overdo it. A 2–3in (5–8cm) layer of organic mulch, such as composted leaves or shredded bark, is beneficial. Never apply soil over the roots of an established tree since this may alter the finely balanced supply of oxygen to the tree's roots and adversely affect its health.

Major tree pruning

Trees that have been neglected or have grown too large for their position should either be cut down or, if still fundamentally healthy, they may be renovated. Except in a confined space or sensitive urban situation, felling a tree is easier and cheaper than renovation and also allows a more suitable tree species to be planted in its place. In urban areas in particular, tree surgery is almost always best carried out by a qualified arborist – sometimes referred to as a "tree surgeon."

Major tree pruning covers not only felling but also crown reduction, lifting, and thinning. Crown reduction, or more drastic pollarding (see p.36), reduces the overall size of a mature tree's canopy. Crown lifting increases the height of clear trunk by removing large lower branches and is most often necessary where branches overhang a street or driveway. Crown thinning removes congested growth; it is a valuable option where a tree is casting heavy shade or blocking a view. Thinning branches to let in dappled sunlight can often mean that an area of garden or a window view is reclaimed without the necessity of losing a fine ornamental tree.

It must be emphasized that none of these jobs is by any means straight-forward, requiring crucial decisions about the tree's structure based on special knowledge and experience.

TREE MADE UNSAFE BY DAMAGE
Storm or lightning damage within the crown of a large tree must be assessed and dealt with using expert knowledge and techniques.

Without this knowledge, pruning may result in a dangerously unstable tree.

Amateur work has additional pitfalls. Mistaken or misguided attempts to improve a tree by cutting off branches are, of course, impossible to rectify, whereas skillful tree surgery should result in a tree that is pleasing to the eye for many years to come. This should not

only further deter the amateur but also highlight the importance of using reputable, preferably certified professional firms or individuals. Shoddy work nearly always entails more expense and often risks the loss of the tree. Using a professional arborist can most often save the life of your tree.

Skillfully performed tree surgery is never inexpensive, but the outlay is repaid by much more than the actual labor. Before the work is undertaken, an arborist will advise on what should be done (and whether any alternatives are feasible), how long it will take, what the effects will be, as well as what future work might be needed and when. As well as being qualified to carry out specialty work, the arborist should also dispose of all lopped or felled wood.

The services of a consultant arborist can also prove invaluable when local authorities have an interest in legally protected trees. A site visit can sort out numerous other minor problems, and alert an owner to such factors as subsidence and soil heave – details that perhaps would not occur to a lay person.

The real cost of using a professional arborist should be assessed, therefore, in the light of all of these benefits, but be sure to check before work begins that any liability for damage or compensation claims is the responsibility of the firm or individual, and that they have adequate insurance coverage.

CROWN LIFTING
Sections or all of some lower branches are removed to create more room below the tree, for example to allow a bus to pass freely below, or to expose a street light that has become hidden in the branches.

CROWN THINNING AND REDUCTION
These operations are often combined to reduce the size of a tree and allow more light and air to penetrate through the crown, reducing wind resistance and stress from wide-spreading, heavy branches.

COPPICING AND POLLARDING

Some trees (and many shrubs) tolerate hard pruning on a regular basis and respond by producing vigorous new growth that is often of considerable ornamental value in the garden. The techniques of coppicing and pollarding used in this kind of pruning are among the most ancient horticultural practices.

Coppicing is the regular, sometimes annual, cutting back of a tree to ground level to obtain vigorous, new young stems. These were traditionally cut in winter to be used for firewood, basketwork, barriers, and as poles. There is evidence of coppicing dating back to Neolithic times; in England and northern France, where this type of woodland management was popular, coppice survives that is at least 600 years old. Coppicing can prolong tree life indefinitely when the cuts are clean and fast-healing, as produced by ancient tools such as billhooks and axes. Roughly sawn coppice is unlikely to be so long-lasting.

A similarly renewable supply of wood was produced by pollarding, but here the shoots arose from the head of a clear tree trunk, from which all branches had been cut away. This elevated form of coppicing freed the land below to provide pasture for grazing animals – a very early form of dual land use.

PRUNING FOR ORNAMENTAL STEMS

Today, gardeners use coppicing and pollarding mainly for ornamental effect, and also to grow trees in less space than is normally necessary. Only a limited number of trees will tolerate such hard treatment: disease resistance is crucial to enable continual recovery from wounds. Coppicing and pollarding are chiefly

COLORFUL YOUNG STEMS
This pollarded willow with its bright new shoots brings winter and early spring color into the garden. Pollarding on a low trunk produces a plant of shrublike proportions, but developing a clear trunk, as here, of 4–5ft (1.2–1.5m) raises the new stems well above other border plants.

used to produce, either on the ground or at eye level, crops of young stems that, when bare in winter, bring welcome color to the garden. Some willow (*Salix*) and dogwood (*Cornus*) species are the trees most commonly managed in this way because their young stems are often vividly colored, from bright yellow to scarlet to dusky purple. The stems are not cut back until the spring in order to have the longest possible display.

PRUNING FOR ORNAMENTAL FOLIAGE

Unusual foliage effects can be achieved by coppicing trees such as *Ailanthus*, *Cotinus*, and *Paulownia*. Directing energy into new shoots results in lush, enlarged leaves. Sometimes the leaf shape and color of juvenile foliage is very different, as with eucalyptus. Some flowers will be lost, since most trees flower on mature wood, unless, like *Buddleja*, flower buds form on this year's wood.

DEVELOPING A POLLARD (LEFT)

Buy or train a suitable young tree (such as this willow) with a well-branched head on a clear stem of about 6ft (2m). Once established in its planting site, but before its stem has a diameter much more than 4–5in (10–13cm), in late winter or early spring saw through the main stem just above the lowest cluster of branches. Cut these back to 1–3in (2.5–8cm) of the main stem. Treat the resulting mass of shoots as an established pollard.

ESTABLISHED POLLARD (RIGHT)

To maintain the effect, prune every one to three years. In late winter or early spring, shorten all stems to within ½–¾in (1–2 cm) of the main stem. Use sharp tools and make sure that the enlarged head of the pollarded main stem is not damaged. As the tree matures the new shoots may be overcrowded: remove some in spring, and discard as seen any shoots that appear on the main stem or at the base of the tree.

PRUNING TO RESTRICT SIZE

Coppicing and pollarding greatly restrict the size of a tree: a full-size *Paulownia*, for example, can easily reach 80ft (25m), whereas coppicing will confine it to the space necessary for a large shrub (although it can still grow to 10ft/3m in a single season). Bear in mind, though, that the tree will still have a large root system. Provided there is sufficient space for their root run, trees such as *Catalpa* and *Cercis* can be grown as small, attractively mop-headed, lush-leaved specimens. Pollarded trees – planes and lindens in particular – are popular for street use, although they are often not completely pollarded to the head of the trunk, but lopped: their main branches are shortened to form a larger framework from which new shoots will grow. This leaves a larger crown, more in proportion with the tall trunks necessary if traffic is to run beneath. Lopping often looks clumsy in a garden setting; crown reduction (*see p.35*) is usually more suitable.

PRUNING TO REJUVENATE

Pollarding and heading back can be used to save a tree that is far too large for safety or for its situation. Some English oaks are estimated to have lived for more than 400 years since losing their original limbs through natural "branch drop." Yew trees, too, rejuvenate remarkably well after severe pruning. Pollarding or coppicing may be the

HAZEL COPPICE

In late winter or early spring, cut all growth to a few inches above ground level; never sever shoots below the soil surface or injure the swollen, woody base of the tree. It is from here that new shoots will develop. The new growth springs from the outer edges of the coppice "stool." The new shoots can be thinned if they are too dense. Cut stems out at the base, rather than shortening them, to maintain a natural effect.

After pruning (below)

Regrowth in spring (right)

solution for a tree that has been left an eyesore through losing much growth to wind damage. Sometimes, after coppicing, a single stem can be selected and grown on to form a replacement leader from which a new crown can be developed (*see Eucalyptus, p.64*). When used on large established trees, these techniques should only be undertaken

by a professional arborist (*see also* Major tree surgery, *p.35*).

Coppicing also makes it possible to protect some trees from winter damage. Cutting back trees such as bay and eucalyptus to the basal stumps (often called the "stool") before hard weather sets in makes them easy to cover, for example with straw.

PRUNING FOR FOLIAGE EFFECT

Instead of forming a tall tree, this Acer negundo 'Flamingo' lights up the border with its fresh, cream-splashed variegated foliage, an effect created by pollarding to a very low stem. The leaves of many trees are at their most attractive on the newest growth.

SUITABLE ORNAMENTAL TREES

ACER PENSYLVANICUM 'ERYTHROCLADUM' Produces attractive young red stems.
AILANTHUS Restricts size, and produces larger leaves (*see p.53*).
CARPINUS BETULUS Coppicing can be used to create informal hedging.
CATALPA BIGNONIOIDES Pollarding can be used to retain an overgrown or damaged tree (*see p.57*).
CERCIS Pollarding restricts size and brings flowers down to eye level (do not cut back every year).
EUCALYPTUS Selected species (*see p.64*) respond by producing attractive juvenile foliage and a shrubby form.
FAGUS SYLVATICA Restricts size, or produces multiple stems for use in hedging.
PAULOWNIA Restricts size and produces attractive large leaves (*see p.78*).
PLATANUS X ACERIFOLIA Pollarding reduces size of crown, particularly of street trees (*see p.80*).
QUERCUS Prolongs life of unsafe trees.
SALIX Many species produce attractively colored young stems (*see p.86*).
TAXUS BACCATA (yew) Rejuvenates old trees, or produces multiple stems for hedging.
TILIA Pollarding restricts crown size; coppice red-twigged lindens such as *Tilia platyphyllos* 'Rubra'.
TOONA SINENSIS 'FLAMINGO' Produces attractive pink juvenile foliage.

PLEACHING

Pleaching is the weaving together of the branches of a row of trees. Combined with formal trimming, it creates a hedge with an intricate branch structure on a freestanding row of clear trunks. It is a horticultural art with a long history: in Tudor England, pleached avenues were status symbols, showing off the numbers of gardeners the landowner was able to employ.

Pleached rows and avenues are enjoying a revival today, despite requiring almost constant attention throughout their lives. The trees traditionally used for this most labor-intensive form of tree pruning are lindens, hornbeams, beeches, and hollies, though most trees that tolerate clipping are suitable. A strong and well-constructed framework is needed until the row is fully established; for hornbeam and beech, this may be about 15 years.

BUILDING THE SUPPORT

The main support posts for each tree's trunk must be driven at least 2–3ft (60–90cm) into the ground, and be as tall as the intended finished hedge. For the best effect, spacing between posts should be about 8ft (2.5m). Endposts will be needed a short distance from the first and last tree, so that the framework can support the entire extent of their growth. Horizontal wood strips or, for a less obtrusive effect, wires, attached or tightly stretched between the posts, form the horizontal framework to which the lateral branches will be tied.

FORMATIVE PRUNING AND TRAINING

Start with three- or four-year-old trees with strong, straight central leaders, already partially cleared as for a standard (*see p.28*), and with laterals at or near the height of the lowest wire. These

TRADITIONAL PLEACHING
Lindens, hornbeams, and beeches are the most commonly pleached deciduous trees. Using different beech cultivars with varying leaf color (left) creates a tapestry effect. The closely woven branches (below) have ornamental value in winter.

laterals need to be growing in as flat a plane as possible. Plant in late autumn or early spring, pruning away any shoots below the bottom wire or strip, and those growing at right angles to the framework that cannot be tied in. Tie the remaining laterals along the wood strips or wires.

Throughout the following and subsequent growing seasons, pinch or rub out shoots that appear on the clear trunks or that will grow away from the framework. Tie in the leader as it extends, and weave and tie in suitably placed shoots as they grow to form an evenly spaced network. Weave along the

strips or wires; as growth develops, the gaps between will narrow. In winter, remove badly placed growth and shorten long shoots to encourage branching.

ESTABLISHED PLEACHED TREES

When a densely woven screen has been established it can be clipped just as an ordinary hedge (*see p.44*). Keep rubbing out shoots on the trunks and remove dead, diseased, or damaged growth as seen, always taking the opportunity to weave and tie in laterals if there are gaps. Fertilize the trees lightly in spring to make up for removing so much foliage, and to keep them in good condition.

PLEACHED ARCHES AND TUNNELS

The upper parts of two trees can be intertwined to create an arch, freestanding or spanning a gap within a hedge. Attach a hoop of thick wire to tall stakes supporting the trees. Gently pull and tie their leaders over it; suitable laterals and sideshoots are then tied together and pruned to develop a solid bridge. More elaborately, pairs of young trees may be trained over a series of arched supports and their branches pleached to form a tunnel (*see also Laburnum, p.70*). Supports must be permanent, so the framework must be solid and of a long-lived material that is either unobtrusive or decorative – iron is the traditional choice. Pruning may be time-consuming, shoots above the top of the arch being especially difficult to reach.

A "PLEACHED" EFFECT

For a labor-saving alternative to pleaching, once the framework has been covered, prune the previous season's growth by at least half each winter to encourage branching (*as left*), tying in awkward growth. This will form a "hedge on stilts" that can be clipped (*see also* Hedges, *p.44*).

FORMATIVE TRAINING, PLEACHED TREES

PRUNING ON PLANTING, WINTER

1 Having constructed a strong framework, plant a three- or four-year-old tree in front of each post, aligning as many laterals as possible parallel to the framework. Tie in the leader, adding extra ties during the subsequent growing season as it develops.

2 Wherever possible, tie lateral branches securely along an adjacent wire or lath.

3 Remove any laterals that are growing outward and cannot readily be secured to a wire or lath.

4 Cut back to the main stem any laterals that are growing below the bottom wire or lath.

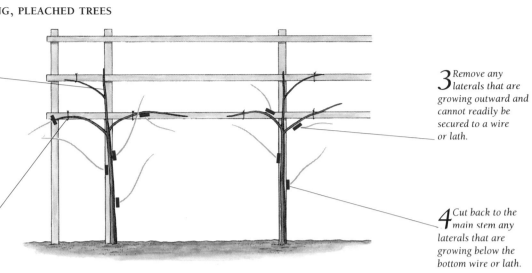

YEAR 2, WINTER

1 Once the leader reaches the top wire or strip, start to train it horizontally. Train a suitably placed lateral along the top lath on the other side. For even development, train all leaders in the same direction.

2 Shorten any long laterals back to a strong sideshoot, and sideshoots back to two or three buds to encourage new, vigorous growth to cover the framework.

3 Throughout the growing season, pinch out all new shoots except those that are growing sideways or can be pulled across and trained sideways. While still pliable, intertwine and tie these laterals within the framework so that all the spaces are filled in.

4 Remove any new growth on the clear trunks.

YEAR 3, WINTER

1 Cut back to a bud all new shoots that extend beyond the limits of the supporting framework, at the edges or at the top. For the best formal effect, keep the line of cuts perfectly straight.

2 Weave together and tie in suitably placed shoots. As the gaps between the tiers narrow, shoots from above and below can be drawn and tied together.

3 Where shoots are growing away from the horizontal surface of the row (that is, sticking out at the front or back) cut back to a sideways-facing bud.

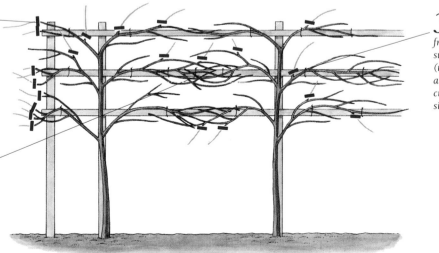

CONIFERS

Most conifers are cone-bearing, evergreen trees with needlelike or scalelike leaves. A few, however, such as larches (*Larix*) and dawn redwood (*Metasequoia*), are deciduous, and the deciduous ginkgo (*see below*) is very uncharacteristic, with broad, veined leaves. Conifers offer a wide range of size, habit, form, and color; it is best to choose one that will not outgrow your garden or dominate other plantings.

Most conifers produce strongly upright and dominant leaders, giving rise to a typical conical habit. With few exceptions, they are best grown with minimal pruning. Once mature, pruning is best avoided unless absolutely essential – for example, to repair damage or to remove reverted or wayward growth. Like all trees, however, they benefit from initial training to avoid problems that will be difficult to rectify as the tree matures.

Unless planting special cultivars with, for example, dwarf or fastigiate habits (*see facing page*), it is often best to start with seed-raised plants. Cuttings taken from lateral shoots often continue to grow sideways, like the branch they were taken from, and it is very difficult to train them as upright, central-leader specimens. This is particularly true of spruces (*Picea*), firs (*Abies*), and pines (*Pinus*); yews (*Taxus*) and larches (*Larix*) are very variable in this respect. Members of the Cupressaceae (such as *Chamaecyparis*, *Cupressus*, and *Thuja*) are less prone to atypical growth when raised from cuttings.

CONIFER
PLANTING PLAN
As a group, conifers require little pruning or training. They offer a wide range of shapes and sizes, often with a dense, compact habit that enhances their clean outlines. With careful selection, they prove invaluable in creating low-maintenance plantings with strong contrasts of form, texture, and color.

BUYING AND PLANTING

Before planting conifers, it is vital to ensure that the plant is not pot-bound and has a healthy system of fibrous roots. Discard pot-bound plants ruthlessly, since they are seldom able to produce a strong root system. This leads to poor anchorage and weakens growth, so that failure, at some later stage in the development of the tree, is certain. It is important to transplant carefully to minimize damage to the fibrous roots. Feeding and mulching well after planting will help the plant to establish well and quickly. Conifers are very prone to transplant shock (*see p.25*). For best results, plant young trees 1–3ft (30–90cm) tall.

Do not stake conifers; they rely on movement of the main stem in the wind to produce strong supporting tissue in the stem and a sound root system.

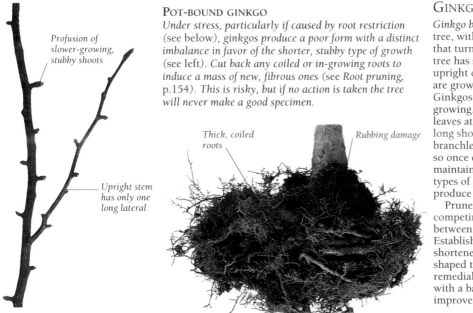

Profusion of slower-growing, stubby shoots

Upright stem has only one long lateral

Thick, coiled roots

Rubbing damage

POT-BOUND GINKGO

Under stress, particularly if caused by root restriction (see below), ginkgos produce a poor form with a distinct imbalance in favor of the shorter, stubby type of growth (see left). Cut back any coiled or in-growing roots to induce a mass of new, fibrous ones (see Root pruning, p.154). This is risky, but if no action is taken the tree will never make a good specimen.

GINKGO BILOBA

Ginkgo biloba is an elegant deciduous tree, with bright green, fan-shaped leaves that turn butter-yellow in autumn. The tree has several variants, with either upright or semipendulous branches: all are grown as central-leader standards. Ginkgos form two kinds of shoot: slow-growing, short, spurlike growths with leaves at the tip, and rapidly growing, long shoots with well-spaced, alternate branchlets that become upright or nearly so once established. A healthy tree maintains a balance between these two types of growth; a tree under stress may produce unbalanced growth (*see left*).

Prune young trees only to remove competing leaders when dormant between autumn and early spring. Established trees dislike pruning, and shortened shoots often die back. Poorly shaped trees can rarely be improved by remedial pruning, but feeding in spring with a balanced general fertilizer may improve growth.

TRAINING AND PRUNING

Timing is important when pruning conifers. Many are very resinous, and bleed copiously when cut. Bleeding is most profuse during active growth, which begins in early spring, often with a second flush in summer, so do not prune at these times. Pruning in autumn to midwinter keeps bleeding to a minimum.

TRAINING A LEADER

Most conifers produce a strong central leader, and many naturally re-form a leading shoot if damaged in juvenility or early maturity. If damage occurs, select and train in a replacement leader as soon as possible (*see below*). In most species, it is unusual for dual leaders to form in response to damage when young. A leader lost later in life, however, often results in the formation of dual leaders, particularly as many conifers produce shoots in "whorls" – clusters of three or more, arising at about the same point on the stem. Many pines produce dual leaders in response to damage, even when young. Remove one (*see right*) to produce a single-stemmed tree and to avoid dangerous narrow forks at maturity.

Not all conifers have a single main stem. *Metasequoia glyptostroboides* often develops multiple leaders but continues to form an upright tree without intervention. Some shrublike conifers, including many junipers, are grown for their tight habit. If they develop a loose upper canopy with several leaders, tie these in with rubber tree ties or with netting to maintain a dense habit, and to protect them from snow or wind damage. (*Continued on p.42.*)

DWARF CONIFERS

Dwarf conifers are propagated vegetatively from sports (natural mutations) of the "normal" tree. Sports are often selected for a prostrate, congested, or fastigiate habit, or, in many dwarf conifers, for the retention of soft, needlelike juvenile foliage that differs markedly from the more scalelike leaves of the adult plant. Pruning is usually unnecessary. Sometimes, however, the plant produces growth that reverts to the normal habit – strongly upright shoots on a prostrate plant, for example (*see right*) – which spoils the form and may eventually become dominant. All such reverted growth must be cut out to maintain the distinctive shape and habit for which the plant has been selected.

REMOVING REVERTED GROWTH
Cut out at the point of origin any shoot that exhibits atypical growth, masking the cut within the remaining foliage.

COMPETING LEADER
To maintain a single-stemmed, central-leader tree, it is essential to remove competing leaders as soon as possible. Cut out the weaker or more crooked shoot cleanly at its base.

REPLACING A BROKEN LEADER

DAMAGED TREE *On young plants, a broken leader can be replaced with a strong lateral that, even if growing horizontally, can be tied in to assume the dominant, vertical role.*

1 Remove all damaged growth, cutting it back cleanly to a strong shoot, preferably of upright habit, that can be trained to replace it. The resulting small wound will heal quickly.

2 Insert a stake carefully through the center of the tree, or tie it to the main stem. Tie in the replacement shoot. Remove the stake once the new leader is growing strongly upward.

(Continued from p.41.) Some conifers, such as *Cedrus deodara*, produce a pendulous leading shoot, known as a "dropper." During rapid growth the terminal bud is "lowered" and protected by several lateral buds. At the end of the growing season, the shoot straightens and the leading bud resumes its place at the top of the vertical shoot. Do not prune or straighten a dropper; in most cases, this will suppress growth.

CLEARING THE TRUNK

Before clearing the trunk, consider the ultimate shape, size, and habit of the mature tree. This will dictate the extent and height of trunk clearance. Most members of the Cupressaceae, and species such as *Abies lasiocarpa* that produce a skirt of foliage to the ground, are best with lower branches retained. Conifers such as *Pinus bungeana* have beautiful bark, but make unattractive "lollipop" trees if cleared too high. Thin the lowest whorls of branches so that the bark can be seen without spoiling the overall form of the tree at maturity. Spruces with a semipendulous or pendulous habit, such as *Picea abies* and *P. breweriana*, need the lowest whorls of branches removed so that the remaining foliage is just clear of the ground. Many others need a taller clear trunk to show off their form. Once the tree is growing strongly, clear the first 3ft (1m) as the tree reaches 8–10ft (2.5–3m) tall, cutting branchlets cleanly back to the trunk to leave small scars that will heal quickly. Over the next few years, clear the trunk to 6ft (2m), then proceed according to the height of the mature tree; one that reaches 70ft (20m), for example, looks well with a trunk of 12–20ft (4–6m). With maturity,

---

HARD PRUNING

Conifers that respond well to pruning back into older wood include:
CEPHALOTAXUS
CRYPTOMERIA
CUNNINGHAMIA
SEQUOIA
TAXUS
TORREYA
and young specimens of:
ARAUCARIA
METASEQUOIA
TAXODIUM
Most of the Cupressaceae, including *Chamaecyparis*, *Cupressus*, and *Thuja*, respond well to regular trimming of young growth, and can be trimmed as formal hedges (*see p.44*), provided that training and pruning is initiated from the start; as with many other conifers, they will not break from older wood.

DEALING WITH SPLAYED-OUT GROWTH

1 Wind, heavy snow or ice, or occasionally the weight of an upright branch, may cause growth to splay out. Check that the branch has not split; if undamaged, it can be tied back in.

2 Tie the growth in, using soft material in case the tie is forgotten as growth extends. Use soft tarred twine, a rubber tree tie, or, ideally, nylon tights or a stocking.

DEALING WITH DEAD PATCHES

1 Remove completely all shoots bearing dead or scorched foliage (inset). Unless the damage is very minimal, this will leave an unsightly hole, especially in formally shaped trees and hedges.

2 Insert a stake into the body of the tree, tying it securely to a main stem or branch, then draw neighboring branches over and tie them in. Though the stake may be temporarily visible, new growth will soon disguise it and the hole.

THINNING

To thin congested growth, first clear away dead matter and other debris, then remove crowded shoots cleanly at their bases, thus disguising the cuts within the foliage. Avoid exposing bare, brown inner branches, since they seldom produce new shoots.

many conifers lose their lowest whorls of branches naturally by "shading out." All dead or dying branches should be removed as seen.

CONGESTION

Many conifers accumulate dead wood, produce congested growth, and hold leaf litter within the canopy. This is often unattractive, and may increase the risk of winter damage by trapping heavy snowfall. In highly resinous species, the accumulation of debris can pose a fire risk in hot summers, especially in dry climates. All dead material should be removed regularly. Where branch whorls are very congested, judicious thinning (see facing page, below) will reduce the risk of snow damage. On mature trees this is best done by a professional arborist.

SNOW AND WIND DAMAGE

Conifers grown for their tight form can be damaged by the effects of wind and snow. Remove lying snow to avoid the risk of damage and splaying out of branches. Splayed-out growth can be tied in (see facing page, above). If the branch is broken, remove it, and, to disguise the gap, reposition adjacent branches and tie them in using rubber tree ties or soft tarred twine. This avoids exposing internal branches only partially clothed with foliage, which seldom resprout. If damage is confined to the extremities of the branch, remove only the affected growth and allow unaffected branches to grow out to restore the shape. Patches of dieback or wind scorch can be remedied in a similar way (see facing page, center), but can be more difficult to deal with, since damage occurs (and may recur) on the colder, more exposed side of the plant. Cold and exposure inhibit the regrowth that is necessary to restore the canopy. Young trees may be best moved to a more sheltered situation. Otherwise, provide extra wind protection, perhaps by planting shelter plants or erecting a temporary screen, as they regrow.

RENOVATION

With a few exceptions (see Hard pruning, facing page), conifers do not regenerate freely from old wood and, in most cases, renovation is limited to the removal of dead or dying branches. Where trees have become too tall for their situation, removal and replacement is the best option. Removal of the top usually results in a mutilated appearance. Many of the Cupressaceae tolerate hard clipping of young growth, and new growth will rapidly mask the cuts. Yew (Taxus baccata) does tolerate hard pruning, but then needs careful shaping to restore its form.

PALMS AND PALMLIKE PLANTS

Palms need minimal training, and little or no pruning. They grow from the center of their single or several stems, and if the growing tip is removed, the palm dies; there are no growth buds lower down on the stem. It is, therefore, difficult to restrict size by pruning. In cool climates, many palms are grown as young plants in the home or greenhouse. If they become too large, they are usually discarded; new plants are easily grown from seed. With suckering palms, such as Chamaerops, height and spread can be controlled removing very tall or excess suckers. Some, such as Chamaedorea elegans, produce aerial roots on the stem. Reduce height by air-layering the stem, then replanting the rooted top.

GROOMING PALM TRUNKS

Most palms benefit from "grooming" to remove dead leaves. In cool climates, this is done mainly for cosmetic effect. In hot climates it is more important, since an accumulation of dead leaf bases can be a fire hazard. Where dead leaves persist, cut them off close to their base at any time of year, leaving the stubs to create a neat pattern. Do not cut them right back to the stem; a naked stem is unsightly and more susceptible to damage. Wear sturdy gloves, especially for those with spiny leaf bases, such as Livistona australis. Many palms produce a protective fibrous covering on the trunk, which is also best left in place; it will be shed naturally as the plant matures.

REMOVING SPENT YUCCA FLOWER
Remove spent flower spikes in spring, cutting them back close to their point of origin in the center of the rosette.

CUTTING BACK DEAD PALM LEAVES
Cut dead leaf bases back almost to the stem to leave a neat stub. Do not overclean the stem by removing all vestiges of the leaf.

PALMLIKE PLANTS

A number of plants resemble palms in that they bear their leaves in rosettes, either basally or at the tips of stems. They include aloes, agaves, cordylines, phormiums, and yuccas. They do not, however, produce all growth from a single growing point, and often possess dormant buds that produce shoots after damage or pruning, forming new rosettes lower on the stem. In general, they need pruning only to remove dead leaves, or to cut out faded flower stems.

Cordylines and yuccas sometimes suffer frost damage when grown at their limits of hardiness. When any danger of hard frost has passed and new growth begins to appear in spring, cut damaged branches back to just above the newly formed shoots. Apply a balanced fertilizer and a mulch to help produce vigorous new growth. Both genera respond well to hard pruning and renovation; cut back to suitable sideshoots or basal shoots, or even to ground level, if necessary. To create a multibranched specimen, remove the growing point before growth begins, then feed and mulch.

Rosette-forming plants such as agaves and aloes readily produce new offsets to replace damaged growth. Remove over-large or damaged offsets carefully to avoid breaking the new shoots that are growing underneath. Alternatively, root young offsets as cuttings and discard the mother plant.

The pruning of slow-growing plants, such as the cycads, Pandanus, and Xanthorrhoea, is best restricted to the removal of dead leaves and spent flower stems. They may produce new growth, but recovery is very slow.

HEDGES

Hedges and screens play an important role in the structure and character of a garden, as well as having a variety of practical uses. Hedges provide privacy, create boundaries, and screen unsightly views. They can provide shelter from wind or strong sun, and filter out noise and dust from nearby roads. Hedges may also provide food and shelter for wildlife. The types of plants you choose will depend on the style of the garden, and the size, position, and purpose of the planned hedge. Is it to be informal or formal, evergreen or deciduous, flowering or not? A hedge is a long-term project, so it is vital to make the right choice from the wide range of suitable trees and shrubs. Make sure that your chosen species is suited to your climate, site, and soil, and keep plants growing vigorously and evenly by good soil preparation and cultivation.

FLOWERING HEDGE
This attractive Chaenomeles bears flowers and fruit on lateral shoots from old wood. Trimming to shape the hedge encourages the production of more flowering and fruiting spurs. In some cases, as with holly (Ilex), berries will be sacrificed by pruning.

INITIAL PRUNING AND TRAINING

Consider the desired height and spread of the hedge, and the speed of growth of your chosen species. Fast-growing plants provide rapid results, but in general slow-growing plants live longer, make dense hedges, and, when established, do not need such frequent clipping.

Evergreen hedges eventually provide privacy, shelter, and a uniform backdrop to other plantings throughout the year. However, although a deciduous hedge may be bare and leafless in winter, most species will still "filter" wind, providing a degree of shelter. In very exposed sites, this filtering effect can have advantages over dense, thick evergreens, which may

cause strong winds to "jump" the hedge and swirl violently beyond it.

Deciduous species offer a changing display throughout the year, attractive in spring and summer when in full leaf, perhaps with the additional ornamental value of flowers and fruit. Some hedging plants, such as *Fagus sylvatica*, have leaves that change color in autumn and do not fall, persisting through the winter. A number of deciduous species, such as fuchsia, can provide temporary or seasonal hedging. In areas where they are marginally hardy, they will die back in winter but will produce long flowering displays throughout the season.

STARTING A HEDGE
Buying plants in bulk usually entails accepting a "mixed bag" of young specimens. Do not try to prune each for balanced regrowth; simply alternate weaker plants with strong ones. If possible, do not stake hedging plants. If in a very exposed, windy site, use posts and wires (see left), positioned on the windward side of the plants, so that they are not blown against the wire, risking damage to the bark.

PRUNING ON PLANTING
Prepare the ground to a width of 2–3ft (60–90cm). Space plants 1–2ft (30–60cm) apart, depending on the vigor of the chosen species. For dwarf hedges space plants about 4–6in (10–15cm) apart. Plant in straight lines: staggered double rows are not now recommended, because growth becomes crowded and dead wood can accumulate.

The degree of pruning on planting depends very much on the chosen plants and the desired effect. Flowering shrubs for an informal hedge can be pruned lightly as for freestanding specimens (*see p.155*). Most evergreens also need only minimal pruning; shorten only overlong lateral shoots in the first few years (*see also* Evergreen trees, *p.27*). Let leaders grow on to the desired height.

For more formal shaping, prune plants such as beech (*Fagus*) and hornbeam (*Carpinus*) moderately to stimulate balanced regrowth. Do not simply "even up" young plants; you are likely to induce the reverse effect. Prune strong shoots lightly and weak ones hard. Shorten vigorous leaders and laterals by no more than one-third and weaker growth by up to two-thirds of its length.

Vigorous plants with a strongly upright habit, such as privet (*Ligustrum*) and hawthorn (*Crataegus*), need hard pruning to encourage growth to bush out at the base. Cut them back to within 6–12in (15–30cm) of ground level in late spring, and clip back laterals again in late summer. During the second winter or early spring, cut back hard again, removing at least half of the previous season's growth.

Establishing and maintaining hedges

Once hedging plants are established, regular pruning or clipping must be initiated and maintained to form a balanced outline and to keep growth dense and healthy. The frequency, timing, and degree of pruning depend mainly on the style of hedge and the species chosen.

INFORMAL HEDGES

An informal hedge is basically a screen of small trees or, more commonly, shrubs. The timing and techniques of pruning, if required, are much the same as for individual specimens. The main difference is that regular pruning should be accompanied by gentle shaping of the outline. Remove misplaced growths, and trim back annually to keep within bounds. For flowering and fruiting hedges, the timing of pruning is critical if the next season's display is not to be spoiled.

SEMIFORMAL HEDGES

Evergreens suitable for semiformal hedges, such as *Prunus lusitanica*, *Aucuba*, and *Garrya*, need only minimal pruning (*see* Evergreen trees, p.27, and Evergreen shrubs, p.157) to create solid but natural-looking shapes and outlines. Many have large, glossy leaves that are spoiled by cutting with hedge trimmers or shears; the cut leaves will turn brown and become unsightly. In these cases, trim with pruners (*see right*) and, if necessary, a pruning saw.

For flowers and fruit, choose shrubs such as *Pyracantha*, *Forsythia*, and *Chaenomeles*, which bear their flowers on laterals or spurs from older wood, rather than terminally on growth that will be removed by trimming.

FORMAL HEDGES

Plants used for formal hedges must have a dense habit of growth and be tolerant of close clipping. The aims of pruning and training are to ensure dense growth from the base to the top, and to produce a neat outline.

From the early stages, the hedge sides should be cut at a slight angle (known as the "slope"), with the base as the widest point. The aim is to produce a tapered outline, with a flat or gently rounded top, which will be less vulnerable to damage by snow or strong winds. Snow will fall away down the sides of a tapered hedge; high winds will be deflected down its sloping sides, thus causing minimal damage to the hedge. In addition, a slope permits more even distribution of light from the top to the bottom, reducing foliage loss at the base from "shading out." Dwarf hedges and parterre plantings (continued on p.46)

INFORMAL HEDGE

This fuchsia hedge will provide color throughout summer, but offers no interest when it dies back in winter. Many gardeners are willing to accept a dull winter appearance in order to enjoy the changing seasonal displays offered by flowering deciduous hedges.

SEMIFORMAL HEDGE

Hedges with large, shiny leaves, such as laurel, should be trimmed with pruners. Ideally, individual shoots should be cut back to within the foliage canopy to disguise the pruning wounds. Pruning with a hedge trimmer or shears will damage the leaves and cause unsightly browning. Since the foliage is the main feature of many formal evergreen hedges, it is important to keep it neat.

FORMAL HEDGE SHAPES

This hornbeam hedge has been pruned to taper at the top, making sure that light reaches its lower flanks.

This yew has been cut into a classic formal A-shape, tapering gently to a neat, flat top.

Sloping sides and a rounded top give this conifer hedge a softer, but still very neat, outline.

(continued from p.45) do not need a slope and look best with vertical sides.

A level top is achieved by cutting to a straightedge or garden line stretched between stakes. It is important to use a guide when clipping low hedges too, since unevenness is just as visible when looking down as when viewing from eye level. Conifers and many evergreens increase their height only by means of their apical shoots, so in most cases, only the laterals are pruned in the formative years. Do not shape the top until the desired height is reached.

MAINTENANCE

Once the size and slope have been achieved, the hedge simply needs trimming to shape, using a straightedge or garden line as a guide. Most formal hedges are trimmed twice annually: when dormant and in midsummer for deciduous hedges; in late spring and late summer for evergreens. Yew (*Taxus*) needs only one summer clipping. For most conifer hedges, this regular trimming is particularly important to maintain a dense surface, since shoots seldom break freely from older wood.

Most formal hedges are cut with shears or an electric trimmer. Make sure that electric trimmers are fitted with a ground fault circuit interrupter, and do not use them in damp conditions. Avoid lifting an electric trimmer above shoulder height; use a sturdy stepladder or scaffolding when cutting tall hedges. Always wear gloves and goggles (*see also* Tools and equipment, *p.17*).

To maintain strong, even growth, all hedges need an annual application of balanced fertilizer and mulch in spring.

TRIMMING HEDGES

USING SHEARS *When using shears to trim a hedge, keep the blades parallel to the line of the hedge to make sure that the surfaces of the top and sides are cut level and flat.*

USING A TRIMMER *If you use an electric trimmer, keep the blade parallel to the hedge and use a wide, sweeping action so that you do not cut into the hedge and damage the outline.*

SHAPING A HEDGE

USING A LINE *To achieve a level top, stretch a taut string horizontally between two upright posts to act as a guideline for the highest point of the hedge, then cut the top of the hedge along this line.*

USING A TEMPLATE *To taper the top, cut a template of the required shape. Place the template on the hedge and cut, following the line of the template, moving it along as you proceed. Then cut the sides.*

CHANGING DISPLAY *Once the catkins fade, Garrya elliptica can be formally clipped.*

RECOMMENDED HEDGING PLANTS

EVERGREEN, FORMAL
CARISSA
ELAEAGNUS
ESCALLONIA
EUONYMUS
GRISELINIA
ILEX
LAURUS
LONICERA NITIDA
MYOPORUM
OSMANTHUS
  DELAVAYI
PHILLYREA
PRUNUS
  LAUROCERASUS,
  P. LUSITANICA
For conifers,
  see p.40.
 	
**EVERGREEN,
SEMIFORMAL**
ACACIA
ACALYPHA
ACMENA
ATRIPLEX
AUCUBA
	BERBERIS DARWINII,
	  B. X STENOPHYLLA
	BOUVARDIA
	BRUNFELSIA
	CARISSA
	CASSINIA
	CEANOTHUS
	COTONEASTER
	  LACTEUS,
	  C. STERNIANUS
	DESFONTAINEA
	DURANTA
	GARRYA ELLIPTICA,
	  G. X THURETII
	MURRAYA
	MYOPORUM
	NANDINA
	OLEARIA
	PIERIS
	TAMARIX
	
	DECIDUOUS, FORMAL
	ACER CAMPESTRE
	CARPINUS
	FAGUS SYLVATICA
	LIGUSTRUM
		**DECIDUOUS,
		SEMIFORMAL**
		ALNUS
		CORYLUS
		COTONEASTERS
		PRUNUS X BLIREANA,
		  P. CERASIFERA
		  'PISSARDII' and
		  var. 'NIGRA'
		
		FLOWERING HEDGES
		BERBERIS
		CAMELLIA
		CHOISYA
		ESCALLONIA
		FORSYTHIA
		FUCHSIA
		IXORA
		GREVILLEA
		HIBISCUS
		MYRTUS
		OLEANDER
		RIBES
		ROSA
		TAMARIX
		VIBURNUM
			FRUITING HEDGES
			ARONIA
			PYRACANTHA
			ROSA RUGOSA
			SYMPHORICARPOS
			
			BARRIER HEDGING
			BERBERIS (some)
			CHAENOMELES
			ILEX
			PONCIRUS
			PRUNUS SPINOSA
			PYRACANTHA
			ULEX
			
			**DWARF
			HEDGES/EDGING**
			BUXUS
			DAPHNE MEZEREUM
			LAVANDULA
			PODOCARPUS ALPINUS
			ROSMARINUS
			SANTOLINA
			SARCOCOCCA
			RHODODENDRONS
			  (dwarf)

RENOVATION

Given regular maintenance and feeding, most hedges will remain healthy and in good shape for many years. In time, however, hedges may gradually edge their way beyond bounds, obscuring pathways, encroaching on a border, or becoming too tall and casting shade on other parts of the garden.

A number of hedging plants respond very well to hard renovation pruning, even when they have been neglected and become severely overgrown. They include beech (*Fagus*), hawthorn (*Crataegus*), hornbeam (*Carpinus*), holly (*Ilex*), *Lonicera nitida*, and yew (*Taxus*). The renovation of most conifer hedges (*see right*) is limited to the tying-over and patching of holes (*see p.41*), and in the long term it may be better to consider removing and replacing them with young plants.

WHEN TO RENOVATE
For best results, deciduous hedges should be renovated in midwinter, and evergreen ones in midspring. Where drastic renovation is necessary, renovate each side of the hedge in different years (*see below, left* and *center*) to avoid overstressing the plants. Reducing height (*see below right*) should also be a separate operation; allow a complete growing season for recovery. In the growing season before first pruning, feed and mulch well in spring, to encourage vigorous growth. Follow each pruning operation by a further application of fertilizer and mulch, to replenish the plants' food reserves and ensure strong

RENOVATING CONIFER HEDGES
Conifers (*see pp.40–43*) are ideal plants for hedging in many ways. However, they may pose problems if they are neglected. Initial training followed by regular trimming is especially important to maintain a dense, even surface. If neglected, the usual result is a bare, open center with a fringe of foliage at the extremities. The hedge then becomes prone to splitting or collapse in heavy snow or strong winds. A few conifers, especially yew (*Taxus*), respond well to hard pruning, but many do not readily produce shoots from old wood. Branches can be tied over to conceal holes (*see p.41*), but in the long term, replacement will eventually become necessary.

SECTION THROUGH CONIFER HEDGE
Regularly trimmed conifers have a dense, even surface, but are leafless within; most will not produce new shoots from this old, bare wood.

regrowth. The surfaces that are not subjected to hard renovation pruning should be pruned in the usual way.

RESTORING THE OUTLINE
To re-create a dense, even surface, both the top and sides of the hedge need to be cut back to at least 6in (15cm) less than the final desired width and height. Where hedges are very thin and patchy, it may be necessary to cut back almost to the main stems to stimulate more vigorous regrowth. When reducing the height of very long hedges, it may be easier to paint on an indicator line that identifies where to cut, using whitewash or a commercial white-line marker that

will not damage the plants, and which will be removed during pruning. In most cases, a straightedge or garden line should be used as a guide to reinstate the hedge's new, clean edge. When reshaping the sides, do not forget to taper them, restoring the slope (*see p.45*). To re-create a uniform surface, it is essential that each plant in the hedge is cut back to the same width. Check this at regular intervals.

Renovation pruning inevitably results in ugly, bare areas and wounds, but, provided that you feed and mulch the hedge well, regrowth should be sufficiently rapid to hide these wounds within one or two growing seasons.

REDUCING THE WIDTH OF AN OVERGROWN HEDGE

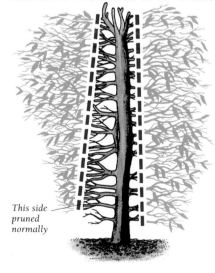

This side pruned normally

This side now cut back hard

REDUCING HEDGE HEIGHT

Top growth is thin and lanky

Hedge was shortened to here once before

FIRST YEAR *In the first year, cut one side of the hedge back hard, almost to the main stems if necessary (right side). Prune the other (left) side as is usual for the plant.*

SECOND YEAR *In the second year, the renovated surface has produced dense regrowth. Cut the unrenovated surface back hard, by the same amount as the other side.*

To re-create a dense, uniform top, reduce the height to at least 6in (15cm) below the desired height. Cut back harder where upper portions are open and patchy.

TOPIARY

A form of training to create living garden "sculpture," topiary is a garden art that has been popular since Roman times. Traditionally used to produce strongly architectural and geometric shapes in formal gardens, it has been developed to include birds, animals, and unusual, even whimsical, features such as giant chess pieces and trains.

Different styles of topiary may be used to create a variety of effects. Imaginative forms express personal style and add a humorous or bizarre touch to a garden. Using topiary for geometric shapes such as cones, obelisks, and columns provides a strong, structural element in a design. This type of topiary has uses both in formal gardens, perhaps to frame a vista or form an avenue, and in informal gardens,

as a contrasting foil for less structured planting. A hedge top can be used for topiary, clipping it into birds, spheres, or cubes, for example. Topiary is also effective in containers: use a single container plant as a centerpiece, a pair to flank a doorway, or several to line a path.

Many plants are suitable, including traditional, long-lived evergreens such as yew (*Taxus*), bay (*Laurus nobilis*), and boxwood (*Buxus*), and less common ones like *Osmanthus*, *Berberis,* and *Phillyrea*. Simple, short-lived shapes can be created using *Artemisia abrotanum* or *Santolina chamaecyparissus*. The impatient gardener can achieve almost instant topiary effects by training climbers, such as ivy (*see p.272*), on wire forms.

TOPIARY SHAPES AND EFFECTS

BASIC DESIGN
Simple geometric forms, such as a cone, obelisk, or pyramid, lend a formal elegance to the smallest garden or courtyard. They are easy and economical to produce, since they require no intricate training, and can usually be created by clipping single young specimens. Use small-leaved plants, such as boxwood or conifers, to achieve a dense surface and neat, sharp outline.

POODLE
More complex symmetrical shapes, such as the traditional tiered "cake-stand" or "poodle" topiary form, are also relatively simple to create if you have a steady hand and eye. The easiest way is to "carve" the tiers out of a bushy young shrub. A fixed-length line attached to the central stem is used as a compass, to ensure that each tier has an even circumference.

SPIRAL
A spiral effect is formed in two stages, and will take several years to complete. First train the shrub against a central stake, and clip to form a vertical cylinder. In the third year, using pruners and a wire spiral as a guide, begin shaping the spiral from the bottom up. The stakes and wires are removed when the spiral reaches its full height.

STEM EFFECTS
Eye-catching effects can be created using a combination of simple training and pruning techniques. This shrub has been trained as a standard (*see p.165*), but its young, flexible leader was first trained around a sturdy stake, so that it grew up in a spiral (*see p.51*). The formal "mop" or "lollipop" head is then shaped and kept compact by regular trimming with pruners.

NOVELTY ANIMAL
This hunting hound is one of any number of unusual designs that can be created using topiary techniques. It is formed around a permanent guide frame of chicken wire and metal laths, anchored in the ground at the hedge base, which provides both strong support and a shape toward which to work. A bundle of strong shoots is left unclipped to grow out from the hedge top. While still flexible, they are trained and tied in to the frame (*see also p.50*), and encouraged to cover the wire so that, eventually, the wire is completely disguised. The form is clipped with shears and pruners.

CLIPPING TO CREATE SHAPES

Plants used for topiary must have a dense habit, produce pliable growth, and respond well to clipping. If a close, dense surface and sharp outline is required, they should also have small leaves. It is essential to check that the species selected is suitable for your soil type and that it is completely hardy in your climate. Precise forms and close-textured surfaces are quickly spoiled by dieback caused by cold and wind damage or unsuitable soil conditions.

TRAINING AND SHAPING

Topiary requires precise clipping using techniques that are slightly different to those used for normal hedge cutting. It is important that tools are kept perfectly sharp at all times. Complex forms need a combination of clipping and training and tying in to a guide frame, preferably with tarred soft twine that will eventually rot. Take time when clipping and shaping, especially in the formative stages, and stand back frequently to check for discrepancies. Do not cut too much in one place since it may spoil the symmetry of a design for a whole season until replacement growth appears. Work from the top downward and from the center outward, moving from side to side to ensure balance and symmetry.

Rounded topiary pieces are easier to produce and maintain than sharp-edged, geometric shapes, and are usually cut freehand. To produce a sphere, first trim the top of the plant and then cut a channel down both sides around the circumference. Cut a second channel at

SIMPLE GEOMETRIC SHAPE

The simplest topiary design is one that is closest to the natural shape of the plant. This young boxwood tree is first clipped roughly into shape. In the following year, the bush is clipped into a neat cone, using stakes and wire as a guide. The finished plant needs clipping two or three times a year, depending on growth rate, to retain a sharp outline.

90° (at a right angle) to the first to leave four distinct quarters to be trimmed. Use the tips of the shears rather than the flat of the blades to cut curved surfaces.

Geometric topiary should have precise symmetry, flat, even surfaces, and sharp, angled or squared edges. However, such perfection is more difficult to form and maintain than rounded shapes. Even if you have a good eye, you will need to use levels, straightedges, guide lines,

and a plumb line for vertical surfaces to make sure the cut is precise and even. Clipping, with the flat edges of the shear blades held parallel to the surfaces, needs to be accurate in order to maintain a well-defined shape. Gradually adjusting discrepancies may entail clipping the entire surface again. Use shear tips, pruners, or single-handed trimmers to shape intricate niches and corners.

DETAILED GEOMETRICAL SHAPE USING A FRAME

1 *Make frameworks for large topiary pieces from strong materials, since they will be in place for many years, perhaps permanently. Clip a young plant (a yew is shown here) as necessary to keep it within the framework.*

2 *Pinch out shoot tips until the entire frame is filled with bushy growth. Then clip to shape in late summer, following the outline of the framework and pinching shoots that do not yet extend beyond it to encourage density.*

3 *When mature, the plant will form a dense bush and cover the framework. It needs regular clipping, at least twice during the growing season, following the lines of the frame to maintain the precise outline of the design.*

TRAINING TO PRODUCE IRREGULAR SHAPES

The forming of complex designs is limited only by the gardener's patience and imagination. Intricate forms need a combination of clipping and intensive training, and may take several years to complete. It is, however, very rewarding to watch the gradual growth and development of the final form.

Irregular topiary designs need a sturdy framework that will be used as a guide form to train and tie in to, as a template for clipping, and as a support for the finished sculpture. Use strong materials such as metal laths or heavy-duty fencing wire to form a "skeleton," and chicken wire and finer gauge wire to form more precise detail. For free-standing or hedge-top forms, anchor the framework firmly into the ground. Use temporary stakes and lines as necessary during formative shaping. To tie in shoots, use tarred soft twine that will eventually rot away. Avoid using wire to tie in since it may eventually constrict stems as they increase in girth. For intricate clipping, use shear tips, pruners, or single-handed trimmers.

Whether working to a design from scratch, or adding to an existing hedge top, the shoots to be trained should be young and sufficiently pliable to bend around the framework. Tie them in regularly throughout the growing season, and check previous ties to make sure that they are not rubbing or constricting growth. As shoots reach the desired length, pinch out their tips to encourage branching. Use the resulting sideshoots to fill in the body of the design. It is best to select only well-placed young shoots to fill in, and to cut or rub out the remainder at an early stage. If left to develop, they may have to be pruned out at a later stage, thus leaving awkward gaps or holes.

CREATING A TOPIARY BIRD

FINISHED BIRD *Topiary birds and animals are most successful if the outline is stylized and simple, since this makes clipping more feasible. Aim to produce a characteristic pose rather than fine detail.*

1 In the first year, insert a fan-shaped stake support at an angle to form the tail. Select well-placed shoots and train and tie them in to the stakes with soft twine. Tip back weaker shoots to stimulate their growth.

2 During the growing season, prune back the trained-in shoots by up to one-third of their length, cutting to a leaf, to encourage dense, compact growth that will form a solid mass of foliage without holes or gaps.

3 In the second year, insert a supporting stake for the head. Select three strong shoots, and tie them to the stake to start forming the head. Trim the tail and pinch out shoots on the body. Unwanted shoots can be removed, as here, or (right) brought across to bulk out the tail.

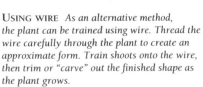

USING WIRE *As an alternative method, the plant can be trained using wire. Thread the wire carefully through the plant to create an approximate form. Train shoots onto the wire, then trim or "carve" out the finished shape as the plant grows.*

4 In the third year, tie down the strongest shoot at the head to form the curve of the beak. Continue trimming to gradually shape the body more precisely and to keep the tail growth dense. Once the shape is formed, clip regularly, at least twice during the growing season.

ORNAMENTAL STEM EFFECTS

A "mop-head" standard, such as those made of boxwood, bay (*Laurus nobilis*), or weeping fig (*Ficus benjamina*), can be enhanced by special stem effects. These add a novel dimension to plain, formal heads of foliage. Attractive forms, like the spiral "barleysugar" stem or braided stems shown right, are easily created using simple training techniques on flexible young stems. To form a barleysugar stem, train one or two young shoots around a strong cylindrical pole. Braided stems are formed simply by plaiting three young stems together. They will eventually form a strong natural graft, fusing where they touch, but will need the support of a strong stake until growth hardens sufficiently to support itself.

PRODUCING TRAINED STEM EFFECTS

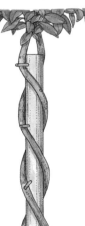

BARLEYSUGAR STEM *Use a sturdy wooden pole with dowel pegs inserted in a spiral along its length. Train one or two stems around the pole, holding them in place by looping them beneath the dowels. Remove the pegs and the pole in sections when stem growth has hardened.*

BRAIDED STEM *Form a braided stem simply by braiding together three flexible young shoots. Select the strongest three on a multistemmed young plant, and remove the remainder. Single-stemmed plants can be cut back hard to produce multiple stems (see p.30).*

MAINTAINING TOPIARY

Once a topiary feature is established, it will need frequent routine clipping during the growing season. The time between cuts will depend on the rate of growth, and on the vigor of the species. An intricate, geometric design in boxwood may need to be cut at four- to six-week intervals. Trim as soon as any new growth begins to appear uneven.

If a perfect finish is not required throughout the year, two cuts during the growing season are usually sufficient for a shaped effect, depending on the plant used. Yew, for example, needs to be cut only once a year, boxwood (depending on the cultivar) usually needs to be cut twice, and *Lonicera nitida* three times.

Clip plants at the appropriate time of year. Do not clip bushes after early autumn since any young shoots produced in response will not ripen

sufficiently to withstand low winter temperatures. In warm climates where growth may be almost continuous, regular trimming will be needed.

Weeding, watering, and mulching are vital to keep topiary in good condition. Since clipping is intensive, it is important to apply additional balanced fertilizer two or three times during the growing season to ensure vigorous regrowth.

In regions that experience regular snowfall, topiary forms should be netted in winter to prevent splaying out and breakage of branches under the weight of snow. Brush snow off all flat surfaces to take the weight off the plant.

RENOVATION

With regular attention to clipping, feeding, mulching, and watering, most problems can be avoided. Where

renovation becomes necessary, however, it will only be successful for species that regenerate freely from old wood, such as boxwood (*see below left*).

If topiary specimens have been left unclipped for one or two years, regular clipping should restore the original form within the season. Where topiary has been neglected for several years, the shape may have been lost. Prune hard in the first spring to restore the outline, and clip more precisely in the following two or three seasons to restore a dense, even surface. Feed with a balanced fertilizer and water the plant thoroughly to aid its recovery.

DAMAGED GROWTH

If a leader, a section, or a branch has been damaged or broken, cut it back cleanly with pruners. Alternatively, it may be possible to manipulate nearby shoots by tying them in to fill the gap (*see Conifers, p.42*). Where damage is severe, and the shape has been badly disfigured, it may take several years before regrowth is sufficient to repair the damage. In this case, especially where designs are abstract or free-form, it may be possible to form a new design out of the remains of the old one, thus avoiding the problem of gaps in the original shape.

The foliage of some evergreens may be scorched or die back in hard winters. New growth in spring will usually disguise the damage, but trim it back if it is unsightly, carefully following the outline of the shape as closely as possible. Occasionally, shoots will not regenerate to fill gaps. If growth is poor or slow, check for pests or diseases and take appropriate action, or consider whether damage to the root system is being caused by poor drainage or other unsuitable conditions.

RESTORING BOXWOOD TOPIARY

DAMAGED GROWTH *If dead patches appear in established topiary forms, they must be cut back hard to healthy living wood. Check that pests, diseases, or unsuitable soil conditions are not the cause; if so, they must be rectified.*

REPLACEMENT GROWTH *Provided that the plant is well fed and watered, new shoots emerge on old wood when cut back hard. It will take several years to restore the original form if damage is extensive, as shown here.*

DICTIONARY OF ORNAMENTAL TREES

A

ACACIA FLOWERS
Deadheading a young acacia with pruners after flowering directs the plant's energy into the production of compact, branching growth.

ACACIA MIMOSA, WATTLE

Trees or large shrubs that are valued for their delicate foliage and fragrant clusters of soft, fluffy, usually yellow flowerheads, mostly borne in late winter and early spring on wood formed in the previous growing season. In frost-free climates acacias are used as specimen plants and as hedges and windbreaks. In general, no acacias are cold-hardy, although *A. dealbata* and *A. baileyana* can be grown outdoors in zones 9 and 10. Acacias are also excellent greenhouse plants.

WHEN TO PRUNE Soon after flowering. Remove frost-damaged growth in late spring once prolonged frosts are past.

TRAINING AND PRUNING Train as central-leader standards (*see p.28*), clearing the trunk to 3–6ft (1–2m). Vigorous species (*A. longifolia, A. dealbata*) may be cut back hard when young to form multi-stemmed trees (*see p.30*), suitable for growing in the shelter of a wall.
  Prune young plants after flowering, cutting to a sideshoot or to two or three buds beyond the spent flowered shoot to encourage compact growth. Prune *A. dealbata* directly after flowering.
  Keep pruning of established plants to a minimum. *A. cultriformis, A. saligna,* and *A. verticillata,* however, tolerate moderate clipping and may be used as informal hedges (*see p.44*). Most acacias resent hard pruning and cannot be renovated successfully. Suckering species, which include *A. dealbata* and *A. melanoxylon,* may regenerate.

ACER MAPLE

Useful and ornamental trees valued for their autumn foliage color and delicate flowers. Many of the smaller maples branch low, a habit that is also induced by pruning. Those with attractive bark are usually grown with clear trunks. Snakebark maples are prone to canker; affected growth must be cut out if possible.

WHEN TO PRUNE Winter, when fully dormant; maples "bleed" sap badly at other times. Small cuts, to remove reverted shoots, for example, may safely be made in late summer/early autumn.

A. DAVIDII (ZONES 6–8)

PÈRE DAVID'S MAPLE, SNAKEBARK MAPLE

Elegant, deciduous tree with white-striped green or purplish bark and handsome foliage, coloring orange and yellow in autumn.

15 | 50
m | ft

TRAINING AND PRUNING Train as a central-leader standard (*see p.28*), then let the tree branch naturally at 3–5ft (1–1.5m), or prune to form a multistemmed tree on a low trunk (*see below*). Clear the trunk or trunks to about 5ft (1.5m) to display the bark. As the crown develops, remove crossing shoots and twiggy growth that obscure the bark on the trunk and main branches. Established trees need minimal pruning. Renovation is rarely successful: hard pruning seldom produces shoots that are strong enough to form a new branch framework.

A. NEGUNDO (ZONES 2–9)

BOX ELDER, MANITOBA MAPLE

20 | 70
m | ft

Spreading, deciduous tree with yellow-green or reddish flowers. Golden-leaved or variegated cultivars may be coppiced or pollarded for larger leaves (*see facing page and p.36*).

TRAINING AND PRUNING Train as a central-leader standard (*see p.28*) with a clear trunk of 5–6ft (1.5–2m). As the crown develops, the leader will naturally lose dominance. No further special pruning is required. Remove any green shoots on variegated cultivars. If epicormic shoots develop where wind-damaged branches are removed, retain only one or two to develop into replacement branches.

A. SACCHARINUM (ZONES 3–9)

SILVER MAPLE

30 | 100
m | ft

Large, deciduous tree with a graceful habit. Its brittle branches may be damaged by strong winds.

TRAINING AND PRUNING Train as a central-leader standard (*see p.28*) with a clear trunk of 6–8ft (2–2.5m) to display the bark and allow the branches to form "skirts" around the trunk. Retain the leader for as long as possible, removing any competing shoots. Lightly thin established trees every three to five years to reduce wind and ice damage.

PRUNING TO FORM A MULTISTEMMED TREE ON A LOW TRUNK (ACER DAVIDII)

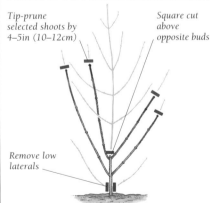

Tip-prune selected shoots by 4–5in (10–12cm)

Square cut above opposite buds

Remove low laterals

YEAR 1, WINTER *Prune a young feathered tree to about 20in (50cm) above two pairs of strong shoots. Remove lower laterals and prune the selected shoots to induce branching.*

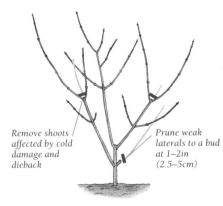

Remove shoots affected by cold damage and dieback

Prune weak laterals to a bud at 1–2in (2.5–5cm)

YEAR 2, WINTER *Young maples are prone to dieback and cold damage: cut it out, pruning to healthy buds or to the shoot's point of origin. To stimulate weak stems, prune hard.*

POLLARDED ACER NEGUNDO
Cut back to a framework in winter for larger leaves and a shrubby habit. Variegated cultivars grown from cuttings may be less prone to reversion than grafted plants.

OTHER MAPLES
A. CAMPESTRE Training should consist only of staking and the removal of badly placed or crossing shoots. When established, keep pruning to a minimum.
A. CIRCINATUM As for *A. campestre*.
A. GRISEUM As for *A. davidii*.
A. JAPONICUM As for *A. campestre*.
A. PALMATUM As for *A. campestre*.
A. PENSYLVANICUM As for *A. davidii*.
A. PLATANOIDES Although seedlings develop naturally as central-leader standards, train grafted garden cultivars to form compact branched-head standards (*see p.28*) with clear trunks of 4½–6ft (1.35–2m). When established, keep pruning to a minimum. Remove green shoots on variegated cultivars. Renovation is rarely successful.
A. PSEUDOPLATANUS As for *A. platanoides*
A. RUBRUM As for *A. saccharinum*.
A. RUFINERVE As for *A. davidii*.
A. SACCHARUM As for *A. saccharinum*.
A. SEMPERVIRENS As for *A. campestre*.
A. TATARICUM subsp. GINNALA As for *A. campestre*.

AESCULUS *HORSE CHESTNUT, BUCKEYE*

Deciduous, large trees and big, shrubby, suckering species. The trees are trained as central-leader standards from seedlings or grafted cultivars. Early training is crucial to form a strong structure that will support the heavy, spreading branches. Allow plenty of space for larger species; they are often lopped, ruining their form, having been misplaced in small gardens.

A. HIPPOCASTANUM (ZONES 3–7)

COMMON HORSE CHESTNUT

Handsome, heavy branched tree with yellow- or red-centered white flower "candles" in early summer, followed (except in the double-flowered 'Baumannii') by lustrous nuts ("buckeyes") in spiny casings.

WHEN TO PRUNE After leaf-fall, from autumn until midwinter. Minor pruning may be carried out in summer.

TRAINING AND PRUNING Train as a central-leader standard (*see p.28*) with a clear trunk of 6–10ft (2–3m) or more to accommodate the downward-sweeping lower branches when mature. Maintain the central leader for as long as possible to produce a tall trunk with evenly spaced framework branches.

Keep pruning of established trees to a minimum. Epicormic shoots that develop around pruning wounds will not make sound replacement branches. Rub them out as soon as seen. On older trees, cut out any vertical shoots on horizontal branches to avoid unbalanced growth. Hard pruning should always be done by a professional arborist.

OTHER AESCULUS
A. X CARNEA As for *A. hippocastanum*. When training, remove all laterals making narrow V-angles with the main stem (*see p.12*) since this hybrid is prone to structural weaknesses. Mature trees may produce unsightly burrs (corky, cankerous growths) on the bark. Do not remove them – they will not heal well.
A. INDICA As for *A. hippocastanum*, but clear the trunk to about 5–6ft (1.5–2m). The cultivar 'Sydney Pearce' is grafted.
A. X NEGLECTA As for *A. indica*.
A. PARVIFLORA Large, suckering shrub to 10ft (3m) forming a dense thicket that may be thinned, if desired, as for the shrub *Amelanchier stolonifera* (*see p.175*).
A. TURBINATA As for *A. hippocastanum*.

Terminal flowers

Pair of opposite buds

OPPOSITE BUDS
All horse chestnuts have opposite buds; if the leader is lost and a pair of shoots develops, select one to train vertically and remove the other as soon as the new leader is established.

Remove lower shoots to clear main stems

Remove any cold damage

YEAR 3, WINTER *Remove low laterals on main stems to display the bark. If necessary, remove inward-pointing laterals from main stems to prevent overcrowding in the center.*

AILANTHUS (ZONES 4–8)

Ailanthus altissima (syn. *A. glandulosa*) is a pollution-tolerant, vigorous, upright, deciduous tree that may reach 100ft (30m), with bold leaves, gray bark, and, on female trees, red-brown fruits. Suckering and self-seeding may cause problems. Train seed-raised plants or suckers as central-leader standards (*see p.28*), pruning when dormant to produce a clear trunk of 6–10ft (2–3m). If the leader is lost or cut out, the resulting suckers can be thinned to develop a multistemmed tree. Keep pruning of mature trees to a minimum.

A. altissima responds vigorously to annual or biennial coppicing (*see p.36*), producing new shoots 6ft (2m) or more in height with large, striking leaves. To renovate, coppice and then select a single stem to train as a central leader.

OTHER ORNAMENTAL TREES
ADANSONIA Training is generally unnecessary. Established trees have no special pruning needs.

AGONIS Training is generally unnecessary and pruning when established is best kept to a minimum.

ALBIZIA *MIMOSA, SILK TREE* (ZONES 6–9)

Large, mainly semi-deciduous trees with feathery foliage and pink, yellow, or white "powder-puff" flowers. Most commonly grown species are fast-growing trees that in cool climates must be grown under glass. Warm summers are essential for reliable flowering and to ripen wood well so that it can withstand cold.

WHEN TO PRUNE Spring, as growth begins.

TRAINING AND PRUNING Train as branched-head standards, letting the leader divide, or pruning it if necessary to induce branching (*see p.28*), at 4–6ft (1.2–2m). Established trees generally need no pruning, but in colder climates frost-damaged growth may need removing in spring. *A. julibrissin* tolerates pruning to restrict size: cut back last year's growth to four or five buds, or 3–4in (7–10cm) of the old wood. It can also be pollarded (*see p.36*); if renovating this way, new shoots must be carefully selected to re-create a branch framework.

ALNUS *ALDER* (ZONES 3–7)

Small trees grown for their catkins and foliage, and for their tolerance of a wide range of soil conditions, including very wet soils. Most alders are pyramidal in habit, naturally developing straight trunks with well-spaced branches. Although usually trained with a central leader, many species, including *Alnus incana* and *A. japonica*, will naturally develop as multistemmed trees – a suitable form for informal plantings and windbreaks. *A. glutinosa*, the European alder, is a waterside tree of narrowly pyramidal habit but often multistemmed and spreading. *A. incana*, the gray alder, is similar but with gray downy leaves. Its cut-leaved cultivar 'Laciniata' and the yellow-leaved 'Aurea' may be grown from cuttings or grafted.

WHEN TO PRUNE After leaf-fall in autumn until midwinter. Minor pruning may be carried out safely in summer.

TRAINING AND PRUNING To form a central-leader standard (*see p.28*), clear the stem to 5–6ft (1.5–2m). Lower laterals are often shed naturally by *A. cordata*, *A. firma*, and *A. rubra*. With species (such as *A. incana* and *A. japonica*) that tend to branch from the base, select and train a single main stem as early as possible, if a standard is required. Otherwise, let them develop naturally as multistemmed trees or, if necessary, prune them to the base (*see p.30*) to produce this form. Established trees have no special pruning needs, but respond to hard pruning if necessary.

ARBUTUS (ZONES 7–9)

Evergreen trees with dark foliage, warm-toned bark, clusters of white flowers, and red strawberry-like fruits. Although they tolerate pruning, none transplant well, so plant as young as possible, with shelter from cold, dry winds; *Arbutus* are tender when young (but regenerate well after cold damage). They generally need minimal training. *A. menziesii*, *A. andrachne*, and *A. x andrachnoides* need firm support until well established, or they may lean over with age.

A. MENZIESII

MADRONA

One of the most attractive species, with large flower clusters and smooth, peeling, red-brown bark. It forms a tall, spreading tree with a branched head, although it often retains a central leader some way into the crown.

WHEN TO PRUNE Spring, as soon as any danger of frost is over.

TRAINING AND PRUNING Stake newly planted trees well, and allow to develop naturally, removing low laterals as for a standard tree (*see p.28*) to display the bark on the trunk, if required. Cut frost-damaged growth back hard once live growth is clearly distinguishable.

Established pruning is best kept to a minimum, although the careful removal of low branches is tolerated if a taller trunk is desired. As the tree matures, small branches within the canopy die off naturally and should be cut out as seen.

OTHER ARBUTUS
A. ANDRACHNE, A. X ANDRACHNOIDES As for *A. menziesii*.
A. UNEDO (strawberry tree) Commonly a tall shrub (which can be allowed to develop naturally), but can make a small tree in favorable climates. To produce a tree, train and prune as for *A. menziesii*.

B

BETULA *BIRCH*

Deciduous trees, popular in cooler regions for their graceful habit, autumn color, and ornamental bark. They are vulnerable to bracket and rot fungi. Hard pruning is not recommended.

WHEN TO PRUNE Birches bleed heavily; prune only when dormant, from late summer to before midwinter.

B. PAPYRIFERA (ZONES 2–6)

PAPER BIRCH, CANOE BIRCH

An elegant tree, which spreads with age and whose zigzag shoots droop at the tips. It has yellow autumn color and white peeling bark.

TRAINING AND PRUNING Train as a feathered tree (*see p.27*), or as a central-leader standard (*see p.28*) with a clear trunk of 6ft (2m). Once established, little pruning is needed. In autumn, remove twiggy shoots on the trunk and main branches that obscure the bark.

B. PENDULA (ZONES 2–6)

EUROPEAN WHITE BIRCH

Semiweeping tree with delicate foliage and silvery peeling bark, up-right when young and spreading with age, with branchlet tips that are usually pendulous. The leaves turn a fine clear yellow in autumn.

RAISING THE HEIGHT OF A NATURALLY WEEPING STANDARD (BETULA PENDULA 'TRISTIS')

It is essential to keep the leading shoot staked until the wood has hardened sufficiently for the stem to remain rigid. As the tree grows, tie the leading shoot to a vertical cane attached to the main stake. Continue tying in as growth proceeds until the leader reaches the required height. The weeping crown may then be allowed to develop naturally. Remove any low laterals that develop on the main stem.

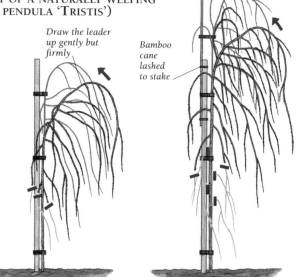

Draw the leader up gently but firmly

Bamboo cane lashed to stake

TRAINING AND PRUNING Train as a central-leader standard (*see p.28*), clearing the trunk to 6ft (2m), or as a feathered tree (*see p.27*). To create a multistemmed tree, cut back either close to ground level (*see p.30*), or to about 1–2ft (30–60cm) from the ground, as for *Acer davidii* (*see p.52*). Established trees have no special pruning needs; as for all birches, hard pruning is not recommended.

B. PENDULA 'TRISTIS' (ZONES 2–6)

WEEPING BIRCH

Narrow-crowned, elegant, strongly weeping tree, usually top-grafted at a height of about 6–7ft (2–2.2m). It is also possible to grow the tree on its own

25 | 80

m | ft

BETULA NIGRA
River birches (zones 4–9) with colored, peeling bark are striking in winter when grown with clear trunks, as multistemmed specimens (as left) or in small groups. For a group planting, place three seedlings, evenly spaced, in the same, large planting hole, and train each as a central-leader standard.

trunk, from softwood cuttings or low-grafted stocks, in which case very careful vertical training of the main stem to the required height is essential to overcome its naturally pendulous habit.

TRAINING AND PRUNING Train and, when established, maintain as a weeping standard (*see p.28*), removing any shoots below the graft union. If a taller tree is desired (*see above*), the leading shoot, which is flexible when the wood is still young, may be trained in the early years to extend the height of the trunk up to 10–12ft (3–4m).

OTHER BIRCHES
B. ALBOSINENSIS Highly ornamental, peeling orange-red bark.
B. ERMANII, B. 'INVERLEITH', B. 'JERMYNS', B. PLATYPHYLLA, B. SZECHUANICA, B. UTILIS var. JACQUEMONTII (including 'Grayswood Ghost' and 'Silver Shadow') As for *B. papyrifera*.
B. MEDWEDIEWII Naturally densely branched: no special training or pruning.
B. NIGRA As for *B. papyrifera*, although the stem frequently divides naturally at 2–3ft (60–90cm) into two to four stems, forming a multistemmed tree on a short trunk.
B. PENDULA 'YOUNGII' Deciduous, mushroom-shaped tree, commonly sold as a weeping standard top-grafted at 6–7ft (2–2.2m). Train as a weeping standard (*see p.28*). This cultivar has a strong weeping habit and, left to develop naturally, may form a squat dome that is broader than it is tall. Its height can be extended up to 25ft (8m) by vertical training of one of the leading shoots (there may be several bud-grafts), as for *B. pendula* 'Tristis' (*see above*).
B. PUBESCENS As for *B. pendula*.

BRACHYCHITON
BOTTLE TREE, FLAME TREE

Large, fast-growing, evergreen or summer-deciduous trees (sometimes with swollen trunks) that require frost-free conditions, though mature plants of some species withstand short periods of light frost (zone 10). In subtropical regions, they are grown as central-leader standards and used as shade and street trees. In cold areas, they can be grown under glass, although they need careful shaping and pruning to keep within bounds. Some flowers will be lost, since they are borne only on older wood.

WHEN TO PRUNE After flowering. Plants grown under glass may also be pruned when dormant, soon after leaf-fall.

TRAINING AND PRUNING Brachychitons usually form a naturally strong central leader, making them easy to train. They can be trained as a feathered tree (*see p.27*) or as a standard (*see p.28*), clearing the trunk gradually to about 10ft (3m). Once established, specimens grown outdoors need little further pruning. Plants grown under glass will need, and will tolerate, regular pruning as necessary to restrict their size.

OTHER ORNAMENTAL TREES
ALECTRYON Training and pruning are generally unnecessary.
ALLOCASUARINA See Casuarina, p.57.
AMHERSTIA Train as a central-leader standard (*see p.28*). Keep pruning thereafter to a minimum.
ANGOPHORA As for *Eucalyptus* (*see p.64*)
BANKSIA Tree species have no special needs, although they tolerate shaping when young. For shrub species, *see p.177*.
BARKLYA (BAUHINIA) SYRINGIFOLIA As for *Albizia julibrissin* (*see facing page*), but prune after flowering.
BAUHINIA As for *Albizia julibrissin* (*see facing page*), but prune after flowering. See also Climbing Plants, *p.263*.
BOLUSANTHUS Allow *B. speciosus* to develop either as a single-stemmed or multistemmed tree. Low laterals may be removed to clear the trunk. Pruning when established is generally unnecessary.
BOMBAX Train as a standard, allowing the leader to branch at about 6ft (2m). Established trees tolerate, but generally need, little pruning.
BROUSSONETIA As for *Morus* (*see p.76*).
BROWNEA As for *Albizia julibrissin* (*see facing page*), but prune after flowering.
BUCKINGHAMIA Train as a central-leader standard (*see p.28*). Keep pruning thereafter to a minimum.
BUTEA *B. monosperma* is best left to develop its untidy, congested habit naturally. Tolerates hard cutting back to the swollen rootstock if required.

C

CARPINUS HORNBEAM

Strong, deciduous trees with year-round interest: catkins in spring, winged fruits and foliage color in autumn, and silvered bark in winter. *Carpinus betulus*, the European hornbeam, is the most often grown. The cultivar 'Fastigiata' is conical when young, but assumes a flamelike outline with age. Hornbeams are usually grown as feathered trees or central-leader standards. Easily trained and very responsive to pruning, they are also ideal for pleaching and hedging. *C. caroliniana* branches freely from the base, so while it is ideal as a hedge, choose *C. betulus* or *C. orientalis* for pleaching or for hedges "on stilts."

WHEN TO PRUNE From late summer to midwinter, to avoid severe bleeding.

TRAINING AND PRUNING Train and prune either as feathered trees (*see p.27*) or central-leader standards (*see p.28*). Established trees need little attention. To use as a hedge, *see p.44*. To pleach, *see p.38*. *C. betulus* 'Fastigiata' looks best as a specimen central-leader standard: clear the stem to 3–6ft (1–2m).

Hornbeams tolerate hard pruning, if necessary, but this may result in twiggy growth that, while ideal for hedging, will not develop into strong replacement branches for a tree unless thinned to strong, well-spaced shoots.

CARPINUS BETULUS 'FASTIGIATA'
This upright tree should be trained and pruned as for the European hornbeam.

CARYA HICKORY

Hickories are known as typical American trees. They are relatively fast-growing and elegant and naturally develop long, straight, single trunks and shapely, full crowns, usually conical but sometimes broad and spreading. Fall foliage color varies from golden yellow to rusty-red in different species. *Carya illinoinensis*, the best nut-bearing species (*see* Pecan, *p.148*), is hardy from zones 5 to 9. Ornamental species include *C. cordiformis*, *C. glabra*, and *C. ovata*.

It is best either to sow seed or to plant seedlings as young as possible in the final position. Hickories rapidly produce long taproots and do not transplant well from containers unless long pots have been used that allow the root to develop naturally. Galls may develop on mature trees but, although unsightly, they will not cause serious long-term damage.

CARYA FLOWERS
Even if the climate is too cool for nuts to develop, hickory trees have great ornamental value.

WHEN TO PRUNE Hickories bleed heavily if pruned in spring, so prune only when fully dormant in autumn or early winter.

TRAINING AND PRUNING Grow as feathered trees (*see p.27*), or as central-leader standards (*see p.28*) with a clear trunk of 6ft (2m). Little pruning or training is necessary, since most species adopt these forms naturally. Keep pruning of established trees to a minimum. Renovation is seldom effective.

CASSIA SHOWER TREE

A huge genus of trees, shrubs, and sub-shrubs, of which only a few are grown in gardens, mainly for their very beautiful and long-lasting flowers. Most will grow outdoors only in frost-free climates.

C. FISTULA (ZONE 10)

GOLDEN SHOWER, INDIAN LABURNUM

Deciduous or semi-evergreen tree, suitable for outdoor cultivation only in tropical areas, where it is valued as a street tree and lawn specimen. In spring, the tree bears pendent racemes of small, fragrant, cup-shaped, bright yellow flowers, followed by dark brown pods up to 2ft (60cm) in length. Grown as a central-leader standard, it develops an ovoid crown.

WHEN TO PRUNE Prune young plants when dormant, and established trees after flowering, if necessary.

TRAINING AND PRUNING Train as a central-leader standard (*see p.28*), clearing the trunk in the early years to about 6–10ft (2–3m). Established specimens need little pruning other than to remove shoots that will grow to cross others. Cassias tolerate hard pruning well, but are so easily raised from seed that replacement is a preferable option.

CASSIA FISTULA
Tree species of Cassia, such as C. fistula, look best trained with a tall clear trunk, echoing their natural habit in their native forest environment.

OTHER CASSIAS
C. CORYMBOSA (syn. SENNA CORYMBOSA) *See* Dictionary of Ornamental Shrubs, *p.184*.
C. GRANDIS As for *C. fistula*.
C. JAVANICA As for *C. fistula*.

CASTANEA
CHESTNUT

The trees in this summer-flowering, deciduous genus form spreading, increasingly stately, domed canopies. Their creamy flowers are followed by spiny fruits that may enclose edible nuts. Most species thrive in areas with high summer temperatures; *C. sativa* alone grows well in cool climates.

Chestnut trees are grown as central-leader standards. Some species sucker freely, and respond vigorously to hard pruning. Chestnuts were traditionally coppiced for fencing poles; today, coppicing has largely saved *C. dentata* (the American chestnut) from extinction by chestnut blight, which attacks only mature growth; the continually renewed young stems are resistant to the disease.

C. SATIVA (ZONES 4–8)

SWEET CHESTNUT, SPANISH CHESTNUT

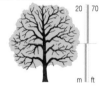

Broad, imposing tree with toothed leaves and gray-brown to brown strongly ridged bark. This species grows well in zone 5 where *C. dentata* has been replaced by the smaller, blight-resistant *C. mollissima*, grown for its nuts (*see p.148*).

WHEN TO PRUNE When dormant, in early winter or early spring.

TRAINING AND PRUNING Train as central-leader standards (*see p.28*), gradually producing a clear trunk of 6–10ft (2–3m). It is important to ensure a balanced, evenly spaced branch system when young, since a lopsided framework of heavy branches is prone to wind and storm damage. Established specimens need little pruning. Remove reverted shoots from variegated cultivars in late summer. Mature trees may lose large limbs, and crown thinning (*see p.35*) or reduction may be needed. Any such work on these heavy-limbed trees should be carried out only by a professional arborist.

OTHER CHESTNUTS
C. ALNIFOLIA, C. PUMILA Shrubby, suckering species best allowed to develop their thicketlike habit naturally. Tolerate thinning as for *Amelanchier stolonifera* (*see p.175*).
C. MOLLISSIMA *See* Chestnuts, *p.148*.

CATALPA *BEAN TREE*

Tall, deciduous trees with spreading crowns and handsome, large leaves, and erect panicles of purplish pink or white blooms in summer, followed by long, dark brown pods that persist through the winter. Catalpas are tolerant of hot, dry environments and diverse soil conditions.

Catalpas are usually trained initially as central-leader standards, although the crown usually branches naturally as it develops. They are best planted at one or two years old: older specimens may develop large heads, which will be out of proportion to the root ball. Catalpas respond well to hard pruning and make good pollards.

C. BIGNONIOIDES (ZONES 5–9)

EASTERN CATALPA, INDIAN BEAN TREE

A handsome tree bearing white flowers with yellow-striped and purple-spotted throats in late summer. The foliage, often purple-tinted when young, is particularly attractive in the golden-leaved cultivar 'Aurea', which is often pollarded to increase the size of its leaves. Mature catalpas can reach heights of 30–40ft (9–12m).

WHEN TO PRUNE When dormant, between autumn and late winter or early spring.

TRAINING AND PRUNING Train as a central-leader standard (*see p.28*), clearing the stem to 4–6ft (1.2–2m). The leader can then be allowed to branch and produce a low, open, spreading crown, mature specimens often being broader than tall. If you have purchased a trained tree whose head seems too large for its root ball, the crown should be thinned on planting (*see also p.25*) to leave a framework of only four or five main branches.

Established trees need little pruning, although heavy branches may need shortening or removal to balance the framework. This should be done by a professional arborist.

Catalpas respond to very hard pruning (to no lower than 1–2ft/30–60cm); to redevelop a branch framework, retain only the strongest, best-placed new shoots from the regrowth. To maintain as a pollard, cut back annually or every two years (*see p.36*) in late winter.

OTHER CATALPAS
C. SPECIOSA As for *C. bignonioides*.

POLLARDED CATALPA BIGNONIOIDES
This tree, suffering from dieback, was pollarded to a framework at about 4ft (1.2m) and has regenerated well, responding with a mass of vigorous young growth that has been carefully thinned (see p.32).

OTHER ORNAMENTAL TREES
CALODENDRUM *C. capense* needs little pruning other than to cut back over-long shoots after flowering to maintain its naturally neat outline *See also* Evergreen trees, *p.27*.
CALPURNIA Treat *C. aurea* as for *Albizia julibrissin* (*see p.54*), but prune after flowering, if required.
CARRIEREA Train *C. calycina* as a feathered tree (*see p.27*), pruning soon after leaf-fall in autumn as necessary. Established trees have no special pruning needs.

CASUARINA Pinelike evergreens that develop as feathered trees but may be pruned to clear the trunk (*see* Central-leader standard, *p.28*). Otherwise, little pruning is necessary. *C. stricta* and *C. glauca* tolerate clipping, and make good hedges (*see p.44*).
CEDRELA *See Toona, p.90*.
CEIBA *C. pentandra* naturally forms an upright, single-stemmed tree with no special training or pruning needs. It will tolerate fairly severe pruning if required.

CELTIS *HACKBERRY, NETTLE TREE* (ZONES 2–9)

Medium-sized to large, deciduous trees with alternate leaves and well-spaced, horizontal branches that droop at the tip. Most are best grown as single-stemmed, central-leader trees. Poor growing conditions and transplantation shock may result in the loss of the leading shoot, which may be difficult to replace. If possible, purchase seed-raised specimens, since these are easier to train than grafted plants. Plant as young as possible, in a site sheltered from cold and wind, and use only a low-nitrogen fertilizer. The trunk must be cleared of laterals while the tree is young, since, with the exception of *C. occidentalis*, hackberries are prone to decay and to form cavities, which large wounds made later in the tree's life will encourage.

C. OCCIDENTALIS

COMMON HACKBERRY

Deciduous, spreading tree with pointed, sharply toothed, lance-shaped leaves and insignificant flowers that are followed by purple-black fruits.

15 | 50

m | ft

WHEN TO PRUNE When growth resumes in early spring. Winter pruning may lead to canker in some species. Remove dead wood in summer.

TRAINING AND PRUNING Train as a central-leader standard (*see p.28*), aiming to clear the stem to about one-quarter of the young tree's overall height after the first two growing seasons. In far northern climates, retaining the leader is difficult, but possible with patience. Once the required length of stem has been cleared, little further pruning is needed. Rub out water shoots (*see p.32*) that develop around pruning wounds when they are young, to avoid having to make future unnecessary cuts.

Mature trees may produce vigorous, vertical shoots, which, if allowed to develop, increase the load on the horizontal branches. Cut them out to the base as soon as possible: if upright branches are well established, however, they are best left in place to avoid large pruning wounds. For this reason, too, renovation is rarely successful.

> **OTHER CELTIS**
> C. CAUCASICA, C. AUSTRALIS,
> C. LAEVIGATA As for *C. occidentalis*.

CELTIS OCCIDENTALIS
Celtis are best trained as standards, with a clear trunk to raise their near-horizontal, spreading lower branches above ground level.

CERATONIA *CAROB, LOCUST BEAN* (ZONES 9–11)

Ceratonia siliqua is an evergreen tree bearing long, leathery pods that have a variety of culinary uses. It prefers a Mediterranean-type climate and is very drought-tolerant. There are grafted cultivars selected for their potential to bear heavy crops of pods. Carobs are usually trained with a short trunk to make harvesting easier. While top-growth is slow in the first year, carobs quickly develop a long taproot. Young trees sold in long pots or bags that let the root grow naturally will establish more quickly than older, pot-bound ones.

WHEN TO PRUNE Winter to early spring.

TRAINING AND PRUNING Prune to form a multistemmed tree on a 2–3ft (60–90cm) trunk as for *Acer davidii* (*see illustrations, p.52*). Young trees will tolerate shaping cuts if growth is uneven and straggly: remove branch leaders and shorten sideshoots to make a more compact, bushy crown. Mature trees tolerate trimming to restrict their size, but do not remove too much growth in any one year: the pods are borne on new sideshoots springing from older laterals.

CERCIDIPHYLLUM

6 | 20

m | ft

Cercidiphyllum japonicum (katsura tree) is a graceful, deciduous tree, usually forming a conical crown when young, with evenly spaced, upright branches, and sublaterals that become pendulous toward the tips. Its paired, heart-shaped leaves are noted for their autumn color (which is best on acid soil).

Hardy from zones 4 to 8, *C. japonicum* does better in moist soils. It grows naturally as a broad-spreading, multi-stemmed tree or, equally attractively, with a single central leader. Individual trees determine their own growth habit from a very early age; do not attempt to train or prune them into a different form. *C. japonicum* forma *pendulum* is treated as for the species.

WHEN TO PRUNE Autumn to late winter, when dormant. Remove dead wood and cold-damaged growth in late spring.

TRAINING AND PRUNING Trees that naturally adopt a multistemmed habit begin to branch at or near ground level at an early age, and need little formative pruning. Remove the lowest laterals when young only where access is necessary. If young plants naturally produce a central leader, train as a central-leader standard (*see p.28*) and clear the lowest two or three whorls of branches to about 5ft (1.5m), to enhance the treelike character. Established trees need little further pruning. They do not respond well to hard pruning.

CERCIDIPHYLLUM JAPONICUM
Allow young trees that branch early to develop naturally as multistemmed trees. Use a short angled stake (see above) to support very low-branching specimens.

CERCIS *REDBUD, JUDAS TREE*

Deciduous trees and shrubs with alternate leaves, grown for their purplish-pink or white flowers and foliage that colors well in autumn. *Cercis canadensis* 'Forest Pansy' has dark red-purple leaves. The pealike flowers appear on older wood before or as the leaves emerge. Redbuds thrive and flower most freely in areas with long, hot summers. All develop long taproots and are very susceptible to transplant shock, which may cause the leader to die back, so plant as young as possible, preferably in spring as the buds begin to break. Weak or damaged wood is vulnerable to canker; cut affected growth well back into healthy wood in late summer.

EARLY FLOWERS
Cercis are unusual among trees by flowering directly on bare branches.

C. CANADENSIS (ZONES 4–9)

REDBUD

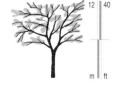

Deciduous, often multistemmed, bushy tree with spreading branches, purple or pink flowers, and heart-shaped leaves. It is beautiful as a specimen tree.

WHEN TO PRUNE Prune and remove any frost-damaged shoots in early summer.

TRAINING AND PRUNING Train and, if necessary, prune to create a multistemmed tree on a trunk of 2–3ft (60–90cm) as for *Acer davidii* (*see p.52*). Select three to five strong laterals, well-spaced around the main stem, to form a framework. The natural tendency is for stems to cluster, forming tight, V-shaped crotches that are easily split by strong

winds. The resulting damage renders the tree susceptible to rot.

Established trees have no special needs; they do not respond well to renovation. Purple-leaved cultivars, such as 'Forest Pansy', and variegated cultivars, such as 'Silver Cloud', may be coppiced or pollarded (*see p.36*), first allowing the plant to establish for two or three years. Do not prune yearly unless the plant is growing vigorously.

> **OTHER CERCIS**
> C. SILIQUASTRUM Train as a feathered tree (*see p.27*) or clear the stem to about 3ft (1m). For a small garden, can also be trained as a multistemmed tree as for *C. canadensis*. Established trees need no special pruning, but can be completely renovated by cutting back hard and selecting, at most, five strong, young stems to form a new framework.
> C. CHINENSIS Shrubby species; needs no special training or pruning. May be wall trained (*see Magnolia grandiflora, p.74*).
> C. OCCIDENTALE As for *C. siliquastrum*.
> C. RACEMOSA As for *C. canadensis*. Thrives only in areas with hot summers and mild winters.

CINNAMOMUM *CAMPHOR TREE* (ZONES 9–10)

The evergreen *Cinnamomum camphora* grows to 40ft (12m) or more. Its single trunk usually branches early, resulting in a low canopy formed by competing, near-upright limbs. Prune in summer, after the first flush of rapid growth. Train as a central-leader standard (*see p.28*) with a clear trunk of about 6ft

(2m). If branching is allowed before this length of trunk is cleared, crown lifting (*see p.35*) may be necessary in later years to allow access under the tree. Established trees have no special pruning needs, though they renovate well. To restrict size under glass, treat as for *Camellia* (*see p.182*).

CLADRASTIS *YELLOW-WOOD*

Deciduous trees and shrubs grown for their form, flowers, autumn color, and beautiful, smooth, beechlike bark. The wisteria-like flowers are produced in profusion only every two or three years. Cladrastis rapidly develop long taproots, and must be planted young.

C. LUTEA SYN. C. VIRGILIA

YELLOW-WOOD, VIRGILIA

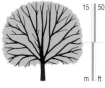

A deciduous tree (zones 4 to 8) with alternate leaves and white flowers, forming a broad, flattened, dome-shaped canopy with heavy branches. Formative pruning is vital: it is essential to avoid creating a low-branching or multistemmed branch structure that will become unsafe. The wood is brittle, and narrow, V-shaped crotches, especially those with included bark (*see p.12*), frequently split. The resulting damage usually lets in decay, leading to the decline of the tree. Because of the potential for structural weaknesses, do not plant this species close to buildings or busy streets.

WHEN TO PRUNE Midsummer.

TRAINING AND PRUNING Train as a central-leader standard (*see p.28*), clearing the trunk to about 5–6ft (1.5–2m). Make sure that the remaining laterals are evenly and well spaced, and remove any that grow at narrow angles to the main stem. Established trees have no special pruning needs. They do not respond well to renovation: the wood is prone to splitting, and damaged branches are best removed by a professional.

> **OTHER CLADRASTIS**
> C. PLATYCARPA As for *C. lutea*, but is less prone to structural weaknesses. Makes a much smaller tree in cooler areas.
> C. SINENSIS In continental climates and mild maritime climates, as for *C. lutea*. In cooler regions, it forms a much smaller tree that is best allowed to develop naturally.

> **OTHER ORNAMENTAL TREES**
> CHORISIA Train as a central-leader standard (*see p.28*) with a clear trunk of 6ft (2m) to accommodate the spreading branches. Renovates well.
> CITHAREXYLUM Train as a central-leader standard (*see p.28*) with a clear trunk of 5–6ft (1.5–2m). When established, little pruning is required. May be tip-pruned
>
> in summer to restrict growth and will tolerate harder pruning if necessary.
> COCCOLOBA No special training or pruning required.
> COLVILLEA Train *C. racemosa* as a central-leader standard (*see p.28*) with a clear trunk of 4½–6ft (1.35–2m). Maintain the leader through the crown for as long as possible.
>
> CORDIA Train as a central-leader standard (*see p.28*) with a clear trunk of 4½–5ft (1.35–1.5m). Established trees have no special pruning needs.
> CORDYLINE See Palms and palmlike plants, p.43.

CORNUS *DOGWOOD, CORNEL*

Trees in this mainly deciduous group are grown for their form and foliage, and for the showy bracts that surround the inconspicuous flowers.

C. CAPITATA

BENTHAM'S CORNEL

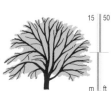

Tiered, evergreen or semievergreen tree with dark leaves, pale yellow bracts, and strawberry-like fruits. In cool climates it usually grows as a smaller, multistemmed tree or large shrub.

WHEN TO PRUNE Autumn to early spring.

TRAINING AND PRUNING In mild regions, can be grown as a feathered tree with a single trunk (*see p.27*). In cold and exposed areas, it is best allowed to develop naturally as a multistemmed tree, thinning if necessary to ensure a well-spaced framework of branches. To wall train, *see p.74*. Keep pruning of established trees to the minimum.

C. CONTROVERSA (ZONES 4–8)

GIANT DOGWOOD

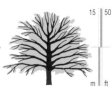

Picturesque, deciduous tree with a tiered habit, white bracts, red-purple autumn color, and red shoots in winter. It could be used as a street tree, since it will grow well enough in urban areas.

WHEN TO PRUNE Autumn to early spring.

TRAINING AND PRUNING Train as a central-leader standard (*see p.28*) with a clear trunk of one-quarter to one-third of the young tree's height. Does not respond to hard pruning.

C. KOUSA (ZONES 5–8)

CHINESE DOGWOOD

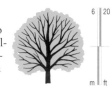

Bushy, deciduous tree best allowed to develop as a central-leader or branched-head standard with minimal attention.

WHEN TO PRUNE Autumn to early spring. Remove dead wood after flowering.

TRAINING AND PRUNING Clear a short trunk, to 2–3ft (60–90cm), then keep pruning to an absolute minimum. When removing dead wood, take care not to damage the twiggy, flowering growth. Does not tolerate hard pruning.

CORNUS CONTROVERSA
Most dogwoods make beautiful free-standing small trees. Those that develop a tiered habit with age, such as Cornus capitata, C. controversa, *and* C. florida, *can be fan-trained on a partially sunny wall (see also* Magnolia grandiflora, *p.74).*

OTHER DOGWOODS
C. ALTERNIFOLIA Equally attractive allowed to develop as a multistemmed feathered tree, or trained as a standard as for *C. controversa,* clearing the trunk very slowly to 3–5ft (1–1.5m). In the first two or three years, limit pruning to the removal of competing leaders and strong low laterals.
C. 'EDDIE'S WHITE WONDER' Best left to develop naturally with minimal attention. Also recommended for wall training (*see Magnolia grandiflora, p.74*).
C. FLORIDA As for *C. kousa,* clearing a short trunk (*see p.28*) to 2–3ft (60–90cm) if desired. Shading and cold damage may spoil the form, resulting in an untidy, multistemmed tree that should not be pruned in an attempt to improve it.
C. NUTTALLII As for *C. controversa,* with a clear trunk to about 5ft (1.5m). A short-lived tree, and prone to dieback; does not respond well to hard pruning and is best replaced.
See also Dictionary of Ornamental Shrubs, *p.188.*

CORYLUS *HAZEL*

While the shrubby hazel species are valued for their nuts, trees in this deciduous genus are grown for their foliage and erect habit, and for the yellow, male catkins borne in late winter and early spring on bare branches with attractively rugged bark. The tiny female flowers fringe the trees in a red haze in early spring.

C. COLURNA (ZONES 4–7)

TURKISH HAZEL

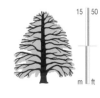

Conical tree with spreading, rather twisted branches, best grown with a clear trunk to display the bark.

WHEN TO PRUNE Winter, when dormant.

TRAINING AND PRUNING Train as a central-leader standard (*see p.28*), gradually clearing the trunk to about 6ft (2m). Always remove competing leaders as soon as possible. Established trees need little pruning other than to remove occasional suckers at the base. They respond well to hard pruning.

OTHER HAZELS
C. AVELLANA, C. MAXIMA *See* Dictionary of Ornamental Shrubs, *p.189*. Grown for edible nuts, *see* Hazelnuts and Filberts, *p.149*.
C. AVELLANA 'PENDULA' Weeping cultivar usually top-grafted onto a clear stem at about 6ft (2m) to form a weeping standard. To maintain this tree form, *see p.28*. Prune in winter.
C. JACQUEMONTII As for *C. colurna*.

CORYLUS COLURNA
A pleasing tree structure, with a straight trunk and well-spaced branches, makes the most of the ornamental value of shaggy hazel bark in winter.

+ CRATAEGOMESPILUS *BRONVAUX MEDLAR* (ZONE 6)

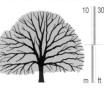

This tree is a deciduous graft hybrid between *Crataegus* and *Mespilus*, grafted on to *Crataegus* stock. It is grown as a branched-head standard, forming a round-headed tree bearing clusters of white flowers in profusion during late spring and early summer, followed by medlarlike fruits.

WHEN TO PRUNE Autumn to early spring. Summer pruning may also be necessary.

TRAINING AND PRUNING Train with a clear trunk of no more than 6ft (2m) (*see p.28*), then allow the crown to branch naturally. Pruning of established trees should be minimal, since it can create an imbalance between the two genetically distinct tissues of which the tree is composed. Shoots consisting of tissue from only one of the parent species occasionally develop. These need not be removed unless very vigorous, when they should be cut back by up to one-third in summer, so that they do not become dominant. Does not respond well to renovation measures.

CRATAEGUS

Deciduous, usually thorny trees, often with a congested branch structure, useful as a barrier hedge that may be clipped after leaf-fall, or pruned more informally on a two- or three-year cycle to obtain more flowers and fruits, which are borne on older wood (*see Hedges, p.44*). Tree-forming species tend to branch from the base, but are easily trained as standards (which may be trimmed into formal "lollipop" shapes).

WHEN TO PRUNE Between autumn and early spring.

C. CRUS-GALLI (ZONES 3–7)

COCKSPUR HAWTHORN

Small tree with a widely spreading, often flat-topped crown, white flowers, and red fruits. The leaves turn orange in autumn. It is an ideal standard tree for a small garden.

TRAINING AND PRUNING There is usually a strong central leader that can be allowed to lose dominance as the crown develops. Clear two or three whorls of lower branches (*see p.28*) as the tree reaches semimaturity to give a clear trunk of about 6ft (2m). Established trees need little pruning.

C. PHAENOPYRUM (ZONES 3–8)

WASHINGTON HAWTHORN

Round-headed tree, with fragrant white flowers and bright, glossy red fruits that color in autumn and often last through the winter. It is best trained as a central-leader specimen, but can also be left to

CRATAEGUS BLOSSOM
The flowers are followed by fruits ("haws") that may be orange, red, yellow, blue, or black.

develop more naturally as a multistemmed tree. This late-blooming species is often grown as a shrub form; excellent as a single specimen plant near buildings, hedges, and borders. The sharp thorns may present a problem.

TRAINING AND PRUNING *C. phaenopyrum* has a strong tendency to branch from the base. To obtain a treelike form, it is best to purchase a whip (*see p.24*) and feed in the first three years with nitrogenous fertilizer in early spring to encourage vigorous, more upright growth that is easier to train. Do not start to remove any laterals until after planting in the final location, then clear the trunk gradually (*see p.28*) to about 5–6ft (1.5–2m). Mature trees need little pruning. Crown congestion is natural; remove only badly rubbing branches. Overthinning may cause branches to twist and tear in high winds. Responds well to hard pruning.

OTHER CRATAEGUS
C. DOUGLASII, C. OXYACANTHA, C. TANACETIFOLIA As for *C. phaenopyrum*.
C. X DUROBRIVENSIS Shrubby in habit, with no special pruning needs.
C. X PERSISTENS As for *C. crus-galli*. In cool climates, thin young trees on planting to reduce the risk of cold damage.
C. X PRUNIFOLIA (syn. C. PERSIMILIS 'PRUNIFOLIA') As for *C. crus-galli*.

X CRATAEMESPILUS

Crataemespilus grandiflora is a vigorous, deciduous hybrid valued for its weeping habit, profusion of white flowers in late spring, and autumn color. Grown as a central-leader standard, it makes a beautiful specimen, up to 25ft (8m) tall.

Train as a central-leader standard (*see p.28*), pruning when dormant. Although the laterals are horizontal when young, they will become increasingly pendulous with age, so clear the trunk to about 6ft (2m) so that they do not form an unsightly skirt of foliage around the base. Does not respond well to hard pruning.

CYPHOMANDRA

Cyphomandra betacea (tamarillo, tree tomato) is a small, evergreen tree (zone 10) with pink-tinged flowers borne on new growth, followed by egg-shaped, fleshy red fruits, edible only when fully ripe and cooked. Grown widely in tropical to warm temperate regions, in cool climates it needs a heated conservatory or greenhouse. Seedlings develop an erect, sparsely branched habit, while trees grown from cuttings are more bushy and spreading.

WHEN TO PRUNE In early spring, just before new growth begins.

TRAINING AND PRUNING Over the first two or three years, aim to create an open, branched crown on a clear stem to a height of about 20–30in (50–75cm). Let the leader break at this height to form a broad, open head. Young trees grow fast; if they reach 5ft (1.5m) before producing laterals, prune back to a strong bud at about 3ft (90cm) from the ground to stimulate branching.

To promote the production of flowering wood and contain tree size if necessary, prune established trees annually, cutting back one in three of the fruited laterals to the main branches. Take care since branches are brittle. Mature trees may require staking or bracing since the root system is fibrous and relatively shallow. Tamarillos have a productive life of about eight years, so replace rather than renovate old trees.

OTHER ORNAMENTAL TREES
CORYNOCARPUS Evergreen (*see p.27*) with no special needs; if desired, the trunk may be cleared to 6ft (2m).
CYDONIA See Quince, *p.121*.

D

DAVIDIA DOVE TREE

Davidia involucrata is a deciduous tree (zones 6–8) of elegant habit with graceful, pendent white bracts that are produced from late spring on the previous year's growth. The growth habit is very distinctive, with long terminal shoots and very short, almost spurlike sideshoots. It is the longer growths that must be used to create the branch framework. Davidias are best grown as central-leader standards with a tall trunk, so that the bracts hang down. Formative training is vital during the first five or six years. A multistemmed tree cannot be transformed by pruning into a central-leader standard. Trees may naturally lose their leaves unevenly in autumn: this should not be mistaken for dieback or disease.

WHEN TO PRUNE Autumn to early spring.

TRAINING AND PRUNING Train as a central-leader standard (*see p.28*) with a clear trunk of 6–10ft (2–3m). The tree

DAVIDIA INVOLUCRATA
Davidia is also known as the ghost tree or handkerchief tree; all of its common names are inspired by its large, white bracts.

naturally forms a strong central leader surrounded by strongly upright laterals. These can usually be allowed to grow without check unless very vigorous, upright laterals overtake the leader. If these are allowed to develop, they result in an undesirable multistemmed crown; remove them, or tip-prune by up to one-quarter. If the leader is damaged, select and train in a long lateral as a replacement (*see p.26*).

Established trees need no special attention. They do not respond well to hard pruning and are reluctant to branch, so a poor form is hard to rectify.

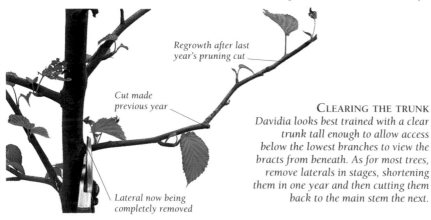

Regrowth after last year's pruning cut

Cut made previous year

Lateral now being completely removed

CLEARING THE TRUNK
Davidia looks best trained with a clear trunk tall enough to allow access below the lowest branches to view the bracts from beneath. As for most trees, remove laterals in stages, shortening them in one year and then cutting them back to the main stem the next.

DELONIX FLAME TREE, ROYAL POINCIANA

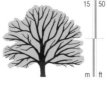

Delonix regia is a deciduous tree (zone 10) widely grown in sub-tropical and tropical regions for its red flowers. Its broad crown makes it an ideal shade tree. Plant as young as possible: if the long taproot is damaged, the tree may be unstable when mature.

WHEN TO PRUNE Late winter, before the new flush of growth begins in spring.

TRAINING AND PRUNING Train initially as a central-leader tree, with a clear trunk to a height of about 6ft (2m). The leader quickly loses dominance and cannot be maintained. To support the spreading crown, main framework branches must be well spaced around the trunk. In the early years, select about five strong laterals arising from different, evenly spaced points, and remove the remainder. Provided that formative pruning is carried out early, little further pruning is necessary. *Delonix* will respond to renovation, but replacement is preferable.

DIOSPYROS PERSIMMON

Elegant, spreading trees, grown for their attractive form and foliage that often colors well in autumn. In warm climates, some species are grown for their fruits (*see* Persimmon, *p. 131*).

Train as central-leader standards (*see p.28*) with the trunk clear to a height of 4–6ft (1.2–2m), allowing the semi-pendulous branches to sweep almost to ground level. Prune between autumn and early spring. In cool maritime climates, where trees need a well-lit site to develop a good form, the leading shoot of *D. virginiana* (zones 4–9) is sensitive to frost damage when young. Plant in a sheltered site; if the leader is damaged or lost, select and train in a new leader as soon as possible. When established, *Diospyros* need little pruning and do not respond well when cut back hard.

DOMBEYA (ZONE 10)

Small, fast-growing, bushy trees, bearing pendent flower clusters in winter or early spring on wood made the previous year. They can only be grown outdoors in warm, frost-free climates, where they are best allowed to develop naturally as feathered trees (*see p.27*), needing little pruning. Make any shaping cuts in early summer. Specimens grown in a warm conservatory tolerate pruning to restrict size. Grow as a tallish pollard (*see p.36*) to display the flowers at eye level (*see also Brugmansia, p.179*). Cut back flowered shoots by about one-third in spring or early summer. Most dombeyas respond vigorously when pruned hard.

DOMBEYA X CAYEUXII
Dombeyas tolerate pruning to restrict size, but grow them tall enough to display the appearance and fragrance of the flowers.

E

EMBOTHRIUM *CHILEAN FIREBUSH* (ZONES 9–10)

Embothrium coccineum (Chilean firebush) is a small, evergreen or semievergreen tree grown primarily for the abundance of vivid red flowers produced along its branches in late spring or early summer. Often suckering in habit, it is usually grown as a multistemmed tree, but in mild, damp, maritime climates may also be trained with a central leader. It tolerates frosts and coastal conditions, but must have shelter from cold, dry winds.

WHEN TO PRUNE Late summer, after flowering. Remove dead wood in spring.

TRAINING AND PRUNING In most areas, *E. coccineum* is best allowed to develop naturally with little or no pruning, resulting in a multistemmed specimen with each stem arising from below ground. In mild, damp climates, where

EMBOTHRIUM COCCINEUM
The previous year's wood flowers at the same time as extension growth is being made from the shoot tip.

growth is rapid, avoid congestion at maturity by selecting three to five strong stems to provide a framework that is left clothed with laterals to ground level. On exposed sites, also thin out young stems, by about one in five, to reduce wind resistance. To grow as a single-stemmed specimen, train as a central-leader tree (*see p.28*) with a clear trunk to a height of about 5ft (1.5m). Newly planted trees need initial staking but root growth is vigorous and plants stabilize quickly. Remove basal suckers as seen.

Because of the suckering habit, multi-stemmed trees may develop into a mass of vertical stems sparsely furnished with thin horizontal laterals, and overcrowding may result in dieback and rot. Remove dead stems with a sharp spade, cutting them out from below ground, thus leaving room for new, replacement growth that will emerge from the roots. It is also possible to grub out old plants, leaving young stems to regenerate from the periphery of the original plant.

EMMENOPTERYS (ZONES 7–9)

Emmenopterys henryi is a deciduous tree of open habit with slender branches and rough, attractive bark. Its terminal clusters of white flowers are produced freely only in areas with long, hot summers. In cool climates, provide a warm, sheltered, sunny site.

WHEN TO PRUNE Between autumn and early spring.

TRAINING AND PRUNING Train as a central-leader standard (*see p.28*). If the leader is damaged by cold, it is difficult to train in a replacement but not impossible with patience. Once established, pruning is best kept to a minimum. Young plants tend to put on extension growth at the expense of an increase in girth, giving a rather spindly appearance. Pruning will not improve this habit; the tree naturally becomes less spindly with maturity. It does not respond well to hard pruning, tending to produce a proliferation of soft, cold-sensitive growth.

ERYTHRINA

Hardy in zones 9 and 10, usually thorny trees bearing racemes of brilliantly colored, pealike flowers.

E. CRISTA-GALLI (ZONES 9–10)

COCKSPUR CORAL TREE

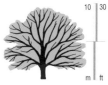

Deciduous, up-right, small, bushy tree, grown in warm climates as a spreading, heavy-branched, central-leader standard. In cooler climates it is best planted against a warm, sunny wall. It may die back to ground level in winter, regrowing as a rounded, untidy shrub that produces brilliant crimson flowers.

WHEN TO PRUNE When fully dormant, between autumn and early spring.

TRAINING AND PRUNING In warm climates, train as a central-leader standard (*see p.28*). Once established, little pruning is needed except to remove dieback. In cool climates, the inevitable loss of the leader results in shrubby growth that is best cut back annually (*see* Coppicing and pollarding, *p.36*) when dormant. Mulch to protect the base from cold.

> **OTHER ERYTHRINAS**
> E. CORALLODENDRON In warm climates, as for *E. crista-galli*. In cool conditions grows naturally as an open shrub with no special pruning needs.
> E. VARIEGATA (syn. E. INDICA) Needs minimal training and pruning.

ERYTHRINA CRISTA-GALLI
In colder areas, cut all stems back to a low framework each spring, before growth begins.

OTHER ORNAMENTAL TREES
DILLENIA Develops naturally as a branched-head standard, similar to *Catalpa bignonioides* (*see p.57*).

DOCYNIA As for *Malus baccata* (*see p.75*). Tolerates pruning well.
EHRETIA Train with a clear trunk to

about 4ft (1.2m), then let the crown branch. Responds well to hard pruning.
ELAEOCARPUS *See* Evergreen trees, *p.27*.

EUCALYPTUS *EUCALYPT, GUM TREE* (ZONES 9–10)

A huge genus of evergreens, ranging in habit from large forest trees to shrubby "mallees" that produce slender stems from a tuberous rootstock (lignotuber). They are grown for their habit, often fragrant flowers (rarely produced in cool climates), aromatic foliage, and peeling, mosaic bark in shades of cream, gray-pink, and soft green. Most thrive only in frost-free climates; *E. gunnii*, *E. dalrympleana*, *E. parvifolia*, and *E. pauciflora* thrive if sheltered from cold, dry winds and given a deep winter mulch. Some species naturally form attractive, informal, multistemmed trees. Others are trained as central-leader standards, although the leader may lose dominance as the tree matures. Many develop crooked trunks even if staked when young; poorly formed trees can be cut back hard and retrained (*see below*). This treatment is also the best course for trees that have suffered damage or extensive dieback, often caused by cold or strong, particularly salty, winds. All eucalypts tolerate hard pruning, and several are often grown as pollarded or coppiced shrublike specimens for their attractive juvenile foliage.

WHEN TO PRUNE Winter to spring, when new growth begins, after any danger of late hard frosts in cool climates.

E. DALRYMPLEANA

MOUNTAIN GUM

Fast-growing eucalypt with gray-green leaves that are bronze-tinted when young and mosaic bark that gradually turns white.

25 | 80

m | ft

TRAINING AND PRUNING Train as a central-leader standard (*see p.28*) with a clear trunk to about 6ft (2m). Many specimens grow naturally as central-leader trees; lower limbs can be removed just as they start to die back. Maintain a strong leader up to early maturity.

Established trees need little attention; even large, heavy, horizontal branches are usually sound. If necessary, new branches can be developed by hard pruning and then thinning the dense regrowth to reduce wind resistance and the likelihood of breakage. *E. dalrympleana* can be pollarded or coppiced when young, but other species are better suited to regular cutting back.

E. GUNNII

CIDER GUM

Can be grown as a central-leader standard, or as a pollard or a coppiced shrub with perpetually juvenile leaves. A row of coppiced shrubs, with alternate specimens cut back each year, makes an attractive hedge.

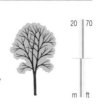

20 | 70

m | ft

TRAINING AND PRUNING Train as a tree as for *E. dalrympleana*. Poorly formed or damaged trees should be replaced or completely renovated (*see below*), rather than having individual branches removed. To produce and maintain a pollarded or coppiced specimen, *see p.36*. Cut back all new growth annually or every other year in early spring. Pollarding or coppicing is best initiated from the start, rather than used on overlarge or damaged mature trees.

EUCALYPTUS FOLIAGE
Many eucalypts have juvenile (center) and adult foliage that is quite different in form.

OTHER EUCALYPTS
E. CAESIA subsp. MAGNA (syn. E. 'SILVER PRINCESS'), E. CITRIODORA, E. FICIFOLIA, E. GLOBULUS, E. LEUCOXYLON, E. PARVIFOLIA, E. URNIGERA As for *E. dalrympleana*.
E. CINEREA, E. EREMOPHILA, E. LEHMANNII As for *E. gunnii*.
E. COCCIFERA As for *E. dalrympleana*, to display the bark well. In cooler climates, may adopt a stunted or shrubby habit.
E. KRUSEANA Small shrubby species needing minimal pruning; frost-hardy, ideal for conservatories.
E. MACROCARPA, E. TETRAPTERA Best allowed to develop a multistemmed, open habit with minimal pruning.
E. PAUCIFLORA As for *E. citriodora*.
E. PAUCIFLORA subsp. NIPHOPHILA As for *E. gunnii*.
E. RUBIDA As for *E. dalrympleana*.

RETRAINING A CENTRAL LEADER (EUCALYPTUS GUNNII)

BEFORE PRUNING (SPRING)
Eucalypts often grow crooked and may need staking for support. It is better to renovate, a process best repeated every five or six years.

Reducing top growth first for safety, saw stem straight across here (see Felling a small tree, p.33).

YEAR 1, SUMMER

1 *Select and stake a strong stem for vertical growth. Ties must be secure but allow some movement.*

2 *Cut all other new stems back to the ground or the stump.*

Vigorous regrowth has typical vertical habit

YEAR 3, SUMMER

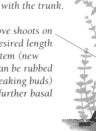

1 *Let a crown of branches develop at the desired height, removing only crossing shoots or laterals making narrow V-angles with the trunk.*

2 *Remove shoots on the desired length of clear stem (new growth can be rubbed out as breaking buds) and any further basal growth.*

EUCRYPHIA

Elegant trees, some upright, some multi-stemmed, grown for their glossy foliage and beautiful, four-petaled flowers. Hardy in zones 9 and 10, in cooler areas they benefit from a sheltered site. They generally need little pruning or training and do not respond well when cut back hard. Pruning may be necessary to counter the effects of cold and cold winds.

E. X NYMANSENSIS

Columnar, evergreen tree with slender, upright branches and few laterals. The form develops naturally, but is difficult to maintain if the tree is exposed to prolonged cold; even mature trees may be extensively damaged by hard frosts or cold winds. Careful pruning and feeding (*see p.15*) may restore the form.

WHEN TO PRUNE Spring, if required.

TRAINING AND PRUNING Little or no formative pruning is required. To restore winter damage, cut back dead and damaged growth into living wood just above a suitable lateral. If possible, reduce all other branches to the same height. New growth quickly adopts the upright habit and requires little further attention except to thin if overcrowded.

OTHER EUCRYPHIAS
E. CORDIFOLIA, E. LUCIDA, E. MOOREI Columnar evergreens; may develop a shrubby habit in cold regions and need an open but sheltered site. Need minimal attention. Remove dead wood in spring.
E. GLUTINOSA Needs little training, usually growing naturally with a central leader and lower branches that may sweep down and then grow upward as they touch the ground. On windy sites, the crown may become distorted; corrective pruning in spring (*see p.34*) will restore the form if the tree is still young. Avoid pruning mature trees.

OTHER ORNAMENTAL TREES
EUCOMMIA Elmlike tree (*see Ulmus, p.91*) best trained as a central-leader standard (*see p.28*). It is hard to replace a lost leader. Prune when dormant, keeping cuts as small as possible. Does not renovate.
EUPTELEA Usually develops naturally as a multistemmed tree (*see p. 30*); trunks may be cleared to 30–36in (75–90cm) if desired, as for a birch (*see Betula, p.57*). When established, sparse-leafed older wood can be removed in the dormant season to encourage new growth.

F

FAGUS *BEECH*

Deciduous trees with dense, spreading crowns and long, straight, smooth-barked, silver-gray trunks, grown for their habit, fresh green leaves (some cultivars have rich purple foliage), and copper and golden autumn color. They make fine specimens for parkland, avenues, and large gardens. *F. sylvatica* is ideal for formal hedging.

F. SYLVATICA (ZONES 4–7)

COMMON BEECH, EUROPEAN BEECH

Stately tree with pendulous lower branches and dense foliage, conical when young and domed with age. It is shallow-rooted, and trees must be well trained to avoid instability in high winds. Can be grown as a clipped hedge (*see p.44*).

WHEN TO PRUNE Autumn to early spring. Prune hedges in winter, or midsummer if they show any signs of disease.

TRAINING AND PRUNING Allow young trees to develop initially as feathered trees (*see p.27*). The lower laterals protect the young bark of these forest natives from sun scorch. Removing laterals early may also encourage dual leaders. When the tree is six to eight years old, growing with a strong, distinct central leader, clear the trunk (*see p.28*) over four or more years, ideally always removing laterals before they reach 2½in (6cm) in diameter. Small wounds seal quickly, leaving no obvious stem blemish. A clear trunk of 8–10ft (2.5–3m) lets the pendulous lower branches fall to just above ground level. As the crown develops, remove any strongly upright laterals that may compete with the leader. Pruning of mature trees (rarely necessary) should be carried out only by a professional.

FAGUS SYLVATICA 'PENDULA'
This strongly weeping cultivar, when purchased, may have already developed laterals to below soil level. Shorten them to an outward-facing bud.

OTHER BEECHES
F. JAPONICA, F. ORIENTALIS As for *F. sylvatica*.
F. ENGLERIANA Multistemmed tree (*see p.30*), often dividing just above ground level. Needs no special pruning.
F. GRANDIFOLIA As for *F. sylvatica*. More effort is required to maintain a central leader. Planting as young as possible and light fertilizing will help.
F. SYLVATICA 'DAWYCK' Fastigiate form (*see p.20*), needs no pruning.
F. SYLVATICA 'PAGNYENSIS' Usually sold grafted; keep pruning to a minimum.
F. SYLVATICA 'PURPUREA' (Purple or Atropurpurea group) As for *F. sylvatica*, but where possible remove any shoots that revert to green foliage.
F. SYLVATICA 'ZLATIA' Train as a standard (*see p.28*) with a clear trunk to 6–10ft (2–3m), then let the broad, multistemmed crown develop naturally.
F. SYLVATICA 'PENDULA' The weeping beech may adopt two habits. If young trees have sturdy, horizontal branches with slender, pendulous laterals, treat as for *F. sylvatica*. The other form (*see above*) has a distinctive narrow crown, with stems that ascend, then droop, clothed in long, pendent laterals. These laterals will root on touching the ground to produce a distinctive and unusual mature form of great size (*see below*). To encourage this, the trunk should not be cleared and pruning kept to a minimum.

MATURE WEEPING BEECH
In time, the narrow-crowned form of Fagus sylvatica 'Pendula' may form a monumental specimen with several generations of layers radiating from the parent tree.

FICUS *Fig*

Ornamental tree species in this large and varied genus (for climbers, *see p.271*) are often used as shade trees in warm to tropical regions, or, in cooler climates, as foliage plants for the house or heated conservatory. *Ficus carica*, which will tolerate cool-climate conditions, makes a handsome tree but is more commonly grown for its edible fruits (*see Figs, p.138*). Tropical species grow into giant trees with a buttressed trunk and a tangled mass of aerial and surface roots; when grown under cover they are far less energetic, and their size can be restricted by pruning. Young plants benefit from training, but the naturally erratic, congested branch structure, and the bleeding of latex sap, makes pruning of mature trees very difficult. In warm climates *F. benjamina* is used for hedges (*see p.44*) and is wall trained (*see p.74*).

WHEN TO PRUNE Late winter, or at any time in frost-free regions.

TRAINING AND PRUNING In tropical climates, train initially as central-leader standards (*see p.28*) and maintain the leading shoot for as long as possible, clearing the trunk to 6–10ft (2–3m). The leader is often lost early, and is difficult to replace. Allow ample space for growth, and keep pruning of established specimens to a minimum. Remove any plain green shoots on cultivars with variegated or marbled foliage. Under glass or in the home, prune at any time to confine to the allotted space. Ficus respond well to hard pruning, and even relatively large wounds are soon hidden by new growth.

FICUS BENJAMINA
When grown as a small house or green-house plant, trunks can be braided for an ornamental effect (see Topiary, p.48).

FRANKLINIA *Franklin tree* (ZONES 6–9)

Franklinia alatamaha is a small, deciduous tree grown for its large white flowers and scarlet autumn color. It grows and flowers best in areas with long, hot summers and mild winters, reaching 20ft (6m) in eastern North America. It grows naturally as a single- or multistemmed tree, and needs little formative pruning. Any that is necessary should be carried out when the tree is dormant, between autumn and early spring. As the tree matures, lower branches may eventually form secondary leaders. Do not shorten them: they will form a broad, structurally sound crown. Once established, prune only to remove any dead wood in summer and carry out other routine tasks (*see p.31*). Can be renovated by cutting to the ground in late winter.

FRAXINUS *Ash*

Handsome, deciduous trees grown for their attractive foliage and impressive stature. Some, notably *F. ornus*, have attractive flowers or, like *F. americana*, color well in autumn.

WHEN TO PRUNE Between autumn and early spring, when dormant.

F. AMERICANA (ZONES 3–9)

WHITE ASH

A large tree with heavy branches, and one of the most attractive trees for autumn color. It must have a strong central leader that persists through the crown: forked trees may be unsafe.

TRAINING AND PRUNING Needs little formative pruning, naturally forming a vigorous leader that remains dominant as the crown develops. Train with a clear trunk (*see p.28*) of about 10ft (3m). Prune mature trees only to remove wind damage. Mature ashes produce fast-growing water shoots (*see p.32*) from wounded tissue, especially around large cuts. Rub out as soon as seen; if allowed to develop, they are prone to breakage. Does not respond well to hard pruning.

F. EXCELSIOR 'PENDULA'

Weeping standard, top-grafted onto a clear trunk of, usually, 5–6ft (1.5–2m) in height (zones 4 to 8). The growth habit is congested and, unless checked, crossing or rubbing branches may fuse, hiding structural defects and rot within ripples of bark. Framework branches must be carefully selected when young.

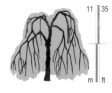

TRAINING AND PRUNING Train and maintain as for any weeping standard (*see p.28*). In the early years, remove

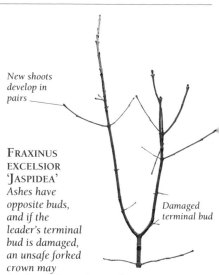

New shoots develop in pairs

FRAXINUS EXCELSIOR 'JASPIDEA'
Ashes have opposite buds, and if the leader's terminal bud is damaged, an unsafe forked crown may develop. Select only one shoot and train it in vertically as the new leader (see p.26).

Damaged terminal bud

crossing branches, and also the weaker of any two that twine together, since one or sometimes both may die from suppression. Try to achieve evenly spaced branches around the graft union. Does not respond well to hard pruning. Do not thin too much since gaps in the canopy will spoil the outline.

OTHER ASHES
F. ANGUSTIFOLIA (syn. F. OXYCARPA) 'RAYWOOD' Popular as a street tree, and so usually trained as a central-leader standard. However, is equally attractive as a feathered tree (*see p.27*). Otherwise, as for *F. americana*.
F. EXCELSIOR 'HESSEI' Hardy in zones 4 to 6, forms broad spreading shape at maturity. As for *F. americana*.
F. EXCELSIOR 'MONSTROSA' Fasciated form, needs little pruning.
F. ORNUS Naturally forms a clear stem and needs minimal training and pruning.
F. PENNSYLVANICA (zones 3–9) Train as a central-leader standard. Develops a spreading habit with an irregular crown at maturity. Excellent street, park, or lawn tree.

G

GLEDITSIA HONEY LOCUST

Deciduous, spiny trees, grown for their elegant form and divided foliage that often turns yellow in autumn. Honey locusts are tough, well adapted to difficult sites, and make fine urban or street trees.

G. TRIACANTHOS (ZONES 3–9)

HONEY LOCUST

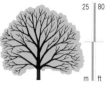

In its native North America, may reach 180ft (55m) in height. There are many forms and cultivars. Most cultivars, such as the golden-leaved 'Sunburst' (with its tiered habit, a fine specimen for a small garden) are treated as for the species. Thorns present a problem in the species, but all the cultivars are thornless. *G.* 'Moraine', *G.* 'Perfection', and *G.* 'Sunburst' are generally graceful in outline and fairly resistant to disease. *G. triacanthos* var. *inermis* is a fast-growing tree with an open, spreading crown. It tolerates a range of conditions and is both drought and salt-tolerant.

WHEN TO PRUNE Late summer to midwinter.

TRAINING AND PRUNING Train as a central-leader standard (*see p.28*) with a clear trunk to a height of about 6ft (2m). *G. triacanthos* naturally produces a vigorous leader and needs little formative pruning. Established trees tolerate light pruning, but this is rarely necessary.

OTHER GLEDITSIAS
G. 'HALKA', G. 'IMPERIAL', G. 'MAJESTIC', G. 'SHADEMASTER', G. 'SKYLINE' As for *G. triacanthos*.

GREVILLEA SILK OAK

Frost-tender evergreens (*see also* Dictionary of Ornamental Shrubs, *p.197*) grown for their habit, foliage, and spidery flowers, produced reliably only in warm conditions (zones 9 and 10). *G. robusta*, which can attain a height of 110ft (35m) or more, is widely grown: in cool areas in pots under glass; wall-trained as a foliage plant in mild maritime climates; or as a street tree or garden specimen in warm temperate or subtropical climates.

WHEN TO PRUNE Early summer as growth slows down (in mature trees, after flowering).

TRAINING AND PRUNING In warmer areas, grow as feathered trees (*see p.27*) or as central-leader standards (*see p.28*) with a clear trunk to a height of 6–10ft (2–3m). It is difficult to train in a replacement for a damaged leader, and without a leader the tree is likely to develop an unsound branch system. To wall-train, *see p.74*. Avoid pruning mature trees

GREVILLEAS AS POT PLANTS
Tree species of Grevillea can be grown from cuttings to make short-lived potted plants under glass in cooler climates. They will not flower, but the fernlike leaves are attractive.

unless absolutely necessary. Large pruning wounds are disfiguring and are seldom disguised by new growth. If crown lifting becomes necessary (*see p.35*), remove complete limbs rather than shortening branches.

H-I-J

HALESIA SILVER BELL

Showy, deciduous, small trees grown for their snowdroplike flowers and winged fruits. Most color yellow in autumn. Although they can be allowed to develop naturally into multistemmed trees, they display their flowers and sweeping branches better with a short trunk. Despite a naturally irregular habit, they generally require little pruning.

H. TETRAPTERA (ZONES 4–8)

CAROLINA SILVER BELL

Halesia tetraptera (syn. *H. carolina*) is a small tree with spreading, even slightly pendulous, lower branches that often furnish the tree with foliage to the ground. It prefers a sunny position.

WHEN TO PRUNE Autumn to early spring.

TRAINING AND PRUNING Several stems often develop from the base: it is best if the strongest stem is selected and trained as a single trunk and then allowed to branch low, at about 20–30in (50–75cm).

Established trees have no special needs. If they do not flower well, prune out older wood in early spring to stimulate new growth that will bloom in the next year. On old, congested plants, thin out the oldest flowered growth directly after flowering. Never attempt to lift the crown of established specimens since this will spoil the graceful outline.

OTHER HALESIAS
H. DIPTERA No special pruning needs.
H. MONTICOLA Forms a much taller tree than *H. tetraptera*. Until four years old, prune only to remove competing leaders, then train as a central-leader standard (*see p.28*) with a clear trunk of about 5ft (1.5m). Routine pruning of established trees is unnecessary. Poorly formed or poorly flowering trees can be treated as for *H. tetraptera*. Lower branches can be removed from older trees (*see also* Crown lifting, *p.35*).

OTHER ORNAMENTAL TREES
FIRMIANA Train as a central-leader standard (*see p.28*).
GEIJERA Maintain *G. parviflora* as a weeping standard (*see p.28*). Laterals can be pruned back, when dormant, to pendulous sublaterals to enhance the weeping form.
GINKGO See Conifers, *p.40*.
GORDONIA Related to *Camellia* and needs similar treatment (*see C. japonica, p.182*), whether grown outdoors or under glass.
GYMNOCLADUS Train as a central-leader standard (*see p.28*) with a clear trunk of about 6ft (2m). Established trees have no special pruning needs.

HOHERIA

Small, evergreen or deciduous trees with attractive, alternate leaves, bearing large white flowers on the current season's growth in late summer or early autumn. They are generally hardy to about 23°F (–5°C), but in cooler areas the evergreens, in particular, are best grown in the shelter of a warm, sunny wall. If protected at the roots, deciduous species badly damaged by cold often regenerate from the base in spring.

H. POPULNEA (ZONES 9–10)

LACEBARK

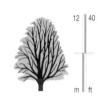

Spreading evergreen with narrow, glossy, dark green leaves, white flowers, and, when mature, brown and white flaking bark. Grows naturally as a multistemmed tree, branching freely from the base.

WHEN TO PRUNE Late spring.

TRAINING AND PRUNING Needs little, if any, formative pruning. Restrict growth of trees against walls, if necessary, by removing overly long branches to well within the tree to maintain an informal outline. This species responds well to hard pruning: old, ragged, or poorly formed specimens can be rejuvenated by severe cutting back.

OTHER HOHERIAS
H. GLABRATA Grows naturally as a bush tree needing minimal pruning. Hard cutting back, in early summer, is tolerated, but it is better to replace an old, poorly shaped specimen than to attempt renovation.
H. LYALLII Train as a central-leader standard (*see p.28*) with a clear stem of 3–5ft (1–1.5m), pruning in early summer. Established trees need little further pruning, other than routine removal of dead wood.

IDESIA (ZONES 6–9)

Idesia polycarpa is a small tree (it grows much taller in Mediterranean-type climates) grown for its red, pealike fruits and its tiered, open crown – a habit it achieves only on fertile, slightly acid soil in a sheltered, sunny site. Grow as a feathered tree or as a central-leader standard (*see p.28*) with a clear trunk to a height of 3–8ft (1–2.5m). Prune, if necessary, when the tree is dormant. Do not cut back hard; the water shoots (*see p.32*) that result will not make sound replacement branches.

ILEX *HOLLY*

Evergreen and deciduous trees and shrubs grown for their glossy foliage and berries, borne on female trees when males grow nearby. Variegated cultivars of *Ilex aquifolium* and *I.* x *altaclerensis* have gold or silver markings either around the leaf margins or as a central blotch. The second type (*see right*) is more prone to reversion. The evergreens are widely grown as formal hedges (*see p.44*) and in clipped shapes (*see* Topiary, *p.48*), although clipping hedges and topiary removes most of the berrying wood. Even informal, freestanding specimens benefit from an occasional shaping cut; take care when doing so, however, since overzealous pruning may spoil their form.

I. AQUIFOLIUM (ZONES 6–9)

COMMON HOLLY, ENGLISH HOLLY

Evergreen, densely branched, pyramidal tree, with usually spiny, glossy dark foliage and bright red berries. The smaller cultivars of shrublike proportions can be pruned as for the larger ones. The weeping 'Pendula' is a bottom-grafted tree that, unlike many pendulous trees, is compact and dome-forming, naturally producing more height at its center. It is easy to select and train in a central leader, which is best cleared to display the habit to advantage.

WHEN TO PRUNE Mid- to late summer. Clip hedges and shaped trees in late summer, when new leaves are firm and glossy, but before the shoots have fully ripened and become hard to cut. If pruned before midsummer, a second flush of uneven regrowth may occur, thus spoiling the clean outlines created.

ILEX X ALTACLERENSIS 'LAWSONIANA'
The foliage of variegated holly cultivars may have either colored blotches or edges.

TRAINING AND PRUNING Train as a feathered tree or central-leader standard (*see* Evergreen trees, *p.27*). Young hollies are vigorous, frequently forming competing leaders. Rapid extension growth sometimes fails to ripen fully before the onset of winter and is then susceptible to cold damage – cut back to live wood in spring. Maintain or improve the natural pyramidal shape by removing any vigorous, protruding branches, cutting back to well within the crown to hide the cuts.

Train 'Pendula' with a clear trunk to about one-third of the height of the young tree, so that the branches will weep to just above soil level. Maintain as for any weeping standard (*see p.28*). Common holly responds vigorously to to hard pruning, even into old wood. Thin regrowth if necessary.

OTHER HOLLIES
Most evergreen hollies, including
I. X ALTACLERENSIS and I. LATIFOLIA, are pruned as for *I. aquifolium*.
I. X ATTENUATA (and other American hybrids), I. OPACA and other species *See* Dictionary of Ornamental Shrubs, *p.203*.

JACARANDA (ZONE 10)

Very vigorous, evergreen or semideciduous trees grown for their fernlike foliage and vivid blue flowers produced in spring (at the same time as leaf fall) and sometimes in autumn. They form tall trees with branches so widely spaced that they look vulnerable to wind damage, but in fact, this rarely occurs. Unlike many fast-growing trees, they produce strong, flexible wood and are long-lived. Outdoors, they look best with a clear trunk and well-spaced branches. Jacarandas grown under glass form smaller trees that are best left feathered, allowing flowers to be appreciated at close quarters.

WHEN TO PRUNE Winter, when dormant.

TRAINING AND PRUNING Train as central-leader standards (*see p.28*), clearing the trunk to up to 20ft (6m) as desired, or under glass as feathered trees (*see p.27*). Trees usually branch at 6–10ft (2–3m). Remove any vigorous, vertical laterals. If allowed to develop, they will form narrow crotch angles that are prone to splitting. Responds well to hard pruning.

JUGLANS WALNUT

Large, deciduous trees grown for their stately habit, beautiful bark, and big, pinnate leaves that, in some species, emit a sweet scent when crushed. *J. regia* makes a fine ornamental tree and is also grown for its edible nuts (*see p.149*), which ripen well only in long, hot summers. If a walnut tree is not to be cultivated primarily for its nuts, *J. nigra* is an easier tree to grow, particularly in continental climates. Many walnuts are important timber trees.

Walnuts are intolerant of root disturbance and pruning and must be planted young, as one- or two-year-old trees, with as large a root ball as possible, to minimize stress when transplanting. Do not purchase pot-bound, container-grown specimens since these are very difficult to establish. Cultivars are grafted on seedling understock.

Young walnut wood is made up of hollow compartments of very soft pith. If incorrectly pruned, this tissue is very prone to dieback and, in severe cases, cavities may form (*see p.33*). When pruning, it is very important not to leave stubs that will die back. Walnuts also bleed profusely, so pruning must be kept to a minimum. Certain species should not be pruned at all.

WHEN TO PRUNE Midsummer to before midwinter. Do not prune in late winter or spring as the sap rises early and will bleed profusely.

J. NIGRA (ZONES 4–9)

BLACK WALNUT

A large tree that naturally forms a central leader, giving it a distinctive pyramidal habit when young. It 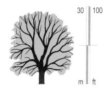 spreads widely in maturity, with lower branch tips that are more or less pendulous, furnishing the tree with foliage almost to ground level.

TRAINING AND PRUNING Train as a central-leader standard (*see p.28*). It is important to remove laterals from the trunk when the tree is young to reduce the risk of cavities and stem blemish. Keep pruning of established trees to a minimum (*see also J. regia*). Does not respond well when cut back hard.

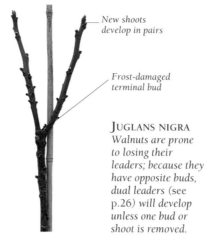

JUGLANS NIGRA *Walnuts are prone to losing their leaders; because they have opposite buds, dual leaders (see p.26) will develop unless one bud or shoot is removed.*

New shoots develop in pairs

Frost-damaged terminal bud

J. REGIA (ZONES 6–9)

ENGLISH WALNUT

Naturally forms a rounded canopy with heavy branches and little twiggy growth, giving a solid appearance. It is valued for its timber and for edible nuts that ripen reliably only in warm climates. Most cultivars are treated as for the species. Thin the crown of *J. regia* 'Pendula', a weeping standard (*see p.28*), when young to avoid congestion in maturity.

30 | 100
m | ft

TRAINING AND PRUNING Train as a central-leader standard (*see p.28*). In cooler climates, the leader is easily lost to cold damage: cut back to a healthy shoot in summer and train it in. It is vital when removing cold damage to cut well into healthy, solid wood. Clear the trunk early in the tree's life to reduce the risk of cavities forming. Pruning of established trees should be kept to a minimum. If a damaged branch must be removed, it is imperative that the branch collar be left intact (*see p.12*). The tree does not respond well to hard pruning.

OTHER WALNUTS
J. AILANTHIFOLIA, J. CINEREA As for *J. regia*.
J. CALIFORNICA, J. HINDSII, J. MICROCARPA Best allowed to develop naturally into small, shrubby, multistemmed trees. *See also* Walnuts, *p.149*.

K

KALOPANAX (ZONES 4–8)
CASTOR-ARALIA

Spiny, deciduous tree that grows naturally with a central leader and short, well-spaced, near-horizontal branches. Young trees are prone to cold damage. New shoots flower terminally, then develop spurlike sublaterals with whorls of leaves. Plant young, since transplant stress may cause dieback. Trees can take three years to produce laterals. Train as a central-leader standard (*see p.28*), clearing the trunk to 6–10ft (2–3m) by rubbing out shoots as they emerge. This reduces the risk of decay entering the soft, pithy wood. Keep pruning of established trees to a minimum.

KOELREUTERIA

The deciduous, sun-loving golden-rain tree (zones 5–9) is prone to dieback 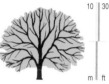 in shade. An open habit that lets in light is to be encouraged. Koelreuteria is fast-growing and short-lived, and the pithy wood is susceptible to rots, especially canker. Do not feed on planting in fertile soils; the resulting sappy growth will be susceptible to disease and cold damage. Train as a central-leader standard (*see p.28*), pruning when dormant, but do not remove laterals until they begin to die back as a result of shading. Never tip-prune to encourage dense growth. Keep pruning of established trees to a minimum; they do not respond to hard pruning.

10 | 30
m | ft

KOELREUTERIA PANICULATA *The foliage turns butter-yellow in autumn, especially after a long, hot summer. In warm climates, the flowers are followed by distinctive bladderlike fruits.*

OTHER ORNAMENTAL TREES
HOVENIA Train as a central-leader standard (*see p.28*). Established trees need minimal attention.

HYMENOSPORUM Train *H. flavum* with a clear trunk initially (*see p.28*), then allow the crown to branch naturally.

KIGELIA As for *Brachychiton* (*see p.55*).
KNIGHTIA As for *Hovenia* (*see left*).

L

+ LABURNOCYTISUS

Small, deciduous graft hybrid between *Cytisus* and *Laburnum*, often unstable due to poor root formation. Plant as young as possible, and use a short stake to strengthen the stem (*see p.23*). Use guy wires on established specimens with weak stems. Train as a central-leader standard (*see p.28*) with a clear stem to 5–6ft (1.5–2m), then allow the leader to lose dominance, letting a branched head develop naturally. Prune during the dormant season or very lightly in mid- to late summer. Once the tree is established, prune only if necessary. Remove suckers and uncharacteristically vigorous shoots within the canopy at once, since these will be pure laburnum; if allowed to develop, they will suppress the hybrid. Renovation should be avoided: hard pruning upsets the tissue balance and may lead to a proliferation of pure laburnum growth.

+ LABURNOCYTISUS ADAMII
Two genetically distinct tissues form a single plant that bears three types of flower at once: yellow laburnum, purple broom, and these pink flowers that are a mixture of both. The foliage is mostly laburnum-like, but branches of Cytisus *may occur within the canopy.*

LABURNUM *GOLDEN CHAIN TREE* (ZONES 5–7)

Small, deciduous trees, grown for their pendent racemes of bright yellow flowers. They respond well to training and regular light pruning to maintain trained forms. Although usually grown as free-standing specimens, laburnums are very beautiful trained to form an arch. They are fast-growing when young, but tend to be short-lived. They resent transplanting, so plant as young as possible. Check containerized plants for root restriction and do not purchase if pot-bound. All parts are poisonous.

L. ANAGYROIDES

COMMON LABURNUM

Vigorous, spreading tree that flowers profusely in late spring and early summer. Named cultivars,

such as *L. anagyroides* 'Aureum', with golden leaves, and 'Erect', with ascending branches, are grafted and are treated as for the species; rootstocks may sucker.

WHEN TO PRUNE Late summer to before midwinter, to avoid bleeding of sap.

TRAINING AND PRUNING Grow as a feathered tree, or train as a central-leader standard (*see p. 28*) to show off the pendulous flowers to best effect. Aim for a balanced head and a clear stem of about 5ft (1.5m) by the third year, since the removal of larger laterals usually leads to the formation of cavities. Avoid pruning established specimens except for spur-pruning (*see below*) of trained forms. If removal of dead wood is necessary, try to avoid cutting back to living tissue, since this will breach the tree's natural defenses (*see p.11*). On grafted or budded cultivars, rub out

immediately any buds that break below the graft union. Renovation is seldom successful; replace old or poorly formed specimens.

Training of laburnums to walls and arches (*see below*) is relatively easy but must be maintained and combined with both renewal and spur pruning each year to encourage free flowering.

> **OTHER LABURNUMS**
> L. ALPINUM As for *L. anagyroides*.
> L. ALPINUM 'PENDULUM',
> L. ANAGYROIDES 'PENDULUM'
> Maintain as top-grafted weeping standards (*see p.28*).
> L. X WATERERI 'VOSSII' Voss's laburnum, usually sold as a grafted, central-leader standard; choose young trees with neat, sound graft unions. Train and prune as for *L. anagyroides*. Remove suckers or buds that appear below the graft union.

FORMING A LABURNUM TUNNEL

FORMATIVE TRAINING
Plant one- or two-year-old feathered trees in two rows along the structure at 6–10ft (2–3m) intervals. Train over the framework of the arch, tying in early in the season while the wood is still supple. Where insufficient laterals are produced to fill in the sides of the framework, tip back the leading shoot to encourage laterals to break. Trees pictured right are shown at various stages of development.

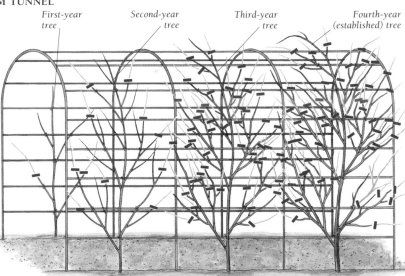

First-year tree   Second-year tree   Third-year tree   Fourth-year (established) tree

ESTABLISHED PRUNING
Once the basic branch framework is established, prune annually at the end of the growing season to reduce the density of growth and allow the production of flowering spurs. Remove dead or badly placed branches, and select replacement shoots where possible to fill in gaps. Shorten the remainder of the current year's shoots to two or three buds of the framework branches; this will encourage spur production.

LAGERSTROEMIA

Crape myrtles are deciduous and evergreen, multi-stemmed trees or shrubs (zones 7–9) grown for their terminal panicles of large pink, red, purple, or white flowers that are produced from mid- to late summer on the current year's growth. The leaves color well in the autumn (shortly after flowering is over) but may drop quickly if the weather is cold. Although some species tolerate cold winters, crape myrtles thrive and flower well only in areas with long, hot summers and mild winters. In cooler zones, they can be grown in a well-lit cool greenhouse or conservatory.

WHEN TO PRUNE Autumn to early spring.

TRAINING AND PRUNING Train as a single or multistemmed tree (see p.30), selecting one to five strong shoots to form main stems arising at or near ground level. These will support a proliferation of slender, flowering laterals and sublaterals if desired. Once the framework is established, prune one in three of the laterals and sublaterals back to the framework. This stimulates new growth that ripens to bear flowers from mid- to late summer. Plants grown in frost-free climates need little further pruning. In cooler areas and under glass, especially in northern areas with short growing seasons, thin to allow light and air into the center of the tree to discourage disease.

LAURELIA CHILEAN LAUREL

L. serrata is a small, evergreen tree (zone 10) grown mainly for its attractive foliage, which is spicily scented when crushed. Although the mature tree is cold-hardy, young growth is not. The densely leafy older branches may break in strong winds, so plant in a warm, sheltered site. It grows naturally with a strong leader and is best grown as a feathered tree (see p.27), pruning in summer, after flowering.

Laurelias need little training or pruning. If necessary, restrict spread by cutting back branch leaders by up to one-third of the season's growth. They are suitable for training against a sunny wall (see Magnolia grandiflora, p.74). They regenerate well if pruned hard, but the dense regrowth may need thinning to reduce wind resistance. If branches are broken by winds, cut back to sound wood. Crown thinning (see p.35) may be needed to reduce future wind resistance.

LAURUS BAY

Slow-growing evergreens with aromatic foliage, sometimes grown as dense shrubs and as hedges. Bay trees are grown both for their culinary use and for their formal ornamental value.

L. NOBILIS (ZONES 8–9)

BAY, BAY LAUREL, SWEET BAY

A dense, low-branching tree with leathery leaves used in cooking. It grows naturally as a central-leader tree, looking best with branches retained almost to ground level. Bay lends itself to topiary, responding well to pinch pruning and clipping. Bays make excellent container plants and are trained as cones, pyramids, or "lollipop" standards. In cooler climates, except in very mild areas, these need winter protection; foliage is susceptible to wind scorch.

WHEN TO PRUNE Train young plants in spring, just before new growth begins. Clip or trim shaped plants in summer.

TRAINING AND PRUNING Train as a feathered tree (see p.27). Upper laterals rarely compete with the leader, eventually forming near-horizontal branches. Once established, pruning is best kept to a minimum. Clip formally shaped specimens (see Topiary, p.48, and also Hedges, p.44) with pruners, not shears. If wind scorch or dieback occurs, wait until late spring, when defoliated branches often leaf out again. If they do not, cut back to live wood, concealing cuts within the canopy. New shoots will develop to fill in gaps. Although tolerant of severe pruning, bays are slow to recover and regrow. Large wounds are therefore very obvious, so heavy pruning

should be a last resort. Occasionally, strong winds cause trees to develop unevenly. In early summer, prune correctively (see p.34), but as lightly as possible, to restore a balanced shape. Thereafter, trim lightly and regularly in summer to encourage a dense habit.

> **OTHER LAURUS**
> L. AZORICA As for *L. nobilis*. Hardy in mild areas that experience only light frosts, if given the protection of a sheltered, sunny wall.

Year 1

Year 2

Stem cleared of shoots

Remove basal suckers

LAUREL TOPIARY
To form a small standard, prune a young straight-stemmed plant back to a cluster of laterals, shortening these to outward-facing buds. As new shoots develop, tip-prune each to a bud facing in the direction in which growth is desired, building up a compact head.

LEUCODENDRON

Leucodendron argenteum (silver tree) is a columnar, evergreen tree or large shrub (zone 10), grown for its silver-gray foliage and tiny yellow flowers with silver bracts, produced from autumn to spring and followed by curious, conelike fruits. In cooler climates, it is suitable for a greenhouse. Plant as young as possible. Trees are usually short-lived but easily raised from seed. In warm climates, train as a feathered tree (see p.27), leaving laterals almost to ground level. Prune, as necessary, in early summer. For established specimens and for those grown under glass, pruning should be kept to an absolute minimum, since this tree is prone to infection and dieback.

> **OTHER ORNAMENTAL TREES**
> LAGUNARIA Train as a central-leader standard (see p.28). Tolerates pruning if required, for example, to restrict size when grown under glass.

LINDERA *SPICE BUSH*

Aromatic trees and large shrubs grown for their form and foliage. They prefer a sunny, sheltered site (zones 4–9), and can be wall-trained. Young growth may be prone to frost damage, but linderas usually regenerate well.

L. PRAECOX

Small deciduous tree that can also be coppiced for attractive large leaves (but few flowers).

WHEN TO PRUNE Autumn to early spring.

TRAINING AND PRUNING In mild climates, train as a central-leader standard (*see p.28*) with a clear trunk to 4–5ft (1.2–1.5m). In cooler climates, will develop naturally as a multistemmed tree (*see p.30*). As a multistemmed tree, it is suitable for wall training; if necessary, prune to within 12in (30cm) of the ground when dormant (*see p.30*), and select three to five well-placed, upright shoots from those that develop to form the main stems. Tie these in (*see p.74*), fanned out over the allotted space, as growth proceeds. The slender, flowering laterals need little pruning other than to removing long outward-growing shoots. This will stimulate water shoots (*see p.32*): rub them out as they emerge. Remove shoots from the base promptly or train in if needed to replace an older branch. Linderas respond well to hard pruning if needed. Cut coppiced trees (*see p.36*) back to 12–20in (30–50cm) every other year in early spring.

> **OTHER LINDERAS**
> L. BENZOIN, L. OBTUSILOBA Shrubby species that need little pruning. Respond well to renovation if carried out over two or three years (*see p.160*).

LIQUIDAMBAR

Sweetgum trees are deciduous, with maplelike leaves, and are valued for their autumn color and attractive bark. All are relatively intolerant of root disturbance, so plant when young. Older trees are usually ready-trained, central-leader standards (although some species look equally attractive as feathered trees). They establish more successfully if the lower laterals are removed before transplanting to reduce water loss through transpiration. Avoid pot-bound, container-grown specimens; plants are intolerant of root pruning, especially if planting in autumn. None respond well to hard pruning in cooler climates.

L. STYRACIFLUA (ZONES 5–9)

AMERICAN SWEETGUM

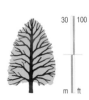

Broadly pyramidal tree with drooping branches at maturity, grown for its glorious autumn colors of scarlet, crimson, and purple. It is the hardiest and most widely grown liquidambar.

WHEN TO PRUNE When dormant, from late autumn to early spring. Remove dead wood in late summer.

TRAINING AND PRUNING Train as a central-leader standard with a short trunk (*see p.28*); any competing leaders must be removed as soon as seen. Remove lower

LIQUIDAMBAR STYRACIFLUA
Brilliant autumn foliage color makes this variegated cultivar a striking specimen tree, particularly against a dark background.

branches to allow the drooping branches to descend to eye level, so that the autumn color can be appreciated at close quarters. However, this is not a good city tree; it drops its spiny fruits and needs a large area for root development.

> **OTHER LIQUIDAMBARS**
> L. FORMOSANA, L. ORIENTALIS Prone to cold damage and competing leaders when young: train as a feathered tree (*see p.27*) until at least 20ft (6m) tall. Only then clear the trunk, if desired, by about 12in (30cm) each year over four or more years.

LIRIODENDRON

Deciduous trees grown for their pale green, tuliplike flowers in midsummer, and for their foliage, which turns deep gold in autumn.

L. TULIPIFERA (ZONES 4–9)

TULIP TREE

Fast-growing, vigorous tree; in its native eastern North America, it is considered aristocratic and beautiful. In temperate climates, it is ideal for gardens, often growing larger than 100ft (30m) and forming a dense, more rounded crown; it may also lose the characteristic semipendulous nature of its mature branches.

WHEN TO PRUNE When dormant, from autumn to early spring. Remove dead wood when the tree is in full leaf.

TRAINING AND PRUNING L. tulipifera usually forms a strong central leader and little formative pruning is required. In warmer continental climates, remove laterals gradually in the early years to clear the trunk (*see p.28*) to about one-third of the overall height of the young tree. In cool, maritime climates, delay the removal of laterals until the tree is well established. Aim to clear the trunk to about 6–10ft (2–3m).

Keep pruning of established trees to a minimum because the wounds are vulnerable to wood-rotting organisms. If branch removal becomes necessary, seek professional advice.

> **OTHER LIRIODENDRONS**
> L. CHINENSE Plant as young as possible. Train and prune as for L. tulipifera.
> L. TULIPIFERA 'FASTIGIATUM' Fastigiate form (*see p.20*) best left branched to the ground. Needs little or no pruning.

LOMATIA (ZONE 10)

Small to medium-sized evergreen trees. Frost often nips terminal buds, resulting in bushier growth. They are pruned after flowering. Let L. ferruginea form a multistemmed tree (*see p.30*). L. hirsuta looks best as a single stemmed, feathered tree (*see p.27*) but if the leader is damaged, it cannot be replaced; allow a multistemmed form to develop, with five to seven main stems. These trees have no special pruning needs once established. They can also be wall-trained, as for *Lindera* (*see above*).

LUMA (ZONES 9–10)

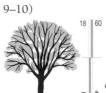

Luma apiculata (syn. *Myrtus luma*, *M. apiculata*, *Myrceugenia apiculata*) is an evergreen tree or shrub of variable habit, but usually with upright laterals that droop at the tip with maturity, and elegant, pendulous sublaterals. It is grown for its aromatic, leathery, glossy green leaves and small, cup-shaped white flowers, borne from late summer to early autumn. Its attractive, cinnamon-colored bark peels to reveal a creamy gray inner surface. In mild, almost frost-free areas it is grown as a central-leader standard, but in cooler regions, where it seldom reaches more than 20ft (6m) in height, it is more successful, and equally attractive, as a multistemmed tree.

WHEN TO PRUNE Spring, before new growth begins.

TRAINING AND PRUNING In mild areas, train as a central-leader standard (*see p.28*), removing lower branches progressively to about 5ft (1.5m). The leader is not strongly dominant, so remove competing shoots as soon as

LUMA APICULATA
Cup-shaped flowers are followed by spherical, red fruits, darkening to purple. Both are set off well by the dark, glossy foliage. 'Glanleam Gold' is a variegated cultivar with yellow-splashed leaves.

possible. In cool climates, allow to develop as a multistemmed tree (*see p.30*), branching at the base or from a low trunk; if necessary, select only three to five of the strongest shoots to form a well-spaced framework of main stems. Once trees are well established, thin laterals within the crown to produce an open-centered canopy that will reveal the bark. Mature trees rarely require attention. If needed, thin branches of established specimens better to display the bark and drooping habit; however, this is unlikely to be necessary provided that trees have been well trained.

LYONOTHAMNUS *CATALINA IRONWOOD* (ZONE 10)

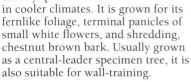

Lyonothamnus floribundus is an exceptionally graceful evergreen tree. It prefers frost-free conditions and is usually quite small in cooler climates. It is grown for its fernlike foliage, terminal panicles of small white flowers, and shredding, chestnut brown bark. Usually grown as a central-leader specimen tree, it is also suitable for wall-training.

WHEN TO PRUNE Spring, before new growth begins.

TRAINING AND PRUNING Train as a single-stemmed, feathered tree (*see p.27*), leaving well-spaced branches to ground level. These produce both upright and pendulous, whippy sublaterals on the same branch. Prune only to thin

congested branches. Removal of too much growth stimulates vigorous water shoots (*see p.32*) that spoil the crown. Once the framework is established, little further pruning is required.

These trees do, however, tolerate drastic pruning and respond well. Cut neglected or overgrown plants back almost to the ground in spring. As for *Eucalyptus* (*see p.64*), select the strongest of the resulting shoots as a new leader and remove the the rest of the shoots. Repeat formative pruning as described above.

Once the central leader and main, horizontal laterals are trained in (*see Magnolia grandiflora, p.74*), the most effective way of growing lyonothamnus against a wall is to allow only those sublaterals that have a pendulous habit to develop, thus creating a curtain of foliage. Remove any upright laterals annually in mid- to late summer, after flowering.

M

MAACKIA

Small, deciduous trees grown for their pinnate foliage and spikes of small, white pea-flowers borne in late summer. Makes a good street or container tree.

M. AMURENSIS (ZONES 3–7)

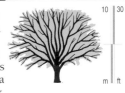

A spreading tree often grown as a multistemmed specimen. It can also be trained as a standard with a short clear trunk and an open, rather sparse crown.

WHEN TO PRUNE Autumn to early spring.

TRAINING AND PRUNING If left to develop naturally, *M. amurensis* will form an attractive single-stemmed tree that needs little or no pruning. To produce a more treelike form, select and train a central leader, removing lower branches (*see p.28*) to a height of at least 30–36in (75–90cm). If the leader is lost, the crown will open out quickly, providing little opportunity for selecting and training a replacement. Established trees do not respond well to hard pruning.

OTHER MAACKIAS
M. CHINENSIS As for *M. amurensis*. If forming a central-leader tree, tip-prune any competing leaders.

MACLURA *OSAGE ORANGE*

Maclura pomifera is a spiny, round-headed, deciduous tree (zones 4–9) with very hard wood, bearing yellow-green, orangelike fruits. It is grown as a central-leader tree or as impenetrable, informal hedging or barrier plantings. Its milky sap can be harmful: wear gloves when pruning. Prune when dormant, from autumn to early spring. Train as a feathered tree (*see p.27*). Little pruning is needed. The leader loses vigor early and a broad, congested crown develops that should not be thinned. For a hedge or screen, plant 20–36in (50–90cm) apart to restrict height and width. If necessary, shear back hard in winter. (*See also Hedges, p.44*.)

OTHER ORNAMENTAL TREES
LITHOCARPUS As for *Quercus ilex* (*see p.84*).
LITSEA See *Neolitsea* (*p.77*).

LOPHOMYRTUS As for *Luma* (*see above*).
LOPHOSTEMON Treat *L. confertus* (syn. *Tristania conferta*) as for *Luma* (*see*

above), training as a central-leader standard. Withstands hard pruning well.

MAGNOLIA (ZONES 4–8 OR 9)

Large genus of trees and shrubs grown for their showy, often fragrant flowers. Early-flowering species may be marred by late frosts; most species need protection from strong winds. Plants grown on poor soil seldom make well-shaped specimens.

In general, avoid pruning established magnolias unless essential. Many species bleed and should only be pruned from summer to before midwinter. Where light pruning (making cuts no more than ⅘in/2cm in diameter) is necessary to shape young plants or restrict growth, prune in midsummer those that flower before or with the new leaves in spring. Prune the late-flowering species, which bloom after new leaves are produced, in spring as new growth begins. Many magnolias break from old wood and respond well, if necessary, to hard pruning at the correct season. Recovery is slow: trees usually direct their energy into wound healing in the first year, producing heavy new growth only in subsequent years. The more vigorous may produce sappy water shoots (see p.32) around cuts, which must be removed.

M. CAMPBELLII (ZONES 7–9)

Deciduous tree, bearing usually pink flowers from late winter to mid-spring. It is sometimes low-growing and sprawling, but more commonly a well-branched, pyramidal tree with a strong central leader. Grafted plants (usually cultivars) tend to branch earlier than seedlings, and often develop lower, broad crowns.

WHEN TO PRUNE Early to midsummer, when the leaves have expanded fully.

TRAINING AND PRUNING To train a single, straight-stemmed, pyramidal tree, select a vigorous, unbranched whip (see p.24). It is important that the leader grows without check for the first four or five years. Remove only damaged growth and competing leaders: harder pruning will stimulate vertical shoots that rise up through the center of the tree, spoiling its form. Grafted plants tend to branch low in the early years; if low laterals become overlong, particularly if the central leader is weak, shorten them by two buds (these are on stubby "pegs").

Once the central leader is well established, remove lower branches over two to four years (depending on vigor). Little further pruning is required. To fill a gap if a branch is lost, select a suitable shoot from the cluster that arises around the wound. Remove the rest, and rub out new buds as they emerge. Tip-prune the new shoot in early spring to promote

TRAINING MAGNOLIA GRANDIFLORA AGAINST A WALL

YEAR 1, FIRST SUMMER AFTER PLANTING

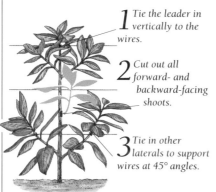

1 Tie the leader in vertically to the wires.

2 Cut out all forward- and backward-facing shoots.

3 Tie in other laterals to support wires at 45° angles.

YEAR 2, SUMMER

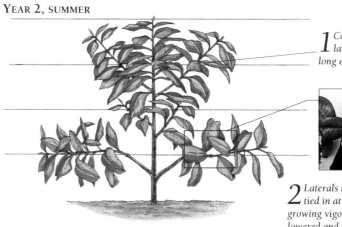

1 Continue to tie in new laterals at 45° when long enough.

2 Laterals that were previously tied in at 45° are now growing vigorously and can be lowered and tied in horizontally.

YEAR 3 AND THEREAFTER, SUMMER

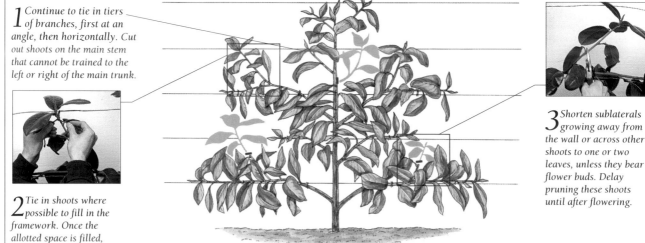

1 Continue to tie in tiers of branches, first at an angle, then horizontally. Cut out shoots on the main stem that cannot be trained to the left or right of the main trunk.

2 Tie in shoots where possible to fill in the framework. Once the allotted space is filled, pinch out shoot tips.

3 Shorten sublaterals growing away from the wall or across other shoots to one or two leaves, unless they bear flower buds. Delay pruning these shoots until after flowering.

Magnolia kobus

branching; in the following spring cut back the vertical portion of the shoot to the best-placed, outward-growing side-shoot, and remove others. Rub out unwanted shoots as they emerge.

To renovate completely, cut back all branches to a main framework (preferably over two or three years). Select and train in new shoots as above.

M. GRANDIFLORA (ZONES 6/7–9)

SOUTHERN MAGNOLIA, BULL BAY

Evergreen with large leaves and creamy white, late summer flowers. In its native southern United States, where it may reach 80ft (25m), it is a dense, conical tree. In cooler climates it has an open, shrublike habit and is usually trained against a wall (preferably sunny and sheltered), where a central leader can be retained to a good height.

WHEN TO PRUNE Spring, as growth begins, and in summer if wall-training.

TRAINING AND PRUNING In areas with long, hot summers and mild winters, it forms a strong central leader and needs little pruning other than to shorten lanky young branches, if necessary, to maintain the conical outline. To wall-train in cooler climates, *see facing page*. Renovate as for *M. campbellii*.

OTHER MAGNOLIAS
M. DELAVAYI As for *M. grandiflora*.
M. DENUDATA (syn. M. HEPTAPETA) As for *M. grandiflora*, which it resembles, though it is better suited to cool climates.
M. KOBUS Spring-flowering; pyramidal when young, then spreading to form a broad-crowned tree. Grows naturally with a strong leader; little training is needed. Prune lightly after flowering in midsummer if necessary. Older trees sometimes produce water shoots within the canopy: remove as seen. Renovate as for *M. campbellii*.
M. SALICIFOLIA Prune lightly after flowering in midsummer. Train as a central-leader standard (*see p.28*) with a clear trunk to about 3–5ft (1–1.5m). Needs little or no pruning once established. Renovate as for *M. campbellii*. For other species, *see Dictionary of Ornamental Shrubs, p.208*.

MALUS CRABAPPLE

Small to medium-sized deciduous trees grown for their spring blossoms, their foliage and fruits, and, in some cases, autumn color. Crabapples look equally attractive as standards or feathered trees. Bottom-grafted cultivars such as 'Donald Wyman' and 'Jewelberry' are usually purchased as trained central-leader standards.

WHEN TO PRUNE Autumn to early spring. Light pruning may be needed to remove water shoots in summer.

M. BACCATA (ZONES 2–7)

SIBERIAN CRAB

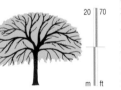

Spreading tree with heavy branches, with white flowers followed by red or yellow fruits. It is best grown on its own roots: grafted specimens, even if well trained, often lean over with age.

TRAINING AND PRUNING Grow initially as a feathered tree (*see p.27*). The tree usually sheds lower branches naturally. If not, remove only a single whorl in each year. Harder pruning stimulates vertical shoots within the canopy: these should be removed because they will form an unattractive secondary crown.

Once established, try to avoid hard pruning: it often leads to branch dieback due to fungus infection.

M. FLORIBUNDA (ZONES 5–8)

Spreading tree with a dense natural branch structure, grown for its profuse pale pink flowers. Some forms have a shrubby habit, while others grow naturally with a strong central leader.

TRAINING AND PRUNING Specimens that exhibit shrubby growth at an early age cannot be trained as trees. Let them develop naturally with several main stems clothed to the ground with branches. Train those that produce a leader with a clear trunk (*see p.28*) to 3–5ft (1–1.5m), then allow the crown to branch, removing only badly placed or crossing branches to form a well-spaced framework and alleviate the naturally congested habit that develops with age. Once the tree is five years old, little further pruning is required. It does not respond well to hard pruning.

MALUS 'BUTTERBALL'
Crabapple cultivars bear fruits in a range of colors, all attractive to foraging birds.

M. TSCHONOSKII (ZONE 6)

A beautiful specimen tree for smaller gardens, with a distinctive pyramidal habit, white flowers, greenish yellow fruits, and vibrant autumn foliage color.

TRAINING AND PRUNING Field-grown trees tend to produce unsubstantial root systems, so a short stake is essential to build this up (*see p.23*). The tree grows naturally with a central leader and semi-upright or upright branches, needing little formative pruning. If the leader is lost and a new one is trained in, shorten vigorous upper laterals by four buds so they do not compete. Low branches can be retained or cleared to a height of 5–6ft (1.5–2m). No other pruning is required.

OTHER MALUS
M. 'BEVERLY', M. 'CALLAWAY', M. 'CENTURION', M. 'CORALBURST', M. 'DAVID', M. 'HARVEST GOLD', M. 'CATHERINE', M. 'MARY POTTER', M. 'PROFUSION', M. 'RED JADE', M. 'SNOWDRIFT', M. 'WHITE ANGEL', M. 'WINTER GOLD' Little pruning is needed; remove occasional water shoots in the crown and suckers from below the graft union.
M. HUPEHENSIS Naturally forms a central-leader standard with ascending branches. Needs little pruning.
M. SARGENTII Naturally multistemmed and wide spreading, but can be trained as a central-leader standard. Needs little further pruning.

MELALEUCA
HONEY MYRTLE, PAPERBARK

Medium-sized evergreens with dark, glossy foliage and "bottle-brush" flowers. Hardy in zone 10, they need a sunny site. They benefit from shaping when young, but little further attention is necessary. They do not respond well to hard pruning and are better replaced than renovated.

WHEN TO PRUNE Late winter or early spring. Shrubby melaleucas such as *M. hypericifolia* tolerate trimming to shape and to limit size after flowering.

TRAINING AND PRUNING Most are best left to develop a multistemmed form with minimal pruning. They make attractive semiformal hedging or screening if regularly trimmed; shoots will not break from old, bare wood. *M. linariifolia* may be left to grow naturally but displays its erect habit and flowers better when only three strong main stems are selected (*see p.30*). Remove any laterals that show strong horizontal growth to encourage an upright profile. Grow *M. styphelioides* as a single-stemmed, feathered tree (*see p.27*); once established, remove low branches, if desired, to about 5–6ft (1.5–2m) to display the papery bark.

MELALEUCA NESOPHILA
These pink-mauve flowers are borne terminally in spring on last year's shoots.

MELIA (ZONES 7–10)

Melia azedarach (chinaberry) is a round-headed, deciduous tree bearing panicles of star-shaped, lilac-pink flowers in spring, followed by orange-yellow fruits. Train as a central-leader standard (*see p.28*), pruning between autumn and early spring. Maintain the leader for as long as possible and aim to clear the trunk to a height of about 6ft (2m). Young trees produce well-spaced branches with long internodes and few sublaterals, creating an open, spindly habit. Clearing the trunk in the early years encourages closer branching higher on the trunk.

MELIOSMA (ZONES 7–9)

Uncommon deciduous trees and shrubs, bearing pyramidal clusters of small, honey-scented flowers in early summer. Tree species – *M. alba* (syn. *M. beaniana*), *M. oldhamii*, and *M. veitchiorum* – are grown as central-leader standards. They are fully hardy, but soft growth made late in the season may suffer cold damage.

WHEN TO PRUNE Spring, as growth begins, or lightly in early summer.

MICHELIA (ZONES 8–9)

Evergreen trees related to *Magnolia*, grown for their fragrant flowers in late winter or early spring.

M. DOLTSOPA

Evergreen or semi-evergreen tree with a broad, rounded crown, attractive as a standard or multistemmed tree. It is suitable for outdoor cultivation only in sheltered gardens in mild climates. The magnolia-like flowers open in early spring from buds set in the previous autumn; they will be damaged by cold weather.

WHEN TO PRUNE Spring, as new growth begins.

TRAINING AND PRUNING Train as central-leader standards (*see p.28*) with a clear trunk to 5–6ft (1.5–2m). Even when young, *M. oldhamii* characteristically forms a single stem and short, stubby laterals that may take several years to develop as proper branches. Grown either as a tree or as a shrub, the sparse habit that results is natural and will not be improved by pruning. Established trees need little pruning and do not respond well when cut back hard.

TRAINING AND PRUNING Minimal formative pruning is needed to produce a multistemmed specimen (*see p.30*); the young tree will branch naturally from ground level. To train as a central-leader tree (*see p.28*), remove competing stems and clear a single trunk to a height of about 2½–3ft (75–90cm). As the tree matures, the leader loses dominance, resulting in a multistemmed crown with upright, then spreading branches.

Keep pruning of established trees to a minimum; they do not respond well when cut back hard.

OTHER MICHELIAS
M. FIGO As for *M. doltsopa*. Will tolerate light trimming in spring to shape or restrict size.

MORUS MULBERRY

Fast-growing deciduous trees grown for their gnarled, picturesque habit. With age, they form a broad, open crown of great character. Fruits are prolific but messy. Mulberries have brittle, fleshy roots; plant with care.

WHEN TO PRUNE When fully dormant, from autumn to early winter, to avoid bleeding of sap.

M. ALBA (ZONES 4–8)
WHITE MULBERRY

Morus alba (syn. *M. bombycis*) forms a wide, rounded head of heavy branches supported on a stout trunk, often of impressive girth. Although a less attractive tree than the black mulberry (*M. nigra*), the fruits do not stain paving as they drop in autumn. The most picturesque specimens often have

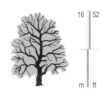

structural defects, usually the result of neglect in their formative years. A "prematurely aged" specimen can be deliberately created by pruning (*see below*) so that the tree will almost certainly develop weak lower limbs that will eventually require propping.

'Pendula' is a bottom-grafted, naturally weeping tree that will not form a central leader unless a shoot is specifically trained for the purpose.

TRAINING AND PRUNING Train as a central-leader standard (*see p.28*) with a clear trunk to about 5ft (1.5m). To create a prematurely gnarled, spreading crown, remove the leader when the tree is four or five years old and allow the tree to develop its own form without further pruning. To produce a structurally strong specimen, it is essential that the leader is maintained for as long as possible, preferably to a height of about 20ft (6m). No further pruning is needed. As the tree matures, the growth of lateral branches will

N-O

NOTHOFAGUS *SOUTHERN BEECH*

Evergreen and deciduous trees grown for their botanical interest and fine-textured foliage. Usually grow rapidly and may be damaged by high winds.

N. DOMBEYI (ZONES 8–9)

Open branch, evergreen tree with toothed, glossy, dark foliage and an elegant, horizontally branching habit.

WHEN TO PRUNE Late spring, after the first flush of rapid spring growth.

TRAINING AND PRUNING Train as a central-leader tree (*see p.28*) with a clear trunk to a height of 5–6ft (1.5–2m). If lower branches are retained, the result is a skirt of foliage around the base of the tree that restricts access beneath. The tree tends to form dual leaders and often continues to do so into early maturity. If allowed to develop, these will form weak crotches. Remove the weaker of the two leaders as seen. Established specimens need little pruning. Lower branches that reach ground level may begin to grow upward, thus forming a skirt of foliage. Remove the lowest branches, if necessary, to permit access beneath.

N. OBLIQUA (ZONE 8)

ROBLÉ BEECH

Vigorous deciduous tree with horizontal branches, pendulous at the tips. The silver-gray bark becomes furrowed and reddens with age, and the leaves color well in autumn. Hardy to about 5°F (-15°C), *N. obliqua* is not suited to exposed sites: the fast-growing crown creates a wind-resistant "sail" that cannot be supported by the roots, and trees often blow over.

WHEN TO PRUNE Autumn to early spring.

TRAINING AND PRUNING Train as a central-leader standard (*see p.28*) with a clear trunk to a height of 10ft (3m). It is vital to maintain a single, strong leader. The rapid growth and weight of mature branches create a high risk of dangerous structural weakness if narrow forks are allowed to develop. With maturity, lower branches become very heavy and produce long, pendulous sublaterals, usually to ground level. If access beneath the tree is necessary, remove the sublaterals. Entire lower branches must only be removed by a professional.

NOTHOFAGUS PROCERA
The branchlets of many southern beeches make a distinctive herringbone pattern.

OTHER SOUTHERN BEECHES
N. ANTARCTICA Grow as a feathered tree (*see p.27*). Trees often lose their central leader early, but this is not a problem.
N. BETULOIDES As for *N. dombeyi*, except that the tree can be left covered with laterals to the ground.
N. PROCERA (syn. N. ALPINA, N. NERVOSA) Hardy in zone 8, but needs shelter from cold, dry winds or a misshapen tree will result that pruning or training cannot rectify. Train as for *N. obliqua*, but with a clear trunk to about 12ft (4m). Support with a short stake (*see p.23*). Ties may need several adjustments during the growing season. If the leader is lost, it is usually replaced naturally by vigorous growth from a lateral branch. If not, train in a replacement (*see p.26*). Established trees need little pruning and do not respond well to hard pruning.

Leader must be trained vertically

Laterals shortened to outward-falling shoots

MORUS ALBA 'PENDULA'
If growing this strongly weeping tree in a container, prune to restrict size and enhance the cascading effect: shorten branches to an outward-growing lateral.

naturally exceed that of the leader, forming a characteristic broad crown. Keep subsequent pruning to a minimum. Remove any epicormic shoots (*see p.32*) periodically. Trees are not easily renovated by drastic cutting back; they respond by producing a mass of water shoots (*see p.32*). Prop lower branches (*see p.33*) if necessary.

To train *M. alba* 'Pendula', insert a stake on planting and tie in a flexible young shoot to form a leader. Extension growth will be strongly arching. Toward the end of the growing season, before the wood is fully ripe, straighten the leader and tie in to the support. Repeat over several years, until the tree reaches a height of about 15–20ft (5–6m). During this period, gradually clear the trunk to a height of about 5ft (1.5m). Thereafter, the crown can be allowed to weep naturally. Keep pruning of established trees to a minimum.

OTHER MULBERRIES
M. NIGRA, M. RUBRA *See* Mulberries, *p.137.*

OTHER ORNAMENTAL TREES
MANGLIETA Treat *M. insignis* as *Magnolia campbellii* (*see p.74*). Do not prune hard.
MAYTENUS Plant young. For a multi-stemmed tree (*see p.30*), remove the central stem when young. For a single-stemmed, feathered tree (*see p.27*), select the strongest stem and remove others. When established, pendulous growth may rest on the ground or become congested. Thin lateral branchlets only. No other pruning is needed. Hard pruning encourages water shoots and may result in a shrubby, less attractive habit.
MELICYTUS *M. ramiflorus* can be grown in a cool greenhouse or conservatory. Needs little pruning other than to tip back laterals, when dormant, to shape.
MESPILUS See Medlar, *p.120.*
METROSIDEROS Usually grows as a large-limbed, multistemmed tree. Little pruning is required.
MYRTUS See Luma, *p.73.*
NEOLITSEA (syn. LITSEA) Train with a clear trunk (*see p.28*) of about 3ft (1m), then allow the tree to branch to form a broad, leafy, and usually structurally sound crown. Established specimens need little pruning and do not respond well to renovation.

NYSSA *TUPELO, BLACK GUM* (ZONES 3–9)

Deciduous trees with attractive foliage and spectacular autumn color. Climate influences their growth habit and form: in warm climates with hot summers it is possible to grow them as central-leader trees; in cool, temperate climates the leader is frequently lost, and it is best to train from the start as multistemmed trees on short trunks.

N. SYLVATICA (ZONES 3–9)

BLACK GUM, SOUR GUM

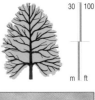

Deciduous tree grown for its form and for its stunning autumn color. It is extremely

NYSSA SYLVATICA
A clear trunk allows lower branches to spread, creating a striking "starburst" effect, particularly in autumn.

intolerant of transplanting, so plant only one- or two-year-old trees. Transplant shock may be fatal, but if container-grown and moved when small, the tree will reestablish well.

WHEN TO PRUNE When dormant, between autumn and early spring.

TRAINING AND PRUNING In warm climates, train as a central-leader standard (*see p.28*), but do not start to clear the trunk until the second year; then remove laterals gradually over four or five years to a height of 6ft (2m). Hard pruning too early may induce early branching in the crown. To create a treelike form it is vital that the leader remains dominant in the early years. Reduce any vigorous laterals that compete with the leader by up to one-third of their length. If the leader is lost or damaged, it is very difficult to replace; it may be better to allow the tree to develop as a multistemmed specimen (*see below*).

In cool climates, create a multi-stemmed form on a short trunk by tip-pruning a newly planted whip to promote branching. Select four or five strong laterals to form framework branches. Remove the lowest laterals so that the trunks are clear to 24–36in (60–90cm).

Little further pruning is needed. The spreading limbs of semimature and mature trees sometimes produce fast-growing upright shoots that grow through the canopy, spoiling the form of the tree (especially in winter). Remove as seen. *Nyssa* tolerate pruning when necessary to tidy growth, restrict spread, or thin a congested canopy (*see* Renovation, *p.34*).

OTHER NYSSAS
N. SINENSIS (zones 7–9) As for *N. sylvatica*.

OXYDENDRUM *SOURWOOD, SORREL TREE* (ZONES 5–9)

Oxydendrum arboreum is a deciduous tree grown for its slender terminal panicles of greenish-white flowers in late summer, and brilliant red, yellow, and purple autumn color. Treelike growth occurs only in areas that experience hot summers, where it is grown as a central-leader specimen. In areas with cool summers, it will develop naturally as a bush or multistemmed tree. Plant trees in their final location as young as possible; transplant shock often results in the loss of the leading shoot. They prefer an open, sunny site. Shade and competition from other vegetation will produce a distorted or

offset canopy, which is best accepted; the sourwood is intolerant of pruning.

WHEN TO PRUNE When dormant, between autumn and early spring.

TRAINING AND PRUNING Plant a young, well-feathered tree. In areas with hot summers, grow as a feathered tree (*see p.27*), and clear a short trunk gradually over time. It is rarely possible to replace a lost leader, and if loss occurs, trees should be allowed to branch and grow naturally. Once established, pruning is best kept to a minimum. Does not respond well when cut back hard.

P

PARROTIA

Parrotia persica (Persian ironwood) is a deciduous tree (zones 4–8) grown primarily for its spectacular gold and crimson autumn color. It is variable in habit, being either treelike or shrublike, but in continental climates the tree form predominates. In shrublike forms, the leader is quickly lost and laterals adopt a horizontal or even pendulous habit. This results in a wide-spreading specimen, seldom more than 12ft (4m) in height and usually broader than it is tall. This form resists all attempts to train an upright leader. In treelike forms, which may reach 40ft (12m) in height, the leading shoot continues to grow, apparently suppressing short laterals, which become increasingly thick with age. Transplant when small. Their habit does not become apparent until

---

PAULOWNIA

Fast-growing, deciduous trees grown for their handsome foliage and foxglovelike spring flowers. All need long, hot summers to ripen the pithy stems, increasing hardiness and reliability of flowering. Even in continental climates, young plants are best raised under glass, or protected for at least the first winter. In colder areas, young growth and flower buds, which develop in autumn, are often lost to frost; paulownias can alternatively be grown as foliage plants by cutting back hard to produce vigorous shoots with very large leaves. These are best overwintered under glass.

P. TOMENTOSA SYN. P. IMPERIALIS

ROYAL PAULOWNIA, PRINCESS TREE

Broadly columnar tree (zones 5–9) with pink-lilac flowers, grown as a central-leader standard (although climate usually dictates growth habit) or as a coppiced or pollarded nonflowering shrub.

WHEN TO PRUNE Winter or early spring.

TRAINING AND PRUNING Train from an early age as a central-leader standard (*see p.28*), but clear the trunk, to a height of about 3–5ft (1–1.5m), where possible by rubbing out buds before they shoot

PARROTIA PERSICA

Parrotias have a curious self-grafting habit: branches that touch will in time fuse together, adding interest to the tree in winter, when its attractive patchwork bark can also be clearly seen.

specimens are three or four years old, so they are best planted in a site where either form will be acceptable.

WHEN TO PRUNE Autumn to early spring.

TRAINING AND PRUNING Shrublike specimens need no formative pruning. Do not thin or shorten laterals, since this will lead to congested growth.

With treelike forms, train as a naturally branched-headed standard (*see p.28*), clearing the trunk to about 5ft (1.5m), then allowing the crown to branch. If necessary, shorten pendulous tips to allow access beneath and display the bark. Established specimens need no regular pruning and are better replaced than renovated. Older trees may be grafted: remove any suckers (*see p.32*).

---

rather than by removing laterals: their branch collars (*see p.12*) are often poorly formed and even if left intact, may not prevent the onset of decay. The leader is often lost – not always to cold – and the crown branches early. In areas with hot summers, the leader can usually be replaced with a vigorous lateral. In areas with cooler summers, numerous lateral buds produce competing leaders, resulting in a natural shrubby growth. Once established, prune only to remove

dead wood or cold damage. Paulownias tolerate hard cutting back but are then best maintained as coppiced or pollarded specimens (*see below and p.36*); cut back annually in winter or early spring.

> **OTHER PAULOWNIAS**
> P. FARGESII, P. FORTUNEI As for *P. tomentosa*.

New shoots will grow up to 8ft (2.5m) in height

Smooth and bevel edges of cut with a pruning knife

Pruning encourages large leaves

PAULOWNIA TOMENTOSA

Paulownias can be grown as foliage plants, with much larger, "tropical"-looking leaves, by cutting back hard each year; this also enables them to be grown in containers in colder climates, either in greenhouses or conservatories, or as summer bedding plants.

PHELLODENDRON

Small to medium-sized, deciduous trees (zones 3–7) with a broad crown of well-spaced, spreading branches; most have rugged, corky bark. The leaves, pale green in spring, assume striking yellow tints in autumn. Young cork trees need moist, loamy soil and a sheltered but sunny site to produce a good form; fine specimen trees are rare in colder areas. Prune when dormant. Train as a central-leader standard (*see p.28*) with a clear trunk to about one-third of the young tree's height. Do not damage the leader; it is difficult to replace. The crown branches early, forming a flattened dome. Prune mature trees only to remove dead wood.

PHYTOLACCA (ZONE 10)

Phytolacca dioica is a vigorous evergreen that will grow outdoors only in frost-free climates. Train as a central-leader standard (*see p.28*) with a clear trunk of 6–10ft (2–3m). Prune in winter or early spring, before growth begins. The leader often branches early, and by early maturity the crown usually increases more rapidly in spread than in height. Established trees need little pruning.

PISTACIA

In warm climates, *P. chinensis* forms a tall tree with a long, straight trunk and a broad, domed crown, but in cool climates is often more shrubby: a sheltered site may help produce a treelike form. Train as a central-leader standard (*see p.28*) with a short, clear trunk, pruning in winter. A lost leader is difficult to replace, and the resultant shrublike habit is best accepted. Established trees need little pruning and do not respond well to hard pruning. Drying winds may cause die-back that in turn results in a proliferation of growth, which should be thinned. To grow *P. vera* for its nuts, *see p.148*.

> **OTHER ORNAMENTAL TREES**
> OLEA *See* Olive, *p.146*.
> OSTRYA As for *Carpinus* (*see p.56*).
> PARKINSONIA No special pruning needs.
> PELTOPHORUM Train as a central-leader standard (*see p.28*). Established trees have no special pruning needs.
> PERSEA *See* Avocado, *p.147*.
> PICRASMA *P. quassioides* grows naturally as a multistemmed tree (*see p.30*). It needs little pruning, other than to clear low laterals, in the early years, to about 24in (60cm).
> PLANERA As for *Ulmus* (*see p.91*).

PLATANUS *PLANE TREE, SYCAMORE*

Large, stately, deciduous trees with dense foliage, popular in urban areas throughout the cool temperate world: they thrive in polluted environments. Planes develop heavy branch structures, and even if well trained they may become unsafe. However, most respond vigorously to hard pruning. Planes grown as street trees are often pollarded, giving them a compact crown atop a tall, clear trunk that allows for traffic below.

WHEN TO PRUNE Autumn to early spring.

P. X ACERIFOLIA (ZONES 4–8/9)

LONDON PLANE

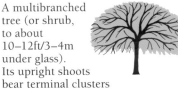

Platanus x acerifolia (syn. *P. x hispanica*, *P. x hybrida*) attains huge dimensions in continental climates, but is often of only medium height in cooler regions. Young trees are vigorous, with a strong central leader and short, well-spaced laterals. The tree looks attractive with foliage to the ground or with a tall, clear trunk. Variegated cultivars may revert (*see p.32*); remove any plain green-leaved shoots.

TRAINING AND PRUNING For a central-leader standard (*see p.28*), clear the trunk to up to 10ft (3m). To produce a tree clothed to the ground, remove laterals below 4ft (1.2m) and allow downward-pointing sublaterals to develop. Because branches grow heavy, it is essential to maintain a strong leader and develop a sound framework. Badly damaged young trees are better replaced. Occasionally, horizontal branches produce upright shoots that will become structurally dangerous "secondary leaders," so remove strongly upright sublaterals as seen.

Established trees need little further pruning. Planes in need of renovation must be dealt with only by a professional.

P. OCCIDENTALIS (ZONES 4–9)

SYCAMORE

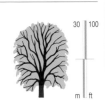

Similar to *P. x acerifolia*, but has a more spreading habit, with massive, crooked branches and broader leaves. The smooth bark flakes off in large, irregular pieces to expose the lighter inner bark, giving an attractive mottled appearance.

TRAINING AND PRUNING Train as a central-leader standard (*see p.28*) with a clear trunk to 6–10ft (2–3m). As the crown develops, keep only evenly and well-spaced laterals. Mature specimens need little or no pruning, but removal of dead twigs enhances the natural form. Over-thinning results in a mass of vigorous growth that increases wind resistance and thus instability. Disinfect pruning tools frequently to avoid spreading canker. For specific renovation needs consult a professional arborist.

OTHER PLANES

P. ORIENTALIS Broadly columnar in continental climates, but rarely achieves a good form in temperate zones. Prune as for *P. x acerifolia*.

CROWN REDUCTION
The crown of a plane that has outgrown its situation, or is casting too much shade, can be reduced by professional arborists (see also Major tree surgery, p.35).

LOPPING
Street planes are frequently disfigured by crude pruning techniques. Full pollarding, taking all branches back to the head of the trunk, is more attractive in a garden setting.

PLATYCARYA (ZONES 6–8)

Platycarya strobilacea is a small, deciduous tree with catkinlike flowers followed by conelike fruits. A member of the walnut family, its wood has soft pith. Although hardy in zones 6 to 8, young growth may be damaged by late spring frosts, and it is often difficult to replace a lost leader. Train and prune as for *Juglans* (*see p.69*).

PLUMERIA *FRANGIPANI*

Tropical, deciduous trees with fleshy branches and fragrant, waxy flowers. In cool areas they may be grown in a greenhouse or conservatory in full light.

P. RUBRA (ZONE 10)

FRANGIPANI

A multibranched tree (or shrub, to about 10–12ft/3–4m under glass). Its upright shoots bear terminal clusters of foliage and branch to produce an open, flat-topped crown. The soft wood is prone to rot and shrinks at the site of cuts, hampering wound closing. Pruning is therefore best kept to a minimum.

WHEN TO PRUNE Early spring.

TRAINING AND PRUNING Train initially as a central-leader standard (*see p.28*) with a clear trunk to 3ft (1m). The leader is rapidly lost as the naturally branched head develops, and pruning will not aid its retention. Established trees need little further attention. Replace trees rather than attempt major renovation. When grown under glass, size may be restricted by cutting growth back to a shoot or branch junction.

OTHER PLUMERIAS

P. ALBA As for *P. rubra*.

POLIOTHYRSIS

Deciduous tree that grows and flowers best in areas with long, hot summers. Train as a central-leader standard (*see p.28*) with a clear trunk of 3–5ft (1–1.5m). The leader is easily lost; in the first year or two, a spring feed of high-nitrogen fertilizer, which induces vigor and inhibits branching, makes training easier (although it increases the risk of cold damage). Mature trees need no special pruning. Avoid cutting back hard into old wood.

POPULUS *POPLAR*

Usually fast-growing, hardy, deciduous trees, grown for their stature and foliage and for their tolerance of a wide range of conditions. Although often considered brittle, most poplars are very wind-resistant. The wood is flexible, and well-trained trees rarely split. The exceptions are those susceptible to bacterial poplar canker, such as *P. x canadensis* 'Eugenei' and *P. wilsonii*. Canker is untreatable but there are resistant clones. Prune species vulnerable to canker, which gains entry through wounds, in summer when wounds seal most quickly. Prune suckering species in summer also, to check the regrowth of suckers and water shoots (*see p.32*). Prune other poplars in autumn, since many begin growth in late winter or early spring and bleed badly if pruned then.

P. ALBA (ZONES 3–8)

WHITE POPLAR, ABELE, SILVER-LEAVED POPLAR

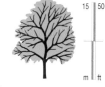

Short-lived tree grown for its foliage and autumn color, best as a central-leader standard or in barrier plantings, where it may also be allowed to develop its natural suckering habit. 'Pyramidalis' is best trained as a feathered tree (*see p.27*); train 'Globosa' initially with a central leader, which will soon be lost as the crown begins to spread; it needs little further pruning.

WHEN TO PRUNE Late summer or early autumn.

TRAINING AND PRUNING To train as a central-leader standard (*see p.28*), clear the trunk to a height of about 5–6ft (1.5–2m). Remove any basal growth and suckers in late summer. Trees grown as standards do not respond well to severe pruning. To grow as barrier plantings, allow suckers to develop; a proportion usually die before the clump becomes congested. Suckering clumps are easily regenerated by hard pruning.

P. X CANADENSIS (ZONES 3–6)

CANADIAN POPLAR

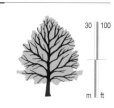

Group of hybrids, including some with golden leaves ('Aurea'), and columnar types such as 'Eugenei', 'Robusta', and 'Serotina', the black Italian poplar. All are potentially very large trees, and neglect of formative pruning will ultimately result in a dangerous tree.

POPULUS X CANDICANS 'AURORA'
This variegated poplar, with cream-blotched leaves, makes an attractive foliage plant when coppiced or pollarded.

WHEN TO PRUNE As for *P. alba.*

TRAINING AND PRUNING Aim to produce a straight-stemmed tree with light, even branching. Train as a central-leader standard (*see p.28*) with a clear trunk of 6–10ft (2–3m). The leader must be maintained at least into early maturity; never allow competing leaders to develop. Remove laterals that are not evenly and well spaced and shorten any upright growth that develops at branch tips by about one-third. Established trees need little pruning. It is rarely worth renovating an old tree; they are susceptible to rot, and respond to hard pruning by producing a mass of water shoots that do not form sound branches.

P. LASIOCARPA (ZONES 3–7)

CHINESE NECKLACE POPLAR

Grown primarily for its attractive habit and heart-shaped leaves with downy undersides. Young trees naturally produce a strong central leader surrounded by stout, vigorous, upright shoots; with maturity, the lower branches become almost horizontal, creating a round-headed tree.

WHEN TO PRUNE As for *P. alba.*

TRAINING AND PRUNING Train as a central-leader standard (*see p.28*), with a clear trunk of 5–6ft (1.5–2m). Little further pruning is required. The leader is strongly dominant, and despite their vigorously upright habit, the topmost laterals seldom form competing leaders, so do not shorten or remove them. Does not respond well to renovation.

P. NIGRA VAR. ITALICA

ITALIAN POPLAR, LOMBARDY POPLAR

Probably the best-known fastigiate tree (*see p.20*), widely planted as a windbreak or visual screen in the open landscape (zones 3 to 9). The cultivar 'Plantierensis' is similar, but branching lower and with a denser, slightly broader crown. It makes a more effective screen and is less prone to canker.

WHEN TO PRUNE As for *P. alba.*

TRAINING AND PRUNING Grow as a feathered tree (*see p.27*). Although little formative pruning is needed, cutting young laterals back to 4in (10cm) results in bushier growth that is useful for a screen. Although the leading shoot always appears to be under threat from competing laterals, actual dual leaders are very rare. Avoid pruning established trees hard; they cannot be renovated.

OTHER POPLARS

P. BALSAMIFERA (syn. P. TACAMAHACA) As for *P. trichocarpa.*
P. X CANDICANS 'AURORA' Commonly grown as a central leader or branched-head standard (*see p.28*). Remove suckers regularly during summer. Can also be coppiced annually or biennially, in late winter (*see p.36*), to produce a large-leaved, multistemmed shrub.
P. DELTOIDES (cottonwood) Fast growing, tolerant and adaptable, hardy from zones 2 to 9. Develops a broad, vase-shaped habit, often with open, spreading branches.
P. MAXIMOWICZII As for *P. trichocarpa.*
P. TREMULOIDES (quaking aspen) Widely distributed throughout North America, fast growing, highly tolerant of all soils and conditions. Good yellow leaf color in autumn. Needs little, if any, training or pruning.
P. TRICHOCARPA Easily trained as a central-leader standard (*see p.28*) with a clear trunk to a height of 6–10ft (2–3m). Prune in late summer or early autumn. Remove suckers in summer. Little further pruning is required. Does not respond well to renovation.
P. WILSONII Very susceptible to canker: do not prune unless absolutely essential. To clear the trunk, to about 5ft (1.5m), rub out buds on the lower stem before they shoot. The upright habit of the laterals can lead inevitably to weak branch crotches and breakage.

PRUNUS

A huge and complex genus of deciduous and evergreen trees and shrubs, grown for their attractive bark, foliage, fruits, and flowers, and for crops such as plums, cherries, and almonds. The pruning of nearly all ornamental *Prunus* is best kept to an absolute minimum. Where formative pruning is necessary, it should be done as early as possible, aiming to create well-formed trees that will need little further attention in later life. Keeping pruning wounds small, and pruning in midsummer reduces the risk of diseases such as silver-leaf (*see p.123*). In common with the stone fruits, ornamental *Prunus* are sometimes affected by gummosis (*see p.123*).

P. AVIUM (ZONES 3–8)

MAZZARD CHERRY

Deciduous tree grown for its white spring flowers. With the exception of the dwarf 'Nana', which needs no pruning, cultivars, including 'Pendula', are treated as for the species. Most produce surface roots that sucker freely.

WHEN TO PRUNE Summer is best but not essential. Remove dead wood in summer and suckers in early spring.

TRAINING AND PRUNING Train as a central-leader standard (*see p.28*) with a clear trunk to 5–6ft (1.5–2m). Remove suckers by rubbing out. Established trees need little further pruning other than removing dead wood; they do not respond well when cut back hard.

ROOTSTOCK SHOOTS ON P. 'UKON'
The growth of epicormic shoots (see p.32) on clear trunks (here below a top-graft union) is a common problem with Prunus.

P. CERASIFERA (ZONES 5–8)

CHERRY PLUM, MYROBALAN

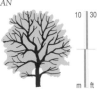

Deciduous tree grown for its profuse, highly fragrant, pinkish flowers, followed by bronze to dark purple foliage. It is grown as a branched-head standard, but also makes an attractive flowering hedge.

WHEN TO PRUNE Midsummer. Prune established hedges after flowering.

TRAINING AND PRUNING Train initially as a central-leader standard (*see p.28*) with a clear trunk to a height of at least 5ft (1.5m). Horizontal branches often throw up vigorous, vertical shoots. Remove these or shorten by one-third to avoid competition with the leader. The leader breaks by early maturity, resulting naturally in a dense, congested crown. Pruning of established specimens is best kept to a minimum, since it stimulates the growth of epicormic shoots that spoil the crown. They do not respond well to renovation.

To grow *P. cerasifera* as a hedge, plant young trees or whips at 3ft (1m) spacings during the dormant season. Tip back the leading shoots in midsummer to encourage branching. In subsequent growing seasons, clip back the new growth by about one-quarter to one-third in midsummer until the required dimensions have been achieved. Once established, clip annually in early summer, immediately after flowering. Overgrown hedges respond well to renovation by hard pruning, preferably spread over three years (*see* Hedge renovation, *p.47*).

P. DULCIS (ZONES 7–9)

ALMOND

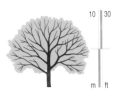

Deciduous tree, valued in cool temperate gardens for its mass of white, pale pink, or rose pink flowers in late spring. The nuts (almonds) ripen fully only in Mediterranean-type climates. The lightly branched crown casts only dappled shade, permitting underplanting. Single trees look splendid against a dark background, and group plantings make an exceptionally beautiful garden feature. Trees are usually raised by budding on to plum rootstocks, and are often sold as whips (*see p.24*).

TOP-GRAFTED JAPANESE CHERRY
Always choose young trees with neat, sound graft unions: never cut or pare graft points that have become unsightly with age.

Rootstock suckering can be a problem. Almonds are susceptible to peach leaf curl (*see also* Peaches, *p.132*).

WHEN TO PRUNE Prune and remove dead wood in midsummer. Remove suckers in early spring.

TRAINING AND PRUNING Train as a central-leader standard (*see p. 28*) with a clear trunk to a maximum height of 5ft (1.5m). Remove suckers from the rootstock in early spring by rubbing out or, if necessary, paring with a sharp pruning knife (*see* Suckers, *p.32*). Established trees need little further pruning. They commonly produce twiggy growth in early maturity, usually resulting in increased flower production. Thinning of the crown is unnecessary and usually spoils the tree's habit. To wall train, *see* Peach fan, *p.134*.

P. SATO-ZAKURA GROUP

JAPANESE FLOWERING CHERRIES

These complex hybrids, probably all derived from *Prunus serrulata*, form one of the most important groups of flowering trees in the temperate world (zones 5 and 6). They vary enormously in growth habit and character. They include fastigiate forms such as 'Amanogawa'; weeping ones such as 'Kiku-shidare' (syn. 'Cheal's Weeping'); the stiffly ascending 'Kanzan' (syn. 'Sekiyama'), and the largest-flowered of all, 'Taihaku', the great white cherry. All are grafted and, depending on the cultivar, are grown variously as central-leader, branched-head or weeping standards. Most need little pruning.

WHEN TO PRUNE Immediately after flowering or in early winter.

YOUNG P. 'AMANOGAWA'
To encourage strong, upright branches and reduce the risk of wind damage, in the first year loop them loosely around a cane or stake with strips of burlap, netting, or soft twine.

TRAINING AND PRUNING In general, do not prune unless absolutely essential. If removing dead wood or crossing or rubbing branches, the tree's natural habit, whether fastigiate, spreading, or weeping, should be enhanced and not compromised by pruning operations. All pruning must be undertaken early in the tree's life. *P.* 'Kanzan' will naturally form a short trunk, displaying its bronzed young foliage and pink flowers at eye level. Where access beneath the tree is necessary, train early with a clear stem to a height of 5–6ft (1.5–2m). *P.* 'Amanogawa' is strongly upright, but

the branches can be open when young, and will benefit from support (*see left*).
On established trees, prune only to remove any dead, diseased, and damaged wood, and also any suckers that appear below graft unions, pruning in summer. Drastic pruning to renovate a tree is seldom successful.

P. SERRULA (ZONES 5–6)

PAPERBARK CHERRY

A beautiful, deciduous tree grown for its smooth, glossy, mahogany-red bark that peels with age. Small white flowers in spring are followed by red fruits in autumn.

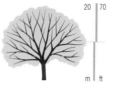

WHEN TO PRUNE Early spring to midsummer. Pruning in spring results in gummosis (*see p.123*) that may cause bark dieback.

TRAINING AND PRUNING Train as a central-leader standard, ensuring well-spaced laterals. Remove unwanted laterals by rubbing out buds before they shoot, to prevent stem blemish at maturity. Train with a clear trunk no taller than 5ft (1.5m). To enhance the bark effect on the lower limbs, clear sub-laterals to within 12–18in (30–45cm) of the main trunk, again by rubbing out buds. Do not prune established trees: it creates wounds that seldom seal fully and results in atypical growth.

OTHER PRUNUS
P. AMERICANA Suckering shrub or small tree. Transplant stress (*see p.25*) increases suckering. Prune in mid-summer. To grow as a tree, train a field-raised whip initially as a central-leader standard (*see p.28*). Remove basal suckers and clear the trunk to one-quarter of the young tree's height by rubbing out buds before they shoot. A branched head will develop naturally.
P. CAROLINIANA As for *P. cerasifera.*
P. 'HALLY JOLIVETTE' May be grown as a multistemmed shrub or small tree (*see p.30*).
P. MAACKII Train as a central-leader standard, clearing the trunk to about 6ft (2m) as for *P. serrula,* rubbing out buds before they shoot. Established trees need no special pruning and do not respond well to hard cutting back.
P. 'OKAME' As for *P. maackii.*
P. PADUS As for *P. avium,* but must be trained early: soon produces vigorous upright growth. Plant ideally at only two or three years old. Older specimens tend to produce dual leaders.
P. SEROTINA As for *P. padus.*
P. SERRULATA See *P. Sato-zakura* group.
P. SUBHIRTELLA var. PENDULA Grown as branched-head standards or multi-stemmed specimens needing little or no pruning. A strong central leader is seldom formed. Clear the stem (*see p.28*) to about 5ft (1.5m), or allow branching from the base.
P. VIRGINIANA 'SHUBERT' As for *P. americana.*
For other species, see Dictionary of Ornamental Shrubs (p.214) and Hardy Fruits (pp.122–136).

CORRECTING UNEVEN GROWTH, TOP-GRAFTED PRUNUS

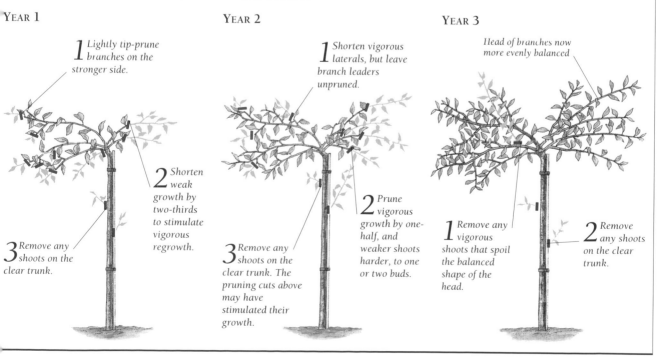

YEAR 1

1 *Lightly tip-prune branches on the stronger side.*

2 *Shorten weak growth by two-thirds to stimulate vigorous regrowth.*

3 *Remove any shoots on the clear trunk.*

YEAR 2

1 *Shorten vigorous laterals, but leave branch leaders unpruned.*

2 *Prune vigorous growth by one-half, and weaker shoots harder, to one or two buds.*

3 *Remove any shoots on the clear trunk. The pruning cuts above may have stimulated their growth.*

YEAR 3

Head of branches now more evenly balanced

1 *Remove any vigorous shoots that spoil the balanced shape of the head.*

2 *Remove any shoots on the clear trunk.*

PTEROCARYA WING NUT (ZONES 5–8)

Deciduous trees grown for their catkins and slender-winged nuts. Though vigorous when mature, they can be frost-tender when young. All develop heavy, spreading branches with pendulous sublaterals. *P. × rehderiana* and *P. fraxinifolia* tend to sucker.

WHEN TO PRUNE Summer. With young trees, delay removing any frosted growth until there is no further danger of cold winds or late frosts. Never prune in autumn; the cambium of the pithy wood shrinks, leading to frost crack.

TRAINING AND PRUNING Train as central-leader standards (*see p.28*). Clear the trunk to one-third of the young tree's height by rubbing out buds before they shoot. It is important to maintain a clear trunk of this height until early maturity. Remove suckers from the base or roots as seen; if a mass build up, removing all simultaneously will stimulate many more to grow. The crown of mature trees may need lifting (*see p.35*) to stop the pendulous sublaterals reaching ground level and rooting to form an unsightly mass of congested growth.

PYRUS PEAR

Deciduous trees with white blossom and alternate-leaved foliage that often colors well in autumn. *P. communis* is grown for its fruit. Some species also have attractive bark. Fireblight (*see p.117*) may be a problem: cut out affected growth and disinfect tools.

WHEN TO PRUNE Autumn to early spring.

P. CALLERYANA (ZONES 5–8)

CALLERY PEAR

Valued for its white spring blossoms, russet-brown fruits, and, especially in areas with long, hot summers, autumn color. *P. calleryana* 'Bradford' has a distinctive pyramidal form; although often recommended as a street tree, the branches frequently form weak crotches that may break. 'Chanticleer' seems less prone to structural weakness.

TRAINING AND PRUNING Train as a central-leader standard (*see p.28*) with a clear trunk of 5–6ft (1.5–2m). For 'Bradford' and 'Chanticleer', retain only evenly and well spaced laterals around the trunk to reduce the risk of branch failure at maturity. Thin established trees to reduce the risk of breakage. They respond poorly to drastic pruning.

P. SALICIFOLIA (ZONES 4–7)

WILLOW-LEAVED PEAR

Grown for its pure white flowers that coincide with new, silvery leaves. Its spreading crown of horizontal branches bears semi- or, in the cultivar 'Pendula', fully pendulous sublaterals, creating a curtain of willow-

PYRUS SALICIFOLIA
The zigzag habit of shoots and sideshoots will disguise light thinning or trimming cuts.

like foliage. Loss of the leader may be due to transplant shock or poor soil. Plant as young as possible.

TRAINING AND PRUNING Train as a central-leader standard (*see p.28*) with a clear trunk to 3–6ft (1–2m), depending on whether foliage to the ground is required (bear in mind that the pendulous habit only develops with maturity). 'Pendula' needs a trunk of at least 5ft (1.5m) to accommodate its fully weeping habit. To avoid congestion at maturity, thin laterals in the early years to create an evenly spaced, balanced framework. Established trees need little further pruning. Though light thinning or trimming is tolerated, trees do not respond well if cut back hard. If growth is vigorous, established specimens may need crown thinning (*see p.35*); take great care not to create gaps in the curtain of foliage since older trees rarely produce replacement growth.

> **OTHER PYRUS**
> P. COMMUNIS See Pears, *p.117*.
> P. USSURIENSIS As for *P. calleryana*.

Q

QUERCUS OAK

An enormous and varied genus of evergreen and deciduous trees, generally slow-growing and noted for their strength and longevity. They are usually grown as central-leader specimens, producing a spreading crown of large, heavy limbs that support smaller, often bushy sublaterals, thus producing the characteristic billowing outline. Deciduous species color well in autumn.

Q. ALBA (ZONES 3–8)

WHITE OAK

Broadly domed, deciduous tree with fissured bark, eventually stately in form, with a trunk of 6ft (2m) or more in diameter. Because of its hard, durable wood, the white oak is one of the most important timber trees. It is distinguished by its distinctive, variably lobed leaves, and its oblong acorns, enclosed for one-quarter of their length in a knobby bowl-like cup.

WHEN TO PRUNE When dormant, in winter or early spring.

TRAINING AND PRUNING Train as a central-leader standard (*see p.28*) with a clear trunk to 8ft (2.5m). In areas with short, cool summers the leading shoot may lose dominance at an early age, resulting in shrubby growth of poor form. To preserve the leader, clear the trunk gradually over three to five years, reducing each limb progressively in two or three stages. Apart from the regular removal of dead wood, established trees need little further pruning. Renovation, including the removal of large dead branches within the canopy, must be undertaken by a professional arborist.

Q. ILEX (ZONE 9)

HOLM OAK

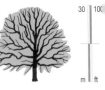

One of the finest of evergreen oaks, forming a broad, rounded canopy, with dark, glossy leaves that are gray-fawn beneath. Young trees, best planted as young as possible, vary in habit from pendulous to fastigiate (usually somewhere in between), often resembling shrubs when young. All, however, produce a central leader. The holm oak tolerates clipping if trained early as a hedge (*see p.44*) or as a large, formally shaped tree.

WHEN TO PRUNE Mid- to late summer, after the first flush of rapid growth.

TRAINING AND PRUNING Train as a feathered tree (*see p.27*), allowing lower laterals to be shed naturally through shading out. The leader barely retains dominance, but do not shorten laterals that appear to compete; these will ultimately form framework limbs. Old specimens often form asymmetrical crowns, but restoration is seldom successful: holes in the crown rarely fill in. Prune established specimens only if essential, for example, to deal with storm damage. This should be dealt with by a professional. The pendulous growth of low branches is attractive, and crown lifting should only be undertaken if essential for light penetration or access.

Q. ROBUR (ZONES 4–8)

ENGLISH OAK

Deciduous tree with a broad canopy of strong, heavy framework branches arising from a trunk that becomes gnarled 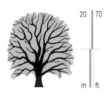 and massive with age. Grown as a central-leader tree, it is suitable for large gardens and open parkland. The cultivars 'Cristata' and 'Filicifolia' and the fastigiate form are best left to develop naturally. *Q. robur* f. *pendula* should be trained as for the species.

WHEN TO PRUNE When dormant, between autumn and early spring.

TRAINING AND PRUNING Train as a central-leader standard (*see p.28*), aiming to clear the trunk to about one-quarter of the tree's overall height by the third or fourth growing season. Little further formative pruning is required. Old specimens may accumulate dead wood, which, if essential, should only be removed by a professional arborist. A proliferation of epicormic shoots on the main stem and lower laterals usually precedes dieback. This does not necessarily herald the end of the tree's life; the English oak can take as long to die as it does to reach maturity. Pollarding (*see p.36*) is an option for renovation.

Q. PALUSTRIS (ZONE 5)

PIN OAK

Elegant tree with often brilliant red autumn color. Although tough, it will not tolerate alkaline soils. It should always be trained as a central-leader standard to show off its unique branching habit.

QUERCUS ROBUR
Mature oaks can often become stag-headed, their "antlers" resulting from the dieback of upper branches. They may survive for years, protected by the natural barriers (see p.11) that plants form between live and dead wood.

WHEN TO PRUNE As for *Q. alba*.

TRAINING AND PRUNING Train as a central-leader standard (*see p.28*) and maintain a clear trunk to approximately one-quarter of the young tree's height until early maturity. In hot-summer climates, retain the leading shoot for as long as possible. In cooler climates the crown usually soon branches but this does not cause problems. Established trees need little further pruning.

OTHER OAKS

Q. ACUTISSIMA (sawtooth oak, zones 6 to 9) As for *Q. alba*.
Q. AGRIFOLIA As for *Q. ilex*.
Q. COCCINEA As for *Q. palustris*.
Q. HEMISPHAERICA (laurel oak, zones 6 to 9) Evergreen until February in the Deep South; makes a good street or campus tree due to its size and habit. Smaller than *Q. virginiana*.
Q. IMBRICARIA (shingle oak, zones 4 to 8) Elegant, medium-growing, to 80–100ft (24–30m). Makes a fine lawn, park, or street tree. As for *Q. palustris*.
Q. MACROCARPA (bur oak, zones 2 to 8) As for *Q. alba*. Excellent park or golf course tree.
Q. PETRAEA In temperate climates can be treated as for *Q. robur*, which it resembles. In wet, acid soils in cold regions, trees grow gnarled and stunted, showing clearly the dwarfing effects of low summer temperatures. In these conditions, such climate-trained trees make interesting specimens and need no pruning.
Q. RUBRA As for *Q. robur*. It is essential to select a straight-stemmed, evenly feathered young tree; the growth pattern, often influenced by climate and site, is set early and pruning cannot change it. Young trees need shelter during their first two winters and will only form a balanced crown where there is no competition from other trees.
Q. VELUTINA (black oak, zones 3 to 9) Native from Maine to Florida and Minnesota to Texas. Black oaks have variable spreads, but can often grow to 60ft (18m) or more. The bark is nearly black on older trunks.
Q. VIRGINIANA (live oak) Massive, widespreading evergreen, extremely long-lived, hardy in warm, maritime climates. Branches form a broad, rounded canopy; useful for park or street tree plantings in the Deep South. Train as a central-leader standard (*see p.28*), pruning in mid- to late summer. Established trees need no further pruning.

OTHER ORNAMENTAL TREES

PTEROCELTIS (zones 5–7) Grows best in areas with long, hot summers, reaching 40ft (12m). In cooler regions seldom retains a central leader and is best allowed to develop naturally, producing a multistemmed tree.

R

RHUS SUMAC

Trees and shrubs, many toxic, grown for their architectural form and foliage that often colors well in autumn. Dense panicles of flowers give rise in some species to conical clusters of fruits.

R. CHINENSIS (ZONES 5–7)

CHINESE SUMAC

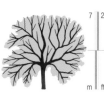

Spreading, suckering, flat-headed tree, useful in large settings or borders. Like much of its family, this species has toxic properties: avoid contact with the sap.

WHEN TO PRUNE Late summer.

TRAINING AND PRUNING Train as a central-leader standard (*see p.28*), clearing the trunk to about 3ft (1m). The leader is lost relatively early and a broad crown soon develops. Little further pruning is required but remove suckers to retain the tree form. Avoid skin contact when pruning. Never burn prunings since the smoke may cause severe skin and internal reactions.

> **OTHER RHUS**
> For other species, see Dictionary of Ornamental Shrubs, *p.217*.

ROBINIA LOCUST

Deciduous, often spiny, hardy trees and shrubs grown for their foliage, flowers, and, in some cases, rugged bark. Nearly all grow vigorously and may produce overly vigorous shoots prone to wind damage. In exposed areas, many are tender when young. Plant in spring and do not feed, since fertilizers stimulate soft growth vulnerable to cold.

R. PSEUDOACACIA (ZONES 3–9)

FALSE ACACIA, LOCUST

Grown for its fragrant flowers in summer, and for its delicate leaves. The wood is brittle and susceptible to wind damage, so good training is essential. Plant as young as possible. Treat most cultivars, including the fastigiate 'Pyramidalis', as for the species. They may be grafted and may sucker. The very similar hybrid 'Idaho' is a small, shrubby tree that is best trained as a central-leader standard. If allowed to develop multiple branches near the base, the tree may break up in storms.

WHEN TO PRUNE Mid- to late summer.

TRAINING AND PRUNING Train as a central-leader standard (*see p.28*) with a clear trunk to about 6–8ft (2–2.5m). It is vital to maintain the leader until early maturity, so remove any competing leaders as soon as possible (*see p.26*). Ensure that laterals are evenly and well-spaced, and remove any upright growth close to the trunk. Narrow crotch angles are invariably structurally weak.

Pruning of established trees is best kept to a minimum. Remove any suckers as early as possible. Large pruning cuts seldom heal well and are prone to rot. In addition, the tree responds with vigorous, thorny, vertical growths, which may become dangerous if allowed to develop. Do not renovate, but fell the tree and, if ungrafted, use as a replacement one of the vigorous suckers that grow from the roots after felling.

> **OTHER ROBINIAS**
> R. BOYNTONII, R. ELLIOTTII, R. HARTWEGII, R. HISPIDA Multistemmed, shrublike growth habit; need little or no pruning.

R. PSEUDOACACIA 'FRISIA'
This cultivar produces a changing foliage display, the leaves turning from clear yellow through lime green to orangy gold in autumn.

S

SALIX WILLOW

A large and diverse genus of mainly deciduous trees and shrubs, grown variously for their habit, catkins, stem color, and foliage (with alternate leaves). Willows are generally very responsive to pruning and many species may be coppiced or pollarded to obtain brightly colored young stems.

WHEN TO PRUNE Autumn to early spring. Remove dead wood in summer. Coppice or pollard suitable species in midspring, just before new growth begins.

S. ALBA (ZONES 2–8)

WHITE WILLOW

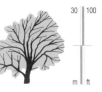

Large, strongly growing tree, often with a rather unshapely crown consisting of upright branches with horizontal sublaterals that bear more or less pendulous shoots. It is one of the best willows for landscape use. Although it naturally produces a strong central leader, structural weakness is common in mature trees, since vigorous shoots tend to arise from the same point on main stems, leading to congested branches. It is essential, therefore, that early training establishes a well-spaced branch system. A number of plants in this group, including S. *alba* 'Britzensis' and 'Vitellina', and S. *alba* var. *sericea*, are coppiced and pollarded to display their attractive bark.

WILLOWS PRUNED FOR STEM EFFECT
Coppicing and pollarding at various heights has produced a striking display of colored stems, welcome in winter.

TRAINING AND PRUNING To grow as a tree, train as a central-leader standard (*see p.28*) but rub out lateral buds before shoots emerge until the trunk is clear to about 6ft (2m). To ensure a balanced branch framework, rub out excess lateral buds to produce evenly spaced, alternate branches as opposed to congested whorls of growth. Once a sound framework is established, little further pruning is needed.

To grow for stem effect, coppice or pollard (*see p.36*) annually or every other year. The length of main stem for pollards can be between 2 and 5ft (60–150cm) depending on the desired effect. This pruning pattern should be established from the start: mature trees respond badly if large wounds are made. Being very susceptible to decay, they rapidly form cavities. The reduction of dangerous limbs on mature trees should be carried out by a professional arborist, but since problems will recur, the best option is to remove and replace old specimens. This is true of most vigorous willows.

S. CAPREA 'KILMARNOCK'

KILMARNOCK WILLOW

Slow-growing, weeping tree, hardy in zones 4 to 8, forming an umbrella-shaped crown and bearing a profusion of male catkins in spring. Plants are usually sold as weeping standards, top-grafted onto a clear stem of about 5ft (1.5m). Although they need little further formative pruning (*see also p.28*), they require annual regulative pruning to prevent the crown from becoming congested, with many branches growing stiffly downward to ground level.

TRAINING AND PRUNING The aim of annual pruning is to remove about 50 percent of the branches to create a light, airy curtain of foliage that will just reach the ground by the end of the growing season. Thin out branches from within the crown to form an open, umbrella-like framework, and then thin the outermost sideshoots, removing them completely. Shorten the remaining branches by approximately half, cutting back to an outward-facing bud.

KILMARNOCK WILLOW
Salix caprea 'Kilmarnock' is valued for its weeping habit, compact form, and profusion of catkins that are first gray, then turn to yellow. Unlike many weeping standards, it benefits from an annual pruning schedule.

In spring, the new flush of growth quickly disguises pruning wounds, and by midsummer the tree is once again clothed to the ground. Remove regularly suckers arising below the graft union.

S. X SEPULCRALIS (ZONES 3–7)

WEEPING WILLOW

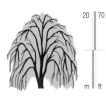

Broadly domed, strongly weeping deciduous hybrid between *S. alba* and *S. babylonica*, valued for its habit and for the brilliant green of its foliage that contrasts well with the yellow-tinted young shoots.

TRAINING AND PRUNING Young plants typically form a strong leader with short, almost stubby, horizontal laterals. Train initially as a central-leader standard (*see p.28*) with a clear trunk to 5–6ft (1.5–2m). As growth proceeds, the leader will eventually be lost so that the crown broadens and assumes its weeping habit. The tree then increases in height by means of a single, upright, whippy shoot that rises above other laterals during the growing season

before adopting a weeping habit the following year: this shoot should never be pruned because of its seemingly atypical early growth habit. In subsequent years, new leading shoots develop on an annual basis, creating a layered crown. Established specimens need little pruning, although occasional crown thinning allows light and air into the center, strengthening the branches. Trees do not respond well to hard pruning.

OTHER WILLOWS
S. ALBA 'TRISTIS', *S.* X PENDULINA As for *S.* x *sepulcralis*.
S. BABYLONICA As for *S.* x *sepulcralis*. Needs a site sheltered from frost when young.
S. BABYLONICA var. PEKINENSIS 'TORTUOSA' (syn. *S.* MATSUDANA 'TORTUOSA') Noted for its contorted branches (*see also p.30*) clothed in narrow, twisted, bright green leaves. It grows naturally as a multistemmed tree with a short trunk, needing little formative pruning, but remove about one in three inward-growing laterals to avoid later crown congestion. Once established, occasional thinning by removing badly placed or crossing laterals stimulates new growth and perpetuates the curious growth pattern. Old trees respond well to hard pruning, but since young trees grow more vigorously, replanting is preferable.
S. CAPREA, *S.* EXIGUA Shrubby, multi-stemmed habit, branching from the base. Cut back hard to the ground to rejuvenate.
S. DAPHNOIDES Naturally forms a well-shaped multistemmed tree, or can be pruned hard for increased stem interest: young growth has purple bark with a plum-colored bloom. Develop as a pollard or coppice as for *S. alba*, then cut back one in three stems every year.
S. FRAGILIS Train as a central-leader standard (*see p.28*), maintaining the leader for as long as possible: the crown will eventually divide and branch naturally.
S. HOOKERIANA Similar to *S. caprea*; may also be trained as a standard as for *S. alba*.
S. UDENSIS 'SEKKA' (syn. *S.* SACHALINENSIS 'SEKKA') Deciduous, shrubby tree grown for its contorted stems, best cut back annually to a framework of branches to stimulate fresh growth with this curious habit.
For other species, see Dictionary of Ornamental Shrubs, *p.218*.

OTHER ORNAMENTAL TREES
REHDERODENDRON *R. macrocarpum* is best as a feathered tree (*see p.27*) but needs little, if any, pruning. Will not renovate.
ROTHMANNIA Train as a central-leader standard (*see p.28*), pruning after flowering or fruiting has finished. Established trees need minimal attention.
SAMBUCUS See Dictionary of Ornamental Shrubs, *p.219*.
SAPINDUS Train as central-leader standards (*see p.28*). Established trees need minimal attention.
SAPIUM Train as a central-leader standard (*see p.28*). Established trees need minimal attention.

SASSAFRAS (ZONES 4–9)

Sassafras albidum is a deciduous tree that seldom achieves its potential height of 100ft (30m) in cool climates, where its growth is usually shrubby. In continental climates, it is easily trained as a central-leader standard (*see p.28*) with a clear trunk to a height of about 1.5–2m (5–6ft). To attain this form in mild maritime climates, shelter from winter winds and cold for the first two or three years. Remove frost-damaged growth in early summer. If the leader is lost, it is best to allow the tree to develop as a multistemmed, suckering shrub. Otherwise no special attention is required.

SCHEFFLERA

The ivy or umbrella trees are tropical and subtropical evergreens grown for their handsome leaves and large clusters of flowers. All are hardy in zone 10, therefore requiring a reliably frost-free climate. Most need little or no pruning. Plants grown under glass will tolerate hard pruning to limit size: cut back growth to a shoot or main branch in early spring before growth commences. For shrub species, *see p.219*.

SCHIMA

Evergreens similar to camellias, hardy in zone 10 and therefore needing reliably frost-free conditions. *S. wallichii* can be grown in tubs in a cool greenhouse or conservatory, as for camellias (*see p.182*). Schimas need little or no formative pruning but tolerate even hard pruning if necessary. Removing frost-damaged growth usually causes shoots to break from old wood, and these can be trained to replace damaged portions of the crown.

SCHINUS

Evergreen, often spiny trees or shrubs grown for their aromatic foliage, small white or yellow flowers, and ornamental fruits. Most need a frost-free climate, but in cooler regions are easily grown in a cool greenhouse or conservatory. *S. polygamus* tolerates light frosts. In warm climates, it needs little pruning or training, growing naturally as a multi-stemmed shrub or small feathered tree. It may also be trained against a warm, sunny wall (*see Magnolia grandiflora, p.74*). Under glass, it will tolerate cutting back to restrict growth. Prune during midsummer when the first flush of new growth has ceased.

SOPHORA *SCHOLAR TREE, PAGODA TREE* (ZONES 4–8)

Trees and shrubs (*see p.220*) grown for their foliage, flowers, and, in some tree species, ruggedly handsome bark. Most grow best in warm climates with hot summers. *S. japonica*, the pagoda or Chinese scholar tree, is widely grown as a street tree. Sophoras that tolerate cool maritime climates may not flower in these conditions. They resent root disturbance, so plant as young as possible.

WHEN TO PRUNE Summer; many species bleed if pruned in late winter or spring.

TRAINING AND PRUNING Train as central-leader standards (*see p.28*) with a clear trunk to a height of 5–6ft (1.5–2m). In continental climates they produce a vigorous central leader, naturally shed lower limbs, and form a sound branch system, so need little formative pruning. In temperate climates, the leader is usually lost early and an open crown develops, with large, heavy, contorted branches arising from near the same point low down on the main stem. These branches may break in strong winds, so it is essential to maintain a leader for as long as possible, and to select laterals in the early years that will form a balanced framework. If the leader is lost, select and train in a replacement (*see p.26*). This is difficult, but possible with perseverance, and is important since the dominant shoot inhibits the production of weak, contorted branches. Established trees need little pruning, and do not respond well to renovation.

SORBUS *MOUNTAIN ASH*

Small to medium-sized, deciduous trees and shrubs, grown for their form and foliage, spring flowers, and autumn fruits and, often, foliage color. They are generally undemanding and need little pruning. They prefer cool climates: *S. alnifolia* and *S. commixta* are better suited to areas with hot summers. Most are ideally planted as unbranched whips (*see p.24*) and trained young. This reduces transplant stress and helps to maintain a strong central leader. Semi-mature trees also establish easily; the intermediate (and most widely sold) tree sizes appear to suffer most transplant shock. Some cultivars may be grafted. Fireblight (*see p.117*) can cause dieback.

WHEN TO PRUNE Autumn to early spring. Remove dead wood in summer.

SORBUS AUCUPARIA
The mountain ash or rowan is noted for the profusion of red berries it bears in autumn.

S. ARIA (ZONE 5)

WHITEBEAM

Dome-shaped tree with upswept branches bearing leathery leaves, white-felted below, and red berries. The canopy often develops an irregular shape on exposed sites; pruning can do little to correct it.

TRAINING AND PRUNING Train initially as a central-leader standard (*see p.28*), removing laterals so that the trunk is clear to a height of 6ft (2m) by early maturity. The crown can then be allowed to branch. Little further pruning is needed. Cannot be renovated as a tree, but if cut to the ground will regrow as an attractive shrubby thicket.

S. AUCUPARIA (ZONES 3–7)

EUROPEAN MOUNTAIN ASH, ROWAN

Usually, a broadly conical central-leader standard, ideal for urban plantings and for small to medium-sized gardens. Prune all cultivars as for the species.

TRAINING AND PRUNING Train as a central-leader standard (*see p.28*) with a clear trunk to a height of 5–6ft (1.5–2m), depending on vigor. Make sure that laterals are alternately and evenly spaced around the trunk, aiming to produce about five main framework branches. This is especially important on fastigiate cultivars such as 'Sheerwater Seedling'.

SOPHORA JAPONICA
Cool climates inhibit flowering, but the attractive foliage has great ornamental value.

Closely spaced branches often constrict the main stem and result in crotches with included bark that are structurally weak. 'Xanthocarpa' tends to lose its leader early: it should be retained at least until the stem has been cleared.

Restrict pruning of established trees to the removal of dead and damaged wood, and of suckers that appear below the graft union on grafted cultivars. Poorly formed specimens are difficult to restore and are better replaced.

OTHER SORBUS
S. AMERICANA As for *S. aucuparia*. Young trees produce ascending laterals: if any compete with the leader, rub out their terminal buds. Hardy to zone 2.
S. CASHMIRIANA As for *S. americana*.
S. COMMIXTA As for *S. aria*.
S. DOMESTICA Train as a central-leader standard (*see p.28*) with a clear trunk to 6ft (2m) so that the horizontal branches, with semipendulous sublaterals, cover the tree with foliage to the ground. Little further pruning is required. Remove accumulated dead wood from old trees.
S. HUPEHENSIS As for *S. aucuparia*, with a clear trunk of 6ft (2m): with age, lower branches adopt a semipendulous habit.
S. 'JOSEPH ROCK' Select young, lightly branched specimens. The form is often spoiled by an overlong trunk. Aim to create a short clear trunk of 3ft (1m), and maintain a central leader until early maturity, when the crown will begin to open up slightly. Little further attention is necessary.
S. REDUCTA *See* Dictionary of Ornamental Shrubs, *p.221*.
S. VESTITA (syn. S. CUSPIDATA) Train as a central-leader standard (*see p.28*), clearing the trunk to 3ft (1m) by the fourth growing season. Established trees need little pruning.

STYRAX *SNOWBELL, STORAX*

Deciduous and evergreen trees and shrubs with alternate leaves, grown for their graceful habit and pendent clusters of white flowers in summer. Most cultivated species are frost-tender when young but vigorous once established. They dislike pruning, and are best left to develop naturally and informally: they are ideal for woodland gardens and other sheltered sites.

S. JAPONICUS (ZONES 5–8)

JAPANESE SNOWBELL

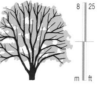

Small, deciduous tree, occasionally a large shrub, with a dense, rounded crown of more or less horizontal branches supporting slender twiggy growth. This is a beautiful and delicate flowering tree, but it dislikes pruning. Training to produce a strong leader relies mainly on the prevention of any check in growth during the early years. Plant as young as possible in early spring, in a sheltered site either in full sun or partial shade.

WHEN TO PRUNE Autumn to early spring.

TRAINING AND PRUNING Aim to produce a central-leader tree (*see p.28*) with a short clear trunk. As the dense crown develops, the lowest laterals begin to die back naturally through shading out. Remove the dying limbs by cutting back to the branch collar (*see p.12*) in early spring. Established specimens need little further pruning and do not respond well when cut back hard.

OTHER STYRAX
S. HEMSLEYANUS, S. OBASSIA In warm climates, as for *S. japonicus*. In cool climates, young plants need an open, sunny site. Grow as multistemmed trees (*see p.30*); despite narrow crotch angles, the strongly upright branches, which rapidly equal the leading shoot in vigor, are structurally sound at maturity. Established specimens need little pruning. The vigorous growth produced in response to hard pruning is likely to be damaged in hard winters.

SYZYGIUM *LILLY PILLY*

Evergreen trees and shrubs needing a moist, warm temperate to tropical climate (zone 10), cultivated both as ornamentals and for their edible fruits (most commonly known as water or water rose apples, or jambolans), which can be used in cooking and preserves. Tree-forming species tend to branch low and form a broad, dense, sometimes irregular crown. Although often left to grow naturally as multistemmed trees (most have a tendency to branch from the base), they are very tolerant of pruning, which can be used to stimulate fruit production. If a more manageable, heavier-cropping tree is desired, create a multistemmed tree on a short leg of 2–3ft (60–90cm), as for *Acer davidii* (*see p.52*), pruning in early spring. Tip-prune any overly vigorous shoots to encourage balanced development. Most species will continue to produce lateral shoots low on the trunk, and these and any water shoots should be removed at an early stage, preferably by rubbing them out by hand as they emerge. When trees are established, remove only crossing, diseased, or dead wood at regular intervals. Root pruning (*see p.101*) or bark-ringing (*see p.106*) are sometimes used to increase the production of vigorously growing but low-yielding trees.

OTHER ORNAMENTAL TREES
SCHOTIA Train *S. brachypetala* as a central-leader standard (*see p.28*). Established trees tolerate pruning to thin and improve the shape if necessary.
SESBANIA As for *Cassia, p.56*.
SINOWILSONIA As for *Hamamelis, p.198*.
SPATHODEA Train *S. campanulata* (syn. *S. wrightii*) as a central-leader standard (*see p.28*). Established trees have no special pruning needs.
STENOCARPUS Evergreen tree (*see p.27*), needs minimal training as a central-leader standard. Established trees have no special pruning needs.

STERCULIA Train as a central-leader standard (*see p.28*). Established trees have no special pruning needs.
STEWARTIA (syn. STUARTIA) Need little or no formative pruning, and are best allowed to grow naturally so that plants produce flowering shoots more or less to ground level. In continental climates the leader is maintained, but in cool areas trees will branch low and become broadly tiered with age. Planting as young as possible in a sheltered site encourages more treelike growth.

T

TAMARINDUS *TAMARIND* (ZONE 10)

Large evergreen with a dense, spreading, rounded crown, grown for its pods in tropical regions. In subtropical areas it is used as a roadside shade tree. It tolerates a range of warm-climate conditions including drought. Young trees are cold-sensitive but older trees are more resistant. Young trees grow slowly, and seedlings rarely bloom until they are at least five to seven years old. Grafted cultivars are preferable, flowering three or four years after planting. They normally require little training or pruning when established. Renewal pruning is carried out as pods are harvested. To restrict size or renew less productive fruiting growth, cut back fruited wood to a well-placed sideshoot. Trees usually respond well to crown reduction (*see p.35*) if necessary.

TOONA (ZONES 5–8)

Toona sinensis (syn. *Cedrela sinensis*) is a handsome, deciduous tree grown in cool climates for its large leaves, unusual habit, and ornamental bark. With a hot summer, it also flowers. Train initially as a central-leader standard (*see p.28*) with a clear trunk of 6ft (2m), pruning when dormant, between autumn and early spring, then allow the crown to branch and the sparse, irregular habit to develop naturally. Established trees need little, if any, further attention and do not respond well to hard pruning.

TILIA *LINDEN, LIME*

Deciduous, usually long-lived trees grown for their stature, foliage, and scented flowers. Some are very tolerant of pruning and training and are often pollarded (*see p.36*) or pleached (*see p.38*); heavily pruned trees may sucker freely. Several species produce large burls that give rise to a mass of upward-growing epicormic shoots. These usually need removing since they can spoil the crown if they develop. At maturity, many lindens accumulate and shed dead wood. Dieback tends to occur from the tips downward, producing a stag-headed effect (*see also Quercus, p.84*).

WHEN TO PRUNE Midsummer or mid-winter; lindens bleed if pruned in spring, late fall, or late winter.

T. PLATYPHYLLOS (ZONES 4–7)

BIGLEAF LINDEN

Stately, deciduous tree with a narrow crown of large, heavy, strongly upright branches. Despite very tight crotch angles with included bark and water pockets, it rarely sheds branches. It is prone to cavities but seldom produces burls or epicormic shoots.

TRAINING AND PRUNING Train as a central-leader standard (*see p.28*), retaining the leader for as long as possible. Clear the trunk to a height of 6–10ft (2–3m) to allow sublaterals to hang down. As the tree matures, upper laterals begin to grow vigorously, frequently resulting in multiple leaders. These are safe in a well-balanced crown. Trees grown in exposed sites may develop distorted crowns, with branches prone to breakage that are dangerously heavy and should be removed only by a qualified arborist. Provided that trees are free from cavities, the crown of overly mature or declining trees may be reduced by a professional (*see* Major tree surgery, *p.35*) to remove heavy dead wood and extend the safe life of the tree.

T. TOMENTOSA (ZONES 4–7)

SILVER LINDEN, EUROPEAN WHITE LINDEN

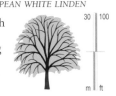

Deciduous tree with a dense, regular crown of ascending branches, its dark leaves felted silver-white beneath.

TRAINING AND PRUNING Train as a central-leader standard (*see p.28*). The tree grows vigorously when young, and although it produces upright upper laterals, these seldom compete with the leader, so do not reduce or remove them. Aim to clear the trunk to a height of 8–10ft (2.5–3m) by early maturity. If allowed to branch low, this species may produce heavy limbs that form sub-canopies which spoil the otherwise regular outline. It will not respond well to renovation.

OTHER LINDENS

T. AMERICANA, T. CHINENSIS, T. X EUROPAEA (syn. T. X VULGARIS), T. INSULARIS, T. MONGOLICA As for *T. cordata*, but easier to train.

T. CORDATA Planting young in fertile soil in a sheltered site aids training, essential for a sound tree. Train very gradually as a central-leader standard with a clear trunk to 6–10ft (2–3m). Delay the removal of laterals until the second or third year, then remove over three or four years, maintaining the leader. Established trees need little pruning (though always remove any shoots on the clear trunk) and do not respond well to hard pruning.

T. X EUCHLORA Readily forms a strong central leader and needs little pruning. Retain the lower laterals to encourage branching to ground level. Established trees naturally begin to exhibit irregular growth that pruning can do little to improve. They do not respond well to hard pruning.

T. OLIVERI Train initially as a central-leader standard (*see p.28*) with a clear trunk of 5–6ft (1.5–2m), then allow to branch to form its broad, domed crown.

T. PETIOLARIS As for *T. tomentosa*. Rub out shoots below the graft union.

PLEACHED LINDENS

Lindens usually grow well after planting, showing little transplant shock; it is therefore possible to buy and plant semimature specimens to hasten the finished result if planning a row of pleached trees.

U-Z

ULMUS *ELM*

Large, mainly deciduous trees, grown for their stature and habit. Since the 1960s, many have succumbed to the fatal Dutch elm disease; elms are now rare in Europe and North America. Some species are prone to branch drop, for reasons that are unclear, usually on warm, still days in midsummer.

WHEN TO PRUNE Autumn to early spring.

U. AMERICANA (ZONES 2–9)

AMERICAN ELM, SWAMP ELM

Distinguished by its serrated, dark green lustrous leaves and upright, vase-shaped form in which the trunk divides into several arched limbs with pendulous branches.

TRAINING AND PRUNING Train as a central-leader standard (*see p.28*), clearing the trunk gradually to about 12ft (4m) by maturity. Mature trees need little pruning. Monitor for Dutch elm disease; remove infected branches.

U. GLABRA (ZONES 4–6)

SCOTCH ELM, WYCH ELM

Deciduous tree with a billowing canopy that may produce burls and epicormic shoots but rarely suckers. 'Camperdownii' (the Camperdown elm) is a top-grafted weeping standard (*see p.28*) noted for its congested, tortuous branch system. 'Pendula' is a straight-stemmed tree, its weeping branches sporting a herringbone fan of sublaterals.

TRAINING AND PRUNING Train as a central-leader standard (*see p.28*) with a clear trunk to about one-quarter of the young tree's overall height. Remove all laterals that are not evenly and well spaced around the stem. Tip-prune any that compete with the leader. Older trees accumulate dead wood, which can be heavy and should be professionally removed, particularly where there is public access beneath the tree. *U. glabra* 'Camperdownii' defies training and pruning. The pendulous sublaterals can be tip-pruned if necessary. Weaker limbs are often strangled by competitors. It is usually possible to remove only the extremities of dead branches. Little further pruning is needed other than to remove any suckers on the clear stem. *U. glabra* 'Pendula' is also impossible to train or prune; let it grow naturally.

U. PARVIFOLIA (ZONES 4–9)

CHINESE ELM

Native to Asia, the Chinese elm is resistant to Dutch elm disease. It may be shrubby when young.

TRAINING AND PRUNING Usually best left to grow naturally; it resists formative training and pruning. In continental climates it can be trained as a central-leader standard (*see p.28*) with a clear trunk to about one-quarter of the young tree's height. Established specimens need little, if any, further pruning. Any shoots that grow on the trunk and mask the attractive bark are best removed.

OTHER ELMS

U. ALATA (winged elm, zones 6-9) As for *U. americana*.
U. X HOLLANDICA Hybrids developed for their resistance to Dutch elm disease, but not without drawbacks: tend to produce heavy, upright branches with narrow crotches; prone to epicormic shoots, root suckers and branch drop. Train as central-leader standards (*see p.28*), clearing the trunk to 6–10ft (2–3m). It is vital to maintain the leader for as long as possible and to reduce or remove any shoots that compete with it. Retain only laterals that are evenly and well spaced around the trunk. Remove epicormic shoots on the trunk as for *U. procera*.
U. PROCERA Suckers profusely and is notorious for branch drop; unsuitable for urban environments. Train as a central-leader standard (*see p.28*), but do not remove lower limbs until they begin to die back naturally. Remove any shoots on the trunk using pruners: tearing increases the risk of infection. Dead wood that accumulates should be removed by a professional to avoid branch drop.
U. PUMILA As for *U. parvifolia*.

ZELKOVA

Deciduous trees with smooth or flaking bark and alternate, toothed, rough-textured leaves. They look best as specimen central-leader standards.

Z. SERRATA (ZONES 5–8)

JAPANESE ZELKOVA

Large, broad-crowned tree with heavy, spreading branches. Resistant to Dutch elm disease. Young trees are prone to frost damage. The leaves turn orange, pink, and yellow in autumn.

WHEN TO PRUNE Late winter. May be lightly pruned if necessary in summer.

TRAINING AND PRUNING Train as a central-leader standard (*see p.28*) with a clear trunk to 10ft (3m) and well spaced framework branches. The lower branches of established trees are often semipendulous and the crown may need to be raised to allow access beneath. Cut back branch tips to a suitable lateral when the tree is in full leaf. Thin branches to form an open structure when young. Branch removal is best left to a professional arborist.

OTHER ZELKOVAS

Z. ABELICEA (syn. Z. CRETICA) Grows naturally as a multistemmed tree (*see p.30*); remove only badly placed branches.
Z. CARPINIFOLIA Train with a clear trunk of 6–10ft (2–3m), then let the stem divide to form an egg-shaped, multistemmed crown. Thin the crown carefully when trees are young or semimature to reduce the risk of later defects: mature specimens do not respond well to drastic pruning.
Z. SINICA As for Z. serrata. Susceptible to canker, so keep pruning to a minimum.

OTHER ORNAMENTAL TREES

TABEBUIA Train as central-leader standards (*see p.28*). Established trees have no special pruning needs.
TECOMA Usually develop naturally as multistemmed trees. Under glass, limit size by shortening the current season's growth by half after flowering. Respond well to hard pruning; thin regrowth.
THEVETIA As for *Nerium* (*see p.209*).
UMBELLULARIA In warm climates, train as a central-leader standard (*see p.28*) with a clear trunk to 6ft (2m). In cool climates, grow as a feathered, multistemmed tree (*see p.30*) in a sheltered site. Branches may have narrow crotches but rarely break. Established trees need little attention.

TREE FRUITS

Whether grown primarily for their cropping potential or for their combined productive and decorative value, tree fruits need careful pruning and training to maintain high-quality yields

There has been a revival of interest in growing fruit trees in the garden, due to an increasing desire not only for fresh, fully flavored fruit, perhaps of more unusual cultivars than those usually found in stores, but also for produce whose culture is known to be free of interference from the application of chemical or preservative treatments. With this revival has come a rediscovery of the traditional pleasures of fruit-growing and of the enormous decorative potential of fruit trees. Nearly all belong to genera that contain trees grown solely for their ornamental value. The choice of a tree that is both attractive and productive justifies the extra attention needed to realize its fruiting potential.

Pruning and training play major roles in fruit tree cultivation. Careful shaping and routine maintenance will maximize yields of high-quality fruit. Many of the tender fruits that grow only in tropical and subtropical climates need little more than basic care and for this reason have been grouped separately (*see pp.140–147*). However, the hardy fruits have always been the focus of great interest in creating more specialized trained forms. While gardeners' aims in developing training methods have been to afford their trees more protection from harsh weather or to create a more formal and decorative effect, commercial fruit growers have been more interested in developing tree forms that are small, compact, and easily managed. To meet these growers' needs, new rootstocks with a "dwarfing" effect were introduced, and these have made perhaps the most significant contribution to the wider growing of fruit trees in the domestic garden. With smaller trees, fruit growing is no longer just the domain of those with large gardens or orchards. When less vigorous trees are grown in compact trained forms, two or even three cultivars can be accommodated in – and make a great ornamental contribution to – a small garden.

FAN-TRAINED APPLE
Fans and espaliers maximize the use of space in a small garden and help to expose the ripening fruits to the warmth of the sun. Wall-training can give additional protection to less hardy fruits, such as peaches and apricots.

PEACH IN BLOSSOM
Although a major orchard crop in many temperate countries, in the coldest temperate zones peaches can be trained and pruned to make attractive small fruiting trees that can be grown in containers and brought under cover for winter protection.

FRUIT TREE FORMS

Most fruit trees can be trained into almost any shape, but several recognized forms have been developed to suit different situations and the habits of individual trees. Some forms are freestanding; others need permanent staking or the support of a wall or wires. Some are grown without restriction on shoot growth; on others, new shoots are pruned to maintain a shape or silhouette. When selecting a form, there are three main factors to consider. First, growth habit: if you want to grow an apple tree against a wall, for example, the espalier form ideally suits the way most apples fruit on short shoots (spurs). Second, consider the space available and the number of trees required for pollination purposes; several cordons can be sited in the space needed by one fan. Third, estimate how much attention you can devote to your tree. Free-growing forms such as the bush and spindle bush are quite easy to shape and need pruning only once a year, in late winter or early spring. More elaborate forms, such as the cordon and espalier, require precise training and need extra maintenance with a pruning program that may stretch over several weeks in summer.

BUSH
A very productive and widely used form, suitable for nearly all tree fruits where space for its considerable spread permits. Framework branches radiate from a trunk that is only 2½–3ft

(75–90cm) tall; the leader is pruned to give a branched-headed, open-centered tree. The branches are evenly and well spaced around and along the upper third of the trunk to give structural strength.

HALF-STANDARD
This is basically a bush tree on a taller clear trunk. A vigorous rootstock is necessary for such a large tree. Because the extra height makes maintenance and harvesting more

difficult, this form is rarely seen in modern orchards or fruit gardens. However, it provides a fine specimen tree of increased stature that looks good in an ornamental garden.

STANDARD
With a clear trunk of 6–6½ft (2–2.1m), standards can only be grown on the most vigorous rootstocks. The crown is formed as for a bush tree, but its spread will be far greater. In most gardens standards

are too big to be feasible. They are, however, in demand for filling in gaps in established orchards to preserve old and valued noncommercial cultivars in traditional form.

PYRAMID
Mainly used for plums because the maintenance pruning required suits their fruiting habit, pyramids have branches that grow largely outward. The tree tapers, allowing

fruits on the lower branches to receive plenty of sun. These are small, compact trees, no more than 6–8ft (2–2½m) tall, easy to site in a small space because they can be planted closely.

DWARF PYRAMID
Modern rootstocks with a very dwarfing effect enable many cultivars of apples and pears to be grown in this small, compact form, no more than 5–6ft

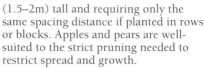

(1.5–2m) tall and requiring only the same spacing distance if planted in rows or blocks. Apples and pears are well-suited to the strict pruning needed to restrict spread and growth.

SPINDLE BUSH
A productive form popular in commercial apple production, the spindle bush – named after the tree's silhouette – has low main branches, creating a broad-based,

conical form. The branches are trained horizontally for heavier crops. Spindle bushes are grown with a sturdy stake, to which wires may be attached to support branches heavy with fruit.

CORDON
A convenient form for apples and pears, since several cultivars can be grown in a small space, on posts and wire, or against a wall. For its size, an oblique cordon is very productive. It is a form widely used to produce fruits of exhibition quality, combining maximum sun exposure with all the vigor of a large root system directed into top growth that is restricted by pruning.

DOUBLE ("U") CORDON
This variation on the single cordon is more usually grown upright. It often grows most strongly at the top of its two main arms, and needs careful corrective

pruning. A double cordon is easier to site against a narrow area of wall than two single, oblique cordons. It is also an ideal form for soft fruits that are spur-pruned, such as redcurrants.

MULTIPLE CORDONS
Cordons with three, four, or more vertical arms need intricate training and maintenance, but the result is as decorative as an espalier. They are suitable for apples

and pears. Three-armed (triple) cordons are inadvisable for certain cultivars because all the vigor is directed into the central arm. A four-armed ("double-U") cordon is preferable.

FAN

A decorative, heavy-bearing
form, suitable for many fruit trees but
particularly for stone fruits such as
plums and peaches, and for figs.
Correctly trained, the main stem
is short, and the ribs of the fan
originate from two low, angled arms.

PALMETTE

A variation on the espalier (*below*) in
which staggered tiers of branches are
angled upward rather than sideways.
It is easier to disguise a slight lack of
symmetry with this less rigid form.

ESPALIER

This form is ideal for apples and
pears, but does not suit stone fruits.
Its decorative impact lies in its formal
symmetry: the pairs of branches
should be as nearly opposite as
possible and of equal length.

STEPOVER

This is a cordon bent almost at right-
angles and then trained horizontally.
Stepovers are usually freestanding,
supported by strong wires. They can
form an attractive low edging to a bed.

ROOTSTOCKS AND TREE SIZE

Fruit trees will not usually breed true
from seed or grow satisfactorily from
cuttings. Thus, fruit trees are
propagated most frequently by
budding or grafting. Because the tree's
growth rate and ultimate size are
largely dependent on the rootstock, it
has a significant bearing on pruning
and training. Traditional vigorous
rootstocks produced large, long-lived
trees that needed little pruning to fruit
year after year. Modern rootstocks
produce much smaller trees that need
more careful pruning and training.

These new rootstocks are clonally
reproduced, so all with the same name
or number will produce trees of nearly
identical size. The more "dwarfing"
their effect, the quicker the tree will

fruit. In most cases they are selections
of the same kind of fruit, but in a few
cases they are of a different genus.

To overcome incompatibility
between a cultivar and its proposed
rootstock, an intermediate length of
stem of a cultivar compatible with
both may be used: there are thus two
graft unions, and these trees are
described as being "double-worked."

Never buy a fruit tree without
making sure that the rootstock used is
suitable for its intended site and form.
Otherwise, you may end up with a tree
that never fulfills your expectations. In
particular, a vigorous tree can never be
made or kept small by pruning; it will
simply respond with more growth and
little or no fruit.

HOW DIFFERENT ROOTSTOCKS AFFECT TREE SIZE

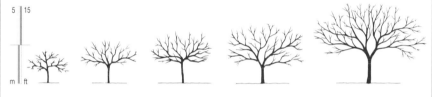

*The same cultivar may be available in a range of tree sizes if compatible with several
different rootstocks. Rootstocks are often given names or numbers that refer to the place
where they were developed: the "M" series for apples, for example, originated at the
horticultural research station at East Malling in southern England.*

FAMILY TREES

It is possible to produce a fruit tree made up of several cultivars growing on a
single root system. These "family" trees have much more than novelty value: the
cultivars may pollinate one another, or may have been selected to fruit in
sequence to supply ripe fruits over a long season. The rootstock must be carefully
chosen, and the cultivars should be of approximately similar growth habit so that
the tree is well balanced. Three cultivars is usual for a bush tree.

FAN-TRAINED FAMILY TREE

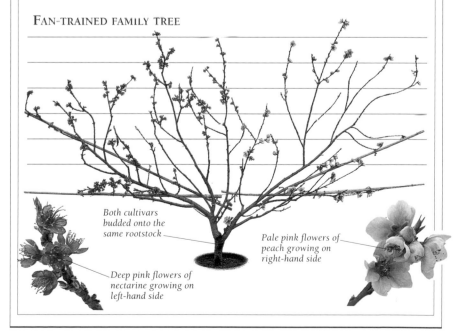

Both cultivars
budded onto the
same rootstock

Deep pink flowers of
nectarine growing on
left-hand side

Pale pink flowers of
peach growing on
right-hand side

BASIC TECHNIQUES

There are three primary aims when pruning and training fruit trees: to influence the direction of shoot growth, ensuring structural strength and the desired tree form; to remove promptly dead, diseased, or damaged wood and prevent crowded or crossing branches, protecting the tree's health; and to maintain a good balance between cropping and growth. Fulfilling these aims should result in a tree that fruits evenly and regularly, with well-spaced branches that bear sound, ripe fruits.

Further aims, secondary to the tree's health, are of great importance to the gardener. The amount of space and the site available will influence the choice of cultivar and rootstock, and the tree form that is chosen. In most gardens, visual appeal will almost certainly be a factor; the extra work demanded by an espalier, for example, is handsomely repaid by its decorative impact.

DIFFERENT APPROACHES TO PRUNING

Choice of tree form dictates a training program that can range from simple to intricate. When pruning mature trees, too, there is a clear distinction between the treatment of free-growing tree forms (bushes, standards, and spindle bushes) and those where shoot growth has to be restricted (such as cordons, pyramids, and fans). With free-growing forms, pruning is used simply to maintain the balance between the number of fruit buds that develop and the amount of growth (which represents future crop potential) that is made. With restricted forms, pruning must also maintain size, shape, and branch structure.

The techniques used will also need to be varied at different times of the year and at different stages in the tree's life. The key is to understand and respond to the growth and fruiting habit not only of fruit trees in general (the "composite tree" below, based on an apple, illustrates some of the terminology), but also of how the chosen fruit and cultivar is affected by your soil, site, and climate.

Fortunately, pruning mistakes with tree fruits can usually be corrected within a year or two. Even a tree that has previously been pruned badly or has been neglected may be restored to years of fruitful life by careful renovation.

DIFFERENT PARTS OF THE FRUIT TREE

GROWTH BUD (APPLE) *Although appearance varies with individual fruits, a narrow, pointed bud will usually develop into a new shoot or a spur. A vigorous tree produces many growth buds; as vigor decreases (normally as the tree matures) more fruit buds (see right) are formed.*

FLOWER BUD (APPLE) *In favorable circumstances, some embryonic growth buds (see left) develop instead into buds that contain flowers, which will be followed by fruits. Flower buds are more obviously rounded and "fat" than growth buds. They often have downy bud scales, particularly on apples, pears, peaches, and nectarines.*

Previous growing season's growth

Two-year-old wood

Lateral
A shoot growing directly from a main stem or branch.

Branch leader
The shoot at the end of a branch that extends its length (this is sometimes referred to as "extension growth"), usually having grown from the bud immediately below a pruning cut. Tree forms with a central trunk, such as a pyramid or spindle bush, have a vertical "central leader."

Spur

Sublateral
A shoot growing from an existing lateral, often also called a "sideshoot."

Older spur system

Main framework branch

Length of clear trunk keeps fruiting branches off ground

Scion (grafted cultivar)

Graft union

Rootstock

Scar of previous year's fruit stalk

GRAFT UNION *At the base of a grafted fruit tree, some 4–12in (10–30cm) from the ground, is a kink, often slightly swollen. This is the point at which the chosen cultivar – the "scion" – was grafted on to the rootstock, and is termed the "union." The union must be above soil level, or roots may grow out of the scion above it, nullifying the stock's dwarfing effect.*

SPUR *On apples and pears, a short length of wood that produces fruit buds for many years. Spurs are usually clustered together, forming complicated, jointed spur systems. This is a natural growth habit for pears and many apples, which is accentuated by "spur-pruning."*

MAKING CUTS

Pruning fruit trees may involve cutting into all types of growth – branches old and new, shoots, and spurs. Clean, sharp tools are essential to making precise cuts that do not leave torn or bruised tissue, which invites disease.

PRUNING YOUNG GROWTH

The simplest way of pruning young shoots, and one that is frequently needed with fruit trees, is to pinch out new growth, either to a leaf or to its point of origin while it is still young and soft. If ripened (woody) shoots need cutting, correct positioning above either a bud or sideshoot is vital; most hardy fruits have alternate buds, so unless cuts are to be made back to a main branch or trunk, they should slope gently.

The loss of buds through pruning damage or dieback is particularly serious in the training of young trees because shoots will not then develop where they were needed. The compromises that are necessary may make shaping the tree more difficult.

PRUNING OLDER WOOD

Professional fruit growers use a technique whereby wood up to 1in (2.5cm) in diameter can be easily cut. Holding the pruners in one hand, use the other to grasp the stem above the blades and very gently push or pull it away from the cutting blade as it begins to bite into the wood. This helps to open up the cut, making the progress of the blades through the wood much easier.

To remove larger sections of branches use a pruning saw or sharp loppers. Removing whole branches needs a special technique to prevent the bark from splitting (for step-by-step

GOOD AND BAD CUTS
Correct cuts are made at a gentle angle just above the bud, sloping down away from it. Leaving a stub of "blind" wood (center right) is particularly undesirable: if infection travels down the stem, you may lose the selected bud and possibly the whole shoot.

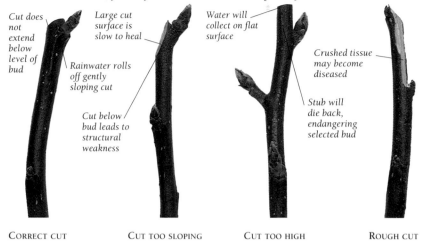

Cut does not extend below level of bud

Large cut surface is slow to heal

Rainwater rolls off gently sloping cut

Cut below bud leads to structural weakness

Water will collect on flat surface

Crushed tissue may become diseased

Stub will die back, endangering selected bud

CORRECT CUT   CUT TOO SLOPING   CUT TOO HIGH   ROUGH CUT

illustrations, *see p.22*). The use of wound paints is not now normally considered necessary (*see also p.22*).

WHEN TO PRUNE

Timing of pruning depends not only on the fruit in question but on the form in which it is grown. In general terms, the pome fruits (those with a core of seeds – apples, pears, quince, and medlar) are pruned when dormant in late winter or early spring, to remove older and less productive wood in favor of new growth and fruiting wood.

However, in some climates, because of a risk of disease if winter-pruned (*see p.123*), the stone fruits (plums, cherries, peaches, and apricots) are pruned in summer. While young trees are being trained, pruning to influence growth can be done in early spring.

TRAINED FORMS

Any fruit tree grown in a controlled, trained form, such as a cordon, pyramid, or fan, will also require additional summer pruning. Whereas the aim of routine pruning is to stimulate growth, this extra pruning consists largely of restricting it, to prevent the season's new shoots from shading the developing fruits and to maintain the size and shape of the trained form. Summer pruning also encourages the tree to produce new fruit buds for the following year.

Emerging sideshoots are pinched out as they develop to prevent over-crowding. Later in the summer, new shoots are shortened – possibly removing as much as 80 percent of the tree's new, long shoots – to maintain the trained form and to create spurs on which flower buds will develop.

CUTTING TO A BUD

Always try to approach with the pruners from the opposite side to the selected bud. This reduces the risk of the bud being damaged by the closing blades.

CUTTING TO A REPLACEMENT SHOOT

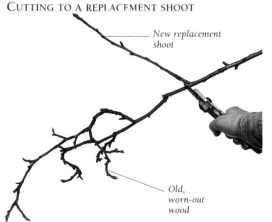

New replacement shoot

Old, worn-out wood

Choose a strong, healthy shoot growing in a direction that will enhance the shape of the tree, and cut in line with this direction of growth. You will be able to make a more controlled, and thus a cleaner, cut if you approach from the opposite side to the shoot.

CUTTING BACK TO A MAIN STEM

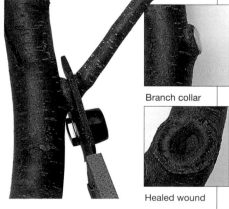

Branch collar

Healed wound

For thicker wood, always use more powerful tools. Cut back to the raised ring, or collar, at the base of the branch (see p.12) so that the wound does not interfere with sap flow up the main branch or trunk.

TRAINING TECHNIQUES

In the first years of a fruit tree's life, the development of new growth is of prime importance. If formative training is neglected in favor of obtaining a quick crop, a tree can quickly lose its shape, especially if on a dwarfing rootstock. The chosen cultivar's growth habit – with upright, spreading, or even drooping branches – may also become so well established that form-training becomes problematic. In the past, when only those rootstocks inducing vigorous growth were available, as many as seven or eight years could be spent in building up the framework of a tree before fruiting commenced. Today, with dwarfing rootstocks, trees may begin fruiting in their third year. However, if a complex form is still being created, it is better to remove any flowers to channel energy into growth.

BUYING YOUNG TREES

Always buy fruit trees from specialty fruit nurseries. They will supply strong, healthy stock that has been well trained from the start and can also offer advice about pollination requirements – whether the cultivar you would like to grow needs another cultivar growing nearby in order to set fruit – and about the suitability of your intended planting site. Try to match the choice of tree form to the natural habit of the cultivar, and use the same criteria to select good specimens as you would for ornamental trees (see p.25). A sturdy, robust young tree is preferable to a lanky one. The position and direction of growth of any laterals is also crucial. A one-year-old fruit tree will either be a clear, upright stem – a "whip" – or will have developed sideshoots to become a "feathered whip." Pruning back the leader and using techniques such as nicking and notching (see p.107) can be used to promote well-shaped growth and encourage laterals to develop where they are needed. Laterals that develop on an unpruned whip may be badly

YOUNG FRUIT TREES (APPLE)

In its first growing season, the tree develops initially as a single stem, or "whip" (see below left), on which laterals may form (when it is known as a "feathered whip"). Some may be suitable for training as main branches. A two-year-old feathered tree (see right) will have plenty of laterals from which to make a selection.

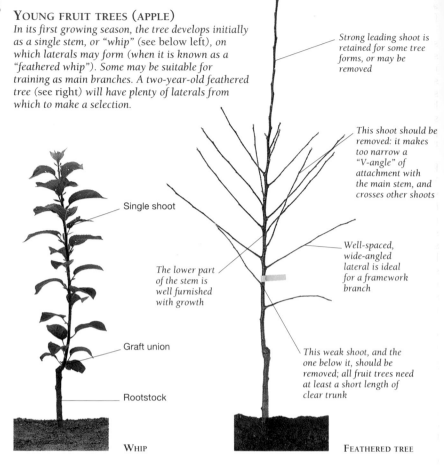

Single shoot

The lower part of the stem is well furnished with growth

Graft union

Rootstock

WHIP

Strong leading shoot is retained for some tree forms, or may be removed

This shoot should be removed: it makes too narrow a "V-angle" of attachment with the main stem, and crosses other shoots

Well-spaced, wide-angled lateral is ideal for a framework branch

This weak shoot, and the one below it, should be removed; all fruit trees need at least a short length of clear trunk

FEATHERED TREE

spaced, upright-growing, and crowded, making it more difficult to train a well-shaped tree.

CREATING THE FRAMEWORK

The first few years are spent establishing the branch framework of the chosen form. First, remove or shorten all shoots that are unwanted. For example, since all fruit tree forms have a length of clear trunk, sometimes just tall enough to keep fruits on the lowest branches off the ground, laterals below this height are always removed. Also remove any laterals forming a narrow V-angle (see

p.12) with the stem. If left they will almost certainly break later under the weight of a crop. Even on a mature tree, shoots that form a narrow fork at the point of origin are best removed.

For free-growing forms – bush, standards, and spindle bush – the shoots selected to form the framework must be well spaced, originating over a length of trunk rather than in a cluster. Select the best of what is already there, pruning to enhance their direction of growth. Some trees produce ample shoots, making selection easy; others, such as tip-bearing apples, do not, and it may take

CORRECTING UNEVEN DEVELOPMENT (FAN)

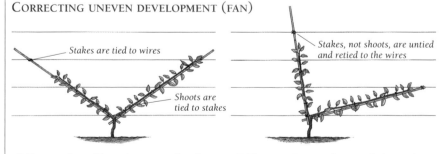

Stakes are tied to wires

Shoots are tied to stakes

1 *Here, one lateral is much stronger than the other, which, particularly at this early stage, reduces the chances of obtaining a symmetrical trained form from the young fruit tree.*

Stakes, not shoots, are untied and retied to the wires

2 *The more vigorous shoot can be lowered toward the horizontal to slow its growth. The weaker shoot can also be raised toward the vertical to increase its vigor.*

3 *Once the two shoots are of equal length (usually by the end of the growing season) they can be returned to their original positions and training can continue.*

a year or two longer to establish a basic framework of well-placed branches.

For more complex forms, the first shoots' position and direction of growth should be controlled from the start: more cuts are made that will stimulate shoot growth where it is needed. Surplus shoots are removed or can be pinched back to two or three leaves; should a selected shoot fail, the buds left on the pinched shoot may provide a replacement shoot to take its place.

PROVIDING SUPPORTS

Young fruit trees must usually be supported, at least until established. For freestanding forms, use a tall stake for pyramids and spindle bushes; these supports will be permanent. Use low stakes, preferably one on each side, with looped ties (see p.23), for bushes and standard trees. These can be removed once the tree is established in its final site: usually after about three years, more if the site is very exposed.

Fruiting branches on freestanding forms, especially the spindle bush, may need extra support if the weight of a good crop threatens to break them. They can be looped up – "maypoled" (see below) – with soft twine or ribbons cut from soft plastic netting, which will not damage young bark, either tied around a strong upper branch or nailed to the tree's supporting stake.

Walls and fences must be equipped with horizontal wires held at least 2in (5cm) from the surface, allowing air to circulate behind the tree. Tie shoots

to bamboo stakes attached to the wires at the desired angle. These act like splints, keeping the tied-in shoots straight and preventing them from rubbing on the thin wire. Once shoots are hardened and woody they can then be tied directly onto the wires and the stakes removed.

UNEVEN DEVELOPMENT

On fruit trees, an occasional shoot often develops far more quickly and strongly than others. When training free-growing forms, and on all mature trees, remove overvigorous upright shoots completely in summer. Where removal of a selected shoot would set back complex training (for example, to form the arms of an espalier where shoots are needed at precise points), correct uneven development (see facing page, below) by lowering the vigorous shoot to an angle nearer the horizontal: this will slow its growth, enabling the others to catch up. When they have done so, return the lowered shoot to its original position. Conversely, raising a weak shoot will encourage it to put on more growth. Shoots on stakes and wires are easily adjusted (see facing page, below); on free-standing trees, use soft twine or plastic netting strips, attached to the stake or pegged into the ground with wire bent into hoops.

TRAINING FOR FRUITING

While horizontal growth is less vigorous than upright growth, it is more fruitful and should be encouraged. Some trained

TIED-DOWN BRANCH RELEASED

Tying down the branch to a more horizontal angle has encouraged fruits to form all along the length of this branch. When the branch does not spring back, but stays naturally at its lower angle, the tie can be removed.

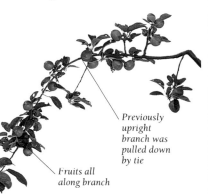

Previously upright branch was pulled down by tie

Fruits all along branch

forms were developed specifically to exploit the principle of horizontal training – for example, the espalier and spindle bush. On the latter in particular, upright shoots are best tied down by late summer, before they mature and become rigid, to increase flower bud formation (see also Apples, p.110). On trees with whippy long growths, particularly plums, long shoots can be pulled down and tied to the stake or main stem, a process known as "festooning" (see below). This technique, producing good crops on small trees, was in use long before dwarfing rootstocks became available.

Pound a nail into the stake to keep strings from slipping down

Sideshoots have developed all along length of branch

Branches once tied down by their tips now remain in position

MAYPOLING
The central stake or, as here, another stake lashed to the original low stake, forms an anchor point for loops of string or netting that support branches heavily laden with fruit.

FESTOONED PLUM
Whippy branches are carefully arched over and tied in below, using soft twine, in late summer. In early spring the ties are released but the branches stay bent, conferring the advantages of horizontal training.

Pruning techniques

Mature fruit trees can expend energy in two ways – in putting on more growth, and in producing fruit. Trees in the wild usually achieve a natural balance, but those that have been grafted onto different rootstocks (or are being grown in a less than natural form), may have this equilibrium disrupted. The skill of fruit tree management lies in using pruning and training to restore and influence the balance between growth and the formation of flower buds. This routine pruning usually takes place in late winter or early spring (in summer for stone fruits in some regions) and is applied to all fruit trees; the additional pruning necessary to maintain restricted trained forms is explained in their individual entries (*see pp.104–139*).

HARD VERSUS LIGHT PRUNING
To maintain the size and balanced shape of a mature tree, the most important rule is to prune weak growth hard and stronger growth lightly. After hard pruning, the root system has far fewer buds to serve, so these have a much greater growth potential, resulting in strong new shoots. Little or no pruning will leave a smaller ration of nutrients per bud. Hard pruning overall will result, therefore, in strong new growth but few fruits; general underpruning may be followed by an abundance of small fruits, exhausting the tree at the expense of the young growth that would bear future crops.

ADJUSTING THE BALANCE
The degree of pruning must be varied: pruning weak growths hard will encourage them to grow into worthwhile shoots; pruning vigorous shoots lightly, or not at all, results in little growth, encouraging their buds to develop into flower buds instead. The exact mix and severity of pruning is entirely dependent upon the state of the tree – whether it is lacking in vigorous new growth or is growing vigorously but fruiting lightly – and on where new growth is needed to replace older wood nearing the end of its useful life.

FRUITING HABIT
In general, younger wood produces finer fruits, but tree fruits vary in the age at which a shoot begins to bear fruit, and in the length of time it remains useful. Some, such as sour cherries, peaches, and nectarines, fruit only on the young shoots of the previous summer; others, such as apples and pears, fruit mainly on two-year-old and older shoots and spurs. (Year one produces the shoot, year two should initiate some flower buds on the shoot, and these then flower

and fruit in year three; this wood from then on produces more flower buds.) Plums, sweet cherries, and apricots fruit mainly on two-year-old and older wood, but also bear a few fruits at the base (the oldest part) of one-year-old shoots. For all fruits, routine pruning must be tailored to give a good mix of useful wood of different ages.

GROWTH PROBLEMS

If growth is poor, check the tree thoroughly, taking all possible factors into consideration. A disease such as canker (*see p.102*), competition from grass and weeds, and lack of feeding are common causes. If new apple trees are

planted where old ones grew, for example, poor growth may be due to a soil problem known as Specific Apple Replant Disease. (Exchanging planting-hole soil at planting time with soil from another area of the garden helps to prevent it.) Once the problem has been resolved, hard pruning can be used to encourage strong new growth.

Conversely, if growth is very strong and the tree is slow to fruit, consider whether it has been fertilized too heavily or pruned too severely. Lighter pruning may curb overly vigorous trees, as may planting grass under the tree to give it some competition. On apples and pears only, another option is bark ringing (*see pp.106*). For other trees, or as a last

RESPONSE TO PRUNING – WEAK SHOOTS
With light or no pruning, weak shoots develop flower buds but do not grow much longer. Moderate pruning encourages growth and allows some flower buds to develop, while hard pruning stimulates strong growth.

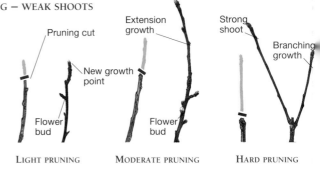

LIGHT PRUNING   MODERATE PRUNING   HARD PRUNING

RESPONSE TO PRUNING – STRONG SHOOTS
Left unpruned, or at most lightly tip-pruned, strong shoots produce some extension growth and several flower buds; moderate pruning will increase branching and reduce the flower-bud count; hard pruning induces still stronger growth at the expense of flower buds. Hard pruning can be used to encourage growth on young trees or, on mature trees, to stimulate replacement growth that will fill a gap caused by, for example, removal of a diseased branch.

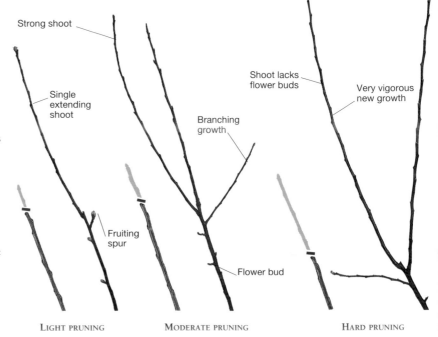

LIGHT PRUNING   MODERATE PRUNING   HARD PRUNING

resort for apples and pears, vigor can also be limited by pruning the root system, reducing the amount of nourishment the tree can absorb.

ROOT PRUNING

Young trees are most easily root pruned by being lifted and replanted in winter. Dig a trench around the tree, 2–2½ft (60–75cm) from it, and carefully undermine and undercut the root system. Strong tap roots must be cut with a pruning saw, but try to leave fibrous roots undamaged. Replant and stake the tree securely. Mulch the following spring.

On large trees, root pruning *in situ* (*see right*) is a major operation that should be spread over at least two years. Staking afterward is helpful, but is rarely possible; guy wires (*see p.23*) pegged outside the trench may be useful.

If a tree is still overly vigorous, there may be a simple explanation – that it is on a more vigorous rootstock than at first thought and still attempting to grow into its final, mature size before starting to fruit. If you can accommodate a larger tree, this will not pose problems; if you cannot, replace it.

FRUITING PROBLEMS

Poor crops may be caused by any of the factors responsible for poor growth (or by the lack of a suitable pollinating cultivar), or they may result from overpruning that has suppressed the development of flower buds in favor of vigorous new shoots. Adjusting the degree of pruning should help. In some regions birds may also be to blame; smaller trained forms, such as the pyramid, and wall-trained trees are much easier to net. Heavy crops of

ROOT PRUNING A FRUIT TREE

To avoid stressing the tree too much, only half of the root system is pruned each year. In the first winter, mark a half-circle about 4ft (1.2m) from the tree and dig a trench 12–18in (30–45cm) deep along it.

Saw through large roots you encounter when digging, taking out the section that crosses the trench. Replace the soil, firming it well, and mulch in spring. Repeat the operation on the other side of the tree the following winter.

small, unsatisfactory fruit can again be countered by adjusting the pruning level, but an important aid to this is fruit thinning (*see below*), which will not only produce a better crop of fewer but finer fruits but also help to prevent, in apples and pears, the onset of a problem known as biennial bearing.

BIENNIAL BEARING

An overheavy crop, frost damage to buds, disease, or underfeeding can all trigger biennial bearing, particularly in apples and pears: the alternation of a heavy crop (on years) with a light crop or no crop at all (off years). In the winter following an "off" year, prune as usual but leave unpruned as many one-year-old shoots as possible. These will

not fruit the next year but will develop plenty of flower buds for the following one – the next expected "off" year. The following winter (after the heavy-cropping "on" season), again leave these shoots (now two years old) unpruned, but prune one-year-old shoots back hard, so that two years later (in the next "on" year) these will bear moderate rather than heavy crops, breaking the biennial cycle.

Another cure for biennial bearing is fruit thinning. The young fruits must be drastically reduced in the year of expected heavy cropping to break the cycle. If a tree is very large, thinning, at flower or fruit stage, can be done on one or two branches only, but will have to be repeated for many years.

BLOSSOM THINNING

To counteract biennial bearing, within a week or 10 days after flowering, remove nine out of every 10 blossom trusses. Pinch or cut out the open flowers with scissors, leaving the rosette' of leaves intact.

FRUIT THINNING

BEFORE THINNING *If all of these crowded fruits are allowed to develop, they will be small and poorly flavored. The weight of such a heavy crop may also break the branch, so future crops will also be affected.*

AFTER THINNING *The thinned fruits are large and well ripened. A moderate crop will also ensure a balance between the formation of new flower buds and growth for future regular cropping.*

RENOVATION

Neglect is the chief cause of a fruit tree requiring renovation. However, a fruit tree can also need renovating because it has been overpruned, stimulating a mass of vigorous, congested growth that, if allowed to develop, tends to be unfruitful and prone to disease. Always, therefore, resist the temptation to prune neglected trees hard. Renovate carefully and gradually, over several years.

First, decide whether the tree is worth keeping. Even if its crop is of no interest, a fruit tree that is sound and healthy may well, once renovated, be an attractive garden feature. You could also seek expert advice about the possibility of "grafting over" – converting the tree, by specialized grafting, to another cultivar. However, if it is riddled with disease, especially canker, it should be grubbed out and discarded. Do not plant another fruit tree on the site.

The same strictures concerning safety apply as when renovating ornamental trees (see p.34). Never use a chainsaw without the correct training. Renovate at the same time as you routinely prune the tree in question: late winter or early spring for most fruits; late spring or summer for stone fruits. Although many

CANKER
Some apples suffer badly from this disease. Heavily infected trees should be grubbed out and discarded. Otherwise, cut below all infected growth until clean, healthy wood is reached, and then disinfect tools.

CROWDED AND CROSSING BRANCHES
Overcrowding causes a buildup of stagnant air, and, where branches touch, rubbing can lead to damage and an entry point for disease. Of the crossing pair, retain the younger or healthier growth, if possible.

growers still use wound paints to "seal" large cuts, recent research has shown them to be unnecessary and often counterproductive (see also p.22).

NEGLECTED TREES
Some problems due to neglect are common to all trees, while others are more specific to certain fruits; an apple,

for example, may have overgrown spur systems. Tackle problems systematically over two or three years. Removing too much growth in one season stresses the tree and leads to excessive regrowth; many large cuts also attract infection. No more than a quarter of the crown should be removed each year. The number of years renovation will take

RENOVATING A NEGLECTED FRUIT TREE (APPLE) OVER TWO YEARS

BEFORE RENOVATION *In the first year, remove dead, diseased, and damaged wood. Remove, or shorten to a replacement shoot or branch, crowded and crossing branches. In the second year, improve fruiting potential: shorten overlong and unproductive growth to a replacement shoot, and thin regrowth from the sites of previous cuts. On apples and pears, reduce congested spur systems (see Spur thinning, p.105).*

AFTER RENOVATION *Two years later, the tree has a well-spaced crown of strong framework branches on which fruiting growth has plenty of room to develop. Routine pruning for the fruit can now be introduced: on this apple, long, young shoots now need shortening to start the formation of fresh spur systems. To keep new growth balanced, prune weak shoots hard and vigorous shoots lightly.*

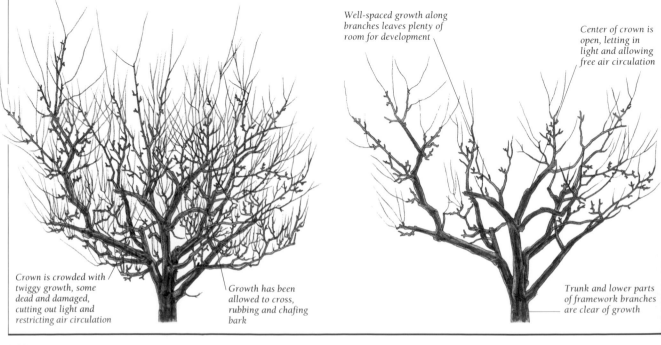

Well-spaced growth along branches leaves plenty of room for development

Center of crown is open, letting in light and allowing free air circulation

Crown is crowded with twiggy growth, some dead and damaged, cutting out light and restricting air circulation

Growth has been allowed to cross, rubbing and chafing bark

Trunk and lower parts of framework branches are clear of growth

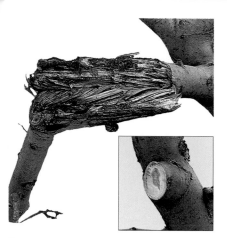

BROKEN BRANCH

Branches broken by wind or weight may split length- or crosswise. Here, on the cut surface, water penetration is still visible, but this is as far back as the cut can safely be made without damaging the branch collar.

will vary depending on the tree's size and condition. Concentrate first on restoring health rather than obtaining a crop. As well as dead, damaged, or diseased wood and crowded, crossing growth, there may be low, spreading branches that are best removed. Remove branches correctly (*see p.22*), and never tackle overly large jobs yourself. Once unwanted and unproductive wood has been removed, the normal annual pruning routine can be reestablished.

Succulent "water shoots" (*see also p.32*) may emerge in profusion around large pruning cuts. Check the tree every two weeks in summer, and rub these shoots off by hand as they sprout.

OVERPRUNED TREES

A tree whose branches are severely lopped will have produced a mass of shoots that must be thinned over several years (*see right*) to develop worthwhile fruiting branches. Careful treatment is necessary to restore a balance between wood of different ages, so that the normal cycle of pruning can be resumed. Always err on the side of underpruning, or the problem will recur.

RESTRICTED TRAINED FORMS

The more specialized the trained form, the more difficult it is to rescue, particularly if growing on a dwarfing rootstock: these trees are far less able to withstand neglect than larger specimens. If the framework can still be discerned, it is worth attempting to reduce growth and thin any congested spur systems until the condition of the main branches can be properly assessed. If they seem sound, and the response in the following growing season is good, routine pruning can be resumed. If not, replace the tree.

RENOVATING AN OVERPRUNED TREE (PEAR) OVER THREE YEARS

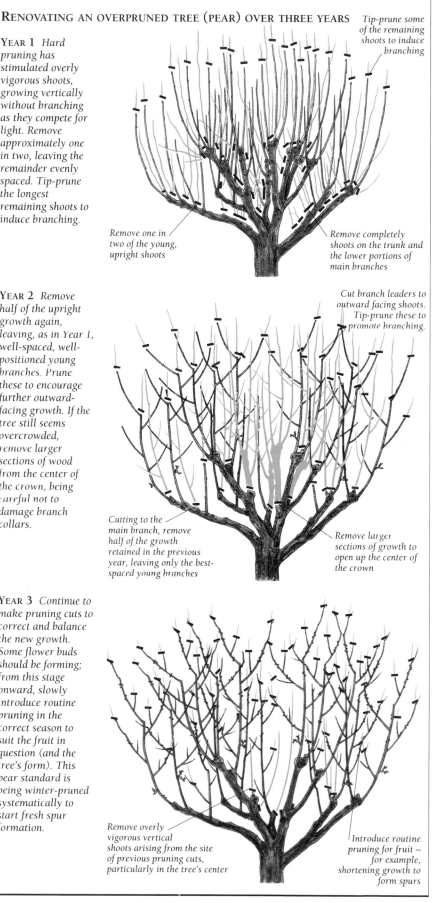

YEAR 1 *Hard pruning has stimulated overly vigorous shoots, growing vertically without branching as they compete for light. Remove approximately one in two, leaving the remainder evenly spaced. Tip-prune the longest remaining shoots to induce branching.*

Tip-prune some of the remaining shoots to induce branching

Remove one in two of the young, upright shoots

Remove completely shoots on the trunk and the lower portions of main branches

YEAR 2 *Remove half of the upright growth again, leaving, as in Year 1, well-spaced, well-positioned young branches. Prune these to encourage further outward-facing growth. If the tree still seems overcrowded, remove larger sections of wood from the center of the crown, being careful not to damage branch collars.*

Cut branch leaders to outward facing shoots. Tip-prune these to promote branching.

Cutting to the main branch, remove half of the growth retained in the previous year, leaving only the best-spaced young branches

Remove larger sections of growth to open up the center of the crown

YEAR 3 *Continue to make pruning cuts to correct and balance the new growth. Some flower buds should be forming; from this stage onward, slowly introduce routine pruning in the correct season to suit the fruit in question (and the tree's form). This pear standard is being winter-pruned systematically to start fresh spur formation.*

Remove overly vigorous vertical shoots arising from the site of previous pruning cuts, particularly in the tree's center

Introduce routine pruning for fruit — for example, shortening growth to form spurs

HARDY FRUITS

Tree fruits that can be grown outdoors in most cool temperate climates are divided into those that are hardier, such as apples, pears, and plums, and those that require, ideally, the protection in winter of a sheltered wall or greenhouse, such as figs. While the latter fruits grow and fruit well in hot climates, the hardier fruits need a period of winter cold to flower and hence set fruit. This "chilling requirement" is usually expressed as a number of hours below a given temperature. For all tree fruits, an important

requirement may be for another cultivar to be grown nearby to act as a pollinator. However, fruit trees can now be grown in a range of sizes and forms. Even a small garden has room for two or three cordons; alternatively, a "family tree" (*see page 95*) could be considered.

Regular and correct pruning and training is essential for all of these trees to maintain their health and shape and to ensure quality crops. Their fruiting habits vary, and this has a significant bearing on both timing and techniques.

APPLES (ZONES 3–9)

MALUS SYLVESTRIS VAR. DOMESTICA

The apple, with its variety of colors and flavors, long season of ripening, culinary and preserving potential, tolerance of different climates, and ease of training, easily ranks among the most popular and widely grown fruits. Its fresh green leaves, spring blossoms, and handsome bark and fruits give it enormous decorative value too, and it is probably the top choice as a single fruit tree in any ornamental garden.

It is also a major commercial crop. The apple has always been at the forefront of fruit research and development, resulting in a wider range of rootstocks, tree forms, and cultivars than for any other fruit. Popular cultivars are available as bushes and trees that will grow to anything from 5 to 15 feet (2–5m) or more. Moreover, recent interest in traditional cultivars

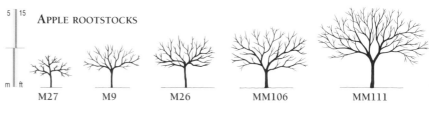

APPLE ROOTSTOCKS

M27　M9　M26　MM106　MM111

and in conserving old orchards of large, standard trees is increasing the availability of older cultivars, considered by many to have the best flavors.

GRAFTING AND ROOTSTOCKS

Choice of rootstock will determine not only the size of the apple tree but also the forms into which it can be trained: it would be very hard, for example, to grow a tree on the vigorous MM111 stock into a cordon; the dwarfing M27 will never make a tree of much more than head height. It is vital to decide first in what situation and form you want your apple to grow, next to

determine the best rootstock, and only then to look at the choice of cultivars (and their pollination requirements) available on those rootstocks. Any good specialty fruit nursery will offer advice.

FRUITING HABIT

Most apples are "spur-bearers," fruiting on wood that is in its third year or older, in the form of short, fruit-bearing shoots known as spurs. Their main branches are fairly evenly and well clothed with flower buds, spurs, and new shoots. However, a minority of cultivars tend to produce, instead, clusters of fruit at or near the tips of longer shoots, with far fewer spurs and greater lengths of bare wood between the buds and shoots. These are known as "tip-bearers"; some cultivars are markedly tip-bearing, others partially so. It is crucial to determine whether your apple is tip- or spur-bearing (for examples of tip-bearers, *see facing page*), and to vary the pruning regime in favor of the fruiting habit. This fruiting habit also influences the forms in which the apple may be trained: tip-bearers do not make good cordons or espaliers, where a closely and evenly distributed crop along a fairly short length of main branch is required.

All apple trees vary in their growth and fruitfulness, and pruning needs to be tailored to suit the individual tree. Only experimentation and experience will determine what degree of pruning and which combination of methods gives the best results for your trees.

TIME OF PRUNING

Apples start into growth early in the year, flowering in midspring. The main pruning season is late winter or early spring, after the harshest weather is over. Trained forms need extra pruning in summer to maintain their shape by restricting new growth.

MODERN APPLE ORCHARD
Apple trees are grafted in the nursery. During the past 70 years, primarily British research into the dwarfing effects of various rootstocks has had an enormous influence on their cultivation. With the advent of tree forms suitable for ever-smaller spaces and closer planting, new formative training and annual pruning systems have had to be developed to create and maintain the new forms.

WINTER PRUNING

The routine pruning of spur-bearing apples ("spur-pruning") consists of shortening laterals to stimulate short, fruiting sideshoots. Growth from these will in turn be shortened, thus building up the familiar, knobby spur systems. Only the lusher branch leaders are not pruned, since pruning would encourage even more vigorous extension growth (diverting energy from fruit formation) – unless the cultivar has a tendency to tip-bearing, which is best prevented. Continual spur-pruning inevitably leads, after some years, to congested growth, and this will need thinning.

Tip-bearers should not be spur-pruned since it will remove the wood on which fruits form. Instead, each year cut back a proportion of older fruited shoots (*see* Renewal pruning, *below*), either completely or to one or two buds, leaving the remainder unpruned to bear the crop for that year. After these shoots have borne fruit for a few years, they are removed in favor of the new growth stimulated by the pruning cuts on other shoots. All of the tree's fruiting wood is thus renewed over a period of years.

An overcrowded spur-bearing apple will also benefit from moderate renewal pruning, particularly if the tree produces numerous laterals.

REGULATED PRUNING

On large, mature trees, especially of very vigorous cultivars such as 'Bramley's Seedling', 'Blenheim Orange', and 'Newton Wonder', the annual pruning of individual shoots is impractical. Instead, remove a large section of branch or even a complete limb. Always select unproductive, crossing, or congested growth to prune out; never remove too much growth in any one year.

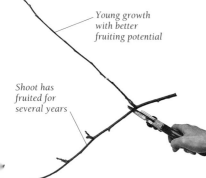

Young growth with better fruiting potential

Shoot has fruited for several years

RENEWAL PRUNING
On tip-bearing apples, prune some older fruited shoots each year, cutting to a strong young shoot or a low bud or, where growth is crowded, removing the shoot completely. This keeps the crown open, and ensures the continual production of young fruitful shoots.

TIP-BEARING APPLE CULTIVARS
While most apple cultivars fruit on spurs, a few fruit either exclusively or partially at the tips of shoots, and pruning must be adjusted.

TIP-BEARERS
'Cornish Gillyflower'
'Irish Peach'
'Tydeman's Early Worcester'
'Worcester Pearmain'

PARTIAL TIP-BEARERS
'Bramley's Seedling'
'Blenheim Orange'
'Discovery'
'Epicure'
'Golden Noble'
'Lord Lambourne'
'St. Edmunds Pippin'

Spur-bearing habit (*left*)

Tip-bearing habit

SPUR-PRUNING

Pruning the laterals stimulates the production of flower buds near their bases. The apples then develop close to main branches (reducing the risk of breakage under crop weight). Prune the weaker laterals harder to encourage even regrowth.

1 *Cut back long laterals to five or six buds, weaker ones to two or three. Shorter shoots can be left unpruned.*

2 *Cutting to a bud, prune branch leaders by a quarter to one-third of the previous season's growth, unless (on spur bearers only) they are very vigorous.*

SPUR-THINNING

BEFORE THINNING *After several years of spur-pruning, spur systems become congested and overcrowded, and fruits will not have room to develop fully.*

These spur systems have become crowded and overgrown

AFTER THINNING *The older, more complicated growth is cut out, leaving younger wood where possible. Weak systems are removed completely to alleviate overcrowding.*

Overgrown, congested spur systems have been reduced in size

Weak spur system has been removed completely

SUMMER PRUNING

The more formally trained ("restricted") apple tree forms, such as cordons, fans, and espaliers, must be pruned in summer to restrict growth and encourage fruit buds to form. The technique used is known as the Lorette system. In warm climates, the full system is used. All new shoots 6–9in (15–22cm) long are shortened to 2in (5cm) as their bases become woody. Pruning continues throughout summer, not only of shoots produced in the first flush of growth, but also of the shoots stimulated by the first round of cuts ("secondary growth"). These are shortened to ¾in (2cm).

In colder areas, such as northern Europe, the Lorette system is modified to discourage secondary growth, which may be vulnerable to cold damage. Pruning does not start until the basal third of a new shoot has turned woody, and growth is slowing down. Timing will depend largely on the weather. The shoots will become ready for pruning over a two- to three-week period. Leave unpruned any shorter than 9in (22cm) long.

To further discourage secondary growth, a few vigorous shoots may be left unpruned to act as "sap-drawers": any nourishment still traveling up the tree late in the season will be drawn into these shoots, rather than causing any more buds to develop into new shoots. Shorten sap-drawers in the spring. If secondary growth does occur, prune it back to a bud at the base in midautumn.

Other measures that may need to be undertaken during the growing season are fruit thinning (see p.101) if a heavy crop sets, and fruit or blossom thinning to counteract biennial bearing. Bark ringing (see below) may also be used as a last resort in midspring to discourage a tree that always makes excessive summer growth at the expense of flowers and fruits. It *must* be done correctly or the tree may be damaged, even killed. If it must be repeated, wait a few years.

SUMMER PRUNING

BEFORE PRUNING
New laterals have grown rapidly on this espalier, and are now ripening from the base upward. If the new growth is not shortened, trees can rapidly outgrow their site, and the trained form will be lost. The foliage on new shoots also tends to shade the fruits from the ripening sun.

1 Shorten new shoots growing directly from the trunk or main branches to three leaves above the basal cluster of leaves.

2 Prune sideshoots from existing laterals or spurs back to one bud above the basal cluster of leaves.

Basal cluster of leaves

AFTER PRUNING
The espalier branch is visibly restored, and more sun can reach the ripening fruits. Pruning cuts made in summer also stimulate the development of future flower buds.

BARK RINGING

Strip of tape used as guide

1 With a sharp knife, circle the trunk almost completely with two parallel cuts ¼in (6mm) apart (up to ½in/12mm on larger trees) leaving a small uncut "bridge" of bark. Incisions should penetrate down to the wood.

2 Carefully and cleanly remove the band of bark, levering it up and out with the blunt edge of a pruning knife. Do not make an entire circle; this restricts the flow of nourishment to the crown of the tree, eventually killing it.

3 Bind insulating tape around the wound to stop it from drying out and to assist healing. Seal the wound completely, but do not push the tape in so that it adheres to the cut surface. Remove it when scar tissue begins to form.

FORMATIVE TRAINING

Pretrained young apple trees are available, but they are also relatively simple to train yourself into a range of forms (*see following pages*). Buying young trees is much less expensive, especially if several are required. In addition, one- or two-year-old trees are quick to establish, suffering less of a growth setback caused by transplant shock.

BUYING WHIPS
Starting with one-year-old trees is the most economical option. If you can contact a specialty nursery to select your own trees, so much the better. A well-feathered whip (already furnished with strong laterals) gives a head start, but if you choose to buy whips (single stems), select good, straight specimens; it is usually worth sacrificing height in favor of a sturdy stem with plenty of healthy buds. Professional training techniques can be used right from the start to influence the position and direction of shoot growth to suit the intended trained form.

In order to build up a good, thick trunk, whips are often cut back in their first year. If the intended tree form is to have a central trunk (for example, a pyramid), a new leader is trained in. Many more forms require no central leader, but well-positioned, strong, low branches. When a whip is cut back, the natural result is for the upper buds to develop into vigorous upright shoots, competing to become the new leader. These are not ideal for branches because they will be growing at a narrow V-angle to the stem and may split when mature and heavy. Fruit growers use nicking (*see above*) to counteract this

NICKING AND NOTCHING

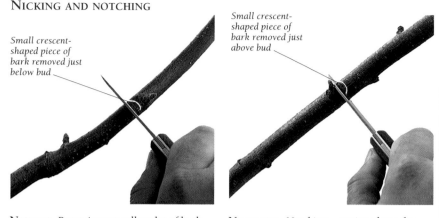

NICKING *Removing a small wedge of bark below a bud weakens its growth by restricting the supply of nutrients; it may develop into a flower bud or a small shoot. Energy is directed instead into shoots in more desirable positions.*

NOTCHING *Notching – cutting above the bud – stimulates a shoot's growth. It is used mainly to encourage shoots to grow low down on a stem, or to obtain shoots in positions desirable for form-training.*

undesirable growth habit. Nicking below the two topmost buds once the leader is cut back (*see below*) allows only weak growth from them. Lower buds grow strongly to compensate, and at wide angles, because of shading by the stub of stem above them. Any growth that does develop from the two top buds can be pinched back. The stub can be cut back to just above the topmost lateral in the following winter.

The result is a short trunk well furnished with evenly spaced laterals of equal vigor that make wide angles to the stem, desirable both for strength and for the structure of many tree forms.

Notching – nicking above the bud – is a similar technique that can be used to encourage a shoot to break where it is needed – for example, to fill a gap in a fan. If shoots are not wanted in a

particular place, an alternative to nicking is to keep pinching back to two leaves any growth that develops.

BUYING FEATHERED TREES
A year's advantage can be gained by buying feathered trees, either whips or two-year-olds (*see p.98*). Choose strong, straight stems with plenty of wide-angled laterals to give room for training. Less ideal specimens should be pruned to redress any imbalance: prune weaker growth hard, and strong growth less. If one shoot is markedly stronger, it is always best to cut it out completely to avoid any imbalance in future growth. Where only one or two laterals exist, or laterals are spindly or unequal in size, it is better to cut them back hard to one or two buds from their bases and virtually start again, treating the tree as a whip.

USING NICKING TO PRODUCE LOW, WIDE-ANGLED LATERALS FOR FAN-TRAINING (APPLE)

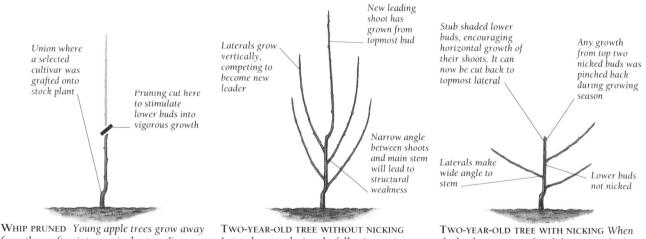

WHIP PRUNED *Young apple trees grow away from the graft point as a single stem. For many tree forms, this is cut back to thicken the main stem and encourage lateral shoots to grow from low buds.*

TWO-YEAR-OLD TREE WITHOUT NICKING *Laterals grow during the following spring and summer, but naturally tend to adopt a vigorous, vertical habit, undesirable for structural safety and for many trained forms.*

TWO-YEAR-OLD TREE WITH NICKING *When the leader is removed and the top two buds are nicked, the young tree develops well-positioned, wide-angled laterals, ideal for framework branches of forms such as a fan.*

APPLE BUSH

The bush is one of the most useful apple tree forms, and also one of the easiest to train and maintain. A wide range of rootstocks and thus of heights for the mature bush is available, although to accommodate their spread, even the smallest dwarf rootstocks need to be planted at least 6ft (2m) apart.

FORMATIVE TRAINING

The aim is to create a branched, open-centered crown, with eight to ten branches radiating from a short trunk, about 24–30in (60–75cm) tall. Start in late winter or early spring with a young feathered tree (see p.107) that has three or four strong, wide-angled laterals between 2ft (60cm) and 3ft (90cm) from the ground. The laterals should be as well spaced as possible, both along the length of the trunk and around it, to give the bush strength and symmetry.

The leader is pruned back and the laterals shortened to encourage branching. The next winter, the strongest and best placed of these shoots are selected and shortened to build up the main branch framework. At this stage, cut to outward-facing buds to give the bush an open center.

In the third winter, tip-prune branch leaders to encourage the bush to fill out. Adjust other pruning depending on whether the cultivar is a spur-bearer or tip-bearer (see p.104). Shorten laterals on spur-bearing apples to start building up the stubby, fruiting spur systems.

ESTABLISHED PRUNING

As the bush becomes established and begins to fruit, pruning thereafter is necessary only in winter, and should complement the fruiting habit of the tree, whether spur- or tip-bearing. Some trees vary between the two; experimentation may be necessary to see which method, or combination of methods, is most successful.

An open center to the bush is still desirable, as it allows air, light, and sunshine to penetrate. However, as the bush matures, branches will gradually become lower and more spreading under the weight of fruits. Some pruning cuts should encourage the development of a few strong, more upright growths eventually to replace them, or the bush will splay out and the spreading branches may eventually break.

APPLE BUSH, WINTER PRUNING ON PLANTING

1 Prune back the leader to just above the topmost of three or four strong laterals.

2 Shorten laterals by two-thirds of their length. Cut to upward-facing buds on more horizontal shoots and outward-facing buds on upright shoots.

Well-spaced lower laterals radiate outward like spokes of a wheel

Short trunk will keep lower fruiting branches clear of ground

Short stake

YEAR 2, WINTER

1 Shorten laterals selected to become main branches by half.

2 Prune shoots not required for main branches to four or five buds.

3 Remove shoots that are badly spaced, crossing, or making narrow V-angles with the stem.

YEAR 3, WINTER (SPUR-BEARERS)

1 Shorten branch leaders by a quarter of the previous season's growth.

2 Prune strong laterals to four to six buds, and weak ones harder (to stimulate growth), to two or three buds.

Adjust tree tie as trunk thickens

3 Cut out badly placed shoots completely.

YEAR 3, WINTER (TIP-BEARERS)

1 Shorten branch leaders by a quarter of the previous season's growth.

Leave all sideshoots unpruned, unless badly placed or crossing

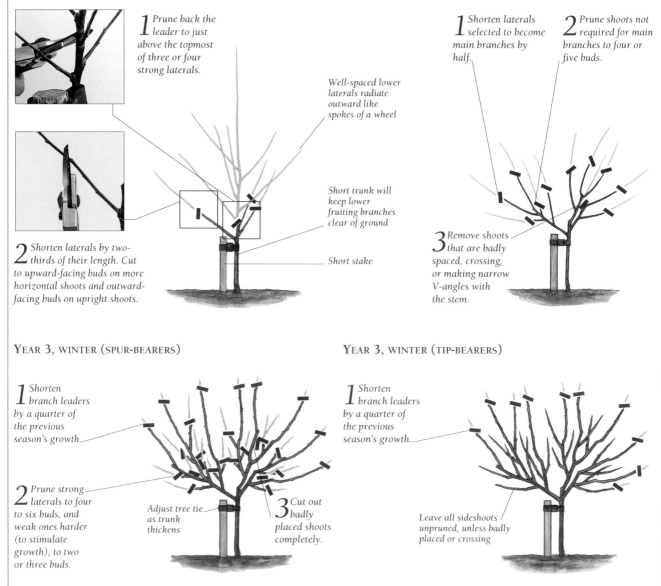

Established apple bush, spur-pruning (for spur-bearers) in late winter

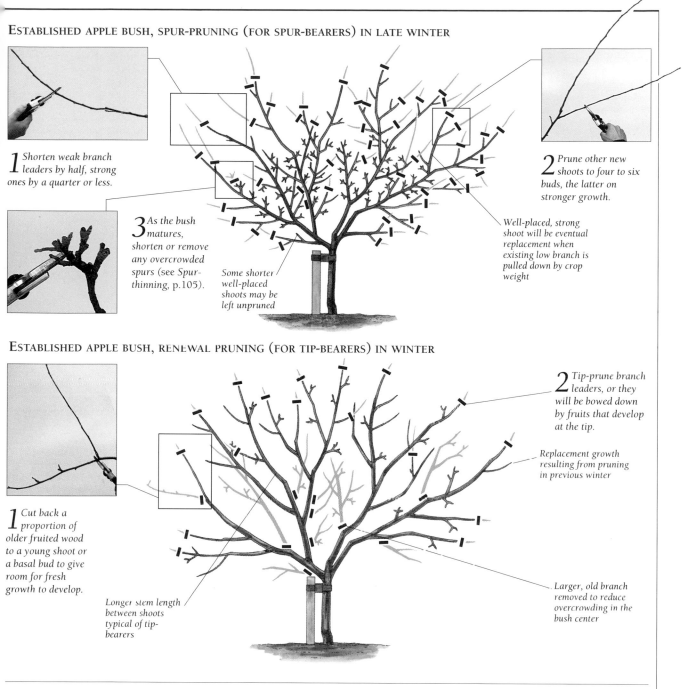

1 *Shorten weak branch leaders by half, strong ones by a quarter or less.*

3 *As the bush matures, shorten or remove any overcrowded spurs (see Spur-thinning, p.105).*

Some shorter well-placed shoots may be left unpruned

2 *Prune other new shoots to four to six buds, the latter on stronger growth.*

Well-placed, strong shoot will be eventual replacement when existing low branch is pulled down by crop weight

Established apple bush, renewal pruning (for tip-bearers) in winter

2 *Tip-prune branch leaders, or they will be bowed down by fruits that develop at the tip.*

Replacement growth resulting from pruning in previous winter

1 *Cut back a proportion of older fruited wood to a young shoot or a basal bud to give room for fresh growth to develop.*

Longer stem length between shoots typical of tip-bearers

Larger, old branch removed to reduce overcrowding in the bush center

Standard apple trees

The height and spread of standard and half-standard trees, and the relative difficulties in pruning, spraying, and picking them, means that they are used less frequently in domestic gardens, although they are occasionally required to fill gaps in older orchards. Vigorous rootstocks are used, and the trees may take up to eight years to bear fruit – creating the clear stem takes two years alone.

Beginning with a young feathered tree (*see p.107*), the leader is not pruned but staked, grown on, and gradually cleared

of laterals just as for an ornamental standard tree (*see p.28*). Standards (*above left*) need a clear trunk of at least 6ft (2m), and half-standards (*above right*), 4½ft (1.35m).

Once the desired length of clear stem is achieved, the leader is pruned back and the crown of the tree built up exactly as if it were a bush (*see facing*

page). The tree's extra vigor, derived from the rootstock, will produce a crown proportionate to the height of the tree. Because the branches will be larger and heavier, it is extremely important for the tree's safety that they make wide angles to the trunk; choose laterals carefully to develop the main branch framework.

Once established, these trees are usually better served by regulated pruning (*see p.105*) – the removal of large portions of branches – than by spur- or renewal pruning. However, if the tree is sluggish in making new growth, spur- or renewal prune as for a bush.

APPLE SPINDLE BUSH

The spindle bush is a small tree form that was developed in Holland as a way of maximizing crops while minimizing labor costs. 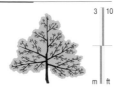 Although popular with commercial growers, it is rarely seen in home gardens, perhaps because of its rather ungainly appearance. It requires careful formative training. When established, it needs both winter renewal pruning and some work in summer, but it repays this attention with a heavy, early-ripening, and easily harvested crop in a very small space.

The basic spindle bush framework consists of a central trunk 6–7ft (2–2.2m) tall with four main branches, or arms, radiating out like the points of a weathervane about a third of the way up. The silhouette is thus broadly conical, something like that of an old-fashioned spinning top.

Upper branches on the central trunk above the arms are not permanent, but pruned hard after carrying one or two crops and replaced by younger shoots, so that they never grow large enough to overshadow the lower fruits.

All lateral growth – the main branches and their sideshoots, and those growing from the trunk – is pruned and trained so that it is as nearly horizontal as possible.

FORMATIVE TRAINING

Young spindle bushes are rarely offered for sale outside the wholesale trade, so it is more than likely you will have to train one yourself. The starting point is, ideally, a feathered whip (*see p.107*) with four good, strong laterals of equal vigor between 24 and 36in (60–90cm) up the stem. (An effective spindle can be made with three arms, but a proportion of the potential crop is lost.) It is essential that the laterals make as wide an angle as possible to the main stem. The tree will need a sturdy, permanent, 6ft (2m) stake.

Initial training concentrates on the development of the arms: pruning cuts will often need to be made to downward-pointing buds to encourage near-horizontal growth. Tying down (*see also p.99*) in summer also plays an important role. Use thick string or strips of plastic netting that will not cut into the young bark. The ties should not be removed until the branches show no tendency to spring upward when the tension is slackened.

While the tree is developing, the central leader is shortened each winter.

APPLE SPINDLE BUSH, WINTER PRUNING ON PLANTING

1 Prune the leader to a bud at about 3ft (90cm), 3–4in (7–10cm) above the topmost selected lateral.

2 Shorten the three or four laterals chosen to form branches by half, cutting to downward-facing buds.

3 Remove completely any additional weak and low-growing laterals.

YEAR 1, LATE SUMMER

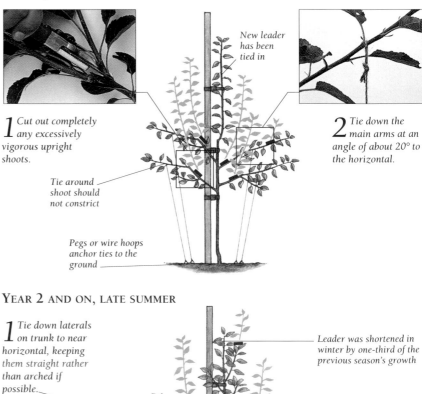

1 Cut out completely any excessively vigorous upright shoots.

New leader has been tied in

Tie around shoot should not constrict

Pegs or wire hoops anchor ties to the ground

2 Tie down the main arms at an angle of about 20° to the horizontal.

YEAR 2 AND ON, LATE SUMMER

1 Tie down laterals on trunk to near horizontal, keeping them straight rather than arched if possible.

2 Remove over-vigorous upright shoots on competing laterals.

Leader was shortened in winter by one-third of the previous season's growth

3 Check ties on the main arms – if the stem does not spring upward when they are loosened, the ties may be removed.

Aiming for a straight trunk, a new leader is retrained and tied in until the tree reaches a height of 6–7ft (2–2.2m). Then, delay pruning the leader until late spring to discourage regrowth.

ESTABLISHED PRUNING AND TRAINING

Tie down laterals on the trunk and main branches each summer so that they grow horizontally. Staples hammered into the tree's stake make convenient anchor points, as do any of the stronger, lower branches. Remove completely any vigorously upright growth that resists tying down, since it will shade the developing fruits and spoil the tree's shape.

Once fruiting begins, the young fruiting branches on the upper length of the trunk are also winter-pruned using the renewal system, as for a tip-bearing bush (*see p.105*). These branches should never get too big; they should ideally have no more than a three- or four-year lifespan. Growth along the lower, permanent arms is managed with a combination of renewal pruning and spur-pruning (*see p.105*) in winter. To maintain a constant height, cut the new leading shoot at the top of the tree back to one or two buds each year.

ESTABLISHED APPLE SPINDLE BUSH, WINTER PRUNING

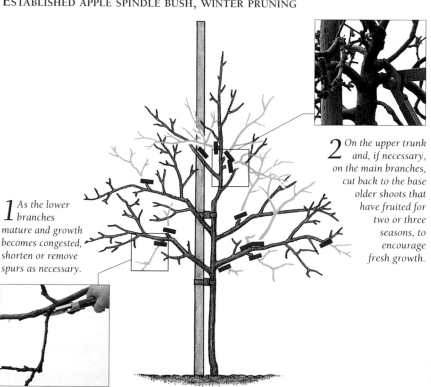

1 As the lower branches mature and growth becomes congested, shorten or remove spurs as necessary.

2 On the upper trunk and, if necessary, on the main branches, cut back to the base older shoots that have fruited for two or three seasons, to encourage fresh growth.

APPLE DWARF PYRAMID

The dwarf pyramid is a small tree whose compact form is made possible by dwarfing rootstocks and maintained largely through regular summer pruning. Branches are progressively shorter from the bottom to the top of the tree, and radiate from a central trunk to form a narrow pyramidal shape. Because so much shortening of growth is needed to restrict size and prevent overcrowding, the dwarf pyramid is a form best suited to spur-bearers (*see p.104*). It is also an ideal compact form for pear trees.

FORMATIVE TRAINING

Start with a well-feathered young tree (*see p.107*) and train as for a pear dwarf pyramid (*see p.118*).

ESTABLISHED PRUNING AND TRAINING

As for a pear dwarf pyramid (*see p.118*). When summer pruning, follow the Lorette system (*see p.106*); it is particularly important with this form to check the growth of vigorous upright shoots high up on the central stem. Winter pruning largely consists simply of shortening leading shoots at the top of the tree, if necessary, and reducing or removing old, crowded growth.

APPLE DWARF PYRAMID

Provided that they are well maintained, dwarf pyramids are suitable for close, almost hedgelike planting at 4–5ft (1.2m–1.5m) apart. They need permanent staking or, if to be grown in a row, a sturdy system of posts and wires.

APPLE CORDON

A cordon consists of a single main trunk, along which laterals are both summer- and winter-pruned to form fruit-bearing spur systems. The form is best suited to spur-bearing cultivars (*see p.104*). Cordons are ideal for a small garden; they can be spaced at only 2½ft (75cm) from each other in rows 6ft (2m) apart.

The more oblique the angle at which they grow, the better; cordons fruit more evenly along their length if grown this way. If vertical growth is preferred, consider training a double cordon (*see facing page*). There are apples advertised to grow in single-stemmed, columnar form, often sold as container trees under a variety of names. It is often said that they require no pruning, but they are often capable of reaching heights of up to 15ft (5m), with vigorous lateral growth. They may require just as much pruning as a traditional cordon, and they are available only in a limited range of cultivars.

FORMATIVE TRAINING

Cordons need strong horizontal support wires, held by vine eyes or wood strips 4–6in (10–15cm) away from a wall or sturdy fence, or strung tautly (using turnbuckles) between 7ft (2.2m) concrete posts. Start with a feathered

APPLE CORDON, WINTER PRUNING ON PLANTING

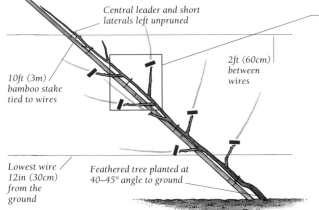

Central leader and short laterals left unpruned

10ft (3m) bamboo stake tied to wires

2ft (60cm) between wires

Lowest wire 12in (30cm) from the ground

Feathered tree planted at 40–45° angle to ground

Prune laterals longer than 4in (10cm) to three or four buds from the base.

YEAR 1, SUMMER (MODIFIED LORETTE SYSTEM)

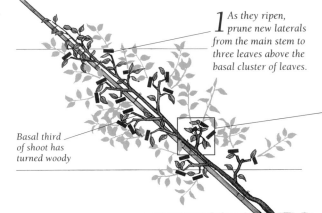

1 As they ripen, prune new laterals from the main stem to three leaves above the basal cluster of leaves.

Basal third of shoot has turned woody

2 Prune sideshoots from existing laterals to one leaf to begin forming fruiting spur systems.

ESTABLISHED APPLE CORDON, SUMMER (MODIFIED LORETTE SYSTEM)

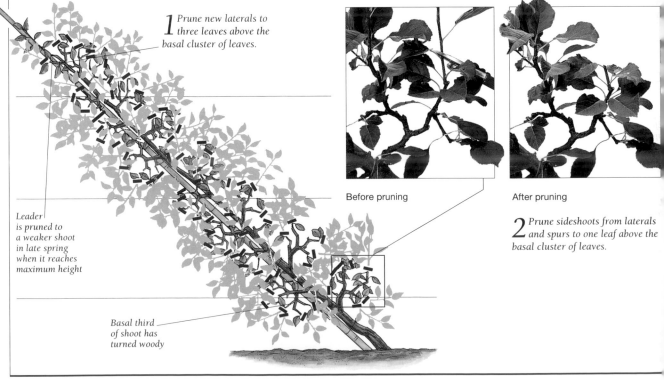

1 Prune new laterals to three leaves above the basal cluster of leaves.

Leader is pruned to a weaker shoot in late spring when it reaches maximum height

Basal third of shoot has turned woody

Before pruning

After pruning

2 Prune sideshoots from laterals and spurs to one leaf above the basal cluster of leaves.

whip or two-year-old tree with plenty of well-spaced laterals (*see p.107*). Plant it at a 45° angle, tying its main stem onto a bamboo stake, which in turn is lashed diagonally to the wires so that the bark is not damaged. The first stage in developing fruiting spurs is to shorten long laterals, and this is repeated over subsequent summers. The central leader is not pruned until it reaches the top wire; then, cut it back to a weaker shoot, pruning in late spring to discourage regrowth.

ESTABLISHED PRUNING

The laterals, including the leading shoot, are summer-pruned following the Lorette system (*see p.106*), either full or modified depending on climate. As the cordon matures and spur systems become more complicated, they will need simplifying and thinning in winter (*see also Spur-thinning, p.105*). Conversely, if by late spring a length of the cordon remains bare, notching (*see p.107*) above an eye, or latent bud, may stimulate the bud into growth.

ESTABLISHED CORDON, WINTER

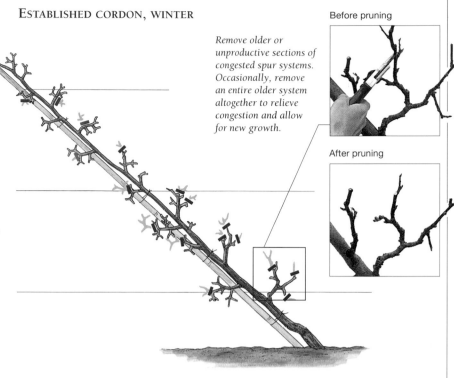

Remove older or unproductive sections of congested spur systems. Occasionally, remove an entire older system altogether to relieve congestion and allow for new growth.

Before pruning

After pruning

APPLE, MULTIPLE CORDONS

Double ("U") and four-armed (double-"U") cordons need careful training but look attractive, and are very productive. Triple cordons, with three arms, are not recommended for apples since the central arm tends to grow much more vigorously than the outer two. Achieving a good shape depends on having laterals develop precisely where they are needed to form the main arms, so it is easiest to start with a whip, using nicking and, if necessary, notching

2.5 | 8

m | ft

(*see p.107*) to produce shoots in the required positions. All multiple cordons require horizontal wires with bamboo stakes tied in diagonally and vertically on which the arms can be trained. Multiple cordons need a more vigorous rootstock than single cordons.

TRAINING AND PRUNING

A double cordon is formed as below (*see also Redcurrant cordons, p.238*). From its third summer, growth on the vertical arms is pruned as for a single cordon.

For a four-armed cordon, first create a double cordon, but do not train the arms vertically until they are at least 2–2½ft (60–75cm) apart. The following winter, cut both arms back to the lowest pair of good buds facing to the left and right on the vertical part of the stem. From each, a pair of arms can then be grown on and managed as for a double cordon.

DOUBLE APPLE CORDON, FORMATIVE TRAINING

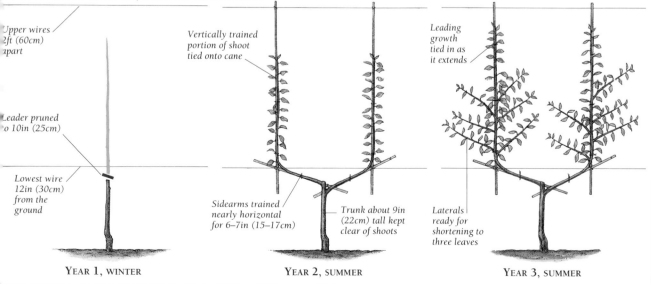

Upper wires 2ft (60cm) apart

Leader pruned to 10in (25cm)

Lowest wire 12in (30cm) from the ground

Vertically trained portion of shoot tied onto cane

Sidearms trained nearly horizontal for 6–7in (15–17cm)

Trunk about 9in (22cm) tall kept clear of shoots

Leading growth tied in as it extends

Laterals ready for shortening to three leaves

YEAR 1, WINTER

YEAR 2, SUMMER

YEAR 3, SUMMER

APPLE ESPALIER

Espaliers need firm support: a wall, a strong fence, or concrete posts, with horizontal wires 18–24in (45–60cm) apart (*see also* Apple cordon, *p.112*). Since much of an espalier's charm lies in its formal symmetry, it must be trained and maintained with care. Always use a spur-bearing cultivar (*see p.105*). Two-tiered espaliers can be used as low, fruit-bearing "fences"; for more than three tiers, a vigorous rootstock must be used.

FORMATIVE TRAINING

Precise early training is easiest from a whip (*see p.107*), but a feathered tree with one or two pairs of nearly opposing laterals will have a head start (if it also has a strong upper shoot, cut to it and train it in as the new leader).

Each winter, the central leader is cut back to just above where the next tier of branches is wanted in order to direct energy into laterals that will break from buds just below the cut. The topmost shoot – the new leader – is tied in vertically. The two below it are first trained diagonally on stakes to keep them growing strongly. (The two laterals that will form the top tier will need stakes that extend above the top wire.) At the end of the growing season, both stake and shoot are lowered to the horizontal. If one of a pair of laterals is growing less strongly than the other, raise it again temporarily (*see* Correcting uneven development, *p.98*), or shorten it, to stimulate its growth.

When the espalier has filled its allotted space, cut back the central leading shoot and branch leaders to one bud in late spring or summer to discourage regrowth.

APPLE ESPALIER, YEAR 1, WINTER

Cut the leader back to a good bud 2–3in (5–7cm) above the first wire. This bud will produce the new leading shoot.

Angled cut

Shoots from buds below wire will form first tier of branches

YEAR 1, SUMMER

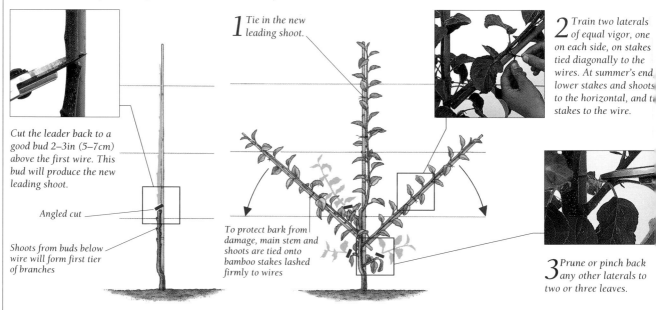

1 *Tie in the new leading shoot.*

To protect bark from damage, main stem and shoots are tied onto bamboo stakes lashed firmly to wires

2 *Train two laterals of equal vigor, one on each side, on stakes tied diagonally to the wires. At summer's end, lower stakes and shoots to the horizontal, and tie stakes to the wire.*

3 *Prune or pinch back any other laterals to two or three leaves.*

YEAR 2 UNTIL ALL TIERS ARE FORMED, WINTER

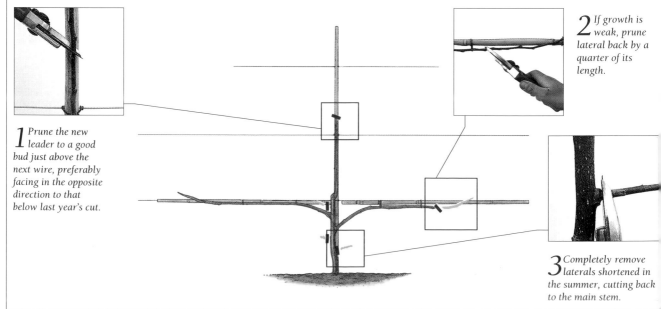

1 *Prune the new leader to a good bud just above the next wire, preferably facing in the opposite direction to that below last year's cut.*

2 *If growth is weak, prune lateral back by a quarter of its length.*

3 *Completely remove laterals shortened in the summer, cutting back to the main stem.*

ESTABLISHED PRUNING

An espalier establishes gradually. On a three- or four-tiered tree, the lower branches are likely to be fruiting before the topmost limbs are fully formed. As each tier is being created, those below will be producing sideshoots that are summer-pruned (see p.106) to form fruiting spurs. As spur systems develop and become more complex, use winter pruning to relieve overcrowding (see below). Regular summer pruning is vital, otherwise the central stem will direct energy into strong upper growth at the expense of the lower tiers. If the top tiers tend to be more vigorous in spite of summer pruning, thinning shoots on their spurs after growth has started will restore a balance.

YEAR 2 UNTIL ALL TIERS ARE FORMED, SUMMER

1 Train in new leading shoot vertically.

2 Select and train laterals to form the next tier as in Year 1.

3 Prune shoots on the lower branches back to three or four leaves.

4 Shorten any other laterals on the stem by two-thirds of their length.

ESTABLISHED APPLE ESPALIER, SUMMER (MODIFIED LORETTE SYSTEM)

1 Prune all new laterals from the main arms to three leaves above the basal cluster.

2 Shorten all sideshoots to one leaf.

Once all tiers have been formed, leading shoot is removed

3 Remove completely any overvigorous, upright shoots on the arms and especially on the main stem.

Growth on lower arms tends often to be less vigorous than on top tier

Basal third of new shoots has ripened

ESTABLISHED ESPALIER, LATE WINTER

By the time the top tier of an espalier is fully established, lower arms will also have begun to need winter pruning (see also p.105) to thin congested spur systems built up by spur-pruning. This thinning should subsequently be carried out where necessary every year.

Prune away old or unproductive sections of overcrowded spur systems. If spur systems themselves are too close together, remove one or two completely.

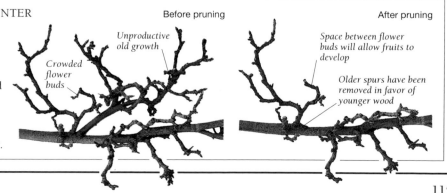

Before pruning

Unproductive old growth

Crowded flower buds

After pruning

Space between flower buds will allow fruits to develop

Older spurs have been removed in favor of younger wood

APPLE FAN

The fan form was traditionally used to wall-train plums and other stone fruits. Stone fruits are not suitable for training as espaliers, because such a rigid, closely pruned form does not exploit their fruiting habit well. However, apples are just as well suited to more informal training, and a fan, if well formed, does not need quite such rigorous attention to pruning as does an espalier. It may also be more productive.

Fans can sometimes be bought pretrained, but avoid purchasing one whose branches radiate outward from a central stem, rather than upward from two low arms: a central trunk draws the tree's energy upward so that the top growth in the center of the fan grows much more vigorously than the rest.

FORMATIVE TRAINING
As for a peach fan (see p.134), but because there is no risk of silver-leaf disease as with stone fruits, the pruning can be carried out in winter as for an

FAN-TRAINED APPLE
Fans can be grown on freestanding systems of posts and wires, but these must be very well built to withstand the considerable wind resistance offered by such large, flat trees.

apple espalier. Use string tied vertically between wires to provide plenty of attachment points for shoots.

ESTABLISHED PRUNING
Once the framework has been formed, growth on the ribs of the fan is summer- and winter-pruned as for a single cordon (see p.112). Remove excessively vigorous

shoots that develop during the summer, unless they can be used in the following winter to replace a worn-out branch. Overgrown spur systems will need thinning as for a cordon (see p.112).

Fans can carry heavy crops, and efficient and well-timed fruit thinning (see p.101) is essential to avoid the onset of biennial bearing (see p.101).

APPLE STEPOVER

These are low, horizontal cordons, most often seen grown in series (usually along the edge of a bed or path), reaching to touch the trunk of the next tree in line. Use spur-bearing cultivars (see p.104), as they are more suited to the necessary regime of summer and winter pruning. It is essential to start with a very young whip, so that the stem has the necessary flexibility to withstand being bent over.

This must be done gradually and very carefully, flexing and tying the stem farther down (with twine to a peg in the ground) in stages over the entire first growing season.

As laterals develop, shorten them to three leaves from the basal cluster to start building up fruiting spur systems. When the leading shoot attains the desired length, shorten it to a bud. The shoot that develops can be treated as any other lateral.

Established stepovers are summer- and winter-pruned as for a single, oblique cordon (see p.112). Growth may be more bushy at the "trunk end" of the stepover, and may require more thinning in late winter or early spring.

APPLE STEPOVER
To give support to a row of stepovers, space sturdy 2ft (60cm) posts approximately 5ft (1.5m) apart and tightly stretch strong wire horizontally between them, attaching it about 2in (5cm) below the post tops.

APPLE PALMETTE

The palmette is a variation on the espalier, with tiers of branches trained at a 40° angle to the ground. It is often seen in commercial orchards in southern Europe where, once formed, it is allowed to grow quite freely, but in cooler climates summer pruning is necessary to allow more sun to reach the lower parts of the tree.

These trees are very rarely offered for sale, but can easily be trained. Both formative and established pruning and training are exactly as for an espalier (see p.114), with one crucial difference: the laterals trained to form branches are never lowered from their initial, angled position to the horizontal, but are left to grow permanently at a 40° angle. Remember to check and, if necessary, loosen ties as the girth of the branches expands. A wall or fence with supporting horizontal wires, or posts and wires in the open, will be necessary.

PEARS *PYRUS COMMUNIS* (ZONES 4–9)

Although they are cool-climate fruits requiring cold winters (the "chilling requirement"), pears generally require warmer, more sheltered conditions than apples. Among the wide range of cultivars (mostly dessert fruits) there are trees to suit all areas in a cool climate, but hardiness varies with cultivar. However, since pears flower earlier than apples, cold, wet weather at flowering time can cause pollination problems and consequently a smaller crop.

For shelter, pears are often grown in wall-trained forms such as cordons, fans, and espaliers. Preformed young trees are widely available, but pear forms are easily trained in the same way as apples. Cordons are doubly popular because they allow two cultivars or more – essential for pear pollination – to be grown in a small area. Wall training also displays to good effect the decorative qualities of pear trees: furrowed bark, a stubby, gnarled habit with age, showy clusters of blossoms, autumn leaf color, and fruits that vary as greatly in shape and color as they do in flavor. Bushes and dwarf pyramids – small, compact trees ideal for a sheltered spot – are also popular forms.

ROOTSTOCKS AND GRAFTING

Like apples, pear cultivars do not come true from seed and are propagated by grafting. Choice of rootstock is not as easy or as wide as for apples. In some countries, pear seedlings and the related *P. calleryana*, an ornamental tree, are used as rootstocks. Selections of quince are more widely used, largely because they produce small, manageable trees that fruit from an early age. 'Quince A' is moderately vigorous, 'Quince C' less

PEAR IN FRUIT
Pears are among the most attractive of fruit trees, their profuse white blossoms followed by fruits that may develop yellow or red tints as they ripen. The foliage, too, often displays bright autumn color. Even if its fruits are of little interest, an old pear tree, with its furrowed bark and gnarled habit, is a valuable ornamental feature.

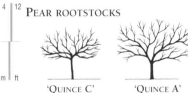

PEAR ROOTSTOCKS

'QUINCE C'   'QUINCE A'

so; the latter is preferable for growing vigorous cultivars such as 'Doyenne du Comice'. The choice of trained form may also dictate the rootstock to be used. One disadvantage of quince rootstock is its incompatibility with a number of pear cultivars. The solution is a form of grafting known as double-working (*see*

also *p.95*), in which two grafts are made using an intermediate length of a mutually compatible cultivar to bridge the gap between the stock and the scion.

GROWTH AND FRUITING HABIT

Pears grow in a similar way to apples and also fruit on two-year-old and older wood. However, a typical pear tree has a more upright growth habit than most apples, and it usually also has a marked natural tendency to form spur systems. Without regular thinning, these tend to become crowded. Some cultivars, such as 'Doyenne du Comice' and 'Beurré Hardy', are very vigorous, and their longer shoots need only light pruning in their early years. Trees that do not grow well, developing nothing but congested, short growths, are usually suffering from a problem in cultivation (often nitrogen deficiency).

There are very few tip-bearing, rather than spur-bearing, pear cultivars (*see p.104*); if one of these is chosen, follow the advice given for pruning tip-bearing apples (*see p.105*).

TIME OF PRUNING

All pears need pruning in late winter or early spring. For highly trained forms, summer pruning to restrict growth and maintain the tree's shape is essential. Winter pruning consists of spur-thinning and the removal of larger portions of branches in favor of younger growth (*see Regulated pruning, p.105*). Pear trees often set a large crop and fruit or blossom thinning (*see p.101*) are often advisable. (*Continued on p.118.*)

FIREBLIGHT

Additional pruning of pears may be necessary if they are attacked by the potentially fatal bacterial disease fireblight, to which all *Pyrus* (and, to a lesser extent, some *Malus*) are prone. In some areas of the US, the growing of pears is severely restricted because of this vulnerability. The symptoms of fireblight need watching for in summer; affected growth must be pruned back to at least 2ft (60cm) below any signs of disease, and tools dipped in disinfectant afterward.

PEAR WITH FIREBLIGHT
Blackened, scorched leaves, as if a fire had been burning under them, are the main indication of fireblight. The affected growth must be cut out completely as soon as possible.

(*Continued from p.117.*) Summer pruning of trained trees is identical to that for apples, following, depending on climate, either the full or modified Lorette system (*see p.106*), but usually timed a week or two earlier.

SPUR-THINNING

Spur systems build up both naturally and with pruning, becoming more complex with age. Without regular thinning, they become congested and encroach upon neighboring systems on the branch, crowding the fruits. On older trees, the removal of an entire system with a saw or loppers is the best way to start opening up growth on the branch. Then use pruners to thin the remaining spur systems.

Pears require greater levels of nitrogen than apples; light fertilizing in spring may be desirable.

SPUR-THINNING, PEARS

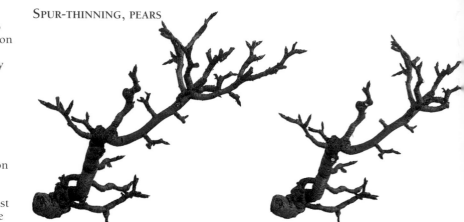

BEFORE THINNING *Start by removing obviously dead, weak, or worn out, budless spurs, then continue by thinning wherever growth is crowded.*

AFTER THINNING *Spur-pruning shortens and thins growth until only strong, productive spurs remain and there is space for fruits to grow and receive plenty of ripening sunlight.*

PEAR DWARF PYRAMID

The pear's fruiting habit (it naturally forms spurs on which fruits are borne) makes it ideal for this neat, small form. As with apples, pear dwarf pyramids can be planted quite closely, with only 6ft (2m) needed between trees. When trees are planted closely, good formative training and regular summer pruning is even more essential to prevent this compact

tree form from getting out of hand. Use 'Quince A' rootstock, or 'Quince C' for more vigorous cultivars.

FORMATIVE TRAINING

While the shape is being formed, pruning concentrates on overcoming the upright growth habit to reduce vigor and form an open branch structure around a strong central trunk. Choose or train a young feathered tree (*see Apples, p.107*) with good, wide-angled laterals, and encourage this growth habit by cutting to outward-facing buds on the undersides of the shoots. Establishing

strong lower branches is the first priority; dominant vigorous shoots on the upper part of the stem should be removed. The tapering pyramid shape ensures that all parts of the tree receive sun and air, with no overshadowing.

ESTABLISHED PRUNING

Summer pruning follows the full or modified Lorette system, depending on climate, as for apples (*see p.106*), but usually timed a little earlier. Late winter pruning consists of spur-pruning (*see p.105 and above*) and also of shortening the leading shoot, if necessary.

PEAR DWARF PYRAMID
Close planting helps keep these trees small through root competition. Hedgelike planting is attractive, but pears should not be used as a windbreak, or fruiting will suffer.

PEAR DWARF PYRAMID, YEAR 1, WINTER

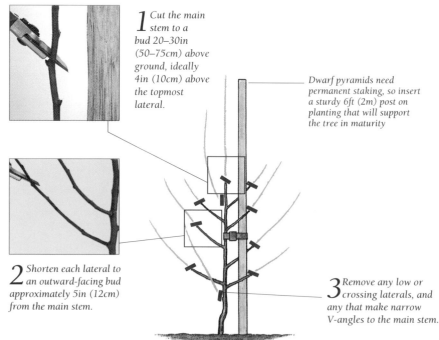

1 Cut the main stem to a bud 20–30in (50–75cm) above ground, ideally 4in (10cm) above the topmost lateral.

Dwarf pyramids need permanent staking, so insert a sturdy 6ft (2m) post on planting that will support the tree in maturity

2 Shorten each lateral to an outward-facing bud approximately 5in (12cm) from the main stem.

3 Remove any low or crossing laterals, and any that make narrow V-angles to the main stem.

YEAR 1, SUMMER

Prune back vigorous upright shoots so that only one bud remains, particularly on the upper part of the tree.

If new leader does not grow straight and vertical, tie it to stake

YEAR 2, WINTER

1 *Shorten the central leader to a bud, to leave about 10in (25cm) of the new growth. Repeat each year until the tree reaches the desired height.*

Bud faces in opposite direction to previous year's cut to help keep trunk straight

2 *Prune new laterals and branch leaders to 6–8in (15–20cm), cutting to a downward- and outward-pointing bud to create an open branch structure.*

3 *Prune sideshoots to two or three buds to begin the formation of fruiting spur systems.*

YEAR 2 AND ON, SUMMER (MODIFIED LORETTE SYSTEM)

1 *Prune new growth on branch leaders back to five or six leaves.*

Leading shoot left unpruned

2 *Prune new shoots arising directly from the trunk or main branches to three leaves beyond the basal cluster.*

Basal cluster of two or three leaves

3 *Prune sideshoots from winter-pruned laterals (spurs) to one leaf beyond the basal cluster.*

Basal third of shoot has ripened

YEAR 3 AND ON, WINTER

1 *To maintain the desired height, shorten leader to one bud of the summer's growth. (This pruning can be delayed until midspring to discourage regrowth.)*

2 *Reduce overgrown spurs and, as trees mature, thin out spur systems where overcrowded.*

OTHER PEAR TREE FORMS

PEAR BUSH

This is the most commonly grown unrestricted pear form. Formative training is as for an apple bush (*see p.108*). Many pear cultivars are more upright in habit than apples and therefore may need more encouragement to form open-centered bushes. Cutting to outward-facing buds, or tying down young shoots into a more horizontal position with twine pegged into the ground (*see also p.99*), will help. It is important to train shoots when young, since pear wood becomes inflexible as it ages. If the chosen cultivar is growing too fast to achieve a compact, bushy shape, prune more lightly or not at all to curb regrowth.

Established bushes will form spurs naturally, but this can be encouraged by spur-pruning. Considerable spur-thinning (*see p.105*) and occasional regulated pruning – removing older sections of branches where young growth exists to develop in its place (*see also p.105*) – will be necessary in winter.

STANDARD

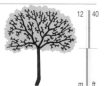

These are trained and pruned as for apple standards (*see p.109*), although established trees will need more spur-thinning. As with apples, these large trees are rarely feasible for a domestic garden, but they may be required as specimen trees or in an older orchard. Only a pear rootstock would provide the necessary vigor; a specialty fruit nursery should be able to offer advice.

CORDON

A pear cordon can easily be sited in a sheltered position and is trained and pruned as for an apple cordon (*see p.112*). Pears are difficult to train as stepovers – low, horizontal cordons – because pear wood lacks the flexibility of apple wood, which can be bent at a 90° angle.

ESPALIER

A pear espalier is trained and pruned as for an apple (*see p.114*), although it may need more spur-thinning in winter. On a sheltered wall, pear espaliers can be extremely productive. For two or three tiers, choose a very dwarfing rootstock; for more, a less dwarfing rootstock.

FAN

Pear fans, trained and pruned as for an apple fan (*see p.116*), are rarely seen but can be very successful and decorative. A moderately dwarfing rootstock is best.

MEDLAR *MESPILUS GERMANICA*

The medlar has fruits of somewhat esoteric interest, since they are only considered edible once they have, to all intents and purposes, rotted. They are then made into preserves. However, like the crab-apple, the medlar makes a handsome ornamental tree, with distinctive flowers and fruits and bright autumn color.

Medlars are hardy in zones 6–9, and are self-fertile, so only one tree is necessary for a crop. The fruits are borne on spurs from older wood, but these form naturally and spur-pruning is unnecessary.

The natural habit of the tree is spreading, even pendulous in some cases, and a short, clear trunk gives the most attractive shape. Training is as for an ornamental branched-head standard (*see p.28*) with a clear trunk of at least 3–4ft (1–1.2m). Once a strong, well-spaced branch framework has been established, however, only minimal pruning is required thereafter, removing a small proportion of older fruited wood in winter if growth is overcrowded. Medlars do not renovate well; hard pruning stimulates a mass of vertical shoots that spoil the tree's appearance.

MEDLAR TREE AND FRUIT
The fruits need to be fully ripened on the tree, then picked and stored, stalk upward, in a cool, dark place until the flesh turns soft and yellowish brown. The correct term for this is "bletted," not rotten, fruit.

QUINCE *CYDONIA OBLONGA* (ZONES 5–9)

The quince, with its downy, intensely aromatic, apple- or pear-shaped fruits, is normally grown as a large bush, but may be trained as a fan or palmette, as for apples (*see p.116*). Cultivars grown for fruit are usually grafted onto either the 'Quince A' or 'C' rootstocks used for pears (*see p.117*). Although the quince is self-fertile, it is claimed, but not proven, that growing two cultivars ensures better fruiting.

Growth habit is untidy, and suckering quite common. Fruits are produced on naturally forming spurs and at the tips of one-year-old shoots. Winter pruning is standard practice for quinces.

QUINCE BUSH

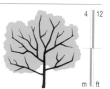

Left to its own devices, a quince will form a multistemmed tree that will gradually become more dense and thicketlike; it will need constant thinning if it is to continue to fruit well. A well-trained bush form with a short, clear trunk and strong, well-placed and well-spaced main branches is a much more easily managed tree, needing only minimal routine attention. Starting with

a young feathered tree, the branch framework is developed along the same lines as for an apple bush (*see below and p.108*). As the tree matures, growth will become untidy and crowded; vigorous shoots can be shortened (*see below*) to prevent congestion building up, or more informal pruning, removing some older wood (*see also p.105*), can be used to relieve congestion and keep the center of the bush open. Never prune too hard in any one year or vigorous regrowth will be stimulated. Congested spur systems should also be thinned, and suckers from the base or on the clear trunk should be removed.

QUINCE BUSH, YEAR 1, WINTER

1 *Making an angled cut just above a healthy bud, prune back the central stem to a bud about 3ft (90cm) from the ground.*

2 *Prune upper laterals by two-thirds of their length, cutting just above an upward-facing bud.*

3 *Remove any laterals arising from the stem less than 2ft (60cm) from the ground.*

YEAR 2, WINTER

Cut to outward-facing buds

1 *Shorten the new leading shoot to about 4ft (1.2m) from the ground, cutting to just above a strong lateral.*

2 *Prune branch leaders and laterals back by one-third of their length.*

3 *Shorten any strong, vertical shoots to a bud that will produce a shoot that grows away from other branches.*

YEAR 3 UNTIL ESTABLISHED, WINTER

The quince's growth habit is erratic; remove any growth that crosses other shoots or develops in unwanted directions.

Fruiting spurs start to form naturally

ESTABLISHED QUINCE BUSH, WINTER

1 *Thin congested spur systems, removing older, less productive sections to make space for younger growth.*

2 *Tip-prune branch leaders to encourage fruiting spurs on young wood.*

3 *Occasionally (not every year) remove an older branch, particularly low down or in the center of the tree, to relieve congestion.*

4 *Occasionally (not every year) spur-prune a proportion of new, upright shoots. cutting back to two or three buds.*

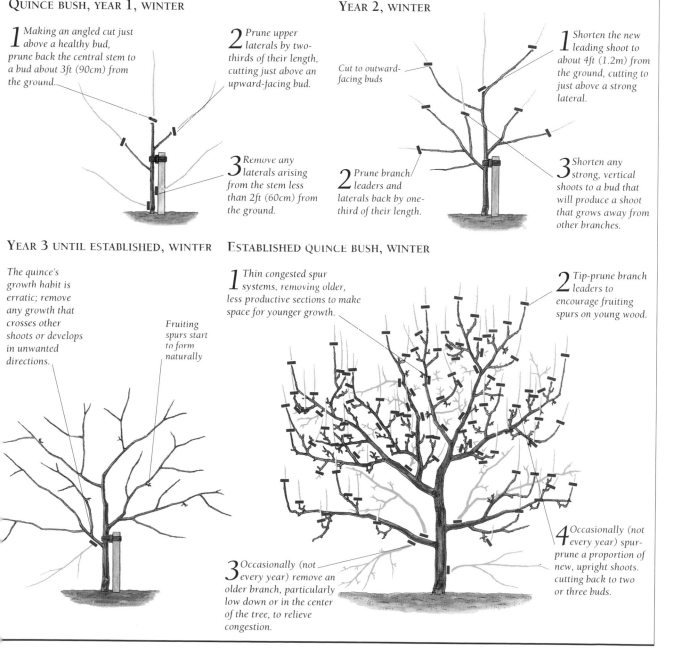

PLUMS *PRUNUS* SPP. (ZONES 5–9)

The superior flavor of fresh-picked plums, the huge variety of fruits, and the decorative qualities of the trees make plums a popular garden choice. For cool climates there are European plums, gages, bullaces, and damsons (*P. domestica* and *P. domestica* subsp. *insititia*), while warmer regions suit the earlier-flowering types – the mirabelle and the Japanese or salicine plum (*P. salicina*, syn. *P. triflora*).

Although plums have complex pollination requirements, they make excellent small trees with less rigid pruning requirements than apples or pears, making the siting and planting of two or even three compatible pollinators easy, even in a small garden.

Plums flower early in the year, and so are vulnerable to late frosts; in some regions the early buds appeal to birds, causing severe damage. A small, easily netted tree in a sunny position is ideal. As with apples, the bush is the most productive and widely grown form, but pyramids are also popular. The spindle bush is a similar compact form that requires less maintenance pruning. Wall-training, for extra shelter and sun, may be advisable in colder areas. Plum trees are unsuited to the pruning required to maintain cordons and espaliers, so the fan form is used.

Fans grown flat against walls or on open posts and wires are easy to net against birds, as are compact tree forms such as pyramids. This is an important factor in areas where birds are a nuisance; the damage they cause to unnetted trees may necessitate removing branches and rebuilding tree frameworks.

The risk of disease may also be a factor in choosing tree forms. Plums are susceptible to serious infections (*see* Plum problems, *facing page*) that gain entry through pruning wounds, especially if made in winter (*see* Time of pruning, *right*). Forms that require only light pruning, such as the bush and spindle bush, therefore run less risk of being affected by disease.

PLUM IN FRUIT
Trees in the plum group, such as this 'Shropshire Damson', fruit all along the length of young shoots, so these are not spur-pruned as they would be on apple and pear trees. On restricted forms, such as the pyramid and fan, some shortening of growth (summer pruning) is necessary to maintain the form and expose the fruits to light.

PLUM ROOTSTOCKS

| 'PIXY' | 'ST. JULIEN A' | 'BROMPTON' | 'MYROBALAN B' |

ROOTSTOCKS AND GRAFTING

All plum trees are grafted, and suckering (*see p.32*) may be a problem. For small gardens, rootstocks such as 'St. Julien A' or the dwarfing 'Pixy' are suitable, particularly for compact trained forms. 'Brompton' and the cherry plum rootstock, 'Myrobalan B', will produce a large tree or extensive fan. On all rootstocks, damson cultivars develop into smaller trees than other plums.

Stake plum trees for the first growing season if the plants are unsteady. It is vital that the stake and ties do not chafe and damage the stem, creating an entry point for disease.

FRUITING HABIT

Plums fruit at the base of one-year-old shoots and along the length of two-year-old and older stems. This young growth is therefore not routinely pruned back as on apples and pears, since the newest, most vigorous stems will bear a good crop. Once a strong framework has been formed, therefore, free-growing trees such as the bush or spindle bush require minimal pruning. More pruning is necessary on trained forms simply to maintain their shape.

Plums can fruit heavily, and thinning (*see p.101*) is often needed. A single fruit requires 3–4in (7–10cm) of branch space, depending on the cultivar, to expand fully.

TIME OF PRUNING

Pruning plums in winter is dangerous because silver-leaf disease and cankers may gain entry through the wounds. Pruning tasks usually performed in winter for other fruits are therefore delayed until early spring or until midsummer in regions where canker is a problem. It is safer to remove diseased and damaged wood as seen. Remove dead wood in late summer or autumn, while the tree is still in leaf and it can easily be identified.

The techniques of nicking and notching used for apples and pears should not be used on any stone fruit because the wounds formed may allow the entry of disease. For most plum tree forms, it is advisable to start not with a whip, but with a feathered young tree trained by a specialty nursery.

Plant plums trees in late winter, before they start into growth. Do not make pruning cuts until the buds break.

PINCHING PLUM SHOOTS
Pruning wounds on plums should be as small as possible, reducing the cut surface area that is exposed to possible infection. Whenever possible, control growth at an early stage by pinch-pruning, using finger and thumb to nip out the soft tips of shoots. If plums are inspected regularly (once every week or two during the growing season), unwanted growth can be pinched out promptly, rather than being allowed to become woody and require cutting with pruners.

PLUM PROBLEMS

No plum is immune to silver-leaf disease, although some cultivars are more resistant than others. Affected growth must be cut back as soon as seen until the cut surface is perfectly clean. Discard prunings and disinfect pruning tools. Like all stone fruits, plums are also susceptible to gummosis; a gumlike substance oozes from the bark, and is often found around the fruit pits. The gum itself is harmless but is a sign of stress caused by disease, damage, or adverse soil conditions.

Gummosis on one branch probably indicates a local infection, and the branch should be removed. Gummosis on the trunk or in the crotch of main branches indicates a more serious problem: seek professional advice to cure it.

Elongated, flattened cankers that exude gum, accompanied by distorted growth, indicate the presence of bacterial canker. To treat plum trees affected by this condition, cut back to healthy wood, discard prunings, and disinfect tools.

Silvered foliage of plum affected by silver-leaf disease

PLUM BUSH

Starting with a well-feathered whip, the aim is to produce a well-spaced, open-centered crown with three or four main branches on a clear trunk of at least 2½ft (75cm). Once established, no routine pruning regime in either spring or summer is required. Instead, in early summer, remove twiggy, damaged, unproductive, crossing, or crowded growth, cutting back to a replacement shoot or to the point of origin. With naturally spreading cultivars (such as 'Victoria'), such cuts should be made to upward-growing shoots; horizontal branches will start to droop and may break under the weight of fruit.

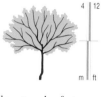

PLUM BUSH, YEAR 1, EARLY SPRING

Angled cuts

1 *Shorten three or four well-spaced laterals by two-thirds, to an outward-facing or, on more horizontal shoots, upward-facing bud.*

3 *Shorten low or narrow-angled laterals to two buds. Pinch back any subsequent growth to two leaves throughout the season.*

Check ties regularly to avoid damage through chafing

2 *Cut the leader back to the highest of the selected laterals, ideally about 3ft (90cm) from the ground.*

YEAR 2, EARLY SPRING

1 *On each lateral, shorten two or three strong sub-laterals by half to a bud pointing in a direction that will produce an open-centered crown.*

2 *Remove completely any weak, badly placed or narrow-angled shoots.*

Well-placed shorter growth can be left unpruned

3 *Remove completely low laterals that were pruned, then pinched back in the previous year.*

If further shoots emerge on trunk, rub them off

2ft (60cm) stake does not chafe lowest branches

YEAR 3, SPRING TO EARLY SUMMER

1 *Prune horizontally growing or weak branch leaders by a quarter in early spring, cutting to a bud facing in the direction where new growth will fill in gaps in the branch framework.*

2 *Remove badly placed, overly vigorous new shoots that develop.*

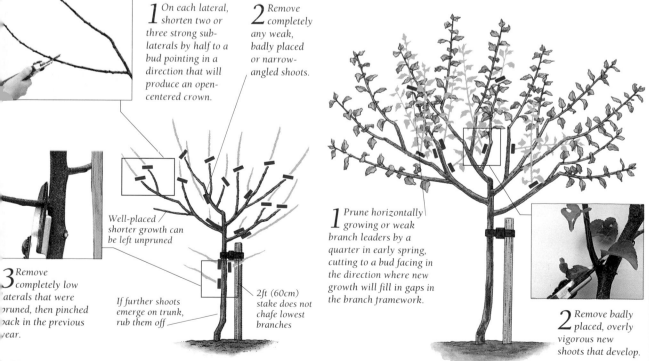

PLUM PYRAMID

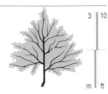

The plum pyramid is ideal for a small garden, especially if the dwarfing 'Pixy' (6ft/2m) rootstock is used. Although it needs regular pruning to keep the compact form, a tree that is well trained from the start is easy to maintain. This form, in which numerous branches radiate from a central stem, suits all types of plums, although those of very upright habit are more difficult to control, because the lower branches must remain dominant and not be shaded by growth above. If you are planting several trees, space those on 'Pixy' 8–10ft (2.4–3m) apart (these trees must be staked permanently) and on 'St. Julien A', 10 12ft (3–1m) apart.

STARTING WITH A WHIP

Whips should be cut to a strong bud 5ft (1.5m) from the ground. Let the top bud grow to extend the central leader, but rub out the two or three immediately below, since they will develop at a narrow angle and tend to be too vigorous, competing with the leader. At the end of the first year the tree should have a good complement of laterals and be equivalent to a feathered whip: formative training can then begin.

FORMATIVE TRAINING

Although it is possible to start training a pyramid from a whip, it is easier to begin with a feathered tree, since all but its lowest laterals can immediately be used in the first stage of branch formation. Trees will also fruit sooner. Because so many laterals are retained, there is no need, as on a bush, to shorten and then remove unwanted growth, in order to retain foliage to assist stem thickening.

The aim, when developing the branch framework, is to create a "Christmas tree" shape, so cut to buds whose direction of growth will achieve this structure and outline. While the tree is being formed, encourage branching by

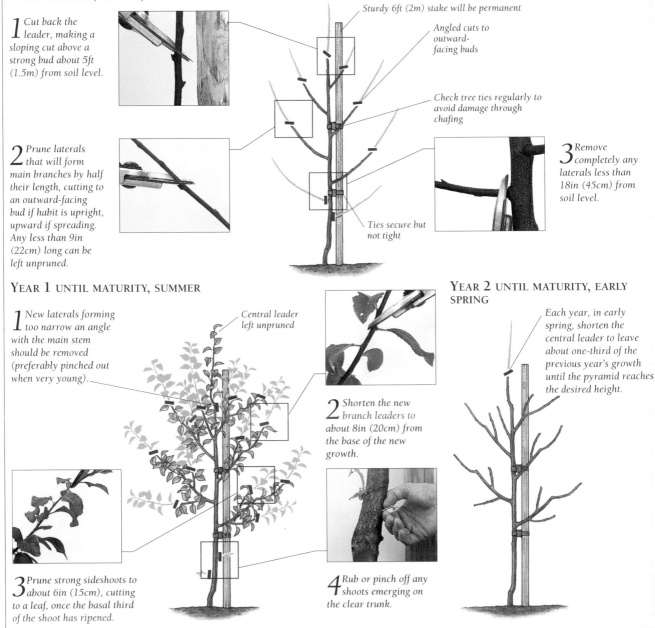

PLUM PYRAMID, YEAR 1, EARLY SPRING

1 Cut back the leader, making a sloping cut above a strong bud about 5ft (1.5m) from soil level.

2 Prune laterals that will form main branches by half their length, cutting to an outward-facing bud if habit is upright, upward if spreading. Any less than 9in (22cm) long can be left unpruned.

Sturdy 6ft (2m) stake will be permanent

Angled cuts to outward-facing buds

Check tree ties regularly to avoid damage through chafing

Ties secure but not tight

3 Remove completely any laterals less than 18in (45cm) from soil level.

YEAR 1 UNTIL MATURITY, SUMMER

1 New laterals forming too narrow an angle with the main stem should be removed (preferably pinched out when very young).

Central leader left unpruned

2 Shorten the new branch leaders to about 8in (20cm) from the base of the new growth.

3 Prune strong sideshoots to about 6in (15cm), cutting to a leaf, once the basal third of the shoot has ripened.

4 Rub or pinch off any shoots emerging on the clear trunk.

YEAR 2 UNTIL MATURITY, EARLY SPRING

Each year, in early spring, shorten the central leader to leave about one-third of the previous year's growth until the pyramid reaches the desired height.

shortening the central leader each spring until the desired height is reached. Meanwhile, summer pruning of all sideshoots, once the bases of the shoots have become woody, produces a compact shape and promotes fruitfulness.

ESTABLISHED PRUNING

Once the tree reaches the desired height, delay the annual pruning of the leader until late spring to discourage regrowth, shortening it to 1in (2.5cm) of the previous season's growth. Summer pruning must be carried out annually or the pyramid form will be lost. It is particularly important to strictly control growth on the upper part of the tree, or it will shade fruit on the lower branches. Very vigorous upright shoots on the upper branches are best removed completely. The annual shortening of growth will inevitably lead to overcrowding in the center of the tree: thin out less productive wood to ease congestion.

Fruit thinning (see p.101) may be necessary, but even so, pyramids can bear heavy crops for their size. If the weight of fruit is dragging a branch downward, prop it with a cleft stick, or use maypoling (see p.99) to give the branch support. Shorten this branch to an upward-facing shoot after fruiting.

ESTABLISHED PLUM PYRAMID, SUMMER

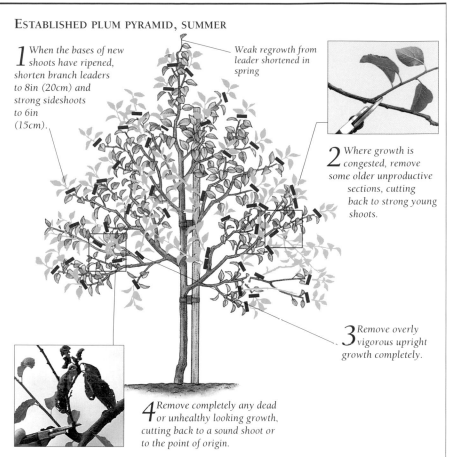

1 When the bases of new shoots have ripened, shorten branch leaders to 8in (20cm) and strong sideshoots to 6in (15cm).

Weak regrowth from leader shortened in spring

2 Where growth is congested, remove some older unproductive sections, cutting back to strong young shoots.

3 Remove overly vigorous upright growth completely.

4 Remove completely any dead or unhealthy looking growth, cutting back to a sound shoot or to the point of origin.

PLUM SPINDLE BUSH

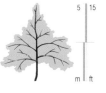

Spindle bushes, particularly of plums, are more often seen in commercial orchards than in gardens. However, once correctly trained, the basic spindle shape – a broad-bottomed cone, with three or four permanent low branches and a central stem, along all of which short, fruiting branches are renewed from time to time – is easy to maintain. This form therefore combines the compact form of a pyramid (although spindles need a little more space than pyramids) with the less formal pruning requirements of a bush.

FORMATIVE TRAINING

Start with a young feathered tree (preferably on 'St. Julien A' rootstock) that has three or four well-spaced laterals making wide angles to the main stem, between about 2ft (60cm) and 3ft (90cm) from soil level. Neither these nor the central leader are cut back when pruning in the first spring after planting. Instead, remove any laterals below 2ft (60cm), any that make narrow angles to the main stem, and any upper shoots

that are more vigorous than the selected shoots or that threaten to crowd them.

Formative training then continues as for an apple spindle bush (see p.110). Pruning and tying down branches to form the spindle shape largely takes place in summer, which is a safe time to prune plums. However, whereas for apples the leading shoot is cut back in winter, delay pruning a plum's leader until spring to minimize the risk of insects or diseases entering the wound.

ESTABLISHED PRUNING

Prune when established and tie down branches as for an apple spindle bush (see p.110), but for a plum all cuts should be made only in early summer. Growth on a plum will be more vigorous: as the trees become more mature, the removal of quite substantial sections of growth will become essential, particularly on the upper part of the central trunk. If the branches that are trained to grow out horizontally extend too far they may snap under the weight of fruit. It is safer to shorten them to a sound but less vigorous replacement shoot. Maypoling – supporting branches with ties of twine or strips of netting nailed to the top of the stake (see also p.99) – to take the weight of the crop is an alternative.

STANDARDS AND HALF-STANDARDS

A full standard plum tree is not recommended for a domestic garden since the height makes maintenance very difficult. A half-standard is preferable if a tree form is desired. Both will require an area 20ft (6m) in diameter. To provide the necessary vigor to produce a taller tree, use 'Brompton' or 'Myrobalan B' rootstock; on very rich soil, 'St. Julien A' is possible for a half-standard.

The trunk is cleared of branches as for an ornamental tree (see p.28), but formative pruning must not take place until buds break. Once the trunk is cleared to the desired height (about 4ft/1.2m for a half-standard, 6ft/2m for a standard), the crown of branches is developed as for a plum bush (see p.123), except that in the first spring, the laterals selected to become framework branches should be shortened by one-third, not half. Subsequently maintenance is as for a plum bush.

PLUM FAN

2.5 | 8

m | ft

Fan-training on a sunny wall is an ideal method, in cool climates, for growing fine dessert plums and gages. They will be less susceptible to spring frost damage, and the ripening fruits are protected from poor weather conditions. Equip walls with horizontal wires about 12in (30cm) apart, threaded through vine eyes (see p.246). Trees on 'St. Julien A' rootstocks will need an area 12ft (3.6m) wide by 8ft (2.5m) in height, those on 'Pixy' about 2ft (60cm) less each way. In warm areas fans can also be trained on open post-and-wire fences. Remember that suitable pollinating cultivars should be planted nearby. Even self-fertile cultivars fruit better with cross-pollination.

FORMATIVE TRAINING

Plant a young feathered tree with two strong, low laterals, preferably of equal vigor, growing in a horizontal plane. Tie the laterals onto angled bamboo stakes secured to the horizontal wires at 40–45°. The angle of either stake can be adjusted if one lateral is more vigorous than the other (see Correcting uneven development, p.98). These two initial "arms" are cut back to stimulate the growth of sublaterals, and from these shoots a selection can be made to form the "ribs" of the fan. All unwanted shoots are pruned out or, preferably, pinched back when young to one or two leaves; these help to feed the tree and are possible reserve sources for new shoots should the chosen shoots be damaged.

When selecting the ribs, aim for even development on each side. Choose a shoot to continue extending each arm, at least two on the upper side of each arm, and at least one from below. These lower ribs are crucial: without them, you will not achieve full coverage of the fan's base, since natural growth is always vertical. To encourage branching and thus establish the framework quickly, shorten the ribs in the early spring of the second and third years (see also Peach fan, p.134) to leave 24–30in (60–75cm) of the previous year's growth.

ESTABLISHED PRUNING

Once the fan's framework is filled out, the emphasis of pruning changes, from stimulating growth to controlling it and avoiding overcrowding. Initially this is done by pinching very young shoots out with thumb and forefinger. First, pinch those growing directly out and away from, or toward, the wall. Others should be thinned in spring to about 4in (10cm) apart. Later in the season they are shortened (see facing page), and again once the fruits have been picked.

On older trees, areas of the fan will become crowded and can be thinned in spring or early summer. Spread this work over the years to keep cuts to a minimum in any one season. As the tree achieves full fruiting potential, fruit thinning (see p.101) will be necessary.

TRAINING FROM A WHIP

If the young tree has only weak or badly placed laterals, cut back to a bud about 18in (45cm) from ground level to stimulate vigorous laterals. When a suitable pair is 18in (45cm) long, proceed as shown right.

PLUM FAN, YEAR 1, EARLY SPRING

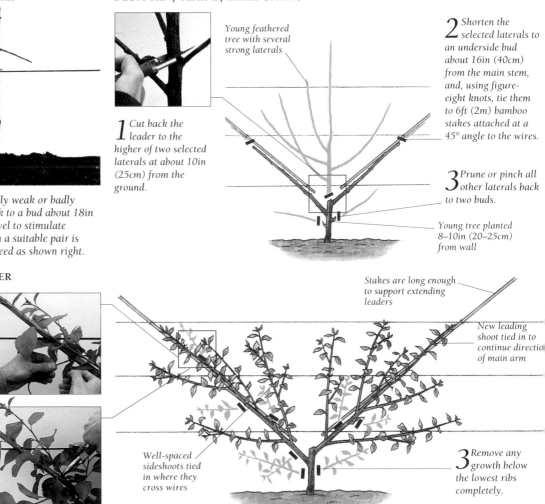

Young feathered tree with several strong laterals

1 *Cut back the leader to the higher of two selected laterals at about 10in (25cm) from the ground.*

2 *Shorten the selected laterals to an underside bud about 16in (40cm) from the main stem, and, using figure-eight knots, tie them to 6ft (2m) bamboo stakes attached at a 45° angle to the wires.*

3 *Prune or pinch all other laterals back to two buds.*

Young tree planted 8–10in (20–25cm) from wall

YEAR 1, MIDSUMMER

1 *Tie in selected ribs, and, where necessary, fan out and tie in well-spaced, well-placed sideshoots.*

2 *Cut or pinch back surplus sideshoots to one leaf.*

Stakes are long enough to support extending leaders

New leading shoot tied in to continue direction of main arm

Well-spaced sideshoots tied in where they cross wires

3 *Remove any growth below the lowest ribs completely.*

ESTABLISHED PLUM FAN, SUMMER

1 Tie in laterals, using soft twine tied in figure eights, to fill gaps in the framework.

2 When they have 9–12 leaves, cut or pinch back to five or six leaves laterals not required to fill in the framework, later pinching out any regrowth.

3 Cut out any worn-out wood and any badly placed, unhealthy, or excessively vigorous and upright new shoots.

PRUNING AFTER FRUITING

In early autumn, after harvesting, prune back to three leaves all the shoots that were shortened to five or six leaves earlier in the summer.

ESTABLISHED PLUM FAN, SPRING

Thin new growth by pinching out shoots until the remainder are 4in (10cm) apart (see also Peach fan, p.131).

New shoots in narrow branch forks are particularly likely to cause congestion.

LATE SPRING TO SUMMER

As the new growth develops, remove badly placed young shoots growing out from the horizontal plane or inward toward the wall. Shorten to a bud or shoot any that grow across other stems, or any branch leaders that exceed the allotted space.

Sweet and Duke Cherries *Prunus avium* hybrids (zones 4–8)

Sweet cherries are hardy in the above zones, but in colder areas crops will not ripen fully unless trees are trained against a sunny wall. In warmer regions they make excellent bushes, formed and pruned as for a plum bush (*see p.123*). Most cherries need another compatible cultivar nearby to ensure pollination.

Duke cherries, probably hybrids between the sweet and sour cherry (*see facing page*), have the growth and fruiting habit of a sweet cherry and are trained and pruned in the same way.

Grafting and Rootstocks

Although dwarfing rootstocks – 'Inmil' and 'Canil' – are still under trial, the rootstock 'Colt', while not dwarfing, has made it possible to grow sweet cherries in domestic gardens. Even so, a bush

Cherry Rootstocks

'Colt'   'Malling F12/1'

Sweet Cherry Fan, Early Summer

1 Tie in new shoots where they can fill spaces in the framework. Tying string vertically between wires provides more attachment points.

will be too big to net easily against birds, and a fan will need a wall or fence 8ft (2.5m) in height by 15ft (5m) wide. Larger old trees and fans are probably growing on 'Malling F12/1', a vigorous, now largely superseded, stock.

Growth and Fruiting Habit

Like plums, cherries fruit at the base of the previous season's shoots and on older wood. Fruit thinning is never needed. Cherry branches are sturdy and are rarely weighed down by fruit; bushes do not, therefore, tend to splay out as they age – so it is important when pruning to maintain an open center. The heavier branches are also liable to break if they make narrow V-angles (*see p.12*) with the main stem or branch. Remove any shoots with narrow forks.

Time of Pruning

As with other stone fruits, winter-pruned cherries are susceptible to silver-leaf disease (*see* Plums, *p.122*): pruning must be delayed until bud-burst in spring when training a young tree (plant in autumn to midwinter), and summer for established trees. Remove dead, diseased, or damaged growth as soon as seen.

Sweet Cherry Fan

A fan on a sunny wall gives excellent results in cool climates and is also easy to net against birds. Formative pruning is carried out at bud-burst in spring, and the form is maintained by summer pruning in two stages: once in late spring to early summer, and again after fruiting. The framework is built up as for a plum fan (*see p.126*), on a support system of wires and stakes. It may be possible to select not just two but four laterals on a feathered whip, and develop the framework more quickly.

Once the framework is established (*see below*), pruning is also as for plums: shorten growth to stimulate fruiting and keep the fan flat against the wall, and thin crowded growth, occasionally removing old growth in favor of young shoots. Where the fan exceeds its allotted space, cut leaders back to sideshoots.

Leave branch leaders unpruned until allotted space is filled

2 Once they have 8–12 leaves, pinch or cut back to six or seven leaves all other new shoots, pinching any subsequent growth on them to one leaf. After fruiting, shorten these shoots again, to three leaves (see also Plum fan, p.126).

SOUR CHERRIES *PRUNUS CERASUS* HYBRIDS (ZONES 4–8)

The pruning requirements of the sour cherry differ from those of the sweet cherry and are more demanding and complicated than for sweet cherries. However, sour cherries are much easier to grow in colder climates and in small gardens. The trees are less vigorous and mostly self-fertile; even if the fruits do not ripen to finest quality in a poor summer, they are always excellent for cooking and preserving. In cooler zones, a good crop can be obtained from a bush (*see below*) in a sunny position, or from a fan (*see p.130*) trained on a wall – not necessarily one receiving full sun. 'Morello' is the most popular and widely available cultivar; there are inferior variants of this cultivar, so buy from a reliable specialty fruit nursery.

ROOTSTOCKS AND GRAFTING

There are no dwarfing rootstocks, so sour cherries are not suitable for tiny gardens. The rootstock normally used is the semivigorous 'Colt', also used for sweet cherries. While it produces a manageable bush tree, about 10–12ft (3–4m) tall and a fan that is 7ft (2.2m) high and 12ft (4m) wide, it is too vigorous for the smaller trained forms used for plums. Sour cherry pyramids are occasionally seen, but they are mostly grown experimentally and need an impractical amount of maintenance.

GROWTH AND FRUITING HABIT

Unlike most fruits, the sour cherry fruits almost exclusively on shoots that were produced the previous year. The aim of annual pruning, therefore, is to cut out some of the wood that has fruited each year to provide more space for existing young growth and further stimulate the production of new shoots.

Sour cherries can fruit in their third or fourth year, so keep this in mind when training young trees. Always cut to a pointed growth bud, rather than to a fat flower bud, to obtain a shoot growing from the intended point and in the planned direction. If there is no suitably placed single growth bud, a triple bud (a growth bud flanked by two flower buds) will do (*see also* Peaches, *p.132*). Rub the flower buds away to direct all available energy into the new shoot.

TIME OF PRUNING

As with other stone fruits, winter-pruned cherries are susceptible to silver-leaf disease (*see* Plums, *p.122*), so pruning must be delayed until bud-burst in

HARVESTING CHERRIES

Use scissors to snip off the fruit rather than picking by hand. The stalks are tough, and pulling them from the stem late in the season can leave small tears in the bark that will be open to infection in autumn.

spring when training a young tree, and spring and/or summer (*see below*) for established trees. Cut out diseased or damaged growth as soon as seen. In colder areas, sour cherries may not be ready to harvest (*see above*) until very late summer.

SOUR CHERRY BUSH

The aim is to create a well-structured, compact yet open crown on a short trunk. Cherries are spreading trees, and this needs to be kept in mind when pruning. Allow for a crown 12–15ft (4–5m) in width.

FORMATIVE TRAINING

As for a plum bush (*see p.123*), pruning in spring. Take care to cut to growth or triple buds, not to flower buds (*see* Growth and fruiting habit, *above*).

ESTABLISHED PRUNING

Prune partly in spring, as buds burst, and again after fruiting. On older trees, cut back one or two branches or sections of branches each year to encourage new growth, otherwise fruiting will gradually become limited to the periphery of the tree. This pruning is best done in spring, when growth buds can often be seen low down on shoots and branches. It can, however, be delayed until after fruiting (*see right*), when up to a quarter of the fruited shoots are also cut back to a new shoot. Leave those that have made plenty of fresh growth beyond the fruited portion, unless it spoils the shape of the tree: this growth will fruit well next year.

NEWLY ESTABLISHED SOUR CHERRY BUSH, PRUNING AFTER FRUITING

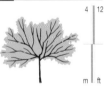

1 Cut back one in four fruited shoots to a replacement shoot near their base.

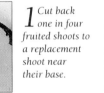

2 Shorten to a side-shoot or leaf any overly vigorous upright growth that will crowd the center or put load-bearing stress on a branch as it matures.

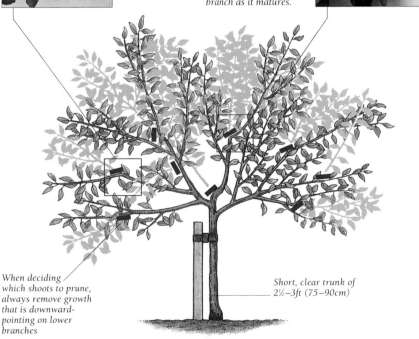

When deciding which shoots to prune, always remove growth that is downward-pointing on lower branches

Short, clear trunk of 2½–3ft (75–90cm)

SOUR CHERRY FAN

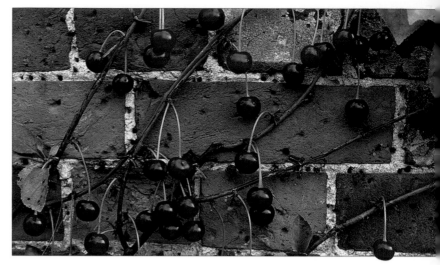

A sour cherry fan, like a peach fan, is one of the more demanding fruit tree forms to develop and maintain successfully. It can be grown either on walls and fences equipped with horizontal wires, or on an open system of posts and wires. Because many of a fan's shoots need to be tied in at an angle, space wires closely (6in/15cm apart) or tie lengths of string vertically between wires to provide plenty of attachment points. Sunny sites are preferable but not essential, provided the site is airy, although a sunless site can increase the risk of disease in very wet years. Covering the fan with netting or muslin from late winter to bud-burst will protect buds from birds, and also to some degree against frost damage.

FORMATIVE TRAINING
Pruning and training to build up the framework of the fan is as for a peach fan (*see p.134*).

SOUR CHERRY FAN
A tree trained on a sunny wall can produce fruits ripe enough to be eaten raw, but even after a poor summer, in a less favored site, the fruits will be excellent for cooking and preserving.

ESTABLISHED PRUNING
Pruning when established is also as for a peach fan, since both fruits crop on one-year-old shoots. The aim is to control growth to maintain the form, while maximizing crops in both current and future seasons. The fan is pruned in late spring or early summer (*see below*) to favor, as far as possible, one-year-old shoots on which fruits are developing. After harvesting, the fruited wood is removed (*see facing page*) to allow the following year's fruiting shoots to develop. On older fans, less productive, older parts of branches can be cut out in summer and new growth tied in to fill gaps.

ESTABLISHED SOUR CHERRY FAN, EARLY SUMMER

1 *Remove shoots growing into the wall or across other shoots.*

2 *Where necessary, thin the remaining new shoots until they are 4in (10cm) apart. On each shoot where fruits are forming, retain one sideshoot below the lowest fruits, and one farther up. These will replace the fruited shoots when they are cut away.*

ESTABLISHED SOUR CHERRY FAN, PRUNING AFTER FRUITING

1 *Cut back each fruited shoot, either to the lower replacement shoot or, if there is room to tie in both, to the upper "reserve" shoot.*

2 *Tie in the replacement shoots to fill in the fan framework, spacing them evenly. These shoots should fruit next year.*

3 *Cut out any shoots growing toward the wall or fence, or across other shoots, which have grown since the spring.*

PERSIMMON *DIOSPYROS KAKI* (ZONES 6–9)

The Japanese or Oriental persimmon is the *Diospyros* species most widely grown for its fruit. To bear crops, it requires not only cool winter weather to meet the "chilling requirement" but also, for edible fruits, a long, hot summer; persimmons fruit on the current season's shoots, so these must grow before the fruits can form. Cultivars are usually grafted; suckering from the rootstock can be a problem. Most cultivars bear only female flowers. Without a pollinator, fruits may be small and seedless.

TRAINING AND PRUNING

Fruiting persimmons can be trained as for ornamental species (*see Diospyros, Dictionary of Ornamental Trees, p.62*), reaching 40ft (12m) in height with a rounded canopy composed of upright branches. However, persimmons grown primarily for crops are usually trained as smaller, multistemmed trees on a short, clear trunk of about 2ft (60cm), as for an ornamental tree (*see Acer davidii, p.52*). Let dwarf cultivars develop naturally, but remove, in the early years, any badly placed shoots or those making narrow angles with the trunk. Good formative training is crucial for all persimmons;

the branches tend to be brittle and may break under a heavy fruit load. Branches with wide crotch angles are essential; select only the strongest laterals making the widest angles with the main stem to form main branches. Remove all weak branches.

Because selection of shoots must be so rigorous, it can take five years to build up the framework of the tree. Routine pruning is not normally necessary (nor does the tree tolerate heavy pruning

well). Trees often produce an abundance of twiggy growth; if the center of the tree becomes crowded, lightly thin in winter to promote air circulation and to let more sunlight reach the fruits.

In cool climates, remove any winter-damaged growth in summer. In warm areas, fruit thinning is normally recommended to ensure a good quality crop. Thinning in the "on" year may solve any problems with biennial bearing (*see p.101*).

PERSIMMON

The persimmon makes a small tree in cooler regions, with an attractive habit and dark, shiny leaves that color well in autumn. Although it cannot be wall trained formally, this persimmon has been planted close to a wall for shelter, giving the fruits a better chance of ripening.

PEACHES AND NECTARINES *PRUNUS PERSICA* (ZONES 5–10)

Peaches and nectarines are downy and smooth-skinned forms of the same fruit, the latter preferring slightly warmer conditions. Sunny, reasonably dry summers are essential to produce good crops; in cooler climates peaches may be grown under cover. Nearly all cultivars are self-fertile. In areas with wet or uncertain weather, pollination may be erratic or poor; this can be improved by hand-pollination. Select cultivars that are well adapted to local conditions.

PEACHES IN COOL CLIMATES
Peaches flower in very early spring and should be protected from frost. A south-facing wall is an ideal site. Correct pruning is a vital factor in successful pollination. If growth is congested, the flowers are inaccessible to the few pollinating insects abroad at this time of year. In cool, wet climates, peaches are also vulnerable to peach leaf curl, a serious fungal disease prevalent in damp conditions. Control is by spraying, but if infection occurs, pick off and discard the affected leaves (new ones will grow). Repeatedly infected growth will become unproductive and may have to be removed.

GRAFTING AND ROOTSTOCKS
Grafting is widely used to obtain desired cultivars, to determine tree size, and to give resistance (as with the Australian 'Nemaguard') to disease. Grafted trees will fruit two or three years after planting. Plum rootstocks are widely used and, to

TRIPLE BUD

Some fruits, including peaches, often produce a growth bud that is flanked by two flower buds. The growth bud may not necessarily produce a shoot unless stimulated by pruning.

PEACH ROOTSTOCKS

'ST. JULIEN A'   'BROMPTON'

a lesser extent, peach seedlings. Double-working (*see p.95*) on the dwarfing 'Pixy' rootstock may prove successful in some areas. Also, there are several genetically dwarf cultivars, which fruit well in a warm, sunny site.

Peaches and nectarines can produce worthwhile seedling trees, though fruits will differ in quality from the parent. These trees usually grow vigorously and take five to eight years to fruit.

FRUITING HABIT
Like sour cherries, peaches and nectarines fruit on shoots that grew the previous year. The aim of pruning,

therefore, is to remove fruited growth and encourage new shoots. When pruning to induce a new shoot, take care to cut to a pointed growth bud, not to a plump flower bud. If necessary, cut to a triple bud (*see above*) and remove the two flower buds on either side of the growth bud. Unless many flowers have been damaged in bad weather, peaches and nectarines will almost always require some degree of fruit thinning (*see below*).

TIME OF PRUNING
Like plums, peaches and nectarines are vulnerable to diseases such as silver-leaf disease (*see p.122*) and canker. It is important, therefore, to usually prune in late winter or early spring. The aim of spring pruning is to make sure there is a constant supply of well-placed young shoots each year. Carry out formative pruning in early spring, as buds burst. Established bushes and fans can be pruned as shown in the summer.

DWARF PEACH
Dwarf peach cultivars such as 'Garden Lady' naturally make very small trees without grafting. Although the fruits resemble those of larger cultivars, the stems and foliage have a curious, congested growth habit that some find unattractive. Fruit thinning is particularly necessary on dwarf trees.

FRUIT THINNING, PEACHES AND NECTARINES

1 Where fruit set is heavy, thin first in midspring to leave one or two fruits per cluster.

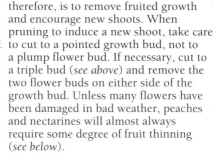

2 If necessary, thin again when fruits are about the size of walnuts to leave fruits about 6–9in (15–22cm) apart (the closer distance for nectarines and for peaches in warmer areas).

PEACH BUSH

Plant a feathered whip in autumn or winter, but delay making any pruning cuts until early spring. Allow 12ft (4m) for the tree's spread. Seedling peaches may be allowed to develop naturally into an informal bush, but it is easier to control size and achieve a well-trained tree using a grafted cultivar.

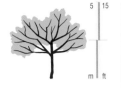

FORMATIVE TRAINING

With a grafted cultivar, a bush is formed in much the same way as a plum bush (*see p.123*), aiming for a crown with 8–10 main branches on a short, clear trunk. If using a seedling, pruning should be minimal, removing only dead, diseased, and damaged wood until fruiting begins, and then should be as for an established bush (*see below*).

ESTABLISHED PRUNING

Once the bush is established, prune annually in early spring. The aims are first to maintain a healthy, strong, open-centered bush, then to maximize fruiting potential by removing older wood in favor of new growth. Keep the crown as open as possible while retaining some new growth in the center of the bush, so that branches bent down by crop weight can be shortened to an upward-pointing replacement shoot.

YEAR 2, EARLY SPRING

1 On each main branch, select two or three strong, well-placed shoots and prune them to half their length. Cut just above outward-facing buds.

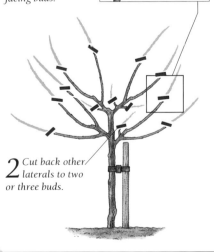

2 Cut back other laterals to two or three buds.

PEACH BUSH, YEAR 1, EARLY SPRING

1 Select three or four laterals to form the main branches, and prune back the leader to just above the topmost one.

2 Prune the selected laterals by about two-thirds of their length, cutting to an outward-facing bud.

3 Prune any laterals below those chosen back to the main stem.

Clear trunk of 2½–3ft (75–90cm)

PEACH BUSH, YEAR 1, SUMMER

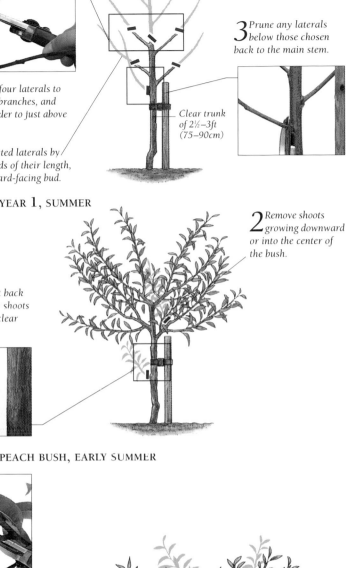

2 Remove shoots growing downward or into the center of the bush.

1 Pinch off or cut back to the stem any shoots growing from the clear trunk.

ESTABLISHED PEACH BUSH, EARLY SUMMER

1 Cut back one in four of the shoots that fruited last year to a replacement shoot, ideally upward- and outward-facing. Remove first those that have been bent down by fruiting.

2 With fruits now developing, older, unproductive wood can be identified. Remove it, together with any crowded or crossing growth.

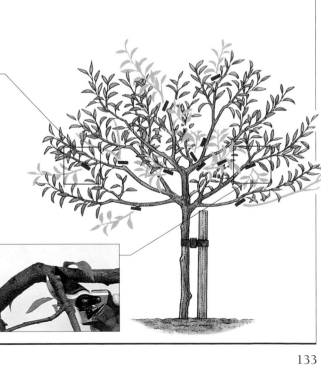

PEACH FAN

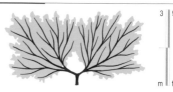

A correctly trained peach fan has two short main arms, one on each side, from which ribs radiate outward and upward. To support it, equip the wall with the same arrangement of horizontal wires used for a plum fan (see p.126). In colder areas, a sunny outdoor wall is essential to produce regular, ripe crops. In greenhouses, support wires need to be held at least 9in (22cm) away from the glass to allow air to circulate and prevent sun scorch. Start with a young feathered tree of a grafted cultivar, planted in autumn or winter about 6–9in (15–22cm) from the wall. The wall needs to be at least 6ft (2m) tall, and 12–15ft (4–5m) wide for a peach on 'St. Julien A'; 15–20ft (5–6m) on 'Brompton'.

FORMATIVE TRAINING

The fan's main branch structure is formed just as for a plum (see p.126). Use bamboo stakes tied between the wires to "splint" young shoots securely at the desired angle. The angle can be adjusted temporarily if shoots are growing with unequal vigor (see Correcting uneven development, p.98). When branches are mature, remove the stakes and tie in directly to the wires. As the framework of the fan fills out, tie lengths of tarred string or garden twine between wires to provide plenty of tying-in points for young shoots. Always keep the fan well tied-in to prevent growth from shading the fruits. Pinch out surplus new shoots where the wires are well covered to stimulate growth where there are gaps to be filled.

ESTABLISHED PRUNING

Once the fan framework has been established, the growth of new shoots not required to fill in gaps in the framework needs to be controlled to avoid overcrowding. Starting in spring, the shoots should be systematically thinned when they are no more than a cluster of leaves.

First, remove shoots growing toward the fence and any that seem excessively vigorous. Then, on each fruiting shoot (now in flower), select one strong sideshoot at the base, which will take the place of the fruited wood when it is cut back, and another shoot farther up as insurance if the lower one fails. These shoots are retained (though later tip-pruned), while all other sideshoots are pinched back to one leaf.

As the new shoots grow, shorten any that overlap fruiting wood and cannot be tied in where they will be out of the way. After the tree has cropped, each fruited shoot is cut back to its replacement, unless it is needed to fill a gap. In this case, tie it in to become part of the permanent framework. Older wood does tend to become bare, so if a branch in the framework produces few new shoots, it can be cut out, providing there are some strong, young fruited shoots to tie in to take its place.

PEACH FAN, YEAR 1, EARLY SPRING

1 Select two laterals to form the main arms: one on either side, about 10–12in (25–30cm) from the ground. Cut out the leader just above the higher one.

2 Shorten each arm to about 15in (38cm), cutting to just above a strong, upward-facing bud.

3 Tie each arm to a bamboo stake attached at an angle of about 40° to the horizontal wires.

4 Cut back to one bud other laterals below the two main arms. (The remaining buds can provide reserve shoots should a main arm be lost.)

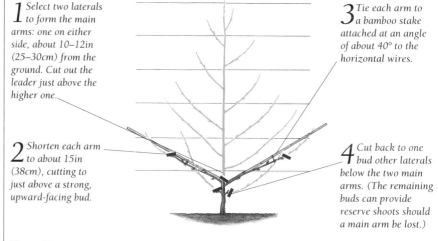

YEAR 1, SUMMER, AND YEAR 2, SPRING

On each side, select "ribs": tie in the new branch leader in the same direction as the original arm and, ideally, two well-spaced shoots on the upper side of the arm and one below. Pinch or cut back all other shoots to one leaf. The following early spring, prune the ribs by a quarter of last year's growth to encourage further branching. Cut to a bud facing in the direction where there is space to be filled.

YEAR 2, EARLY SUMMER

1 Tie in well-placed sideshoots as they develop, adding stakes where necessary, to build up an evenly spaced framework.

2 Cut out completely any badly placed or inward- or outward-growing shoots.

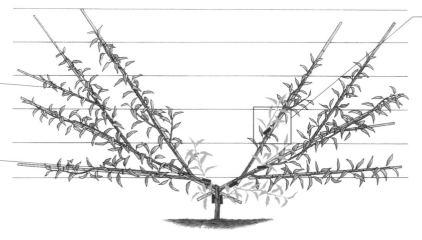

3 Now that the main arms are safely established, prune any previously shortened laterals below the main arms back to the stem.

YEAR 3, EARLY SPRING

Cut back each rib's leading shoot by a quarter of last year's growth to stimulate further growth and extend the branch framework.

YEAR 3, SPRING

Thin young sideshoots to 4–6in (10–15cm) apart by pinching out unwanted shoots, removing first those growing toward the wall or across another shoot.

YEAR 3, EARLY SUMMER

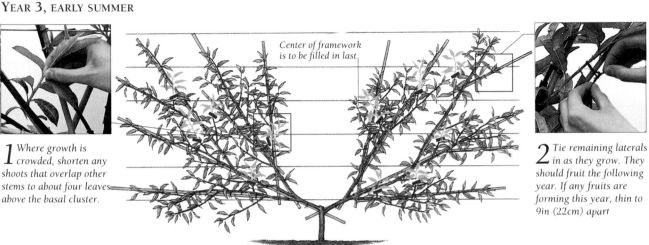

Center of framework is to be filled in last

1 Where growth is crowded, shorten any shoots that overlap other stems to about four leaves above the basal cluster.

2 Tie remaining laterals in as they grow. They should fruit the following year. If any fruits are forming this year, thin to 9in (22cm) apart

ESTABLISHED PEACH FAN, SPRING

1 Remove completely shoots growing toward the wall, and those that will otherwise grow to cross other shoots.

2 Leaving a shoot below the lowest flower and another in reserve farther up, pinch to one leaf all other sideshoots on flowering shoots.

3 Thin all other shoots to 4–6in (10–15cm) by pinching surplus shoots out completely.

ESTABLISHED FAN, SUMMER UNTIL AFTER FRUITING

When the replacement and reserve shoots on each fruiting stem are 18in (45cm) long, pinch out their tips, and pinch any sideshoots that form to one leaf. Shorten any other shoot that grows across another. Thin fruits if necessary (see p.132). After fruiting (see also Sour cherry fan, p.130), cut back each fruited shoot to its replacement near the base, and tie in the shoot. If there is room to retain and tie in the reserve shoot as well, cut to this shoot instead.

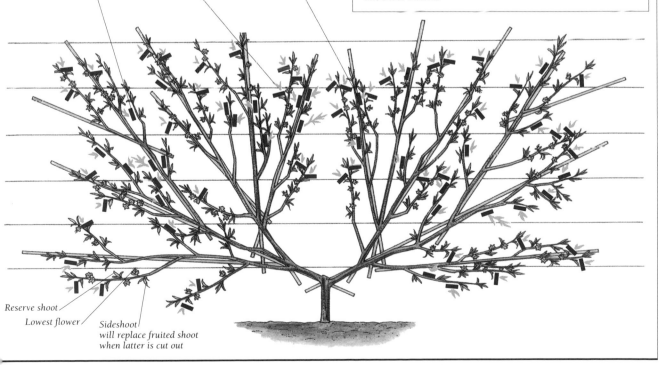

Reserve shoot

Lowest flower

Sideshoot will replace fruited shoot when latter is cut out

APRICOTS *PRUNUS ARMENIACA* (ZONES 4–10)

Apricot trees flower very early in the spring, so they grow best given a sunny site, protected from strong winds. Dry, sunny summers are needed for successful fruiting.

Always seek advice from a local specialist before buying. Apricots are fussy trees, and if they fail to do well this can be less to do with pruning, training, or cultivation than to a dislike of some aspect of their site or the prevailing climate. This may show up as dieback: pruning may cure the symptom but not the cause. Fruiting levels can also be affected by bad weather at pollination time; if the crop is sparse, much more growth will be made. This will need to be controlled by pruning, preferably at an early stage, or branches will become overcrowded. Where there is a danger of late frost, do not plant on a warm, south-facing wall. This will force the flowers out early, thereby increasing the danger of frost damage.

GRAFTING AND ROOTSTOCKS

While a variety of rootstocks are used where apricots are grown commercially, the plum rootstock 'St. Julien A' is widely used for garden trees. Both peach and apricot seedling rootstocks are also compatible. Dwarfing rootstocks are not usually available.

FRUITING HABIT

Apricots fruit like plums: the crop is born on two-year-old and older wood, but also at the base of one-year-old shoots. In warm climates, apricots fruit prolifically and fruit thinning (*see p.101*), to 3in (7cm) apart, will be necessary.

TIME OF PRUNING

As with all stone fruits, prune as buds burst when training a young apricot, and in summer when the tree is established. Never prune in early winter, when the risk of infection by diseases (*see* Plum problems, *p.123*) is at its greatest.

APRICOT FAN

An apricot fan requires a wall or fence at least 8ft (2.5m) high by 15ft (5m) wide. The first years of training are as for a peach (*see p.134*). It is more likely, with apricots, that a selected shoot will be lost and a replacement, arising from the stubs of unwanted shoots that were pinched back, will need to be trained in.

Once established, prune as for a plum fan (*see below and p.126*). Shorten, rather than remove, shoots to fill gaps, leaving their bases intact to fruit the following year. Relieve crowding by removing older sections of branches, filling gaps with strong new shoots.

ESTABLISHED APRICOT FAN

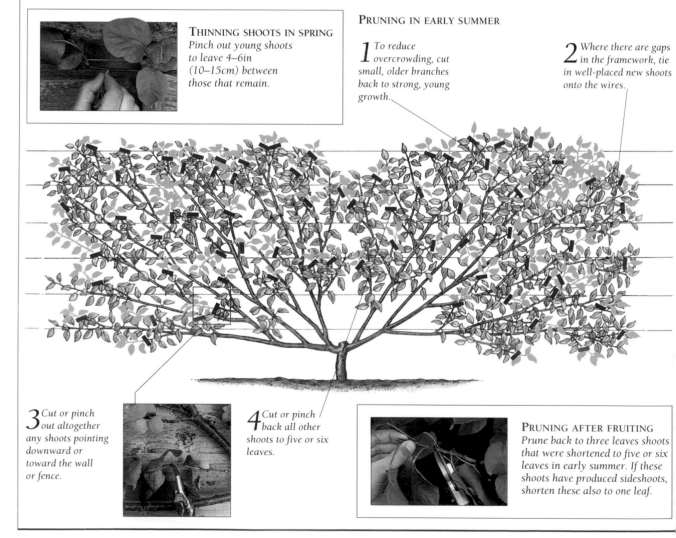

THINNING SHOOTS IN SPRING
Pinch out young shoots to leave 4–6in (10–15cm) between those that remain.

PRUNING IN EARLY SUMMER

1 To reduce overcrowding, cut small, older branches back to strong, young growth.

2 Where there are gaps in the framework, tie in well-placed new shoots onto the wires.

3 Cut or pinch out altogether any shoots pointing downward or toward the wall or fence.

4 Cut or pinch back all other shoots to five or six leaves.

PRUNING AFTER FRUITING
Prune back to three leaves shoots that were shortened to five or six leaves in early summer. If these shoots have produced sideshoots, shorten these also to one leaf.

MULBERRIES MORUS SPP. (ZONES 5–8)

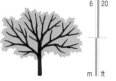

Mulberries grown for fruit include *Morus nigra*, the black mulberry, *M. rubra* and its hybrids, and *M. alba*, the white mulberry (*see also Morus*, Dictionary of Ornamental Trees, p.76). Mulberries are long-lived, fast-growing trees. They need cold winters and hot summers in order to fruit well, but start into growth late, so that frost rarely damages the flowers. The flowers are self-fertile, and the fruits are borne on second-year and older wood.

Mulberries are also sometimes grown in containers but will never grow large enough to obtain a worthwhile crop. Summer-pruning new shoots to five leaves helps keep them compact, and tying down branches to the horizontal (*see p.99*) can increase crops.

WHEN TO PRUNE

Only in early to midwinter, when fully dormant, to avoid bleeding. Older trees, however, may still bleed copiously, so only prune established trees if absolutely necessary, to remove diseased or damaged wood; remove dead wood in summer. The roots also bleed, so do not root-prune on planting.

TRAINING AND PRUNING

Later pruning can be kept to a minimum if the tree is well formed. Train a young tree (*see right*) with a clear trunk of about 5ft (1.5m) to accommodate the spreading branches when mature. Unwanted laterals on the main stem should be shortened in their first year, then removed in the next.

To produce a large, structurally sound specimen tree, retain a central leader to about 20ft (6m) by removing competing leaders, thereby allowing the crown to develop naturally. However, if ease of maintenance and harvesting is desired, a smaller, more compact tree can be produced. Prune the leader to just above the topmost of three or four strong laterals, 4½–5½ft (1.35–1.7m) from the ground. From these, develop a framework of 8–10 branches as for an apple bush (*see p.108*). Then allow the crown to develop naturally, keeping pruning to a minimum. Any unwanted new shoots are best rubbed or pinched out promptly.

Mulberries may have a tendency to lean over, but crown lifting or reshaping is not recommended. If possible, prop or brace low branches where necessary rather than removing them; combined with the gnarled habit, this adds to the tree's picturesque appeal.

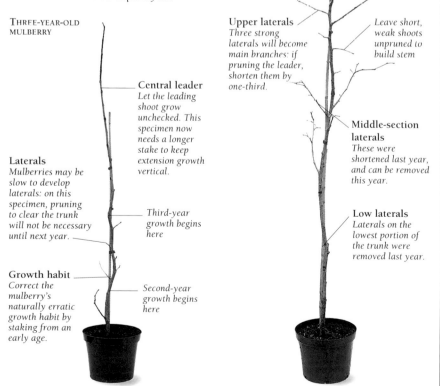

ESTABLISHED MULBERRY TREE
Although mulberries are very long-lived, their gnarled habit can make them look prematurely aged, increasing their ornamental value. The fruits ripen in early to midsummer.

TRAINING A YOUNG MULBERRY

Young mulberries are not difficult to train. Young whips are slow to develop "feathers," or laterals, and the tree may be three or four years old before pruning to clear the stem, as for any ornamental standard tree (see p.28), needs to start. Once a clear stem is achieved, either let the crown develop naturally or, for a more compact tree, prune the leader and upper laterals (see right) as for an apple bush in this and the subsequent year.

THREE-YEAR-OLD MULBERRY

Central leader
Let the leading shoot grow unchecked. This specimen now needs a longer stake to keep extension growth vertical.

Laterals
Mulberries may be slow to develop laterals: on this specimen, pruning to clear the trunk will not be necessary until next year.

Third-year growth begins here

Growth habit
Correct the mulberry's naturally erratic growth habit by staking from an early age.

Second-year growth begins here

FIVE-YEAR-OLD MULBERRY, PART-WAY THROUGH TRAINING

Central leader
If a small tree is desired, prune the leader back to here. If not, continue staking for as long as possible.

Upper laterals
Three strong laterals will become main branches: if pruning the leader, shorten them by one-third.

Leave short, weak shoots unpruned to build stem

Middle-section laterals
These were shortened last year, and can be removed this year.

Low laterals
Laterals on the lowest portion of the trunk were removed last year.

FIGS *FICUS CARICA* (ZONES 7–10)

Figs ideally need long, hot summers to bear heavy crops. In warm countries, figs are grown as informal bush or half-standard trees, with trunks of about 2–4ft (60–120cm). In cool climates, unless they have a favored site and are pruned to be very open in habit (to let in light), trees or bushes seldom bear well. Growing under glass is difficult unless the root run is severely restricted. By far the most usual outdoor tree form for cool climates is the fan; even this may not fruit well every year, and winter protection, in the form of netting filled with straw, is advisable.

ROOT RESTRICTION

Fig cultivars are raised from cuttings, not grafted, but a dwarfing effect can be achieved by restricting the root system,

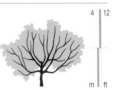

SUMMER PRUNING
Pinch out the tips of young shoots when they have made five or six leaves.

either by growing in pots or, in open ground, planting in a brick- or concrete-lined pit, 2ft (60cm) square, with a layer of broken bricks at the bottom, not a solid base.

FRUITING HABIT

The fig has an unusual fruiting sequence. Figs at three distinct stages of development may be present simultaneously. First to ripen are figs that overwintered in leaf axils as "embryo" fruits from the previous season. Following these are fruits that form in the spring on new growth and, in hot climates, develop to ripeness as the main crop late in summer. Meanwhile, embryo fruits for the next year's crop are forming near the tip of the new shoots.

In hot climates, this cycle results in a long fruiting season. In cool climates, the summer season is not long or hot enough for fruits to develop and ripen in a single year. The only fruits to ripen and become edible will be those that overwintered as embryos from the previous year. Pruning is therefore concentrated on encouraging embryo figs to form, and giving these the best ripening conditions in their second year.

TIME OF PRUNING

Figs are pruned yearly in early spring, once any danger of prolonged frost has passed. In cool climates, summer pruning is also necessary: all new shoot tips are pinched back to five or six

Embryo figs develop in leaf axils

Last year's fruit, now ripening

Scar of fallen leaf

This year's fruit

FRUIT DEVELOPMENT, FIGS
On this unpruned shoot, a fig at the base that overwintered from last year is now ripening. Above it, figs that formed this spring will be the next to ripen, providing the summer is long and hot enough. Embryo fruits for next year are starting to form at the shoot tip.

leaves. This lets in more light, and also helps to reduce the production of the second crop of unwanted figs. With its growth checked by tip-pruning, the shoot will not produce many fruits but will start into growth again, producing sideshoots from its leaf axils. At the end of the growing season, the fruits in the leaf axils of these sideshoots will still be only at an embryonic stage, and may overwinter successfully. Any larger, but still green fruits on the main shoot will not survive. Pick them off to direct the tree's energy into the more worthwhile fruits.

FIG BUSH

Start with a two-year-old fig with three or four well-spaced laterals of equal vigor arising from the main stem, at a height of 1½–3ft (45–90cm) from the ground. Planting and pruning in late winter or early spring (in cool climates, once severe weather is over), form a basic bush framework as for an apple bush (*see* p.108), with 8–10 main branches arising at or near the trunk.

Prune established fig bushes in spring and, in cool climates, in early to mid-summer. In cool climates, spring pruning cuts should be made (*see right*) with the aim of keeping the bush as spreading and open in habit as possible. In warm climates, the reverse is true: cut spreading branches to upright shoots, and leave growth in the center to give protection from sun scorch. In cool climates, pinch-prune new shoots in summer (*see* Summer pruning, *above*).

ESTABLISHED FIG BUSH, SPRING (COOL CLIMATE)

1 *Cut back any frost-damaged shoots to healthy wood.*

2 *Thin out badly placed shoots and, to let in sunshine, overcrowded growth, particularly in the center of the bush.*

All pruning cuts have been made to encourage an open, spreading habit. In warm climates, denser growth is preferable

3 *Cut any leggy, bare shoots or old branches back to one bud, or 2–3in (5–8cm), to encourage new growth.*

Clear trunk of 1½–2ft (45–60cm)

Balanced crown with 8–10 well-spaced branches

FIG FAN

A fig fan has the same branch structure as other fruit fans, but its main ribs must be farther apart to allow for the fig's much larger leaves. A wall at least 7ft (2.2m) high and 12ft (4m) wide is required, with strong horizontal wires.

FORMATIVE TRAINING

Start with a sturdy, two- or three-year-old fig. If its laterals are weak or badly placed, the best course is to start again: remove them and prune the leader to 16in (40cm) to stimulate strong lateral growth the following year.

Develop the branch structure as for a peach fan (*see p.134*). If the laterals are sturdy, prune away only a few inches; prune weaker ones harder, to about half their length. Aim to produce about six main ribs on either side over two or three winters, tying in laterals to fill out the framework. As soon as there are

more laterals than are needed for tying in, start summer-pruning them to maintain the flat fan form and encourage fruit formation.

ESTABLISHED PRUNING

Fans must be pruned in spring and, in cool climates, early to midsummer. When spring-pruning, it is important to remove some older wood, and shorten a few young shoots back to one bud, in order to encourage new growth. However, any excessively vigorous, or in colder areas overcrowded, laterals should be removed.

ESTABLISHED FIG FAN, SPRING

1 Once any risk of prolonged frost has passed, cut any frost-damaged shoots back to their point of origin.

2 On each rib, cut back two or three young shoots to one bud to encourage fresh growth that will develop embryo fruits.

3 Tie in remaining well-positioned shoots so that they are evenly spaced over the fan. In summer, pinch out new shoot tips once they have 5–6 leaves.

4 Prune shoots that grow toward the wall or across another shoot to their point of origin or to a well-placed sideshoot.

5 Cut back a proportion of old wood (perhaps one side branch on either side of the fan) to one bud or node and tie in newer shoots in its place.

GROWING FIGS IN CONTAINERS

Figs in pots, which can be moved into shelter for winter protection, can be grown as standards, but with a clear trunk no more than 15in (38cm) high, to make them stable. They may also be grown in a more compact multistemmed form. This is produced by cutting a two- or three-year-old fig down to ground level, then selecting up to 10 of the best shoots that grow up from the base. In subsequent springs, cut away three or four stems

to the base (in later years, always removing the oldest or weakest), letting new growth replace them and removing any surplus basal growth. Shoots on these stems are summer-pruned as for any fig; remove only those that cross and rub against each other in the center of the plant. These figs need light root pruning every other spring (*see* Root pruning a container-grown shrub, p.154). They generally need yearly repotting.

CONTAINER-GROWN FIG
Prune at the base to maintain a multi-stemmed form. Summer-prune all sideshoots.

TENDER FRUITS

Many of the frost-tender tree fruits need a completely frost-free climate. Others may survive light frosts, but will then fruit poorly or not at all. Although all tender fruits benefit from initial training, regular pruning is not always needed (and can be inadvisable in hot, humid climates), and these trees are grown in much more free-growing forms than the hardy fruits. Training is more comparable to that of ornamental trees, and pruning when mature is often limited to the removal of dead, diseased, or damaged wood, possibly with light pruning at or after harvesting. Most are better replaced than renovated.

Many tender fruits can be grown successfully under glass in cold climates. They may flower in a heated conservatory or greenhouse but, given the relative shortness of the summer season and reduction in hours of sunshine, fruits are unlikely to develop. The most satisfactory group to grow under glass is the citrus fruits (see p.142), highly ornamental plants that will tolerate pruning to size and shape and, given the right conditions, will produce a small crop of fruits in most years. They make attractive container plants too, and if grown this way can be brought out of doors in summer to decorate terraces and patios.

ATEMOYA, CHERIMOYA, & CUSTARD APPLE
ANNONA SPP.

The cherimoya (*Annona cherimola*), the true custard apple or bullock's heart (*A. reticulata*), and the hybrid atemoya (called custard apple in Australia) are closely related. The atemoya and cherimoya thrive in tropical highlands and subtropical areas but will tolerate lower temperatures, shedding their leaves during dry or cool periods. The true custard apple prefers tropical, humid conditions with a cool but frost-free winter period.

Untrained trees may give good yields but will be structurally weak. They fruit on both old and new wood.

WHEN TO PRUNE During the dormant or dry season; for custard apples, at the end of dormancy as buds break. Light pruning may also be needed during the growing season and after fruiting.

TRAINING AND PRUNING These fruits are best trained as multistemmed trees on a short trunk (see p.30). Prune the young tree back to about 3ft (1m), and let only three or four laterals develop. When these have grown to about 2ft (60cm), tip-prune them and let a new branch leader and two well-spaced sideshoots develop on each. These trees only develop shoots from buds just under the leaves once the leaf is shed, so removing strategically placed leaves, leaving the leaf-stalk on, can induce well-spaced laterals to grow where they are desired. Shorten vigorous, vertical shoots to an outward-facing bud or sideshoot.

When established, prune only to remove damaged, diseased, crossing, or crowded growth; hard pruning stimulates excessive growth at the expense of flowering shoots. Atemoyas and cherimoyas may develop vigorous, nonflowering shoots; prune these by up to a third during the growing season to stimulate more flowering sideshoots.

ATEMOYA
Untrained trees grow with an erratic and weak branch structure; vigorous shoots tend to grow long and leggy, branching sparsely, and may break under the weight of crops.

JACKFRUITS
This jackfruit has been allowed to develop naturally into a tall tree that fruits all the way up the trunk and on main branches. A smaller, trained tree is easier to harvest.

BREADFRUIT, JACKFRUIT *ARTOCARPUS* SPP.

The breadfruit (*Artocarpus altilis*) grows best in wet, tropical lowland areas, while the jackfruit (*Artocarpus heterophylla*) tolerates a drier and cooler climate; it fruits well in many frost-free areas between the tropics but is very sensitive to soil waterlogging, cold, and drought.

Breadfruit trees will grow to up to 100ft (30m), naturally developing a well-branched, spreading crown. The branches are brittle and easily damaged. The jackfruit grows to a height of 50–70ft (15–20m), with a dense, sometimes irregular crown that spreads with age.

Vegetatively propagated plants fruit in three or four years. Both trees crop better where two cultivars pollinate each other.

WHEN TO PRUNE When established, as fruits are harvested.

TRAINING AND PRUNING Once young plant are well established in their planting site, prune back the leader to the topmost of three or four laterals that will form main framework branches on a short, clear trunk; remove all other laterals. Shorten excessively vigorous or leggy branch leaders by about one-third, and, with the very upright breadfruit cultivars, bend and tie down laterals (see p.99) at an earl stage to ensure an open crown.

Once the framework is established, shorten fruited shoots after harvesting to stimulate the growth of shoots that will flower the following year. Otherwise, keep pruning to a minimum. Mature tree sometimes require thinning to prevent leafy growth becoming too dense and shading the fruits; crowded branches restrict access for harvesting.

STAR FRUIT
AVERRHOA CARAMBOLA

The star fruit, or carambola, grows well in tropical and subtropical regions, although mature trees can withstand light frosts for short periods. Evergreen in the tropics, it is sometimes semievergreen in the subtropics and is relatively slow-growing, with a short trunk and an initially pyramidal, then bushy, rounded crown. The branches of some cultivars have a drooping habit. Named cultivars, sometimes grafted, are preferable. They may flower within two or three years of planting; fruiting is irregular, but two main crops are obtained in some areas. Trees usually require pollination by another cultivar.

In warm temperate areas, with liberal feeding and watering, plants may be grown in either containers or beds in full sun in a heated greenhouse or conservatory, with minimum summer temperatures of 72°F (22°C).

WHEN TO PRUNE After harvesting.

TRAINING AND PRUNING Train as a multi-stemmed tree (see p.30), pruning back to 12–18in (30–45cm) from ground level, then selecting four to six main stems. Some cultivars grow strongly upright, and branch crotch angles may be narrow; to counteract this, tie down branches for a single growing season with twine pegged into the ground (see p.99) so that a more open crown is formed. As the tree develops, shorten vigorous branch leaders by one-third to encourage a branching habit.

Little further pruning is needed. Low-hanging, weak, and crossing growth should be regularly removed, together with any damaged or diseased wood.

YOUNG STAR FRUIT TREES
Most cultivars of these small, slow-growing, multistemmed trees need another cultivar planted nearby for pollination purposes.

PAPAYA CARICA PAPAYA

Although popularly referred to as a tree, the papaya (pawpaw, tree melon) is, botanically, a tall, slender arborescent herb, with a single, thick, usually unbranched trunk on which the fruits are borne. It has a productive lifespan of only four or five years. It is widely grown in subtropical to tropical regions. For fruits to form, both male and female plants are usually needed, although some self-fertile cultivars are available.

Papayas need a sheltered site in full sun, plentiful rainfall throughout the growing season, and good drainage. A tropical climate is ideal, although some cultivars withstand minimum temperatures of 60°F (16°C). These may be grown in greenhouses in warm temperate regions. Plants under glass may not fruit reliably: high levels of light during the summer and temperatures that never fall below 68°F (20°C) are needed. Even self-fertile cultivars will need to be hand-pollinated. Papayas make attractive ornamentals, however; pruning back the leader will induce a less vigorous, branched habit.

Papayas are usually propagated from seed. Young plants grow rapidly to a height of 12–20ft (4–6m), normally fruiting within two years. The fruits may be produced at any time of the year.

WHEN TO PRUNE After harvesting.

TRAINING AND PRUNING The single stem of the papaya rarely branches naturally, and initial training is therefore normally minimal. Branching may be induced, to restrict height and make harvesting easier, by removing the terminal shoot, tip-pruning the leader after the first harvest. Trees that have become too tall to harvest or have outgrown their space, for example under glass, may be cut

PAPAYA FLOWERS AND FRUITS
The flowers are produced in the leaf axils; both the leaf and leaf-stalk are shed as the plant grows upward, and the fruits gradually increase in size.

back to half their height or, to renovate completely, to within 32–36in (80–90cm) of ground level; they usually respond well, producing several shoots from dormant basal buds. Train the strongest stem vertically at first with a short stake, and remove the others at the base. These can then be used as cuttings for propagation. Male trees pruned in this manner sometimes produce female flowers and fruits in a form of sex reversion.

STAR APPLE CHRYSOPHYLLUM CAINITO

This large, evergreen tree prefers a humid, tropical environment with well-distributed rainfall and high temperatures throughout the year; in subtropical areas such as southern Florida, it requires protection from cold winds for the first two or three years after planting.

Star apples may grow to a height of 100ft (30m), developing a dense, broad canopy. Propagation is usually by seed, but grafting (onto selected rootstocks of star apple) is successful, as is air layering. The flowers are insect-pollinated and are usually self-fertile. Star apples need minimal training and pruning. They usually develop naturally as multistemmed trees (see p.30) on a short trunk of 2–3ft (60–90cm); select only three main framework branches to allow light to penetrate the canopy. Thin inward-growing laterals if necessary to avoid a congested crown at maturity. Limit pruning of established trees to the removal of crossing or weak shoots, and any damaged or diseased growth. Remove any water shoots (see p.32) that develop at the sites of pruning cuts.

CITRUS FRUITS

The genus *Citrus*, like *Prunus*, contains a great many species grown for fruits, the most popular being oranges, lemons, grapefruits, and limes. There are other citrus fruits from different genera, including kumquats (*Fortunella*) and calamondins (× *Citrofortunella microcarpa*), both ideal for growing under glass, or in containers to be given winter shelter, in cooler climates. They are often grown purely for their ornamental value.

Citrus fruits grow well in almost any frost-free climate, and in areas with hot summers, such as Mediterranean countries or Florida and Texas, the mature wood can survive light frosts. In cool climates, trees can be moved into a sheltered spot for the summer; cool night temperatures improve the fruit color.

GROWTH AND FRUITING HABIT

In frost-free climates the growth cycles of most citrus trees usually last for four to six weeks, with up to five cycles per year under good growing conditions. It is therefore quite normal for flowers and fruits to be present on branches at any one time. Trees become dormant at temperatures below 55°F (13°C), or in dry or drought conditions (the onset of rain or resumption of watering usually results in flowering within four weeks).

TIME OF PRUNING

Prune at any time in warm, frost-free climates. Elsewhere, prune young trees from spring to late summer; spring gives regrowth time to ripen before cold weather sets in. Established trees can be pruned at or after harvesting.

FORMATIVE TRAINING

For ease of harvesting, fruiting citrus trees are grown as bush trees (*see facing page*), with a domed, open-centered

LEMON FRUITS AND FLOWERS
While most fruits have distinct growth cycles, those of a lemon are much more likely to overlap, so that flowers and fruits may be present on the tree simultaneously.

crown on a clear trunk no shorter than 20in (50cm) to keep fruits from touching the soil. Where trees are grown as ornamentals, particularly in containers, they look better as small branched-head standards (*see p.144*), with a clear trunk of 3–5ft (1–1.5m). The trunk is cleared gradually of growth, as for any ornamental tree (*see p.28*), so that the foliage nourishes the stem and protects the young bark from sun scorch.

Once the desired height of clear trunk has been achieved, the crown is formed in much the same way. Select only three or four upper laterals as the main branches; these should be of about equal length, making crotch angles of at least 40° to the main stem.

To develop a symmetrical and compact crown, shorten branch leaders again at the beginning of the growing season in spring or, alternatively, while the trees are semidormant during the winter period. The main branches should each give rise to two or three sublaterals that will, in turn, produce two or three shoots. Continued shortening of branch leaders promotes this neat, bushy habit. A second light pruning may be carried out during the growing season, if necessary, to remove any new shoots growing across other growth, or into the center of the tree.

Shoot from rootstock should be pinched out

GRAFTING AND ROOTSTOCKS

Many citrus trees come true from seed and are easy to raise as seedlings. In general, these are more vigorous than grafted plants, lemons in particular. They often have a greater degree of resistance to diseases such as root rot. However, seedling citrus are generally less productive and do not start to crop until about six years old, whereas grafted trees may begin to flower within two or three years of grafting. Most citrus species and cultivars can be successfully bud-grafted onto a range of rootstocks that can be used to modify tree vigor, fruit yield and

RECENTLY GRAFTED CITRUS
This young citron has been grafted on to Meyer's lemon, a useful rootstock that confers tolerance of lower temperatures.

quality, resistance to disease, and tolerance of low temperatures. Some combine several properties: the widely used Troyer citrange, for example, results not only in smaller trees but also confers some resistance to attack by root nematodes. Kumquat trees are usually grafted onto trifoliate orange (*Poncirus trifoliata*) for its dwarfing effect and cold-resistance; this rootstock also reduces fruit acidity when used for grapefruits.

In general, the chosen rootstock can affect the degree of pruning that is required, particularly where a dwarfing type of rootstock is used, and expert advice in these cases is invaluable. Always choose a plant that is grafted onto dwarfing stock if the tree is to be grown in a container.

TRAINING A CITRUS BUSH

STAGE 1

When a young, unbranched plant is about 3–4ft (90–120cm) high, prune it to just above a leaf at about 2ft (60cm) from the ground.

STAGE 2

1 Select three or four strong laterals to form framework branches, shortening each to about 12in (30cm).

2 Pinch out any low shoots that develop on the stem, but retain single leaves.

ESTABLISHED PRUNING

In general, prune mature trees as lightly as possible. An exception can be made for some cultivars of lemon grown on a vigorous rootstock. These cultivars have a predominantly upright habit and may require fairly severe pruning, when mature, to encourage lateral branching.

On grafted citrus, suckers are likely to arise from below the graft union. All citrus also tend to produce water shoots on their main branches. These should all be removed as soon as they appear. Inward-growing shoots should also be removed or cut back to an outward-facing bud since, shaded by other growth, they are unlikely to produce flowers. As with all fruit trees, any diseased or dead branches should be regularly removed, as should any crossing branches that could cause damage by chafing.

Fruit thinning is rarely required, particularly with overlapping crop cycles when only a proportion of shoots are fruiting, while others are in flower. Remove the first-formed fruits from trees in containers, to promote growth.

When harvesting, prune each fruited shoot back to the next young shoot, since it will not fruit again. Always harvest with pruners: citrus fruits pulled from the tree so that their calyx is damaged or left behind will quickly rot. Pulling fruit off may also bruise the rind.

RENOVATION

Citrus trees usually respond to hard pruning, if necessary. On older trees, an unproductive branch or section of branch can be removed. Do not remove more in any one year. Unlike many fruit trees, citrus trees, in general, have limited reserves of carbohydrates in their stem tissues, and excessive pruning is therefore likely to set back growth and fruiting. If several shoots arise around a cut, select only one or two of the best placed to develop as main branches.

STAGE 3

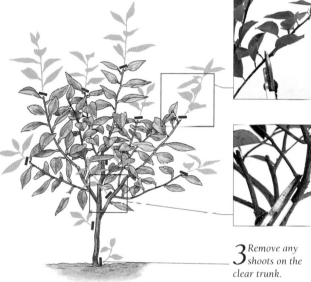

1 Shorten the new branch leaders by one-third of their growth, and tip-prune strong sideshoots by three or four leaves.

2 Remove sideshoots growing across other shoots or into the center of the bush.

3 Remove any shoots on the clear trunk.

YOUNG, ESTABLISHED CITRUS BUSH

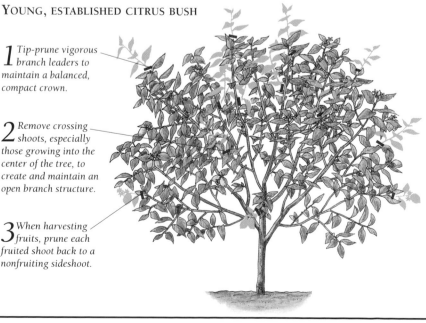

1 Tip-prune vigorous branch leaders to maintain a balanced, compact crown.

2 Remove crossing shoots, especially those growing into the center of the tree, to create and maintain an open branch structure.

3 When harvesting fruits, prune each fruited shoot back to a nonfruiting sideshoot.

CITRUS FOR COOLER CLIMATES

Tangerines, mandarins, and satsumas are, in general, more cold-tolerant than sweet oranges and also more drought-resistant. The lime *Citrus aurantiifolia* 'Tahiti' (syn. 'Persian') is more cold-tolerant than 'Mexican'. The Meyer lemon (presumed to be a hybrid between *C. limon* and the mandarin orange) is a small, fairly cold-tolerant plant, very suitable for growing in containers. Kumquats are also excellent container plants. They usually remain semidormant during autumn and winter but grow vigorously during spring and summer. Although they normally make shrubby trees up to 12ft (4m) high, their

FROST DAMAGE
Prune back to completely healthy growth, cutting to a leaf so that a new shoot may develop from its axillary bud.

size can be restricted under cover by pruning in winter to remove much of the previous season's growth.

CITRUS IN CONTAINERS

When growing citrus trees in containers, feed young plants regularly each month during the growing season (*see p.15*). This is essential to promote strong and healthy branch development. During this period of active growth, any water shoots or suckers, which grow from the rootstock, must be removed (*see p.32*) as soon as they develop.

Other pruning should take place in the early part of the year, particularly if the plants have been semidormant during the winter. At this time, shorten any shoots that have been cold-damaged (*see left*). For well-established plants, reduce watering to a minimum for three or four weeks during the early part of the summer to promote flower initiation when watering resumes.

Make sure there is adequate ventilation, particularly during the summer months, and avoid excessive humidity, which encourages disease. Shade and low levels of light reduce yields. Mature plants in containers may be transferred to a sunny outdoor site, protected from wind, during the summer.

Repotting should be carried out very carefully, in early spring, in order not to interrupt the growth cycle. Light pruning may follow repotting. Established trees grow best in large tubs.

**CITRUS STANDARD
IN CONTAINER**
This calamondin has been trained as a standard largely for ornamental effect, although its small orange fruits can be crystallized or used in preserves.

TRAINING A CITRUS STANDARD

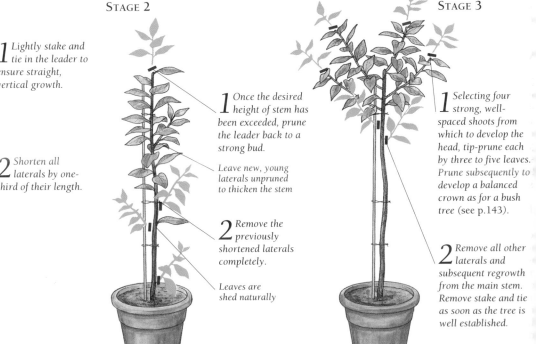

STAGE 1

1 Lightly stake and tie in the leader to ensure straight, vertical growth.

2 Shorten all laterals by one-third of their length.

STAGE 2

1 Once the desired height of stem has been exceeded, prune the leader back to a strong bud.

Leave new, young laterals unpruned to thicken the stem

2 Remove the previously shortened laterals completely.

Leaves are shed naturally

STAGE 3

1 Selecting four strong, well-spaced shoots from which to develop the head, tip-prune each by three to five leaves. Prune subsequently to develop a balanced crown as for a bush tree (see p.143).

2 Remove all other laterals and subsequent regrowth from the main stem. Remove stake and tie as soon as the tree is well established.

DURIAN *DURIO ZIBETHINUS*

Durians, grown chiefly in tropical Southeast Asia, need high humidity and rainfall, with a definite dry season. A pollinating cultivar is usually required. Seedling trees may grow to 100ft (30m); grafted trees rarely achieve half this height. Young trees have a pyramidal shape that gradually becomes more irregular. Let trees develop naturally, pruning only to remove or shorten vigorous upright shoots, since vertical growth rarely fruits. Thin the more horizontally growing branches, on which most flowers form, to avoid crowding and crossing growth. Remove epicormic shoots (*see p.32*) on the trunk and main branches. Established trees need minimal attention. Thin fruitlets four to six weeks after flowering, to leave one or two fruits per panicle. Overlarge trees respond well to crown reduction (*see p.35*) to a height of about 30ft (10m).

DURIAN IN FRUIT
The famously malodorous durian fruits form along the length of horizontal branches.

LOQUAT IN FLOWER
In suitable conditions, flowers, followed by fruits, are borne on the current year's growth, mainly in terminal clusters, from about four years after planting. For ease of harvesting, choose one of the more compact cultivars, grafted onto a dwarfing rootstock.

LOQUAT *ERIOBOTRYA JAPONICA*

Loquats tolerate light frost, but require frost-free conditions with warm summers to fruit. Cold winters may reduce flowering. Many cultivars also require a pollinator. Train as a multistemmed tree (*see p.30*) on a short, clear trunk; shorten branch leaders by about one-third of their length, if necessary, to encourage branching. Prune just before trees start into growth. Established trees need no special pruning; to harvest, remove entire fruit clusters, cutting back to a bud or shoot. This may stimulate numerous sideshoots: thin by removing, not shortening, shoots if growth becomes crowded, particularly in the center. Keep the short trunk clear of growth. If a heavy crop is set, thin fruit by removing the tip of each fruit cluster.

LITCHI *LITCHI CHINENSIS*

The litchi, or lychee, is a slow-growing, evergreen tree. It has a dense, symmetrical, domed canopy; some cultivars have branches with a spreading, semipendent habit. Most cultivars do not grow to more than 30–40ft (10–12m) tall. Lychees need a subtropical climate, with a cool, dry winter season and hot summers with relatively high humidity.

WHEN TO PRUNE When harvesting.

TRAINING AND PRUNING Trees naturally branch from the base, but training is recommended to ensure a well-structured multistemmed tree. Choose a young, feathered tree that has three or four well-spaced, wide-angled laterals between 1 and 2ft (30–60cm) from the ground, and prune back the leader to the topmost lateral. It is essential that laterals make wide V-angles with the main stem, otherwise mature branches may split away from the trunk. Remove any laterals less than 1ft (30cm) from the ground. Some cultivars develop long, semipendent branches, and these should be shortened by about 1ft (30cm) to stimulate fruiting sideshoots.

Mature trees rarely need pruning. When the clusters of fruit are harvested, shorten the fruited shoots by about 1ft (30cm) to stimulate the growth of new laterals that will fruit the following season. Remove dead and weak branches within the crown at the same time.

Older trees, and particularly those that have been damaged by frost, will respond well to hard pruning; this will result in both increased fruit size and yield. In some regions, trees that are not fruiting will, provided that they are well established, healthy, and vigorous, respond to bark ringing (*see p.106*); always seek local expert advice before using this technique.

MANGOSTEEN *GARCINIA MANGOSTANA*

The mangosteen prefers the climate of its native Southeast Asia. Seedling trees are usually grown. Tree height is very variable, from 20 to 80ft (6–25m); crown reduction (*see p.35*) is often necessary.

Mangosteens are best pruned soon after harvesting; they may flower twice a year. Little training or pruning is required, except to remove inward-pointing and strongly upright branches, both on young and maturing trees, to encourage a tiered habit. Remove low branches that touch the soil. Over-crowded trees with very dense foliage fruit only at the tips of branches; thinning will increase light penetration into the tree canopy. Spread the work out over several seasons; heavy pruning at any one time is not recommended.

YOUNG MANGOSTEEN TREE
Mangosteens grow slowly when young, with a straight trunk, symmetrically branched to form a pyramidal crown. Fruits are borne after 8–10 years at the tips of mature shoots.

MANGO *MANGIFERA INDICA*

Mangoes are well-branched, evergreen trees with an oval, dome-shaped, open crown. The form develops naturally, but training will ensure a strong branch structure. Mangoes need a tropical or subtropical, damp climate with a distinct dry or cool season. Wetter conditions encourage growth at the expense of fruiting. Seedlings take seven or eight years to fruit, but grafted cultivars usually flower in the third year after planting. Dwarfing rootstocks are available that restrict height to 22–30ft (7–10m), enabling mangoes to be grown under cover, given a warm, humid atmosphere.

WHEN TO PRUNE When young, between growth flushes, then after the main crop.

TRAINING AND PRUNING All mangoes benefit from formative training. Aim to form a bush tree, as for an apple (*see p.106*), with a clear trunk of about 3ft (1m) and a well-spaced crown formed by three to five framework branches with wide crotch angles. All weak laterals should be removed; mango fruits are heavy and will break branches that are not strong and structurally sound. Fruits should be thinned or removed for the first two years of flowering; later, fruit thinning is rarely necessary.

Established trees need no routine pruning. Remove any low or crossing shoots. Branch leaders may be shortened by one-third to promote branching or to restrict the size of vigorous cultivars. Older trees can be reinvigorated by pruning out inward-pointing branches and thinning out crowded growth and some of the terminal shoots.

MANGO FRUITS
Fruits are heavy and borne in drooping clusters; the branch framework must be stron

RAMBUTAN
NEPHELIUM LAPPACEUM

The rambutan, native to Malaysia and Indonesia, is grown in many lowland tropical regions. Temperatures below 50°F (10°C) severely limit growth. Trees are prone to damage by strong winds.

Seedling rambutans grow to 40–70ft (12–20m) tall, with a canopy that spreads to about two-thirds of their height. Vegetatively propagated cultivars, which fruit earlier, are pruned and trained to grow only to 12–40ft (4–12m); they may have an erect, but more usually a spreading habit. Flowers are produced mainly at the shoot tips.

WHEN TO PRUNE After harvesting.

TRAINING AND PRUNING Trees tend to be dense and crowded if unpruned, so early training is essential to ensure a regularly spaced branch framework that lets in air and light. Aim to form a bush tree, as for an apple (*see p.106*). Prune a one- or two-year-old feathered tree on planting to 2–3ft (60–90cm) from ground level, just above three or four evenly spaced, vigorous laterals that make wide V-angles with the main stem. Three months later, shorten these laterals by about one-third of their length to encourage sideshoots.

Once the main framework has been established, minimal pruning is required. Remove water shoots (*see p.32*), diseased or dead wood, and any branches that are crossing or growing too close to the ground. The remains of the fruited panicles can be removed after harvesting to stimulate new fruiting shoots.

OLIVE *OLEA EUROPAEA*

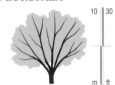

Olives are slow-growing evergreens, widely grown in Mediterranean-type climates. They need cool winters to fruit, though they will be damaged by temperatures below 14°F (–10°C). In temperate climates they need the protection of a sunny wall, and seldom grow taller than 12ft (4m). They can be grown as nonfruiting trees in cool climates, if brought under cover for winter. They tolerate pruning well, and their size can be restricted. Self-fertile cultivars are available. Trees normally fruit four or five years from planting, and may remain productive for 100 years or more. Fruits are borne on one-year-old wood, often on the periphery of the tree canopy; trees should be given ample space and have open crowns that allow sunlight to penetrate.

WHEN TO PRUNE Early spring.

TRAINING AND PRUNING Stake well on planting. In Mediterranean climates, train with a clear trunk of 3–4ft (1–1.2m). The crown often branches naturally; prune to induce branching at about 5ft (1.5m) if necessary, and select three or four well-spaced laterals to form framework branches. Then let the dense, twiggy crown develop with minimal pruning. Trees usually recover from light frost damage if cut back to live wood.

When established, remove only old and unproductive wood in order to stimulate new shoots that will flower the following year, and thin overcrowded growth in the center of the crown to let in sun, if necessary. Trees can be maintained at a height of 12–15ft (4–5ft) for ease of harvesting by pruning branch leaders to replacement shoots each year. Use the same technique to restrict growth of tub-grown trees. Olives respond well to hard pruning, and can be completely renovated by pruning to ground level; either select a new leader (*see Eucalyptus, p.64*) or allow a small, shrubby form to develop.

Olives can also be wall trained, tying in evenly spaced growth (*see also Magnolia, p.74*) to form a fan framework. Pruning back outward-growing and badly placed shoots will stimulate young, twiggy growth with attractive, fresh foliage.

OLIVE TREE
The central leader and branch leaders can be pruned low to form a smaller, branching crown, enabling olives to be grown in tubs.

Avocado (alligator pear) *Persea* spp.

The three types of avocado – Mexican, Guatemalan, and West Indian – prefer, respectively, a semitropical, subtropical, and tropical climate. All need plenty of light. Most form large trees, although size can be restricted by pruning. There are cultivars that do not grow to more than 15–20ft (5–6m) tall. Seedlings will not fruit until at least five years old, and their fruits are often poor. Grafted cultivars may flower in their third year; some rootstocks also give resistance to root rots and tolerance of lower temperatures.

Avocados generally have a spreading habit, although some cultivars have a more conical silhouette. Extension growth is made from terminal buds, and there are two growth flushes per season. They are virtually evergreen. Lateral buds may be shed during dormant periods, often leaving flowers clustered at the tips of branches. Two or more trees often fruit better than single trees.

The Mexican cultivars are the most cold-tolerant and can grow well in sunny, open, but sheltered sites where temperatures do not fall below 55–59°F (13–15°C). They will grow under glass in temperate areas, although light levels may still be too low for flowering (hand-pollination will be necessary). They dislike root disturbance.

When to prune After fruiting.

Training and pruning Little initial training is needed; laterals may be shortened by up to half their length to induce branching, if needed; retain as much foliage as possible to protect the young bark from sun scorch. When established, prune only to remove damaged, diseased, crossing, or crowded growth, or to tip-prune any vigorous upright shoots to encourage a more spreading, branching habit. Branches are brittle, and buds and shoots are

AVOCADO
Avocados tend to flower and fruit at the tips of existing branches, and then make new extension growth.

easily damaged; be extremely careful when pruning. Harvest fruits using a sharp knife or pruners to cut the stalk about ½in (1cm) from the fruit.

Trees that have grown too large for comfortable harvesting may be "headed back" (*see* Crown reduction, *p.35*), preferably after harvesting.

Guava *Psidium guajava*

A native of the American tropics, and widely grown in tropical and subtropical regions, the guava is a multi-stemmed tree, often equal in both height and spread, with a tendency to sucker and branch close to the ground. Grafted cultivars fruit more reliably than seedling trees. The guava may flower two or three times per year. Fruits start to form two or three years after planting on new shoots from mature wood. Regular, careful pruning keeps plants productive.

When to prune After main harvesting periods.

Training and pruning The main aim is to allow full sunlight penetration to the center of the canopy. Train as a multi-stemmed tree with four or five strong, well-spaced main stems; if the young tree reaches 3ft (1m) without branching, prune it back to 20in (50cm) to encourage low laterals (*see p.30*). Three months later, shorten each of these by about half its length, and thin inward-growing sideshoots to prevent over-crowding. When established, remove suckers from the rootstock and shoots on the clear stem. After harvesting, tip-prune branch leaders and vigorous laterals to encourage a compact habit and stimulate the growth of further flowering shoots.

Pomegranate *Punica granatum*

A multistemmed or bush tree, probably native to Iran but very adaptable to a wide range of frost-free climates. It fruits best in semi-arid climates with hot summers and cool winters. Here, trees are deciduous or semievergreen; they are evergreen in humid tropical areas.

Seedling pomegranates are very variable; choose trees grown from cuttings or lifted suckers. Fruits form four or five years from planting, ripening over five to seven months. Trees flower either once or twice a year, depending on climate. They are often

POMEGRANATE
Harvest with pruners to avoid damaging the spur, so that it may fruit the next year.

self-fertile, but growing two together can improve fruit-set. Fruits are borne on short spurs that remain productive for three or four years. Remove some old, unproductive wood annually to encourage new fruiting growth. Overpruning is likely to reduce crops.

Pomegranates will grow well and flower profusely, occasionally fruiting, in full sun in a heated greenhouse. They tolerate pruning to restrict size.

When to prune In the dormant season.

Training and pruning Train as a multi-stemmed tree on a short leg (*see p.30*); if the young tree does not branch low, prune it to 24–30in (60–75cm) to encourage laterals to develop. Remove any less than 8in (20cm) from the ground, and select four or five of the remaining shoots, choosing the strongest and most widely spaced. For the next three years, shorten the leading shoots by about one-third of the previous season's growth, to develop a branched framework.

On established trees, annual pruning is confined mainly to shortening a small proportion of older branches to encourage the development of new shoots. Pomegranates have a strong tendency to sucker at the base of the stem; remove as seen unless a replacement for a main stem is needed, in which case train on a young, well-placed shoot.

NUTS

Most nuts are borne on trees or bushes. Some, such as walnut, chestnut, and pecan, grow very large, forming handsome specimens suitable for big gardens or parks. Hazelnut and filbert bushes are more suited to the small garden. As with fruit trees, nut trees will only produce if successfully pollinated, sometimes by another cultivar; even nut trees that produce both male and female flowers on the same plant may not do so simultaneously.

Only hazelnuts and filberts grow and bear well in any cool temperate region; chestnuts, almonds, and walnuts need warmer and more favorable conditions to bear nut crops – although even then they may not do so regularly. In climates with milder winters, pistachios and pecans can be grown, whereas the macadamia, brazil, and cashew need tropical conditions.

Although hazelnuts and filberts will bear more heavily if regularly pruned, nuts in general need minimal pruning. Early training will ensure well-shaped, sound trees, but subsequently little attention is needed beyond those routine tasks (*see p.31*) that keep any tree in good health.

CASHEW *ANACARDIUM OCCIDENTALE* (ZONE 10)

The cashew grows in tropical regions with definite dry seasons, such as India and East Africa. It is evergreen, with a wide, spreading crown. Lower branches, often nearly horizontal, may reach 20ft (6m) and are liable to break in high winds. Both seedlings and higher-yielding grafted clones are used. Seedlings grow most rapidly and quickly develop very long roots.

The aim is to develop an open-centered, multistemmed crown on a short, clear trunk of about 3ft (1m). Prune a young feathered tree back to a height of 4ft (1.2m), selecting four or five laterals to form the main branches (*see also Acer davidii, p.52*). These may be tipped back to induce additional branching if necessary. Established trees have no special pruning needs.

YOUNG CASHEW TREE
Trees require a short, clear trunk to accommodate the low, spreading branches.

Cashews may also be pollarded (*see p.36*) at 20–30in (50–75cm) from the ground. The tree bears again in two or three years. In Australia, in commercial "hedgerow" plantings, when the foliage of trees in adjacent rows almost meets, alternate rows are pollarded.

BRAZIL *BERTHOLLETIA EXCELSA* (SYN. *B. NOBILIS*)

The Brazil or para nut grows wild in the Amazonian forests and is also planted in Southeast Asia where climatic conditions resemble those of the lowland rainforests. The trees are tall and densely furnished with branches about a quarter of the way up, giving a narrowly conical form. Bearing begins when trees are 10–20 years old; the nuts take a year to ripen. Wild trees are normally left unpruned, but young trees can be encouraged to branch lower, at a height of 3–6ft (1–2m), by pruning back the main leader and subsequently shortening the main framework branches at regular intervals.

PECAN *CARYA ILLINOINENSIS*

Many species of *Carya* make fine ornamental trees in cool climates (*see* Dictionary of Ornamental Trees, *p.56*). To bear well, however, the pecan, a vigorous, erect, deciduous tree, needs a fairly dry, subtropical or warm temperate climate with a hot summer and a distinct cold but frost-free season (zones 6–9).

Choose a selected cultivar, grafted on to seedling stock, that will set nuts after about five years. Pecans quickly develop a long taproot: choose very young specimens sold in long pots or bags, and transplant carefully. Never buy an old containerized tree because the root system will not establish satisfactorily.

WHEN TO PRUNE From autumn to midwinter. Trees bleed sap profusely if pruned in spring.

TRAINING AND PRUNING *Carya illinoinensis* looks best trained as a central-leader standard, although it may be kept as a feathered tree. Do not tip-prune laterals, either when training or as the tree matures; the separate male and female flowers are both borne on shoots that have grown from terminal buds in the previous growing season.

Established trees have no special pruning needs and dislike hard pruning.

CHINESE CHESTNUT *CASTANEA MOLLISSIMA*

The Chinese chestnut matures into a small tree prized as an ornamental specimen (*see* Dictionary of Ornamental Trees, *p.57*). The Chinese chestnut is resistant to chestnut blight, an affliction that can be fatal to other chestnut species. This blight has made the native American chestnut (*C. dentata*) all but extinct. Chinese chestnuts are not self-fertile, and two different varieties are necessary to provide cross-fertilization. The trees are hardy in zones 4–8(9).

Training and pruning are the same as for an ornamental tree (*see p.57*): train as a central-leader standard, selecting only laterals that will form well-placed framework branches making wide V-angles to the trunk. Heavy branches on old trees may become unsafe.

CHINESE CHESTNUTS
Seed-grown trees will produce edible nuts after about four or five years.

HAZELNUTS AND FILBERTS *CORYLUS AVELLANA, C. MAXIMA* (ZONES 5–8)

Hazelnuts and filberts make attractive large, ornamental shrubs (*see* Dictionary of Ornamental Shrubs, *p.189*), but also bear well, even in cool climates. When trained and regularly pruned, their habit is more compact, and bearing improves markedly. There are many self-fertile cultivars available. Both hazelnuts and filberts grow well from seed; suckers can also be carefully uprooted and used for propagation.

WHEN TO PRUNE Late winter. When trees are bearing, this will coincide with pollen production from catkins; shaking the branches when pruning helps to pollinate the female flowers. Established trees are also "brutted" in summer.

TRAINING AND PRUNING Aim to form an open-centered bush on a clear stem of about 18in (45cm). Choose a young tree with three or four strong laterals at around this height. Prune the leader back to the topmost of these, as for an apple bush (*see p.108*), and shorten the selected laterals to 9in (22cm). Remove all other laterals. In the next two years, let 10–12 well-spaced shoots develop to form main branches, tip-pruning them if they are slow to branch. Remove any growth below the main branches.

On established trees, in late summer, partly break ("brut") long, vigorous shoots halfway along their length. Leave short, twiggy growth, since this usually carries the female flowers that will develop into nuts. The following winter, prune the broken ("brutted") shoots back to three or four buds. The year-on-year effect will be to build up spur systems, which will from time to time need reducing, with a saw or loppers, to a short stub on the main branch, from which new shoots should develop. As bushes age, also remove a worn-out branch or two where strong new growth exists to replace it.

BRUTTED HAZELNUT SHOOTS
Long, vigorous shoots often bear no female flowers, so will not bear nuts. Breaking them partially (see above) retains their foliage to give the plant vigor, which is then diverted into female flower production on shorter, spurlike shoots.

WALNUT *JUGLANS REGIA* (ZONES 6–9)

English walnuts may not bear in cool temperate regions unless summers are warm. Sites prone to late spring frosts should be avoided. Seedlings take 10 or more years to bear, and nut quality is unpredictable, so always choose a named cultivar, grafted onto black walnut (*Juglans nigra*) or the Californian black walnut (*J. hindsii*). Although commercial growers, particularly in California, develop open-centered walnut bushes (using suitable cultivars), a central-leader tree with a clear trunk of 4–6ft (1.2–2m) looks far better in a garden setting. Train as for an ornamental tree (*see p.69*).

MACADAMIA *MACADAMIA* SPP.

Macadamias are native to the Australian tropical rainforest, and although they will tolerate light frosts, they need a hot growing season and lots of rain. They are evergreen, with a dense, upright habit. Training should aim to produce a central-leader tree with a clear trunk of about 3ft (1m) and well spaced, spreading side branches. Young macadamias tend to produce leaves and shoots in whorls of three; if these develop, select one to form a main branch and cut the other two back to ½in (1cm); shoots from the buds on these stubs will develop into horizontal, flowering shoots. In South Africa growers repeatedly prune back the central leader of young trees at intervals of 16–20in (40–50cm) to produce tiers of horizontal branches. Established trees need minimal pruning.

MACADAMIA TREE
Branches develop naturally with narrow crotch angles and may split in high winds.

PISTACHIO *PISTACIA VERA*

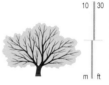

This deciduous tree needs hot summers and cool, frost-free winters to bear (zones 9–10). A sunny site is essential; lower branches die if shaded. It is much easier to train a grafted plant into a well-formed tree. Stake the leader carefully, maintaining it for at least 3ft (1m) before allowing the crown to branch and develop. Keep further pruning to a minimum. Cuts do not heal well or quickly, and pruning checks growth. To combat a straggly habit, growth may have to be thinned and branches shortened. (*See also* Dictionary of Ornamental Trees, *p.79*.)

ALMOND *PRUNUS DULCIS*

The almond is an attractive tree (*see* Dictionary of Ornamental Trees, *p.82*) that requires a Mediterranean-type climate to bear satisfactorily. To produce an easily maintained nut tree, choose a grafted cultivar and train as a bush tree or wall-train as a fan, just as for a peach or nectarine tree (*see p.134*). A suitable pollinating cultivar must be nearby.

For an established bush, pruning should be minimal; remove a little unproductive wood in late winter or early spring. Prune an established fan as for a peach fan (*see p.135*).

ORNAMENTAL SHRUBS

Attractive, well-shaped, healthy growth gives all shrubs greater ornamental value, in addition to flowering and fruiting displays that are enhanced by correct pruning at the right time

Many of the most successful low-maintenance plantings rely on carefully chosen shrubs whose well-shaped forms and healthy growth give pleasure all year. For these plants, light pruning to shape and the routine removal of dead, diseased, or damaged growth is the only pruning necessary to maintain handsome, vigorous specimens. However, for many popular shrubs, proper care and cultivation involves not only training and maintenance but also regular pruning that enhances ornamental characteristics such as flowering and fruiting. The aim of this pruning is to remove older, less productive wood in favor of that which will flower or fruit more profusely, while promoting healthy new growth for future displays – in effect, hastening and controlling the natural cycle of decay and renewal found in nature.

An enormous range of shrubs exists to fill any site or fulfill any requirement in the garden. They vary widely in size, vigor, and growth habit, and also in productive lifespan – always a factor to bear in mind when deciding whether to renovate a neglected or overgrown plant. Because the choice is so large, it should always be possible to select plants that not only are well suited to your climate and conditions but that will also fulfill your ornamental requirements and expectations within the available space. Unless being trained for some special effect, shrubs generally look best where their natural habit and vigor can be expressed fully. Careful choice and siting of shrubs will ensure that pruning enhances, rather than restricts, their growth.

EUPHORBIA CHARACIAS SUBSP. WULFENII
The long stems of this euphorbia grow in one year and flower in the next. It does not need pruning, but its appearance is greatly improved if the old, flowered stems are removed in favor of the new basal growth.

WALL-TRAINED FREMONTODENDRON
Special training and pruning techniques can be used to grow shrubs in a variety of ways. This meticulously wall-trained fremontodendron, frost-tender in colder climates, benefits from full sun, shelter, and reflected warmth, and it responds with a profusion of flowering growth.

BASIC TECHNIQUES

The routine pruning of a typical selection of garden shrubs entails cutting through stems of all sizes, from pinching young shoot tips to removing old, woody stems. A range of good-quality, well-maintained tools (*see p.16*) – a knife, sharp pruners, loppers, and a pruning saw – is essential to maximize the benefits of pruning.

As with all plants, primary pruning tasks include the removal, as soon as seen, of dead, diseased, and damaged growth, and of unwanted growth such as reverted shoots and suckers (*see* Routine tasks, *facing page*). Formative pruning not only gives a shrub a good start but may also be desirable throughout its life. In ideal conditions, shrubs usually develop a balanced, even shape. Many factors, however, can unbalance growth: disease, damage, or lopsidedness caused by a shaded planting position, competition from other plants, or a prevailing wind. Making well-positioned pruning cuts (and, if possible, removing the cause of the problem) is the key to restoring a balanced outline. Understanding flowering and fruiting habits, and how to maximize displays while maintaining health and vigor, gives an added dimension to the pruning of many shrubs. Pruning to enhance flowering or foliage effect should always respect the shrub's natural growth habit and, if possible, improve it.

TYPES OF CUT

As a general rule, where possible, remove unwanted growth while still young. However, pruning shrubs often involves cutting woody growth, and cuts should be made with as much care as when pruning trees, giving the shrub the best chance of rapid recovery. Pruning cuts should always be clean; torn and bruised tissue heals slowly and is more likely to allow harmful organisms to gain entry, which may endanger the whole plant. Also, cuts should always be as small as possible. Large wounds take longer to heal over, meanwhile remaining open to disease.

WHEN TO PRUNE

While formative and renovation pruning are usually best carried out while a shrub is dormant, the optimum time to prune an established shrub nearly always depends on its flowering habit. The age of the shoots on which flowering occurs is critical. Shrubs that produce flowers on the current season's shoots should be pruned *before* these develop, in late winter or early spring. Those that produce flowers on the previous season's growth, that is, on older shoots, are best pruned *after* flowering, giving new growth time to develop before overwintering and flowering in the following year.

POSITIONING THE CUT

Shrubs with buds that grow opposite one another should be cut squarely across the stem (*see above left*). Stems with an alternate arrangement of buds or shoots should be cut at an angle (*see above right*). When cutting to a replacement stem or shoot, cut squarely across the stem parallel with the direction of the new stem.

Pruning cuts should be made as close to the bud or shoot as possible without physically damaging it. If made too close, a bud may become desiccated and die, or a sideshoot might break off or

CUTTING TO OPPOSITE BUDS

On a shrub with opposite buds, cut squarely just above a pair of strong buds or shoots. If only one shoot is desired (for example, to form a central stem or an outward-facing branch), rub off the bud that is not facing in the desired direction of growth.

crack in windy conditions. But if the cut is made too far away, the resulting stub of stem without active buds will die back and become a site of infection. Sometimes the main stems of shrubs need to be cut near the base, where no buds are visible. However, the cut should stimulate dormant buds near the ground into life, and new shoots will emerge. If there is then a stub of wood left, it can be removed.

Always anticipate the kind of growth the shrub will make in response to the cut. As with all plants, hard pruning promotes stronger regrowth than light pruning. When correcting the shape of a shrub, cut back weak shoots hard and strong growth lightly. When shortening growth, it is particularly important to envisage the direction of shoot growth that will result from the position of your pruning cut, or the result will be a poorly shaped plant with crossing stems and a crowded center.

CUTTING TO AN ALTERNATE BUD

Select a healthy bud pointing in the direction in which you require a shoot to grow. From the side opposite the bud, cut at an angle to just above where the bud joins the stem. Do not angle the cut too steeply; this makes a larger wound that takes longer to heal.

PINCHING OUT SHOOT TIPS

Pinch out the shoot's soft growing tip to just above a leaf or pair of leaves

Soft shoot tips can be pinched out cleanly with finger and thumb. Removing the terminal bud of the shoot (see p.13) stimulates buds lower down the stem into growth, to produce a bushy, well-branched plant.

ROUTINE TASKS

Minor pruning tasks to correct common problems may become necessary from an early stage. Dead, diseased, and damaged growth and crossing stems (*see p.154*) should always be removed, as should reverted shoots and suckers on grafted plants, however much this appears to denude a young plant of growth. Always carry out routine tasks as soon as a problem is noticed.

DEADHEADING

Deadheading (*see right*) is not essential, but for some shrubs it can improve their appearance, stop them from self-seeding, and, by preventing them from expending energy on setting seed, stimulate further growth and flowering.

REVERSION

Variegated cultivars occasionally produce shoots bearing plain green foliage. This may be a response to stress or to heavy pruning. Variegated growth tends to be less vigorous since the leaves contain less chlorophyll (essential in energy production); the more vigorous green-leaved growth should be removed or it will dominate the plant.

SUCKERS

The natural habit of many shrubs is suckering; new growth from ground level increases the plant's size and spread, and replaces stems that grow old and die. If the plant is congested or overgrown, it is the older stems that should be removed, not this vigorous young growth (unless, as is sometimes possible, the plant is being trained with a single stem). However, some shrubs are grafted, and shoots (continued on p.154)

DEADHEADING FLOWERING SHRUBS

Spent flower clusters

Non-flowered shoot

SINGLE FLOWERS
On some shrubs, such as rhododendrons, new shoots develop from buds just under the flowers, so pinch out only the flower head, taking care not to damage any growth below.

FLOWER CLUSTERS *Use pruners on shrubs such as buddlejas and lilacs (Syringa) to shorten flowered shoots to buds or young sideshoots; these should be stimulated into flowering, either later in the season or the following year, depending on time of pruning.*

REMOVING REVERTED SHOOTS
Cut out any plain green shoots on variegated shrubs as they are noticed. If not removed, green-leaved shoots may quickly dominate the shrub, being more vigorous than variegated growth. Cut the entire reverted shoot back to its point of origin.

IDENTIFYING AND REMOVING SUCKERS

Broadly oval, mid-green leaves on desirable cultivar

Smaller, unevenly margined, pale green leaves on the sucker

Normal growth

Sucker

IDENTIFYING SUCKERS (LEFT) *A shoot from the top growth of a desirable cultivar of* Hamamelis mollis *is easily distinguished from a shoot that has been produced below the graft from the rootstock, the vigorous but seldom blooming* Hamamelis virginiana.

REMOVING SUCKERS (RIGHT) *Ideally, suckers should be rubbed off by hand while they are still young and soft. If they have thickened, however, pull them off sharply at their point of origin, either on the stem or on a carefully uncovered root. Try to remove all growth with a single tug; if fragments remain, nip them off with a sharp knife (see inset), without enlarging the wound.*

(*continued from p.153*) that emerge from below the graft union, either low on the trunk or from the roots, will be growing from the rootstock and not from the more desirable grafted plant (the scion). These must be removed if the usually weaker scion is not to be overwhelmed.

CROWDED AND CROSSING BRANCHES

Dense growth is desirable for barrier plantings of shrubs such as *Berberis*, and also for shrubs trained as hedges and topiary. However, for other plants, relieving congestion by removing a few stems or taking out a whole branch prevents the development of a dark, dank environment within a shrub that will encourage pests and diseases.

Do not let any shoots grow across and rub against other stems. Chafing damage provides a potential entry point for disease, and the plant may suffer structural problems when the stems develop and thicken (*see right*).

DEAD, DISEASED, AND DAMAGED GROWTH

If there is a clear demarcation between live and dead wood, cut to just above this line. If, however, there is no clear distinction between healthy and unhealthy tissue, cut into completely healthy wood, to a suitable bud or shoot. If the cut surface is discolored, cut further down until it is clean.

Jagged stem ends resulting from storm or other damage should be cut cleanly across to a bud or shoot. If damage is extensive, this might be the time to reshape or rejuvenate the shrub (*see* Renovation, *p.160*). Frost-damaged growth should not be removed until the risk of prolonged hard frost is over, because it provides some protection for the undamaged growth below.

CROSSING BRANCHES

This well-established hamamelis shows the dangers of allowing crossing branches to develop. Here, one branch is taking the weight of another, causing a split to develop on a main trunk. If the load-bearing branch breaks, the one resting on it is liable to break too, and the shrub will be badly damaged. Crossing branches should never be allowed to develop like this, but renovation (see p.160), or bracing or propping the load-bearing branch (see p.32), may help the plant to recover.

Branch crosses, touches, and weighs down on branch beneath

Severe split developing at branch crotch

REMOVING DEAD WOOD

Natural demarcation

Cut squarely across here

If the plant has formed a natural barrier to isolate dead wood (see p.11), it will continue to protect the rest of the plant; cut just above it to remove the bulk of the dead tissue.

FROST DAMAGE

Cut back to completely healthy growth

With this recent frost damage, there is no clear dividing line between affected and healthy growth. Cut well back to a bud, leaf, or shoot on completely healthy growth.

GROWING SHRUBS IN CONTAINERS

Many shrubs grow well in containers; in colder climates, container-grown tender shrubs can be brought under cover for the winter. As they grow, these plants will need repotting in spring until they are in the largest feasible container, after which they should be top-dressed. After a few years, however, they may appear to be lacking in vigor. Lift the shrub carefully from its container (*right*) to check that the root ball has not become congested. If it has, both the top-growth and root system must be pruned; reducing the amount of top-growth the roots must support will help the plant develop new fine feeder roots.

ROOT PRUNING A CONTAINER-GROWN SHRUB

1 *Using a hand fork, tease out a tightly packed root ball, working away as much of the old compost as possible without probing right into the center of the root system.*

2 *Prune coarse and damaged roots by up to two-thirds, and repot using fresh compost. Prune the shrub to reduce top growth overall by one-third.*

INITIAL TRAINING

Most shrubs are bought as young, partially trained plants from nurseries and garden centers (*see p.156*). They will have been propagated in a variety of ways. However, many gardeners propagate their own shrubs, most using simple vegetative methods such as taking cuttings and layering. It is never too early to start training the young plants in order to achieve strong, well-shaped, mature specimens.

CUTTINGS

Like seedlings, softwood and semimature cuttings tend to grow as single stems. Some branch naturally, while in others the apical bud is more strongly dominant, and the shoot must be pruned to encourage side buds to develop into shoots (*see below*).

A hardwood cutting should develop several stems from buds along the length of the cutting. A root cutting may also develop several stems from adventitious buds along the portion of root. If the shrub is to grow with a single, central stem and a conical form (as for *Abutilon vitifolium*), train the topmost shoot vertically, staking lightly with a split stake, and remove the other shoots, either by rubbing out as they emerge or by cutting back. If, however, a bushy, multistemmed form is desired, all well-placed, healthy shoots can be retained.

LAYERING

The stems of some shrubs root naturally where they touch the ground; others may be more deliberately "layered," by nicking through the bark of a stem, then anchoring it under the soil, encouraging it to root at this point. When the latter method is used, the shoot tip should be trained more or less vertically up a light stake so that the new plant develops with an upright main stem. But, with naturally layered stems, the young plant is likely to have an obliquely growing main stem. This may be correctable by angled planting and light staking. If not, cut to a low, upward-facing bud and train the new growth vertically.

GRAFTING

Shrubs that are difficult to propagate in other ways may be grafted. Young bud-grafted plants will grow away with a single stem; if a section of stem is grafted, multiple shoots may develop from its several buds. These plants can be treated exactly like cuttings. However, any developing buds or shoots below the graft point must be rubbed off as soon as they are noticed.

PRUNING VERY YOUNG SHRUBS

As growth develops, young plants may be lightly pruned to influence their future shape. Tip-pruning – either pinching out soft shoot tips, or cutting back long leading or lateral shoots by no more than one-third – can be used to encourage branching growth (*see below, center*) that will result in a bushy habit.

Do not leave recently pruned young plants in hot sun, for example, on a greenhouse bench; the previously shaded tender young bark may scorch.

In colder climates, do not prune plants that are outdoors after midsummer; the growth that is stimulated will not have time to mature fully and will be particularly vulnerable to cold damage when winter sets in.

DECIDUOUS CUTTINGS

The young Forsythia (below left) is growing vigorously upward as a single stem and may take some time to branch, which is ideal if a tall plant of upright habit is desired. However, if its growing tip had been removed early in the growing season, it would have developed as has the other young plant (below right): two vigorous sideshoots have grown, laying the foundations of a more branched, bushy habit. Because neither shoot has absolute dominance, other lower buds are also stimulated, promoting further basal growth.

EVERGREEN CUTTING

Evergreens like this Ceanothus are much more likely to branch naturally low down, and form a balanced, in this case conical, shape. Such plants rarely need pruning in their first year.

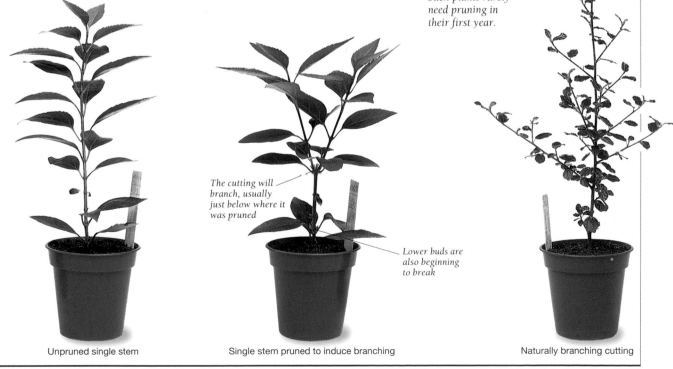

The cutting will branch, usually just below where it was pruned

Lower buds are also beginning to break

Unpruned single stem

Single stem pruned to induce branching

Naturally branching cutting

BUYING YOUNG SHRUBS

Young shrubs are increasingly sold as
container-grown specimens, though
bare-rooted and root-balled plants are
available. Choose plants that have
vigorous, healthy growth and, if
grafted, a strong, streamlined union
(*see right*). The root system should also
be large enough to support the top-
growth; an unbalanced root-to-shoot
ratio is one of the principal reasons for
poor growth after planting. Container-
grown shrubs are particularly likely to
have extensive top-growth compared to
their root system. Plants that have been
encouraged to flower heavily as a sales
feature should be avoided or deadheaded as soon as possible.

BARE-ROOTED AND ROOT-BALLED SHRUBS
These shrubs must only be planted in
the dormant season; autumn is best, in
order that the root system may become
at least partly established before the
next growing season. They should be
planted as soon as possible after
purchase. First, inspect the roots, and
cut any damaged portions cleanly
away. This should be done in the shade
and out of the wind to avoid drying out
fine, fibrous roots, which die very
swiftly when deprived of moisture.

CONTAINER-GROWN SHRUBS
Container-grown shrubs may be
planted at any time of the year.
However, make sure that the shrub has
really been grown in its container and

not just lifted and potted up for sale;
such plants should only be planted in
the dormant season.

Usually, good container-grown
plants should not require root pruning,
but if any roots are damaged, cut them
back. Light initial staking may also be
necessary. These plants are often raised
massed closely together, with pots
touching, and so may develop tall
vertical stems. When sold individually,
they lose their mutual support and the
stems sometimes flop outward.

PRUNING ON PLANTING
Do not buy plants that are generally
in poor condition (*see below right*).

A well-chosen, healthy young plant
(*see below left*) should need no pruning
except perhaps to pinch-prune or
shorten any overlong shoots to
encourage a balanced shape to develop,
as for any young plant (*see p.155*). If
there are one or two minor defects they
may be rectified on planting. Remove
any damaged or weak shoots or dead
tips, along with unnecessary stakes and
ties. Remove any flowered shoots to
direct energy into new growth rather
than seed formation. If the top-growth
seems too ample compared to the root
system (*see right*), reduce it by up to
50 percent. This can be done in two
ways: by shortening all stems, which
will result in a bushy habit, or by
cutting some stems to the base, to
encourage taller, more upright growth.

GRAFT UNION
*The union is the point
at which rootstock and
scion were joined*

GRAFTED SHRUBS
*Check grafted shrubs, such as this
Hamamelis, for a sound union; the scion
and rootstock should join smoothly,
without forming a kink in the stem.*

CORRECTING ROOT-TO-SHOOT RATIO

*Top-growth
is ample and
vigorous
compared to
small size of
root system*

*This plant will establish
more quickly if its top growth is reduced,
either by shortening all stems by half, or
by removing the two shoots on the left.*

SELECTING SHRUBS FOR PURCHASE

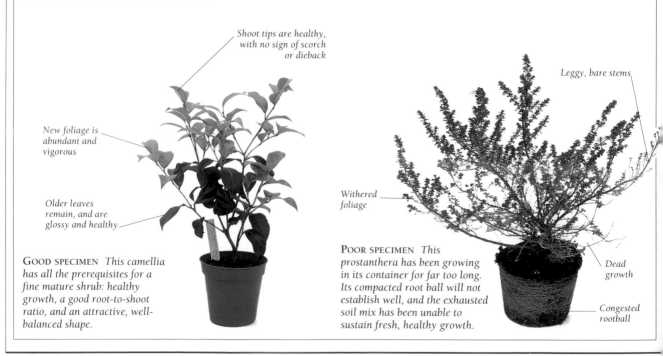

*Shoot tips are healthy,
with no sign of scorch
or dieback*

*New foliage is
abundant and
vigorous*

*Older leaves
remain, and are
glossy and healthy*

GOOD SPECIMEN *This camellia
has all the prerequisites for a
fine mature shrub: healthy
growth, a good root-to-shoot
ratio, and an attractive, well-
balanced shape.*

Leggy, bare stems

*Withered
foliage*

POOR SPECIMEN *This
prostanthera has been growing
in its container for far too long.
Its compacted root ball will not
establish well, and the exhausted
soil mix has been unable to
sustain fresh, healthy growth.*

*Dead
growth*

*Congested
rootball*

FORMATIVE PRUNING

As young shrubs grow, any routine tasks, such as the removal of dead, diseased, or damaged growth (*see pp.153–154*), should be dealt with as needed. Once shrubs have had a growing season in which to establish in their planting site and have become dormant, they may be pruned further to influence their future shape and the development of their ornamental features. On freestanding plants this could mean light corrective shaping, or pruning back hard to start developing a low framework, or tip-pruning to produce a dense, bushy habit. Shrubs that are being grown for special effects have special training needs: for wall training, stem and foliage effects, or training as a standard, *see pp.162–165*; for topiary, *p.48*; for hedging, *p.44*.

DECIDUOUS SHRUBS

Deciduous shrubs are much more likely to benefit from formative pruning than evergreens, which naturally tend to grow in an even, compact shape (*see below*). The pruning requirements of the shrub when mature should be anticipated when pruning young plants. It is important that shrubs that are to become permanent features of some stature (usually flowering on second-year or older wood, such as *Weigela* and *Philadelphus*) develop with an open center. Overcrowding will restrict airflow and light penetration. Remove any crowded or crossing stems or shorten them to strong buds or young shoots that face in directions where growth can be accommodated.

Many shrubs that flower on the current season's growth are cut back to a low framework each year, particularly in colder climates, and these shrubs (such as *Caryopteris*, *Buddleja davidii*, and deciduous *Ceanothus*) should be pruned hard right from the start to build up a base of strong, woody stems that will support vigorous new growth each year (*see also Hydrangea paniculata, p.202*). This framework is usually near ground level, but if extra height is desired, a taller framework can be developed by more moderate pruning.

EVERGREEN SHRUBS

The object of formative pruning of an evergreen shrub is to ensure a healthy plant and develop its symmetrical shape, or whatever other outline is required, with the minimum amount of pruning.

Start by cutting out any cold-damaged growth, as well as any badly positioned stems. Then remove weak and straggly stems, and lightly tip-prune, if necessary, any overlong stems to balance the shrub's outline.

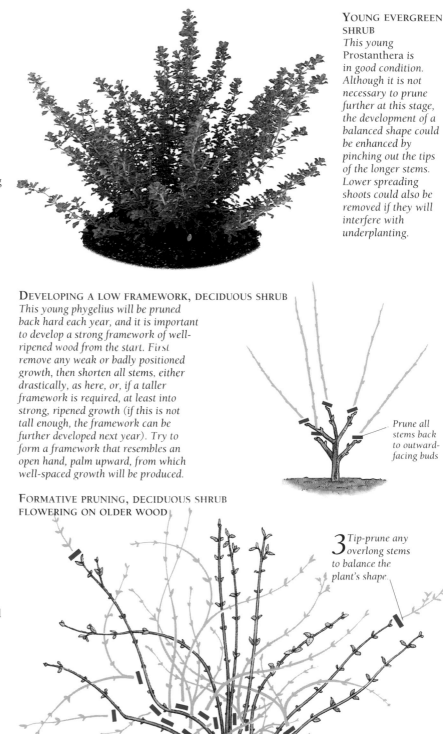

YOUNG EVERGREEN SHRUB
This young Prostanthera is in good condition. Although it is not necessary to prune further at this stage, the development of a balanced shape could be enhanced by pinching out the tips of the longer stems. Lower spreading shoots could also be removed if they will interfere with underplanting.

DEVELOPING A LOW FRAMEWORK, DECIDUOUS SHRUB
This young phygelius will be pruned back hard each year, and it is important to develop a strong framework of well-ripened wood from the start. First remove any weak or badly positioned growth, then shorten all stems, either drastically, as here, or, if a taller framework is required, at least into strong, ripened growth (if this is not tall enough, the framework can be further developed next year). Try to form a framework that resembles an open hand, palm upward, from which well-spaced growth will be produced.

Prune all stems back to outward-facing buds

FORMATIVE PRUNING, DECIDUOUS SHRUB FLOWERING ON OLDER WOOD

3 Tip-prune any overlong stems to balance the plant's shape.

2 Remove all growth that crosses the center of the plant, by cutting it back either to its point of origin or to a well-placed bud or sideshoot.

1 Remove all weak, spindly growth to its point of origin or to ground level.

Early pruning is invaluable in forming a well-shaped, uncluttered, healthy mature shrub. Remove unwanted stems while they are still relatively small in diameter and while the plant is young and its healing potential is at its greatest.

PRUNING ESTABLISHED SHRUBS

Without pruning, shrubs will deteriorate over the years; dead and congested growth will build up and encourage disease, and wayward growth will develop to result in a misshapen plant, perhaps prone to structural damage. Extensive renovation pruning (*see p.160*) can largely be avoided, however, if routine tasks (*see p.153*) are attended to promptly. These include the removal of dead, diseased, and damaged growth, as well as crossing stems, reverted shoots, and suckers.

SHRUBS WITH NO SPECIAL PRUNING NEEDS
Some shrubs, such as most daphnes, neither need nor will tolerate anything more than this minimal attention. Others, including many evergreens, need minimal attention but will tolerate harder pruning if necessary, for example to remove a branch that has grown across a path, or to renovate (*see p.160*). Some shrubs need minimal pruning when grown as "natural," freestanding specimens, but require extra pruning every year if being grown in special

ways. *Cornus alba*, for example, makes an attractive, branching shrub of some stature when allowed to develop with minimal pruning, but if being grown for the winter effect of its brightly colored young stems (*see* Special stem and foliage effects, *p.164*), it is pruned hard each year to create a shrub of quite different habit, with a mass of vigorous, upright, unbranched stems.

The time taken to reach overmaturity is also important. Many shrubs, such as most *Berberis*, grow and flower well with only minimal pruning for several years, but then reach a stage where they would be strongly reinvigorated by hard pruning. Others will reach a point where no amount of pruning can encourage them to make vigorous young growth; these plants have simply reached the end of their productive lives and should be replaced. Remember, too, that pruning cannot improve the growth of a plant that is not suited to the local climate and soil conditions.

However, in spite of all these qualifications, there are a great many

shrubs that benefit from regular pruning that is in addition to any routine attention. This regular pruning removes older wood in favor of new, vigorous growth, on which the best flowers and foliage are produced.

Although some general principles can be applied to broad shrub groupings (*see below and facing page*), most plants have needs relating to their individual growth habits (and individual specimens will not always conform to the general requirements for that plant). These individual requirements are given in the Dictionary of Ornamental Shrubs (*see pp.174–225*). When pruning, keep in mind that the way in which you position cuts will affect the future direction and vigor of growth. Always use the annual pruning of a shrub as an opportunity to restore, if necessary, a well-balanced framework and an open center.

WHEN TO PRUNE
While routine tasks such as the removal of damaged growth should be attended to as soon as the problem is noticed, the

PRUNING AN ESTABLISHED DECIDUOUS SHRUB THAT FLOWERS ON OLD WOOD

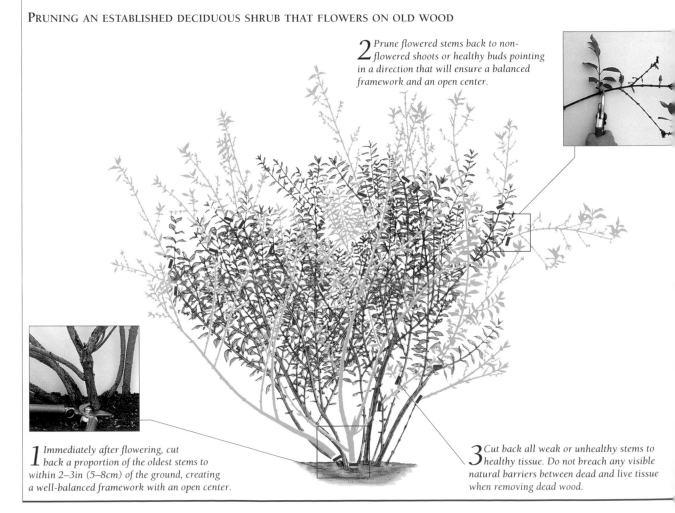

2 Prune flowered stems back to non-flowered shoots or healthy buds pointing in a direction that will ensure a balanced framework and an open center.

1 Immediately after flowering, cut back a proportion of the oldest stems to within 2–3in (5–8cm) of the ground, creating a well-balanced framework with an open center.

3 Cut back all weak or unhealthy stems to healthy tissue. Do not breach any visible natural barriers between dead and live tissue when removing dead wood.

timing of pruning intended to enhance ornamental features is critical. If you prune a shrub correctly but at the wrong time, you may remove all the wood that would have flowered in the following season.

Where shrubs flower on new wood (mostly deciduous species, but including such gray-leaved evergreens as lavender), pruning in early spring will direct extra energy into the remaining buds, so that fewer but better flowers are produced. On deciduous shrubs that flower on the previous year's wood, pruning directly after flowering will promote the growth of strong flowering shoots for the following year.

Evergreens should generally be pruned in spring, after any danger of severe cold has passed; pruning scars are then easily disguised by growing foliage. Delaying pruning until summer may be necessary for shrubs that bleed sap profusely. Flowering evergreens may also be pruned lightly after flowering, to remove older, flowered wood, to trim to shape, or in regions that experience heavy snow to thin dense growth on which snow and ice could accumulate, and cause breakage.

PRUNING AN ESTABLISHED SHRUB THAT FLOWERS ON NEW WOOD

Prune back all the stems to a low framework, taking care not to damage any promising new shoots at the base. This santolina has already been trimmed over once, in the autumn, to remove straggly growth that wind and the weight of snow might force to splay outward, causing damage in the center of the shrub.

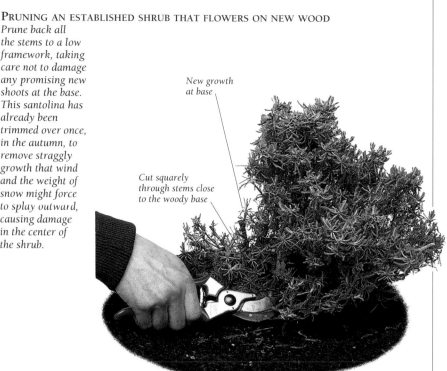

New growth at base

Cut squarely through stems close to the woody base

PRUNING AN ESTABLISHED EVERGREEN SHRUB

1 Immediately after flowering, deadhead all flowering stems, cutting back to healthy, outward-pointing buds or non-flowered shoots.

2 Prune out any diseased, damaged, or dead wood, or straggly growth, using sharp pruners, loppers, or a pruning saw.

3 Remove shoots to thin out congested areas and any badly positioned stems that spoil the balanced appearance of the shrub.

RENOVATION

Many neglected and overgrown shrubs, typically producing few flowers and with crowded growth cluttered by accumulated dead wood, will respond well to hard pruning. Provided that the plants are healthy, hard pruning is an effective way of giving them a new lease on life. There are also several popular shrubs that tend to outgrow their space despite regular pruning – lilac (*Syringa*) and Portugal laurel (*Prunus lusitānica*), for example – but they can be pruned hard to bring them back within bounds.

A surprisingly large number of plants will tolerate drastic renovation, in which all growth is cut back to near ground level or to a low framework of stumps (*see facing page*), and will respond rapidly with vigorous young growth. This is the most convenient way of dealing with shrubs, such as *Berberis*, that have dense, tangled habits and whose spiny stems are difficult to thin out. However, other shrubs are slow to make new growth and are better renovated in stages. Grafted plants require special care because the desirable grafted plant (the scion) will be lost if the cut is made below the graft union. Even if not all the scion is removed, severe pruning may stimulate the growth of vigorous shoots from the rootstock, and if these are not removed they will become dominant.

RENOVATION OR REPLACEMENT?

Deciding which plants to renovate very commonly forms part of a general garden renovation. It may be necessary to lift shrubs, either to remove perennial weeds and otherwise improve the soil, or to move them to preferred positions. This is best done at the beginning of the dormant season, and is usually much easier if the plants are cut back first.

It is not worth attempting to reinvigorate plants that are sickly. If a diseased shrub cannot be treated to bring it back to health, it is better to replace it entirely. It also has to be recognized that all plants have a finite life. Even plants that tolerate hard pruning when vigorous may not do so when old. It is thus a wise precaution to propagate from favorite plants so that you have replacements.

Although rare plants and particularly fine specimens are almost always worth salvaging, it is often more sensible to replace common, fast-growing shrubs than to attempt to rejuvenate them.

WHEN TO RENOVATE

Deciduous plants are normally best renovated in their dormant season, between autumn and early spring, and evergreens just as they are coming into growth in spring. The disadvantage of losing a season's display is offset by the more vigorous response that shrubs usually make in spring. However, pruning can also be carried out at the normal season for that shrub. Those that flower in spring and early summer, such as mock orange (*Philadelphus*), can be renovated immediately after flowering.

STAGED RENOVATION

If there is any doubt that a shrub will respond to drastic renovation, the operation should be carried out in two or three stages. Many evergreens, in particular, will often make only weak growth if all or most of the foliage is removed in a single pruning operation, but will respond well when the pruning is carried out over several years. Even plants that can tolerate heavy pruning in a single operation are sometimes worth renovating over two or three years simply for the sake of their appearance. The garden will continue to look reasonably well furnished if some growth is retained.

In the first year, remove up to half of the stems at ground level, or cut back to a framework of main branches, first removing dead, damaged, and diseased

REINVIGORATING A NEGLECTED OR OVERGROWN SHRUB (PHILADELPHUS)

1 *First remove completely any dead, damaged, or diseased stems, then cut back up to half of the oldest stems to within 2–3in (5–8cm) of ground level.*

2 *Shorten the remaining stems by half, cutting to a healthy bud or vigorous sideshoot, aiming to produce a compact but open-centered plant.*

3 *Remove or shorten to a bud any sideshoots from main stems that are growing across the center of the shrub, or crossing and rubbing against other stems.*

wood and crossing and rubbing stems. Then target the oldest, least productive growth. Any remaining old stems may be shortened by up to a half, the cut being made to a well-placed bud or vigorous shoot, usually one facing out from the center of the shrub. During the following growing season the shrub will probably produce a number of vigorous new shoots from below the main cuts, and these may need thinning. The following year, cut back half the remaining old stems to ground level or to framework branches, shortening the rest if appropriate; these last old stems should be cut back in the next year. Thereafter revert to the normal pruning appropriate to the individual shrub.

DRASTIC RENOVATION

Several, mainly deciduous, shrubs respond well when cut back drastically in a single operation. Unlike the regular hard pruning practiced for ornamental effects on shrubs (*see p.164*) and trees (*see p.36*), where the aim is continually to renew fresh, young growth, only strong stems should be carefully selected from the regrowth to redevelop a main framework of branches.

It is usually easier to cut back the main branches if side branches are removed first. The main branches should be cut straight across, usually 12–24in (30–60cm) above ground level and always above any graft union (this slightly swollen area is generally around 6in/15cm above ground level). To avoid a heavy branch tearing, cut first about 12in (30cm) above the desired final cut (*see Removing a branch, p.22*). Do not

STAGED RENOVATION (YEAR 2) OF AN EVERGREEN SHRUB (RHODODENDRON)

Main stem cut back in first year

1 As in the first year, remove some old main stems, cutting back half of those that remain to just above ground level or the graft union. Repeat in year 3 so that all main stems are renewed.

2 As new shoots emerge around previous main pruning cuts, thin out surplus growth to leave only two or three of the strongest and best-placed young stems.

treat cut surfaces with preservative or with wound paint; these now are not generally recommended (*see also p.22*). Shrubs should be well fed and mulched to ensure that they regrow vigorously.

Although at the time of pruning the buds from which regrowth will develop are not usually visible, a healthy shrub

will produce numerous shoots from the pruned stumps in the growing season following drastic pruning. In the next dormant season, thin these to leave two or three strong, well-placed shoots per stump. Remove any further surplus growth from the base and any suckers from the rootstock of grafted plants.

DRASTIC RENOVATION OF A DECIDUOUS SHRUB (SYRINGA)

1 When renovating a large shrub with heavy branches, reduce the top-growth before cutting back main stems.

2 Cut back all main stems, making straight cuts across branches to form a low framework 12–24in (30–60cm) above ground level.

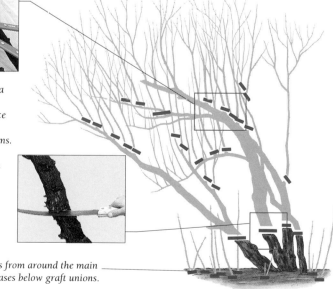

3 Remove all suckers from around the main stems or at their bases below graft unions.

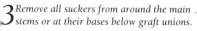

REGROWTH AFTER HARD PRUNING
Healthy and vigorous shrubs will produce many new shoots from the stumps in the first growing season after drastic pruning. In the following dormant season, thin these to two or three strong, well-placed stems per stump that will grow to form a new framework.

WALL TRAINING

There are, in addition to climbing plants, a great number of shrubs that can be grown successfully against walls and fences. This not only gives an alternative form of display for the shrub, but it can also increase the range of plants that may be grown. In a small garden, for example, training or tying in against a wall allows shrubs to be accommodated that might be too large grown as freestanding specimens. In colder regions, many shrubs that are not hardy enough to thrive in the open garden may be grown successfully close to a sunny, sheltered wall.

INFORMAL AND FORMAL WALL TRAINING

Some shrubs, including many of the slightly frost-tender plants, are best planted close to, but not right up against, the wall, and allowed to develop naturally, with long stems tied in loosely at strategic points. This informal support enhances the ornamental value of many shrubs with naturally open habits, often producing a cascading display of foliage and flowering shoots. Other shrubs lend themselves to more formal training and pruning, producing structured, fan-shaped or tiered arrangements of stems carrying blossoms or berries. To achieve a particular effect, however, account must be taken of the

WALL-TRAINED PYRACANTHA
The arching main stems of pyracanthas lend themselves to training in to a wall or fence, showing the berries off to maximum effect.

plant's natural habit, and the pruning that is used must relate to the shrub's specific needs. Individual pruning requirements are given in the Dictionary of Ornamental Shrubs (*see pp.174–225*).

Shrubs trained against walls or fences need similar supports to those used for climbing plants (*see p.246*). Plants will be in position for many years, and, unlike flexible-stemmed climbers, they

will be difficult to detach to allow for maintenance. It is important, therefore, to make sure that walls and fences are in good condition before training shrubs on them. Use durable materials to provide a sturdy means of attachment for the plant, such as trellises or a system of wires to which stems can be tied, keeping them slightly away from the wall to allow free air circulation.

INITIAL WALL TRAINING OF A SHRUB (CEANOTHUS)

1 *Removing any original stakes or ties, tie the plant in to the support, starting with main stems, then well-placed laterals.*

2 *Remove, or shorten to one or two buds, any stems growing directly outward or inward toward the wall that cannot be tied in.*

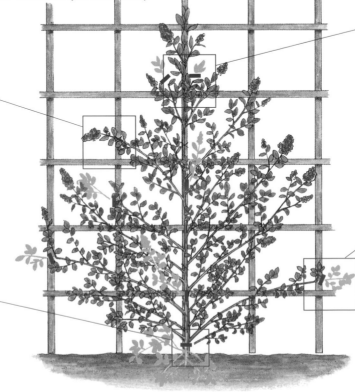

3 *Pinch out the tips of young forward-growing shoots to encourage sideways branching.*

4 *Shorten the longest laterals by a few buds particularly where growth is sparse, to stimulate branching and balanced coverage.*

PRUNING ON PLANTING

Plant at least 12in (30cm) from the base of the wall, avoiding the dry rainshadow area of soil. If the wall is old, it may have shed lime-rich mortar, making the site unsuitable for acid-loving plants. If planting a bare-root or balled-and-burlapped shrub, position the plant so that the roots can be spread to grow away from the wall. With a container-grown shrub, rotate it until you find the position where as much well-placed growth as possible can be tied in.

Initial pruning depends on the shrub's requirements and the desired effect. To make an informal fan of an open shrub such as *Ribes speciosum*, little pruning may be required other than the removal of weak or badly placed stems before spacing out remaining stems and tying them in. For a more formal fan of *Prunus triloba* 'Multiplex', for example, the ideal is to start with three to five strong stems radiating evenly from a main stem. Single-stemmed specimens of suitable plants should be cut back hard on planting to stimulate the growth of several stems that can be tied in to trellises, or to stakes attached obliquely to wires. It is also possible to train some single-stemmed shrubs in an espalier or palmette form, with tiered branches extending horizontally or obliquely on each side of a vertical main stem.

ESTABLISHED WALL SHRUBS

Although individual shrubs will be pruned in different ways at maturity, some requirements are common to all wall-grown plants. Tie in new shoots promptly and check all ties regularly, loosening them before they become tight. Remove or shorten shoots growing into or away from the wall that cannot be trained in. Tie in laterals to fill gaps, stimulating growth by pruning if necessary. Where the form allows (as with a fan) aim gradually to replace old wood with vigorous new stems. Further pruning, perhaps to maintain close, formal coverage of the wall or to enhance flowering, may be possible or desirable (*see* Dictionary of Ornamental Shrubs, *pp.174–225*). Some shrubs, including *Chaenomeles* and *Pyracantha*, can be spur-pruned as for apples and pears (*see* Apples, *p.105*) to give a particularly dense display.

Ribes
sanguineum

SHRUBS SUITABLE
FOR WALL TRAINING

BUDDLEJA CRISPA, B. FALLOWIANA,
    B. MADAGASCARIENSIS
CEANOTHUS (evergreen species)
CESTRUM ELEGANS
CHAENOMELES
CHIMONANTHUS PRAECOX
COTONEASTER HORIZONTALIS
CYTISUS BATTANDIERI
FORSYTHIA SUSPENSA
FREMONTODENDRON
FUCHSIA ARBORESCENS
PIPTANTHUS NEPALENSIS
PRUNUS MUME, P. TRILOBA 'MULTIPLEX'
PYRACANTHA
RIBES SANGUINEUM, R. SPECIOSUM
VITEX AGNUS-CASTUS, V. NEGUNDO

PRUNING AN ESTABLISHED WALL-TRAINED SHRUB (CEANOTHUS)

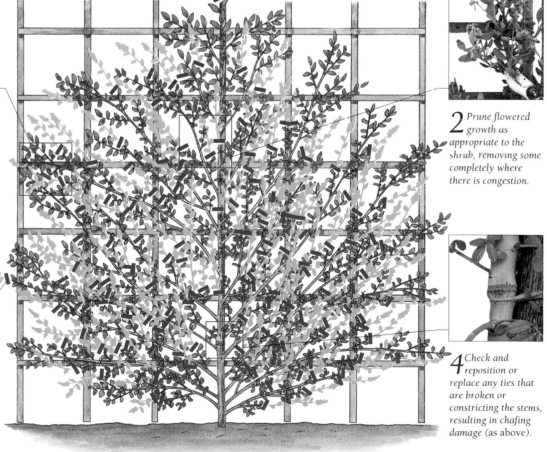

1 Tie in new growth where possible (as shrubs mature, older, less productive framework stems may be removed to make way for younger growth). Shorten weak shoots (above) to stimulate stronger growth.

2 Prune flowered growth as appropriate to the shrub, removing some completely where there is congestion.

3 Shorten stems where the shrub is reaching the limits of its allotted space.

4 Check and reposition or replace any ties that are broken or constricting the stems, resulting in chafing damage (as above).

SPECIAL STEM AND FOLIAGE EFFECTS

A number of shrubs and trees, for example, willows and hazels, have traditionally been regularly pruned hard for the practical purpose of obtaining a renewable supply of strong but pliable young stems for use in fencing and weaving. Coppicing, in which growth is regularly cut back to near ground level, and pollarding, cutting to the head of a single stem, are traditional techniques of woodland management that can be adapted to produce special ornamental effects in some trees (*see p.36*) and shrubs. Regular hard pruning, either to near ground level (as with the *Cornus, below left*) or to a low head or frame-work (as with the *Eucalyptus, below right*), can be used to renew young stems that are more colorful and decorative than older wood, as with willows (*Salix*). It may also perpetuate attractive juvenile foliage or induce extra-large leaves (as with the *Cotinus, above right*).

Only use shrubs for which regular hard pruning is recommended (*see Dictionary of Ornamental Shrubs, pp.174–225*). To produce a display from ground level, cut back hard each year while the shrub is young, so that a strong woody base is formed. If a taller plant is required, a clear stem or several clear stems can be developed as for a standard (*see facing page*) and, at the desired height, a "head" or a stubby framework of older growth may be developed. Once the base or framework is established, young growth may be cut back to it at intervals of between one and five years, depending on the plant. Many shrubs that may be pruned hard flower on old wood, so if the plant is cut back annually, the floral display will be lost; the stem or foliage effect is usually more than adequate compensation. However, the young growth of other plants, such as *Salix irrorata*, maintains its ornamental value for several years, allowing it to mature and flower before being pruned again. Alternatively, only one in two or three stems can be cut back each year, resulting in a mixture of growth of different ages.

COTINUS PRUNED FOR FOLIAGE EFFECT
Cultivars of Cotinus coggygria *and* C. obovatus *with purple foliage produce larger leaves when pruned hard, making their vivid orange-red autumn color particularly striking.*

SUITABLE SHRUBS
BERBERIS Several, such as *B. dictyophylla,* have attractive young stems with a white or purplish bloom.
CORNUS Red, yellow, or bright green young stem colors; the red stems of *C. alba* 'Sibirica' are particularly vivid.
COTINUS Handsome foliage (*see above*).
PHILADELPHUS The yellow foliage of *P. coronarius* 'Aureus' is enhanced.
RUBUS White young stems of *R. thibetanus* are attractive in winter.
SALIX Strong young stem colors, some, as on *S. irrorata,* with attractive bloom.
SAMBUCUS Leaves are more finely cut and brightly colored in, for example, *S. racemosa* 'Plumosa Aurea'.

CORNUS PRUNED FOR STEM EFFECT
In early spring, just before growth begins, cut all shoots down to within 2–3in (5–8cm) of ground level with sharp pruners or loppers (here on Cornus stolonifera *'Flaviramea').*

EUCALYPTUS, JUVENILE GROWTH
Many Eucalyptus (*see Dictionary of Ornamental Trees, p.64*) *make attractive shrubs if regularly pruned back hard.*

TRAINING SHRUBS AS STANDARDS

Growing a shrub as a standard on a clear stem brings its decorative features up to eye level and often gives it a formal effect. Such shrubs are popular container plants, or are used to give height to a small border while allowing underplanting. Only certain plants are suitable (see Dictionary of Ornamental Shrubs, pp.174–225), although shrubs that cannot be trained in this way from the start are sometimes top-grafted onto the tall stem of a stock plant, giving the same effect. The head of both trained and grafted standards is developed and maintained in exactly the same way.

Top-grafting is a skilled job usually carried out in the plant nursery, and grafted standards are usually bought ready-formed. However, for other plants a leading shoot can be trained up from an early age to form a clear stem, following exactly the same principles as for an ornamental tree (see p.28).

Staking will be necessary, sometimes permanently. At first, a bamboo stake will suffice; a mature standard needing support must have a wooden stake that reaches a point just below where the head branches. Use spacers (see p.23) to keep the stake clear of the stem.

TRAINING TO FORM A CLEAR STEM

Select a strong shoot as the leader (see below) and stake it to ensure straight, vertical growth. Just as for a tree, the central stem should be cleared in stages, first shortening, then removing laterals, so that some foliage is always retained. This will allow the plant to manufacture food that will help to build a strong central stem. Once the leader has reached the desired height, generally 3–5½ft (1–1.7m), allow three more sets of buds to develop above this height before pinching out the terminal bud. Removing the shoot's growing tip will encourage the growth of shoots from the lateral buds below that will form the main framework branches of the head.

DEVELOPING AND PRUNING THE HEAD

After the first growing season, or if a newly grafted shrub has been purchased, shorten laterals by about half. The aim when pruning subsequent growth should be to build up a dense, well-balanced head, by cutting to well-positioned buds and pruning weak shoots harder to stimulate stronger growth where necessary. Remove any badly placed shoots (although some crossing growth is unavoidable) and any growth from the clear stem or at the base of the plant. This is particularly important on top-grafted plants, when such growth will be from the more vigorous rootstock. Never remove too much growth from the head of such grafted plants at any one time because this could encourage the rootstock to sprout more vigorously.

As for any shrub, cut out any weak, dead, or diseased stems as seen. Further pruning should be undertaken at the same season and broadly in the same manner as if the shrub had been grown as a bush, if necessary pruning harder to maintain a neat and balanced head.

STANDARD PYRACANTHA

INITIAL TRAINING AND PRUNING

1 Remove any competing leaders or strong, well-developed laterals to concentrate growth into a single, vertical leading shoot.

2 Shorten weaker laterals, removing them in the following year so that the portion temporarily retained feeds and builds a strong main stem.

FORMING A BUSHY HEAD

Leader has been pinched out just above desired height of clear stem

1 As laterals are allowed to develop, tip-prune the young shoots to encourage a compact, branching habit.

2 Pinch out any shoots that grow on the clear stem. Single leaves may be left to nourish the plant; they will be shed naturally as the plant matures.

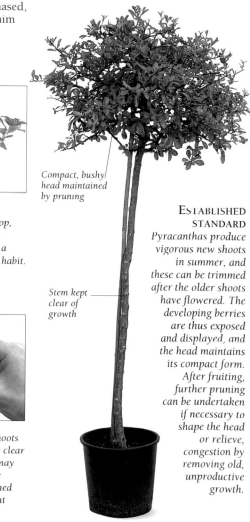

Compact, bushy head maintained by pruning

Stem kept clear of growth

ESTABLISHED STANDARD
Pyracanthas produce vigorous new shoots in summer, and these can be trimmed after the older shoots have flowered. The developing berries are thus exposed and displayed, and the head maintains its compact form. After fruiting, further pruning can be undertaken if necessary to shape the head or relieve, congestion by removing old, unproductive growth.

BAMBOOS AND GRASSES

Bamboos, grasses, rushes, and sedges cannot be trained, nor can pruning generally be used to form the shape of the plant or restrict height and spread. When pruning cuts are necessary, individual leaf-blades and canes are always removed at or close to the base, and never shortened; this ruins the plants' appearance. The chief value of these plants in the garden lies in their informal, upright, or arching habit.

BAMBOOS

As a general rule, bamboos – with the exception of dwarf species – do not need much in the way of pruning. In spring, any broken, badly cold-damaged, or discolored canes can be removed at the base. Loppers or a saw, and heavy protective clothing, are essential.

If a clump has become too dense and overbearing for its position, it can be thinned in spring or late summer (*see below left*) to let air and light into the center. Thinning also displays well those species that have colored stems, or those in which the young canes are the most attractive. A very few bamboos will flower once the canes are several years old; beware of removing them too early. To restrict the spread of bamboos, however, an actual physical barrier (*see below right*) is necessary to contain the invasive roots. It is particularly important to install this type of barrier if growing a line of bamboos as a hedge or screen, since the extent of the planting can thus be strictly contained.

Most bamboos can be renovated by cutting all canes to the ground.

DWARF BAMBOOS
Unlike full-sized species, dwarf bamboos respond well to the same treatment as grasses – that is, clipping to within

PRUNING GRASSES *Shear the clump close to the ground, then pick out any debris to let light and air into the base of the plant. Many species have razor-sharp leaves, so always wear thick gloves.*

6in (15cm) of the ground each spring to encourage new growth with fresh young foliage. Pruners will probably be needed to cut the tough stems.

GRASSES, RUSHES, AND SEDGES

These plants benefit from annual pruning, removing weather-buffeted old foliage and flower stems in favor of fresh, vigorous new growth. Deadhead annual grasses to prevent self-seeding, but leave the fading flower heads of perennial species for winter display. As these die back or are broken by winter winds, they can be trimmed to neaten the plant. In spring, cut the plant back to just above the ground. This work is best done with shears, although a scythe can be used on large clumps, providing you are experienced in using one safely. When

growing species that are not fully hardy in colder climates, leave this pruning until mid- to late spring so that the dead plant matter protects the new growth from any late frosts. When pruning, however, be careful not to damage the soft tips of young growth. Make a first shear 12in (30cm) from the ground and then clear away the shorn material, so that you can see into the heart of the plant clearly when making the final cuts.

To restrict spread, grasses are usually lifted and divided in spring when they exceed their allotted space. The split-off pieces can be used for propagation. Tufted grasses that build up from a central crown are the least invasive.

Cut grasses for drying while the inflorescences are still furled up, then let them gradually open and dry in a cool, well-aired room.

THINNING ESTABLISHED CLUMPS OF BAMBOO

BEFORE THINNING *Wearing heavy gloves and using loppers, first remove dead and damaged canes, then cut out the oldest ones at the base until the desired effect is achieved.*

AFTER THINNING *Without damaging new shoots, clear away debris at the base to relieve congestion further, let in light and air, and allow young canes to grow unchecked.*

RESTRICTING THE SPREAD OF BAMBOO

Dig a trench around the clump, deeper than the main body of the root system, chopping through and removing peripheral roots. Insert a barrier of, for example, slates or rigid plasti

PINCH-PRUNING

Sometimes known as "finger-and-thumb pruning," pinch-pruning is a technique that is occasionally used on a wide range of plants to produce bushy growth by nipping out soft shoot tips. However, when repeatedly applied to suitable plants, the technique can be used, particularly when combined with training on stakes or wire frames, to produce many decorative shapes. Some plants are used for flowering displays, others for foliage effect. With flowering plants, the repeated pinching effectively delays flowering, because the shoot never has time to form a flower bud at its tip; instead, energy is diverted into producing sideshoots. When pinching ceases (usually about two months before flowering is desired), the "last" set of shoots, because they all started into growth at the same time, all flower at the same time, giving a spectacular display. The plants that are used fall into the category known as subshrubs: short-lived plants – such as fuchsias, coleus (*Solenostemon*), and certain types of chrysanthemum – that become woody at the base with herbaceous top-growth. In colder climates many pinch-pruned plants are grown and displayed in greenhouses and conservatories, although they may be brought out for the summer months.

CHARM CHRYSANTHEMUM
For a labor-saving "pinch-pruned" effect, use this group of chrysanthemums, which grow naturally as even mounds. They need no pruning except to pinch back wayward shoots.

FUCHSIA FAN
Fuchsias make delightful standards and pillars, but can also have their shoots spread out and tied in to a framework of stakes to make a two-dimensional fan display (*see p.173*). Cascade chrysanthemums and coleus also make attractive fans with a more solid effect.

COLEUS STANDARD
Coleus, like fuchsias, are often seen as standards (*see p.169*), with clear stems and dense heads created by regular pinch-pruning. *Pelargonium, Heliotropium, Abutilon* x *hybridum* and *A. megapotamicum, Felicia, Lantana,* and *Argyranthemum* will also make standards of varying heights and sizes.

CHRYSANTHEMUM SPHERE
Cascade chrysanthemums (*see above right*) grow vigorously, and three or four plants will cover a large wire balloon frame. Growth is tied in wherever there is space to be filled, and surplus shoots pinched, to form impressive flowering spheres (*see p.172*). Using stakes and wire netting of various gauges, frames can be made in different shapes and carefully covered with growth to create floral "sculptures."

HELICHRYSUM POODLE
Small-leaved plants give a neat outline for this novel variation on the standard. Cascade chrysanthemums, with their fine foliage, give good results, while foliage helichrysums create a quick "topiary" effect. The leading shoot is trained up a stake, and sideshoots are either pinch-pruned regularly to encourage bushing out to a ball shape, or pinched out to create the "waists" between the balls.

CASCADE CHRYSANTHEMUM
This is a name for a special group of cultivars with flexible stems, finely cut foliage, and small but profuse flower heads. The plants need support, and are readily trained on stakes and wire; they can easily be persuaded to grow down a stake (*as above*) and pinch-pruned to form, viewed from the front, a "cascade" of flowers (*see p.170*).

GERANIUM PILLAR
Three plants grown up central stakes, regularly pinched, will make an impressive pillar (*see p.171*). Geranium (*Pelargonium*) flowers do not last as long as those of cascade chrysanthemums, which can also be used. More flowers will form if flower clusters are picked off as they fade.

ARGYRANTHEMUM CONE
Most plants on which pinch-pruning is used lend themselves to forming a natural, conical shape (*see p.171*). As for a pillar, three plants grown together will produce more impressive results than one, and the more abundant growth makes it easier to pinch selectively to form a symmetrical shape.

BASIC TECHNIQUES

Pinch-pruning will be familiar to anyone who has grown, for example, fuchsias and chrysanthemums, where the technique known as "stopping" is commonly applied to young plants. It is also used by chrysanthemum exhibitors to obtain top-quality blooms at a desired time (*see below*). To achieve a pinch-pruned display, however, special care and patience are needed. Pinching, though in itself a simple technique, must be repeated at frequent and regular intervals throughout the growing season. No tools are usually required, although on plants with hairy stems, such as helichrysums, a pruning knife can be used to make neater cuts.

CARE AND CULTIVATION

In general, always choose named cultivars that are bred for their vigor and flowering performance, such as *Fuchsia* 'Swingtime', or for attractive leaf color, such as the coleus *Solenostemon* 'Pineapple Beauty' or *Helichrysum petiolare* 'Limelight'. Always use plants grown from cuttings to obtain named cultivars and, in the case of coleus (grown only for its leaves), to obtain plants that are more shy to flower than seedlings. Pot young plants on regularly, from 3in (7cm) to 5in (12cm) and then into at least 9in (22cm) pots to give the mature plant stability. Do not pinch-prune a week or so before or after potting to enable root systems to reestablish well.

Plants must be healthy in order to respond well to this technique. Site plants growing under glass in a well-lit, well-ventilated place; the dense growth is vulnerable to mildew in a stagnant atmosphere. Pick off discolored leaves as seen. Feed young plants with a fertilizer high in nitrogen to stimulate growth. When pinching stops, switch to a high-phosphorous feed to stimulate flower development or, in coleus, to allow the leaf color to develop fully. Do not feed flowering plants while they are overwintering.

TRAINING FRAMES AND SUPPORTS

Bamboo stakes, wire and wire netting, both large- and small-gauge, and soft twine or raffia for tying in young stems are the most commonly used materials for frames and supports. They can be used to create many variations on the shapes described on the following pages. The head of a pinch-pruned standard needs no frame, but is formed entirely by bushy growth, pinch-pruned to create and maintain an even shape. However, no subshrub can, in one season, produce a stem sturdy enough to support the head, so staking is required.

PINCH-PRUNING

Removing the shoot tip breaks its apical dominance (see p.13); side buds, often latent in leaf axils, are stimulated into activity and develop into shoots. If these in turn have their tips pinched out, and so on, the effect is a proliferation of growth. When applied regularly to entire plants, pinch-pruning can be used to form and maintain densely growing, compact, and, with training, decorative shapes.

Pinching stimulates shoots from the top buds and further down the stem

1 *With finger and thumb, pinch out the tip of the shoot just above an opened leaf. Remove only the very tip to stimulate the maximum number of buds into producing sideshoots.*

2 *Side buds will break and develop into shoots. When these have developed two to four leaves (or two pairs), repeat the process.*

3 *Further shoots will break from the original stem as well as from the sideshoots. The plant gets progressively bushier. It will not flower until you stop pinching and let shoots develop normally; shoots usually need 8–12 weeks of unchecked growth before producing a terminal flowering bud.*

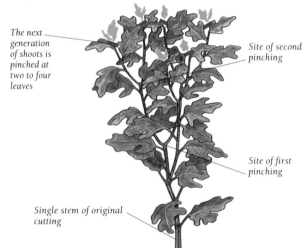

The next generation of shoots is pinched at two to four leaves

Site of second pinching

Site of first pinching

Single stem of original cutting

SHOW CHRYSANTHEMUM BLOOMS

To obtain flowers of this quality, growers pinch-prune young plants, then allow shoots to develop, disbudding as buds form. For single blooms, all side buds are removed; for spray chrysanthemums, the strong central bud is pinched out so that side buds develop evenly.

PINCH-PRUNED STANDARD

Many subshrubs can be trained as standards, including those that do not naturally tend to form one single stem. Coleus (*see below*) are very easily trained, and cascade chrysanthemums and fuchsias are also popular; with the latter, young plants that have their leaves arranged in whorls of three, rather than in pairs, should always be used if possible, since they give much better, bushier results. More interest can be gained from experimenting with plants in addition to those mentioned on these pages. However, check examples before attempting to imitate them; some of the more unusual standards seen, such as ivy-leaved geraniums, may have not been trained, but top-grafted.

The height of the clear stem and head will vary according to the plant used and, to a degree, on personal preference; the most pleasing appearance, in general, results if the depth of the head occupies one-third to half of the total height. The density of the head will also vary with the intervals at which growth is pinched, and also with the plant's size of leaf compared to its internodal distance; a vigorous coleus cultivar, with large, closely spaced leaves, can be used to form a solid "lollipop" head, but a heliotrope will have a much looser, less formal head of growth.

In the early stages of training, growth is restricted to one single stem that will grow strongly upward. If it breaks, fails, or (rarely) develops a flower bud, before the desired height has been achieved, pinch or cut back to a healthy leaf and train in the resulting new shoot (there will be an unavoidable slight kink in the stem). Once the desired height is reached, pinch-pruning is used to encourage growth at the top of the stem to bush out, forming the head.

STAGE 1

Pot a vigorous, single-stemmed cutting into a 10in (25cm) pot, inserting a stake, and tie the young stem in vertically with soft twine or raffia, taking care not to damage either the stem or the leaves. Feed well, but do not remove any growth until the plant has had a week or so to reestablish.

STAGE 2

Until the desired height is reached, pinch out all sideshoots that develop, but retain the large leaves from whose axils they sprang. This foliage will nourish the plant and thicken the stem. Keep tying in the main stem at regular intervals as it grows upward.

STAGE 3

When the leader is at least 8in (20cm) taller than the desired height of clear stem, pinch out the shoot tip.

FINISHED STANDARD

STAGE 4

At the head of the plant, pinch-prune all new shoots when they have two to four leaves, until a bushy head is formed. Pinch out any shoots that develop on the main stem.

On flowering plants, stop pinching 8–12 weeks before flowers are desired. Foliage plants such as this coleus can continue to be pinched to maintain a neat shape. When plants start to deteriorate, use them to provide cuttings for next year's displays.

Leaves have been shed naturally from main stem; if not, they may be picked off carefully

CHRYSANTHEMUM CASCADE

Only chrysanthemums described as cascading types are suitable for cascade training. Despite their name, they will grow vertically if not trained down a stake. A raised shelf, about 5ft (1.5m) high, is needed to train the plant; well-grown and trained cascades can be 6ft (2m) long. The entire training process takes almost a year, ending with a flowering display that lasts for several weeks in late autumn. It is common practice then to overwinter the plants, taking cuttings from them in late winter to start again.

Start with cuttings taken in late winter, or very young, single-stemmed purchased plants. In colder climates, protection under glass will be needed to propagate and begin training the plants. They can be brought outdoors as soon as the possibility of late frost has passed. Initially, the leading shoot of the young plant should be trained straight upward. Pinch out the tips of any sideshoots to start encouraging the effect of a bushy column. At 12 weeks old, downward training, at an angle of about 45°, begins (*see below*). At this stage, the plants are now put into their final, 10in (25cm) pots, since repotting will be impossible once the stakes are in position and the plants placed on the shelf. The leading shoot is trained downward; if by any chance it breaks, cut it cleanly back to a leaf and train in the shoot that grows from the axillary bud as the new leader. Pinch-prune all other growth throughout summer until early autumn, four weeks before flowers are required. When pinching for the last time, pinch the main stem once to halt downward growth. Once pruning stops, the shoots will grow, develop flower buds, and flower. Though they will survive outdoors, cascades are usually displayed in a well-ventilated greenhouse or conservatory, sheltered from bad weather that might spoil the flowers.

STAGE 1, LATE SPRING

Plant the 12-week-old rooted cutting in a 10in (25cm) pot, forming a soil-mix slope so that the plant lies at a 30° angle to the horizontal. Add more soil and firm it around the root ball, watering in well. Planted like this, the main stem will be easier to train downward.

Keep plant tied to its original stake, otherwise it will try to grow vertically

STAGE 2, FOUR WEEKS LATER

Stake rests on pot, with its tip propped on floor

1 *Insert a short, sturdy, vertical stake in the center of the pot. Lean an 8ft (2.5m) stake from the floor against the pot, and lash it to the vertical stake to form a firm, downward-pointing support at an angle of about 45°.*

2 *Untie the main shoot from its original stake and lower and tie it in to the new one. Carefully tie in at the base, then the tip, then the middle.*

STAGE 3: SUMMER TO MIDAUTUMN

Every time two leaves on a new shoot or sideshoot have fully unfurled, pinch out the shoot's growing tip between finger and thumb. Continue to tie in the leading shoot; never pinch it out.

Scar of previous pinching

STAGE 4, MIDAUTUMN

Four weeks before flowers are desired, pinch out the leading shoot once, then stop pinching altogether to let flower buds develop. Remove the stakes and move the plant to its display site.

FINISHED CASCADE

The display should last for several weeks in a sheltered, well-ventilated environment. The plant will benefit from a high-phosphorous fertilizer and generous watering as required. Water early in the day.

PILLARS AND CONES

Geraniums, fuchsias, and even naturally spreading plants such as *Helichrysum petiolare* can be trained upright and pinch-pruned to form dense cones and pillars that, with careful cultivation, can last for several years. While a single well-pinched plant will make a small, solid cone in a single season, three plants will result in a 4–5ft (1.2–1.5m) display. A pillar of this height will need a little more attention to keep the sides vertical, and may need pinch-pruning over two growing seasons in order to obtain the necessary density of foliage at the top. In colder climates, plants can be moved outside after the danger of frost has passed, either onto a patio or planted out as summer bedding. The plants can then be brought back under glass to overwinter. In spring, trimming and pinching is resumed as new growth begins.

STAGE 1, EARLY SPRING

Starting with rooted cuttings or single-stemmed young plants, tie the leading shoot in vertically and let sideshoots develop.

Spreading helichrysum stems must be drawn up carefully

STAGE 2, SIX TO EIGHT WEEKS LATER

1 *Plant three young plants in their permanent 9in (22cm) pot and retie each to a new stake.*

2 *Pinch or cut back sideshoots to a bud or leaf, so that none extends beyond the width of the pot.*

STAGE 3: THROUGHOUT SUMMER

1 *To produce a cone, tie the stakes together to form a "wigwam." Keep tying in the leading shoots. If a leader breaks, choose a strong shoot below and tie that in. If desired, add extra height by sliding in longer stakes or, for a cone, one long, central stake.*

2 *Pinch all shoots back every week, developing a conical shape, or to a columnar outline for a pillar. Pillars must be pinched more often (every two or three days) on the top half to make the plant as bushy in the upper regions as it is at the base.*

Shoots on this side have been pinched

Shoots on this side are yet to be pinched

STAGE 4

Leaders now tied in to one central stake

When the plants reach the desired height and shape, pinch out the leaders. Then stop pinching flowering plants altogether, except to remove any vertical shoots that grow at the top, to allow flowering shoots to develop all over the plants.

FINISHED CONE

This helichrysum cone has been left to grow out for an informal display, and will flower. However, since helichrysum foliage is of more ornamental value than its flowers, the cone may be pinched further, or trimmed with shears, for a "topiary" effect.

Leaves at base that discolor should be picked off

Pot has been placed in a 12in (30cm) clay pot for display and stability

CHRYSANTHEMUM SPHERE

Cascade chrysanthemums, which make plenty of growth, are the subshrubs most commonly used to cover large wire balloon frames, usually seen with climbing plants trained around them (*see p.246*). When in full flower a large sphere can be 6ft (2m) in diameter.

A big pot is needed to give stability. It is best to erect the frame around the young plants. A frame can be made in many ways: one of the easiest is made from large-mesh chicken wire, with squares of about 7in (20cm). Cut eight strips from the wire, each one square across and six squares long, leaving prongs of wire at each end so that the strip forms a "ladder." The lower prongs can be pressed into the soil around the edge of the pot, and the ladders bent over to form the globe. The upper prongs can be twisted around each other and around sturdy central bamboo stakes.

The most difficult part of the operation is drawing the plants' stems across to cover the framework evenly; they are fleshy and snap very easily. While the main stems are trained upward, their sideshoots are pinched to produce more and more lateral growth, which can be tied in where necessary to conceal the framework completely by late summer, after which shoots can be allowed to develop and flower.

STAGE 1, LATE SPRING

Plant four 12-week-old cuttings, each with several main stems, in an 18in (45cm) pot, angling them slightly outward.

STAGE 2

1 *Using wirecutters, or the wirecutting notch on a pair of pruners, cut eight "ladders" (see above) from chicken wire.*

3 *Remove the plants' original stakes, and very gently fan out and tie in the main shoots so that they are evenly spaced around the framework.*

2 *Insert four stakes vertically in the center of the pot in a square. Insert the wire ladders around the pot, bringing them to the top in a curve and twisting the upper prongs around the stakes.*

4 *Very carefully, tease all loose shoots through the framework so that they can be tied to the outside of the sphere.*

STAGE 3

Keep tying in the main stems, pinching their tips when they reach the top of the frame. Pinch out the tips of all other shoots once two leaves have unfurled, tying in growth laterally until the frame is well furnished with bushy growth. In early autumn, stop pinching to let flowering shoots develop. In cool climates, if plants are outdoors, bring them under cover.

FINISHED SPHERE

The sphere will flower in about eight weeks, and the display will last for about six weeks.

PINCH-PRUNED FAN

Coleus (*Solenostemon*) are ideal plants for training in a fan shape; their growth is strong and bushy, needing only the support of a skeleton of stakes, which are soon hidden by growth. Cascade chrysanthemums, argyranthemums, and fuchsias are also suitable, though they need the extra support of a "backing" of chicken wire netting on the framework. It may only be possible to obtain growth dense enough to conceal the framework on one side.

The fan shape is one of the easiest to produce. However, as with fruit tree fans, it is most important not to let the main stems grow upward and outward too soon, or the lower areas of the fan will prove difficult to cover. Always pinch-prune young plants right from the start, encouraging them to form bushy mounds before forming the fan.

COLEUS FAN
The brilliant foliage of many coleus cultivars provides a lasting display. Pinch out any flower buds that form.

STAGE 1

Plant two vigorous coleus cuttings in the same 10in (25cm) pot. Pinch out the growing tips, then pinch all subsequent shoots that develop until the plants are about 10in (25cm) tall. Then pinch only on two opposite sides of the plants, developing a flattened shape.

SUPPORTING FRAMEWORK

When the plants are about 20in (50cm) tall (see left), they will need the support of a framework, made from stakes arranged and tied as a fan. For plants with more slender stems and less vigorous growth than coleus, attach a semi-circle of wire netting to the skeletal frame.

STAGE 2

Use as many ties as possible to create firm support

1 *Carefully insert the stakes that form the fan's ribs, and tie in crossbars to brace them.*

2 *Tie in stems wherever possible, gently drawing some growth down to the horizontal.*

STAGE 3 (SIDE VIEW OF FAN)

Growth is dense and bushy on both sides

Let all growth that extends toward the perimeter of the fan grow out, tying in at regular intervals. Continue pinching all shoots on the flat faces of the fan. Once the frame is covered, pinch all growth to maintain the shape and stimulate fresh, young leaves.

DICTIONARY OF ORNAMENTAL SHRUBS

A

ABELIA (ZONES 6–9)

Mainly evergreen or, in colder climates, deciduous shrubs of arching, twiggy habit that are frost-tolerant if given a warm, sheltered position. Most flower in summer on the previous year's wood and may flower again later in the season on the earliest of the current season's growth. Abelias regularly produce new growth from low down and thus benefit from moderate replacement pruning. All but dwarf forms are suitable for training against walls, especially *A. floribunda*.

WHEN TO PRUNE Spring, after the last frost, and summer, after flowering.

TRAINING AND PRUNING If wall training (*see p.162*), tie in branches promptly before they arch over. Spring pruning consists of removing dead or damaged growth. After flowering, remove some old wood (this is not as necessary for *A. triflora*), cutting back up to one in four flowered stems to strong, new shoots or to the ground. To renovate, cut all stems to the base in early spring.

ABELIOPHYLLUM

Korean abelia-leaf (*A. distichum*) is a deciduous shrub, bearing white flowers in early spring on the previous year's

growth. Stems may root where they touch the ground. It is hardy in zones 5 to 8. In colder climates it should be given a sheltered site; training against a sunny wall will encourage flowering.

WHEN TO PRUNE Spring, after flowering. Tie in wall-trained plants and prune to shape throughout the growing season.

TRAINING AND PRUNING Prune free-standing shrubs as for *Forsythia* (*see p.196*), cutting some old wood back to vigorous shoots low down. To renovate, cut back to a low framework of branches. To train on a wall (*see p.162*), select strong shoots to make an informal framework. Once established, cut back one in two or three of the flowered shoots to low replacement shoots or buds low down. As plants mature, remove any old branches with few laterals and train in replacements.

ABUTILON

Evergreen, semievergreen, and deciduous shrubs that in cooler climates need a sheltered position and frost protection; several are best grown under glass. Some may be grown as standards. Abutilons flower on the current season's growth. They flower over a long period but are relatively short-lived.

A. MEGAPOTAMICUM (ZONES 8–10)

TRAILING ABUTILON

Evergreen shrub, flowering from spring to autumn; the cultivar 'Variegatum' has yellow-mottled leaves. Its long,

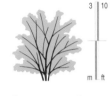

slender stems and readiness to produce growth from the base make it suitable for wall training.

WHEN TO PRUNE Early to midspring.

TRAINING AND PRUNING On freestanding shrubs, shorten the previous season's growth by one-third. Cut bare branches back to strong shoots or buds near the base. To produce larger leaves on variegated plants, prune hard each year (*see p.164*). Young, healthy plants respond well to cutting back hard. Wall train (*see p.162*) as an informal fan, tying young growth to bamboo stakes attached to wires (*see also* Tree Fruits, *p.98*). Once a framework is established, occasionally remove old wood in favor of strong young replacement shoots, tying these in to fill in gaps.

A. X HYBRIDUM 'SOUVENIR DE BONN'

The natural habit (left) is tall and spindly. Pruning when young will encourage bushier growth (right).

Laterals have developed

Tip of shoot was removed here

A. 'KENTISH BELLE'
This hybrid can be treated as for Abutilon megapotamicum; *wall training displays its flowers attractively, and the wall gives its slender growth shelter, warmth, and support.*

A. VITIFOLIUM (ZONES 8–9)

Fast-growing, evergreen shrub bearing masses of purplish-blue to white flowers in late spring and early summer. In

colder climates it may be damaged by severe frosts. It can be allowed to grow as a multistemmed shrub, but training with a central leader enhances the pyramidal form and gives it stature.

WHEN TO PRUNE Summer, after flowering.

TRAINING AND PRUNING Train initially with a central stem (*see p.155*). If this leader is broken, train in a replacement (*see p.26*) and cut back laterals by two-thirds. Do not prune established plants, except to remove dead, diseased, or damaged growth. Cutting back hard ruins the plant's natural form by encouraging too much lateral growth, and should be avoided. Deadheading can increase the vigor of the plant.

OTHER ABUTILONS
A. X HYBRIDUM As for *A. pictum*. Many cultivars break readily from the base if pruned hard annually in spring.
A. X MILLERI As for *A. megapotamicum*.
A. PICTUM (syn. A. STRIATUM) In colder climates, ideal for a greenhouse or as summer bedding. Can be grown as an upright plant with a central leader; the stem may be cleared to form a standard (*see* Pinch-pruning, *p.169*). Can also be grown as a bushy shrub (*see left*); shorten the main stem by about half and laterals to 3–4in (8–10cm) in midspring.
A. X SUNTENSE As for *A. vitifolium*.

ACALYPHA (ZONE 10)

Chenille plants are evergreen shrubs and perennials with attractive foliage, some with interesting flowers. They may be grown outdoors only in tropical areas, as freestanding bushes or as informal hedges. In colder climates they need a frost-free position, and are best grown in pots under glass. Acalyphas require little pruning except to remove wayward shoots, but can be cut back by up to a third in midspring to restrict growth. This will also result in larger leaves. They should not be cut back harder.

ALLAMANDA (ZONE 10)

Allamanda schottii (syn. *A. neriifolia*), the bush allamanda or golden trumpet, is an evergreen shrub with dense growth and yellow flowers from summer to autumn, followed by spiky seed capsules. It needs subtropical conditions. It responds well to pruning. Pinch-prune young plants (*see p.168*) to encourage bushy growth. Trim established plants from late winter to spring, cutting stems back by 2–5in (5–12cm) or more. During the growing season, shorten long stems to maintain a balanced plant. For other species, *see* Dictionary of Climbing Plants, *p.262*.

ALOYSIA (ZONE 10)

Aloysia triphylla (syn. *Lippia citriodora*), or lemon verbena, is a medium-sized evergreen grown more for its lemon-scented leaves than the white flowers borne on the current season's growth. In cooler climates it needs a sunny site and protection with a mulch in winter.

WHEN TO PRUNE Midspring.

TRAINING AND PRUNING In cooler climates prune main stems to strong buds about 12in (30cm) from ground level. In warm climates allow a woody framework to develop, then shorten growth to buds 2–4in (5–10cm) from the old wood. From spring to early summer pinch out shoot tips for leafy, bushy growth. May also be informally wall trained (*see p.162*) or grown as a standard (*see p.165*).

AMELANCHIER

The shadbush (or serviceberry) is a large, deciduous shrub or small tree. It bears white flowers in mid- to late spring and is noted for its beautiful autumn leaf color. *A. canadensis* also produces edible berries. Amelanchiers may grow as multistemmed bushes (the natural habit of most species), or may sometimes be trained as a small tree. The spreading, vigorously suckering species, such as *A. stolonifera*, are grown as dense, thicketlike shrubs.

A. LAMARCKII (ZONES 5–9)

Deciduous, upright, multistemmed shrub that can be allowed to develop naturally with minimal pruning. It may also be trained with a short trunk to form a small, branched-headed tree.

WHEN TO PRUNE Winter, when dormant, or after flowering in late spring.

TRAINING AND PRUNING If grown as a multistemmed bush, thin young plants lightly to create an open, informal vase shape; left unattended, main stems that are too close together tend to twist around each other as they mature. To renovate neglected, overcrowded specimens, cut congested, intertwined stems back to ground level.

For a tree-like form, select the strongest, straightest stem and clear a short trunk of 2–5ft (0.6–1.5m) as for a central-leader tree (see p.28), then allow

AMELANCHIER STOLONIFERA
Prune in winter if growth is crowded, removing one of every three stems.

AMELANCHIER LAMARCKII
A light, open form enhances the display of autumn color in multistemmed specimens.

a branched head to develop, selecting laterals to create an open, evenly spaced branch framework. In the dormant season, remove any shoots that have developed on the clear trunk.

A. STOLONIFERA (ZONES 4–7)

A suckering, woodland shrub, suitable for a large border or wild area of the garden. Unpruned, it tends to spread and will eventually form an impenetrable thicket.

WHEN TO PRUNE Winter, when dormant.

TRAINING AND PRUNING No routine pruning is required. If established plants are congested, cut out up to one in three of the stems every two or three years, removing them to the base (*see left*). More drastic thinning, retaining only the strongest young shoots, can be used to renovate neglected specimens.

OTHER AMELANCHIERS
A. ASIATICA Train with a treelike form as for *A. lamarckii*.
A. CANADENSIS As for *A. lamarckii*; if berries are desired, prune in winter only.
A. CONFUSA, A. x GRANDIFLORA As for *A. lamarckii*.

OTHER ORNAMENTAL SHRUBS
ACACIA See Dictionary of Ornamental Trees, *p.52*.
ACCA (syn. FEIJOA) No special needs; if necessary, prune ornamentals after flowering, and fruiting plants in winter.
ADENANDRA No special pruning needs. May be trimmed to shape after flowering.

AGAVE See Palms and palmlike plants, *p.43*.
ALANGIUM No special pruning needs. Will break from old wood if cut back hard.
ALOE See Palms and palmlike plants, *p.43*.
ALYOGYNE Frost-tender. Tip-prune young plants (*see p.155*) to encourage bushiness. Shorten main stems and laterals by one-third

in spring, keeping a woody framework. *A. huegelii* (lilac hibiscus) may be cut back harder into old wood.
ANDROMEDA As for *Erica carnea* (see p.193).
ANISODONTEA Frost-tender. Regular pinch-pruning will keep plants compact and bushy. Tolerates hard pruning to renovate.

ARALIA DEVIL'S WALKING STICK (ZONES 3–7)

Deciduous shrubs with very thorny stems, producing handsome, pinnate leaves and showy panicles of white flowers. Aralias usually make large, suckering plants with upright stems and short laterals, but they sometimes naturally form small, sparsely branched trees. They should be pruned in early spring, before the onset of growth. Let young aralias develop naturally, removing only dead, diseased, damaged, or badly placed growth. When plants are established, keep pruning to a minimum. The buds break late and can appear lifeless until quite late in the season; do not mistake this for frost damage. If a late, hard frost does damage the tip growth, prune back to a stubby lateral showing healthy growth. When grown with a single trunk, any suckers should be removed as they appear (see p.153). Reverted shoots on variegated cultivars (which may also appear as suckers) should also be promptly removed (see p.153). Old plants will not respond to hard pruning.

ARALIA ELATA 'VARIEGATA'
Reverted, green-leaved growth may appear as suckers, and these should be removed.

ARGYRANTHEMUM

Argyranthemum frutescens (syn. *Chrysanthemum frutescens*), the marguerite, is an evergreen subshrub (zone 10) with attractive white, yellow, or pink daisylike flower heads all through summer. In colder temperate climates it is often pot-grown for summer bedding, the young plants overwintering under glass. Increase the flowering potential and encourage a rounded shape by pinching out the tips of young shoots two or three times in spring (see p.155) and also by dead-heading regularly. Argyranthemums are also suitable for growing as standards, formed and maintained by pinch-pruning (see p.169). Train up a clear single stem, then form a bushy head by repeatedly pinching out the tips of lateral growths.

ARONIA CHOKEBERRY

Two species (and one hybrid between them) of medium-sized, deciduous, suckering shrubs (zones 4 to 8), related to *Pyrus* and *Sorbus*. They bear clusters of white flowers in spring on growth made the previous season, followed by fine autumn color, often early in the season, and black or red fruit, according to the species; these berries persist into midwinter. Left unpruned, the shrub will not produce many new central growths to maintain a naturally rounded shape, and will gradually spread by suckering away from the main rootstock. When established, remove one in three of the older stems each year, pruning in winter to late spring. To restrict spread, prune off suckers around the shrub below ground level. Suckers can also be dug up and transplanted for propagation. Although old plants sometimes respond by producing vigorous new shoots when pruned hard, renovation is generally not worthwhile.

ARTEMISIA WORMWOOD

A genus that includes a number of shrubs and subshrubs, grown for their attractive and aromatic foliage. They thrive in a sunny, well-drained site. Regular pruning is needed to prevent the plants from becoming bare and leggy at the base and to promote bushy growth. Most can be cut back into old wood. The yellowish flower heads are seldom attractive; pinch the inflorescences out as they develop to maintain the fine foliage.

A. ABROTANUM (ZONES 5–8)

SOUTHERNWOOD, LAD'S LOVE, OLD MAN

Deciduous subshrub with sweetly aromatic, gray-green foliage. Plants tend to become straggly; pruning them encourages bushy growth. Plants that have become leggy and bare at the base can be renovated by hard pruning.

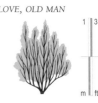

ARTEMISIA 'POWIS CASTLE'
Cut back to a low framework each year to renew the fresh, young foliage.

WHEN TO PRUNE Early spring, after any danger of severe frost is past.

TRAINING AND PRUNING The first spring after planting, cut all the stems back to 1–2in (2.5–5cm) from the ground to stimulate strong new growth. Encourage bushiness by regularly pinching out shoot tips. On established plants, clip the previous season's growth back by up to half every year. To renovate, cut all stems back hard.

A. 'POWIS CASTLE' (ZONES 6–9)

Mound-forming, evergreen shrub with filigree, silver-gray foliage. Since it is the young growth that is the most attractive, prune the plant annually to maximize the effect. It is pruned harder than *A. abrotanum*, because the foliage has a tendency to die back on older wood, leaving leggy, bare stems.

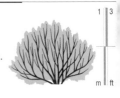

WHEN TO PRUNE Early spring, after any danger of severe frost is past. In warm climates, can be pruned in autumn.

TRAINING AND PRUNING Pinch out the shoot tips of young plants to encourage bushy growth. Cut back annually to a low framework of main stems, as for other gray-leaved shrubs (see p.158). Discard old plants that cease to make vigorous new growth; they do not renovate well and are better replaced.

OTHER ARTEMISIAS
A. ARBORESCENS, A. LUDOVICIANA, A. NUTANS (syn. SERIPHIDIUM NUTANS), A. TRIDENTATA (syn. SERIPHIDIUM TRIDENTATA) As for *A. abrotanum*.

ATRIPLEX SALTBUSH (ZONE 9)

Attractive foliage plants, including some annuals and perennials as well as a number of evergreen or semievergreen, gray-green shrubs that are noted for their tolerance of coastal sites. With age they tend to develop into straggly, open shrubs; keep them compact by annual pruning in spring. Either clip over the whole plant with shears, removing one-third of the previous year's growth, or, for a more natural outline, trim with pruners. With trimming, *A. halimus* maintains a dense enough habit to be used as a hedge.

AUCUBA (ZONES 6–10)

Evergreen, rounded shrubs, several with variegated or spotted leaves; the female plants often bear showy fruit in autumn. The most commonly grown species is *A. japonica*, all of whose cultivars are similar in growth habit and are usually used in shrub borders or as specimens grown in tubs. They are also popular for dense, semiformal hedging, particularly since they tolerate heavy shade. Aucubas are naturally dense in growth and rounded in habit, but they are prone to dieback and also have a tendency to become bare at the base.

WHEN TO PRUNE Midspring, after the winter display of berries. Nonfruiting plants, or those on which berries are not desired, may be pruned in winter.

TRAINING AND PRUNING The first spring after planting, cut back the previous year's growth by one-third of its length to encourage a more bushy habit. As the plant becomes established, remove any overvigorous, canelike shoots that spoil its shape. Cut back any shoots that show signs of dieback (this may be caused by drought), either to strong, completely healthy buds or to the main stem. Hedges should be trimmed with pruners (*see p.46*), rather than clipped, to avoid unsightly damage to the large glossy leaves; shorten the previous year's growth by about one-third until the hedge is established, then trim over with pruners each year to keep compact and to the desired height. Aucubas that have become bare at the base may be rejuvenated by hard pruning in stages (*see p.161*), cutting one in three of the main stems back to the base each year.

AUCUBA JAPONICA
Prune wayward stems to well within the plant's outline, so that cut marks are hidden.

AZARA (ZONE 9)

Evergreen shrubs and trees grown for their leaves and their dense yellow flower heads. In warm climates they may be grown as freestanding shrubs that need only minimal pruning. They are sometimes grown as hedging, in which case they may be trimmed over in autumn (or in midspring in colder areas) as for *Escallonia* (*see p.194*). In cooler climates they are reliably hardy only if given the protection of a warm wall; fan-train them (*see p.162*) and prune in late spring to remove any frost damage. Small-leaved species, such as *A. microphylla*, may be clipped into geometric shapes (*see Topiary, p.48*), but this will be at the expense of the flowers. Established azaras respond well to hard pruning in late spring, producing new growth freely from old wood.

B

BANKSIA (ZONE 10)

Australian genus of tropical and subtropical, evergreen shrubs or small trees with cylindrical or globelike flower spikes. Banksias need frost-free conditions but make good potted plants under glass in colder climates. They need little pruning but may be trimmed lightly to restrict size. Like *Eucalyptus* (*see p.64*), some banksias have a swollen base (lignotuber) from which new shoots grow if the shrub is pruned hard.

WHEN TO PRUNE After flowering.

TRAINING AND PRUNING Confine pruning of established plants to shortening the previous season's growth if this is necessary to limit size. *B. integrifolia*, *B. menziesii*, and *B. spinulosa* should resprout if cut back into old wood, but *B. coccinea* and *B. ericifolia* will not respond well if cut back below green foliage. It is better to replace a plant that has become leggy or has outgrown its space than to attempt renovation.

BANKSIA ERICIFOLIA
The spikes of flowers and the needlelike foliage are popular with flower arrangers.

BARLERIA (ZONE 10)

Barleria cristata, the Philippine violet, is a tropical, evergreen, medium-sized shrub with pale violet or white, tubular flowers and a long flowering season. Pinch out shoot tips of young plants to encourage branching. Shorten long, flowered stems by about one-third to encourage future flowering growth. It may also be grown as a hedge (*see p.44*), in which case trim after flowering.

OTHER ORNAMENTAL SHRUBS

ARCTOSTAPHYLOS No special pruning needs. Prostrate species tolerate trimming in summer after flowering, but fruit is lost.
ARDISIA Evergreen (*see p.159*); prune lightly in spring only if necessary.

ARISTOTELIA No special pruning needs. Can be wall trained, pruning in spring.
ASIMINA No special pruning needs.
ASTARTEA No special pruning needs. Trim to shape if necessary after flowering.

BACCHARIS As for *Atriplex* (*see above*).
BAUERA No special pruning needs. Trim lightly after flowering if necessary.
BEAUFORTIA No special pruning needs.

BERBERIS *BARBERRY*

Shrubs that vary in size from dwarf to large; some are semiprostrate or mounding in habit, while others are upright or arching. They have yellow or orange spring flowers followed by red or black fruit. Many deciduous species have fine autumn color. Berberis are dense in habit and tolerant of most situations and soils. The thorny ever-greens are popular for barrier plantings and for formal or informal hedges; they are most easily clipped with shears, because of the thorns, but look more attractive if pruned more selectively with pruners. A few deciduous berberis, such as *B.* x *ottawensis* and cultivars of *B. thunbergii*, may be regularly coppiced (*see p.36*) or cut back to a low framework of permanent branches for larger and more vividly colored leaves, and for attractively colored young stems. Those grown for their autumn color should not be pruned in this way, since the best leaf color is usually produced on mature wood.

Berberis respond well to renovation, and even healthy plants that have not been neglected or become too large benefit from being cut back hard every seven years or so. When pruning, always wear thornproof gloves and clothing.

B. DARWINII (ZONES 8–9)

DARWIN'S BARBERRY

Evergreen, arching shrub, often used for informal hedging or in mixed shrub borders. Deep orange-yellow flowers, borne on the previous season's growth, are succeeded by bluish purple berries. It has a naturally dense habit with arching stems, which is best preserved by minimal pruning. However, it can become very large, eventually flowering and fruiting only on the periphery of the plant; it responds well to drastic cutting back.

WHEN TO PRUNE After flowering, in early summer, provided that fruit is not required. Otherwise, prune in autumn or winter, after fruiting.

TRAINING AND PRUNING Specimen plants in shrub borders need minimal pruning. To renovate, cut back all stems to within 12in (30cm) of the base in late winter, although flowers will be lost the following season. Plants grown as an informal hedge should not be clipped, or the berries will be lost. Fruited stems can be shortened in winter to keep the hedge reasonably compact.

BERBERIS DARWINII
Berberis that are outgrowing their site should grow back vigorously if cut back hard.

B. THUNBERGII (ZONES 4–8)

JAPANESE BARBERRY

Deciduous shrub with many cultivars of varying habit, grown mainly for foliage that turns brilliant orange-red in autumn. It is popularly grown as a hedge, though at the expense of the flowers if clipped. It benefits from thinning each year, removing some growth to the base. Thinning dense growth also displays the foliage better. Some cultivars, such as 'Aurea' and 'Rose Glow', can be cut back hard each year to enhance the effect of spring foliage.

WHEN TO PRUNE Mid- to late winter. Remove dead wood in midsummer when it can be clearly distinguished.

TRAINING AND PRUNING Thin the plant and stimulate new growth by cutting out one in five of the stems each year, to the base or to a strong shoot low down. To cut back regularly for foliage effect, *see p.164*. Renovation is as for *B. darwinii*.

> **OTHER BERBERIS**
> B. BUXIFOLIA As for *B. darwinii*.
> B. X CARMINEA As for *B. thunbergii*.
> B. HOOKERI As for *B. darwinii*. Neat, dense, upright habit.
> B. LINEARIFOLIA As for *B. darwinii*.
> B. X OTTAWENSIS As for *B. thunbergii*. 'Superba' is vigorous and recommended for regular hard pruning (*see p.164*), producing red young stems and purple-green leaves.
> B. X STENOPHYLLA As for *B. darwinii*. As an informal hedge it can be cut back hard in early summer, after flowering.
> B. TEMOLAICA As for *B. thunbergii*. Cut hard back for the best stem effect.
> B. WILSONIAE As for *B. thunbergii*.

BORONIA (ZONES 9–10)

Woody evergreens of varying size, grown for their aromatic foliage and flowers. Some will survive light frost when mature, but are much better grown under glass in colder climates. Pruning helps to maintain vigor and bushiness, and increases the number of flowers. Boronias are usually short-lived.

B. MEGASTIGMA

BROWN BORONIA, SCENTED BORONIA

Slender, evergreen shrub with powerfully fragrant, bell-like brown flowers borne along the stems in late winter and spring. Named cultivars with other flower colors are available.

WHEN TO PRUNE After flowering, in late spring.

TRAINING AND PRUNING Pinch out shoot tips on planting to encourage bushiness and flowering shoots. After the first flowering season, cut back flowered shoots hard, but do not leave any stems without foliage. In subsequent years shorten flowered shoots by about one-third. To renovate, cut back all stems by half in late spring; conditions need to be ideal for a good response.

> **OTHER BORONIAS**
> B. DENTICULATA Intolerant of heavy pruning, but may be cut back lightly after flowering to maintain vigor.
> B. FLORIBUNDA As for *B. megastigma*: on established plants, reduce lanky flowered stems by half.
> B. HETEROPHYLLA As for *B. megastigma*.
> B. MOLLIS Requires minimal pruning.
> B. SERRULATA As for *B. megastigma* but, once established, cut out one or two of the oldest branches. When shortening other stems, do not cut back beyond the foliage into bare wood.

BOUVARDIA (ZONE 10)

Deciduous, semievergreen, or evergreen shrubs, grown mainly for their flowers, which are borne on new wood in terminal cymes. They are frost-tender, and should be grown under glass in winter in colder climates. Prune in late winter, removing dead and weak wood, and cutting back stems that have flowered by half to three-quarters. Pinch-prune (*see p.168*) the resulting new growth until midsummer, to encourage bushiness. Cut any old, unproductive wood back to ground level.

BRACHYGLOTTIS (ZONES 9–10)

Evergreen, usually mound-forming shrubs, formerly classified under *Senecio*; most have attractive silvery-gray foliage and bear terminal clusters of daisylike, yellow flower heads on the previous season's growth in summer. Hard pruning results in a finer foliage effect, but will be at the expense of the flowers. Most prefer a sunny aspect but tolerate windy coastal conditions. In shady or damp sites, however, they may become leggy. In colder climates plants are often damaged by frost, and a heavy fall of snow can break the rather brittle branches.

B. 'SUNSHINE' (DUNEDIN HYBRID)

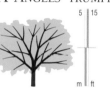

Spreading shrub with gray leaves that are white beneath, and yellow flower heads in summer.

WHEN TO PRUNE Midspring, when any danger of severe frost has passed and with the onset of new growth.

TRAINING AND PRUNING Plants grown on coastal sites and in warm climates tend to adopt a rounded habit without regular pruning. In colder climates growth may be spreading; cut back any wayward stems and frost-damaged growth. Established plants may also be clipped to shape after flowering. Prune hard to renovate damaged plants, cutting back to active buds on older wood. Plants must be in good health for renovation to be successful; old plants are best replaced.

> **OTHER BRACHYGLOTTIS**
> All other Dunedin Hybrids are pruned as for B. 'Sunshine'.
> B. ELAEAGNIFOLIA Minimal pruning.
> B. HUNTII Requires minimal pruning.
> B. LAXIFOLIA As for B. 'Sunshine'.

RENOVATING B. 'SUNSHINE'
'Sunshine' will respond to drastic pruning, but the regrowth will be slow on old plants such as this one, shown here in midsummer after hard pruning in spring. It is usually preferable to replace an old plant with a young specimen, which will quickly make vigorous growth.

BRUGMANSIA *ANGELS' TRUMPETS* (ZONE 10)

Semievergreen or evergreen shrubs or small trees formerly classified under *Datura*. They are grown for their large, fragrant, trumpet-shaped flowers, which are borne in summer to autumn. Most are shrubs or small trees. They need frost-free conditions. In warm climates moderate pruning encourages plants to flower freely. Brugmansias grow well under glass in colder climates, as bushes or as standards (*see p.165*); they need regular pruning to restrict size while stimulating flowering growth. Softer growth may may die back in winter, but plants will usually regenerate the following spring. Wear gloves when pruning; toxic alkaloids are contained in the leaves and the flower heads.

WHEN TO PRUNE Late winter, before the onset of growth.

TRAINING AND PRUNING Cut back the previous season's growth to within 6in (15cm) of ground level or to framework

BRUGMANSIA PRUNED HARD
Brugmansias make vigorous new spring growth after hard pruning, so their size can be restricted if required.

stems; these may consist of stubby branches on a clear trunk (*see above*). Deadhead faded flower heads in summer. Brugmansias respond well to renovation, and a plant that has outgrown its allotted space may be cut back hard before spring growth begins.

BRUNFELSIA

Evergreen shrubs or small trees with glossy leaves, grown for their sometimes fragrant flowers, borne on the previous season's growth. The flowers are blue, often fading to lavender, then white (or sometimes yellow), so that flowers of several colors can be seen simultaneously. They will grow outdoors only in frost-free gardens, but grow well under glass.

B. PAUCIFLORA (ZONES 9–11)

YESTERDAY-TODAY-AND-TOMORROW

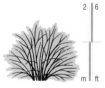

Spring-flowering, with a spreading habit, particularly when grown in shade. Suitable for wall training.

WHEN TO PRUNE Spring, after flowering.

TRAINING AND PRUNING To encourage young plants to branch and develop a more compact habit, pinch out the growing tips of shoots. Pruning should be light, to maintain bushiness; cut back straggling branches to shape the plants. To wall train, *see p.162*.

> **OTHER ORNAMENTAL SHRUBS**
> BOENNINGHAUSENIA Subshrub that may be cut down by frost. Prune all growth to the base in spring.
> BOWKERIA No special pruning needs.
> BRACHYSEMA No special pruning needs.
> BREYNIA No special pruning needs.
>
> BRUCKENTHALIA Related to *Calluna* and *Erica*, but less vigorous. Pinch back the shoots of young plants by about one-third in the first spring to promote denser growth. When established cut back after flowering, as for *Erica carnea* (*see p.193*).
>
> **OTHER BRUNFELSIAS**
> B. AMERICANA Dislikes pruning and should be left to develop naturally; it may form a small tree. Trim after flowering in summer if necessary.
> B. LATIFOLIA As for B. *pauciflora*. Naturally more open in habit.

BUDDLEJA

Adaptable, mainly deciduous shrubs, grown for their fragrant flowers and elegant, often arching habit. They are usually grown as freestanding shrubs, but some species and cultivars look attractive grown as standards or trained against walls. Some buddlejas flower on new wood, others on shoots from older wood, and this determines their pruning requirements: the former may be cut back hard each year, while for the latter a permanent branch framework (for example, fan-trained on a wall) should be developed.

B. ALTERNIFOLIA (ZONES 5–9)

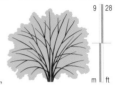

Deciduous shrub with arching, pendent stems, along which, in early summer, clusters of scented, lilac flowers are borne on the previous season's wood.

WHEN TO PRUNE Midsummer, immediately after flowering.

TRAINING AND PRUNING Allow the plant to develop naturally, or train it as a standard (*see below and facing page*) or on a wall (*see p.162*). In all cases, the aim is to maintain a balanced shape and renew flowering wood. Cut back the flowered stems to healthy buds or non-flowering sideshoots. Neglected but healthy specimens can be cut back hard.

B. DAVIDII (ZONES 5–9)

BUTTERFLY BUSH

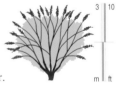

Vigorous shrub that produces terminal racemes of flowers on the current season's growth in summer. Unpruned, it tends to become a leggy, tangled mass of live and dead stems, flowering less freely. Hard annual pruning produces the best flowers, on vigorous stems that will grow to 6–8ft (2–2.5m) in height in a single season. It self-seeds prolifically, so it is best, although not essential, to remove spent flower heads promptly (*see p.153*). This should also result in a second, smaller flush of flowers in late summer.

WHEN TO PRUNE Early spring, with the onset of new growth, and after any danger of hard frosts.

TRAINING AND PRUNING In the first spring cut out weak growth and shorten the main stems to start developing a low

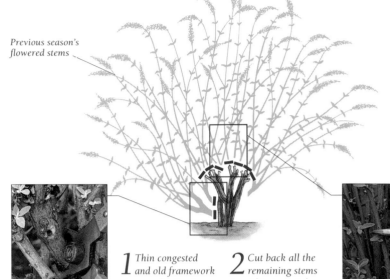

Previous season's flowered stems

1 *Thin congested and old framework stems and cut out any that are producing badly positioned growth.*

2 *Cut back all the remaining stems to within two or three pairs of healthy buds of the woody framework.*

framework 6–18in (15–45cm) high (*see also p.157*). For a plant positioned at the back of a border or elsewhere where extra height is needed, the framework may be taller, up to 4ft (1.2m) high. In the spring of subsequent years prune back to this framework, cutting back the previous season's growth to leave only two or three pairs of buds (*see above*). Shorten any new growth from the base by three-quarters or remove entirely if plants are too dense. As plants mature, remove with loppers or a saw any dead or old, unproductive sections of the stubby framework. Deadhead with pruners as the flowers fade, cutting to a

pair of strong shoots. On windy sites, shorten the top-growth by about one-third in autumn. Neglected plants usually respond well to hard pruning.

B. GLOBOSA (ZONES 7–9)

ORANGE BUTTERFLY BUSH

Medium to large, semievergreen shrub with orange flower clusters on terminal shoots from the previous season's wood. Shoots often retain their foliage through the winter. *B. globosa* is

INITIAL TRAINING OF BUDDLEJA ALTERNIFOLIA AS A STANDARD

When purchased, most plants will have been pruned to develop a bushy habit (left). Remove up to three-quarters of the top growth (right) to leave a single stem, furnished with laterals to strengthen the leader as it grows upward. Train as for a standard (see p.165).

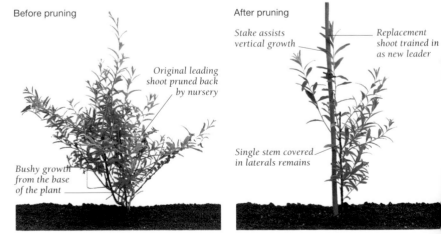

Before pruning

Original leading shoot pruned back by nursery

Bushy growth from the base of the plant

After pruning

Stake assists vertical growth

Replacement shoot trained in as new leader

Single stem covered in laterals remains

apt to become bare at the base and is best grown at the back of the border, with smaller plants in front. Pruning is seldom required; it may be needed to offset the shrub's naturally ungainly habit, but should be done selectively, or the next year's flowers will be lost.

WHEN TO PRUNE Late winter, before fresh growth begins.

TRAINING AND PRUNING Remove any dead or poorly growing shoots. Wayward stems can be shortened by about one-third (although this will remove the flowering tip). Large branches that flower only very high up may be cut back into old wood. Although the next season's flowers will be lost, the plant will recover quickly and produce vigorous shoots that will flower in the next year.

B. MADAGASCARIENSIS (ZONE 10)

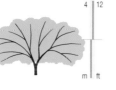

Frost-tender, vigorous, scandent, evergreen shrub. In colder climates it is best wall trained in a very sunny, sheltered site, or grown under glass. Its trailing foliage is silvery on the underside, and panicles of small, yellow, fragrant flowers are borne in winter.

WHEN TO PRUNE Spring, immediately after flowering.

TRAINING AND PRUNING If grown as a freestanding plant, *B. madagascariensis* tends to develop into a large, spreading, untidy mound of shoots, and even in warm gardens is most commonly given support by wall training (*see p.162*). From early to midspring, cut back shoots that have flowered to a bud or vigorous young shoot.

OTHER BUDDLEJAS
B. AURICULATA Evergreen. In cool climates it benefits from wall training, as for *B. madagascariensis*. Prune freestanding shrubs as for *B. alternifolia*.
B. COLVILEI Prune after flowering, as for *B. alternifolia*, but more lightly.
B. CRISPA As for *B. davidii*; it looks better if a taller framework of stems is developed, rather than being cut down to near ground level. Also lends itself to wall training (*see p.162*).
B. FALLOWIANA As for *B. davidii*. In colder climates it benefits from being grown in the shelter of a sunny wall, or trained informally against it.
B. SALVIIFOLIA As for *B. davidii*.

ESTABLISHED BUDDLEJA ALTERNIFOLIA STANDARD, AFTER FLOWERING

1 Remove any old or weakened, unproductive growth, particularly where crowding the center.

2 Cut back the long flowered stems, to nonflowering, preferably upward- and outward-growing shoots where possible; otherwise cut to a healthy bud.

Clear trunk raises up trailing, flowering branches

BUXUS *BOXWOOD*

Tough, evergreen shrubs or small trees, with neat, small, rounded leaves, that are ideal as formal hedges (*see p.44*) or to use in topiary (*see p.48*). They respond well to clipping and break easily from old wood. All are frost-tolerant, although *B. balearica* may be damaged by hard frosts. Heavy snow and ice, if allowed to accumulate, may damage large specimens. The pruning of *B. sempervirens* cultivars should be guided by, and cannot alter, their habit of growth, which ranges from dwarf and prostrate to large and upright. *B. balearica* is large, with a more open habit, but may be kept compact by regular pruning.

WHEN TO PRUNE Mid- to late summer. Renovate in late spring.

TRAINING AND PRUNING Grown as an informal shrub, boxwood requires little pruning, but cut back overlong growths to within the bush, so that the cut is masked. Keep plants at the desired height by trimming long shoots. Cut hedging plants and topiary specimens back hard while young to encourage bushy growth. Trim mature plants closely. Old or snow-damaged plants will make vigorous new growth if cut back to within 6–12in (15–30cm) of the ground. Remove any branches touching the ground that have rooted.

BUXUS SEMPERVIRENS (ZONES 6–8)
If using boxwood for topiary or formal edging, plant young specimens to a depth slightly below the nursery soil mark; this will stimulate growth from the base of the plant.

OTHER ORNAMENTAL SHRUBS
BUPLEURUM Has no special needs, but tolerates pruning and makes a good informal hedge. Trim in late spring. Mature specimens can be cut back hard if they become too dense and twiggy.

C

CAESALPINIA (ZONE 10)

Shrubs and scandent climbers with attractive foliage and flowers, best wall trained or grown under glass in colder climates. Pinch out the main shoot tips of young plants to encourage bushiness. Prune freestanding specimens after flowering only to restrict growth. Prune established wall-trained plants in spring, cutting back the previous year's growth to 2–3in (5–8cm) of the framework.

CALLICARPA BEAUTYBERRY

Medium-sized, deciduous shrubs, grown for the clusters of bright violet fruit borne along the stems in autumn and through the winter. They sometimes flower on new as well as on second-year wood. Some are hardy, while others, such as *C. rubella*, need frost-free conditions. The plants are bushy, making plenty of growth from the base. They need regular thinning to prevent congestion, cutting older stems to the base.

C. BODINIERI VAR. GIRALDII

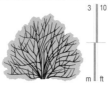

Bushy shrub (zones 6 to 8) with tiny lilac flowers in summer followed by dense clusters of violet fruit.

WHEN TO PRUNE Early spring, after any danger of prolonged frost has passed, but while the plant is still dormant.

TRAINING AND PRUNING Each year, remove up to one in five of the stems completely, cutting them back to the base. Prune back any branches broken by the weight of fruit as soon as seen, either to a strong new shoot on the unbroken part of the stem, or to a shoot at the base of the plant. Callicarpas usually respond to hard pruning. Plants that appear to have been killed by frost may resprout if the dead growth is cut back to ground level in early spring.

> **OTHER CALLICARPAS**
> C. RUBELLA As for *C. bodinieri*.

CALLISTEMON BOTTLEBRUSH (ZONE 10)

Bushy or open and arching, evergreen shrubs bearing distinctive red or yellow "bottlebrush" flowers on new growth. They will grow in open sites only in warm climates; in colder areas they need the protection of a sunny wall (species of arching habit may be loosely tied, but not rigidly trained, to the wall), or may be grown or overwintered under glass.

C. CITRINUS

CRIMSON BOTTLEBRUSH

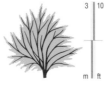

Evergreen, arching shrub with long, red flowers that are borne at the ends of new shoots in summer.

WHEN TO PRUNE Summer, immediately after flowering.

TRAINING AND PRUNING Tip-prune young plants (*see p.152*) to encourage bushy growth. If planting in the shelter of a wall, no special pruning or training is required; simply tie in long stems at a few strategic points, where necessary, and allow the plant to grow upward and outward. Mature plants require little pruning, but to prevent them becoming straggly, older wood can be cut back to young shoots. These should usually be growing upward or outward, the aim being to enhance the naturally arching habit. Callistemons will respond well to the removal of some older wood, but such pruning should be staged over two to three years, and not more than one in two of the stems should be cut back in any one year.

> **OTHER CALLISTEMONS**
> C. 'HARKNESS', C. 'MAUVE MIST',
> C. PHOENICEUS, C. RIGIDUS As for
> *C. citrinus*.
> C. SIEBERI Minimal pruning required.
> C. VIMINALIS Larger, weeping habit, needs little pruning. Is also attractive tied loosely in against a wall.

CALYCANTHUS (ZONES 5–9)

Sweetshrubs are deciduous, summer-flowering plants, with aromatic foliage and brownish red or purplish flowers that have strap-shaped petals. None requires regular pruning other than to remove unhealthy, weak, or wayward shoots. They produce new shoots freely from the base. In spring, before growth starts, thin if necessary by cutting out up to one in three old stems at the base. Neglected specimens can be renovated by cutting out all but the youngest stems in spring.

CAMELLIA RETICULATA CULTIVAR
This beautiful single-flowered camellia must be grown under cover in colder climates.

CAMELLIA

Long-lived evergreen shrubs, with often large, roselike flowers in late winter or early spring. Many are frost-tolerant and can be grown in any climate, although the flowers are susceptible to damage by hard frosts; others are best grown under glass in colder climates. They may also be grown as wall shrubs, although sites exposed to morning sun should be avoided, since the sun's warmth early in the day may damage buds or flowers frosted overnight. Most benefit from formative pruning, since young plants often develop leggy shoots; pruning when established can also encourage a denser growth habit. Some camellia cultivars are genetically unstable and may "sport back," producing stems that bear flowers of a different color. Young reverted growth, which may be useful for propagation, should be removed in spring, but large, old branches (on, for example, inherited plants) may be left.

C. JAPONICA (ZONES 7–9)

JAPANESE CAMELLIA

The species itself is seldom grown, but there are many cultivars of very variable habit. Most need little attention.

CARAGANA PEASHRUB

Deciduous shrubs with pinnate leaves and usually yellow pea-flowers, borne on short shoots on second-year growth. Prune young plants lightly to encourage a bushy habit. No further pruning is required. *C. arborescens* (zones 2–7) can be trained up as a standard (*see p.165*); its weeping cultivar 'Pendula' is usually top-grafted onto a clear stem.

YOUNG CAMELLIAS

Young plants develop a great variety of forms; moderate pruning on planting will help to produce a balanced shape.

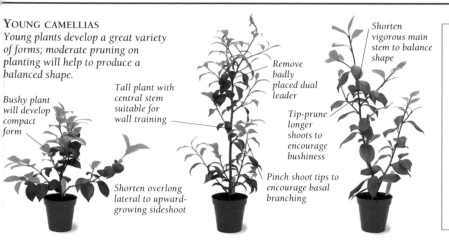

Bushy plant will develop compact form

Tall plant with central stem suitable for wall training

Shorten overlong lateral to upward-growing sideshoot

Shorten vigorous main stem to balance shape

Remove badly placed dual leader

Tip-prune longer shoots to encourage bushiness

Pinch shoot tips to encourage basal branching

OTHER CAMELLIAS

C. CHRYSANTHA (syn. C. NITIDISSIMA) As for *C. sasanqua*.
C. X HIEMALIS As for *C. japonica*. This hybrid may also be used for hedging (*see p.44*).
C. LUTCHUENSIS As for *C. sasanqua*.
C. RETICULATA As for *C. japonica*. Prone to legginess, so benefits particularly from formative pruning.
C. X WILLIAMSII As for *C. japonica*. Deadheading is not necessary, since the spent flowers are shed naturally.
C. OLEIFERA As for *C. japonica*. Hardiest of the camellias, to zone 6.

WHEN TO PRUNE Spring, after flowering, but before growth buds break.

TRAINING AND PRUNING Prune young plants (*see above*) to shape and to encourage bushy growth, reducing thin, leggy shoots by two or three buds or cutting them out entirely. Established plants need minimal pruning, though the previous season's growth can be cut back to just above the old wood. This pruning encourages a bushy, free-flowering habit and can also be used to restrict size: for example, of plants grown under glass. Deadhead after flowering: the flowers persist on the plant and are unsightly.

Camellias can usually be renovated by hard pruning. In early spring, cut large branches to 2ft (60cm) above ground level (or harder, if they are healthy). Spread the work over three years,

cutting back one in three main branches each year. The pruned growth may not show signs of new life until midsummer, but then a mass of shoots normally develops (*see below right*); these should be thinned to develop new framework branches (*see also p.32*).

C. SASANQUA (ZONES 6/7–9)

Shrub that needs frost protection (ideally under glass) in colder climates. It may be open in habit and can be loosely or espalier-trained on a north wall.

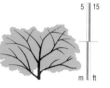

WHEN TO PRUNE Spring, before growth buds break.

TRAINING AND PRUNING Unless it is intended to sprawl over a bank or low wall, *C. sasanqua* may benefit from the support of either a central stake, around which branches can be "maypoled" (*see* Tree Fruits, *p.99*), or a wall (*see p.162*); to produce a formal espalier framework on a wall, *see Magnolia grandiflora, p.74.* Once this is formed, the plant needs minimal attention. Shorten any wayward branches that threaten the balanced shape of a specimen back to a healthy lateral. Remove entirely old branches that no longer flower. If renovation is needed, treat as for *C. japonica*.

RENOVATION OF C. JAPONICA
Camellias respond well, although slowly, if branches are cut back hard.

CAMELLIA SASANQUA
This fast-growing species may have an open growth habit, requiring it to be supported. Here it is tied in to a central post, the branches drawn up to display the flowers.

All stems have been cut back hard after flowering

By late summer the pruned branches are producing new growth

OTHER ORNAMENTAL SHRUBS

CALCEOLARIA Pinch out young shoot tips of *C. integrifolia* in spring to encourage bushy growth. Established plants may become open and straggly. This species breaks well from older wood if hard pruning is needed to rejuvenate old specimens, although it is usually best to renew such plants.
CALLIANDRA To contain the spreading

habit, cut stems back by up to two-thirds after flowering. Grows well in containers.
CALLUNA Single species of evergreen, bushy shrub (*C. vulgaris*), but with many cultivars, most pruned in the same way as *Erica cinerea* (*see p.193*). Dwarf cultivars such as 'Foxii Nana' should not need pruning, but untypical overlong shoots should be cut back to their point of origin as seen.

CALOTHAMNUS No special pruning needs.
CALYTRIX Tip-prune young plants. Lightly prune back flowered shoots after flowering.
CANDOLLEA See Hibbertia, *p.200.*
CANTUA For *C. buxifolia*, see Dictionary of Climbing Plants, *p.267.*

CARISSA (ZONE 10)

Evergreen, medium to large, often dense shrubs, with fragrant flowers in summer; *C. macrocarpa* (syn. *C. grandiflora*) bears edible fruit. They can be grown outdoors only in frost-free gardens, where thorny species are popular as barrier hedging, responding well to close clipping after flowering. *C. macrocarpa* and its cultivars may be grown in pots under glass in colder climates. Cut out weak, twiggy growth in early spring. Wayward shoots on freestanding shrubs may be cut out during the growing season as for *Aucuba* (*see p.177*).

CARPENTERIA (ZONES 7–9)

Carpenteria californica, the tree anemone, is an evergreen shrub, with white flowers borne in summer on the previous year's wood. Although frost-tolerant, it benefits from shelter in colder climates. It is an upright, leggy plant, and needs selective hard pruning to remove older wood weakened by repeated flowering.

WHEN TO PRUNE Spring, immediately after flowering.

TRAINING AND PRUNING As plants mature, remove branches (no more than one in three) that have become exhausted by flowering, cutting them out at the base. More drastic pruning is possible, but recovery takes a long time, so it is better to replace old plants.

CARPENTERIA CALIFORNICA
Carpenterias are best grown against a wall in colder climates, but should be tied in loosely, rather than formally wall trained.

CARYOPTERIS *BLUEBEARD*

Deciduous shrubs, with grayish foliage and blue flowers on the current season's growth in late summer and autumn. They are best pruned back annually to a low framework to prevent them from becoming bare at the base and to encourage the production of flowering shoots. In cold winters, most of the previous year's growth usually dies back.

C. X CLANDONENSIS (ZONES 6–9)

Upright, bushy shrub with bright blue flowers, produced at the ends of shoots and in leaf axils. The many cultivars are all pruned in the same way.

WHEN TO PRUNE Mid- to late spring, as the buds are breaking (when dead wood is more obvious), and when severe frosts are no longer expected.

TRAINING AND PRUNING Develop a low framework (*see also p.157*) by pruning young plants hard in the first spring after planting. In subsequent years shorten all stems by at least three-quarters of the growth made the previous year, cutting to within 1in (2.5cm) of the older wood. Do not cut into the established framework, since plants will very rarely produce new shoots from old wood. To renovate neglected specimens, cut stems back in spring to the lowest active buds that can be seen. Plants are unlikely to survive more drastic pruning.

> **OTHER CARYOPTERIS**
> C. INCANA, C. MONGHOLICA As for *C. x clandonensis*.

PRUNING CARYOPTERIS IN SPRING
Prune back nearly all of the previous year's growth, but do not cut into old wood.

FLOWERING IN SUMMER
These vigorous, arching shoots grow and bear terminal flower heads in a single season.

CASSIA *SENNA, SHOWER TREE* (ZONE 10)

Deciduous or evergreen, medium-sized shrubs (some now included in *Senna*), grown for their usually yellow pea-flowers and handsome foliage. Few withstand frost; they should be grown under glass in colder climates.

C. CORYMBOSA SYN. SENNA CORYMBOSA

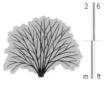

A semievergreen or evergreen shrub or small tree needing warm, frost-free conditions. Rich yellow flowers are borne in late summer on the current season's growth. In cooler climates grow on a sheltered, warm wall or under glass.

WHEN TO PRUNE Spring, when growth is starting.

TRAINING AND PRUNING In warm climates keep pruning to the minimum. In cooler climates establish a framework of stout growth as for *Caryopteris* (*see above*), then prune back to within two or three buds of this framework annually to encourage flowering shoots. The same applies to wall-trained specimens (*see p.162*); cut back the season's growth to within two or three buds of a permanent framework of branches.

> **OTHER CASSIAS**
> *See* Dictionary of Ornamental Trees, *p.56.*

CEANOTHUS

Deciduous and evergreen shrubs grown for their dense clusters of mainly blue flowers; they are often referred to as "California lilac." Those that flower on new growth are frost-tolerant enough to be grown in the open in mild climates. Evergreens are often wall trained. The age of wood on which plants flower determines the time of pruning. Prostrate species need minimal pruning.

C. 'AUTUMNAL BLUE' (ZONES 9–10)

Bushy evergreen with blue flowers, in late spring on the previous year's growth, and in autumn on the current season's shoots. In areas where winters are severe, it is best grown against a sunny wall.

WHEN TO PRUNE Spring.

TRAINING AND PRUNING Tip-prune young plants (*see p.155*). When established, lightly cut back the previous season's growth of freestanding specimens. Train plants on walls informally (*see p.162*), tying in shoots promptly. Prune the previous season's growth by one-third to half, and cut back or remove shoots growing into or out from the wall. Old or neglected freestanding specimens are best replaced. Gradually tie in new shoots to replace old branches on a wall-trained shrub, pruning back sideshoots on the replacement stem by one-third to a half.

C. 'GLOIRE DE VERSAILLES'

Deciduous (zones 7 to 10), with pale blue flowers from midsummer to early autumn on the new growth.

WHEN TO PRUNE Early to midspring.

TRAINING AND PRUNING Shortening the previous season's growth each year (*see above right*), at first to establish a framework, then pruning back to these framework branches, produces the best flowering display. To renovate, cut all growth back to near ground level.

TRAINING AND PRUNING A DECIDUOUS CEANOTHUS

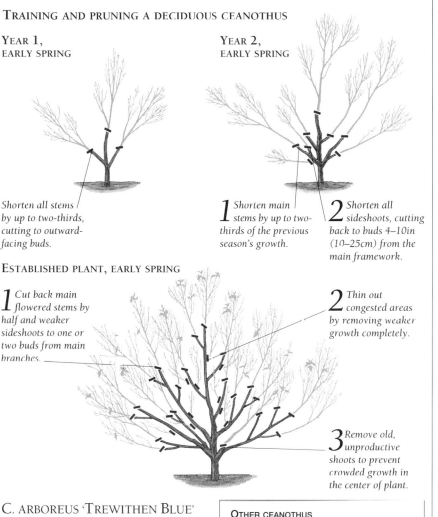

YEAR 1,
EARLY SPRING

Shorten all stems by up to two-thirds, cutting to outward-facing buds.

YEAR 2,
EARLY SPRING

1 Shorten main stems by up to two-thirds of the previous season's growth.

2 Shorten all sideshoots, cutting back to buds 4–10in (10–25cm) from the main framework.

ESTABLISHED PLANT, EARLY SPRING

1 Cut back main flowered stems by half and weaker sideshoots to one or two buds from main branches.

2 Thin out congested areas by removing weaker growth completely.

3 Remove old, unproductive shoots to prevent crowded growth in the center of plant.

C. ARBOREUS 'TREWITHEN BLUE'

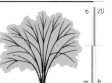

Evergreen (zones 8 to 10) with blue flowers in spring and early summer on the previous season's wood.

WHEN TO PRUNE Midsummer, after flowering.

TRAINING AND PRUNING Establish as for C. 'Autumnal Blue'. Thereafter, cut back longer flowered shoots by one-third to half after flowering. For more bushy growth, trim them again lightly later in summer. To grow as a wall shrub, *see p.162*. Neglected specimens are difficult to renovate because growth does not break from older wood.

OTHER CEANOTHUS

C. 'BURKWOODII' As for C. 'Autumnal Blue'.
C. 'CONCHA' As for C. arboreus 'Trewithen Blue'.
C. X DELILEANUS cultivars (inc. 'Marie Simon', 'Henri Desfusse', 'Perle Rose') As for C. 'Gloire de Versailles'.
C. DENTATUS and var. FLORIBUNDUS As for C. arboreus 'Trewithen Blue'.
C. IMPRESSUS As for C. arboreus 'Trewithen Blue'. Popular for wall training, growing outward from the wall to give a magnificent cascading effect (pruning back outward growing stems too rigorously will ruin this); it therefore needs very sturdy support.
C. THYRSIFLORUS 'SKYLARK' As for C. arboreus 'Trewithen Blue'.

OTHER ORNAMENTAL SHRUBS

CARMICHAELIA No special pruning needs. Grow against a sunny wall in cool climates.
CASSINIA No special pruning needs.
CASSIOPE As for Erica carnea (see p.193).

CASTANOPSIS No special needs, but breaks from old wood if hard pruning is necessary.
CENTRADENIA Pinch out shoots of young plants; trim to shape after flowering.

CEPHALANTHUS No special needs.
CERATOPETALUM If necessary to restrict growth, prune C. gummiferum in mid- to late summer.

CERATOSTIGMA (ZONES 6–9)

Deciduous, semievergreen, or evergreen shrubs (and some perennials) grown mainly for their striking blue flowers, borne in late summer and autumn in terminal clusters on the current season's shoots. Most should be grown in a sheltered spot since they are not fully hardy in colder climates. In cold winters they will usually die back, sometimes to the ground, depending on the harshness of the winter. Prune in midspring: remove any dead wood and shorten all other stems to 1–2in (2.5–5cm) from the ground. In mild climates where plants retain a woody framework, prune as for *Caryopteris* (*see p.184*).

CESTRUM (ZONES 8–10)

Deciduous or evergreen shrubs with attractive flowers borne on the current year's growth, and sometimes on side-shoots from the previous season's wood. A few (such as *C. parqui*) are hardy enough to be grown outside in cooler climates, in a sheltered site, and others may be grown in pots under glass. Cestrums usually have an open habit, so when young, tip-prune (*see p.155*) long shoots to encourage bushiness. May be wall trained (*see p.162*). In early spring, thin by removing two- or three-year-old stems at the base. Top-growth of plants outdoors in colder climates is usually killed in winter; cut back hard in early spring, and fresh growth will be produced from ground level.

CHAENOMELES *FLOWERING QUINCE, JAPONICA*

Deciduous, twiggy shrubs that flower in early spring and produce quincelike fruits in autumn. They may be grown as freestanding shrubs, but often flower better if trained as formal or informal fans against walls and spur-pruned. Pruning in summer helps limit damage by aphids and sooty mold, since any affected young leaves are removed. All chaenomeles are pruned in the same way. *C. speciosa*, which has a naturally dense habit, makes a good informal hedge, and clipping results in the formation of more flowering spurs. Some species are thorny.

Sideshoots left unpruned

Sideshoots pruned to two or three buds

PRUNING FOR FLOWERING
Unpruned Chaenomeles *stems (left) produce few, if any, flowers; spur-pruning stimulates profuse flowering (right).*

C. X SUPERBA (ZONES 5–8)

Deciduous, erect, spreading shrub, with many cultivars. The flowers – red, pink, orange, or white – are borne in spring and followed by yellow fruit.

WHEN TO PRUNE Late spring and early summer, after flowering.

TRAINING AND PRUNING Freestanding shrubs require little pruning beyond thinning once mature, but shortening new growth in summer to five or six leaves improves flowering performance. If grown against a wall, select five or six branches and tie in to form the main framework (*see p.162*). In summer prune back breastwood and remove crossing or badly spaced stems. Once established, cut back excess growth in late spring and summer, and form flowering spurs by cutting back all sideshoots to two or three leaves (*see left*). Any late-produced shoots should be pruned in winter to two or three buds. Spur systems will become congested and need reducing, as for apples (*see p.105*). Prune hard in spring to renovate. Drastic cutting back is best done over two or three years.

OTHER CHAENOMELES
C. CATHAYENSIS Very vigorous, often of gaunt habit. As for *C. x superba.*
C. JAPONICA, C. SPECIOSA As for *C. x superba.*

CHIMONANTHUS

WINTERSWEET

Chimonanthus praecox is a deciduous or, in warm climates, semievergreen shrub (zones 7–9), producing sweetly scented flowers in winter once plants are at least five years old. In colder areas the shelter of a warm wall or wall training is advisable to protect flowers against frost.

WHEN TO PRUNE Late winter, after flowering.

TRAINING AND PRUNING Wintersweet is best left unpruned when young, so that mature flowering wood can develop. Once established, little or no pruning is required for a freestanding shrub. If necessary, shoots can be thinned, and older branches can be shortened by 6–12in (15–30cm).

On wall-trained shrubs (*see p.162*) cut back laterals that have flowered to two or three leaves. Cut old, weak, or badly placed branches to the ground in winter or early spring. Renovate by cutting back all stems to 24in (60cm) from the base of the plant. The plant is slow to recover when renovated by hard pruning, and flowering will be delayed by several years.

CHOISYA (ZONES 9–10)

Dense, evergreen, medium-sized shrubs with aromatic foliage and clusters of strong-smelling white flowers in spring. Choisyas are usually tolerant of light frost, and, although prone to frost

CHOISYA TERNATA
Pruning back flowered shoots will encourage a second, smaller flush of flowers.

CISTUS ROCK ROSE

Evergreen, small to medium-sized shrubs (zones 8 to 9), flowering in midsummer. Pruning is best kept to a minimum except when young.

WHEN TO PRUNE Spring.

TRAINING AND PRUNING Prune young plants (*see below*) to encourage bushiness. Established plants need no special attention. Remove dead and frost-damaged wood in early spring. Old, straggly plants do not respond well to being cut back and should be replaced.

Before pruning

After pruning

YOUNG CISTUS X PURPUREUS
Prune the leader and strong laterals back by two-thirds to produce a more bushy plant.

damage in exposed sites, they will usually survive. *C. ternata* (Mexican orange blossom) is very cold-resistant and, though it may show some dieback, will recover. In cold areas species that are less frost-resistant are better grown as potted plants under cover. Choisyas are fast-growing, and naturally form well-shaped bushes without pruning. Established plants need little attention, although cutting back flowered stems (*see left*) encourages a second flush of flowers in autumn. In a mild year, these will continue into the winter. Choisyas are apt to become unruly with age and top-heavy if their sideways spread is restricted. They respond well to hard pruning in spring.

WHEN TO PRUNE Spring, immediately after flowering.

TRAINING AND PRUNING On established plants, cut back the flowered stems by 10–12in (25–30cm) if a further crop of flowers is desired (*see left*). Any frosted shoots should be cut out entirely. If plants are old, misshapen, or badly frost-damaged, prune them hard.

CLERODENDRUM

Genus that includes climbers as well as tall, bushy, deciduous or evergreen shrubs that have showy flowers. Not all species are frost-tolerant.

C. BUNGEI (ZONES 6/7–9)

GLORY FLOWER

Evergreen or deciduous, upright, suckering shrub. It is frost-tolerant, with heart-shaped leaves and heads of fragrant, pink flowers in late summer and early autumn. In cool climates, where it tends to die back in winter anyway, it should be pruned hard to prevent the accumulation of dead wood that may harbor canker.

WHEN TO PRUNE Spring, when the buds begin to break.

TRAINING AND PRUNING In frost-free areas it forms a woody framework. Cut back annually to this at a height of 24–36in (60–90cm). In colder climates cut out old stems completely.

C. TRICHOTOMUM (ZONES 6–9)

HARLEQUIN GLORYBOWER

Deciduous shrub with heart-shaped leaves and fragrant, white flowers followed by blue berries; best grown on a short, clear leg so that its suckering tendency can be controlled. Annual pruning reduces the number of flowers and fruit but increases their size.

CLERODENDRUM TRICHOTOMUM
The suckers that often emerge over a wide area around this species should be removed or transplanted as new plants.

WHEN TO PRUNE Early spring, before buds break.

TRAINING AND PRUNING Train young plants with a single clear stem (*see p.28*), cutting back the leader anywhere between 2 and 6ft (60–180cm). Select five or six laterals to form a branching head. Little further pruning is needed. Injury to the root system can lead to suckers growing around the base. Prevent this by mulching and minimal disturbance of the soil. Remove suckers (*see p.153*) or transplant for propagation.

OTHER CLERODENDRUMS
C. SPECIOSISSIMUM, C. UGANDENSE Bushy evergreens requiring minimal pruning.
For other species, see Dictionary of Climbing Plants, *p.269.*

OTHER ORNAMENTAL SHRUBS
CERCOCARPUS No special needs.
CHAMAEBATIARIA No special needs.
CHAMELAUCIUM Prune *C. uncinatum* after flowering, if necessary to restrict growth, shortening the flowered stems by half.
CHEIRANTHUS *See Erysimum (p.193).*
CHIONANTHUS No special needs.
CHORDOSPARTIUM No special needs, but cut out dead wood in spring.
CHORIZEMA Pinch-prune young plants (*see p.168*). Trim lightly after flowering.
CHRYSOLEPIS No special needs.
X CITROFORTUNELLA As for *Fortunella* (kumquat); *see* Citrus fruits, *p.142.*
CLETHRA Prune those species with a suckering habit as for *Amelanchier stolonifera (see p.175).* Other species should be allowed to develop unchecked; remove old branches in favor of younger growth only when weak and unproductive.
CLEYERA No special needs.

CLIANTHUS *See* Dictionary of Climbing Plants, *p.270.*
CODIAEUM Pinch out tips of shoots to encourage bushy growth. Tolerates being cut back if necessary.
COLEONEMA Heathlike. Trim over lightly in summer, after flowering.
COLLETIA Spiny shrubs with no special pruning needs. Will tolerate being cut back hard to rejuvenate.

COLQUHOUNIA

Evergreen or semievergreen, medium-sized shrubs (zones 7 to 9) with aromatic foliage, and attractive racemes of red, orange, or yellow flowers in late summer that are borne on the current season's wood. Although frost-tolerant, they often die back in severe winters, so in colder areas they should be grown in a sheltered site. The habit is similar to that of *Buddleja davidii*, and in cooler climates plants should be pruned in the same way (*see p.180*). They may also be wall trained (*see p.162*), cutting flowered growth back to a framework. Pinch out young shoot tips in spring if a more bushy habit is desired.

COLUTEA (ZONES 6–8)

Deciduous, small to medium-sized, fast-growing, bushy shrubs with pealike flowers in summer borne on the current season's wood. They may be grown with minimal pruning, their size restricted if necessary by shortening long growths in spring. They may be trained on a short leg as low standards (*see p.165*) or, once plants are growing strongly, regularly cut back hard in the same way as *Cornus alba* (*see right*) to flower into late summer.

CONVOLVULUS (ZONES 8–9)

Convolvulus cneorum, the silverbush, is an evergreen, rounded subshrub with silky, silvery-gray foliage and, through spring and summer, yellow-centered white flowers that are pink in the bud. It is the only commonly grown shrub in a genus that includes annuals, perennials, and climbers. Frost-tolerant, it requires a warm, sheltered situation to thrive. It is naturally mound-forming and needs little pruning. It occasionally produces elongated shoots that are best removed. It is also prone to dieback.

WHEN TO PRUNE Early spring, before buds break.

TRAINING AND PRUNING Allow plants to develop naturally with minimal pruning. Shorten overlong shoots, cutting them back either to the base or to a healthy sideshoot. Any shoots affected by dieback should be cut out to the base as seen. *C. cneorum* is not long-lived, and its response to hard pruning is poor, so it is better to replace old or neglected plants with new, young specimens.

CORNUS Dogwood

The shrubby species, mainly deciduous, are grown mainly for the red, yellow, or green winter color of their stems, but in some cases also for their flowers, fruit, and variegated foliage.

C. ALBA (ZONES 2–7)

RED-TWIG DOGWOOD, TATARIAN DOGWOOD

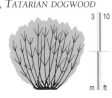

Vigorous, twiggy shrub, with heads of star-shaped flowers in late spring, which are followed by white or pale blue fruits. Young stems are bright red in winter. Hard annual pruning produces the best winter display of stems, but at the expense of flowering growth.

WHEN TO PRUNE Early spring, before buds break.

TRAINING AND PRUNING If growing for flowers and fruit or variegated foliage, allow to develop unpruned. Restrict spread, if necessary, by cutting out one in four old shoots each year. This will also encourage new growth from the base. Neglected plants can be renovated by cutting out old wood at the center of the bush. When cultivars are grown for their stem effect (*see also p.164*), allow the bush to grow unpruned in the first year after planting, then cut all stems back to 2in (5cm) from the ground. In subsequent years cut all stems back to two buds of the previous year's growth.

C. MAS (ZONES 4–8)

CORNELIAN CHERRY

Large, often multistemmed, deciduous shrub that may also be grown as a small standard. Yellow

STAGGERED PRUNING, CORNUS ALBA
Cut back to varying heights to create the effect of a sloping bank rather than a dense mass of regrowth.

CORNUS STOLONIFERA
The bright yellow color of the young stems is striking when they are bare in winter.

flowers appear on the bare wood in winter and early spring. These are followed by rich leaf color and bright red fruit in autumn.

WHEN TO PRUNE Early summer.

TRAINING AND PRUNING Keep pruning to a minimum on multistemmed shrubs. Thin if necessary to keep an open shape and display the flowers better. On variegated cultivars, limited renewal pruning will produce vigorous young shoots. Rejuvenate overgrown shrubs by cutting back to within two buds of framework branches. To produce a standard, train with a clear stem (*see p.165*) to 2–5ft (60–150cm). Competing leaders often break from low on the stem; shorten these to four to six buds.

OTHER CORNUS
C. CHINENSIS As for *C. mas*.
C. OFFICINALIS As for *C. mas*.
C. SANGUINEA As for *C. alba*.
C. STOLONIFERA As for *C. alba*.
For other species, see Dictionary of Ornamental Trees, *p.60.*

CORONILLA (ZONES 8–9)

Crown vetches are small, deciduous or evergreen shrubs and perennials, grown for their attractive foliage and usually yellow flowers. They bloom in spring, or in some cases from late autumn to late spring. Some are not frost-tolerant, but may be grown in cooler climates if given a sheltered site. Restrict pruning to the removal of old, unproductive wood at the base of the plant. Prune the hardier species in early spring, but in cooler climates delay any pruning required of more tender species, such as *C. valentina* subsp. *glauca*, until they have finished flowering, cutting back any frost-damaged wood to healthy shoots. Coronillas are unlikely to survive drastic renovation.

CORYLOPSIS (ZONES 6–8)

Deciduous shrubs of twiggy habit with drooping, catkinlike, yellow flowers borne in winter and early spring on the previous season's wood. They naturally form attractive shapes that are easily ruined by pruning. If it is necessary to restrict size, take old branches out at the base in spring after flowering; trim flowered shoots of wall-trained plants (*see p.162*) at the same time. Otherwise, prune only to remove dead wood.

CORYLUS *HAZEL*

Deciduous, suckering shrubs. Some have attractive foliage while others, such as *C. avellana* 'Contorta', are grown for their twisted stems; all have yellow catkins in late winter or early spring. They may be grown for nut crops.

C. AVELLANA (ZONES 5–8)

EUROPEAN FILBERT, HAZELNUT

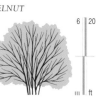

A large, multi-stemmed, cropping species, which is also an attractive ornamental shrub if regularly pruned, especially in its yellow- or purple-leaved forms.

WHEN TO PRUNE Late winter.

TRAINING AND PRUNING Allow the multi-stemmed form to develop naturally. To

COTINUS

Deciduous shrubs and small trees grown for their foliage, smokelike plumes of flowers in summer, and autumn color. Flowers, produced on two- to three-year-old wood, are abundant only during hot summers, so in colder climates cotinus are more often grown for their foliage, the largest leaves being produced on plants that are cut back to a framework. Several cultivars with purple foliage are often pruned hard annually so that they produce much larger leaves than unpruned specimens.

C. COGGYGRIA (ZONES 5–8)

SMOKE TREE, VENETIAN SUMAC

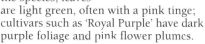

Bushy shrub with many cultivars, all with spectacular autumn color and smokelike inflorescences. In the species, leaves are light green, often with a pink tinge; cultivars such as 'Royal Purple' have dark purple foliage and pink flower plumes.

WHEN TO PRUNE Spring, before growth begins.

TRAINING AND PRUNING To grow as a flowering shrub, keep pruning to a

COTINUS IN BLOOM
Left unpruned, cotinus will flower profusely; cut back annually, they produce larger leaves.

minimum. For a large-leaved effect (*see p.164*), in the first year select three to five strong stems as the main framework, pruning them to 24–36in (60–90cm). In subsequent years cut all the previous year's stems back by about three-quarters, but take care to leave at least two strong buds; harder pruning will produce less vigorous shoots.

> **OTHER COTINUS**
> C. OBOVATUS More treelike, needs little pruning. Hybrids with *C. coggygria*, such as 'Flame', may be pruned hard.

CORYLUS AVELLANA
Regrowth after hard pruning is strong. First year growth is seen on the far right, second-year growth in the center, and third-year growth on the left. Coppicing of hazels (see p.36) is traditionally carried out on a seven-year cycle.

maintain vigor and to balance mature and young growth, each year remove some older wood, occasionally cutting a branch right to the base. To renovate, cut back all stems in late winter. To grow as a cropping bush, *see p.149*. To prune 'Contorta', the corkscrew hazel, *see p.30*.

> **OTHER HAZELS**
> C. MAXIMA (filbert) As for *C. avellana*. Purple-leaved forms are best regularly pruned hard (*see p.164*). See also Nuts, *p.148*.
> *For other species, see* Dictionary of Ornamental Trees, *p.60*.

> **OTHER ORNAMENTAL SHRUBS**
> COPROSMA Evergreens with no special needs. Cut out any frost-damaged growth in midspring.
>
> CORIARIA Cut out dead wood in spring, to ground level if, in cool climates, plants have died back to a woody base.
>
> COROKIA Cut back frosted growth in spring, into old wood if necessary.
> CORREA No special needs.

COTONEASTER

Evergreen and deciduous shrubs, grown for their flowers and red fruit; those that are deciduous often have attractive autumn foliage. They vary widely in habit, some being prostrate while others are large, arching bushes. Although most respond well to pruning, they generally need minimal attention.

C. HORIZONTALIS (ZONES 5–7)

FISHBONE COTONEASTER, ROCK COTONEASTER

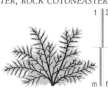

Deciduous, spreading shrub; branches have a rigid habit and a characteristic herringbone arrangement of branchlets, covered in red berries in winter. In open ground it is a mounding, layered shrub, and grows well over low banks. It also looks very effective trained flat against a wall.

WHEN TO PRUNE Late winter.

TRAINING AND PRUNING On freestanding plants, remove only congested and old, sparsely furnished growth, cutting the branches right back to the main stem. To grow against a wall (*see p.162*), choose a young, pliable specimen, and provide initial support for the main branches; stems will then grow flat against the wall. Shorten outward-facing shoots to maintain this form. Fishbone cotoneaster does not respond readily when cut back hard.

C. X WATERERI (ZONES 7–8)

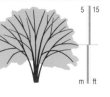

Evergreen or semi-evergreen shrub or small tree; its upright stems have arching laterals. Its small, white flowers are followed by clusters of spherical, red fruits.

WHEN TO PRUNE Winter or midspring.

TRAINING AND PRUNING For a multi-stemmed shrub, develop a framework of four to seven main branches, removing laterals crossing the center of the shrub to reduce later congestion. Thereafter, keep pruning to a minimum. To renovate a neglected specimen, either cut any unwanted stems back to the main branches, or cut all stems back to the base.

COTONEASTER HORIZONTALIS
A species that is particularly effective grown against a wall; the flowers and autumn berries are displayed well by the flat branches with their regular arrangement of branchlets along the main stems. This pattern has gained it the name of fishbone cotoneaster.

OTHER COTONEASTERS
C. FRIGIDUS 'CORNUBIA' As for C. X *watereri*.
C. DAMMERI Small, prostrate shrub; trim wayward shoots in early spring. Responds to hard pruning if necessary.
C. DIVARICATUS Keep pruning to a minimum. Good for informal hedging.
C. FRANCHETII Keep pruning to a minimum.
C. FRIGIDUS As for C. X *watereri*.
C. 'HYBRIDUS PENDULUS' Minimal pruning. Maintain top-grafted standards as for any weeping standard (*see p.28*).
C. LACTEUS Keep pruning to a minimum. Informal hedges may be lightly trimmed.
C. MICROPHYLLUS As for C. *dammeri*.
C. SALICIFOLIUS As for C. X *watereri*.
C. SIMONSII Good for hedging (*see p.44*); can be clipped to a semiformal outline without losing berries. Otherwise, keep pruning to a minimum.
C. STERNIANUS, C. WARDII Keep pruning to a minimum.

CYTISUS *BROOM*

Mainly deciduous shrubs, with yellow flowers in spring or summer. They are fast-growing, though often short-lived, plants that thrive in hot, dry conditions.

C. BATTANDIERI (ZONES 7–8)

MOROCCAN BROOM, PINEAPPLE BROOM

Semievergreen shrub, flowering on the current season's shoots from early to midsummer. It freely produces growth from the base. Needs a warm, sheltered site and may be wall trained.

WHEN TO PRUNE Summer, after flowering.

TRAINING AND PRUNING Freestanding specimens require little pruning, but old wood can be cut out. On wall-trained plants (*see p.162*), occasionally remove

an old framework branch and train in young replacement growth.

C. SCOPARIUS (ZONES 6–8)

Arching shrub, flowering in late spring on the previous year's wood. Although short-lived, annual pruning prevents the seed production that weakens it.

WHEN TO PRUNE Early or midsummer, immediately after flowering.

TRAINING AND PRUNING Pinch out the tips of young shoots for a bushy habit. When established, cut back flowered stems by about two-thirds of the previous season's growth, to a bud or shoot below the spent flowers. It does not break from mature wood; old specimens are best replaced.

OTHER CYTISUS
C. BEANII, C. X KEWENSIS No pruning required, but tolerate light shaping.
C. NIGRICANS Cut back all flowered shoots by about two-thirds in spring.
C. X PRAECOX As for C. *scoparius*.

CYTISUS SCOPARIUS
Regular pruning prevents brooms from becoming too leggy.

After pruning

D

DAPHNE

Evergreen, semievergreen, or deciduous shrubs, grown for their fragrant flowers in early spring. Most are best left unpruned: they are very susceptible to dieback, which pruning can encourage. D. odora (zones 7 to 9) tolerates light trimming to maintain a compact habit, as does D. cneorum (zones 5 to 7). D. mezereum (zones 5 to 8) may withstand the removal of more wayward shoots. It is generally better to layer a wayward shoot of a prostrate daphne than to remove it. In all cases, however, dieback must be removed as soon as it is seen. Remove the entire stem or branch, cutting back to its point of origin, and treat the plant with a fungicide. A few species, such as D. jezoensis (zones 5 to 8), are summer-deciduous; their leaf-fall should not be mistaken for dieback.

DEUTZIA SCABRA
As plants mature, remove some older stems completely to promote younger growth.

DEUTZIA

Medium-sized, deciduous shrubs bearing white or pink flowers in summer on new shoots from the previous year's growth. Like forsythias, they make new growth from the base, developing sturdy stems that support twiggy growth. Prune to encourage a bushy habit and to keep the plants well furnished with productive wood. Pruning should also be carried out to remove any damage by late spring frosts to species such as D. gracilis and D. x lemoinei. Branches whose buds open as small, shriveled flowers due to the effects of frost will not recover satisfactorily, and should be pruned out.

D. SCABRA (ZONES 6–8)

Deciduous, upright shrub with white flowers in summer. The bark becomes attractively shaggy with age.

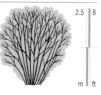

2.5 | 8
m | ft

WHEN TO PRUNE After flowering.

TRAINING AND PRUNING Tip-prune on planting (see p.155). In subsequent years prune to young shoots below the flowered wood. As plants mature, cut out older branches to ground level, or to strong low shoots. To renovate, cut old main stems to the base and shorten others to well-placed sideshoots. Plants take a year or two to flower well again.

DECAISNEA (ZONES 6–9)

Decaisnea fargesii is a deciduous, summer-flowering, upright shrub with racemes of greenish-white flowers and sausage-shaped fruits. It is frost-tolerant, but needs a sheltered site in areas where winters are very severe. Young plants require no pruning. Cut back any old, weak stems on established plants in spring, either to a healthy bud or, if none is available, to the ground. No other pruning is required. Fresh growth that is damaged by a late frost should be cut back in early summer to strong shoots farther down the stems.

DESMODIUM (ZONES 8–11)

Tick trefoils are small, deciduous shrubs (and some perennials), grown for their foliage and racemes of lilac or deep pink flowers, which are borne on the current season's shoots. In cool climates their top-growth is often cut back to ground level in winter by frosts, but plants will generally recover if they are grown in a sheltered site, preferably against a warm wall. In spring, prune all growth back hard close to ground level, as for *Indigofera heterantha* (see p.204). Neglected specimens will also generally respond to such treatment.

DENDROMECON *TREE POPPY* (ZONES 9–10)

Evergreens with open, erect to spreading branches, and gray-green foliage. Fragrant, poppylike, yellow flowers are borne on laterals from the main stems throughout the summer. D. rigida, the tree or bush poppy, may only be grown in cooler climates if given a warm, sheltered site. Its bushy, arching habit makes it suitable for training formally or informally against a south- or southwest-facing wall.

3 | 10
m | ft

WHEN TO PRUNE Early spring, with the onset of fresh growth; prune wall-trained plants in summer after flowering.

TRAINING AND PRUNING After planting, pinch back young shoots to encourage a bushy habit. Once the plant is established, prune only to remove winter-damaged shoots or to shorten weak or bare shoots, cutting them back to a strong, outward-facing sideshoot. Prune wall-trained specimens after flowering, tying young shoots into the framework. Dendromecons may be cut to ground level to rejuvenate them.

OTHER ORNAMENTAL SHRUBS
CRINODENDRON No special needs.
CROSSANDRA No special needs. Shorten flowered stems by half in late winter to promote new flowering growth.
CROTALARIA Cut to the base in spring.
CROWEA Prune lightly after flowering.
CUPHEA Pinch-prune young plants to encourage bushiness, then trim each spring to remove flowered shoots.
CYDONIA See Quince, p.121.
CYRILLA No special needs.
DABOECIA Trim lightly in spring to remove spent flowers.
DAIS Prune lightly in autumn to shape.

DAMPIERA Prune lightly after flowering.
DANAE Prune plants only once established, as for *Kerria* (see p. 204).
DAPHNIPHYLLUM Pinch out the main shoot tips of young plants to encourage low branching. Can be cut back hard.
DARWINIA Tip-prune after flowering to maintain a compact shape.
DATURA See Brugmansia, p.179.
DERMATOBOTRYS No special pruning required.
DESFONTAINEA Do not prune.
DICHOTOMANTHES As for *Cotoneaster* (see facing page).

OTHER DEUTZIAS
D. CRENATA, D. GRACILIS, D. X HYBRIDA, D. X LEMOINEI, D. PULCHRA, D. PURPURASCENS As for *D. scabra*.
D. MONBEIGII, D. SETCHUENENSIS Less vigorous and more compact, needing more moderate pruning. Cut back flowered sideshoots to only one or two buds. Can be wall trained (see p.162).

DIERVILLA (ZONES 4–9)

The southern bush honeysuckle is a deciduous, suckering shrub, similar to *Weigela*, with small, yellow flowers on the current season's growth in summer. It is best pruned hard each year, cutting stems back to a pair of buds about 12in (30cm) from the base in early spring, to stimulate the growth of young stems with attractive bronze foliage. Neglected or overgrown specimens often respond well when pruned back hard, but old plants are better dug up and divided, and young, vigorous portions replanted.

DIPELTA (ZONES 6–8)

D. floribunda is a large, deciduous shrub, grown for its showy flowers in early summer and the peeling bark on mature plants. The natural habit is upright to arching, and strong, new shoots are often produced from the base. Prune after flowering, cutting one in five stems down to the base, selecting first the oldest and any with signs of dieback.

DODONAEA (ZONES 9–10)

Small to medium-sized evergreen shrubs, grown chiefly for their foliage. They may be grown outdoors only in warm climates, but make good pot-plants under glass. Pinch out the growing tips of young plants (*see p.155*) to encourage bushy growth well furnished with young leaves. Established plants may be pruned to shape in late summer and spring. Dodonaeas are good hedging plants (*see p.44*) for warm climates, tolerating windy situations.

DURANTA (ZONE 10)

Evergreen shrubs with arching branches, sometimes spiny. They bear sprays of lilac, lilac-blue, or white flowers from spring to autumn, and poisonous, yellow berries. They are frost-tender, though *D. erecta* (syn. *D. repens*) tolerates light frost. Usually grown as open, multi-stemmed bushes, they are excellent informal hedging plants (*see p.44*). They may also be trained as standards.

WHEN TO PRUNE Spring.

TRAINING AND PRUNING Let young plants develop unpruned, unless training as a standard (*see p.165*). Once established, cut out whole branches if necessary to restrict size. Do not shorten stems; this results in bushy growth below the cut and ruins the habit. Remove any shoots on the clear trunks of standards.

E-F

EDGEWORTHIA (ZONES 8–9)

Paper bushes are small, deciduous shrubs that are best given the protection of a warm wall in cooler areas, since the fragrant, white or yellow flowers are susceptible to frost damage. The papery bark is attractive. The flower heads form in autumn, and the flowers open during late winter and spring. The stems, freely produced from the base, are so thin and supple that they can be tied in knots. Little pruning is needed. Cut any old and unproductive stems out after flowering.

ELAEAGNUS

Large, very vigorous, evergreen and deciduous shrubs, some with highly scented flowers. They make fine specimen plants, and are suitable for hedges or barrier plantings.

E. ANGUSTIFOLIA (ZONES 2–7)

OLEASTER, RUSSIAN OLIVE

Large, spreading, deciduous shrub or small tree with silvery leaves. It bears fragrant flowers in early summer, which are followed by amber fruit in autumn.

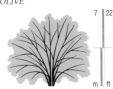

WHEN TO PRUNE If necessary, in midsummer, after flowering.

TRAINING AND PRUNING Allow to grow naturally as a multistemmed bush, or train as a standard (*see p.165*) with a clear stem to a height of 4–5ft (1.2–1.5m). Tolerates hard pruning, so the head of the plant can be maintained in a compact and regular shape.

ELAEAGNUS PUNGENS 'MACULATA'
Remove any shoots with plain green leaves on this variegated cultivar.

ELSHOLTZIA (ZONES 5–8)

Small shrubs, often with aromatic foliage, grown for their flowers, usually produced in autumn on the current season's growth. In warm climates, in early spring cut out one or two old stems at the base, and shorten others to strong buds about 12in (30cm) from ground level. In colder climates they are best given a sheltered position. In severe winters the top-growth is usually killed, and plants should be pruned annually in spring to a low framework of woody growth, as for *Perovskia* (*see p.211*).

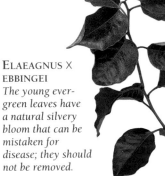

ELAEAGNUS X EBBINGEI
The young evergreen leaves have a natural silvery bloom that can be mistaken for disease; they should not be removed.

E. X EBBINGEI (ZONES 6–9)

Evergreen shrub with silver, scaly leaves and scented flowers in autumn. It does not require annual pruning, but pruning can be used to maintain plants as an informal hedge (*see p.44*). They tolerate coastal locations.

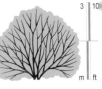

WHEN TO PRUNE Late summer.

TRAINING AND PRUNING Freestanding specimens require only minimal pruning. To keep hedges in check, cut long shoots back to a bud with pruners. Renovate by hard pruning back into old wood.

OTHER ELAEAGNUS
E. COMMUTATA Slow-growing, suckering habit; prune only to remove unwanted growth and excess suckers.
E. GLABRA As for *E. x ebbingei*; long, wayward shoots are frequently produced, especially by young plants.
E. MACROPHYLLA As for *E. x ebbingei*.
E. PUNGENS 'MACULATA' As for *E. x ebbingei*, additionally removing any reverted shoots (*see left*).
E. UMBELLATA As for *E. angustifolia*.

ERICA *HEATH*

Large group of evergreens, ranging in habit from dwarf plants suitable as groundcover to large, treelike plants. Most (but not all) are frost-tolerant. Flowering times occur throughout the year. Most will not break readily from old wood, so only the previous year's growth is usually pruned. Taller species ("tree heaths") may need harder pruning to encourage bushiness.

E. ARBOREA (ZONES 7–8)

TREE HEATH

Evergreen, upright shrub that may become treelike. Formative pruning establishes a good shape; thereafter, only minimal pruning is required, except in colder areas where larger specimens are prone to damage by heavy snowfall; regular pruning creates bushier, more resilient plants. Damaged or overgrown plants respond well to renovation.

WHEN TO PRUNE Early spring, until established; thereafter, in late spring or early summer, after flowering.

ERICA ARBOREA
Unlike most heaths, this species responds very well to hard pruning into old wood.

TRAINING AND PRUNING In the first two or three years, cut back stems by up to two-thirds to promote bushy growth. In later years, pruning is largely unnecessary. Branches may be removed to restrict size, but there will probably be dense, bushy regrowth. In areas that are prone to heavy snow, cut back flowered shoots by about one-third, pruning to emerging shoots, to keep plants compact. Tree heaths will produce new growth if cut back into old wood in later years (*see below left*). It is best to stage renovation over two or three years (*see p.160*).

E. CARNEA (ZONES 6–7)

ALPINE HEATH, WINTER HEATH

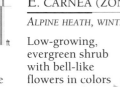

Low-growing, evergreen shrub with bell-like flowers in colors that range from white through pink to red-purple. The flowers are borne in late winter and spring. Several have foliage that colors attractively in winter; some growers prefer to clip the flower buds off these plants in mid- to late winter, because the flower colors clash with the foliage. Annual pruning keeps plants compact, rounded in habit, and free-flowering. They will not break readily from old wood, so only the previous year's growth is shortened.

WHEN TO PRUNE Spring, as the last flowers fade and new growth appears.

TRAINING AND PRUNING Cut stems back to just below the old flower spikes, removing most, but not all, of the previous season's growth. Individual plants look better pruned selectively with pruners, although for large heath beds shearing is much more practical; however, prunings should be cleared away. Old plants that have become straggly are best replaced.

ERICA CARNEA 'WESTWOOD YELLOW'
The golden yellow foliage of this winter heath is attractive all year, with deep pink flowers in the dull days of late winter.

OTHER ERICAS

E. AUSTRALIS As for *E. arborea*, but renovation is likely to be successful only in mild climates.

E. CILIARIS As for *E. cinerea*.

E. CINEREA Prune or trim lightly in early spring, cutting stems back where possible to strong shoots below the spent flower cluster.

E. X DARLEYENSIS As for *E. carnea*.

E. ERIGENA Remove frost-damaged stems in spring, cutting back to new growth. Cut back flowered stems by one-third, to new shoots, after flowering. Should respond to hard pruning provided that some basal growth is retained.

E. LUSITANICA Minimal pruning, in spring if necessary, as for *E. australis*.

E. MACKAIANA As for *E. cinerea*.

E. SCOPARIA Minimal pruning only.

E. TERMINALIS As for *E. arborea*.

E. TETRALIX As for *E. cinerea*.

E. VAGANS As for *E. cinerea*.

E. X VEITCHII As for *E. australis*.

OTHER ORNAMENTAL SHRUBS

DILLWYNIA Trim lightly in spring after flowering.

DIOSMA As for *Agathosma* (*see p.175*).

DIPTERONIA No special needs. Remove any unwanted growth in spring.

DISANTHUS No special pruning needs.

DISCARIA No special needs. Remove any unwanted growth in spring.

DISTYLIUM As for *Hamamelis* (*see p.198*).

DORYCNIUM *D. hirsutum* (syn. *Lotus hirsutus*) is a subshrub; cut back dead and cold-damaged top-growth in spring.

DRIMYS (syn. TASMANNIA) Remove any unwanted growth in spring.

DRYANDRA As for *Banksia* (*see p.177*). Do not cut into old wood.

ECHIUM After flowering, remove spent flower spikes.

ELLIOTTIA No special pruning needs.

EMBOTHRIUM *See* Dictionary of Ornamental Trees, *p.63*.

EMPETRUM As for *Erica carnea* (*see above*).

ENKIANTHUS No special pruning needs. Responds well when cut hard back, as for *Rhododendron* (*see p.216*).

EPACRIS As for *Erica carnea* (*see above*).

ERANTHEMUM No special pruning needs.

EREMOPHILA No special pruning needs.

ERINACEA Minimal pruning only.

ERIOBOTRYA *See* Loquat, *p.145*.

ERIOCEPHALUS No special pruning needs.

ERIOGONUM No special pruning needs.

ERIOSTEMON May be clipped to shape.

ERYSIMUM Pinch out shoots of *E.* 'Bowles Mauve' (syn. *Cheiranthus* 'Bowles Mauve') to encourage bushy growth when young, then trim each year after flowering, cutting flowered shoots back to nonflowered sideshoots.

ESCALLONIA

Evergreen (except *E. virgata*), medium-sized to large shrubs with an arching habit and white, pink, or red flowers, borne mainly on year-old wood in summer and autumn. In cooler climates they may suffer frost damage, but generally recover. Many are suitable as hedges, both formal and informal, although formal trimming reduces the floral display. A few can be trained successfully against walls.

E. 'LANGLEYENSIS' (ZONES 7–9)

Graceful, arching hybrid that is attractive as a free-standing specimen, but it can also be trained against a sunny wall. Bears profuse, deep pink flowers in summer.

WHEN TO PRUNE Summer, after flowering. Renovate in mid- to late spring.

TRAINING AND PRUNING Little formative pruning is required. If training against a wall (*see p.162*), tie in enough stems to form a framework of main branches, removing others. Each year cut back flowered shoots of wall-trained specimens to young sideshoots. Free-standing plants require less rigorous pruning, but cutting out a proportion of flowered wood keeps plants within bounds. Neglected plants usually produce vigorous new growth if pruned hard.

E. RUBRA (ZONES 9–10)

Medium-sized, summer-flowering shrub. Cultivars such as 'Crimson Spire' are excellent for hedging.

WHEN TO PRUNE After flowering; if flowering finishes very late, prune in the next spring. Renovate in spring.

TRAINING AND PRUNING Little or no pruning is required, although plants will tolerate being cut back hard. To maintain an informal outline for hedges (*see p.45*), cut back selected stems to just above vigorous sideshoots.

ESCALLONIA 'LANGLEYENSIS'
Remove growth to well within the plant's outline; shortening ruins the arching habit.

OTHER ESCALLONIAS
E. ALPINA, E. BIFIDA, E. ILLINATA, E. 'IVEYI', E. RUBRA var. MACRANTHA As for *E. rubra*.
E. VIRGATA Keep pruning to a minimum.
Other hybrids, such as 'Apple Blossom' and 'Donard Beauty', are treated as for E. 'Langleyensis', but most are too stiff in habit to be trained against walls.

EUONYMUS

Evergreen and deciduous shrubs. The evergreens, some of which are suitable as hedging in coastal areas, are grown for their foliage, while deciduous euonymus are popular for their autumn color and fruit. Most are frost-tolerant, although some may be damaged by severe cold. Training and pruning varies according to the species and whether plants are grown as freestanding specimens or as a hedge. Some cultivars of *E. fortunei* are effective groundcover and may climb against a support, while others are useful as wall shrubs. Remove plain, green-leaved shoots that appear on variegated plants of any species, cutting them back to their point of origin as soon as seen.

The evergreen species are the most popular as hedges; these should be trimmed with pruners rather than shears (*see p.45*) for a less formal, more attractive outline, and to avoid cutting through leaves, which will turn brown and become unsightly.

To renovate, cut back neglected plants hard, to 12–24in (30–60cm) above ground level; response is generally good.

E. EUROPAEUS (ZONES 4–7)

SPINDLE TREE

Shrub or small tree with fine leaf color in autumn and conspicuous pink capsules that hold orange seeds.

WHEN TO PRUNE Late winter or early spring.

TRAINING AND PRUNING Minimal formative pruning is necessary. Prune established plants only to thin congested growth, cutting out older stems completely to the base to open up the center of the bush.

E. JAPONICUS (ZONES 7–9)

JAPANESE EUONYMUS

Bushy, dense evergreen. Although hardy, its soft, young growth is sometimes damaged by frost.

WHEN TO PRUNE Mid- to late spring.

TRAINING AND PRUNING Little formative pruning is required, but tip-prune hedging plants to encourage bushy growth. Use pruners to cut back whole branches of hedges rather than trimming (*see p.45*). Wall-trained plants require only informal tying in. If necessary, cut out old wood and train in new growth.

OTHER EUONYMUS
E. ALATUS As for *E. europaeus*.
E. FORTUNEI Trim over for denser groundcover, or wall train (*see p.162*) to exploit its creeping, climbing tendency.
E. HAMILTONIANUS As for *E. europaeus*.
E. MYRIANTHUS As for *E. japonica*.
E. NANUS, E. ORESBIUS Minimal pruning required.
E. PHELLOMANUS As for *E. europaeus*.
E. PLANIPES As for *E. europaeus*.

EUONYMUS EUROPAEUS
This reliable species needs pruning only to prevent congestion in the center of the plant.

EUPHORBIA MILKWEED, SPURGE

A wide-ranging genus that includes perennials, annuals, and succulents as well as a number of shrubs, most grown for their foliage and floral bracts. Some are frost-tolerant, others need winter protection in colder climates. Pruning needs vary according to the species, but should always be carried out wearing gloves, since euphorbia stems exude an irritant, milky latex when cut.

E. CHARACIAS INC. SUBSP. WULFENII

MEDITERRANEAN SPURGE

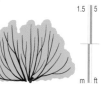

1.5 | 5
m | ft

Evergreen subshrub (zones 7 to 9), with large panicles of greenish yellow bracts in spring and early summer. Stems are biennial, developing in one year and flowering the next. The flowers are terminal, so stems should not be shortened. Once a stem has flowered it will not flower again; remove it to accelerate the natural renewal cycle.

WHEN TO PRUNE Midsummer, after flowering.

EUPHORBIA CHARACIAS
Prune after flowering to strong shoots at the base.

TRAINING AND PRUNING Prune back flowered stems to a strong shoot or bud down low, or to the base of the plant. Strong, developing growth made during the current season that has yet to flower should be left unpruned. Although drastic pruning is rarely necessary, plants will usually regenerate vigorously if all stems are cut back to the base in late winter or early spring. The next season's flowers will be lost, but the plant should flower again in the following season.

E. PULCHERRIMA (ZONE 10)

CHRISTMAS STAR, POINSETTIA

3 | 10
m | ft

Deciduous or evergreen shrub with showy bracts in red, pink, or white. It will grow to a substantial size in the tropics, but is widely grown as a house plant in colder climates, where it is much less vigorous.

WHEN TO PRUNE Spring, after flowering.

TRAINING AND PRUNING Whether grown outdoors or as house plants, cut back hard, removing faded flowered stems to encourage vigorous new growth.

OTHER EUPHORBIAS
E. CAPUT-MEDUSAE Needs no pruning.
E. DENDROIDES Dormant in summer. Minimal pruning needed.
E. INGENS Minimal pruning,
E. MELLIFERA In colder climates, pruning is best kept to a minimum.
E. MILII In warm climates, needs minimal pruning. If grown as an informal hedge, tip-prune all main stems and laterals to encourage branching growth.
E. MYRSINITES As for *E. characias*.

EXOCHORDA COMMON PEARLBUSH (ZONES 5–8)

Deciduous, medium-sized shrubs with a graceful, arching growth habit and racemes of showy, white flowers borne in late spring and early summer on the previous year's wood. Plants may produce numerous basal shoots. Little formative pruning is necessary. Prune established plants annually in late spring, after flowering, to remove weak growth or reduce overcrowding. Cut out to the base of the plant up to one in three old stems and any new shoots that are not required as replacements. Surplus stems can also be cut out in winter. Renovate by cutting out all old stems in spring.

× FATSHEDERA (ZONES 8–10)

Evergreen, medium-sized, sprawling shrub, grown for its large, attractive leaves. Although frost-tolerant, it benefits from shelter or a sunny wall in colder climates. A hybrid of *Fatsia* and *Hedera*, it has characteristics of both a shrub and a climbing plant. If it is to be grown as a freestanding shrub, it needs staking when young; it makes a good standard. However, it is more commonly grown as a wall shrub (*see p.162*), although, unlike *Hedera*, it does not cling, and will need tying in to supports. It looks very attractive trained against a pillar. Its spreading habit also makes it a useful groundcover shrub. In late summer cut back upright shoots to well within the plant's outline. Fatshederas may also be grown as house plants, trained on stakes as for *Hedera helix* cultivars.

OTHER ORNAMENTAL SHRUBS
EUGENIA Evergreen; minimal pruning.
EUPATORIUM (syn. AGERATINA BARTLETTINA) In colder climates cut back to the base in spring; otherwise, needs minimal pruning.
EURYOPS Pinch-prune young plants. When established, prune lightly after flowering.
FEIJOA See *Acca*, *p.175*.

FELICIA Pinch-prune to encourage a bushy, rounded habit. Pinch-pruning may also be used to form decorative shapes such as standards (*see pp.167–173*).
FICUS See Dictionary of Ornamental Trees, *p.66*, and Dictionary of Climbing Plants, *p.271*.
FONTANESIA As for *Ligustrum* (*see p.206*).

FATSIA (ZONES 8–10)

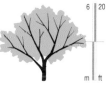

6 | 20
m | ft

The only species is *F. japonica*, the false castor oil plant, a medium-sized, spreading, architectural, evergreen shrub with large, palmlike leaves and clusters of white flowers in autumn, naturally forming a rounded, billowing shape. It tolerates shady situations (or full sun in maritime gardens), but is best given a sheltered position in colder regions. It may be trained against a wall; otherwise pruning is required only to restrict the spread of the plant. Fatsia is also a popular house plant.

WHEN TO PRUNE Midspring.

TRAINING AND PRUNING Formative pruning is not generally necessary, and established bushes usually need little attention. It is best to remove any gaunt or unwanted branches completely: shortening them ruins the plant's naturally graceful habit, and fresh growth will break freely from the base. If trained as a wall shrub (*see p.162*), cut stems growing out too far back to the main branch. Renovate by cutting out old stems completely and retaining only well-placed young growth.

FORSYTHIA

Deciduous, medium-sized shrubs grown for their bright yellow flowers. These are borne in early spring, most profusely on mature, but not aging, wood. Bushy forsythias, such as F. x *intermedia* 'Spectabilis' (zones 6 to 8 or 9), make effective informal flowering hedges. Others of open habit, such as F. *suspensa*

(zones 5 to 8), are suitable for wall training. In large gardens F. *suspensa* may also be grown in closely spaced groups, the stems of the several plants giving each other support.

Forsythias are very adaptable, but if not pruned regularly they often tend to develop into ungainly bushes with long, vigorous shoots at the top, a congested, twiggy center, and a bare base. Their flowering performance also deteriorates.

PRUNING FLOWERED SHOOTS
On established plants, cut back some of the older flowered stems to vigorous, upward- and outward-growing shoots.

WHEN TO PRUNE Midspring, after flowering. Renovate in winter or early spring.

TRAINING AND PRUNING Allow young plants to develop with minimal pruning for the first three years after planting. Thereafter, annually thin out crowded shoots from the center of the shrub, cutting back a proportion of the oldest flowered wood to vigorous shoots (*see left*). In addition, remove one or two old main stems at the base. To wall train (*see p.162*), develop a framework, then cut the flowered shoots back to one or two buds of these branches. Occasionally train in young stems to replace older framework branches. Old and neglected plants can be renovated by hard pruning, staged over two years (*see p.160*).

FREMONTODENDRON

Fremontias are large evergreens (zones 9 to 10) with spectacular, yellow flowers from summer to autumn on the

current season's shoots. They need a sunny position in cooler climates. The stems and leaves bear irritant hairs.

WHEN TO PRUNE After the first flush of flowers in midsummer.

TRAINING AND PRUNING Grow free-standing shrubs with a central leader, supported by a stake. Established plants need only minimal pruning. To wall train (*see p.162*), tie in main stems to form a framework. Only outward-growing shoots need to be shortened, cutting to sideshoots that grow parallel to the wall. Plants are short-lived and dislike hard pruning.

FREMONTODENDRON 'CALIFORNIA GLORY'
Prune back flowered growth where strong shoots exist to replace it.

FUCHSIA (ZONES 6/7–9)

Usually small, deciduous or evergreen shrubs grown for their showy flowers, produced from summer to autumn on the current season's growth. Most are arching or pendulous in habit. They thrive in most soils and situations; some species and many hybrids are tender in colder climates, but are suitable for growing in pots under glass. Fuchsias are versatile plants: some are attractive border plants, while others may be used for an informal, flowering hedge; some may be wall trained, and others pinch-pruned into decorative shapes.

F. MAGELLANICA

LADY'S EARDROPS

Deciduous, upright shrub with red and purple flowers followed by black fruit. As a specimen plant it is usually cut back

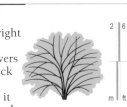

hard annually, but it also makes an attractive, informal, flowering hedge.

WHEN TO PRUNE Early spring, once growth begins. In cooler, exposed sites bushes can be trimmed (shortening stems by one-third) in autumn to reduce the risk of wind damage.

TRAINING AND PRUNING Pinch out the tips of young plants to encourage bushy growth. The following spring and in subsequent years, if top-growth has been killed by frost, cut old stems back to bare wood, being careful not to damage breaking buds at the base. Alternatively, if branches have survived the winter, cut back laterals to the lowest bud.

FUCHSIA HYBRID TRAINED AS A STANDARD
Remove dead growth in spring as new shoots begin to break, and clear the main stem (left).

On hedges, prune back laterals to healthy buds lower down. Straggly or gappy hedging plants may be rejuvenated by cutting right back in spring (*see p.47*). If an entire hedge needs renovating, stagger the pruning by cutting back every other plant one year, the remainder the next.

FUCHSIA HYBRIDS

The many named fuchsia hybrids vary in their hardiness. When grown in the open garden, they are treated as for F. *magellanica*.

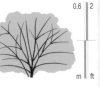

Others that are more tender are usually grown under glass. Many are densely bushy, and can be made more so by

G

FORSYTHIA 'MINI GOLD'
Many cultivars are selected for their profuse flowers, borne on bare branches.

pinch-pruning, while some with an open habit, such as 'Golden Marinka' and 'Swingtime', are well suited to growing in hanging baskets and other containers. Vigorous growers, such as 'Tennessee Waltz', can be trained as standards or fans using pinch-pruning techniques (*see pp.167–173*).

WHEN TO PRUNE Pinch-prune throughout the growing season.

TRAINING AND PRUNING Trailing plants need little attention except to pinch out wayward growth. For a bush, regularly pinching out the tips of shoots (*see p.168*) enhances the development of a dense, well-balanced plant. To train as a fan, *see p.173*; and as a standard, *see p.169*. Bush and hanging-basket fuchsias are often discarded after flowering, having yielded material for cuttings. Fans and standards are usually kept for several years. In colder climates they must be brought under cover for the winter. Trim the plants all over to remove the flowered shoots, but do not prune again until growth begins in spring.

OTHER FUCHSIAS
F. ARBORESCENS Large, frost-tender evergreen; as for *F. magellanica*. Little pruning is necessary, but it will make vigorous regrowth if cut back.
F. BOLIVIANA Minimal pruning. Do not pinch out the tips of shoots.
F. EXCORTICA Large shrub or small tree requiring minimal pruning. Can be trained against a wall (*see p.162*), displaying its attractive bark.
F. FULGENS As for *F. magellanica*.

GARRYA

Evergreen, medium-sized to large shrubs with leathery leaves and attractive catkins (showier on male plants) in winter and spring. They can be grown as freestanding specimens or as informal hedges or windbreaks, or trained informally against a wall of any aspect. Frost may affect catkins.

G. ELLIPTICA (ZONES 8–10)

SILK-TASSEL BUSH

Bushy, dense shrub with gray-green catkins. The cultivar 'James Roof' has the longest catkins.

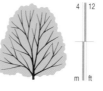

WHEN TO PRUNE Early spring, as the catkins fade, and before growth starts.

TRAINING AND PRUNING Allow free standing shrubs to develop unpruned. To wall train (*see p.162*), prune on planting to one or two framework stems, cutting back laterals growing away from the wall. Once established, cut back badly placed shoots. Renovate overgrown plants by cutting back to framework branches over three or four years (*see p.160*). Regrowth is vigorous.

GARRYA ELLIPTICA
The cultivar 'James Roof'; a freestanding specimen showing off its long catkins.

OTHER GARRYAS
G. FREMONTII As for *G. elliptica*.
G. X ISSAQUAHENSIS As for *G. elliptica*.
G. X THURETII Needs no pruning as a freestanding shrub; if grown as an informal hedge, trim with pruners in late summer.

GENISTA *BROOM*

Deciduous shrubs grown for their pea-like flowers, borne in spring or summer on second-year wood. Most are frost-tolerant, but some need a sheltered site, and all need full sun. Plant as young as possible and trim after flowering to keep plants bushy and compact. *G. aetnensis* (zones 9 to 10) can be grown as a standard (*see p.165*), with a well-staked clear main stem. Hummock-forming species such as *G. hispanica* (zones 8 to 9) may be clipped over after flowering. *G. lydia* (zones 7 to 9) dislikes any pruning. Most brooms are better replaced than renovated.

GREVILLEA *SILK OAK*

Evergreen, summer-flowering shrubs and trees (*see p.67*) with showy, yellow or red flowers over a long period. Hardy in zone 10, some may be grown outdoors in cooler climates if given the protection of a warm, sunny wall. In milder climates they make attractive specimen shrubs, and several are suitable for informal hedging. Tip-prune shoots of young plants (*see p.155*) to encourage bushiness. In colder areas cut out frost-damaged shoots in midspring. Remove stems to their point of origin if necessary to restrict size or when trimming hedges in late summer, after flowering.

OTHER ORNAMENTAL SHRUBS

FORTUNEARIA As for *Hamamelis* (*see p.198*).
FOTHERGILLA As for *Hamamelis* (*see p.198*).
FURCRAEA See Palms and palmlike plants, *p.43*.
GARDENIA As for *Camellia* (*see p.182*).
X GAULNETTYA See *Gaultheria*, below.

GAULTHERIA Little pruning is needed. Remove unwanted suckers (*see p.153*) to restrict spread. Cut back into old wood if plants become leggy.
GAYLUSSACIA As for *Gaultheria* (*see above*).
GEVUINA No special pruning needs.
GRAPTOPHYLLUM No special pruning needs.
GREWIA No special pruning needs.
GREYIA No special pruning needs.

GRINDELIA GUM PLANT

The few shrubby species in this summer-flowering genus (zones 8 or 9 to 10) will grow outdoors in sheltered locations in cooler climates, but are usually cut back by hard frosts. They produce fresh growth each spring, however. In warm climates grindelias have a tendency to become leggy; they will benefit from pruning when young to encourage a branched, bushy habit. Shorten the stems of young plants by one-third in the first spring after planting. Thereafter, keep pruning to a minimum in warm areas. In cooler climates, cut back hard in spring, either to the base or to live wood.

GRISELINIA (ZONE 10)

Evergreen, medium-sized to large shrubs that thrive in coastal conditions, where they are used as windbreaks and informal hedges. They are vulnerable to frost in cold areas inland. Griselinias make new growth freely from the base and branch well, forming naturally rounded shapes, and need no formative pruning. Cut out damaged growth in spring, but otherwise keep pruning of specimen shrubs to a minimum. Clip over hedges carefully in summer, using pruners to prevent damage to individual leaves (see also Hedges, p.44). These plants make vigorous new growth if pruned hard.

GYNURA (ZONE 10)

Tropical, evergreen subshrubs and trailing plants (see p.271), grown for their foliage and winter flowers. In colder climates grow under glass, providing a high level of humidity and some shade in summer. Pinch out the growing tips of young plants to encourage bushiness. Cut all stems back to within 3in (8cm) of ground level in midspring.

YOUNG GYNURA FOLIAGE
Pinch out young shoots to encourage a dense habit and fresh, attractive foliage.

H

HAMAMELIS WITCH HAZEL

Deciduous, large shrubs or small trees, most with good autumn color and red or yellow flowers in winter. All have a similar habit, but some species are suckering and others not. Many named cultivars are propagated by grafting, usually onto the suckering *H. virginiana*. Its suckers hold their leaves longer than the cultivar. Witch hazels are slow-growing and respond slowly to pruning, which should only be necessary if mature plants have outgrown their allotted space.

H. MOLLIS (ZONES 6–8)

CHINESE WITCH HAZEL

Spreading shrub with yellow autumn foliage. Fragrant, yellow flowers are borne in winter.

WHEN TO PRUNE Early spring, as flowers fade but before leaves unfurl. Remove suckers on grafted plants when seen.

TRAINING AND PRUNING Pruning should be kept to a minimum. If it is essential to remove branches, cut back to healthy young growth. Plants are often grafted and these tend to sucker. To remove suckers, see p.153. Plants recover only slowly from major pruning, and on grafted specimens the rootstock may gain dominance.

H. VERNALIS (ZONES 5–8)

VERNAL WITCH HAZEL

Suckering shrub with flowers in winter and spring, and vivid red autumn color.

WHEN TO PRUNE As for *H. mollis*.

TRAINING AND PRUNING Keep pruning to a minimum. Suckers on plants growing on their own roots need only be removed if they become congested or are needed for propagation. Renovate plants by cutting out old wood over two years.

OTHER WITCH HAZELS
H. X INTERMEDIA cultivars, H. JAPONICA
As for *H. mollis*.
H. VIRGINIANA (zones 4–9) Autumn-flowering, but as for *H. vernalis*.

PRUNING HAMAMELIS MOLLIS

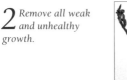

1 *Remove any crossing growth to avoid chafing damage, pruning where possible to a well-placed young shoot.*

2 *Remove all weak and unhealthy growth.*

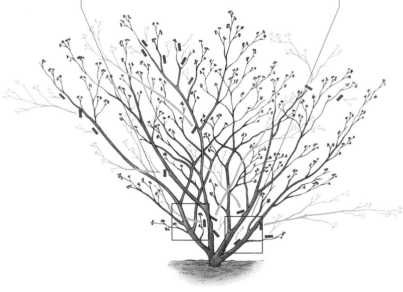

HEBE

Evergreen, prostrate to large shrubs, grown for their flowers and foliage. Some are suitable for rock gardens. The large-leaved hebes are vulnerable to frost damage. However, most hebes break readily from old wood and tolerate even hard cutting back to remove cold- or wind-damaged growth. Shortening lanky stems keeps plants neat, and for many hebes the removal of faded flower spikes helps to keep plants vigorous. Variegated hebes frequently develop reverted shoots with plain green leaves, which will become dominant if not removed early.

H. CUPRESSOIDES (ZONES 8–9)

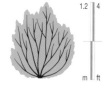

Evergreen grown for its fragrant foliage, and for the rounded habit of the cultivar 'Boughton Dome', rather than for its sparingly produced, pale lilac flowers.

WHEN TO PRUNE Spring.

TRAINING AND PRUNING It is worth sacrificing the insignificant flowers for a compact neat shape, so trim the plant lightly each year. If the plant is

damaged, even if only on one side, cut back the whole plant hard to promote balanced regrowth.

H. PINGUIFOLIA (ZONES 8–10)

Prostrate shrub popular as groundcover, with small leaves, bearing flowers from late spring to summer. It is best known in the white-flowered 'Pagei'.

WHEN TO PRUNE Spring, and in summer after flowering.

TRAINING AND PRUNING In mid- to late spring cut out growth that has been damaged during the winter and any stems that have died back. Use shears to clip plants in summer to remove dead flowers and keep growth compact.

H. SPECIOSA (ZONES 9–10)

Medium-sized shrub with large, glossy leaves and spikes of purplish flowers in summer and autumn.

FROST-DAMAGED HEBE PINGUIFOLIA 'PAGEI'
Cut out completely any localized patches of frost-damaged growth (above left), then trim the whole plant lightly (above right) to stimulate vigorous regrowth.

HEBE 'GREAT ORME'
Prune in spring as for Hebe speciosa, so that there is then time for shoots to grow and flower, from midsummer to midautumn.

In colder temperate regions it is often damaged by frost. It is a parent of many of the finest hybrids, most of which require similar pruning.

WHEN TO PRUNE Mid- to late spring, as the plant begins to make active growth.

TRAINING AND PRUNING Little formative pruning is required, except to ensure balanced growth (*see p.157*). Prune established plants to remove frost-damaged stems and to keep plants within bounds, cutting stems back hard to new shoots if necessary. Plants will tolerate heavy pruning, but it is best to replace old specimens rather than attempt renovation by drastic pruning.

OTHER HEBES
H. ALBICANS As for *H. pinguifolia*.
II. ARMSTRONGII As for *H. cupressoides*.
H. BRACHYSIPHON As for *H. pinguifolia*.
H. DIEFFENBACHII As for *H. speciosa*.
H. X FRANCISCANA As for *H. speciosa*.
H. HULKEANA As for *H. speciosa*.
H. MACRANTHA As for *H. speciosa*.
H. OCHRACEA As for *H. cupressoides*.
H. RAKAIENSIS As for *H. pinguifolia*.
H. SALICIFOLIA As for *H. speciosa*.

HELIANTHEMUM *ROCK ROSE* (ZONES 6–8)

Evergreen, prostrate shrubs for rock gardens or sunny borders, producing cup-shaped flowers in summer. Many named hybrids are available with a range of flower colors. Unpruned, they become straggly, with a buildup of old stems under younger growths.

WHEN TO PRUNE Mid- to late summer, after flowering.

TRAINING AND PRUNING Pinch-prune young plants (*see p.168*) to establish a compact habit. Keep plants neat and encourage repeat flowering by cutting back lightly, pruning stems individually rather than shearing over the whole plant. Plants are short-lived; replace rather than attempt renovation.

OTHER ORNAMENTAL SHRUBS
HAKEA Pinch-prune young plants; apart from occasional shaping cuts, mature plants have no special needs.
X HALIMIOCISTUS As for *Cistus* (*see p.187*).
HALIMIUM As for *Cistus* (*see p.187*).
HALIMODENDRON Minimal pruning.
HEIMIA As for *Fuchsia magellanica* (*see p.196*) but pruning less hard, to 6in (15cm) above ground level.

HELICHRYSUM

Evergreen shrubs and subshrubs that are grown mainly for their foliage. In colder climates several species are frost-tolerant enough to be grown outdoors, although they may suffer frost damage. *H. petiolare* is often used for summer bedding or in containers, and is overwintered as cuttings with protection from frost. All helichrysums respond well to light pruning, which is carried out chiefly to enhance the foliage effect, but not all break readily from old wood.

H. ITALICUM (ZONES 9–10)

CURRY PLANT

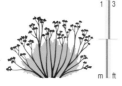

Bushy subshrub with silver-gray, distinctively aromatic foliage and yellow flower heads in summer. *H. italicum* subsp. *serotinum* has densely felted leaves.

WHEN TO PRUNE Spring.

TRAINING AND PRUNING Remove frost-damaged growth and cut back leggy shoots to old wood. Little further pruning is generally needed. Neglected plants usually make vigorous growth if pruned hard in spring.

H. PETIOLARE (ZONE 10)

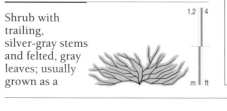

Shrub with trailing, silver-gray stems and felted, gray leaves; usually grown as a

Bushy head developed by pinch-pruning

Clear stem

HELIOTROPIUM HYBRID
Although often grown as an annual bedding plant, heliotrope can be trained up as a standard.

HELICHRYSUM PETIOLARE
Although most frequently grown as a trailing plant, H. petiolare *can also be trained, for example, as a standard. Throughout summer pinch out the tips of shoots to maintain dense growth and a compact form.*

foliage plant, although cream flowers are produced in summer. It can be allowed to trail, or may be staked and pinch-pruned to form decorative shapes such as standards, cones, and pillars.

WHEN TO PRUNE Spring. Pinch back long growths to encourage bushiness throughout the growing season.

TRAINING AND PRUNING Pinch out shoot tips regularly to make a bushy plant, removing unwanted flower buds if they form. For training in special forms such as standards, *see* Pinch-pruning, *pp.167–173*. Plants are not worth renovating.

OTHER HELICHRYSUMS
H. SPLENDIDUM As for *H. italicum.*
H. PLICATUM, H. STOECHAS As for *H. italicum*, but less likely to respond well to hard pruning.

HELIOTROPIUM (ZONE 10)

Heliotropium arborescens and hybrids of which it is a parent are evergreen shrubs bearing fragrant flowers on the current season's wood throughout the growing season. They are tender, but are suitable for summer bedding or growing in pots outside or under glass. They are usually replaced after one, or sometimes two, years. In warm climates keep pruning to a minimum. Pinch out the growing tips of young plants to encourage bushiness. Large plants may need staking. Use pinch-pruning techniques to grow as a standard (*see p.169*); stake a young plant and train up a clear stem, removing all lateral shoots. Pinch out the growing tip at three leaves above the height of clear stem required. Pinch out laterals at the head to encourage bushy growth. If standards are to be kept for a second year, trim over the head in autumn.

HETEROMELES

The single species is *H. arbutifolia* (syn. *Photinia arbutifolia*), the Christmas berry or California holly, a large, evergreen shrub or tree that produces white flowers in late summer, followed by red fruit. It is frost-tolerant (zones 8 to 10), and needs some shelter in colder areas. Bushy and spreading in habit, it is very tolerant of pruning, and may be grown as a multistemmed shrub or with a single trunk. Prune from late winter to early spring. Tip-prune young plants to promote bushy growth. Thin twiggy growth lightly when established, and, if necessary to shape or restrict size, cut branches back to suitably placed laterals. To rejuvenate old plants, cut them back hard to a framework of main branches in late winter or early spring, before growth begins. Heteromeles also makes a good informal hedging plant (*see p.44*).

HETEROMELES ARBUTIFOLIA
This adaptable flowering shrub may be trimmed to shape as required.

HIBBERTIA GUINEA FLOWER

Small to medium-sized, evergreen shrubs with attractive, yellow or orange flowers, usually in spring and summer (some species flower most of the year). Some tolerate light frosts, but others need a completely frost-free climate (hardy in zone 10). Prostrate and semiprostrate species need minimal pruning. Other species may be pinch-pruned when young to promote bushiness. To keep them compact, prune after flowering or between flowering flushes by removing shoot tips and spent flower heads. Thin out any congested growth in spring. *Hibbertia* also includes a number of climbers (*see p.273*).

HIBISCUS

Genus that includes annuals and perennials, as well as a number of deciduous and evergreen shrubs and small trees. They are grown for the large, mallowlike flowers that are borne on the current season's wood in late summer. They need a warm, but not exposed, site and full sun in order to bloom well. Not all can be grown outdoors in colder climates, but tender species may be grown successfully under glass.

H. ROSA-SINENSIS (ZONE 10)

CHINESE HIBISCUS

Evergreen, rounded shrub, of which there are many named selections, grown for its showy flowers, which may be produced throughout the growing season. It needs warm, frost-free growing conditions when grown outside, where it may be used as a hedge or screen, and can make a fine specimen plant for pot culture under glass in colder climates. Prune to restrict the size and spread of pot-grown specimens and to encourage flowering.

2.5 | 8

m | ft

WHEN TO PRUNE Late spring.

TRAINING AND PRUNING Prune young plants lightly if necessary (*see p.157*) to ensure a well-balanced framework of branches. Prune established plants by cutting back main shoots by as much as one-third, and shorten laterals, leaving two or three buds. Dead wood attracts canker, so it should be removed promptly. To renovate completely, remove older branches entirely and cut the remainder back hard. The response is usually good, but if most stems have died back, it is best to replace the plant.

RENOVATING A POORLY SHAPED HIBISCUS SYRIACUS

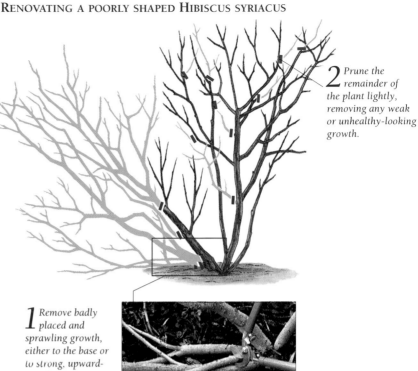

2 Prune the remainder of the plant lightly, removing any weak or unhealthy-looking growth.

1 Remove badly placed and sprawling growth, either to the base or to strong, upward-growing stems.

H. SYRIACUS (ZONES 6–8)

ROSE OF SHARON

3 | 10

m | ft

Deciduous shrub with flowers in a range of colors. It is prone to dieback. The root system sometimes provides an inadequate anchor and plants may become lopsided and sprawling.

WHEN TO PRUNE Late spring.

TRAINING AND PRUNING Prune young plants hard to encourage branching at the base. On established plants pruning is best kept to a minimum, although any

shoots that show signs of dieback should be cut back to live wood. Renovation is as for *H. rosa-sinensis*. Lopsided plants respond well to reshaping (*see above*) if then sheltered from any prevailing wind; otherwise the problem will recur.

OTHER HIBISCUS
H. DIVERSIFOLIUS, H. HETEROPHYLLUS,
H. MUTABILIS As for *H. rosa-sinensis*.
H. SINOSYRIACUS As for *H. syriacus*.
H. TILIACEUS, H. WAIMEAE As for
H. rosa-sinensis.

HIPPOPHAE *COMMON SEA BUCKTHORN* (ZONES 4–7)

Deciduous trees and shrubs, bearing male and female flowers on separate plants. They are grown for their foliage and for the showy fruit on female plants, and do best in an open site. Their natural habit is to form suckering clumps, but they may also be successfully trained as standards. Sea buckthorns can also be used as hedging (*see p.44*), for which they are useful in coastal areas; they tolerate strong, salt-laden winds well.

WHEN TO PRUNE Summer, when it is easiest to distinguish between live and dead wood.

TRAINING AND PRUNING Little pruning is needed, either at the formative stage or when plants have become established. Mature specimens often have numerous twisted branches. If growth becomes crowded, cut unwanted stems to ground level and remove superfluous suckers from around the perimeter of the plant. However, drastic pruning is likely to stimulate the production of numerous suckers. Although plants can be trained as standards (*see p.165*), they tend to develop an irregular head and need careful attention to shaping. Trim hedges in late summer, if needed.

OTHER ORNAMENTAL SHRUBS
HELWINGIA Minimal pruning.
HEPTACODIUM Minimal pruning, in spring if necessary.
HERMANNIA No special needs. Tolerates trimming if required.
HOHERIA In warm climates can be lightly trimmed after flowering. In colder climates delay pruning until spring and cut out any frost-damaged growth. *See also* Dictionary of Ornamental Trees, *p.68*.
HOLODISCUS No special needs. Can be rejuvenated by cutting out one in three stems, as for *Spiraea* 'Arguta' (*see p.221*).
HOVEA Tip-prune young plants, and trim or thin the flowered, twiggy growth lightly after flowering.

HYDRANGEA

Deciduous, medium-sized to large shrubs that flower in late summer to autumn. All respond well to pruning. Some species are woodland plants that require little attention; cultivars of garden origin can be left unpruned but flower better if pruned correctly. Some can be wall trained, although choosing a climbing species (*see p.273*) is a simpler option.

H. MACROPHYLLA (ZONES 6–9)

BIG LEAF HYDRANGEA

Bushy shrub with many cultivars, bearing terminal summer flowers. Some have domed heads of mainly sterile flowers (hortensias or mop-head hydrangeas), others have flat heads with large, sterile flowers on the outside and smaller, fertile flowers in the center (lacecaps). Flowers are borne on the previous season's wood, often satisfactorily with little attention, but regular pruning nearly always enhances flowering.

WHEN TO PRUNE In warm climates prune after flowering. In colder climates leave the old flower heads on over winter and prune in midspring.

TRAINING AND PRUNING Little formative pruning is needed. On established plants (*see above right*) cut back weak, thin shoots and one or two of the oldest stems to the base of the plant. Prune the previous year's flowered branches by up to 12in (30cm), cutting to fat buds; these will produce flowering shoots. Neglected or badly cold-damaged plants may be cut to the base in spring, but there will be no flowers the following summer.

PRUNING HYDRANGEA MACROPHYLLA IN SPRING

2 Shorten the flowered stems to pairs of healthy buds.

1 Cut out one or two old, less productive branches at ground level.

3 Remove weak and spindly stems completely, or if there are strong pairs of buds low down, cut to these.

H. PANICULATA (ZONES 4–8)

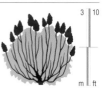

Upright shrub with large panicles of flowers in late summer on the current season's growth.

WHEN TO PRUNE Early spring, before plants start into active growth.

TRAINING AND PRUNING Pruning is not essential, but plants flower much better if pruned back annually to a woody framework (*see below*), as low as 10in (25cm) in exposed positions, but 2ft (60cm) tall or more at the back of a border. In the spring of subsequent years cut all growth back to the lowest pair of buds above this framework. Neglected plants usually respond well if cut back hard to recreate a low framework.

> **OTHER HYDRANGEAS**
> H. ARBORESCENS Minimal pruning, or can be treated as for *H. paniculata*.
> H. ASPERA, H. HETEROMALLA, H. QUERCIFOLIA, H. SARGENTIANA, H. VILLOSA Minimal pruning, in spring if necessary; *H. villosa* wall trains well (*see p.165*).
> H. SERRATA As for *H. macrophylla*.
> For other species, see Dictionary of Climbing Plants, *p.273*.

PRUNING HYDRANGEA PANICULATA TO A LOW FRAMEWORK

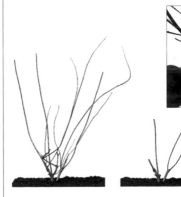

FIRST SPRING AFTER PLANTING *Cut out all but three or four strong stems, and shorten these to 10–24in (25–60cm).*

ESTABLISHED PLANT *Each year, cut the previous season's growth to its lowest pair of healthy buds. Remove any lifeless stubs.*

ESTABLISHED PLANT IN FLOWER *Hard pruning each year results in fewer, but much larger, flower clusters.*

HYPERICUM

Large, diverse genus, containing mostly hardy, vigorous, deciduous and evergreen shrubs of varying sizes, with bright yellow flowers borne over a long period in late summer and autumn. Some make effective groundcover; larger hypericums may be used for an informal flowering hedge. The pruning method depends on the species grown and the purpose for which it is used.

H. CALYCINUM (ZONES 6–8)

AARON'S BEARD, ST. JOHN'S WORT

1.2 | 4
m | ft

Evergreen, low-growing shrub that spreads by means of long stems that creep across or just under the surface of the soil, producing new plantlets. It is suitable for use as groundcover even in dry shade, though it needs to be kept under control. Flowers are borne on the current season's growth, most profusely in a sunny site; annual pruning will produce a crop of fresh leaves and keep the plant within bounds.

WHEN TO PRUNE Early spring.

TRAINING AND PRUNING Cut back all the previous year's growth, either with shears or, for large areas of ground-cover, a lawn mower on the highest setting, or a nylon-line trimmer. To control spread, chop through peripheral roots; this may yield new plantlets.

HYPERICUM FORRESTII
Remove some older wood (below) to leave an open, well-shaped plant (right).

H. FORRESTII (ZONES 7–8)

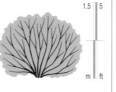

1.5 | 5
m | ft

Evergreen or semi-evergreen, bushy shrub with nearly erect, then arching branches. It can be pruned annually to increase the flowering potential, and benefits from harder pruning every few years. This hypericum and other species of similar habit may be used as hedging plants.

WHEN TO PRUNE Spring.

TRAINING AND PRUNING On freestanding plants remove any old, weak, or thin growth, then shorten the remaining stems back to the base or to strong shoots to keep growth compact. For use as a hedge, *see p.44.* To reinvigorate old or neglected specimens, prune all stems to ground level in spring; plants usually produce vigorous growth in response.

OTHER HYPERICUMS
H. AEGYPTICUM, H. BALEARICUM Rock plants that require no pruning.
H. ANDROSAEMUM As for *H. calycinum,* but cut back only every two or three years.
H. BEANII, H. BELLUM, H. 'HIDCOTE' As for *H. forrestii.*
H. X INODORUM As for *H. androsaemum.*
H. KOUYTCHENSE, H. X MOSERIANUM As for *H. forrestii.*
H. 'ROWALLANE' As for *H. forrestii,* but cut to ground level if damaged by frost.

OTHER ORNAMENTAL SHRUBS
HYMENANTHERA Minimal pruning.
HYPOCALYMMA Prune lightly only if necessary; hard pruning ruins the habit.
HYSSOPUS Cut back hard to near ground level in early spring. Clip hedges lightly in

early to midspring. Neglected plants usually respond well if cut back hard.
ILLICIUM Minimal pruning, but tolerates being cut back in summer after flowering.

I–K

ILEX *HOLLY*

Mostly evergreen trees (*see p.68*) and shrubs with male and female flowers usually carried on separate plants. They are grown for their foliage and the berries borne on female plants in autumn and winter. They are generally tolerant of pollution and maritime conditions, and will grow in sun or shade. Fairly slow-growing, they make fine, free-growing specimen plants but also respond well to pruning, and can be clipped to a formal shape; some species may be used for a formal or informal hedge.

I. OPACA (ZONES 6–9)

AMERICAN HOLLY

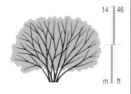

14 | 46
m | ft

Erect, evergreen shrub or small tree with red berries (yellow in *I. opaca* f. *xanthocarpa*) and oval leaves that are a light green and more or less spiny. Needs a continental climate to grow well. In cool maritime climates it will not make a good hedge or bear good crops of berries.

WHEN TO PRUNE Late summer, when the new growth is ripe, or December for holiday decorations.

TRAINING AND PRUNING Little formative pruning is needed, except to encourage a single main stem. Established specimens tolerate pruning, but little is required. Use shears to trim formal hedges from an early age (there is an inevitable loss of berries). Freestanding specimens and hedges tolerate drastic pruning if renovation is necessary (*see p.160*). Stage hard pruning over two or three years.

OTHER HOLLIES
I. CRENATA Bushy, dense species with black fruit. Grown as a specimen shrub, it requires minimal pruning, but is also suitable for topiary and hedging, when it is treated as for *I. opaca.*
I. X MESERVEAE Dark foliage with blue tints; young foliage is most attractive, so it looks good as a clipped hedge. Prune as for *I. opaca.*
I. PERNYI Best grown as a specimen shrub or small feathered tree (*see p.27*) with only minimal pruning.
I. VERTICILLATA Deciduous; minimal pruning required.
For other species, see Dictionary of Ornamental Trees, *p.68.*

INDIGOFERA *INDIGO*

Small to medium-sized, deciduous, multistemmed shrubs that produce pea-like flowers on the current season's growth in summer and early autumn.

I. HETERANTHA SYN. I. GERARDIANA

Medium-sized, arching shrub with racemes of purple-red flowers in summer. Hardy in zones 9 to 10, it reaches its full potential height only in warm climates. In colder climates it may be damaged by hard frosts, and is best pruned hard each spring to stimulate strong young growth.

WHEN TO PRUNE Early to midspring, before the onset of fresh growth.

TRAINING AND PRUNING In warm climates, keep pruning to a minimum. In colder areas, remove weak stems and cut back all others to just above ground level. Neglected specimens will make vigorous new growth if all stems are cut back drastically in spring.

> **OTHER INDIGOFERAS**
> I. AMBYLANTHA As for *I. heterantha*. The woody base can be built up into a low framework to give the plant height.
> I. AUSTRALIS, I. DECORA, I. KIRILOWII Small shrubs; prune as for *I. heterantha*.

INDIGOFERA HETERANTHA
Like other indigos, this species is best pruned back close to ground level in spring when grown in colder climates.

IXORA (ZONE 10)

Small, tender, evergreen shrubs that need a warm, frost-free climate. Flowers are borne on the current season's stems. Ixoras form twiggy plants that can be made bushier by regular pruning. Pinch out the tips of young shoots when they are about 6in (15cm) long. After flowering, remove about half the current year's growth, shaping the plant. Rejuvenate old plants by thinning, then cutting all remaining stems back to about 12in (30cm) from the ground in late winter or early spring.

JASMINUM *JASMINE*

Vigorous, deciduous or evergreen, small to medium-sized shrubs (for climbers, *see p.274*) with an arching habit (zones 6 to 9). All of the shrubby species, such as *J. humile* and *J. parkeri*, bear yellow, starlike flowers in terminal clusters in summer on the previous season's wood. All need pruning to prevent a buildup of old wood. In colder climates more tender jasmines need a warm, sunny wall. Young plants require little pruning. When established, remove one or two old stems after flowering. Drastic pruning of neglected plants is best carried out in spring, but there will be few flowers the following summer.

KALMIA *MOUNTAIN LAUREL*

Evergreen, small to large shrubs (zones 5 to 9) that flower attractively, mainly in early summer. They require very little pruning, but it is worth deadheading the flowers. Specimens that have outgrown their site can be cut back, staging hard pruning over two or three years (*see p.160*).

KERRIA (ZONES 5–9)

Deciduous, vigorous, suckering shrub of medium height with an arching habit, flowering in spring. There is one species in the genus, *K. japonica*, of which the double-flowered form tends to be the more vigorous. Each year, vigorous new stems are produced from ground level, which will flower the following year. Prune to prevent a buildup of old wood and to remove the unsightly faded flower stems.

WHEN TO PRUNE Late spring, after flowering.

TRAINING AND PRUNING Prune the flowered stems either to strong sideshoots or to ground level, aiming to produce a balanced, open shape. Cutting the stems back to different levels encourages new flowering shoots at different heights. If plants are spreading too widely, chop peripheral stems out with a spade: the unwanted suckers can be used for propagation. To renovate, cut all stems back to ground level in spring.

PRUNING KERRIA JAPONICA

1 To maintain vigor, cut out up to one in three stems at ground level in spring each year.

2 Cut back other flowered stems to vigorous young sideshoots where these exist.

KOLKWITZIA *BEAUTYBUSH* (ZONES 5–8)

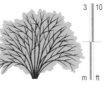

Genus of only one species, *K. amabilis*, a medium-sized, deciduous shrub bearing pink flowers in late spring or early summer on second-year wood.

WHEN TO PRUNE Midsummer, after flowering.

TRAINING AND PRUNING Keep pruning of young plants to a minimum, letting the arching habit develop. Established plants may sucker and freely produce basal shoots. Thin each year to maintain vigor: prune back one in three or four stems, always removing the oldest, cutting either to a low sideshoot or to the base. To renovate, cut old growth hard back to ground level, leaving five to seven strong, young, upright stems.

L

LANTANA (ZONE 10)

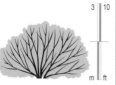

Evergreen shrubs with heads of tubular flowers. The best known, *L. camara*, is a weed in some tropical and subtropical regions, but it and other species are widely grown as bedding or greenhouse plants in temperate areas. They may be trained as standards.

WHEN TO PRUNE Spring; standards under glass may need autumn trimming.

TRAINING AND PRUNING Pinch out the shoot tips of young plants to encourage bushy growth. Use pinch-pruning to train as a standard (*see p.169*); train up a single clear stem and pinch out its tip just above the desired height of clear stem, then pinch-prune laterals to form a bushy head. Plants are often discarded after one season; if standards are to be overwintered, prune laterals at the head back to about 3in (8cm) in autumn.

LAVATERA *TREE MALLOW* (ZONES 9–10)

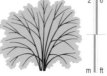

Very vigorous, deciduous shrubs flowering on the current season's growth over a very long period from summer until autumn. They prefer a warm, sunny site. The wood is not strong, and old, heavy branches may split or crack. Lavateras are thus vulnerable to frost and wind damage, but all tolerate hard pruning, which helps to keep bushes neat and improves flowering performance.

LAVATERA 'BARNSLEY'
Prune hard to the base each year once fresh shoots are growing strongly.

WHEN TO PRUNE Spring, after the buds begin to break, and after the last severe frosts. In exposed positions, shorten stems in autumn. During the growing season, cut out any damaged wood.

TRAINING AND PRUNING In spring cut out weak growths and prune all other stems to within 12in (30cm) of ground level (*see below*). During the growing season remove all damaged growth. In autumn shorten stems by up to half their length where there is danger of wind damage. Plants are not long-lived; replace old or neglected specimens.

LAVANDULA *LAVENDER*

Small, evergreen shrubs with aromatic, often gray-green foliage and scented flowers, usually mauve or purple but sometimes white or pink, in summer. Lavenders are best grown in sheltered, sunny sites in well-drained soil, and are useful planted in rows to form a low, flowering hedge. To use as a hedge or as edging, plant 9–12in (23–30cm) apart. Annual pruning keeps specimen and hedging plants compact and clothed with foliage to ground level.

L. ANGUSTIFOLIA (ZONES 6–8)

ENGLISH LAVENDER

Bushy, evergreen shrub with spikes of fragrant flowers in summer. There are many cultivars and hybrids, including 'Hidcote' and the dwarf lavender 'Munstead'.

WHEN TO PRUNE In warm climates prune in autumn, but in colder climates deadhead only in autumn to neaten plants, delaying pruning until spring.

TRAINING AND PRUNING Prune young plants hard to encourage bushy growth. Clip over established plants, removing most of the previous season's growth. If deadheading in autumn, simply remove the long, bare flower stems; leave foliage on the plant over winter to protect young growth buds. Prune hedges in the same way. Plants do not break freely when cut back into old wood. Replace old and neglected specimens.

LAVANDULA ANGUSTIFOLIA
In cool climates, deadhead in autumn to tidy the plant (or harvest the last of the flowers), then prune harder in spring after any danger of frost.

OTHER LAVENDERS
L. DENTATA, L. X INTERMEDIA As for *L. angustifolia*.
L. STOECHAS, L. STOECHAS subsp. PEDUNCULATA As for *L. angustifolia*, although not as hardy.

OTHER ORNAMENTAL SHRUBS

IOCHROMA *I. cyaneum* is tender, but tolerates light frosts. Prune in late winter or early spring, cutting into old wood, reducing growth by one-third to half.
ISOPOGON As for *Kalmia* (*see facing page*), but do not deadhead.
ITEA In warm climates *I. virginica* needs little pruning. Wall train informally as for *Escallonia* 'Langleyensis' (*see p.194*) in colder climates.
JAMESIA No pruning required.
JUANULLOA Scandent shrub; in warm climates, train on a wall or support. As a potted plant, treat as for *Justicia* (*see right*).

JUSTICIA Remove dead growth or cut back flowered stems at the end of winter. In warm areas where all growth survives, shorten all stems by half every two or three years.
KUNZEA Trim lightly after flowering.
LEDUM Minimal pruning.

LEONOTIS *LION'S EAR*

Leonotis leonurus, also known as wild dagga or the minaret flower, is an evergreen subshrub grown for its aromatic leaves and whorls of bright orange-red flowers in summer and autumn. It can grow 6ft (2m) in a year in good conditions. Fully hardy in zone 10, it may survive mild winters in cooler climates. It is also suitable for growing under glass, in full sun, but keep cool in winter.

WHEN TO PRUNE Autumn in warm climates; in cooler climates spring, after flowering.

TRAINING AND PRUNING Tip-prune young shoots to encourage branching. In warm climates cut back the previous season's growth to a low permanent framework. In cooler climates cut all growth to within 6in (15cm) of ground level. Renovate neglected specimens by this method.

LESPEDEZA

Small to medium-sized shrubs, some of which are evergreen in warm climates. The attractive, white to purple, pealike flowers are borne on the current season's wood in late summer or autumn. In warm areas remove some of the old wood each spring. Hardy in zones 4 to 7 or 8, plants may die back in colder climates, even with the protection of a warm wall. Use a straw or similar mulch to protect the roots in winter, and cut down the old stems after any danger of frost has passed.

LIGUSTRUM *PRIVET*

Evergreen or deciduous, medium-sized to large shrubs, grown for their foliage and flowers. Their vigor, tolerance of pollution and a wide range of sites, and good response to clipping make them popular as formal hedges. Prune hedge plants two or three times annually. Some species, such as *L. confusum* and the deciduous or semievergreen *L. sinense* (Chinese privet), are decorative enough to be grown as freestanding shrubs. Privets can also be used in topiary (*see p.48*) or be grown as standards.

L. OVALIFOLIUM (ZONES 6–9)

OVAL-LEAFED PRIVET, PRIVET

Large, vigorous, evergreen or semievergreen shrub with glossy green leaves, and white flowers in summer followed by black fruit. Some cultivars have attractive variegated foliage.

WHEN TO PRUNE Spring.

TRAINING AND PRUNING Keep the pruning of freestanding shrubs to a minimum; no pruning is necessary at planting. Watch variegated cultivars for reverted shoots, removing them as seen (*see p.153*). Cut back young hedging plants on planting to 12in (30cm) above ground level, and cut back new growth by half in each of the following two or three years to ensure dense growth at the base. To train as a standard, *see*

LIGUSTRUM SINENSE 'PENDULUM'
The deciduous Chinese privet is densely branching, with pale oval leaves and large panicles of fragrant white flowers in summer.

p.165. Trim hedges and topiary two or three times between late spring and late summer. Old and neglected privet bushes and hedges can be renovated by hard pruning in spring, but this may cause variegated cultivars to revert.

OTHER PRIVETS
L. DELAVAYANUM As for *L. ovalifolium*.
L. JAPONICUM As for *L. ovalifolium*.
L. LUCIDUM As for *L. ovalifolium*, or grow as a standard (*see p.165*) on a single short stem, no taller than 2ft (60cm).
L. OBTUSIFOLIUM As for *L. ovalifolium*.
L. SINENSE As for *L. ovalifolium*.
L. VULGARE As for *L. ovalifolium*.

LEYCESTERIA

Clump-forming, deciduous shrubs. New stems grow and flower in a single season. The green, bamboolike, hollow stems of *L. formosa* are attractive in winter. Plants need a sunny position and also shelter, since the stems are often broken in strong winds. Plants left unpruned will become congested. Many need subtropical conditions but some are hardy in zone 6.

WHEN TO PRUNE Spring.

TRAINING AND PRUNING Thin out clumps annually, cutting old and weak stems down to near ground level (*see inset, right*). Neglected specimens can be renovated by drastic pruning, cutting back all stems to within 2–3in (5–8cm) of the base. Feed well to aid recovery.

LEYCESTERIA FORMOSA
These shrubs form attractive, arching clumps. Cut some stems back to ground level in spring, since unpruned plants become congested and produce weak growths.

LONICERA *HONEYSUCKLE*

Deciduous and evergreen shrubs, some large, and others low-growing. They often bear strongly scented flowers on second-year wood, followed by showy fruit in some species. They are mostly vigorous and adaptable, usually responding well to pruning. Many are of arching habit, and these may become unruly if left unpruned. Others, such as *L. nitida* and *L. xylosteum*, are more compact and are useful as hedging. Timing of pruning depends on the flowering season and the purpose for which the plant is grown. The genus also includes a number of attractive climbers (*see p.276*).

L. NITIDA (ZONES 7–9)

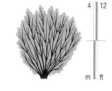

Evergreen, bushy shrub with small, creamy flowers. Its dense habit makes it a useful plant for low, formal hedges. Popular cultivars in varying leaf colors include 'Aurea' and 'Baggesen's Gold'.

WHEN TO PRUNE Trim hedges at least three times between spring and autumn.

TRAINING AND PRUNING Specimen shrubs need minimal pruning. Cut back hedging plants by at least half at planting time, and trim two or three times in the first season. Then cut back annual growth by half until the hedge attains the desired height. Plants that become bare at the base can be renovated by cutting back to 6in (15cm) of the ground in early spring.

L. TATARICA (ZONES 4–8)

Deciduous, arching shrub that bears fragrant white to pink flowers in the previous season's shoots in early summer. The flowers are followed by colorful berries. Can be weedy in some areas.

WHEN TO PRUNE Midsummer.

LONICERA XYLOSTEUM
The fly honeysuckle is a less well-known but neat and attractive species. It is easy to keep in order as an informal screen or hedge.

TRAINING AND PRUNING Cut old and weak stems back to the base of the plant to encourage growth low down that will keep the base well furnished. Shorten up to one in three of the other branches, cutting them back to just above fresh, upright sideshoots, keeping a balanced shape: try not to ruin the natural outline of the plant. Old and neglected specimens can be renovated by being pruned back to a low framework in winter or early spring.

OTHER LONICERAS
L. FRAGRANTISSIMA Prune as for *L. tatarica*, but in late spring, after flowering. Can be wall trained (*see p.162*).
L. KOROLKOWII As for *L. tatarica*.
L. MAACKII As for *L. tatarica*.
L. PILEATA Minimal pruning.
L. X PURPUSII As for *L. tatarica*, but prune in late spring after flowering.
L. SYRINGANTHA (syn. L. RUPICOLA var. SYRINGANTHA) As for *L. tatarica*.
L. XYLOSTEUM As for *L. tatarica*.
For other species, see Dictionary of Climbing Plants, p.276.

LOTUS (ZONE 10)

Genus that contains a few subshrubs, notably the low-growing *L. berthelotii* (coral gem, parrot's beak, pelican's beak), with trailing, silvery stems and striking red flowers in summer. It is tender, needing frost-free conditions, but is widely grown in colder climates, planted out in containers in summer; it may be overwintered under cover. In warm climates it is used in rock gardens or to cover banks. Pinch out the shoot tips of young plants. To encourage fresh growth of established plants and keep the plant neat, cut out some of the old stems in late summer after flowering. Plants overwintered under cover can be cut back hard in spring.

LUCULIA (ZONE 10)

Tender, evergreen, medium-sized to large shrubs with scented, phloxlike, white or pink flowers in winter. Hard pruning encourages plants to flower freely. As soon as flowers fade, cut back flowered wood to within 3in (8cm) of a framework of main branches. Cut hard back in spring to rejuvenate.

LYCIUM *MATRIMONY VINE*

Medium-sized, deciduous and evergreen shrubs of untidy habit and with ornamental berries. Those species that are spiny are often used for formal and informal hedging. *Lycium barbarum* (zones 6 to 9) is a rangy, sparse-blooming plant.

WHEN TO PRUNE Winter. Trim hedges in spring and summer.

TRAINING AND PRUNING Remove dead wood annually and shorten overlong stems, pruning to upright shoots. Plants grown as informal hedges need little pruning. For formal hedges (*see p.45*), cut back at planting to 6–12in (15–30cm) and in subsequent years cut back half the annual growth in mid- to late summer until the desired height is reached. Harder pruning may be needed every three or four years; prune growth close to the base in winter to rejuvenate.

OTHER ORNAMENTAL SHRUBS
LEPTOSPERMUM Minimal pruning. Trim young growth in spring to encourage bushiness; avoid cutting into old wood.
LEUCADENDRON May be moderately pruned, if necessary, after flowering.
LEUCAENA No special needs, but tolerates pruning if necessary.

LEUCOPOGON Minimal pruning.
LEUCOSPERMUM As for *Leucadendron*.
LEUCOTHOE Minimal pruning. If necessary, cut out at the base one or two old stems in late spring, after flowering.
LOMATIA Minimal pruning, but old wood can be cut out in spring.

LOROPETALUM No pruning required, but pinch out shoot tips and trim after flowering if a bushy habit is desired.
LUPINUS Cut off seed heads of *L. arboreus* to stop self-seeding and keep compact.
LYONIA Prune lightly after flowering if necessary.

M

MAGNOLIA

A genus that consists mainly of trees but includes a number of usually large, deciduous and evergreen shrubs. They are grown for their waxy, often fragrant flowers and the graceful habit that normally develops without extensive pruning. They can be grown in sun or semishade, but need some protection from strong wind.

M. X SOULANGIANA (ZONES 4–9)

SAUCER MAGNOLIA

Large, deciduous shrub, popular for its white to purple flowers, borne from midspring to early summer.

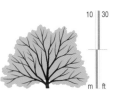

WHEN TO PRUNE Midsummer, when in full leaf. Avoid pruning in spring or early summer, when the wounds will bleed, and in the dormant season, since dieback often affects growth pruned at this time.

TRAINING AND PRUNING After light formative pruning (*see p.157*), little other pruning is needed, unless the brittle wood suffers wind damage. Remove weak growth and tip-prune young shoots. Heavy flowering followed by production of copious seed can reduce the plant's vigor. Remove flowers when faded. Renovate by hard pruning, staged over two to three years (*see p.160*).

> **OTHER MAGNOLIAS**
> M. GLOBOSA, M. SIEBOLDII subsp. SINENSIS, M. WILSONII Only minimal pruning required.
> M. LILIIFLORA As for *M. x soulangiana*.
> M. STELLATA Allow young plants to develop naturally. Renovate as for *M. x soulangiana*, although plants are slow to recover from hard pruning. *For other species, see* Dictionary of Ornamental Trees, *p.74*.

MAGNOLIA X SOULANGIANA
These fragile flowers need shelter from the damaging effect of wind.

MAHONIA

Medium-sized to large, evergreen shrubs. Some are low-growing, spreading plants that make good low cover. The taller-growing species make fine architectural plants. Most mahonias thrive in shade.

M. AQUIFOLIUM (ZONES 6–8)

OREGON GRAPE

Vigorous, low-growing, suckering shrub; the yellow flowers are followed by blue-black berries.

WHEN TO PRUNE Spring, after flowering.

TRAINING AND PRUNING This species spreads by means of suckers, so remove any unwanted growth at the edge of the plant. Shear groundcover plants to just above ground level annually or every two years, to keep them thick. Taller-growing specimens need little pruning, except to remove unwanted suckers. To renovate neglected shrubs, cut old branches back to ground level, leaving young ones unpruned.

M. X MEDIA (ZONES 8–9)

Group of upright shrubs, valued for their whorls of dark, spiny foliage and the yellow flowers produced

MAHONIA X MEDIA
Where stems are overlong, shorten to a sideshoot or a whorl of foliage after flowering.

in autumn and winter. They make large, sometimes strikingly gaunt, shrubs but will tolerate being cut back hard.

WHEN TO PRUNE Spring, after flowering.

TRAINING AND PRUNING No regular pruning is required, but long or old stems that are bare at the base can be cut back to strong growth lower down. Old and neglected plants usually respond slowly, but satisfactorily, when cut back to a low framework 12–24in (30–60cm) from ground level.

> **OTHER MAHONIAS**
> M. JAPONICA As for *M. x media*.
> M. LOMARIIFOLIA As for *M. x media*.
> M. PINNATA As for *M. aquifolium*.
> M. X WAGNERI As for *M. aquifolium*.

MALVAVISCUS (ZONE 10)

Tender, evergreen, sometimes sprawling shrubs, flowering on the current year's wood. *M. arboreus* (sleepy mallow, wax mallow) has tubular red flowers. In cool climates they may be grown in pots under glass. In late winter or early spring cut back the previous year's growth by a half to two-thirds. If the plant is crowded, remove twiggy or old, unproductive stems, but keep the plant's natural, rounded shape. Tolerates harder pruning if required. In warm climates it can be wall trained (*see p.162*), or used as an informal or clipped hedge (*see p.44*).

MELASTOMA (ZONE 10)

Medium-sized, tender, evergreen shrubs and trees, grown for their foliage and white, pink, or purple flowers. Some have edible fruit. *M. affine* is considered a weed in parts of the tropics. Pruning improves the overall appearance and keeps the plants well furnished with new wood. Tip-prune young plants to make them bushy. Prune established specimens, if the fruit is not required, lightly in late winter. Removing some older wood will encourage the production of vigorous new shoots.

MIMOSA (ZONE 10)

This varied, frost-tender genus includes small to medium-sized, evergreen shrubs with attractive leaves, some of which, including *M. pudica* (the humble or sensitive plant), may be grown as annuals in colder climates; they are also suitable for growing in pots. Growth habits vary: the prostrate species should be left to develop naturally, while the bushy types may be pinch-pruned (*see p.168*) when young to encourage dense growth, and may also be trained as standards (*see p.165*).

MIMULUS MONKEY FLOWER

Evergreen shrubs with snapdragon-like flowers in a range of colors borne on new wood from spring to autumn. Hardy in zone 10, they can survive the winter in cooler climates if grown against a warm wall or in a cool greenhouse. Pinch out the shoot tips of young plants to encourage branching. After the first flush of flowers, cut back flowered stems by 4–8in (10–20cm) to encourage further flowers. In late spring shorten all growth by at least half, to a framework for wall-trained plants (see p.165).

MUSSAENDA (ZONE 10)

Tender, evergreen shrubs and climbers that from spring to autumn have striking flowers with colorful bracts at the ends of stems. They require frost-free growing conditions, but may be grown in pots under glass in colder climates. Prune to maintain the production of fresh growth and flowers. Cut off the old flower clusters throughout the flowering season; in winter or spring, when flowering has finished, cut back hard, removing most of the growth made in the previous season. In warm climates mussaendas are often planted en masse or used for an informal hedge.

MYRICA BAYBERRY

Deciduous or evergreen shrubs grown for their aromatic foliage and, in some cases, for their berries. M. gale, the bog myrtle (zone 4), is a deciduous, compact shrub of suckering habit. It needs little or no pruning, but cut any leggy stems to ground level in spring and trim plants lightly. M. californica, the California wax myrtle or bayberry (zones 8 to 10), is a compact evergreen, valued for its wax-bloomed, purple fruit and aromatic foliage. It needs no regular pruning, but it is susceptible to cold and may be badly frost-damaged. In spring cut back damaged growth to live wood or to ground level.

N

NANDINA (ZONES 7–9)

Evergreen, medium-sized shrub with a bamboolike habit of growth. N. domestica, the heavenly or sacred bamboo, bears white flowers in summer, followed, in warm climates or under glass only, by red berries. Several cultivars have fine spring and autumn color. Vigorous specimens freely produce new growth from the base. If young plants are spindly, cut back on planting to stimulate growth. Further pruning is needed only to keep the plant neat. Plants can usually be renovated by cutting back old stems to ground level.

NERIUM OLEANDER (ZONES 8/9–10)

Nerium oleander, the most widely grown species, is a large, evergreen shrub with periwinkle-like flowers. There are many cultivars with flowers in a range of colors, some double. It is tender, and in colder climates needs a very favored site, but will also grow well under glass. The habit is upright and can be ungainly. Oleanders make excellent standards, or can be wall trained or used for informal

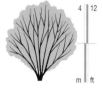

hedges. The sap is toxic, so gloves should be worn when pruning.

WHEN TO PRUNE Late summer to autumn.

TRAINING AND PRUNING Tip-prune shoots of young plants. In warm climates specimen plants require little pruning; shape lightly after flowering, if needed. Prune pot-grown or trained plants annually, cutting back flowered shoots by half and laterals to 4in (10cm). Plants tolerate hard pruning, but may take two years to flower freely again.

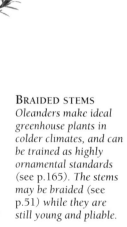

BRAIDED STEMS
Oleanders make ideal greenhouse plants in colder climates, and can be trained as highly ornamental standards (see p.165). The stems may be braided (see p.51) while they are still young and pliable.

NERIUM OLEANDER
In mild climates, oleanders often flower well if grown in the shelter of a sunny wall.

OTHER ORNAMENTAL SHRUBS

MACKAYA Prune lightly in winter, after flowering. Can be pruned hard.
x MAHOBERBERIS Cut straggly stems back to strong shoots in late spring, after flowering.
MALPIGHIA Trim lightly after flowering.
MALVASTRUM As for Anisodontea (see p.175).
MEDICAGO Minimal pruning.
MEDINILLA Prune M. magnifica after flowering to shape. In suitable climates it makes a good hedge (see p.44).

MELIANTHUS In warm climates cut flowered stems out in autumn. In colder climates cut back old growth in spring.
MELICYTUS Minimal pruning.
MENZIESIA Minimal pruning.
MICROCITRUS As for Citrus (see p.142).
MITRARIA Minimal pruning.
MONTANOA Minimal pruning.
MURRAYA After flowering, trim lightly, removing flowered growth.
MYRCEUGENIA If necessary to limit size, prune in spring.

MYRICARIA Shorten flowered shoots to 2in (5cm).
MYRSINE Minimal pruning.
NEILLIA See Stephanandra, p.222.
NEMATANTHUS As for Justicia (see p.205).
NEMOPANTHUS As for Ilex (see p.203).
NEVIUSIA Cut out old wood in summer after flowering.
NICOTIANA Cut back to the base or a low framework after flowering.
NOTELAEA Tolerates shaping.
NOTOSPARTIUM Tolerates renovation.

O-P

OCHNA (ZONE 10)

Tender, evergreen or semievergreen, medium-sized shrubs and trees, grown for their flowers and ornamental fruits. *O. serrulata*, the Mickey Mouse plant, is the most commonly grown; it has yellow flowers in spring and summer, followed by red calyces on which a ring of glossy, black fruit forms. The berried branches are good for cutting. Ochnas need full sun and frost-free conditions (although established plants tolerate light frost), where they may be grown as specimen plants, but they may also be grown under glass in pots. Pinch out the shoot tips of young plants to encourage a bushy habit. Prune established plants lightly in early spring, cutting flowered stems back to strong laterals. At the same time remove dead, damaged, or unproductive wood, and weak, twiggy shoots. In warm climates ochnas may be espalier-trained on walls (*see p.162*), or used as an informal hedge (*see p.45*).

OLEARIA *DAISY BUSH*

Evergreen shrubs of varying size, grown for their foliage and daisylike flower heads, mainly produced in summer. Australasian in origin, most olearias are hardy in zones 9 to 10. In cooler climates, they are often planted in front of a sunny wall (they are not suitable for wall training). They thrive in windy coastal sites, where they usually form compact bushes. Pruning is required only to remove frost damage or to keep plants within bounds, but olearias will make vigorous new growth when cut back. *O. macrodonta* and *O. × haastii* make good informal hedges.

WHEN TO PRUNE Spring, but not before fresh growth emerges.

TRAINING AND PRUNING On young plants shorten the longest shoots to encourage bushiness. Cut young hedging plants back hard (*see p.44*) to encourage dense growth. Once established, allow free-standing specimens to develop unpruned, apart from cutting back any frosted stems beyond the point of damage to healthy, outward-facing buds. To restrict size, prune stems by one-third to half of the previous season's growth, cutting to outward-facing buds. If removing larger sections of branches, cut to well within the body of the plant to hide cut marks. For the pruning of hedges, *see p.45*.

Renovate by cutting back hard into old wood. Response is usually good.

OSMANTHUS

Large, evergreen shrubs, grown for their foliage and small, but fragrant, flowers. Most are hardy. Freestanding specimens do not require regular pruning, but from time to time it may be necessary to keep them within bounds. All tolerate being cut back, even into old wood, but timing depends on the flowering season. Some osmanthus are suitable for hedging, although trimming reduces the floral display.

O. DELAVAYI (ZONES 9–10)

Bushy shrub with glossy leaves and very fragrant, white flowers from mid- to late spring on wood made the previous season. Frost damage is likely in cooler areas; plants benefit from the protection of a warm wall, but are too stiff and slow-growing to train formally.

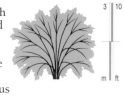

WHEN TO PRUNE Late spring, after flowering. Hedges may be clipped over several times during summer, but in cool climates do not trim them any later than midsummer, or the resulting fresh growth may be vulnerable to frost damage in winter.

TRAINING AND PRUNING Little formative pruning is required (*see* Evergreen shrubs, *p.157*). Prune established specimens only to keep them within bounds and enhance the shape, cutting overlong stems back to a shoot within the body of the plant to hide the cut marks. When given the protection of a warm wall, plants are best allowed to grow naturally, tying in loosely only if necessary. Clip hedges to shape once or twice in a season (*see* Hedges, *p.46*). Rejuvenate old, neglected plants by cutting back hard into old wood; they should respond well.

> **OTHER OSMANTHUS**
> O. ARMATUS, O. FRAGRANS var. AURANTIACUS, O. × FORTUNEI Prune in late spring as for *O. delavayi*.
> O. × BURKWOODII As for *O. delavayi*. Trim hedges in midsummer.
> O. DECORUS As for *O. delavayi*.
> O. HETEROPHYLLUS Prune in late spring. Not suitable for wall training.
> O. YUNNANENSIS As for *O. delavayi*.

PAEONIA *PEONY*

Peonies fall into two groups, the herbaceous, perennial peonies, and the medium-sized, deciduous shrubs known as "tree peonies." The two groups bear similar types of flower. The shrubs include *P. delavayi* var. *lutea*, hardy in zones 6 to 8, with fine, dense foliage, and *P. suffruticosa*, or Moutan peony, which has many beautiful cultivars. Tree peonies are long-lived plants that may be slow to establish. The habit is upright, and older stems may become leggy. Peonies require little pruning, but judicious cutting out of old wood encourages bushier growth. Named cultivars are usually grafted.

WHEN TO PRUNE In summer, after flowering, and in autumn after leaf-fall.

TRAINING AND PRUNING Plants require little formative pruning (*see p.157*). Remove the dead flowers in summer or,

PAEONIA DELAVAYI VAR. LUTEA
The flowered shoots will die back to new growth below after fruiting. Prune back to these shoots in autumn.

if seeds are wanted, the fruiting heads in autumn. Occasionally cut old, leggy stems of mature plants back to ground level. Avoid more drastic pruning, especially of grafted plants.

PAVONIA (ZONE 10)

Evergreen shrubs grown mainly for their attractive flowers. Some need tropical or subtropical conditions, but others tolerate light frosts. The natural habit is open and spreading, so tip-prune young plants (*see p.155*) to make them bush out. Prune established plants lightly in early spring, cutting back any straggling stems. Rejuvenate old, neglected plants by removing some old wood and cutting back the rest by up to half, to well-placed young shoots.

PENSTEMON

Some shrubs in this genus are dwarf or prostrate rock-garden plants that need minimal pruning. The more commonly grown species (sometimes included in *Keckiella*) are woody-based subshrubs bearing attractive flowers in early summer, with an upright habit that is best encouraged by cutting back each year. Hardy in zones 9 to 10, they may suffer frost damage in cooler areas.

WHEN TO PRUNE Spring, after any danger of severe frost has passed, and also after flowering.

TRAINING AND PRUNING In spring, prune any winter-damaged stems back hard to encourage fresh growth from the base. After flowering, shorten flowered stems by half to prevent seed production and encourage further flowering. Cut any stems showing dieback right back to the base: if dieback spreads, plants are usually best replaced, since penstemons do not renovate well.

PEROVSKIA (ZONES 6–8)

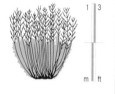

Russian sage is a deciduous shrub with aromatic, gray-green foliage and spikes of blue flowers, borne at the ends of new stems from late summer to midautumn. The top-growth dies back in winter, but new shoots are produced from the woody base the following spring. In cooler climates the dead top-growth provides some protection in winter. Annual hard pruning keeps plants neat and can produce larger, but fewer, flower spikes. Left unpruned, plants become leggy, and old dead wood accumulates.

WHEN TO PRUNE Midspring, as new growth is breaking.

TRAINING AND PRUNING From the first year onward, prune all the previous season's growth back hard, to within

PEROVSKIA ATRIPLICIFOLIA
If regularly pruned, perovskias will produce vigorous flowering shoots from a basal framework for many years.

2–4in (5–10 cm) of the ground initially, and then to the framework of old wood that will gradually develop (*see below*). Old and neglected plants should also respond well to this treatment.

PRUNING AN ESTABLISHED PEROVSKIA

1 *Cut all flowered stems back to within three or four buds of the old wood, varying the height at which you cut.*

2 *Cut away old sections of the framework that produced no new growth last year.*

PERSOONIA (ZONE 10)

Large, evergreen shrubs of Australian origin, with pinelike foliage, terminal spikes of saffron-yellow flowers in summer, and pendulous clusters of edible, green to plum-purple fruit in winter. They will withstand light frosts if grown in a sunny position in well-drained soil. Persoonias may be grown as small trees by training a young plant with a central leader.

WHEN TO PRUNE Autumn, after fruiting.

TRAINING AND PRUNING Do not prune when young, to allow the plant's natural habit to develop. Only light trimming of established plants is needed to thicken the foliage. Wayward shoots may also be shortened to improve the shape. Remove the spent flower heads if fruits are not required; otherwise, prune after fruiting. To grow persoonia as a standard, train up a vigorous stem, removing competing shoots, and then cut back laterals to form a branching head (*see p.165*).

OTHER ORNAMENTAL SHRUBS

OEMLERIA (syn OSMARONIA)
O. cerasiformis is of suckering habit; cut back flowered shoots, and chop around edges to restrict spread if necessary.
OPLOPANAX Spiny. Minimal pruning, if necessary, in spring.
OSBECKIA In spring cut back by half shoots that flowered the previous summer.
X OSMAREA See *Osmanthus* X *burkwoodii* (*facing page*).
OSMARONIA See *Oemleria* (*above*).
OSTEOMELES Freestanding specimens require little pruning. On wall-trained specimens gradually train in young stems to replace old wood, pruning in midsummer.
OXYLOBIUM No special needs. Flowered shoots can be trimmed lightly after flowering. Remove some old wood occasionally.
OZOTHAMNUS Little pruning needed, except to remove frost-damaged growth in spring. Tolerates hard pruning.
PACHYSTACHYS As for *Justicia* (*see p.205*).
PACHYSTEGIA Minimal, as for *Olearia* (*see facing page*).
PALIURUS Minimal pruning as a free-standing shrub. May also be grown as a standard (*see p.165*), and tolerates being cut back hard in the spring.
PARAHEBE Little pruning needed; trim over lightly in summer after flowering.
PARROTIOPSIS Minimal. If necessary, prune lightly in early summer.
PAVETTA Little needed; remove some old wood, after flowering or fruiting.
PENTAS Deadhead and trim lightly in spring. Tolerates hard pruning if necessary.
PERNETTYA See *Gaultheria* (*p.197*).
PETROPHILA No special needs.

PHILADELPHUS

Medium-sized to large, deciduous shrubs, mainly grown for the highly fragrant, white flowers that are produced on the previous season's wood, usually in midsummer. They produce new stems from the base that branch and, after about four years, can become congested, and flowering performance declines. Most philadelphus respond well to pruning, and need regular pruning to maximize their flowering potential. Those grown for their flowers are pruned in the same way, but a few, especially *P. coronarius* 'Aureus', that are grown more for their foliage, are often additionally pruned to enhance this effect at the expense of the flowers.

To encourage young plants to make fresh growth from the base, plant 2in (5cm) deeper than the nursery soil mark.

P. CORONARIUS (ZONES 5–8)

MOCK ORANGE

Medium-sized shrub. The species itself is seldom grown, but it has several popular cultivars with attractive spring foliage. This species can be pruned in several ways, either for flowers or to enhance and prolong the foliage display, which is particularly effective on the gold-leaved 'Aureus', the foliage of which turns green in midsummer.

WHEN TO PRUNE Late summer, after flowering, or for the best leaf effect, prune in late spring, immediately before flowering. Renovate in winter or early spring.

TRAINING AND PRUNING For a flowering shrub, treat as for *P.* 'Virginal'. To enhance and prolong the foliage effect (though this will inhibit flowering), trim over lightly to remove flower buds and to promote further leaf growth. Plants can also be pruned back to a framework in early spring as for *Hydrangea paniculata* (see p.202), feeding the plant generously to maintain vigorous growth. Renovation is as for *P.* 'Virginal'.

P. MICROPHYLLUS (ZONES 6–8)

Small shrub of twiggy habit, with white flowers in early summer. It generally needs little pruning.

WHEN TO PRUNE Summer, after flowering. Renovate in spring.

PHILADELPHUS 'VIRGINAL'
Cut several stems to the ground each year to promote fresh growth with abundant flowers.

TRAINING AND PRUNING Extensive annual pruning is not desirable, but cut back any wayward branches to healthy lower shoots. If the shrub becomes congested, thin growth by cutting some stems down to the base. To renovate, cut back hard to a low framework in spring.

P. 'VIRGINAL' (ZONES 5–8)

Medium-sized shrub, with masses of double, white flowers in early summer. Prune to thin out crowded growth and to maintain peak flowering performance.

WHEN TO PRUNE Late summer, immediately after flowering. Renovate in winter or early spring.

TRAINING AND PRUNING Aim to stimulate young flowering growth while keeping a shrub of balanced proportions. Cut back one in four stems, choosing the oldest, to ground level or to a low shoot. To renovate, cut down all old stems to ground level and shorten any younger vigorous stems by one-quarter to half. If the shrub does not respond with new growth, replace it.

> **OTHER PHILADELPHUS**
> P. 'AVALANCHE', P. 'BELLE ETOILE' As for P. 'Virginal'.
> P. DELAVAYI As for *P.* 'Virginal'.
> P. MEXICANUS As for *P.* 'Virginal', but in cooler regions best grown with the shelter of a warm wall (do not wall train). Cultivars of *P.* x *lemoinei* and *P.* x *purpureo-maculatus* are all treated as for *P.* 'Virginal'.

PHLOMIS

Small, evergreen shrubs and perennials native to the Mediterranean region, with gray-green, sagelike foliage and whorls of hooded, yellow or lilac flowers in summer. *P. fruticosa*, the Jerusalem sage, is a spreading species; *P. italica* is more upright, with pink flowers. Hardy in zones 8 to 10, they may suffer some frost damage, but they usually recover well, making new growth from the base. Regular attention to the removal of damaged and wayward growth helps to keep plants neat and compact. Young, vigorous specimens tolerate being cut back hard.

WHEN TO PRUNE Midspring, when the shrub is in active growth.

TRAINING AND PRUNING Plants require little formative pruning except to remove weak growths and to shorten straggly stems. Established plants need no annual pruning, but benefit from occasional shaping cuts. Shorten any frost-damaged stems, cutting to just above healthy buds. Cut out any weak and old shoots entirely. When branches become leggy and untidy-looking, cut them back to a shoot or bud well within the bush; if this is done regularly, a good shape will be maintained.

Renovate neglected specimens by cutting back hard into the old wood, either to within 3–4in (8–10cm) of the ground or, for a bigger plant, to a taller framework of branches. Recovery is usually good, but phlomis are relatively short-lived: very old specimens are better replaced.

PHLOMIS ITALICA
Only light pruning to remove damaged or wayward growth is needed.

PHOTINIA INCL. STRANVAESIA

Medium-sized to large, deciduous and evergreen shrubs and trees, usually of bushy, upright habit, with white flowers in spring or summer. Hardiness varies with the species. Some of the evergreen photinias have brightly colored young leaves in spring. The deciduous species, which tend to be intolerant of lime, have showy fruit in autumn and attractive leaf color. Photinias do not require regular pruning, but they can be trained as standards, and pruning can also be used to enhance the effect of the striking spring foliage of some of the evergreens.

Photinia x fraseri

P. X FRASERI (ZONES 7–9)

Group of evergreen hybrids with brilliant red young foliage, which pruning can enhance. They may be used as formal or informal hedging.

WHEN TO PRUNE Spring. Clip hedges in spring and summer.

TRAINING AND PRUNING Like many evergreens, needs only minimal formative pruning (*see p.157*). To encourage more bright young leaves, when established, shorten stems by up to 6in (15cm), cutting just above an outward-facing bud. Tip-prune young shoots on hedges to encourage leafy growth. Clip hedges two or three times a year (*see p.46*). To renovate, cut hard back into the old wood. Response is usually good.

P. VILLOSA (ZONES 5–7)

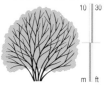

Deciduous shrub, flowering in late spring or early summer, with red fruit and orange-red autumn color.

WHEN TO PRUNE Winter, while dormant.

TRAINING AND PRUNING For a multi-stemmed shrub, allow to develop with minimal pruning. If growth becomes overcrowded, cut stems back to a low shoot where needed. To train as a standard, *see p.165*. Renovate an overgrown shrub by cutting back to a low framework. Thin subsequent growth if shoots are congested.

> **OTHER PHOTINIAS**
> P. ARBUTIFOLIA See *Heteromeles, p.200*.
> P. BEAUVERDIANA As for *P. villosa*.
> P. DAVIDIANA Minimal pruning.
> P. GLABRA, P. SERRATIFOLIA As for *P. x fraseri*.

PHYGELIUS (ZONES 6–10)

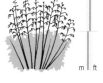

Evergreen and semi-evergreen shrubs or subshrubs, with tubular flowers on the current season's growth in summer to autumn. In colder climates they are usually cut back by severe weather, but normally recover in spring. Plant in a sheltered spot or train on a warm wall.

WHEN TO PRUNE Spring, after the danger of frost has passed.

TRAINING AND PRUNING In warm climates, trim lightly in spring. In cool climates, cut back all frosted stems to healthy buds on live growth, or to the base of the plant. More growth is likely to survive if stems are tied in loosely on a warm wall. To renovate, cut all stems to the ground in spring.

PHYGELIUS 'WINCHESTER FANFARE'
In colder climates, cutting back old stems will stimulate the fresh growth already appearing at the base of the plant.

PIERIS

Small to medium-sized, rounded, evergreen shrubs, with pink or white flowers in spring and, in some species, brilliant young foliage.

P. JAPONICA (ZONES 5/6–8)

JAPANESE ANDROMEDA

Spring-flowering shrub with many cultivars that have brightly colored young leaves; they can be grown in pots.

WHEN TO PRUNE Spring, after flowering.

TRAINING AND PRUNING Like many evergreens, needs minimal formative pruning (*see p.157*). Deadhead annually, and cut out frost-damaged growth promptly. To correct an uneven shape, cut back overlong branches to upright shoots; prune harder on the weaker side. To renovate a neglected specimen, cut back to a low framework. Plants usually recover, even when cut into old wood.

> **OTHER PIERIS**
> P. FLORIBUNDA As for *P. japonica*.
> P. FORMOSA As for *P. japonica*.
> P. FORMOSA var. FORRESTII cultivars As for *P. japonica*.

> **OTHER ORNAMENTAL SHRUBS**
> PHILESIA No pruning required.
> PHILLYREA Allow to grow freely or use to make topiary shapes, pruning as for *Buxus sempervirens* (*see p.181*), but in summer after flowering.
> PHILODENDRON Prune only to restrict size (for example, if growing under glass). *See also* Dictionary of Climbing Plants, *p.280*.
> PHORMIUM *See* Palms and palmlike plants, *p.43*.
> X PHYLLIOPSIS Minimal pruning, if necessary, as for *Erica cinerea* (*p.193*)
> PHYLLODOCE Minimal pruning, if necessary, as for *Erica cinerea* (*p.193*).
> PHYLLOTHAMNUS Minimal pruning, if necessary, as for *Erica cinerea* (*p.193*).
> PHYSOCARPUS Remove up to one in four of the oldest stems in summer after flowering, as for *Philadelphus* 'Virginal' (*see facing page*).
> PIMELEA Minimal pruning, if necessary, in spring.
> PIPTANTHUS Cut out frost-damaged wood in spring, and up to one in four old stems in summer, after flowering. May be wall trained (*see p.165*).
> PISONIA Tolerates pruning, but little is generally needed.

PITTOSPORUM

Medium-sized to large, evergreen shrubs and trees with attractive leaves and fragrant flowers in spring or summer. They are usually neat, rounded, and erect in habit, needing little pruning, and thrive in coastal conditions, where they grow even more dense and bushy. Most are suitable only for warm climates, but tender species may be grown under glass. *P. tenuifolium* and *P. ralphii*, among the hardiest species, are excellent for hedges or screens.

P. TENUIFOLIUM (ZONES 9–10)

TAWHIWHI, KOHUHU

Shrub or tree, with black stems, wavy-edged leaves, and honey-scented, maroon flowers in spring.

WHEN TO PRUNE Midspring, when growth has started. Trim hedges again in midsummer (*see p.44*).

TRAINING AND PRUNING Maintain a single main stem. Established plants require little pruning; trim or thin growth only if necessary. They usually recover well if pruned hard in midspring.

OTHER PITTOSPORUMS
P. CRASSIFOLIUM, P. EUGENIOIDES, P. UNDULATUM As for *P. tenuifolium*.
P. RALPHII As for *P. tenuifolium*, but more regular pruning is needed to keep it compact.
P. TOBIRA As for *P. tenuifolium*, but response to renovation is slower. Can be trained as a standard (*see p.165*).

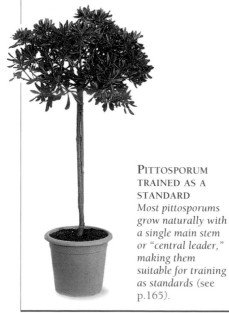

PITTOSPORUM TRAINED AS A STANDARD
Most pittosporums grow naturally with a single main stem or "central leader," making them suitable for training as standards (see p.165).

POTENTILLA

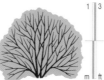

Deciduous, small to medium-sized shrubs of dense, rounded habit. The wiry stems of the current season's growth are covered with wild-roselike flowers over a long period in summer. The many cultivars of *P. fruticosa* and several hybrids range widely in color and are hardy in zones 3 to 7. They are good for low hedges or in rock gardens. Potentillas tend to accumulate old and twiggy shoots; pruning helps to keep them neat and maintains their flowering performance.

WHEN TO PRUNE Midspring; trim in autumn.

TRAINING AND PRUNING Shorten vigorous young shoots by up to half. To tidy plants, trim over lightly after flowering. Cut back the oldest wood to the base and remove weak, twiggy growth. Prune hedges in the same way. Old shrubs sometimes respond well when cut back to a low framework of sturdy branches, but may be better replaced.

PROTEA (ZONE 10)

African genus of evergreen, frost-tender shrubs and trees, grown mainly for their large, striking flower heads. They make handsome specimens in containers or under glass in cooler temperate regions. They require minimal pruning unless it is necessary to restrict their size (for example, when growing under glass); shorten growth in early spring.

PROTEA CYNAROIDES
The king protea may withstand light frosts when established.

PRUNUS *CHERRY*

Small to large shrubs, grown for their flowers and, in some cases, autumn color and fruit. The evergreens make good hedges. Members of this genus are susceptible to various diseases, including silver-leaf, which can gain entry through pruning wounds (*see also* Plum problems, *p.123*). With some exceptions, pruning is best kept to a minimum. Plants are least vulnerable in early summer, when in full leaf. The genus includes many trees (*see p.82*).

P. GLANDULOSA (ZONES 4–8)

DWARF FLOWERING ALMOND

Small, deciduous shrub with upright stems bearing pink or white flowers in late winter to early spring on the previous season's wood. It is best known in cultivars that have double flowers. Plant in a sunny site for the flowering wood to ripen well, otherwise dieback may occur in cold winters. Regular pruning is necessary to maintain the flowering performance. Freestanding specimens should be cut back annually to a low framework.

WHEN TO PRUNE Early spring, immediately after flowering.

TRAINING AND PRUNING In the first year after planting, prune stems back to near ground level. In subsequent years, cut all stems back hard. To train against a wall (*see p.162*), develop a fan of framework stems. Cut out wood that has flowered as soon as blossom fades and tie in replacement shoots. Remove outward-growing shoots annually in midsummer. To renovate, cut all stems back to the ground in early spring. Old plants may not respond well, however, in which case they are best replaced.

P. LUSITANICA (ZONES 7–10)

LAUREL, PORTUGAL LAUREL

Large, evergreen shrub that may become treelike if left unpruned. Slender spikes of small, fragrant, white flowers are produced in summer amid glossy, dark green leaves. It is suitable as a screening plant or an informal hedge and may be grown as a standard on a short clear leg.

POTENTILLA HEDGE
Trimmed plants have a neat, dense habit.

PTELEA (ZONES 4–9)

Large, deciduous shrubs and trees, grown mainly for their aromatic foliage, fragrant flowers, and decorative winged fruit. Pteleas generally require little pruning, but they will tolerate hard cutting back if required. Prune in early to midspring. They have weak root systems, and initial staking of plants is advisable. *P. trifoliata*, the hop tree or water ash, is a low, spreading plant that may be trained as a small standard (*see p.165*), with a single clear stem no more than 2–3ft (60–90cm) high.

WHEN TO PRUNE Late spring or early summer.

TRAINING AND PRUNING Needs no special pruning, except to restrict size if needed: cut overlong shoots well back, to the trunk or a main stem. Specimens trained as standards (*see p.165*) are often trimmed to a rounded shape. Plants break readily from old wood, so if overgrown can be pruned hard back to a framework, or even almost to ground level. One season's new growth is usually enough to hide pruning wounds.

OTHER PRUNUS
P. LAUROCERASUS As for *P. lusitanica*.
P. MUME Allow to develop as a large shrub or small tree with minimal pruning. Remove any dieback promptly.
P. PUMILA Minimal pruning.
P. SINENSIS As for *P. glandulosa*.
P. TENELLA Minimal pruning except to control suckering; usually responds to hard pruning if flowering deteriorates.
P. TRILOBA Minimal pruning. If trained on a warm wall, laterals need to be pruned back to the framework.
For other species, see Dictionary of Ornamental Trees, *p.82, and* Tree Fruits, *pp.122-136.*

PYRACANTHA *FIRETHORN* (ZONES 6–9)

Evergreen, medium-sized to large shrubs, grown for their small, white flowers in early summer, and showy red, orange, or yellow fruit, borne on spurs from the old wood. They may be grown as specimens in a border, but make effective wall shrubs, trained as fans or espaliers. They are dense and spiny, making them also suitable for formal or informal hedging or barrier planting. The close pruning needed to maintain plants as wall shrubs can also be adapted to other formal shapes. Pyracanthas are prone to fireblight (*see p.117*), which must be cut out, although there are disease-resistant cultivars. Wear gloves when pruning; the thorns are long and sharp.

WHEN TO PRUNE Midspring. Wall-trained shrubs can also be pruned in late summer, shortening some new growth to expose the berries. Prune formal hedges in spring, then clip two or three times during the growing season.

TRAINING AND PRUNING Specimen shrubs need little pruning at the formative stage or when established. If wayward or over-vigorous branches ruin the shape, remove them completely. On wall-trained espaliers or fans, form a framework of permanent branches (*see p.162*). Cut back outward-growing shoots and shorten other shoots in spring, although this will mean losing some flowers and berries. In late summer cut back young shoots not needed for tying in to two or three leaves, to expose the ripening berries. Formal hedges need pruning two or three times during spring and summer. Hard pruning can be used to renovate plants, but it may make them more vulnerable to fireblight.

PRUNING A WALL-TRAINED PYRACANTHA, SUMMER

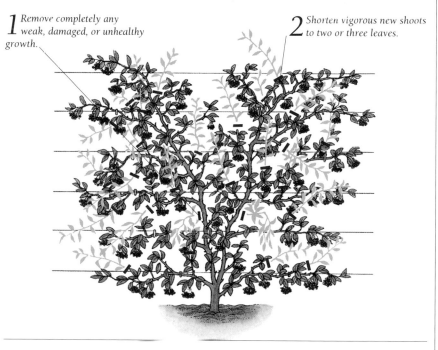

1 *Remove completely any weak, damaged, or unhealthy growth.*

2 *Shorten vigorous new shoots to two or three leaves.*

OTHER ORNAMENTAL SHRUBS
PLECTRANTHUS In warm climates *P. ecklonii* can be cut back hard in early spring, though pruning is not necessary.
PODALYRIA Prune in summer, after flowering, only if necessary.
POLYGALA Cut back long growths in late winter, if necessary.
POLYSCIAS No special needs.
POMADERRIS Tip-prune when young. Trim, if necessary, after flowering.
PONCIRUS Cut back young plants to encourage bushiness. Avoid pruning once established. Trim hedges twice in summer.
PORTULACARIA No special needs.

PROSTANTHERA Tip-prune young plants. Trim established plants after flowering if necessary, but do not cut into old wood.
PSEUDERANTHEMUM Prune in summer after flowering, only if necessary.
PSEUDOPANAX No special needs.
PSEUDOWINTERA Tolerates pruning, although it is rarely needed.
PSORALEA Tip-prune when young. When established, shorten flowered shoots by half after flowering. Do not cut into old wood.
PTEROSTYRAX Prune in summer after flowering, only if necessary.

R-S

RHODODENDRON

Small to large, evergreen, semievergreen, and deciduous shrubs, which include azaleas. They have spectacular flowers, usually in spring; those that are deciduous often have attractive autumn leaf color. Dwarf rhododendrons make good rock garden shrubs, while larger ones may become treelike with age; many are woodland plants and some are suitable for informal hedges. Most are frost-tolerant; the tender species and hybrids may be grown under glass, and some are suitable as flowering house plants.

Most rhododendrons need little pruning, although many tolerate being cut back hard. However, rhododendrons can also be moved, in autumn or spring; transplanting is often a better course than renovation. Many rhododendrons are grafted and suckers should be removed. Older plants may become congested and suffer dieback through lack of light to the center.

R. AUGUSTINII (ZONES 7–8)

Upright evergreen with lavender-blue flowers in spring. Lack of light may lead to dieback in the center.

WHEN TO PRUNE Late spring or early summer, after flowering.

TRAINING AND PRUNING Little formative pruning is necessary. The natural habit of established plants is easily spoiled by pruning; remove only dead, diseased, and damaged wood. Deadhead if practical. Renovate by cutting back hard, leaving a balanced framework of old wood. Response is generally good.

CLIPPED KURUME
AZALEAS IN JAPAN
R. kiusianum is a
parent of these slow-
growing, small-
leaved hybrids,
which in traditional
Japanese gardens
(left) are often
trimmed to form bun
shapes. They are
sometimes grown as
container plants and
bonsai.

R. KIUSIANUM (ZONES 6–8)

A compact semi-evergreen azalea with mauve or purple flowers in late spring. It tolerates clipping.

WHEN TO PRUNE Summer, after flowering. Renovate in spring.

TRAINING AND PRUNING Unless they are to be trimmed closely, plants require little pruning. Tip-prune young plants that are to be clipped, to promote dense growth. Clip over established plants with shears in early summer when flowers fade and, for a formal effect, once more in midsummer. Neglected plants can be renovated by shortening all growth by about half in spring, but old plants are better replaced.

R. LUTEUM (ZONES 6–8)

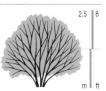

Deciduous, suckering azalea, with fragrant, yellow spring flowers and fine autumn color.

RHODODENDRON
'MRS G. W. LEAK'
Most of the large-flowered hybrids, including this magnificent example, require minimal pruning and are best treated as for R. rex.

WHEN TO PRUNE Summer, after flowering.

TRAINING AND PRUNING Prune young plants lightly to promote a balanced shape. Annual pruning of established plants is not necessary, but to prevent congestion and stimulate flowering, occasionally cut out completely, or to low shoots, one or two of the oldest stems. To renovate, cut back all but young stems in spring.

R. REX (ZONES 7–8)

Large evergreen with red, pink, or creamy flowers in spring. The dark leaves have a buff, felted underside.

WHEN TO PRUNE Early summer, after flowering.

TRAINING AND PRUNING Lightly prune young plants to form an evenly shaped bush. Established specimens will require little to no pruning for many years, but deadhead where practical. Old plants become leggy; this is not easy to rectify by hard pruning, since new growth does not break freely from old, thick branches.

OTHER RHODODENDRONS
R. ARBOREUM As for *R. rex.*
R. CALOPHYTUM As for *R. rex.*
R. HIPPOPHAEOIDES As for *R. augustinii.*
R. MACABEANUM As for *R. rex.*
R. OCCIDENTALE As for *R. luteum.*
R. PONTICUM As for *R. augustinii.*
Suitable for an informal hedge.
R. SINOGRANDE As for *R. rex.*
R. THOMSONII As for *R. rex.*
R. YAKUSHIMANUM HYBRIDS Avoid pruning except to deadhead.
LARGE-LEAVED HYBRIDS As for *R. rex,* but hard pruning may be successful provided that a good length of stem is left above the graft union.
TRIFLORUM SERIES As for *R. augustinii.*
KURUME AZALEAS As for *R. kiusianum.*

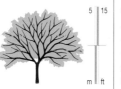

RHUS TYPHINA
Hard pruning produces a display of larger, showier leaves.

RHUS SUMAC

Deciduous shrubs, many of suckering habit, mainly grown for brilliant autumn leaf color. Some can be regularly hard-pruned to enhance the foliage effect. Wear gloves to prune, since the sap is potentially harmful.

R. TYPHINA (ZONES 4–8)

STAGHORN SUMAC

Spreading, suckering shrub that may also be grown as a small standard. The cultivar 'Dissecta' (syn. 'Laciniata') has fine, fernlike foliage, which is enhanced by regular hard pruning.

WHEN TO PRUNE Early spring. Remove unwanted suckers as they appear.

TRAINING AND PRUNING For a shrub, allow to develop naturally. To grow as a standard, train with a clear stem about 4ft (1.2m) in height (*see p.165*). Remove any suckers (*see p.153*). Cut back plants grown for foliage effect each year, either to about 4in (10cm) from the ground or to a low framework of woody stems (*see p.164*). To renovate, cut to the ground, and thin out subsequent new shoots.

OTHER RHUS
R. COPALLINA, R. GLABRA, R. POTANINII, R. x PULVINATA As for *R. typhina.*
R. VERNICIFLUA *See Dictionary of Ornamental Trees, p.86.*

RIBES CURRANT

Shrubs grown for their attractive spring flowers (other species are grown for their fruit). Unpruned plants accumulate old wood, and flowering performance declines.

R. SANGUINEUM (ZONES 6–7)

FLOWERING CURRANT

Vigorous, deciduous shrub with white, pink, or red flowers in spring, borne on the previous year's wood. Grow as a freestanding shrub, or use for an attractive, informal, flowering hedge. Regular pruning encourages the production of fresh, young growth.

WHEN TO PRUNE Mid- to late spring, after flowering. Renovate in late winter.

TRAINING AND PRUNING Cut to the ground one in three or four of the oldest branches, leaving the remainder unpruned. Prune hedges selectively in the same way (shearing hedging plants will impair flowering). Neglected specimens can be renovated by cutting all stems to ground level.

ROSMARINUS ROSEMARY

Evergreen shrubs grown for their aromatic, gray-green leaves and blue spring flowers. *R. officinalis* has many cultivars of varying habit. Upright cultivars can be grown as formal or informal hedges.

WHEN TO PRUNE Early summer, after flowering. Renovate in midspring.

TRAINING AND PRUNING Allow young plants to develop unchecked. Established plants need little pruning except to cut lanky growth back to a main branch or low shoot. Formal hedges should be trimmed twice in the season (*see p.46*). Old, neglected plants are best replaced, but an overgrown, vigorous specimen can be renovated by cutting all stems back by at least half.

R. SPECIOSUM (ZONES 8–9)

FUCHSIA-FLOWERED CURRANT

Medium-sized, deciduous, spiny shrub with drooping, red flowers in mid- to late spring. It is frost-tolerant, but in colder climates it flowers better if grown against a warm wall.

WHEN TO PRUNE Late spring, after flowering.

TRAINING AND PRUNING Prune a free-standing shrub as for *R. sanguineum*, but more moderately. To grow against a wall, train as a fan (*see p.162*); once the framework is established, plants need little pruning except, occasionally, to remove an old framework branch and train in young replacement growth. To renovate a neglected plant, cut all main stems back to about 12in (30cm).

OTHER RIBES
R. ALPINUM Minimal pruning required.
R. ODORATUM As for *R. sanguineum.*
See also Soft Fruits, *pp.234–240.*

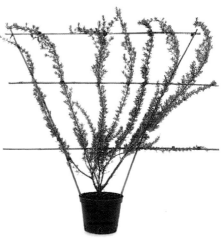

ROSMARINUS OFFICINALIS
With patience, rosemaries can be trained on stake frames – for example, to site container-grown plants against a wall in confined areas.

OTHER ORNAMENTAL SHRUBS
REINWARDTIA Remove shoot tips for a bushy habit. Prune hard after flowering.
RETAMA Deadhead only.
RHAMNUS No special needs. To prune evergreen hedges, clip the previous year's growth back by one-third in spring.
RHAPHIOLEPIS No special needs, but tolerates pruning to shape if necessary.

RHODOTYPOS Prune out some flowered wood in summer, after flowering. In warm climates can be pruned in winter.
RICHEA Very slow-growing; needs minimal pruning. Spent flower heads may be removed.
RICINUS In cool climates, often grown as an annual, but may also be overwintered under glass. No special pruning needs

when young, but support with stakes. Treat mature specimens as for *Fatsia* (*see p.195*).
ROMNEYA Prune in spring. In warm climates, remove up to half of the stems close to ground level; in cold climates, cut all winter-damaged growth back to live wood or to the ground.
RONDELETIA If necessary, prune lightly in spring.

RUBUS BRAMBLE

Scramblers and shrubs, producing new growth each year from the base of the plant. Some are valued for their decorative young stems and foliage; others for the roselike flowers. Some species have edible fruit. All benefit from regular pruning; most *Rubus* are prickly, so wear gloves.

R. 'BENENDEN' SYN. R. X TRIDEL

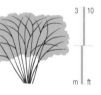

Deciduous, arching shrub, hardy in zones 5 to 7, with peeling bark and white flowers in spring.

3 | 10
m | ft

WHEN TO PRUNE Summer, after flowering.

TRAINING AND PRUNING Requires less drastic pruning than *R. thibetanus*, but annual removal of flowered growth and some old wood (*see below*) is needed to maintain the plant's vigor. To renovate, cut all stems to the ground in spring.

R. THIBETANUS (ZONES 7–9)

GHOST BRAMBLE

Vigorous, deciduous, arching shrub, whose young stems are most attractive when bare in winter. The stems flower in the second year, after which

3 | 10
m | ft

RUBUS COCKBURNIANUS (ZONES 6–9)
Second-year stems are removed in summer after flowering (inset), to leave only the young, white stems for winter display.

they are best removed, retaining only the youngest growth for a winter display of ghostly white stems.

WHEN TO PRUNE Summer, after flowering.

TRAINING AND PRUNING Each year, cut all of the flowered stems to the ground, leaving the current season's new stems unpruned (*see above*).

OTHER RUBUS
R. BIFLORUS, R. COCKBURNIANUS, R. ODORATUS As for *R. thibetanus*.
R. SPECTABILIS Suckers freely and can be invasive. As for *R. thibetanus*.
See also Soft Fruits, *p.230–33*; Dictionary of Climbing Plants, *p.282*.

RUTA RUE (ZONES 5–9)

Small, evergreen subshrubs, grown more for their blue-gray foliage than their unexciting heads of yellow summer flowers. Pruning keeps the plants compact, and can be used to enhance the foliage effect, at the expense of the flowers. Wear gloves for pruning, since the sap is potentially harmful. Prune in early spring: cut back all growth by at least half, to old wood, and remove any weak stems. Neglected plants often respond when cut back to within 6in (15cm) of ground level, but old specimens are best replaced.

SALIX WILLOW

Deciduous shrubs (some dwarf) and trees, grown for their habit, foliage, catkins, and, in some cases, colored bark. Regular pruning of those with attractive young growth ensures a supply of new, strongly colored stems. If the plant is vigorous, all stems can be cut back, as for those large tree willows (*see p.86*) that can be grown as shrubs by coppicing. Other willows need lighter, less regular pruning. Dwarf willows require no special pruning.

S. HASTATA 'WEHRHAHNII'

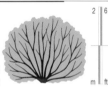

Small, upright shrub with deep purple stems and silver-gray catkins in spring. Prune to maintain a balance between young, colorful stems and older wood with catkins. Hardy in zones 6 to 7.

2 | 6
m | ft

WHEN TO PRUNE After planting, then occasionally in spring after the catkins have faded.

TRAINING AND PRUNING Let young plants develop with minimal pruning. On established plants, occasionally remove one or two of the oldest branches. To renovate, cut all stems back hard.

OTHER SALIX
S. FARGESII, S. MAGNIFICA As for *S. hastata* 'Wehrhahnii'.
S. ELAEAGNOS subsp. ANGUSTIFOLIA (syn. S. ROSMARINIFOLIA), S. GRACILISTYLA, S. PURPUREA No special needs. Prune lightly in winter if necessary.
S. HELVETICA, S. LANATA No special needs.
S. IRRORATA No special needs, but cut back older stems regularly to the base for a display of young, glaucous shoots.
S. REPENS, S. RETICULATA Dwarf species needing only minimal pruning. *See also* Dictionary of Ornamental Trees, *p.86*.

PRUNING AN ESTABLISHED RUBUS 'BENENDEN'

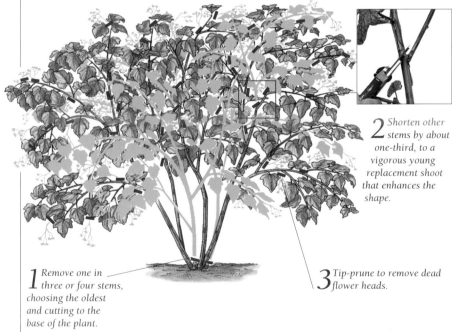

1 Remove one in three or four stems, choosing the oldest and cutting to the base of the plant.

2 Shorten other stems by about one-third, to a vigorous young replacement shoot that enhances the shape.

3 Tip-prune to remove dead flower heads.

SALVIA SAGE

Small, evergreen shrubs and subshrubs in a genus that also includes annuals, biennials, and perennials. The shrubs and subshrubs are grown for their flowers and aromatic foliage, of culinary value in some salvias. Some are frost-tolerant, while others may only be grown in colder climates in the shelter of a warm wall, although they are not suitable for wall training. Regular pruning produces strong, young growth on shrubby sages.

S. MICROPHYLLA SYN. S. GRAHAMII

Ornamental with bright red flowers in late summer and autumn. Hardy in zone 10, in colder climates it may survive winter if grown at the base of a warm wall.

WHEN TO PRUNE Spring, when growth begins.

TRAINING AND PRUNING In warm climates keep pruning to the minimum. In cool climates tip-prune shoots of young plants to encourage branching. When the shrub is established, cut back annually to the framework of woody stems. Neglected plants may respond if cut back hard to near ground level, but are not long-lived in colder climates.

S. OFFICINALIS (ZONES 9–10)

COMMON SAGE

Fragrant shrub with racemes of blue-purple flowers in summer. This culinary herb has various cultivars with purple, variegated, or golden leaves. Unpruned, they become leggy and lose their compact habit.

WHEN TO PRUNE Midspring, and in summer to remove flowers.

TRAINING AND PRUNING Tip-prune after planting (see p.155). If older plants become bare at the base, cut back into the old wood, in effect a form of renovation. Forms grown chiefly for their colored foliage give a better display if trimmed in spring, this regular pruning resulting in neatly rounded bushes. If flowers are produced in summer, trim them off.

> **OTHER SALVIAS**
> S. FULGENS, S. GREGGII, S. LEUCOPHYLLA, S. SESSEI As for *S. microphylla*.

SAMBUCUS ELDER

Medium sized to large, deciduous shrubs, some of which are coarse and weedy. Other elders are grown for their flowers and fruit; some also have highly ornamental foliage. Most respond vigorously to pruning; regular hard pruning also enhances the effect of cultivars grown for their foliage. They are most commonly grown as multistemmed bushes, which become tall and leggy unless pruned. Some strong-growing elders will make good standards when trained with a clear trunk. Hardiness varies with the species.

WHEN TO PRUNE Winter, while dormant. Remove suckers at the base of standards as they appear.

TRAINING AND PRUNING For a large shrub, allow to grow unpruned for a season. Then cut down half the stems to ground level and shorten the remainder by half. Thereafter, shorten one-year-old wood by half and cut back older stems to the ground. More severe pruning, carried out regularly, can be used to enhance the foliage effect of purple and cut-leaf elders, such as *S. canadensis* 'Acutiloba' and 'Aurea', *S. nigra* f. *laciniata*, and the purple-leaved *S. nigra* 'Guincho Purple'. They can be cut back annually (see p.164) to ground level or to a low framework, as for *Buddleja davidii* (see p.180). If the resulting new shoots are congested, thin them early in the growing season.

Use only vigorous species such as *S. sieboldiana* to train as standards (see p.28), clearing the stem to a height of 3–6ft (1–2m). These vigorous elders tend to produce numerous suckers and shoots on the clear stem, which should be removed promptly. Elders are generally short-lived, in spite of the rejuvenating effects that hard pruning can have. Old and neglected specimens are best replaced.

SANTOLINA SPLAYED OUT BY SNOW
Prune back hard into old wood to stimulate fresh, bushy growth.

SANTOLINA (ZONES 7–9)

Small, evergreen shrubs with aromatic, finely divided gray-green leaves, and yellow to white, buttonlike flowers in summer. Unless regularly pruned, plants become straggly.

WHEN TO PRUNE Autumn, after flowering. Prune hard in early spring.

TRAINING AND PRUNING Shorten stems on newly planted santolinas to encourage bushy growth. Trim off faded flowers and long shoots annually in autumn. Every two or three years, as plants become more open and straggly, cut hard back into old wood. Young plants usually respond well, but old specimens are better replaced.

> **OTHER ORNAMENTAL SHRUBS**
>
> RUELLIA No special needs. Prune lightly to shape after flowering if necessary.
> RULINGIA No special needs. May be tip-pruned to encourage a bushy habit.
> RUSCHIA Minimal pruning.
> RUSSELIA Prune some of the oldest stems to the base in winter.
> SARCOCOCCA Minimal pruning, if necessary, in spring.
> SCHEFFLERA As for *Fatsia* (see p.195).
> SELAGO Minimal pruning.
> SENECIO See *Brachyglottis* (p.179), *also*
>
> Dictionary of Climbing Plants (p.283).
> SENNA See *Cassia* (p.184).
> SERISSA Trim after flowering, in autumn.
> SERRURIA As for *Protea* (see p.214).
> SESBANIA As for *Cassia* (see p.184).
> SHEPHERDIA Minimal pruning.
> SIBIRAEA As for *Spiraea* 'Arguta' (see p.221).
> SIDERITIS No special needs.
> SIMMONDSIA No special needs. May be trimmed as a hedge.
> SINOJACKIA Minimal pruning.

SKIMMIA

Small to medium-sized, evergreen shrubs, grown for their neat habit, fragrant spring flowers, and long-lasting red fruit. Fruits are produced on female plants usually only if a male is sited nearby, though a few skimmias are hermaphrodites. Skimmias are naturally compact shrubs, requiring little pruning, but if overvigorous shoots ruin the outline, these can be cut back to well within the bush (to hide the cut) in spring, after flowering. Skimmias will tolerate harder pruning, but old plants are better replaced than cut back hard in an attempt to renovate them.

SKIMMIA JAPONICA (ZONES 6–9)
Cut back overlong shoots that unbalance the neat, rounded shape.

SOLANUM

Large genus containing many scandent or scrambling species (*see* Dictionary of Climbing Plants, *p.283*), and a number of evergreen, semievergreen, or deciduous small shrubs with attractive flowers and, in some cases, fruit. Most of the shrubs are frost-sensitive. In cooler climates they are grown under glass; some, such as the bushy, evergreen *S. pseudocapsicum*, the scarlet-fruited Jerusalem cherry, and its cultivars are treated as annuals. The smaller, evergreen *S. capsicastrum*, the winter cherry, has ovoid, not rounded, orange-red fruit. Those not grown as annuals, whether outdoors or under glass, benefit from being cut back to a low framework in spring.

SOPHORA KOWHAI

Genus that includes not only trees (*see p.88*) but also medium-sized to large, deciduous or semievergreen shrubs, grown for their graceful habit, attractive foliage, and white, yellow, or blue pealike flowers. They require sun; some benefit from shelter and in colder climates are best planted against a warm wall. Allow plants to develop their naturally elegant habit without extensive pruning. Pruning cuts, especially if made in late winter or spring, are likely to bleed sap, and for this reason pruning is best delayed until midsummer.

SOPHORA DAVIDII (ZONES 6–9)
Minimal pruning allows mature, flowering growth to develop.

S. TETRAPTERA (ZONE 8)

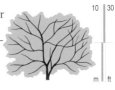

Large, evergreen or semievergreen shrub with golden-yellow flowers in late spring. The buds form in winter, so may be damaged by severe weather. Grown as a freestanding specimen, it may reach treelike proportions. It may also be wall grown for protection in colder climates. Flowers are borne on mature wood, so pruning is best kept to a minimum.

WHEN TO PRUNE Midsummer, when cuts are least likely to bleed.

TRAINING AND PRUNING Allow free-standing shrubs to develop naturally. Tie in shrubs planted against a wall informally and allow to develop with minimal pruning, or train more formally as fans (*see p.162*), although the pruning necessary may delay flowering for five years or more. Hard pruning is likely to be successful only in warm climates.

> **OTHER SOPHORAS**
> S. DAVIDII, S. MACROCARPA,
> S. MICROPHYLLA As for *S. tetraptera.*
> *For other species, see* Dictionary of Ornamental Trees, *p.88.*

SPARRMANNIA (ZONE 10)

African hemp is a large, tender, evergreen, erect shrub or small tree with white and yellow flowers in late spring and summer. It responds well to pruning to restrict size under glass.

WHEN TO PRUNE Summer, after flowering; winter if pruned back hard.

TRAINING AND PRUNING In warm climates, allow freestanding shrubs to develop with minimal pruning. Under glass in colder climates, cut back the flowered growth to sideshoots for a more compact habit. For larger leaves and flowers, cut back hard annually or biennially (*see p.164*). To renovate, cut all growth back to near ground level.

SPARTIUM (ZONES 8–9)

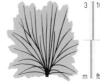

Spartium junceum (Spanish broom) is the only species, a medium-sized, deciduous shrub with erect, rushlike stems, bearing fragrant, yellow flowers from summer to autumn on the new growth. Left unpruned, it tends to become top-heavy. Prune to keep compact and promote a long flowering season.

WHEN TO PRUNE Early spring, when growth begins.

TRAINING AND PRUNING In the first two years, cut back the main stems by half to promote a dense habit. Subsequently every two or three years reduce the previous season's growth to within 1in (2.5cm) of the old wood. Plants may be rejuvenated by hard pruning but replacement is preferable.

SPHAERALCEA (ZONES 9–10)

Globe mallows are small, deciduous subshrubs (evergreen in warm climates), flowering in summer on the current season's growth. They may be grown outdoors in colder climates if in a sheltered, sunny site, but the top-growth is usually killed by frost. They can also be grown under glass. In warm climates, little pruning is generally needed; cut back any overlong stems in spring. In cool areas prune annually to a woody framework or to the base. Replace old plants rather than attempt renovation.

SPIRAEA

Small to medium-sized, deciduous or semievergreen shrubs, some suckering freely, with attractive flowers and, on some cultivars, foliage. Some spiraeas are large and arching in habit, flowering on either old or new growth; others are small and twiggy, flowering on the current season's shoots. Regular pruning, to which all respond well, maintains flowering performance. Timing depends on whether the species flowers on new or old wood.

S. 'ARGUTA' (ZONES 5–8)

BRIDAL WREATH, FOAM OF MAY

Medium-sized shrub with clusters of small, white flowers from mid- to late spring on the previous season's growth. Prune to prevent an accumulation of old, dead wood, and to encourage the production of new stems that will flower the following year.

WHEN TO PRUNE Early summer, just after flowering.

TRAINING AND PRUNING On young plants, cut back flowered stems to strong buds and remove any weak growth entirely. Once established, thin growth by cutting back to ground level one in four of the oldest stems. Remove any weak growth, and shorten the flowered stems by up to half, cutting back to strong shoots. Neglected specimens may respond slowly to drastic pruning. Leaving two or three strong stems unpruned, cut the others back to ground level.

PRUNING SPIRAEA 'ARGUTA'

Thin these dense, twiggy bushes annually by removing some stems at the base, and by shortening flowered stems back to healthy buds or well-placed sideshoots.

S. DOUGLASII (ZONES 5–8)

Vigorous, upright shrub that suckers freely. It produces purplish-pink flowers in mid-summer on the current season's growth. Annual pruning keeps it healthy and encourages new flowering stems.

WHEN TO PRUNE Early spring; deadhead after flowering.

TRAINING AND PRUNING Cut all weak and very old wood back to ground level. Shorten one in three or four of the remaining stems to within two to four buds of the previous year's growth; remove stems entirely where necessary to maintain an open habit. When clumps decline in vigor, use young rooted stems as replacements; cut these back to near ground level on planting.

S. JAPONICA (ZONES 6–8)

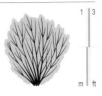

Compact shrub with small heads of usually pink flowers on the current season's shoots in summer. There are many cultivars, some, such as 'Goldflame', with attractive young leaves. Annual pruning keeps plants free-flowering with fresh young foliage.

WHEN TO PRUNE Early spring; deadhead after flowering.

TRAINING AND PRUNING On planting, cut out all weak and old wood. Prune back remaining stems to leave a framework 4–6in (10–15cm) high, and prune to one or two buds of this every year (*see also Perovskia, p.211*). Dwarf cultivars need only be clipped over to shape after flowering. Renovate as for *S. douglasii*.

OTHER SPIRAEAS
S. CANTONIENSIS, S. NIPPONICA, S. PRUNIFOLIA, S. THUNBERGII, S. x VANHOUTTEI, S. VEITCHII As for S. 'Arguta'.
S. DOUGLASII subsp. MENZIESII, S. JAPONICA 'BUMALDA' (syn. S. x BUMALDA) As for *S. japonica*.
S. SALICIFOLIA As for *S. douglasii*.

STACHYURUS (ZONES 7/8–9)

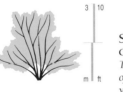

Medium-sized to large, deciduous shrub with an open, spreading habit, flowering in early spring from buds produced the previous autumn. It does not need any regular pruning, but can be lightly renovated by cutting out old, thin growth at the base, and shortening overlong branches by up to a third; new shoots break readily from the base. Prune in spring after flowering.

STACHYURUS CHINENSIS 'MAGPIE'
The pendent clusters of bell-shaped, pale yellow flowers of this variegated cultivar, here seen informally wall trained, open before the leaves in early spring. Buds may be affected by severe winter cold.

OTHER ORNAMENTAL SHRUBS
SORBARIA Prune in late winter, removing one or two old stems and cutting back flowered shoots close to main stems. Remove unwanted suckers (*see p.153*).

SORBUS Remove unwanted suckers from *S. reducta*. See also Ornamental Trees, p.88.

STEPHANANDRA

Deciduous, medium-sized shrubs. They are grown more for their autumn leaf color and the effect of their rich brown stems in winter than for their summer flowers, which are insignificant. Hardiness varies with the species. They form suckering clumps in maturity. In summer, after flowering, thin plants by removing about one in four old stems to the base, then cut back the remaining flowered stems to strong sideshoots, aiming to maintain the natural arching habit. Renovate by cutting all stems back to the base in winter or early spring.

SYRINGA LILAC

Small to large deciduous shrubs, becoming treelike with age, grown for their attractive, usually scented flowers, borne in spring and early summer.

S. VULGARIS (ZONES 3–7)

Common lilacs are vigorous shrubs with white, pink, lilac, or purple flowers on the previous season's wood. They need minimal attention until stems become old, when they respond well to renovation. Cultivars are often grafted and may sucker freely.

SYRINGA MEYERI
This lilac is usually grown naturally as a densely twiggy bush, but it can be trained into an attractive standard shrub, as here.

SYMPHORICARPOS

Deciduous shrubs, with dense, twiggy growth and clusters of showy fruit. Most are suckering plants, useful for low barrier planting and as groundcover. Hardiness varies with the species. For dense cover, prune on planting to 12in (30cm) high. No further pruning is necessary, although old, twiggy growth can be thinned in early spring. If spread needs restricting, in early spring either remove surplus growth to the base or chop it away at the edges with a spade. Renovate by cutting all stems to ground level; on large areas, a nylon-line trimmer may be used.

WHEN TO PRUNE Midsummer, as the flowers fade. Renovate in winter.

TRAINING AND PRUNING Young plants often need light formative pruning (*see p.157*) to encourage the development of a balanced shape. Established plants should be deadheaded carefully, where practical, with pruners (*see p.155*) to avoid damaging the young shoots that will flower next year. Remove suckers as seen (*see p.153*). To renovate, cut back main stems to within 12–24in (30–60cm) of the ground (*see also p.161*). Response is good, and regrowth should be thinned, but flowering will be delayed by up to three years. It is preferable to stagger hard pruning over two to three years.

S. MEYERI (ZONES 4–7/8)

Meyer lilac is a twiggy shrub grown for its panicles of fragrant, purple flowers, which are borne in early summer; there is sometimes a second flush of flowers later in the season.

WHEN TO PRUNE Immediately after flowering.

TRAINING AND PRUNING Bushes are naturally twiggy, and require minimal pruning. *S. meyeri* may also be trained as a standard (*see left, and p.165*).

> **OTHER LILACS**
> S. X JOSIFLEXA As for *S. vulgaris.*
> S. MICROPHYLLA 'SUPERBA' As for *S. meyeri.*
> S. X PERSICA, S. X PRESTONIAE,
> S. REFLEXA, S. YUNNANENSIS As for *S. vulgaris.*

T–V

TAMARIX PARVIFLORA (ZONES 5–8)
This spring-flowering tamarisk should be pruned in summer, to prevent it from becoming straggly.

TAMARIX TAMARISK

Deciduous or evergreen shrubs and trees, grown for their feathery, plumelike branches and pink flowers. In gardens they usually require pruning to keep them compact; they are suitable for an informal hedge, particularly in coastal sites.

WHEN TO PRUNE Tamarisks flowering in early summer, such as *T. parviflora*, are pruned in summer, after flowering. Prune those flowering in late summer, such as *T. ramosissima*, in early spring.

TRAINING AND PRUNING To grow as a well-branched, multistemmed shrub, cut back stems by half on planting and again in the following year. Prune established plants annually, removing weak growth and cutting back flowered stems to strong sideshoots. *T. ramosissima* (zones 3–8) can be pruned hard annually (*see p.164*) to encourage flower production and keep the plant bushy. To use as an informal hedge, cut back plants to 12in (30cm) on planting and tip-prune new shoots in summer to encourage dense growth. Cut back the previous season's growth on established hedges in late winter (*see also* Hedges, *p.45*).
To renovate overgrown specimens and hedges, cut back hard into the old wood. Plants may not flower again for at least two years. Plants grown as standards (*see p.165*) require staking, and the head needs hard pruning at the appropriate time to keep it compact. The new stems will arch gracefully.

THYMUS THYME (ZONES 6–9)

Shrubs and sub-shrubs grown for their aromatic leaves. Some are used as culinary herbs. All thymes are small plants (some are prostrate), requiring full sun; they are suitable for rock gardens or for cracks in paving. Regular pruning keeps them neat and maintains the production of fresh leaves. Cultivars are available that have gold, silver, or variegated foliage. These may produce shoots with plain green leaves.

WHEN TO PRUNE Late summer.

TRAINING AND PRUNING The very prostrate cultivars need no pruning. Lightly trim other thymes with shears or pruners in summer to remove all dead flower heads. On forms with colored or variegated leaves, remove any reverted shoots (*see p.153*) throughout the growing season, cutting them right out to their point of origin. Fresh growth will not break from old wood, so old, neglected plants are best replaced.

THYMUS VULGARIS 'SILVER POSIE'
Lightly trim or clip over this variegated thyme in summer, after flowering.

TIBOUCHINA GLORY BUSH (ZONE 10)

Large, tender evergreens, grown for their foliage and summer flowers, borne on new wood. They may only be grown as free-standing shrubs in warm climates. In cooler climates they may be grown under glass. Pinch out tips of young shoots to encourage bushiness. Cut back flowered shoots to two pairs of buds in spring. Plants can be cut back to a framework and are suitable for wall training (*see p.162*).

ULEX GORSE (ZONES 7–9)

Small shrubs with vicious spines and yellow flowers. Although virtually leafless, their green stems and spines make them appear to be evergreen. They thrive in windy, exposed sites and on poor soil; *U. europaeus* is a serious weed in some countries, including Australia and New Zealand. Planted in rich garden soil, gorse may become leggy, with straggly stems that become bare at the base. Regular pruning keeps plants compact and shapely.

WHEN TO PRUNE The first spring after planting, then in late spring to early summer, after flowering. Renovate in early spring.

TRAINING AND PRUNING If young plants are straggly, encourage them to bush out by shortening all stems by one-quarter to half in early spring (on the small species *U. minor*, just pinch out the tips of the stems). Once established, clip over lightly after flowering to keep growth compact. Shorten wayward stems, if necessary. Renovate plants that

ULEX EUROPAEUS
In favored garden conditions, gorse often becomes spreading and leggy if not regularly clipped after flowering.

have become leggy by cutting back hard into the old wood (*see p.161*), to within 6in (15cm) of the ground if necessary. Response is usually very good.

VESTIA (ZONE 10)

Medium-sized, fast-growing, evergreen shrub, grown for its pale yellow flowers and berries, borne on the current season's wood, and also for its foliage. The single species, *V. foetida*, is usually cut to the ground by hard frosts; it needs a sheltered position in cooler climates. Pinch out the growing tips of young plants (*see p.152*) to encourage branching. In warm climates, prune in late summer as for *Cestrum* (*see p.186*), cutting back growth that has flowered by about half. Each year, cut to the base one or two of the oldest stems so that old growth does not accumulate and crowd young, flowering shoots. To renovate neglected specimens, cut back to ground level or a low framework in early spring. In cooler climates, cut all stems back to the ground in spring.

OTHER ORNAMENTAL SHRUBS

STAPHYLEA As for *Sambucus* (*p.219*). Large species, such as *S. holocarpus*, can be trained as standard trees (*see p.28*).
STRANVAESIA, X **STRANVINIA** See *Photinia* (*p.213*).
STREPTOSOLEN See Dictionary of Climbing Plants, *p.284*.
SUTERA Minimal pruning only.
SUTHERLANDIA Prune lightly if necessary after fruiting. Short-lived; straggly plants are best replaced.
SWAINSONA Cut back each spring to within 12in (30cm) of the ground.
SYCOPSIS Minimal pruning.

SYMPLOCOS No special needs. Shorten over-long stems; when mature, some unproductive old growth may occasionally be removed.
TECOMA See *Tecomaria*, Dictionary of Climbing Plants, *p.285*.
TELOPEA Tip-prune young plants (*see p.155*). After flowering, prune flowered stems to leave 10in (25cm) of the previous year's growth. May be cut back hard to renovate.
TERNSTROEMIA No special needs. Shape lightly in spring if necessary.
TETRAPANAX Deadhead, and remove any suckers; no other special needs.
TEUCRIUM Prune in spring as growth begins,

removing frost damage and trimming to keep compact. Responds well to hard pruning if necessary. *T. chamaedrys* can make a low hedge, clipped in summer.
TURRAEA No special needs. Can be trimmed as a hedge.
UGNI No special needs. Shorten any overlong shoots.
VACCINIUM No special needs; if necessary, trim deciduous species in winter, and evergreens in spring. See also Blueberries, *p.241*.
VALLEA Lightly prune in summer after flowering.

VIBURNUM

Small to large, deciduous, semievergreen, and evergreen shrubs. Some are grown for their fragrant flowers; others have attractive berries in autumn. Habits vary, but all make new growth from the base. Pruning requirements depend on the purpose for which the shrub is grown. Some make fine specimen plants; others that benefit from cross-pollination to produce berries, such as *V. davidii*, are best planted in informal groups. A few lend themselves to formal training and trimming. The timing of pruning depends on the flowering season. All mature viburnums (with the exception of *V. plicatum*) usually respond well to hard pruning.

V. X BODNANTENSE (ZONES 6–8)

Belongs to a group of deciduous, medium-sized, upright shrubs with fragrant, white or pink flowers at the ends of the bare stems in autumn and winter. New stems are regularly produced from the base. Pruning is usually restricted to the removal of old, unproductive wood.

3 | 10

m | ft

WHEN TO PRUNE Early spring, immediately after flowering. Renovate in late spring.

TRAINING AND PRUNING Allow young plants to develop unpruned. On established bushes, cut out up to one in five branches to the base, removing the oldest and weakest. Leave the remainder unpruned: shortening them may affect flowering the following year and ruin the shape of the shrub. To renovate, cut all branches down to the base. New shoots are usually freely produced.

VIBURNUM X BODNANTENSE
Remove up to one in five of the oldest stems at the base to thin this dense, erect shrub.

V. PLICATUM (ZONES 6–8)

JAPANESE SNOWBALL VIBURNUM

Stately, deciduous shrub, with branches held in horizontal tiers. Showy, white, "lace-cap" flowers are borne in late spring and early summer on the previous season's wood. A spreading habit normally develops without extensive pruning, but vigorous, upright shoots that mar the outline may need to be removed.

3 | 10

m | ft

WHEN TO PRUNE Summer, after flowering. Renovate in late spring.

TRAINING AND PRUNING On young plants, keep pruning to a minimum. Strong, upright growths will develop at the centre of the bush, and then branch to form the characteristic tiers. On mature plants, new vertical shoots growing through the tiers may ruin the form and can be removed at their point of origin, unless it is preferable to let them develop to replace old, damaged, or unproductive branches. If reasonably young and vigorous, plants may respond to drastic cutting back to a branch framework in spring, but such pruning usually ruins the form.

V. TINUS (ZONES 8–9)

LAURUSTINUS

Medium-sized, evergreen shrub with heads of star-shaped, white flowers in winter and spring. More compact than many viburnums, it responds well to pruning and can be trained and clipped. It may be grown as a specimen shrub, a standard, or a formal or informal hedge.

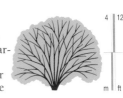

4 | 12

m | ft

WHEN TO PRUNE Early summer, after flowering. Renovate in late spring.

VIBURNUM PLICATUM VAR. TOMENTOSUM
Once the mature form is well established, remove any strongly growing vertical shoots that ruin the distinctive, tiered form.

TRAINING AND PRUNING When grown as a specimen shrub, it may require some formative pruning (*see p.157*) to ensure that the developing shape is well balanced. Once plants are established, keep pruning to a minimum, but remove any overvigorous shoots that ruin the shape, cutting them back to well within the plant's outline to hide where the cuts have been made. To train as a standard, *see p.165*. Hedges (*see p.44*) should be trimmed with pruners to avoid unsightly damage to individual leaves. To renovate a specimen plant, cut back hard (*see p.161*) in late spring. Treat a neglected hedge in the same way.

VIBURNUM TINUS
All viburnums tend to make new growth from the base; if trained as standards, rub out any emerging shoots on the clear trunk as soon as seen.

OTHER VIBURNUMS
V. BETULIFOLIUM As for *V. x bodnantense*, but prune in late winter, after fruiting.
V. X BURKWOODII, V. CARLESII, V. X CARLCEPHALUM Minimal pruning, in midsummer if necessary.
V. DAVIDII Spreading, dense habit, needing minimal pruning; to keep groundcover plants neat, cut back to strong shoots or base of plant. Deadhead male plants; they do not set fruit.
V. FARRERI As for *V. x bodnantense*.
V. LANTANA, V. RHYTIDOPHYLLUM As for *V. x bodnantense*, pruning in late winter.
V. OPULUS As for *V. x bodnantense*.

VINCA PERIWINKLE

Evergreen subshrubs of indefinite spread that make excellent groundcover. The stems are initially upright, then trail, rooting at their tips or where they touch the ground. Blue, white, or purple flowers are produced at varying times of the year. Prune to maintain dense growth, to keep plants within bounds, and to expose the flowers. Occasional hard pruning makes it possible to clear out debris and can improve flowering performance.

WHEN TO PRUNE Spring.

TRAINING AND PRUNING Prune annually to cut back excess growth and any long, straggling stems. When growth becomes congested, trim the whole surface with shears or a nylon-line trimmer.

VITEX CHASTE TREE

Medium-sized, deciduous shrubs and trees (zones 6 to 9) grown for their flowers, borne in summer and autumn on the current season's growth. In colder climates, they require a sheltered position, and do well fan trained against a warm wall (see p.162). Freestanding shrubs require only minimal pruning when young. When established, prune flowered shoots back to spurs on main stems in spring, or cut back hard each year to restrict size. On a wall-trained fan of permanent branches, cut back the previous season's growth to short spurs. Occasionally train in a young shoot to replace an old framework stem.

OTHER ORNAMENTAL SHRUBS
VIMINARIA Prune V. juncea as for *Cytisus scoparius* (see p.190); take care when pruning not to ruin the natural habit.
WEINMANNIA Prune lightly in spring if necessary.
WESTRINGIA No special needs. May be pruned lightly in summer after flowering.
WIGANDIA Prune in spring, cutting out growth that has flowered.
WITHANIA Prune in spring, cutting out growth that has flowered.
XANTHOCERAS No special needs. Tolerates thinning if required.
XANTHORHIZA Suckering and naturally untidy in habit. No special needs.
XANTHOSOMA Minimal pruning needed.
XYLOSMA No special needs, but suitable for wall training or clipping as a hedge or shaped specimen.
YUCCA See Palms and palmlike plants, p.43.
ZANTHOXYLUM Pruning in spring is necessary to remove accumulated dead wood. Some species are spiny.
ZAUSCHNERIA Subshrub; cut back to the woody rootstock in spring.

W–Z

WEIGELA (ZONES 4–8)

Small to medium-sized, deciduous shrubs, grown for the tubular red, white, or pink flowers borne in summer on the previous year's wood. Some also have attractive foliage. All respond well to pruning, which should be used to divert the plant's energy away from seed production and encourage strong new growth.

W. FLORIDA (ZONES 5–8)

Medium-sized shrub with flowers in a range of colors in spring or summer. Regular pruning benefits flower production. Harder pruning can be used to enhance the foliage effect of those cultivars with attractive bronze, purple, or variegated leaves.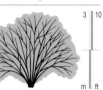

WHEN TO PRUNE Midsummer, after flowering. Renovate in early spring.

TRAINING AND PRUNING Young plants require little formative pruning. When established, each year cut back flowered stems to strong, usually upright, shoots below the faded flowers. Cut out at the base one or two old stems, aiming to maintain a balance between mature and young wood, and remove or shorten overlong new growth that ruins the plant's shape. Yellow- and purple-leaved cultivars may be cut back harder: remove about three-quarters of the old wood entirely and shorten the remaining stems by three-quarters. Cut out any reverted shoots on variegated cultivars (see p.153). To renovate, cut all stems to ground level. Thin the new shoots in midsummer.

OTHER WEIGELAS
W. 'BRISTOL RUBY', 'EVA RATHKE', and other hybrids As for W. florida.
W. HORTENSIS, W. MIDDENDORFFIANA, W. PRAECOX As for W. florida.

PRUNING AN ESTABLISHED WEIGELA FLORIDA

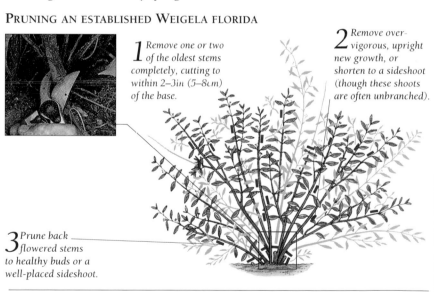

1 Remove one or two of the oldest stems completely, cutting to within 2–3in (5–8cm) of the base.

2 Remove over-vigorous, upright new growth, or shorten to a sideshoot (though these shoots are often unbranched).

3 Prune back flowered stems to healthy buds or a well-placed sideshoot.

ZENOBIA (ZONES 6–9)

Genus of only one species of medium-sized, deciduous or semievergreen shrub, Z. pulverulenta, grown for its fragrant, white summer flowers. Old plants can be cut back hard; pruning promotes vigor and benefits flowering in subsequent seasons. The plant's habit is arching and suckering, and new shoots are freely produced from the base.

WHEN TO PRUNE Midsummer, as the flowers fade. Renovate in midspring.

TRAINING AND PRUNING Young plants require little formative pruning. Once plants are established, prune annually. Cut the flowered stems back to strong shoots. Cut out weak growths completely and, over a period of three years, take out one or two old branches completely, but without ruining the plant's natural habit. To renovate old or neglected, overgrown plants, cut all old wood back to ground level. Response is usually very good.

SOFT FRUITS

Whether grown as bushes or standards, trained as fans or cordons against sunny walls, or forming a decorative fruiting screen, bush and cane fruits need annual pruning to fruit well

A crop of fresh summer fruits is a pleasure that even a small garden can afford. A well-tended, traditional "model" fruit garden may for many gardeners be the ideal, but soft fruits (sometimes called berry fruits) can also be used to great effect in the ornamental garden. Indeed many soft fruits, such as raspberries (*Rubus idaeus*) and blackcurrants (*Ribes nigrum*), have purely ornamental counterparts that are among the most popular of garden plants.

Soft fruits are, generally, cool-climate plants that enjoy sun but dislike humidity and stagnant air. All are self-fertile and are propagated by suckers, layers, or cuttings. None requires grafting, but some can be grafted – for example, to form standards. Most are prone to viruses, and a specialty fruit nursery is always the best source for healthy stock. For some fruits, certification plans ensure that plants are virus-free.

The soft fruits requiring pruning fall into two groups: cane fruits and bush fruits. The cane fruits – raspberries, blackberries, and hybrid berries such as the tayberry – are closely related, as are the bush fruits, gooseberries and currants; the acid-loving blueberry bush belongs to the heather family. The aim of pruning and training is not only to develop and maintain healthy, well-shaped plants but also to establish a gentle cycle of pruning from season to season, removing old or otherwise unproductive wood to encourage

young, strong, fruitful growth to take its place. Left unpruned, all soft fruits will bear, but fruit quality and size decline steeply. Understanding and using the correct pruning and training techniques is the essence of success, ensuring the best possible quantity and quality of fruit and encouraging strong new growth that will fruit in future years. The work and expertise needed may seem daunting at first – incorrect pruning could result in the loss of a season's crop. However, a basic grasp of the fruiting habits of each type makes the various tasks simple and satisfying.

STANDARD GOOSEBERRY
Gooseberries are particularly amenable to pruning and training into decorative forms. A standard gooseberry, as shown here, not only has ornamental value but also raises the fruit-bearing branches to a level at which harvesting becomes less of a thorny and back-breaking task.

RASPBERRIES
The long, whippy stems of raspberries need support; using an organized system of training also makes maintenance, harvesting, and pruning far easier.

SOFT FRUIT FORMS

The cane fruits (raspberries, blackberries, and hybrids such as the loganberry) annually throw up strong new vertical shoots – canes or "rods" – from the base and these replace older fruited canes as they die. Pruning speeds up this natural process and is made easier by careful training of the long, whippy growths. The bush fruits – currants, gooseberries, and blueberries – are naturally shrubby and compact. Most can also be readily trained into a number of forms to take advantage of favored sites. Wall-training suits them well, but the wall must first be correctly wired (*see also p.230*) to let air circulate behind the plants.

Both training and correct pruning can increase yields and also make cultivation easier, particularly for the thorned

plants. Matching the choice of cultivar and trained form to the site is important, particularly for the cane fruits, since they dislike being moved once established.

Pruning must also be tailored to the vigor and growth habit of the chosen cultivar (these vary widely) and its performance on your soil and site. Indiscriminate hard pruning encourages vegetative growth at the expense of fruiting wood. Underpruning results in weak, crowded growth, which leads to increased pest and disease problems, especially if dead wood (such as old raspberry canes) is not removed. The benefits of choosing a trained form are also lost as the shape deteriorates. The longer the neglect continues, the more difficult rescue will become.

SINGLE CORDON
A single stem clothed in fruiting spurs gives a high yield of good-quality gooseberries, redcurrants, or whitecurrants for the space occupied. Cordons can be grown against a wall, but are more usually seen in rows on posts and wires. They may be trained vertically or at an oblique angle. A row of cordons is easily draped with netting, or a block of rows sited within a fruit cage. Measures such as these are essential to protect soft fruits, which are all beloved by birds.

MULTIPLE CORDON
Double ("U"-shaped) triple, and four-armed (double-"U") cordons are popular and ornamental trained forms for red- and white-currants and for gooseberries. Wall-training is necessary for support and to minimize the risk of damage by wind.

MULTISTEMMED BUSH
Blackcurrants and blueberries produce new shoots from the base of the plant each year, forming an upright, multistemmed bush.

BUSH
Red- and whitecurrants and gooseberries are grown as bushes with a crown of frame-work branches on a short trunk or "leg."

STANDARD
A bush on a tall clear stem is produced by grafting a selected gooseberry or red-currant cultivar onto vigorous *Ribes* stock.

FAN
Fan-training redcurrants and gooseberries against a wall not only provides shelter and warmth but also creates a decorative feature.

RASPBERRY CANES
Raspberries sucker freely, and new canes emerge each year over a wide area around the original planting site.

BLACKBERRY AND HYBRID BERRY CANES
Canes develop from a more or less central point. They should be separated and trained apart to receive air and light.

BASIC TECHNIQUES

With the exception of autumn-fruiting raspberries (*see p.233*), all soft fruits crop on wood that is at least a year old. With some – the cane fruits and, to a degree, blackcurrants – wood is routinely cut out after it has fruited once, and on others – redcurrants and gooseberries – it is shortened ("spurred back") to a branch framework, to encourage the formation of new sideshoots that will fruit the following year. On these spur-pruned fruits, the branch framework and spur systems thus build up over the years, and need thinning if growth is not to be crowded.

There are two main pruning periods for soft fruits: winter and summer. Winter is the time to develop and improve the plant's shape, remove badly placed or old, unfruitful wood in favor of younger growth, reduce over-crowding, and open up the center of a bush. Winter pruning should be left until as late as possible in the season so that bird damage to buds can be taken into account when deciding what to cut out. Badly bird-damaged growth, which may not crop well again for two years, should be completely removed. Summer pruning is necessary only for trained forms: to restrict vegetative growth and maintain their shape and structure.

Soft fruits are particularly prone to serious virus diseases. Dig up and discard infected plants before pruning other plants. Remember that pruners and other tools can spread viruses. Disinfect tools by dipping them in alcohol or a 10% chlorine bleach solution, when moving from plant to plant and always once the job is done.

ROUTINE TASKS, BUSH FRUITS (WINTER)

SPUR PRUNING
While gooseberries, redcurrants, and whitecurrants can be grown as a loose, multistemmed bush like a blackcurrant (see below), it is better to develop a permanent frame-work on which growth is pruned to create short, fruiting spurs, somewhat like those on an apple or pear tree.

Cut branch leader to a bud here, to shorten it by about a third of the previous season's growth

All sublaterals are cut to a few buds from base

RENEWAL PRUNING
With bush fruits (particularly black-currants and blue-berries, which are not spur-pruned), a proportion of older wood must be taken out each winter to keep the center open and increase the proportion of the plant formed by one- and two-year-old shoots. These will fruit in the summer, while new shoots that will fruit the following year are developing.

ROUTINE TASKS, CANE FRUITS

CANE PRUNING *Removing fruited canes is the key pruning principle for raspberries, blackberries, and hybrid berries such as tay-berries and loganberries. Cut them straight across at ground level, being careful not to damage young growth that is being retained.*

Figure-eight tie

TYING IN *Canes need secure tying in, particularly if, like those of blackberries and summer-fruiting raspberries, they must survive winter's winds. Regular spacing of the canes improves ripening and makes harvesting and cane pruning (left) easier.*

SUCKERS *All canes begin as suckers developing from adventitious buds on the roots or at the base of the plant. Lightly hoe out those that are too far from the row, or remove them carefully with a portion of root, as above, if wanted for propagation.*

CANE FRUITS

Raspberries, blackberries, and the many hybrid berries bear fruit on short, young sideshoots that develop on long, vigorous, whippy canes that, with the exception of autumn-fruiting raspberry cultivars, grew the previous year. Annual pruning consists of removing old fruited canes so that they can be replaced by new shoots.

All cane fruits are cool-climate plants. Although descended from woodland natives, to produce a fine crop they need a sunny site (blackberries will tolerate some shade). To achieve maximum exposure to the ripening sun, they must be well trained using a method that suits the varying vigor of individual cultivars.

BERRY FRUITS
There are numerous hybrid berries, including the loganberry, tayberry, boysenberry, sunberry, and katonahberry. Some hybrids are crosses between other recognized fruits – the tayberry, for example, is a cross between a blackberry and a raspberry. Others have a more mixed parentage within the genus Rubus.

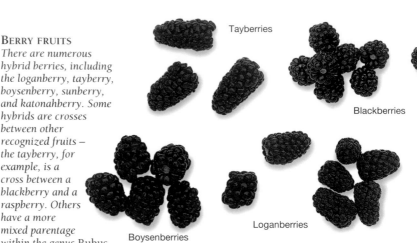

Tayberries

Blackberries

Loganberries

Boysenberries

BLACKBERRIES AND HYBRID BERRIES *RUBUS FRUTICOSUS, RUBUS* HYBRIDS

Blackberries and hybrid berries (which vary in hardiness) can all be cultivated, trained, and pruned in the same way. The aims are always to encourage vigorous, healthy growth; to separate the fruiting canes from the new shoots that appear throughout the growing season; to splay out the fruiting canes to enable the fruits to ripen well and be harvested easily; and to keep the canes clear of the ground to prevent layering. Buy plants from a reliable nursery; these fruits are not normally certified, as raspberries are, against viral diseases. Avoid plants showing signs of infection, such as mottled leaves or dwarfed growth.

TRAINING METHODS A wired wall or fence is the simplest support, but a sturdy system of posts and wires, open on both sides, will suffice. The weaker-growing cultivars, such as the loganberry 'Thornless' can also be trained around a single post. The simplest and most manageable training methods (*see below*)

TRAINING METHODS FOR BERRY FRUITS

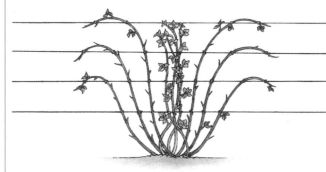

FAN *A compact system for less vigorous cultivars, especially those with more rigid canes. The fruiting canes are spread out, and new canes tied in to the central space as they grow. These are lowered and tied into position once the fruited canes have been cut away (see facing page).*

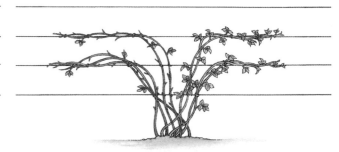

ALTERNATE BAY *Ideal where several plants grow along a long wall. Fruiting canes are trained toward each other in the spaces between plants, or bays, as are the young canes as they grow. All the canes in any bay are therefore fruiting or not fruiting in alternate years.*

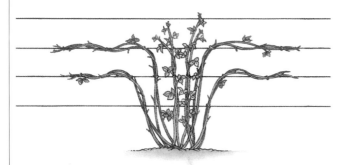

ROPE *Suitable for cultivars with many pliable canes, such as logan-berries. Fruiting canes are twisted into "ropes" and tied along the lower wires; the new canes up the middle and along the top. When the fruited canes are cut out, the new ones are divided between the lower wires.*

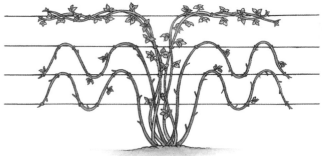

WEAVING *A space-saving method for vigorous cultivars with pliable canes. Fruiting canes are trained in a serpentine manner on the lower wires, new ones up the middle and along the top wire. When the fruited canes are cut away, the new ones are lowered and woven into position.*

keep fruiting and new canes separate; some allow the new canes to be trained directly into their final position as they grow, minimizing handling of prickly stems. Walls and fences should be at least 5–6ft (1.5–2m) high, and wired using bolts or wood strips and staples to keep the wires a little distance away from the wall. For posts and wires, use 8ft (2.5m) posts sunk 24in (60cm) into the ground, with diagonal support struts. Space three or four horizontal wires about 18in (45cm) apart. Depending on the training method, allow at least 10ft (3m) between plants; very vigorous cultivars, such as 'Himalaya Giant', will need space for canes 15ft (5m) or more in length.

WHEN TO PRUNE After planting, then in autumn after fruiting, and again in late winter or early spring. Unwanted canes and suckers can be removed at any time. Always wear gloves for thorned cultivars.

FORMATIVE TRAINING Plants are bought as one-year-old rooted tips (a type of layering). Plant them in early winter or, where the weather is very severe, in early spring. Shorten the original cane to 8–12in (20–30cm) from ground level when first planted to stimulate new basal growth, then cut it out entirely in the first summer. Raising the soil level slightly by mulching also encourages the growth of strong new canes. Tie these in firmly as they develop, using a suitable training method (*see facing page*).

ESTABLISHED PRUNING The aim is to maintain an annual succession of year-old, heavy-cropping canes. Once the last berries have been harvested, all the fruited canes are cut out and the new canes retied into position. If there are not enough new canes to fill the available space, keep a few old ones, cutting sideshoots back to 1in (2.5cm).

As the new canes develop, any weak ones can be removed, particularly if overcrowding seems likely. Pull out any growth springing up too far from the row as soon as seen, or it will quickly become a nuisance. At the end of the winter, tip-prune all canes by about 6in (15cm); if the winter has been severe you may have to remove the entire cane. Canes may be untied and retied in a single bundle on the lowest wire for protection in areas where they might be marginally hardy, then trained out again in spring.

Neglected plants are not easy to deal with. Dig out suckers and rooted growth, and cut away old and tangled canes. Some young canes may be salvageable, and retrained to the support; otherwise, carefully uprooted suckers or layers may be usable as new plants.

NEW GROWTH AFTER PLANTING
The plant's original cane is not used for fruiting. Shorten it to 8–12in (20–30cm) to stimulate new basal shoots. These shoots will fruit in their second season. Remove the stump of the old cane in midsummer.

New canes are supple and green

Previous year's cane is woody and dark

ESTABLISHED BLACKBERRY, PRUNING AFTER FRUITING

1 Cut out the fruited canes at ground level.

2 Separate and tie in (see below) the new canes according to the training method used (see facing page).

TYING IN NEW SHOOTS
Use figure-eight knots to secure the canes firmly to the wires. Choosing a smooth-stemmed cultivar, such as 'Oregon Thornless', makes tying in a less difficult task.

RASPBERRIES *RUBUS IDAEUS* (ZONES 4–8)

Raspberries produce numerous canes that grow directly from a mass of fibrous roots just below soil level. For the best crops, old canes should be cut out after fruiting and replaced by the strongest of the new ones.

There are two distinct types of raspberry: summer- and autumn-fruiting. Cultivation is identical, except for pruning. The canes of summer-fruiting cultivars grow one year and bear the next – after which they are removed at ground level. Autumn-fruiting cultivars, with a longer fruiting season – late summer to the first frosts – are treated much like herbaceous plants: the whole plant is cut back to the ground in late winter, then canes grow and fruit in a single season.

A sheltered site is advisable, and good support is essential for summer-fruiting cultivars, which must survive winter weather. There are variations on an open posts-and-wires system that are widely used (*see right*). Growing against walls or fences is not ideal: the poor air circulation encourages mildew on the fruits, and it is also difficult to tend the row on the wall side. Single posts are not recommended; sun exposure may be poor and harvesting awkward.

Raspberries are very prone to viral diseases, for which there is no cure. Plants showing symptoms – short, weak canes, yellow-blotched foliage, and sparse, small, or distorted fruits – must be dug up and discarded. Any suckers that grow from overlooked root fragments must be removed. Do not replant raspberries for several years where virus-infected ones grew.

SUMMER-FRUITING RASPBERRIES

These are bought as single canes, usually shortened in the nursery to about 2ft (60cm). Having set up a support system (*see above right*), plant at any time from late autumn to early spring, fanning the roots out in a shallow hole to encourage new canes to grow from them.

WHEN TO PRUNE On planting, thereafter in late winter and after fruiting.

TRAINING AND PRUNING Prune the cane on planting, but leave a portion of it intact until early summer so that the foliage it carries helps nourish the new shoots. As the growing season progresses, tie new canes into position. If the odd flower appears this year, pinch it out. Make sure the canes are well supported over winter, tip-pruning them (*see facing page*) as winter ends (unless using the Scandinavian system, *above*). A crop will be borne the following summer.

TRAINING METHODS FOR RASPBERRY CANES

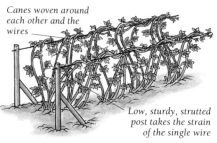

Canes woven around each other and the wires

Low, sturdy, strutted post takes the strain of the single wire

SCANDINAVIAN SYSTEM (ABOVE) *Ideal where a large, sheltered area can be devoted to a quantity of plants, this method is used for less vigorous summer-fruiting cultivars. The canes will not require tip-pruning. Once the system of keeping fruiting and new canes separate is established, it is easy to maintain. Make two parallel rows of low posts 36in (90cm) apart, with about 10ft (3m) between posts in the rows. Use 5ft (1.5m) posts driven 2ft (60cm) into the ground, with diagonal support struts, then stretch a single wire between the tops of the posts. The new canes, while still pliable, are brought to one side or the other and gently woven along the wires and around each other. No more than three or four canes from any one plant should join each "rope," so use only the strongest ones and remove any surplus. Tie in if and where necessary. In the second season, new young canes are left to grow up in the central space between the wires, where they are sheltered and protected from possible damage during harvesting. When the fruited canes are cut away, the replacement canes can be woven into place.*

POSTS AND WIRES (BELOW) *This is a compact, secure method for windy areas. The fruits receive maximum sun. Stretch three wires at heights of 2, 3, and 5ft (75cm, 1m, and 1.6m), either stretched between two endposts or stapled along a line of four or five posts. Tie canes in on one side of the wires; do not weave them in and out or they may rub. New canes may need holding up at first (see Supporting young shoots, facing page).*

POSTS AND NYLON STRING (ABOVE) *The simplest method (here seen from above) is to guide the canes within a loop of nylon string, 18in (45cm) from the ground, stretched and nailed between 6ft (2m) posts. Add an extra loop at 4ft (1.2m) in windy conditions. Add connecting ties between the parallel strings at intervals to stop the canes from slumping or being blown toward one end.*

RASPBERRY, YEAR 1, SUMMER

1 *Tie the new canes to support wires as they grow (see Spacing new canes along a wire, facing page).*

2 *The original cane was shortened to 10in (25cm) on planting. Prune out its stump in midsummer.*

As soon as fruiting has finished, the fruited canes are cut out at the base and the new season's canes tied in. Where there is lots of new growth, retain only the strongest young canes. During the ensuing winter, soft cane tips may be damaged, so in late winter tip-prune to remove any damaged growth.

Canes emerging more than about 8in (20cm) from the row should be removed as seen. Cutting them away at ground level or tracing them back to their point of origin (disturbing the root system) will only encourage more to appear. Instead, hoe them away lightly while they are still young and soft. The exception to this rule is when the suckers are required as new plants; these should be carefully lifted with a substantial portion of root.

Raspberries can be renovated, but they have a useful life of only 12 years or so. If neglected rows seem relatively young and healthy, cut out the oldest canes and tie in the rest. If the crop next summer is small, the plants are probably not worth keeping: they may be too old, or may be fruiting poorly because of viral infection, so plant new canes elsewhere.

AUTUMN-FRUITING RASPBERRIES

Autumn-fruiting cultivars are bought as single canes and planted as for summer-fruiting cultivars (see left). In summer the new canes will both grow and bear their first crop. An annual cycle is maintained by pruning all of the canes to ground level each winter. If they are not cut back, they fruit again, but only on the portion of the cane that did not fruit the previous year. A much bigger crop is gained from strong new canes.

WHEN TO PRUNE On planting, then in late winter when the plants are fully dormant. Do not remove fruited canes after fruiting as for summer-fruiting cultivars, or new growth will appear before the frost, which may destroy it.

TRAINING AND PRUNING Plant and prune initially as for summer-fruiting cultivars (see left). As the new canes grow, shorter cultivars such as 'September' will require no support, but more vigorous ones such as 'Autumn Bliss' need training to guard against wind damage. Since there is no need to keep new and fruiting canes separate, a simple system such as posts and nylon string is suitable (see above left).

At winter's end, but before any sign of growth, all canes are cut to the ground. As the next year's young canes grow, remove weak or damaged growth. Do not tip-prune since much of the fruit is borne at the top of the canes. Replace old plants when fruiting declines.

ROUTINE TASKS, ESTABLISHED RASPBERRIES

CUTTING OUT WEAK SHOOTS *Most cultivars will produce more canes than needed. Removing the spindly ones will concentrate vigor into the canes that remain. Retain about eight strong new canes per plant, pruning out any surplus at the base.*

SUPPORTING YOUNG SHOOTS *Emerging new canes may need extra support before they reach the lowest wire of the system, or because they are too numerous to tie in. Loop string around the support structure and the canes to hold them up.*

CUTTING OUT FRUITED CANES *Prune out all fruited canes at ground level, being careful, with summer-fruiting cultivars, not to damage the current season's new shoots. With autumn-fruiting raspberries, all growth is cut down.*

SPACING NEW CANES ALONG A WIRE *Tie canes no closer than 4in (10cm) apart using a continuous length of string, which is looped around the cane and the wire, then taken on to the next cane, holding each in position.*

LOOPING OVER EXTRA-TALL CANES *Bend very long canes over and tie in again to the top wire while still pliable. At the same time, tip-prune weaker canes to stimulate growth.*

TIP-PRUNING SUMMER-FRUITING CULTIVARS *Unless using the Scandinavian system (see facing page), prune canes at winter's end by about 6in (15cm), to roughly the same height.*

BUSH FRUITS

Although blackcurrants, red- and whitecurrants, gooseberries, and blueberries can all be managed simply by removing, each year, some older, less productive wood in favor of young fruiting growth (like many flowering shrubs), it is worth using different methods for red- and whitecurrants, and gooseberries. These can be spur-pruned to a framework each year, resulting not only in heavier-cropping bushes but also enabling many decorative trained forms to be produced.

BLACKCURRANTS *RIBES NIGRUM*

The blackcurrant is grown as a "stooled" bush – with as many young shoots as possible originating at or near ground level. The bulk of the crop is carried on shoots that grew the previous summer. Some fruit is also borne on two-year-old wood, but a proportion of this is worth sacrificing to make room for new shoots.

Blackcurrants are prone to viral diseases and to blackcurrant gall mite, which spreads reversion virus, so always buy certified plants if possible. Check with your agriculture extension agent for local restrictions. The easily visible "big buds" containing gall mites must be picked off and discarded; badly infested bushes must be dug up and disposed of.

The newest shoots, which will fruit the next year, have smooth bark the color of strong tea

Shaggy gray wood is in its second year and has fruited once, but will bear another, smaller crop. It may also bear strong new shoots for cropping next year

Remaining stalks of the characteristic long, loose bunch, or "strig," of blackcurrant fruits

NEW AND OLD GROWTH
Blackcurrant wood changes color as it ages, providing a valuable recognition aid when pruning. Younger wood, which can be retained, is smooth and pale; older wood, which can be removed, is rough and dark.

BLACKCURRANT BUSH

Blackcurrants are purchased as two-year-old bushes that will crop in the second summer after planting. Choose a healthy specimen that has three or four strong, vigorous shoots. Plant at any time during late autumn and winter, setting the bushes slightly below the nursery soil mark and mulching after planting to encourage basal growth.

WHEN TO PRUNE Winter, as buds begin to burst. Delay the initial pruning of containerized bushes bought and planted in leaf until after leaf-fall. On well-established bushes, "winter" pruning can in fact be started in summer when the fruits are ready to pick. Cutting out whole shoots bearing ripe fruit makes picking easier, and the bush will also benefit from the increased light and air circulation. Winter pruning then consists of tidying up what is left.

FORMATIVE TRAINING The aim is to create a strong, upright, productive bush. First, prune all of the shoots back hard, almost

YEAR 1, WINTER

Well-grown two-year-old plant has several strong shoots

Plant so that nursery soil mark is a thumb's width or so below ground

Immediately after planting, cut back all shoots to one bud above soil level.

YEAR 2, WINTER

Strong new shoots have developed

Remove completely only those shoots that are very weak, or are growing horizontally or downward.

ESTABLISHED BLACKCURRANT BUSH, PRUNING AFTER FRUITING

Strong, two-year-old wood with plenty of new sideshoots is retained

1 *Using loppers or a pruning saw, cut out older wood right down to the base, pruning to a bud where one is visible.*

Low, horizontal branch pruned to a strong upward-growing shoot to restrict spread

2 *Remove any weak or crossing stems.*

Less productive two-year-old wood with few sideshoots is removed

to ground level, to encourage strong young growth in the summer. The next winter, only weak or badly placed shoots should be removed. The remaining strong shoots should bear their first crop the next summer.

ESTABLISHED PRUNING An established bush can be pruned at any time between fruiting and late winter (*see* When to prune, *facing page*). The aim is to cut out as much dark, three-year-old or older wood as possible in favor of young growth with better fruiting potential,

while maintaining the bush's upright habit and shape. Some new growth will originate from near the base of the bush, and some from gray, two-year-old wood. On strong bushes, it may be necessary to cut out up to one-third of this two-year-old wood to reduce overcrowding. On weaker bushes, more of the two-year-old wood with its young shoots should be retained to fill out the bush. No tip-pruning is necessary. Remove low shoots to restrict spread and avoid fruit touching the soil, where it will be damaged by rain and pests.

Neglected blackcurrants can often be renovated successfully; if the bush is more than 10 years old, or seems generally weak or unhealthy, it may be best to replace it. Otherwise cut out as much old wood as possible, keeping only the best strong young shoots – or, if no new wood seems promising, cut all growth down to about 2in (5cm) from the ground. In both cases feed and mulch after pruning and, the following year, thin out the new shoots to 8–12 of the strongest and best. No fruit will be produced until the following year.

PRUNING AN ESTABLISHED BLACKCURRANT BUSH

BEFORE PRUNING *This unpruned bush is crowded; the stagnant atmosphere caused by poor air circulation within the bush's center will encourage disease, especially in a damp year. Light levels will also be low, to the detriment of the fruits.*

AFTER PRUNING *One or two of the oldest branches have been removed at ground level and the remaining growth thinned to relieve overcrowding. The bush is left with a good balance of one- and two-year-old wood.*

RED- AND WHITECURRANTS *RIBES RUBRUM* (SYN. *R. SYLVESTRE*) (ZONES 4–7)

These fruits are comparatively simple to train and prune, particularly in bush form. Because they are spur-pruned to a permanent framework of branches, they are also easy to train and maintain as cordons and fans. Both redcurrants and whitecurrants (the same fruit in terms of cultivation) fruit at the base of one-year-old laterals. These laterals are hard-pruned in winter to form spurs, which will then fruit annually. Unlike blackcurrants, there is no need to replace the fruiting wood each year, and whole branches are taken out only in cases of disease, old age, or overcrowding.

Red- and whitecurrants do not suffer from reversion virus, as blackcurrants do, and certification is unnecessary. They are, however, susceptible to dieback, particularly when old: if this affects a branch, prune it back until a completely clean, white cut surface is exposed. Discard the prunings, and let a suitably placed strong, young shoot grow on to fill the gap. If successive cuts reveal that dieback has affected the main stem, the whole bush must be destroyed. In the US, plant only cultivars that are resistant to white pine blister rust.

RIPE REDCURRANTS
Redcurrant bushes need good formative training and regular pruning to prevent weak and congested growth and ensure good quality fruits.

REDCURRANT BUSH

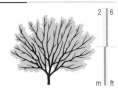

The aim of formative pruning is to produce an upright bush with 8–10 main branches, its center open to let in sun and air. Red- and whitecurrants are usually bought as one-year-old plants grown from cuttings, which will fruit in the second season after planting. Two- and three-year-old bushes are sometimes available and will fruit sooner. Plant in late autumn or winter in well-manured ground, providing shelter from strong winds that may damage new shoots.

WHEN TO PRUNE Winter, as late as possible before bud-burst so that bird damage can be taken into account.

FORMATIVE TRAINING A well-grown one-year-old bush should have three or more vigorous shoots on a short, clear stem, known as a leg. Buds or shoots on this clear leg should be removed, although they are likely to have been rubbed out already in the nursery. The shoots are cut back by half in winter to encourage further strong growths from which the framework of branches can be developed in the second year. The young branches should be staked initially for protection on exposed, windy sites.

REDCURRANT BUSH, PRUNING AFTER PLANTING

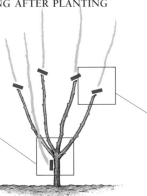

1 *Remove shoots within 4in (10cm) of soil level, cutting them back to the main stem, to make a short, clear leg.*

2 *Prune each shoot to an outward-facing bud (upward, on a drooping shoot) about halfway along its length.*

YEAR 2, WINTER

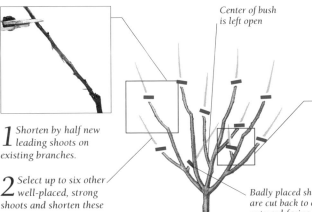

Center of bush is left open

1 *Shorten by half new leading shoots on existing branches.*

2 *Select up to six other well-placed, strong shoots and shorten these by half.*

3 *Cut any weak sideshoots back to one bud to encourage stronger growth.*

Badly placed shoots are cut back to one outward-facing bud

ESTABLISHED PRUNING Each winter, the year's new growth is shortened so that, after pruning, the bush consists solely of its main branches, clothed with short spurs. An old, less fruitful branch may be taken out occasionally; unless the bush seems overcrowded, prune to a new low shoot that will grow to replace it. Choose a replacement shoot that will maintain the open-centered but upright bush shape: low, spreading branches are liable to expose fruits to rodents and other pests on the ground. If growth is vigorous, bushes may also be summer-pruned by shortening the new laterals to five leaves, as for cordons (*see p.238*), but this is not essential.

A neglected but still young redcurrant bush can usually be regenerated, but a bush more than 15 years old, sickly-looking, or infested with perennial weeds, is best dug up, and a replacement planted on a fresh site. To renovate, first remove dead, diseased, or damaged wood, then remove old or badly placed branches, if necessary, to open up the center of the bush. Cut overgrown sideshoots and spurs back to one or two buds. The treatment is best spread over two winters, the eventual aim being to create a bush with a well-spaced structure of 8–10 strong, young branches, whereupon routine pruning as above can begin once more. Always fertilize and mulch after renovation.

ESTABLISHED REDCURRANT BUSH, WINTER

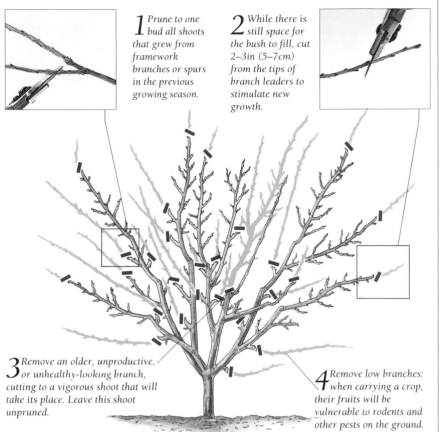

1 Prune to one bud all shoots that grew from framework branches or spurs in the previous growing season.

2 While there is still space for the bush to fill, cut 2–3in (5–7cm) from the tips of branch leaders to stimulate new growth.

3 Remove an older, unproductive, or unhealthy-looking branch, cutting to a vigorous shoot that will take its place. Leave this shoot unpruned.

4 Remove low branches: when carrying a crop, their fruits will be vulnerable to rodents and other pests on the ground.

REDCURRANT FAN

A redcurrant fan takes three years to establish. Laterals on its framework of ribs are pruned to form fruiting spurs. Wire walls and fences as for a cordon (*see p.238*).

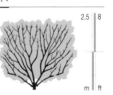

2.5 | 8

m | ft

WHEN TO PRUNE Winter, as for a bush, and also midsummer, to restrict growth.

TRAINING AND PRUNING In winter, plant a one-year-old currant, 6in (15cm) from the wall or fence. Cut the leader back to the topmost of two strong laterals about 6in (15cm) from the ground that can be trained to the left and right, and tie them to two bamboo canes tied to the wires at a 45° angle. Cut each back by half to a downward-pointing bud; remove all other shoots. If one arm grows more vigorously than the other, retie the weaker one nearer to the vertical and the stronger one more horizontally to balance their growth rates (*see Correcting uneven development, p.98*).

During the summer, select three or four well-spaced shoots on each arm (at least one on the underside) to train on

canes as the fan's ribs. Remove vigorous surplus shoots, but keep weaker ones, shortening them to three leaves.

The following winter, shorten the ribs by about half their length and cut their sideshoots back to one bud. During the third summer, fill in gaps, usually in the center, by tying in young shoots. Shorten all sideshoots to five leaves in summer, then to one or two buds in winter. In subsequent years, spur-prune each rib as for a cordon (*see overleaf*). For step-by-step illustrations of forming a fan framework, *see Peaches, p.134*.

REDCURRANT FAN
Redcurrant fans do best with the support and protection of a wall or fence, rather than of posts and wires. This method of training not only ensures maximum sunlight falls on the ripening fruit but also, in the spring, exposes the flowers well to pollinating insects. Wall- or fence-trained fruits are also easy to net against birds.

REDCURRANT CORDONS

A single cordon has one vertical main stem with fruiting spurs along its length. Multiple cordons branch at the base from a short stem, with several upright arms, rather like candelabra. All require a wall, fence, or 6ft (2m) posts with horizontal wires at 12in (30cm) intervals. Single, double, triple, and four-armed cordons should be spaced, respectively, 16, 32, 48, and 60in (40cm, 80cm, 1.2m, and 1.5m) apart.

WHEN TO PRUNE The first spring after winter planting, thereafter in winter, as for bushes (*see p.237*), and midsummer.

FORMATIVE TRAINING Plant a year-old, single-stemmed currant in winter, staking it with a cane tied to the wires. For a single cordon, proceed as shown right.

For a double cordon, cut the leader back in the first spring to the topmost of two nearly opposite laterals. Cut any other laterals back, first to two leaves, then later in the summer to the base. Train the two arms first on stakes fixed at about 30° to the ground – one to the left, one to the right. When their tips are 12in (30cm) apart, start training them vertically on stakes tied to the wires.

For a triple cordon, the leading shoot is trained vertically, and two sideshoots, shortened by half, are trained outward at 30° until the tips are 12in (30cm) from the central shoot, then vertically.

A four-armed (double-"U") cordon needs an extra year's training to produce the branching structure at the base. Using the same method as for a double cordon, train two shoots as near to horizontal as possible before training them vertically when they are 18in (45cm) long. In the winter, cut sideshoots back to one bud, and shorten the vertical portion of each arm to two buds. Train the resulting pair of shoots on each arm as if each were a double cordon.

Thereafter, the arms of all cordons continue to be shortened and trained on as for a single cordon (*right*) until the arms reach their desired height. This gives a firmer main stem. All other shoots are shortened, and the shoots that grow during the summer are then pruned back (*shown top right*) to form spurs that will fruit the next year.

ESTABLISHED PRUNING All cordons are summer- and winter-pruned each year as for a single cordon. In time, older spur systems will need thinning (*see Apples, Spur pruning, p.105*). The leading shoot must also be cut back to a bud to restrict height. Pinch out or shorten shoots growing in toward the wall.

SINGLE REDCURRANT CORDON, PRUNING ON PLANTING, WINTER

1 *Cut back the leading shoot by half its previous year's growth. If a lower shoot is stronger, train this in instead, cutting the main stem back to just above it in the summer.*

Top of original cutting

2 *Cut back other shoots to one bud.*

YEAR 1 ONWARD, SUMMER

When new shoots have at least seven or eight leaves, prune back to five leaves. If they have developed any sideshoots, pinch or cut these back to one bud.

YEAR 2 ONWARD, WINTER

1 *As the cordon grows, prune new growth on the leading shoot by a quarter each winter, always cutting to a bud on the opposite side to last year's cut. When the cordon has reached the top wire, prune back new growth to one bud.*

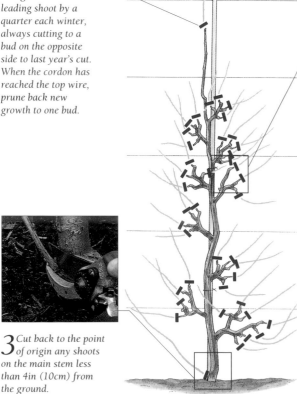

2 *Cut back all the summer-pruned shoots and any new sideshoots to one bud. As the plant ages and spur systems become more complex, cut away old and unproductive sections to relieve overcrowding.*

3 *Cut back to the point of origin any shoots on the main stem less than 4in (10cm) from the ground.*

GOOSEBERRIES *RIBES UVA-CRISPA* (ZONES 5–7)

The gooseberry fruits on year-old shoots and older spur systems. The growth habit of the various cultivars varies between pendent and upright. They are usually grown as open-centered bushes, which can be pruned in two ways: either on a loose renewal basis, or spur-pruned to a permanent framework. This second option makes possible such trained forms as cordons, fans, and standards, which make picking easier. Gooseberries are usually viciously spiny, but nearly thornless cultivars are now available. Many newer cultivars are also resistant to American gooseberry mildew.

Do not grow gooseberries in frost pockets because the early spring flowers may be frost-damaged. A sheltered but airy site, shaded for part of the day, is ideal. As with redcurrants, dieback may be a problem. If it reaches the main stem, the bush must be uprooted and discarded. Otherwise cut affected growth back to completely healthy wood, if possible to a replacement shoot.

This season's growth

One-year-old, fruiting wood

Two-year-old wood

Three-year-old wood

SPUR-PRUNING
The pruning and fruiting pattern of the gooseberry can be seen from this section of stem.

GOOSEBERRY BUSH

Gooseberries are most often bought as one-year-old rooted cuttings, although older plants are sometimes available. The aim is to produce a bush 4–6ft (1.2–2m) tall, with a strong framework of 8–12 main branches on a short leg. Branches should be well-spaced, and the center as open as possible, to aid air circulation and to make picking easier. Choose a strong specimen with at least three good shoots, and plant in autumn or winter, staking initially in exposed sites as the new shoots are fragile.

WHEN TO PRUNE Late winter or just as buds are beginning to burst in early spring; earlier pruning will increase the impact of bird damage. In areas where American gooseberry mildew is troublesome, summer-prune young shoots too, as for cordons and fans. Removing the tips of the shoots, which are most likely to be affected, reduces the spread of the disease.

FORMATIVE TRAINING In late winter after planting, shorten all shoots by about three-quarters of their length; this may already have been done in the nursery, in which case trim by 1in (2–3cm). If the cultivar has a pendent habit, always prune to an upward-pointing bud. Sideshoots should then develop in the following season, from which 8–10 are selected to form the main branches.

GOOSEBERRY BUSH, YEAR 1, WINTER

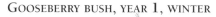

Prune back each shoot by three-quarters to an outward-facing bud (Prune to an upward-facing bud on a cultivar with pendent branches.)

YEAR 2, WINTER

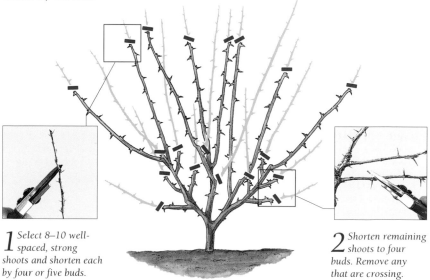

1 *Select 8–10 well-spaced, strong shoots and shorten each by four or five buds.*

2 *Shorten remaining shoots to four buds. Remove any that are crossing.*

ESTABLISHED PRUNING Established gooseberry bushes can be pruned in two ways. Spur-pruning (*right*) – shortening all new growth on a permanent framework of branches – gives a smaller crop of large fruits, while less labor-intensive "regulated" or renewal pruning (*below*) – removing older branches entirely – encourages a heavy crop of small fruit, ideal for preserving. With either method, if larger fruits are required, remove every other fruit in late spring or in early summer, when the thinned fruits may already be large enough to be of culinary use.

A neglected bush less than 12 years old may well repay renovation. In winter, remove strong, vertical shoots from the base of the bush, and shorten trailing growth (which may have layered) to an upward-facing bud. Remove the oldest branches – up to one in four – to reduce overcrowding. After fruiting in summer, you will be able to see which older, less fruitful branches should be removed the next winter, allowing strong, well-placed new growth to take their place.

ESTABLISHED GOOSEBERRY BUSH, SPUR-PRUNING IN WINTER

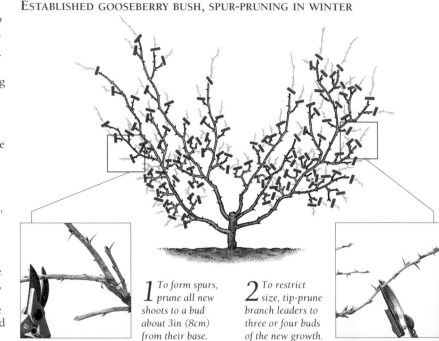

1 To form spurs, prune all new shoots to a bud about 3in (8cm) from their base.

2 To restrict size, tip-prune branch leaders to three or four buds of the new growth.

ESTABLISHED GOOSEBERRY BUSH, REGULATED PRUNING IN WINTER

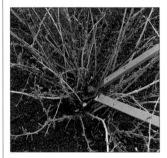

BEFORE PRUNING *Older, less productive or weak branches must be removed to prevent overcrowding and to maintain an open center.*

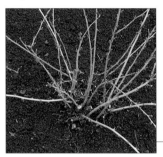

AFTER PRUNING *Branches are well-spaced after the removal of overcrowded growth, allowing light to penetrate and air to circulate freely.*

1 Remove older branches, following the natural growth habit of the cultivar to maintain an upright but open bush.

2 Remove all growth arising from less than 4in (10cm) from the ground.

GOOSEBERRY STANDARD

The selected cultivar is grafted on to vigorous American *Ribes* stock at 3–4ft (1–1.2m), and must be firmly staked. Formative pruning of the head should be as for a bush, aiming to create a balanced, compact yet open-centered crown. This is then pruned as for an established gooseberry bush, using the spur-pruning method to maintain a compact head of branches. Any shoots growing from the clear stem should be rubbed out as seen. Both stake and tie need to be checked regularly, loosening the tie if it is constricting the stem.

GOOSEBERRY CORDON

Gooseberries can be trained and maintained as single, double, or multiple cordons, just as for red-currants (*see p.238*). The winter pruning, however, is less severe, shortening sideshoots to about four buds. As the plants age, spur systems will become overcrowded and thinning will be necessary (*see Apples, Spur-pruning, p.105*).

A row of single cordons that consists of a mixture of cultivars, alternating fruits that ripen to different colors (red, yellow, and green are available), makes a striking display.

GOOSEBERRY FAN

A gooseberry fan against a sunny wall should produce large fruits of dessert quality, especially if they are thinned, removing every other fruit when they are the size of a hazelnut. However, a fan will also produce fruits ripe enough for culinary or preserving purposes on a cool, partially shaded wall. Training and pruning is as for a redcurrant fan (*see p.237*). Good control of gooseberry mildew is essential when plants are trained close to a wall or fence, rather than as freestanding bushes in well-circulating air.

BLUEBERRIES *Vaccinium* spp. (zones 3–8)

The most widely grown blueberry is the highbush type (*V. corymbosum*), an attractive ornamental shrub 6–10ft (2–3m) tall, with stunning fall color. Blueberries can be allowed to develop a permanent framework of branches, since the wood is fruitful for several years.

The dusky navy-blue berries ripen from early to late summer. Select several cultivars that bear at different times throughout the summer to extend the fruiting season. Though self-fertile, blueberries will crop better if grown together to allow cross-pollination.

Highbush blueberries require acid soil but can make successful container-grown shrubs, if given only nonalkaline water and repotted every two to three years (*see p.154*).

The smaller, more spreading rabbit-eye blueberry (*V. ashei*) tolerates slightly higher pH conditions, but still requires acid soil. This species does not produce much fine fruit, but named cultivars and hybrids with *V. corymbosum* bear very palatable berries, and are grown in warmer climates (zones 7–9). They too are attractive plants, particularly since, like the highbushes, they provide a fine display of fall color. *V. ashei* and hybrids are pruned as for a highbush.

Growth bud

Fruit bud

CROPPING BLUEBERRY

Blueberry branches with the potential to fruit heavily can be identified at an early stage, so when pruning in late winter, this can be taken into account when selecting what to remove. The fruit buds are distinctly fatter compared to the relatively insignificant growth buds.

HIGHBUSH BLUEBERRY

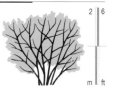

Highbush blueberries are usually sold as container-ized shrubs. They transplant most easily in spring or early autumn. The principle of pruning and renovation is the same as for blackcurrants (*see p.234*). Wood will fruit well from one year until at least four years old, after which it should be removed in favor of younger, more productive wood.

WHEN TO PRUNE Late winter, when fruit buds are readily distinguishable.

FORMATIVE TRAINING The only pruning necessary in the first two years will be to encourage the formation of a strong, well-shaped, open-centered bush. Prune back shoots growing out horizontally and any weak growth, cutting to an upright shoot or low bud where visible.

ESTABLISHED PRUNING Prune out the oldest and weakest wood near the base of the plant to encourage strong new growth and remove any growth spreading out toward the ground. Cut out no more than a quarter of the bush annually. Renovate as for a blackcurrant (*see p.235*) if the plant lacks vigor.

ESTABLISHED HIGHBUSH BLUEBERRY, WINTER

2 *Cut back weak growth to a strong, young shoot.*

1 *Remove unproductive wood close to ground level.*

3 *Either remove any low growth completely or cut it back to a strong, upward-pointing shoot.*

CLIMBING PLANTS

Climbers are one of the most rewarding plant groups; with careful and imaginative training, they can provide year-round displays and combinations of foliage, flowers, and fruits

In the wild, climbing plants evolved their growth habit in order to compete with other plants, scrambling up and over obstacles (including rival plants) in search of air and sunlight. Their energies are concentrated on producing long, fast-growing shoots rather than robust, self-supporting stems. Support and training are very important in order to utilize climbers successfully in the garden. While some climbers develop thick, woody stems with age (when the heavy growth needs substantial support), in general they are unable to support their young growth in an upright position. Unless climbers are to be used as groundcover, they need something to grow up, through, or against.

Climbing plants greatly extend the possibilities of shape, color, and foliage in garden design. They are used particularly to give the dimension of height. In small gardens or confined sites where trees and large shrubs cannot be grown, they can be trained along walls and fences to provide a backdrop to other plantings. Free-standing focal points, such as tripods, arches and pergolas, arbors, and shady bowers, give a new dimension to the garden. Climbers can also be grown over existing garden features: on the walls of a house, up into a tree, or over a hedge. More practically, they can cover an unsightly shed or

other eyesore, or form a "natural" screen on economical materials such as chain-link fencing or cinder block walls. Climbers can also be chosen to set off decorative materials, such as stonework, rustic poles, and wrought iron, and there is enormous opportunity for associating them with other plants, both climbing and otherwise.

TOPIARY EFFECT
Not all climbers are rampant in growth. Training these small ivies over a wire seahorse frame produces decorative "topiary." Small-leaved climbers are best suited to this type of training, where a neat outline is desirable. A frame also enables a climbing plant to be grown as a freestanding specimen, forming a focal point.

COMBINING CLIMBERS
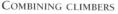
A wigwam arrangement of three rustic poles enables this beautiful combination of roses and clematis to be seen from all sides. The planting also benefits from maximum exposure to sun and free air circulation. Tripods or obelisks covered with climbers add height to border plantings.

TYPES OF CLIMBING PLANTS

Climbing plants have developed a variety of methods by which to support themselves. At the simplest level, they resemble open shrubs with very long, flexible stems that drape themselves over neighboring objects and plants; some have thorns on their stems that act as anchors. At a more specialized level, the growth habit of the stems or leaf stalks (petioles) has adapted to twine around other stems and branches. The shoots usually extend rapidly before leaves develop, so that stems are not weighed down as they seek their next point of anchorage. The most sophisticated climbers have developed additional adaptations that enable them to climb. Some grasp with tendrils onto other stems or branches; others develop adhesive stem roots or suckering pads with which to cling to a sheer surface. It is important to understand the way in which your chosen plants grow in order to provide appropriate support. Other aspects of growth habit must also be taken into account: whether the plant, when fully trained, will be accessible for any necessary pruning (or the support for any maintenance it may need); whether it is of a type where a permanent woody framework can be developed, or whether some or even all growth should be removed at the base each year; and of course the vigor of the plant, and whether this is appropriate to the site and support.

MATCHING CLIMBERS TO SUPPORTS

The method by which plants climb is not directly linked to their pruning needs, but does affect training. Choose climbers whose growth habit complements their intended support. An attractive wrought-iron obelisk, for example, will be so swamped by a vigorous climber such as *Parthenocissus* or hops (*Humulus*) that the cost of such a decorative feature is wasted. If a fuel tank or tree stump is to be masked, however, a densely growing, permanent evergreen is a better choice than a deciduous or herbaceous climber.

It is equally important to choose methods of support, and give additional attention where necessary, that will enable the plant to climb or be trained successfully. For example, whereas ivy will creep up a bare stone wall, a honeysuckle will simply mound up in a heap at the base. However, if the wall is equipped with wires or a trellis, the honeysuckle will, with initial guidance, twine around the wires or struts and climb the support. This is not the case with winter jasmine, which will never make its own way up a vertical support unaided: each stem must individually be tied in to achieve height and coverage. The Dictionary of Climbing Plants (*see pp.262–287*) contains symbols that indicate by which method plants climb.

SCRAMBLING PLANTS

Many climbers do not twine or cling, but simply throw out long shoots that fall or scramble over obstacles. They are ideal for groundcover (*see p.253*) and for smaller host plants (*see p.255*), since they will not wrap and smother the host's stems too closely. They produce a cascading effect (for example, over the top of a wall), because they do not creep back into and around their own growth. Many continually throw up new basal shoots to replace stems or canes that eventually die. In nature the plant uses its own dead stems to climb higher, but in the garden these should be removed because of the risk of disease.

CLINGING CLIMBERS
Ivy (left) will cling to any rough surface with aerial stem rootlets, while Parthenocissus tricuspidata *(above) holds on with touch-activated adhesive pads. Both roots and pads continue to adhere after the death of the stem.*

HOOKED THORNS
Some climbers, such as bougainvillea (right), brambles, and, of course, climbing roses (see p.316), have thorns, sometimes hooked, that support scrambling stems by catching onto the plant's support.

TWINING STEMS
The stems of climbers such as Wisteria *(left) twine around any support that they touch. The stems twine clockwise or counter-clockwise, depending on the species. Climbers with twining stems can grow very rapidly, with vigorous laterals that branch out in search of other supports. Young stems may need to be guided toward supports*

SCANDENT PLANTS

It is difficult to draw a sharp distinction between scrambling climbers and open, long-stemmed shrubs – a habit that is described as "scandent." Some argue that if a plant is unable to twine or cling by itself, it is not a climber at all but simply a very open or prostrate shrub, while some shrubs are so universally wall trained that in many nursery catalogs they are included as climbing plants. Plants such as *Cantua buxifolia*, *Tecoma stans*, and *Streptosolen jamesonii* are the subject of regular debate about their categorization. They have more sturdy growth than, say, *Jasminum mesnyi* (*right*), a scandent plant whose long, thin stems, although tough, are not rigid enough to be self-supporting.

What is certain about these plants is that they all benefit from training. Wall training is the most suitable method; those that can be spur-pruned will create a more formal effect, with dense, two-dimensional coverage. All will need initial training and regular tying in thereafter.

Jasminum mesnyi

TRUE TENDRILS
True tendrils are modified shoots that grow out from a stem, as seen in Passiflora racemosa *(left). These tendrils will twine around any thin support, and then coil up and shorten to tighten their grip. Some tendrils branch and twist in different directions. Many thicken to form a long-lasting hold.*

LEAF TENDRILS
Climbers such as Cobaea scandens *(right) and perennial peas* (Lathyrus) *have leaf tendrils – leaves, or parts of leaves, that have become modified into twining tendrils that reach out in search of support. These plants usually climb unaided rapidly.*

TWINING PETIOLES
On a few climbers, such as Clematis montana *(left), the leaf stalks, or petioles, will wind around each other or any support they meet. Even if the plant is deciduous, the petioles remain on the stem after the leaves are shed. Tying in is needed only to guide and direct growth.*

TWINING AND TENDRIL CLIMBERS
Twining and tendril climbers must be given something to wrap their stems and tendrils around. Walls, fences, posts, and pillars need to be equipped with wires, netting, or a trellis. On a wired wall or fence, tie vertical lengths of string between wires to give more anchorage points and hence achieve denser coverage. Trellises or heavy-gauge wire netting, whether attached to a wall or between posts, are ideal for twining climbers. Tendriled climbers will quickly camouflage plastic netting, chicken wire, or peasticks.

For informal training these climbers are also ideal for growing up into a tree or into other plants: they support themselves and need no tying in. Herbaceous climbers can be given light, seasonal support such as beanpoles or peasticks. The more vigorous and long-lasting plants that develop thick woody stems (such as wisterias) need strong supports; they can also be trained as standards.

CLINGING CLIMBERS
Some climbers develop adhesive roots or pads that cling unaided to masonry, wood, and tree trunks. Adhesive roots form along stems; they do not take in nourishment or water. They are distinct from the long, aerial roots formed by many tropical climbers, which do not adhere (though with age they may harden to prop the plant). Adhesive pads form at the tips of branched tendrils that develop at leaf nodes.

Clinging climbers are best grown directly up or along flat surfaces such as walls and fences, but should be used with caution on house walls. They may loosen old, crumbling mortar; shoots may penetrate under house eaves, or leaves may block gutters and drainpipes. The stems often become thick, woody, and heavy with age. Because stem roots develop only where the plant is in contact with a surface, several of these climbers can be trained as standards.

FIXTURES

A wall- or fence-trained climber is likely to be in position for many years, during which time it will be difficult to do any painting, cleaning, or maintenance of the support. Therefore, any structures must be in good condition before planting; fences, for example, must be treated with nontoxic preservative. It is also essential that the support is capable of bearing the full weight of your chosen climber when mature. Wires and fasteners must be resistant to corrosion and be able to outlast the plant. In areas of high air pollution, wires should be plastic-coated, and fasteners should be made of rustproof metal or plastic. All hardware should be in position before planting.

COVERING WALLS AND FENCES

In sheltered sites, plastic or wooden trellises can be erected between posts to form freestanding screens, or fixed above or against walls and fences. Netting is available in a range of gauges, from open-weave, heavy-duty wire to fine-mesh plastic suitable for lightweight annual or herbaceous climbers. Flexible chicken wire can be used to mold shapes, to soften outlines (to make plants appear to "billow" over a step, for example), or to train topiary forms.

Trellises or netting must not be attached directly onto the surface of a wall or fence; the plant stems cannot twine around it, and a stagnant atmosphere will be created, an ideal environment for disease organisms. The wall or fence may also deteriorate. In order to allow some airspace between the plant and the wall, nail wooden laths to the wall and then fix the trellis panels to them, either with screws or, to allow access to the wall by lifting away both plant and support, with hinges and hooks. The base of a wooden trellis should be at least 12in (30cm) from the ground, to prevent it from rotting.

Wires stretched along a fence or wall should be held about 2in (5cm) away from the surface. They are best spaced 9–12in (23–30cm) apart, depending on the vigor of the climber, and attached by vine eyes or rustproof nails. Vertical wires or twine may be added to form a squared framework, thus improving the plant's coverage of the area.

VERTICAL FEATURES

A permanent structure must be constructed of durable materials. The width and height of an arch or pergola need to be generous; the space under an archway is reduced once plants are established on the framework. In a bed or border, wooden supports should be set in free-draining gravel, not bare soil, to stop the bases from rotting.

USING WIRE NETTING

Here, a clematis has been trained on a spherical wire "balloon," formed by strips of wire netting, one square wide and eight squares deep, that have been buried in the soil around the pot's edge, then brought over and joined at the top. Heavy-gauge galvanized wire netting is one of the most versatile of supports. It can be stapled to wooden laths on a wall as an economical "trellis," and will quickly be disguised by a dense climber such as Clematis montana.

FIXINGS FOR WIRES AND TRELLISES

WIRING WALLS AND FENCES *Vine eyes (above) are the simplest way to hold wires away from the surface of a wall or fence. Use galvanized turnbuckles, or (top) use pliers, to tighten wires.*

RAISING THE HEIGHT OF A FENCE *A strip of trellis on top of a fence is held by metal plates screwed into the fence posts. Short posts with taut or looping wires between them can also be fixed along the top.*

FIXING TRELLIS PANELS TO A WALL OR FENCE

The easiest way to fix trellis panels is to screw 2in (5cm) laths to the fence or wall (left), then screw the trellis to the laths. This leaves airspace behind the plant. If you want to take down the plant and trellis together – for example, from a wall or fence that is painted regularly – use hooks-and-eyes at the top and hinges at the bottom (center and right).

BASIC TECHNIQUES

Early training and pruning is essential to encourage climbing plants to produce plenty of strong shoots that will grow to cover the available space. Guiding or tying in stems to best utilize, direct, and display the available growth according to the training plan is crucial to the final effect. Time and effort spent in developing a good basic framework of stems for permanent climbers will always be amply repaid as the plant matures.

From then on, some climbers need only minimal attention, and these plants should be selected for sites where the mature plant will be difficult to attend to regularly – in the branches of a tree, for example, or high up on a wall. However, climbers may also be pruned to control growth and restrict size, to remove old, less productive growth in favor of young stems, or to increase flowering potential. The amount of time spent cutting overlarge plants back can be minimized if the vigor of the plant is well matched to the site.

Pruning to enhance flowering performance is an annual, sometimes twice-yearly task. It must be carefully timed to complement the flowering habit of the plant. In some genera, such as *Clematis*, different species flower, and thus must be pruned, at different times.

Neglected climbers soon become overgrown and tangled. Old specimens of relatively short-lived plants are best replaced. Otherwise, many plants can be selectively renovated so that the plant is retained as a garden feature. Climbers that respond well to hard pruning may be cut to near ground level, and the resulting new growth trained in again.

TYPES OF CUT

The majority of pruning work on climbers can be done with pruners or with shears because the stems tend to remain small in diameter. However, some climbers do develop thicker, woody growth that will need cutting with loppers or a saw. Climbers with a permanent framework of woody stems, such as *Wisteria* and grapes (*Vitis*), should have each stem spur-pruned individually with pruners. Those that produce a dense mass of spindly growth, such as honeysuckle (*Lonicera*), are often clipped with shears because it is impractical to prune so many stems individually. The exact pruning and training methods depend on the growth and flowering habit of individual species (*see* Dictionary of Climbing Plants, pp.262–287), as does the time of year in which pruning takes place. Always feed and mulch well after pruning.

WHEN TO PRUNE

Overall shaping of deciduous climbers is best done in the dormant season, and evergreen climbers should be pruned in spring, when the cut ends will be quickly disguised by new growth. Those grown for their flowers are additionally pruned either in early spring or after flowering, depending on the age of the wood on which they flower and their season of flowering. In tropical conditions, where climbers may grow continuously, prune during the growing season as necessary to shape them and keep them manageable. More drastic cutting back can be done when plants are dormant, or nearly so.

POSITIONING THE CUT

Climbers that do not lend themselves to overall clipping should have individual stems cut back just above a healthy bud or shoot facing in the direction growth is desired. On stems with alternate buds, always cut at an angle (*see above right*).

CUTTING TO ALTERNATE BUDS

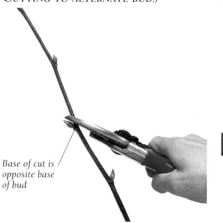

Base of cut is opposite base of bud

On stems with an alternate arrangement of buds or shoots, make an angled cut just above the bud, parallel to its angle of growth, starting from the opposite side.

CUTTING TO OPPOSITE BUDS

Prune stems with opposite buds straight across the stem just above a pair of healthy buds or shoots. Never leave a budless stub of stem that will die back and invite disease.

CUTTING TO A REPLACEMENT SHOOT

Unless you require the stem to follow a radically different direction for training purposes, pruning to shoots that follow the line of the older stem gives a more natural effect.

PRUNING DENSE CLIMBERS

Climbers that produce a dense mass of thin, twiggy stems may have their growth routinely pruned and generally shaped with shears, as here, rather than with pruners.

ROUTINE TASKS

As with all other plants, the pruning of climbers can be divided into essential and nonessential tasks. Some problems will crop up at any time and should be dealt with as soon as they are noticed, while other jobs become necessary as the plant matures: tying in, for example, and thinning crowded growth.

Dead, diseased, and damaged growth should always be removed as soon as seen. Discard diseased prunings, and dip the tools used in household disinfectant. Some climbers flower for a longer season if deadheaded, but this is often impractical where climbers are large or trained up high. Like all pruning that enhances flowering, deadheading is not essential, but should always be undertaken to improve the display if possible. Do not deadhead plants whose fruits are ornamental.

GUIDING IN GROWTH

Guide young, flexible stems of tendril and twining climbers between netting or wires; they will then climb in the desired direction. Shoots are often very fragile.

Very few climbers are grafted, so the attendant problem of suckering from the rootstock is rarely encountered. There are, however, variegated cultivars of many plants, and on these any shoots with plain green leaves should be promptly removed, or they will dominate growth that has the desired foliage variegation.

TRAINING IN STEMS

Guiding and tying in is crucial to climbing plants, particularly wall-trained specimens, both to obtain the desired direction of growth and to encourage maximum coverage of the support. Unless a special effect such as a standard climber (*see p.260*) is being created, the stems of young climbers should be fanned or spread out as much as possible at first. This will encourage twining and tendriled plants to climb up the whole width of the allotted space, rather than straight up the middle. Further growth can be guided or tied in as necessary. With climbers that need regular tying in (those that do not twine with stems or tendrils), early training lays the foundations of an attractive, well-balanced framework, such as a fan. Always train some shoots horizontally or spiraled around the support. Such horizontal training stimulates the production of flowers and fruit (*see* Horizontal training, *p.13*). The shape and structure of the climber are then maintained by pruning and further tying in as needed. Neglected plants will revert very quickly to vertical growth.

Training for good coverage of a framework or support also involves cutting out shoots growing in unwanted directions (for example, inward toward a wall), to stimulate growth in desired

Strong new growth

Dead wood

REMOVING DEAD WOOD

This jasmine shoot has died back to buds that have developed into a pair of vigorous shoots. They are completely healthy, so it is safe to assume that the natural chemical barrier (see p.11) that isolates dead from live wood has formed. Cut back to just beyond the visible line between live and dead wood.

directions. Similarly, weak or straggly shoots should be pruned to concentrate the energy of the plant into young, strong, vigorous shoots.

CHECKING TIES

Ties must be checked regularly to ensure that they are intact and that they are not constricting any stems. Temperate-climate climbers increase their stem diameter rapidly each spring; in tropical or heated conditions, stems expand gradually and continuously. Ties should be loosened before they constrict stems. The stem will become damaged and thus more susceptible to disease or

TYING IN

ACHIEVING MAXIMUM COVERAGE *Early training is essential to obtain good coverage. Where the lower area of a support is to be covered, always fan some shoots out toward the horizontal from the start; gaps at the base can be difficult to fill later.*

FIGURE EIGHTS *Using twine tied in figure eights allows for some stem expansion and buffers the stem against hard surfaces.*

CHECKING TIES *Neglected ties can constrict and eventually bite into stems and may permanently damage the plant.*

it will die above the tie. Chafing can often be avoided by adding extra ties, even on climbers that do not require them for support, to minimize the movement of the stem.

CROSSING AND CROWDED GROWTH

Congestion and crossing growth, always to be prevented with trees and shrubs, are difficult to avoid with climbing plants. If the climber is cut back hard each year, problems are unlikely to accumulate. However, where a permanent framework of woody growth is developed it is vital that main stems are evenly and well spaced (*see facing page, below left*), or they will chafe and eventually become damaged. Shorten excess growth in crowded areas rather than tying it in across other stems.

Once the framework is formed, plants with light, slender stems can be allowed to develop unchecked, since their profusion of stems and density of habit are often precisely the effect that is wanted. Climbers such as honeysuckle and *Clematis montana* that produce a thick blanket of tangled stems over a period of years may be completely cut back to the wall or support to relieve congestion and stimulate vigorous regrowth. Always prune at the correct time for the individual plant to avoid cutting out growth that will flower in the coming season.

With other climbers of sturdier growth, thinning of the stems that develop from the framework is necessary to keep the plant from becoming extremely heavy and growing too far outward from its support and to prevent a dank, lightless environment within the plant. With some plants, thinning may be achieved by the routine pruning that enhances their flowering performance; on plants that are not pruned regularly

DEADHEADING
The dead flower heads or stalks of some climbers, such as this bougainvillea, are unsightly. Where possible, pick or snip them off, being very careful not to damage any new growth.

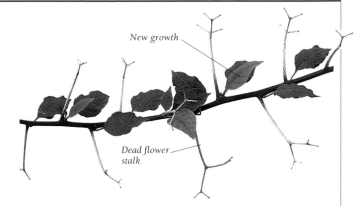

New growth

Dead flower stalk

in this way, it will have to be a job in its own right. The aim should be to prevent congestion from building up, not to wait until extensive pruning is necessary, since this will spoil the plant's appearance. Plants that become mildly congested may be thinned by cutting some stems back – to their point of origin, to a young replacement growth, or to near ground level – to encourage new stems to develop. Some wall and tripod plants can be taken down, laid flat on the ground, selectively thinned, and retrained. If this is not possible, a practical, if unpredictable, method for tangled growth is to cut a few stems, then wait two or three days for their severed top growth to wilt. It is then easier to see and remove the dying stems, then make further cuts as needed.

CLIMBERS UNDER GLASS
It is always important to thin climbers grown under glass in greenhouses or conservatories, since they can be very vigorous. Thinning will increase airflow around the plant, as will training the stems along wires and stakes to keep them from touching the glass. Clear debris such as fallen leaves and flowers

regularly, and keep walls and supports clean and dry. Plants that can be taken outside in warm weather are at less risk from problems arising from lack of air circulation or moisture. More delicate species must be kept under cover all year in colder climates. Despite the fact that they require high temperatures and humidity levels, conservatories and greenhouses should always be ventilated because of the increased risk of pests and mildew in closed environments.

CLIMBERS IN CONTAINERS
Only a relatively small number of true climbing plants are native to temperate regions. Many attractive plants come from tropical and subtropical parts of the world. In colder climates, many tender climbers are popularly grown under cover, often in containers. In these conditions, growth is usually less vigorous. Consequently, these plants, which are often very large in their native habitat, are kept to a manageable size. Plants need regular fertilizing and repotting when necessary (*see p.154*). Containers can be moved outside in summer and then brought inside during the winter months.

THINNING GROWTH

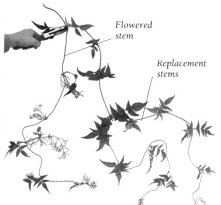

Flowered stem

Replacement stems

THINNING FLOWERED SHOOTS *The routine pruning for flowering of many climbers involves removing flowered shoots, which is often enough to prevent congestion.*

TRACING STEMS *It may not be easy to trace stems to their point of origin. One method is to cut a main stem near the base, then cut and tease out the growth that subsequently wilts.*

SHEARING *Crop densely growing, vigorous climbers back to their support. Once new growth begins, any severed growth that has been overlooked can be seen and picked out.*

INITIAL TRAINING

Wall- or fence-training, as shown on these pages, is the most popular and basic way of training climbers, and many of the principles apply to all types of training. Different plants, however, vary in their individual pruning needs; these are given in the Dictionary of Climbing Plants (*see pp.262–287*).

BUYING AND PLANTING

Choose young plants with sturdy stems and healthy leaves and buds. Remove any dead, damaged, or weak and spindly stems. If only one stem is needed, remove all but the strongest. If strong stems are sparse and more are required, pinch out their tips to encourage branching near the base. However, if there is only one stem (as with many clematis) it is best not to check its growth until after the first growing season. Then, in late winter or early spring, cut it back almost to ground level to encourage new basal growth.

If the climber is to be trained against a wall or fence, plant it at least 9in (20cm) from the structure, if necessary using angled bamboo stakes to lead the shoots toward their support. Climbers can be planted near the base of a post, pillar, or tripod leg, and trained vertically or around the support. It is important to tie in all newly planted climbers, whatever their method of climbing: any twining or clinging habit does not develop until the plant has acclimatized to its new home, and young stems may be damaged by wind if not tied in. Little or no pruning should be needed in the first growing season. As growth proceeds, train shoots to the support in the desired directions. To cover a flat surface, fan them out evenly (*see right*); on a three-dimensional structure, there are several options (*see* Special training, *pp.253–259*).

FORMATIVE TRAINING AND PRUNING

Provided that the climber is not one that is cut down every year, the next few years should be spent developing a sound and well-spaced framework. Sometimes a young stem will break when being trained, so tie in the selected stems before cutting out surplus growth. Where growth is sparse, stems can be shortened to stimulate branching. Shoots growing in undesirable directions (for example, across another stem or outward from a wall) can be carefully repositioned and tied in to spaces while the shoots are still young and supple or shortened or removed. Regular guiding and tying in of growth is essential in the early years to cover the support well; plants will always naturally grow upward rather than sideways.

PRUNING AND TRAINING ON PLANTING

1 Cut any badly placed, weak, or damaged shoots back to their point of origin (here on Jasminum mesnyi) to encourage the development of the strongest stems.

2 Secure the young stems to the support, using twine tied in figure eights (see p.248). If using guiding stakes, tie the shoots to the stakes and secure the stakes to the wires or trellis.

PRUNING TO DEVELOP A FRAMEWORK

1 Where leading shoots grow vigorously without developing sideshoots, shorten them to stimulate branching growth that will cover the allotted space evenly.

2 Shoots that are not required for tying in to develop the main framework may be shortened to three to six buds; this will encourage fresh young sideshoots that, in many plants, will bear flowers.

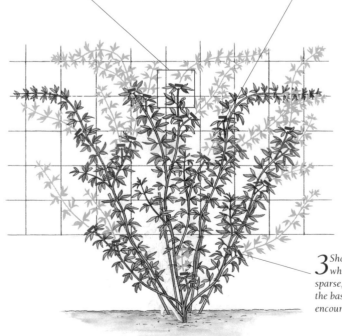

3 Shorten shoots where growth is sparse, particularly at the base of the wall, to encourage branching.

PRUNING ESTABLISHED CLIMBERS

Those climbers that are trained as permanent features against a wall or any other support need a certain amount of maintenance if they are to remain healthy and vigorous. Many tasks should be undertaken as seen (*see* Routine tasks, *p.248*). Others, such as thinning (*see p.249*) and replacement pruning (removing an older section of the framework and tying younger growth into the gap), become necessary as the plant matures. Flowering and fruiting climbers may benefit from additional pruning to enhance their performance. Pruning may also be needed to keep a plant within its allotted area or to maintain the shape of supports such as arches (*see* Special training, *pp.253–261*).

MAINTENANCE PRUNING

Basic, maintenance pruning (*see below*) will keep plants in good condition and encourage vigorous growth, while keeping the plant within bounds. The general principles are illustrated here, but the degree to which the plant is pruned will depend on the individual plant and its vigor and condition. Avoid overzealous pruning; it may result in

SUMMER PRUNING

Climbers that flower on the previous season's wood benefit from pruning after flowering, cutting flowered shoots back to buds or new sideshoots that will become the next year's flowering growth.

excessive growth and few flowers or fruits. Maintenance pruning is generally best undertaken in the dormant season, though the timing varies; evergreens are often pruned in summer, when growth soon disguises unsightly cut marks.

PRUNING FOR FLOWERS AND FRUIT

The pruning of climbers to increase production of flowers and fruits falls broadly into two categories, depending on the age of wood on which flowers are produced. Plants that flower on the previous year's ripened shoots should be pruned, unless fruits are required,

immediately after flowering (*see above*) to allow new shoots to develop before the onset of winter. Vigorous climbers may also be summer-pruned to restrict growth. Plants that flower on the current season's shoots can be pruned in late winter or early spring, at the same time as any maintenance pruning (*see below*). Their shoots are usually spur-pruned – shortened to between three and six buds (depending on the plant), which then develop into flowering shoots.

To prune individual plants correctly and at the best time, *see* Dictionary of Climbing Plants, *pp.262–287*.

MAINTENANCE PRUNING, DORMANT SEASON

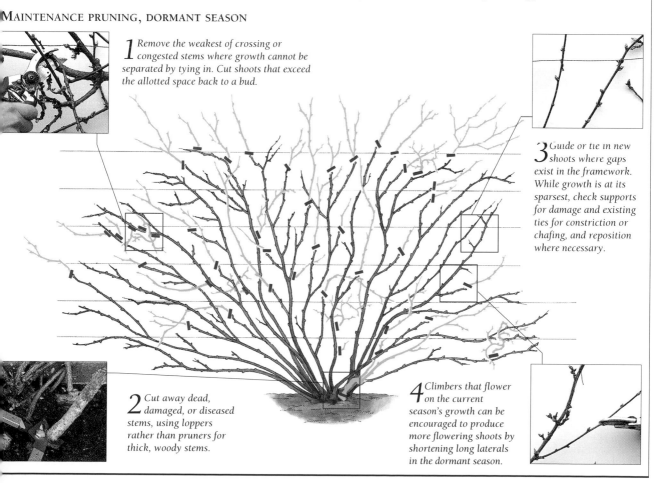

1 Remove the weakest of crossing or congested stems where growth cannot be separated by tying in. Cut shoots that exceed the allotted space back to a bud.

3 Guide or tie in new shoots where gaps exist in the framework. While growth is at its sparsest, check supports for damage and existing ties for constriction or chafing, and reposition where necessary.

2 Cut away dead, damaged, or diseased stems, using loppers rather than pruners for thick, woody stems.

4 Climbers that flower on the current season's growth can be encouraged to produce more flowering shoots by shortening long laterals in the dormant season.

RENOVATION

Neglected climbers soon become overgrown. They also tend to revert to upward growth, which, if it has become woody, may be difficult to retrain. Dense, tangled growth may pull down supports and is likely to be full of dead shoots and foliage. Flowering and fruiting are likely to have declined.

A plant that is moribund, or is suffering badly from disease or pest infestation, is usually not worth renovating. It is best removed and replaced by a vigorous young plant. This may take time to establish, but in two or three years it will make a much better specimen.

Plants that are basically sound, however, can often be renovated. Such work is best done in the dormant season. By far the easiest way to renovate, provided that the plant will tolerate drastic pruning, is to cut the entire plant down (*see right*). Check first that the plant is likely to respond well (*see Dictionary of Climbing Plants, pp.262–287*). Mulching afterward is helpful, but do not overfeed the plant

since regrowth is likely to be vigorous. Tie in the new shoots as they develop.

If the plant will not tolerate drastic treatment (as with many evergreens), or if you are unwilling to sacrifice the effect of the climber for the time needed for it to grow back, stage the pruning over two or three years. In each year, cut only one in two or three of the main stems back to ground level (*see below*).

Detaching a climber from its support and laying it flat on the ground often makes it easier to sort out the tangle of live and dead shoots. This also permits any necessary maintenance work on walls, fences, and wooden supports to be carried out. The disentangling needs to be done with care, since stems are often very stiff or brittle. Many plants wrap themselves so firmly around supports that it is virtually impossible to remove some stems intact.

Clear away debris behind the support, which could harbor pests or diseased material, and tie the climber back onto it, spacing out the remaining shoots and securing them in position.

DRASTIC RENOVATION

Climbers that respond well to hard pruning can be cut back almost to ground level. For many, such as this honeysuckle, it is best not to cut right to the ground, but to leave 1–2ft (30–60cm) of main stem, with plenty of dormant buds that should be stimulated into life and produce strong new stems. These buds will rarely be visible, so simply cut stems across, making clean, angled cuts with loppers or a saw at the appropriate height.

RENOVATING AN OVERGROWN CLIMBER

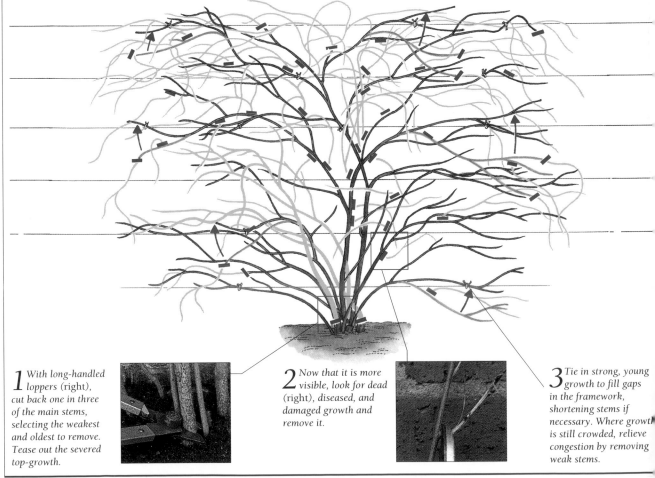

1 With long-handled loppers (right), cut back one in three of the main stems, selecting the weakest and oldest to remove. Tease out the severed top-growth.

2 Now that it is more visible, look for dead (right), diseased, and damaged growth and remove it.

3 Tie in strong, young growth to fill gaps in the framework, shortening stems if necessary. Where growth is still crowded, relieve congestion by removing weak stems.

SPECIAL TRAINING

The shape of a tree or shrub is largely enhanced by well-judged pruning cuts; climbing plants are more versatile in that they can be trained not only on vertical surfaces but also to take on the form of all kinds of supporting structures. The following pages explain and illustrate how to create striking displays by training climbers through host trees and shrubs (*see p.255*); on vertical features and arches (*see p.256*); and up and over pergolas (*see p.258*). It is possible, however, to train climbers into three-dimensional features on much simpler supports, such as basic wire frames, or even, as groundcover, with no support at all.

USING CLIMBERS AS GROUNDCOVER

The dense, trailing growth of many climbers makes ideal groundcover, particularly effective over banks and slopes. Their flowering, fruiting, and foliage displays make a welcome change from the more usually seen range of low-growing shrubs and perennials.

Groundcover plants should provide thick cover yet need little maintenance. Once established, they can be difficult to reach without stepping onto and damaging the long stems or foliage. Laying down a board to work from makes tasks such as clearing away dead matter and prunings much easier.

Ground coverage is most simply achieved by allowing suitable species to trail on the ground, guiding them if necessary with pegs. Pegging down prompts many climbers to root, increasing their vigor and spread. To peg down a climber, space its stems evenly around the planting site and anchor them with short lengths of heavy-gauge wire bent into hoops, looped over each stem and then pushed into the ground. If the pegged stems root they will become firmly anchored and the pegs can be moved elsewhere.

BOUGAINVILLEA HEDGE
In warm climates bougainvillea makes a fine hedge, covering a low framework with dense growth until the supporting structure cannot be seen. Deadheading encourages new growth, so that the surface of the hedge is covered with fresh, young foliage and flowering shoots.

TRAINING OVER A LOW FRAMEWORK

To raise a climber from ground level, train it over a low framework. Insert short posts 3–5ft (1–1.5m) apart over the allocated area. Because the climber will become heavy, the posts must be well anchored; try to have as much post below ground as above. Treat wooden posts with nontoxic preservative. Attach wires or, more simply, wire netting between the posts. Use a wide-gauge netting, with squares large enough to allow you to step into the bed. Staple it to the post tops, not too tightly. (Never rig wiring in cold weather: when the weather warms up, it will expand and go slack.) Tie the stems onto it evenly around the plant using twine in figure-eight knots (*see p.248*), then guide or tie new shoots into place.

Varying the heights of the posts, or using crumpled masses of wire netting at intervals, will create a more interesting "landscaped" effect. The wire structure can be extended to provide seamless cover over garden features such as low buildings or a fuel or propane tank.

CLIMBERS TRAINED AS HEDGES

Training climbers to make an informal hedge requires a strong framework to support plants as they develop. The framework should have ample vertical and horizontal struts or tightly stretched wires. The best climbers to use are those that make thick, woody stems. Ivies (*Hedera*) are ideal, as are *Campsis* (these need a sheltered, sunny site in cool climates) and climbing roses (*see p.316*); in subtropical climates, bougainvilleas and allamandas make good hedges.

To keep hedges neat in outline, tie in or shorten overlong shoots throughout the growing season, in addition to any regular pruning the plant may require.

CLIMBERS IN CONTAINERS

Small frames improvised from wire or wire netting make ideal supports for container-grown climbers. Many climbers are suitable for growing in containers, both outdoors and under glass – use light, nonwoody, short-lived plants with growth that is not too vigorous. (*Continued on p.254.*)

IVY AS GROUND-COVER
Any wall or sloping feature is easily covered by ivy (left). This evergreen, stem-rooting climber is popular because it is so easy to maintain; it may take a year to establish, but thereafter is likely to need only occasional trimming to keep it neatly in place.

RECOMMENDED FOR GROUNDCOVER

AKEBIA
AMPELOPSIS
ANTIGONON LEPTOPUS
CLEMATIS (especially VITICELLA GROUP)
DECUMARIA
HEDERA AZORICA, H. CANARIENSIS, H. COLCHICA, H. HELIX (vigorous cvs.)
HYDRANGEA (climbing species)
LONICERA (climbing species)
RUBUS HENRYI, R. LINEATUS, R. TRICOLOR, R. PENTALOBUS (syn. R. CALYCINOIDES)
SCHISANDRA
SCHIZOPHRAGMA
TRACHELOSPERMUM JASMINOIDES
VITIS

(*Continued from p.253.*) The climbers need support, which can be provided by wire shapes such as hoops, rings, and spheres, or by bamboo stake tripods.

Initial training of climbers on such supports is relatively easy. Climbers with only one main shoot may be cut back hard on planting to encourage new basal growth to train in. Pinch out the shoot tips of annual plants such as rhodochitons and tropaeolums to encourage several stems to form. The leading shoots are guided or tied into place until the structure is covered.

Climbers that produce aerial roots, such as epipremnums, philodendrons, *Manettia luteorubra*, and *Syngonium podophyllum*, should be trained around moss poles, to which they must be tied. The long roots that grow from their stems have little function as supports.

Once plants have reached their desired size or extent, shorten shoots to keep the required shape. Potted plants do not tend to reach the size of those in open ground, so pruning is scaled down accordingly. Many greenhouse plants have tropical origins and in a warm environment may grow continuously, with no specific dormant season; they may be pruned as needed, taking care not to remove future flowering growth.

Flowers can be encouraged on climbers that flower on the previous season's shoots; immediately prune flowered wood back to replacement shoots that will flower the following year. Plants that bloom on the current season's wood should be pruned back to a framework before growth begins.

Climbers that have become too large for their pots can be repotted and root-pruned if necessary (*see p.154*). If too large for their support and situation they may be planted out, if climate permits, or used as propagation material.

PLANTS SUITABLE FOR TRAINING ON MOSS POLES

CISSUS ANTARCTICA,
    C. RHOMBIFOLIA
EPIPREMNUM
HEDERA HELIX CVS.
MANETTIA
    LUTEORUBRA
MONSTERA DELICIOSA
PHILODENDRON SCANDENS
SENECIO
    MACROGLOSSUS
STEPHANOTIS
    FLORIBUNDA
SYNGONIUM PODOPHYLLUM

TRAINING ON A MOSS POLE
Long stem roots from plants such as this epipremnum will probe into a moss pole, which must be kept damp by misting.

PRUNING A CONTAINER-GROWN JASMINUM POLYANTHUM

BEFORE PRUNING *Jasminum polyanthum grows vigorously in warm climates, but in colder climates makes a small potted plant. It benefits from annual pruning after flowering.*

1 *Untie and gently untangle all of the stems, spreading them out around the pot. Take the opportunity now to inspect the frame for damage or instability, or insert a new frame if a*

different form is desired for next year's display. Repot the plant, or top-dress by carefully scraping away a shallow layer of soil and replacing it with fresh soil mix.

2 *Prune all the long, flowered shoots back to nonflowering sideshoots or to a pair of healthy buds.*

3 *Carefully retrain the plant over the frame, gently tying in stems as evenly as possible around the wire form.*

REGROWTH AFTER PRUNING *Feed the plant to obtain vigorous new growth. Guide new growth in horizontally around the frame for coverage and to stimulate flowering sideshoots*

TRAINING CLIMBERS THROUGH HOST PLANTS

A climber growing through a host plant can create striking visual effects. An evergreen climber will give year-round color and foliage contrast to a deciduous host tree; a summer-flowering climber in a spring-flowering host shrub gives twice-yearly blooms.

Host plants must be healthy, strong, and well established. The vigor of the climber and its weight when mature must also be able to be supported by the host. Trees, shrubs, and hedges are all suitable hosts, provided that the climber complements their growth habit and vice versa. Do not choose a shrub that needs extensive annual pruning (the presence of the climber will make this awkward), unless host and climber are pruned at the same time. Hedges are best interlaced with light annual or herbaceous climbers, which will die down and so allow access for clipping. Climbers with tendrils or twining stems are most suitable, because they will attach themselves to the stems of the host. Vigorous plants with adhesive stem roots or pads should be avoided on all but large trees: they blanket the host too closely with growth and can smother it.

CLEMATIS IN HOST
This vigorous clematis, 'Comtesse de Bouchaud', has been encouraged to grow up into a sturdy tree. Host and climber must be well matched in vigor; when two plants grow in such close proximity, one must not dominate the other.

PLANTING AND INITIAL TRAINING

Climbers planted too close to the host will be slow to establish and may lack vigor because of root competition and shading from both light and rain. Plant, ideally, at the perimeter of the crown of the host plant on its windward side, so that the prevailing wind blows shoots into, rather than out of, the host. The climber will make its way toward the sunnier side, so the garden's aspect should be borne in mind when planting.

The climber can be trained up a sturdy rope running up into the host, or be trained up a supporting stake beside the host, then across into its upper branches (this relieves smaller hosts of some of the weight of the plant).

Continuing guidance will probably be needed for the first two or three years after planting, simply by guiding and tying in main stems.

Little pruning may be possible once the climber is fully established; where feasible any weak, dead, damaged, or diseased wood should be removed and crowded growth thinned.

MATCHING HOST PLANTS AND CLIMBERS

Provided that host and climber are matched in vigor and cultivation needs, the final considerations when matching plants are esthetic ones. Colors of flowers and foliage should complement each other, but what constitutes a pleasing contrast or a color clash is always a matter of personal taste.

The "style" of the two plants must also be in keeping. For example, while in warm climates monsteras and bougainvilleas climb into lofty, tropical trees to spectacular effect, an exotic-looking evergreen such as *Berberidopsis* might seem incongruous trained into an apple or pear tree. On these trees, a *Clematis montana* or honeysuckle, for example, would provide the classic "English cottage garden" effect. Vividly colored flowers on a dark background (*see right*) have a sophisticated, urban look, whereas ivies and climbing hydrangeas climbing up wide-trunked trees invoke a more sylvan, woodland mood. Seasons of interest may be chosen to differ or coincide. A summer-flowering honeysuckle bridges the gap between an apple tree's blossoms and its ripening fruits, for example, while the orange and scarlet fruits of *Celastrus scandens* give a special added dimension to the more somber autumn color of *Cornus kousa*.

TROPAEOLUM IN YEW HEDGE
Given acid soil conditions, Tropaeolum speciosum will clamber over hedges, contrasting vividly with dark-leaved conifers. This species "runs" underground, so the flowering stems will emerge and climb at different spots along the hedge from year to year.

TRAINING CLIMBERS ON VERTICAL FEATURES

A strong vertical emphasis is introduced into the garden by training climbers on pillars, arches, tripods, or four-legged structures such as obelisks. Even a simple tripod of three rustic poles provides a strong architectural feature in garden design. Vertical features are especially effective in a border or other open part of the garden away from walls and boundaries.

CHOOSING SUITABLE CLIMBERS

All types of climbers are suitable, provided that their vigor is appropriate to the size of the structure. The selected species should be capable of reaching the top of the structure, and, if strong, tolerant of annual pruning to restrict size. Some, such as *Cobaea scandens*, are easily trained in close to a support, while others, such as honeysuckle, develop into a cascading feature.

If the winter appearance of the plant is immaterial, ideal choices for easily maintained plants are herbaceous species, or those climbers that tolerate severe pruning once their roots are established. These climbers – for example, *Clematis viticella* hybrids – produce numerous basal stems that grow to the height of the structure in

one growing season. Provided that supports are well equipped with attachment points in the shape of wiring, netting wrapped around the posts or the entire structure, or strips of trellis on wide pillars, some of these climbers will, with minimal guidance, make their own way to the top. One disadvantage, compared to plants that are cut back to framework stems each year, is that all of the growth must be untangled and removed. It is much easier to remove the wire support from the structure with the plant still on it, then remove the plant material at ground level. Another solution is to use plastic netting on the structure; then both

netting and plant can be cut away and disposed of. However, this should not be done if you intend to compost the prunings.

If you want a more permanent planting, then, even if the climber is energetic enough to reach the top in one season, it is worth spending two or three years spiraling shoots gradually around the structure to develop a well-spaced framework of stems. Because they are trained toward the horizontal, these stems will produce flowering shoots along their length. These sideshoots will need pruning according to the needs of the individual plant (*see* Dictionary of Climbing Plants, *pp.262–287*).

VIGOROUS HERBACEOUS AND ANNUAL CLIMBERS

ADLUMIA	LABLAB
CANARINA	LATHYRUS ODORATUS, L. LATIFOLIUS
CARDIOSPERMUM	MAURANDYA BARCLAYANA
CIONURA	MENISPERMUM
CLEMATIS VITICELLA HYBRIDS	MINA LOBATA
COBAEA SCANDENS	MOMORDICA
CODONOPSIS	PHASEOLUS
DIOSCOREA	THLADIANTHA
ECCREMOCARPUS	THUNBERGIA ALATA
HUMULUS LUPULUS 'AUREUS'	TRICHOSANTHES
IPOMOEA COCCINEA, I. PURPUREA	TROPAEOLUM MAJUS, T. PEREGRINUM

MIXING CLIMBERS WITH DIFFERENT TRAINING AND PRUNING NEEDS

The requirements of passion flowers (Passiflora) and late-flowering clematis complement each other well. The first is spur-pruned to permanent framework stems, while the second is cut back close to the base. Both are pruned in spring.

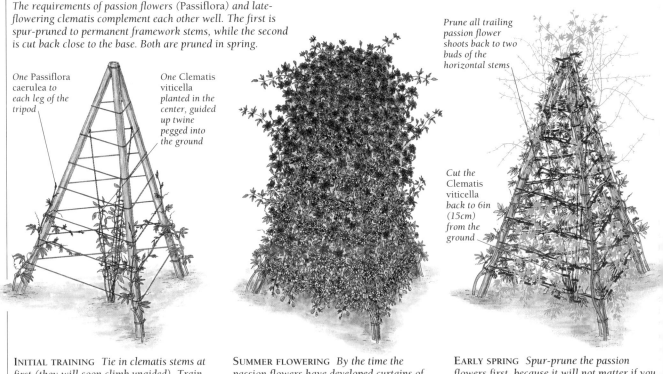

One Passiflora caerulea to each leg of the tripod

One Clematis viticella planted in the center, guided up twine pegged into the ground

Prune all trailing passion flower shoots back to two buds of the horizontal stems

Cut the Clematis viticella back to 6in (15cm) from the ground

INITIAL TRAINING *Tie in clematis stems at first (they will soon climb unaided). Train and tie in laterals from the passion flowers to make permanent horizontal arms along the wires. When they reach the next leg, cut to a bud to stimulate sideshoots.*

SUMMER FLOWERING *By the time the passion flowers have developed curtains of flowering sideshoots from their horizontal arms, the clematis has grown out and over the top, so it will not be affected adversely by the shade cast on its main stems.*

EARLY SPRING *Spur-prune the passion flowers first, because it will not matter if you cut through any clematis stems as well. Once the framework is clear, cut through the base of the clematis stems and tease (never pull) the top-growth out.*

For quick results while long-term planting matures, choose annual or herbaceous climbers, such as *Ipomoea* or *Asarina*. Tender species that can be used as annuals greatly broaden the range of climbers that can be grown in colder climates. Choosing different annuals each year will vary the effect.

TRAINING OVER AN ARCH

An arch – framing a recess, marking a boundary, or spanning a path – can be covered in many ways. Scented climbers can be fully appreciated over arches and arbors. Plants can be mixed to give a succession of flowers and scents, and nonclimbing shrubs introduced to bulk out the lower part of the arch. A woody climber can be trained up one side and over the top of the arch while an annual or herbaceous one climbs up the other. To make the best of the feature, the climbers used must tolerate regular trimming to keep the passage clear. Avoid thorny-stemmed plants, and make sure that the crossbeams are high enough so there is no need to stoop to avoid the flowers.

Plant climbers on the outside of the arch, and then space their shoots out to cover the sides, tying them into position. As growth proceeds, train laterals sideways in order to fill in any gaps. As the climber becomes established, continue to tie in the laterals sideways and extend the main stems across the top of the arch. Once the arch is covered, vigorous vertical shoots must be shortened or tied in.

MIXED PLANTING EFFECTS

Vertical features are ideal structures on which to combine two or more climbing plants to provide either a longer season of interest or eye-catching contrasts of foliage or flowers. Plants can be sited on different sides of a structure and then trained so that their stems entwine, or several plants can be used, one at the base of each leg. With this arrangement, a vigorous climber can also be planted in the center of a structure and trained rapidly up a central, vertical wire or tall stake. Its stems will then cascade from the top of the structure as those of the other plants are climbing up to meet them (*see left*).

It is very easy to cut the wrong stem when trying to prune one of two intertwined plants, so use climbers whose pruning needs are similar or complementary; for example, herbaceous or annual plants on one side and a woody-stemmed, spring-pruned climber on the other. In the latter category, roses (*see p.320*) should not be overlooked because they can provide some of the most charming and floriferous effects, whether planted alone or combined.

TRAINING CLIMBERS ON AN ARCH

Arch of metal with plastic coating is rot- and rustproof

TRAINING HUMULUS LUPULUS 'AUREUS' ON AN ARCH
Plant climbers on both sides of the arch, since stems should not be trained downward. This illustration shows golden hops at two different stages of growth, to demonstrate the changing pruning and training needs.

Plastic netting on the frame is soon disguised by foliage

ESTABLISHED PRUNING Long shoots must be shortened to maintain the arch's form. Flowering plants should be carefully pruned according to their individual needs, or flowering may be impaired. On this vigorous foliage plant, wayward shoots can be trimmed at any time.

Climber planted on outside of arch

INITIAL TRAINING Given adequate support, twining and tendriled plants will climb unaided. To direct their growth, guide young shoots into the wires or netting. Young hop shoots are fleshy and fragile, and must be handled with extreme care.

RECOMMENDED CLIMBER COMBINATIONS
ASARINA with a white-flowered clematis or rose
CLEMATIS VITICELLA with PASSIFLORA CAERULEA
JASMINUM POLYANTHUM with HOYA CARNOSA
LONICERA PERICLYMENUM 'SEROTINA' or 'BELGICA' with CLEMATIS 'JACKMANII' or
    'MADAME JULIA CORREVON'
LONICERA with perennial climbing peas (LATHYRUS LATIFOLIUS, L. NERVOSUS)
RHODOCHITON (annual) through HUMULUS LUPULUS 'AUREUS'
SOLLYA or BOMAREA with SOLANUM JASMINOIDES 'ALBUM'
SOLANUM JASMINOIDES with CLEMATIS 'LASURSTERN' or a blue C. VITICELLA HYBRID
TRACHELOSPERMUM JASMINOIDES with ECCREMOCARPUS SCABER
TROPAEOLUM PEREGRINUM through PLUMBAGO AURICULATA
VITIS VINIFERA 'PURPUREA' with annuals growing through it: sweet peas (LATHYRUS
    ODORATUS) in pale shades or, for a more vivid color contrast, nasturtiums
    (TROPAEOLUM) or black-eyed Susan (THUNBERGIA ALATA)
WISTERIA SINENSIS with a pink-flowered rose, for example 'NEW DAWN'

TRAINING CLIMBERS ON A PERGOLA

A pergola consists of either a series of posts or pillars linked by crossbeams or a row of linked arches. It needs to be sturdy and made of durable materials. A well-placed, well-constructed pergola can be a valuable and integral part of a garden design. Half-pergolas may be butted up to a wall to form a walkway or, if against a house wall, a veranda. Climbing plants are trained up the pillars and along the top, where those with trailing stems or fragrant, pendent flowers are particularly effective.

Allow 10ft (3m) of headroom, especially if you intend to use plants with trailing stems. The structure will need wiring or, for wider pillars, stapled strips of wire netting or narrow panels of trellis. Equip the pergola liberally with supports at the start; it can be a time-consuming and awkward job to add more when plants have grown.

CHOOSING SUITABLE CLIMBERS

Choose climbers that will enhance the structure and complement the materials of which it is made, not obscure it entirely. The objective is to create an open feature, rather than a tunnel of vegetation. Depending on the size of the pergola, one very energetic climber, such as a wisteria, may cover the entire structure, or several less vigorous climbers may be planted, one to each upright. If the pergola is unevenly exposed, plant more shade- or cold-tolerant climbers on the less favored side to match the strong growth of plants on the sunny side.

TRAINING AND PRUNING

There are two ways of training the climbers up the pillars: straight up, or spiraled. Choose the former if you want plants to cover the canopy rapidly, although their stems will become bare at the base. If you want the plants to flower on the pillars as well as over the top, then spiral the stems. Bare stems at the base of established climbers may be concealed by underplanting with shrubs or with light annual climbers, such as nasturtiums and sweet peas.

Once the stems have reached the tops of the posts, spread them evenly over the crossbeams, tying them in position. Prune them according to the individual needs of the plants (*see* Dictionary of Climbing Plants, *pp.262–287*). Long-handled tree pruners are invaluable for snipping off, or hooking down, long stems. If climbing a ladder, make sure it is firmly positioned, and resist the temptation to overreach, particularly above your head or behind you; the job may take longer, but will be much safer, if you climb down and move the ladder.

VERY VIGOROUS CLIMBERS

ACTINIDIA ARGUTA
BIGNONIA CAPREOLATA
CLEMATIS MONTANA
LONICERA
   HILDEBRANDTIANA
POLYGONUM
VITIS COIGNETIAE
WISTERIA SINENSIS

QUICK COVERAGE
Very vigorous climbers will cover a pergola quickly, but their exuberant growth often needs to be checked. Some plants can simply be cropped back to the pergola framework with shears (above) but others need more precise pruning.

Long shoots can be snipped back or tucked into other growth

FREE-FLOWERING CLIMBERS

BOUGAINVILLEA
CAMPSIS
CLEMATIS
LONICERA
PYROSTEGIA VENUSTA
THUNBERGIA
   GRANDIFLORA
WISTERIA

PRUNING FOR FLOWERS
Although some climbers require little, if any, attention to flower freely, others, including Clematis *and* Wisteria, *perform best if regularly pruned.*

Lonicera periclymenum

SHORT CLIMBERS FOR BARE BASES
Where plants have been trained straight up pillars to cover the top quickly, lower stems may be bare. Use small shrubs or short or annual climbers to cover the base of each pillar.

Ipomoea tricolor

FOR PILLAR BASES
HARDENBERGIA VIOLACEA
IPOMOEA TRICOLOR,
   I. LOBATA
LATHYRUS ODORATUS
MANETTIA
RHODOCHITON
SOLLYA
THUNBERGIA ALATA (*left*)
TROPAEOLUM MAJUS,
   T. TUBEROSUM

Posts may be brick, metal, hardwoods, or pressure-treated pine

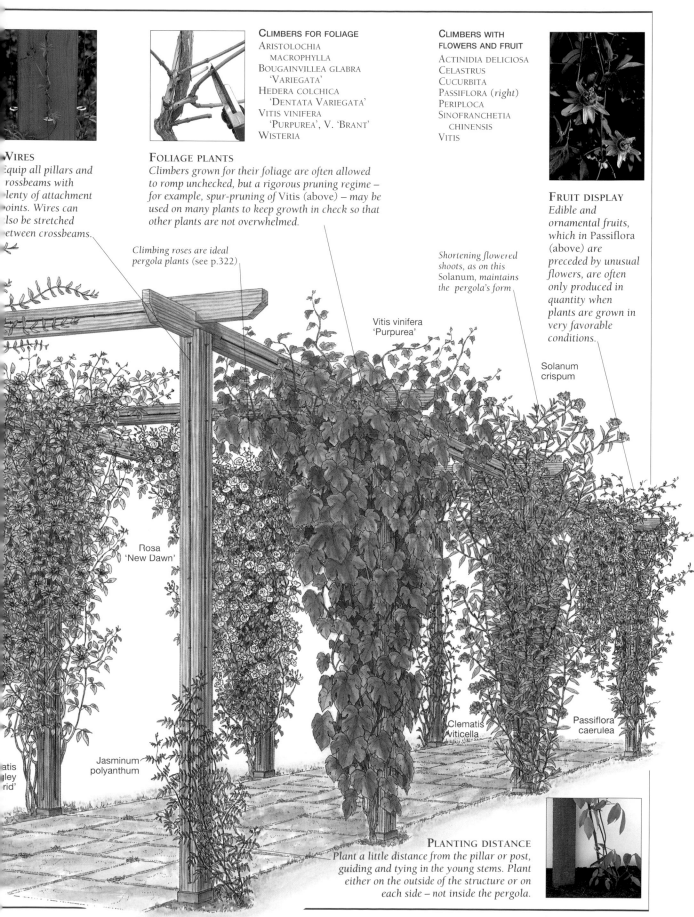

CLIMBERS FOR FOLIAGE
ARISTOLOCHIA
    MACROPHYLLA
BOUGAINVILLEA GLABRA
    'VARIEGATA'
HEDERA COLCHICA
    'DENTATA VARIEGATA'
VITIS VINIFERA
    'PURPUREA', V. 'BRANT'
WISTERIA

**CLIMBERS WITH
FLOWERS AND FRUIT**
ACTINIDIA DELICIOSA
CELASTRUS
CUCURBITA
PASSIFLORA (*right*)
PERIPLOCA
SINOFRANCHETIA
    CHINENSIS
VITIS

WIRES
Equip all pillars and
crossbeams with
plenty of attachment
points. Wires can
also be stretched
between crossbeams.

FOLIAGE PLANTS
*Climbers grown for their foliage are often allowed
to romp unchecked, but a rigorous pruning regime –
for example, spur-pruning of* Vitis (*above*) – *may be
used on many plants to keep growth in check so that
other plants are not overwhelmed.*

FRUIT DISPLAY
*Edible and
ornamental fruits,
which in* Passiflora
(*above*) *are
preceded by unusual
flowers, are often
only produced in
quantity when
plants are grown in
very favorable
conditions.*

Climbing roses are ideal
pergola plants (see p.322)

Shortening flowered
shoots, as on this
Solanum, maintains
the pergola's form

Vitis vinifera
'Purpurea'

Solanum
crispum

Rosa
'New Dawn'

Clematis
Viticella

Passiflora
caerulea

atis
ley
rid'

Jasminum
polyanthum

PLANTING DISTANCE
*Plant a little distance from the pillar or post,
guiding and tying in the young stems. Plant
either on the outside of the structure or on
each side – not inside the pergola.*

TRAINING CLIMBERS AS STANDARDS

Most climbers used as standards can never be completely freestanding. They need a permanent stake of wood or other durable material such as wrought iron, or one of the umbrella frames used for weeping rose standards (*see p.311*).

Climbers that can be spur-pruned to a framework, such as wisteria, are ideal as standards, as are those that tolerate regular pruning, such as honeysuckles and, especially, those climbers with dense, evergreen foliage that can be trimmed without revealing bare growth beneath, such as ivy. Do not use climbers with wispy or wiry stems, particularly strongly twining or tendriled climbers, because they will become very tangled. Plants with aerial roots can be used; these roots normally develop only when the stem touches a suitable surface.

FORMATIVE TRAINING

Plant and stake a young plant with one sturdy stem, removing others if necessary, although several stems can be twisted or braided together (*see Topiary, p.48*). Training (*see right*) initially aims to form a strong, thick trunk, so laterals are cleared only gradually, just as for a standard tree (*see p.28*); the remaining foliage "feeds" and thickens the main stem. Annual shortening of the main stem and training on the new topmost shoot as the new leader also encourages vigorous growth. If the leader is damaged, train in a replacement as for a standard tree (*see p.26*). Once the desired height of clear stem has been achieved, shorten laterals and their

TRAINING A CLIMBER (WISTERIA) AS A 5FT (1.5M) STANDARD

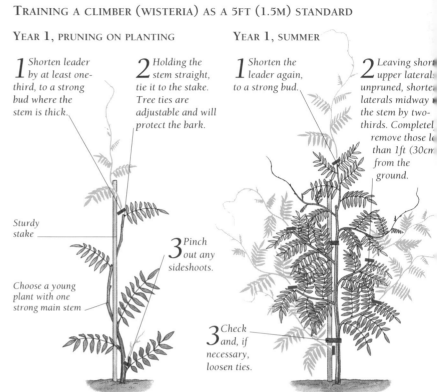

YEAR 1, PRUNING ON PLANTING

1 *Shorten leader by at least one-third, to a strong bud where the stem is thick.*

2 *Holding the stem straight, tie it to the stake. Tree ties are adjustable and will protect the bark.*

Sturdy stake

Choose a young plant with one strong main stem

3 *Pinch out any sideshoots.*

YEAR 1, SUMMER

1 *Shorten the leader again, to a strong bud.*

2 *Leaving short upper lateral[s] unpruned, shorten[s] laterals midway [up] the stem by two-thirds. Completel[y] remove those le[ss] than 1ft (30cm) from the ground.*

3 *Check and, if necessary, loosen ties.*

sideshoots to develop a strong, compact, well-structured framework, with bushy growth, for the head.

PRUNING AN ESTABLISHED STANDARD

Adapt the routine pruning for the individual plant as necessary to maintain

the form. In winter, prune to enhance the shape of the head (pruning harder on a weak side), and remove older wood to reduce congestion. In summer, shorten long shoots to restrict size and encourage dense foliage and, if appropriate, flowers.

WISTERIA STANDARD
Today, standards 5–6ft (1.5–2m) tall are popular for patios and borders, but in the past standards were made much taller, with heads above top-hat or parasol height. Most of the great Victorian *wisteria standards still in existence in British gardens have fragments of metal embedded in them which were once part of their supporting pillars.*

CLIMBING PLANTS SUITABLE TO TRAIN AS STANDARDS

ACTINIDIA ARGUTA, A. KOLOMIKTA
BAUHINIA CORYMBOSA
BEAUMONTIA GRANDIFLORA
BIGNONIA CAPREOLATA
BOUGAINVILLEA GLABRA, B. PERUVIANA
CAMPSIS RADICANS
CLERODENDRUM THOMSONIAE
COMBRETUM GRANDIFLORUM
HEDERA HELIX
HYDRANGEA PETIOLARIS, H. SEEMANNII
JASMINUM POLYANTHUM
LONICERA PERICLYMENUM, L. JAPONICA
MANDEVILLA X AMOENA, M. SPLENDENS
MUSSAENDA ARCUATA, M. ERYTHROPHYLLA
PANDOREA JASMINOIDES, P. PANDORANA
PETREA VOLUBILIS
PLUMBAGO AURICULATA (SYN. P. CAPENSIS)
PYROSTEGIA VENUSTA
SCHIZOPHRAGMA HYDRANGEOIDES
SOLANDRA GRANDIFLORA, S. MAXIMA
SOLANUM CRISPUM, S. JASMINOIDES
STEPHANOTIS FLORIBUNDA
STREPTOSOLEN JAMESII
TECOMARIA CAPENSIS
VITIS AMURENSIS, V. VINIFERA
WISTERIA FLORIBUNDA, W. SINENSIS

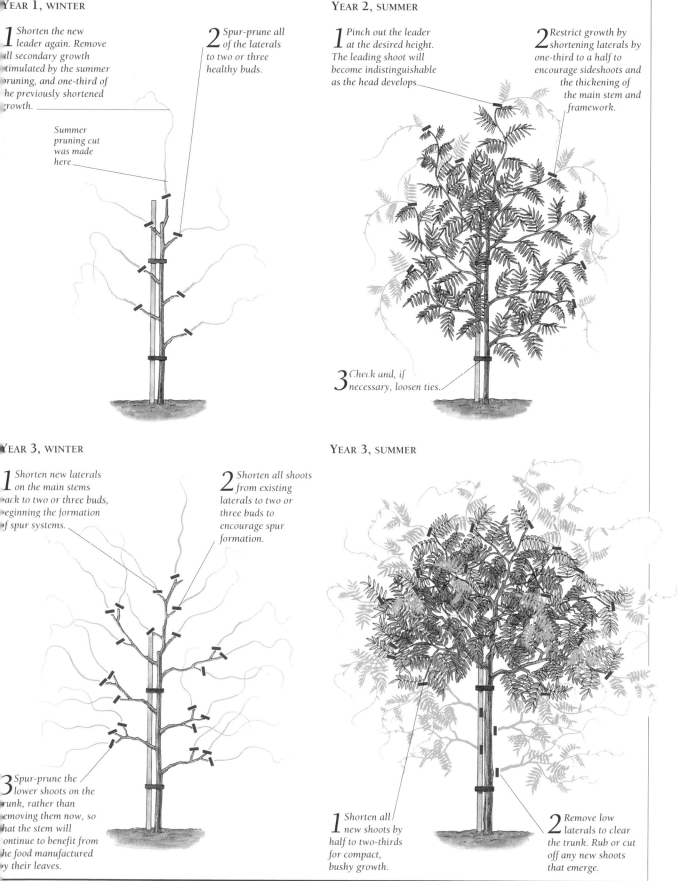

YEAR 1, WINTER

1 Shorten the new leader again. Remove all secondary growth stimulated by the summer pruning, and one-third of the previously shortened growth.

Summer pruning cut was made here

2 Spur-prune all of the laterals to two or three healthy buds.

YEAR 2, SUMMER

1 Pinch out the leader at the desired height. The leading shoot will become indistinguishable as the head develops.

2 Restrict growth by shortening laterals by one-third to a half to encourage sideshoots and the thickening of the main stem and framework.

3 Check and, if necessary, loosen ties.

YEAR 3, WINTER

1 Shorten new laterals on the main stems back to two or three buds, beginning the formation of spur systems.

2 Shorten all shoots from existing laterals to two or three buds to encourage spur formation.

3 Spur-prune the lower shoots on the trunk, rather than removing them now, so that the stem will continue to benefit from the food manufactured by their leaves.

YEAR 3, SUMMER

1 Shorten all new shoots by half to two-thirds for compact, bushy growth.

2 Remove low laterals to clear the trunk. Rub or cut off any new shoots that emerge.

261

DICTIONARY OF CLIMBING PLANTS

A

ACTINIDIA

Mainly hardy, deciduous, twining climbers valued for their alternate, oblong to heart-shaped leaves, splashed with color in some species. Foliage color is best when plants are trained up into the sun, although the base of the plant should be in semishade. They have white, cream, or buff flowers; where plants of both sexes are grown, females produce large, sometimes edible fruits (*A. deliciosa* is the kiwi fruit or Chinese gooseberry). Most species need ample space and the support of sturdy fences, pergolas or strong tripods, or large trees; *A. kolomikta* is a less vigorous species.

ACTINIDIA KOLOMIKTA
Trained on a fully sunny wall, the leaves of A. kolomikta *will color well.*

A. KOLOMIKTA (ZONES 5–8)

Climber grown principally for its large leaves, attractively splashed with creamy pink and white.

WHEN TO PRUNE Late winter or early spring, before growth begins. Shorten overly vigorous or badly placed shoots in summer.

TRAINING AND PRUNING Cut young plants back to strong buds about 12–16in (30–40cm) above ground level to encourage basal growth. Select five to seven strong shoots, tying in as growth proceeds. In the second season, cut back strong laterals by two-thirds of their length, and weaker shoots to one or two buds. Remove any very weak growth. Once established, to keep within bounds, shorten growth by one-third to half of its length, cutting back to a healthy bud. Remove an old main stem at the base occasionally, to encourage new growth. Renovate by cutting all tangled growth back to the framework of main stems in spring.

> **OTHER ACTINIDIAS**
> A. DELICIOSA (syn. A. CHINENSIS) *See* Kiwi fruit, *p.297.*
> A. ARGUTA As for *A. kolomikta.* Much more vigorous and particularly suitable for training through large trees. Pruning established plants trained in this way may prove impractical.
> A. POLYGAMA As for *A. kolomikta.*

AKEBIA QUINATA
Train the chocolate vine where its small, brownish purple flowers and their vanilla scent can be appreciated close at hand.

AKEBIA (ZONES 5–8)

Vigorous, deciduous or semievergreen twiners, with elegant divided foliage and maroon to chocolate-purple flowers followed, after long, hot summers, by pendent, sausage-shaped, violet to gray-purple, edible fruits. Tolerant of sun or semishade, akebias are suitable for walls, fences, or pergolas. Plant as young as possible. Guide young stems into the support, and tie in until they begin to twine. Train and prune as for *Actinidia kolomikta* (*see left*), but prune in late spring, after flowering.

ALLAMANDA (ZONE 10)

Evergreen scramblers with large, paired, glossy leaves and showy flowers. They prefer subtropical conditions; while mature specimens may survive light frost, they are better grown under glass (or in pots that can be brought under cover in winter) in cooler areas. Grow against pillars, walls, or a strong trellis.

WHEN TO PRUNE Late winter, before active growth begins.

TRAINING AND PRUNING After planting, pinch back young shoots to encourage bushy growth, and tie in new shoots to form a framework as growth proceeds. Once established, prune annually by shortening sideshoots to within two or three pairs of buds of the main framework stems. Remove weak, dead, or unwanted growth at the same time. They respond well to hard pruning.

AGAPETES (ZONE 10)

Agapetes (syn. *Pentapterygium*) are scandent, semiscrambling evergreens bearing pendent flowers from winter to spring beneath branches that often have a delightful zigzag growth pattern. All are cold-sensitive. In frost-prone climates, grow them in a humid conservatory, in dappled shade. Train young plants against a wall or trellis. Space out the main shoots to give even coverage, and tie in as growth proceeds. Prune in late winter or early spring to remove badly placed growth if necessary. *A. macrantha* looks better with slightly more formal training than *A. serpens*. Established plants need little pruning, other than to remove weak, dead, or badly placed growth. *Agapetes* do not respond well to hard pruning.

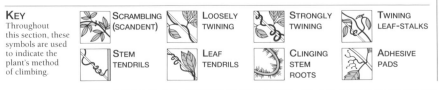

KEY
Throughout this section, these symbols are used to indicate the plant's method of climbing.

SCRAMBLING (SCANDENT)

STEM TENDRILS

LOOSELY TWINING

LEAF TENDRILS

STRONGLY TWINING

CLINGING STEM ROOTS

TWINING LEAF-STALKS

ADHESIVE PADS

AMPELOPSIS (ZONES 4–8)

Deciduous, woody-stemmed, tendriled vines with handsome, pinnate, or lobed leaves. The insignificant flowers are sometimes followed by attractive berries. Vigorous and sometimes weedy in moist, warm regions, *Ampelopsis* are generally too large for small gardens, but are ideal for sheltered pergolas or fences and, with initial support, will scramble through trees. If grown on house walls, cut back in winter to prevent rampant growth from clogging gutters and dislodging roof tiles. Provide initial support by tying in strong young shoots. Subsequent training and pruning is as for *Vitis* (*see p.286*).

ANEMOPAEGMA

Evergreen tendriled climbers (zone 10) with trumpet-shaped flowers, borne during summer at the leaf axils of the current season's growth. They need a humid greenhouse in cool climates. After planting, tip-prune all shoots to encourage strong growth. Tie shoots in as they grow to develop a framework. In later years, shorten all laterals to within two or three buds or nodes of the main stems, and remove weak shoots, pruning in late winter or early spring. If the plant becomes congested, prune also during summer, thinning out surplus stems. Responds well to hard pruning.

ANREDERA (ZONE 9)
MADEIRA VINE, MIGNONETTE VINE

Twining evergreens with racemes of small, fragrant flowers and heart-shaped leaves, often herbaceous, dying down in winter and regenerating from the base in spring. Ideal for pergolas and fences in warm, dry climates; in cooler regions, grow against a conservatory wall or pillar. Training consists only of guiding growth to the support. In late winter or early spring, cut back all of previous year's growth by one-third to half of its length, or if growth has died back, cut almost to ground level.

ANTIGONON (ZONE 10)

Perennial, scrambling evergreens with slender stems, sometimes developing tendrils and racemes of coral pink to red flowers, mainly in summer, but all year in tropical conditions. They will cover buildings, arbors, or large pergolas in tropical and subtropical gardens, but in cooler areas they must be grown under glass. Little training is needed other than to guide new growth into supports. In early spring, cut overly vigorous growth back hard, removing weak, congested, or damaged shoots at the same time.

ARGYREIA (ZONE 10)

Vigorous, woody-stemmed climbers, producing soft annual shoots that die back to a woody framework during winter. The flowers, which open in sunshine from late summer to autumn, are funnel-shaped, pink to lavender or maroon, with distinctive hairy outer bands. Suitable for arbors, pergolas, and trellises in tropical gardens; in cooler climates, plant in a conservatory border in full sun. Provide strong support with wires or a trellis.

ARISTOLOCHIA DUTCHMAN'S PIPE, BIRTHWORT

Vigorous, deciduous or evergreen, twining climbers grown for their extraordinary siphon-shaped, often bad-smelling flowers. Many species, such as *A. elegans* (syn. *A. littoralis*), are subtropical and in cooler areas need warm greenhouse conditions, but *A. macrophylla* (syn. *A. durior*) is hardy in zones 5 to 8. All suit sunny or partly shaded sheltered walls. The large leaves will form a solid, attractive screen if grown on a trellis, arbor, or pergola. Plant in late spring or early summer.

WHEN TO PRUNE Late winter or early spring, or in midsummer after flowering.

TRAINING AND PRUNING After planting, select the strongest shoots and train in to the support. Remove all weak and straggly growth, cutting out close to the

ASARINA (ZONES 9–10)

Asarina (syn. *Maurandia*, *Maurandella*) are scandent to twining, evergreen perennials with soft, diamond- or heart-shaped leaves and pouched flowers in pink and purple (occasionally yellow). *A. barclaiana* is frost-tender; most others tolerate light frosts, and are herbaceous in cool climates. Scrambling types – *A. antirrhinifolia*, *A. erubescens*, and *A. scandens* – need tying to lightweight support such as wires, stakes, or twiggy branches. They need no pruning, other than to cut back dead or damaged growth in spring before growth begins.

WHEN TO PRUNE Late winter, before new growth begins.

TRAINING AND PRUNING Tie in young growth to give well-spaced coverage of the support, and remove excess growth carefully during the growing season, if necessary. In subsequent years, if the previous season's growth has been very vigorous, thin surplus shoots by cutting back to within one or two buds or nodes of the main framework. Responds well to hard pruning if necessary.

TWINING ARISTOLOCHIA STEMS
Aristolochias respond well to hard pruning, producing new shoots that will twine around wires and develop trailing sideshoots.

base. Once established, remove weak growth and cut back long shoots or stems to two or three nodes of the main stems. This can be done annually, in midsummer after flowering or in early spring. Responds well to hard pruning.

OTHER CLIMBING PLANTS
ADLUMIA As for *Asarina* (*see above*).
ARAUJIA Guide twining stems in to the support. Prune only to remove dead or badly placed growth in spring. Responds reasonably well to hard pruning.
ASPARAGUS Treat *A. scandens* as for *Bomarea* (*see p.264*).
ASTERANTHERA As for *Berberidopsis* (*see p.264*).
BAUHINIA On planting, select four or five strong shoots from which to develop a framework on wires or trellis. Once established, after flowering, spur-prune laterals to four or five buds of the framework stems. Do not prune hard.

B

BEAUMONTIA (ZONE 10)

Beaumontia grandiflora (herald's trumpet, Nepal trumpet flower) is a vigorous, evergreen, woody-stemmed, twining climber, grown for its handsome paired leaves and fragrant flowers, borne at the tips of the previous season's growth. It needs a frost-free, temperate climate, or protection under glass, and substantial support, such as thick wires, pillars, or a large tree. After planting, select four or five strong shoots and tie in to the support to give well-spaced coverage. Cut the remaining shoots back to their bases. Once established, prune annually after flowering to thin the plant out; remove weak growth, and prune strong laterals to within two or three nodes of the main framework stems. Beaumontias will respond well to hard pruning.

BERBERIDOPSIS CORALLINA
Glossy green leaves set off the pendent clusters of fleshy, red, globular flowers.

BERBERIDOPSIS

Berberidopsis corallina, the coral vine, is a woody-stemmed, twining and scrambling evergreen (zones 9 and 10). It needs a sheltered, shaded or semishaded wall with wires or trellises, or let it scramble through other plants. It is tender and may die back in hard winters; established plants usually resprout from below ground if protected with a winter mulch.

Guide and tie in young shoots at first; they usually become self-supporting once the plant is established. Cut out weak or dead growth from the base of established plants, pruning in spring after any danger of hard frost has passed. If the interlocking stems become congested, remove the weakest growth, cutting back to a main stem or strong bud. Does not respond well to hard pruning.

BERCHEMIA

Scrambling climbers, with oval, alternate leaves and panicles of white or greenish white flowers, followed by attractive berrylike fruits, blue-black in the vigorous *B. scandens*. They grow best if sheltered from cold winds. On walls and fences, provide the support of sturdy wires or a trellis, or grow through large shrubs or over tree stumps.

B. RACEMOSA (ZONES 6–9)

Deciduous scrambler with heart-shaped leaves that turn yellow in autumn. The late summer flowers are followed by red berries that turn black when ripe. The cultivar 'Variegata' has leaves that are attractively marked with creamy white.

BIGNONIA

Bignonia capreolata (cross vine, trumpet flower) is a vigorous evergreen with orange flowers, climbing by leaf tendrils. In a sunny, sheltered site it will tolerate light frost. Suitable for tall posts; wall-grown specimens need strong wires or a trellis. After planting, select two or three strong shoots as the main framework stems and tie in. In subsequent springs, before growth begins, shorten the previous season's laterals by up to two-thirds, cutting to a strong, well-placed bud. Tie in or remove surplus shoots. To renovate, cut back hard into old wood once any danger of frost has passed.

BILLARDIERA (ZONE 10)

Slender-stemmed, evergreen twiners with attractive flowers and fruits. They need shelter from hot sun and cold winds, and although they tolerate very light frost, they grow best in a completely frost-free climate. In cool climates, they are ideal for a shaded conservatory or greenhouse. Provide support with a light trellis or netting, or grow through shrubs or other, more vigorous climbers.

WHEN TO PRUNE Early spring, or late summer, after fruiting.

TRAINING AND PRUNING Keep pruning to a minimum. Tie in young shoots to provide even coverage of the support. Once established, plants usually need pruning only to remove dead or badly placed growth, but if congested, cut back surplus shoots to within two or three buds or nodes of a main stem.

WHEN TO PRUNE Late winter or very early spring.

TRAINING AND PRUNING Tie in young shoots as growth proceeds, until even coverage of the support is achieved. Once plants are established, prune annually to remove dead or damaged growth, thin out congested shoots, and shorten any stems that have outgrown their allotted space. Responds well to hard pruning.

> **OTHER BERCHEMIAS**
> B. SCANDENS As for *B. racemosa*, but prune in spring, immediately after flowering.

BOMAREA (ZONE 10)

Herbaceous or evergreen, tuberous-rooted, scrambling and twining climbers. They are grown for their clusters of brightly colored, alstroemeria-like flowers. They need a position in full sun and a frost-free climate. Provide upright supports, with wires or trellises, or allow plants to clamber up and through shrubs or other climbers. They need little formative pruning. Herbaceous species, such as *B. caldasii*, die back completely during winter. In spring all dead growth can be cut back to the base. With evergreen species, remove the old, flowered stems after flowering, when the leaves begin to turn yellow.

BILLARDIERA LONGIFLORA
The narrowly bell-shaped, greenish yellow (sometimes purple-tinged) flowers are followed by large, glossy, purple-blue fruits.

BOUGAINVILLEA

Vigorous, deciduous or evergreen, often spiny, woody-stemmed climbers, with ovate or elliptic bright green leaves (zone 10). The insignificant flowers are surrounded by brilliantly colored bracts, mostly in white and shades of magenta, crimson, violet, or purple. They flower on the current season's growth. In warm climates bougainvilleas are very effective grown up large trees or on walls. They need full sun and tend to flower most freely in tropical or subtropical conditions, growing very well under glass. In cool climates, grow in large tubs or bricked-in beds in a warm conservatory; they usually flower better if their roots are confined. *B. glabra* and *B.* x *buttiana* are best for containers, since they flower even when young. All need the support of a sturdy trellis or pillars. They may be trained as standards and spur-pruned annually to restrict size.

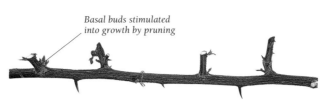

Basal buds stimulated into growth by pruning

WHEN TO PRUNE Late winter or early spring, just before growth begins.

TRAINING AND PRUNING It is essential to develop a well-spaced, strong framework of stems. To train as a climber, prune back hard at first to stimulate strong growth from the base, then tie in shoots as growth proceeds. Tie in only the strongest shoots, removing others; if too many stems are trained in initially, plants will be overcrowded at maturity, especially when confined against a wall (*see below*). In subsequent years, reduce leading shoots by two-thirds to three-quarters of the previous season's growth, cutting back to a strong bud. Cut back

laterals and sideshoots that are not needed to tie in to extend the framework to within two or three buds of the main stems; the shoots that emerge will bear the current year's flowers. Once the framework is established, cut back all the previous season's lateral shoots to two or three buds, to leave spurs about ¾–1¼in (2–3cm) in length. During the growing season, remove weak growth as necessary. Old plants should respond to hard pruning, but are better replaced.

To train as a standard, *see p.260*. Once a balanced head is formed, cut back all the previous season's laterals to within two or three buds of the branch framework each year.

SPUR-PRUNED BOUGAINVILLEA
All sideshoots have been pruned hard to two or three buds.

WALL TRAINING A BOUGAINVILLEA

PRUNING ON PLANTING, SPRING

1 Fan out strong shoots and tie in to form an evenly spaced framework.

2 Shorten all shoots to 6–8in (15–20cm), cutting to just above a healthy bud pointing in such a direction that the new shoots will not cross each other.

YEAR 2 UNTIL ALLOTTED SPACE IS COVERED, SPRING

1 Prune back the previous season's growth by three-quarters, then tie in new leading shoots as they appear.

2 Cut any sideshoots back to one or two leaves or buds to start encouraging the development of flowering spurs.

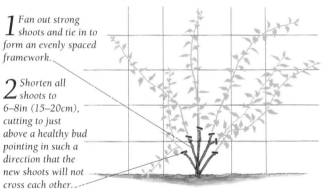

ESTABLISHED BOUGAINVILLEA, SPRING

1 Where shoots exceed the allotted space, cut back to a healthy bud or sideshoot.

2 Where growth is crowded, cut out some older stems, tying in a young sideshoot to fill any gaps in the framework.

3 Spur-prune all other sideshoots to ¾–1¼in (2–3cm), leaving two or three leaves or buds.

ESTABLISHED BOUGAINVILLEA, SUMMER

1 Deadhead as flowers fade, cutting entire flower clusters back to a young, nonflowering sideshoot.

2 As growth develops, tie in new shoots where there is space to do so.

C

CALCEOLARIA (ZONE 10)

Calceolaria pavonii is the only commonly grown climbing species in this varied genus; a robust, evergreen scrambler with a woody base and rather triangular, dark green leaves. It bears showy trusses of pouched, sulfur yellow flowers, sometimes banded with brown-purple, from late summer through to winter on the current year's growth. It makes good groundcover and will also grow well in containers. It needs a completely frost-free climate, and with sufficient rainfall, it will flower well in relatively cool summers; in these conditions it may adopt the habit of a semiwoody subshrub. Provide light support if grown on a wall or in a conservatory.

WHEN TO PRUNE Early spring, before new growth begins.

TRAINING AND PRUNING After planting, pinch back young shoots to encourage the production of vigorous sideshoots that will form framework stems. Train in the new stems to the support, either vertically or over a horizontal framework as groundcover. Subsequently prune established plants annually: trim out weak, dead, or unwanted growth, and reduce the remaining shoots by up to two-thirds of their length, cutting back to a strong healthy bud. Calceolarias respond reasonably well to hard pruning, but old plants should be replaced by strong young ones.

CALOCHONE (ZONE 10)

Calochone redingii is a moderately vigorous, evergreen, scrambling climber with hairy, elliptical leaves and trusses of handsome, red or orange-pink flowers. These tubular flowers are borne in midwinter on growth made during the previous growing season. It must be grown in full light and in warm tropical conditions. Provide the support of wires or a trellis.

WHEN TO PRUNE After flowering, in late winter or early spring.

TRAINING AND PRUNING Pruning is best kept to a minimum other than to remove weak or unwanted growth. Tie in all shoots to the support as growth proceeds. Once the plant is established, prune annually by thinning out overcrowded shoots, cutting back to main stems. It dislikes hard pruning.

CAMPSIS TRUMPET CREEPER, TRUMPET VINE

Vigorous, deciduous, woody-stemmed climbers, often clinging by means of small aerial stem roots. They are grown for their handsome, pinnate leaves and the bold terminal trusses of orange to red, trumpet-shaped flowers, produced on the current season's growth from late summer to autumn. Although frost-tolerant, they need shelter from cold winds and full sun to ripen the wood if they are to flower freely. Grow against a high sunny wall; in Mediterranean-type climates, they thrive on fences or tree trunks.

C. GRANDIFLORA (ZONES 7–9)

CHINESE TRUMPET CREEPER, TRUMPET VINE

Campsis grandiflora (syn. *C. chinensis*, *Bignonia grandiflora*, *Tecoma grandiflora*) has trumpet-shaped, deep orange flowers, yellow within, and up to 3in (8cm) across. It forms few aerial roots, so tie in the main stems to a strong support.

WHEN TO PRUNE Late winter or early spring.

TRAINING AND PRUNING It is essential to establish a strong woody framework. After planting, prune all stems back hard to about 6in (15cm) above ground level to promote vigorous growth. Select two or three of the strongest shoots and remove the rest. Train in to the supporting wires or trellis, and tie in as growth proceeds, until shoots extend fully over the allotted space. In most cases, an area at least 12ft (4m) high is needed. It may take two or three seasons to complete the framework. Once it is established, prune the plant annually, spur-pruning all lateral shoots back to within two or three buds of the main stems. Remove weak or diseased growth entirely. *Campsis* respond well to hard pruning. If a main framework branch is damaged, cut it back to the base, and train in the strongest of the resulting replacement shoots. Renovate by cutting back all growth to within 12in (30cm) of the ground to encourage strong new shoots to break from the base.

OTHER CAMPSIS

C. RADICANS (zone 4) As for *C. grandiflora*, but produces small stem roots more freely and is completely self-clinging once established.
C. X TAGLIABUANA (zone 4) As for *C. grandiflora*.

CAMPSIS X TAGLIABUANA *After spur-pruning in winter (below), new shoots grow and flower in a single season.*

CANARINA CANARY BELLFLOWER (ZONE 10)

Herbaceous, scrambling climbers or trailing perennials, with large, pendulous, bell-shaped flowers of yellow or orange-yellow, handsomely marked with green or reddish lines. They have a tuberous root that can be lifted, removing all top-growth, and stored over winter, as for dahlias. They are frost-tender, preferring a Mediterranean-type climate with dry winters; they may be grown under glass in cooler climates, trained on supports. They flower from late summer to early winter, after which the top-growth dies back. Each year, cut back dead growth close to the ground in spring, being careful not to damage any emerging new growth. Once new shoots are growing strongly, their tips may be pinched out to encourage branching. Guide and, if necessary, tie stems into the support as growth proceeds.

CANTUA (ZONE 10)

Cantua buxifolia (syn. *C. dependens*) is a scandent evergreen with slender stems that look good arching over and through other shrubs, or tied in informally to a wall or pillar. It bears drooping clusters of trumpet-shaped, magenta-red flowers in spring, on the previous season's wood. Frost-tender, it prefers a Mediterranean-type climate.

WHEN TO PRUNE After flowering, in late spring or early summer.

TRAINING AND PRUNING Needs little training or pruning. Tip-prune the shoots after planting to encourage strong new growth. Once established, prune only to shape or remove weak growth. Reduce overcrowding, if necessary, by thinning out old flowered shoots. Does not respond well to hard pruning.

CANTUA BUXIFOLIA
Sometimes known as the sacred or magic flower of the Incas, this South American native needs hot, sunny conditions.

CARDIOSPERMUM

Cardiospermum halicacabum (balloon vine, heart pea, winter cherry) is a deciduous, perennial, scandent climber with slender, woody-based stems and dissected leaves (zone 10). It is grown mainly for its curious, inflated, yellow-green fruits that follow the small summer flowers. The flower clusters produce clinging tendrils. It needs warm, frost-free conditions, but in cool climates can be grown outdoors in full sun as an annual. Provide support with a trellis or twiggy branches, or grow as groundcover. When grown as a perennial, cut back all the previous year's growth by two-thirds to three-quarters of its length in spring.

CELASTRUS *BITTERSWEET*

Deciduous twiners or scramblers grown for their spectacular autumn displays of fruits. Plants of both sexes must be grown together to produce fruit (although hermaphrodite forms of *C. orbiculatus* are available). Bittersweets are tough, energetic, and tolerate semishade. Most are vigorous, needing ample space and strong supports. Generally unsuitable for house walls, but they look good on big garden walls, or festooning garden buildings or large tree stumps. They can also be trained on sturdy pillars or tripods.

C. SCANDENS (ZONES 3–8)

AMERICAN BITTERSWEET

Celastrus scandens is a vigorous, deciduous, twining climber with deep yellow fruits in autumn that split to reveal pink or red seeds.

WHEN TO PRUNE Winter or early spring.

TRAINING AND PRUNING After planting, guide in new growth to the support as growth proceeds. Established plants need little regular pruning, but remove old or badly placed growth and any that arches out too far from the support, cutting shoots back to their base. Trim back overlong laterals to within three or four buds of the main stem, if needed. Overpruning leads to the production of many vigorous, leafy shoots, with fewer flowers and fruits. However, large, old

CELASTRUS ORBICULATUS
Both male and female plants must be grown to obtain these decorative fruits.

branches can be cut back hard to within 12–16in (30–40cm) of ground level and will usually resprout. Train in the strongest new shoots to fill any gaps in the framework, and remove the rest.

OTHER CELASTRUS
C. ANGULATUS, C. RUGOSUS, C. ORBICULATUS As for *C. scandens*. C. GLAUCOPHYLLUS Scandent in habit rather than twining, and thus needs more tying in to its support. Otherwise, as for *C. scandens*.

CIONURA (ZONE 10)

Cionura erecta (syn. *Marsdenia erecta*) is a deciduous twiner with heart-shaped, gray-green leaves and fragrant, five-petaled white flowers during summer. Its fruits split to reveal silky seeds. It grows best in full sun and must have frost-free conditions. The milky sap may cause skin blistering, so avoid contact.

No formative pruning is needed. Tie young shoots in loosely until they begin to twine. Once established, prune after flowering, or in early spring in cool areas, to remove weak or dead growth. Thin overcrowded shoots by cutting them back to their base in early spring. Suitable for use as groundcover. Does not respond well to hard pruning.

CISSUS *GRAPE IVY* (ZONE 10)

Evergreen, woody-stemmed vines, most of which are tendriled climbers. Grape ivies are grown mainly for their handsome, lush foliage. *C. discolor*, the rex begonia vine, needs tropical conditions, but *C. antarctica* (kangaroo vine), *C. rhombifolia* (Venezuela treebine), and *C. striata* (miniature grape ivy) will tolerate cooler frost-free conditions and may be grown under

glass in cool climates or as houseplants. They look good trailing from hanging baskets. All need semishade in summer. Pinch out the growing tips of young plants at intervals to promote bushy growth. They need little pruning once established but, if necessary to restrict size, in spring or summer long growths may be cut back to a healthy bud close to a main branch. *Cissus* respond well to hard pruning.

CLEMATIS *OLD MAN'S BEARD, TRAVELER'S JOY*

Evergreen and deciduous climbers, most with twining leaf-stalks. Flat, cupped, or bell-shaped flowers may be followed, especially in small-flowered species, by silky seed heads. Clematis are best sited so that, while their roots are in cool shade, the top growth can be trained into full sun. It is essential that they are pruned according to the season of flowering and the age of wood that bears flowers; the many species, hybrids, and cultivars fall into three distinct groups (*see below and facing page*).

C. MONTANA (GROUP 1)

Clematis montana (anemone clematis) with its cultivars, such as 'Elizabeth' and 'Tetrarose', is the most vigorous of the deciduous species (zones 5–8) that bear small, flattish, usually single flowers in late spring to early summer on the previous season's ripened growth. They will climb up large walls and trees, or old buildings. They need pruning only when overgrown.

WHEN TO PRUNE Immediately after flowering, if necessary.

TRAINING AND PRUNING Provide sturdy support well equipped with trellises or wires. Pinch out young shoot tips. Young growth is brittle, so tie it in carefully. Keep pruning of established plants to a minimum. Cut back overlong shoots to healthy buds. Remove winter-damaged growth only after any danger of frost has passed. Old, congested plants can be thinned (*see above*) or, for total

OVERGROWN CLEMATIS MONTANA, AFTER FLOWERING

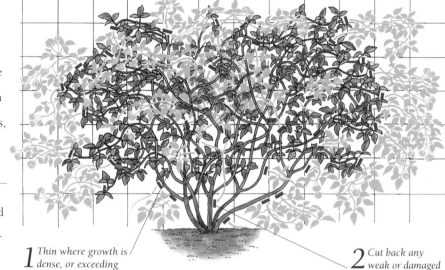

1 *Thin where growth is dense, or exceeding the allotted space, cutting individual stems back to a pair of healthy buds or to their point of origin.*

2 *Cut back any weak or damaged growth to strong buds or to its base.*

renovation, cut back almost to the base, just after flowering, every three years.

C. 'NELLY MOSER' (GROUP 2)

'Nelly Moser' (*see below*) is typical of most large-flowered, deciduous hybrids that have two flushes of flowers, first in early summer on the previous year's wood, then in late summer on new shoots (zones 4–8). With careful pruning, the two can virtually overlap, providing a long, uninterrupted flowering season.

WHEN TO PRUNE Late winter or early spring, before new growth begins.

TRAINING AND PRUNING Early pruning and training is as for *C. montana*. When established, pruning (*see below left*) aims to retain a framework of old wood and also to stimulate new shoots, to maximize flowering. Staggering the pruning, cutting back some shoots to healthy buds later than others, prolongs flowering even longer. However, these hybrids can also be grown with minimal pruning, cutting back hard every three or four years, as for *C. montana*; the first flush of flowers is lost after hard pruning, but the second is greatly enhanced.

C. VITICELLA (GROUP 3)

C. viticella and its cultivars and hybrids, like some large-flowered hybrids (*see facing page*), flower in late summer on growth made in that season. They make new growth from the base each year, so can be cut back hard on a regular basis.

WHEN TO PRUNE Late winter or early spring, when buds show signs of growth.

TRAINING AND PRUNING Early pruning and training is as for *C. montana*. Established plants must be pruned hard each year (*see facing page*), or vigor and flowering performance will dwindle. Cut back to strong pairs of buds about 6–12in (15–30cm) above ground level. If any main stems have been killed by frost, cut them right out; new ones will usually develop from ground level.

ESTABLISHED CLEMATIS 'NELLY MOSER', LATE WINTER/EARLY SPRING

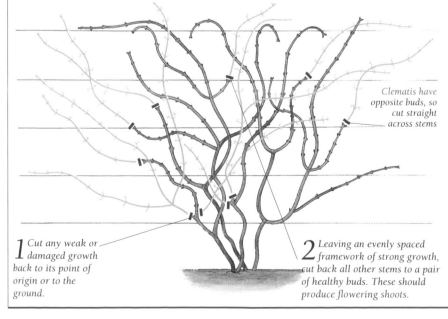

Clematis have opposite buds, so cut straight across stems

1 *Cut any weak or damaged growth back to its point of origin or to the ground.*

2 *Leaving an evenly spaced framework of strong growth, cut back all other stems to a pair of healthy buds. These should produce flowering shoots.*

ESTABLISHED CLEMATIS VITICELLA, LATE WINTER/EARLY SPRING

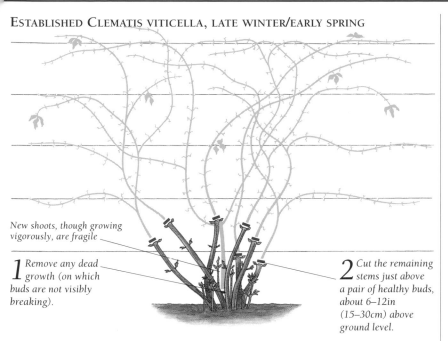

New shoots, though growing vigorously, are fragile

1 *Remove any dead growth (on which buds are not visibly breaking).*

2 *Cut the remaining stems just above a pair of healthy buds, about 6–12in (15–30cm) above ground level.*

OTHER CLEMATIS

GROUP 1
Clematis in this group, like *C. montana*, flower early in the year on wood produced in the previous growing season.

C. ALPINA (inc. 'Columbine', 'Frances Rivis', 'Ruby'), C. 'BLUE BIRD', C. CIRRHOSA (inc. var. *balearica*), C. MACROPETALA (inc. 'Markham's Pink'), C. 'ROSIE O'GRADY', C. X VEDRARIENSIS
Not overly vigorous and rarely need any pruning. If overgrown, thin as for *C. montana*.

C. ARISTATA, C. ARMANDII, C. MARATA, C. PANICULATA, C. PETRIEI
Evergreens whose leaves are prone to wind scorch; they need a sheltered site. *C. armandii* can become heavy and needs substantial support. Train and prune as for *C. montana*. Prune established plants only if necessary to restrict growth.

GROUP 2
Clematis in this group, all large-flowered hybrids, flower first on wood produced in the previous year, then, in late summer and autumn, on the new growth.

C. 'BARBARA DIBLEY', C. 'BARBARA JACKMAN', C. 'BEE'S JUBILEE', C. 'BELLE OF WOKING', C. 'BEAUTY OF WORCESTER', C. 'CARNABY', C. 'COUNTESS OF LOVELACE', C. 'DANIEL DERONDA', C. 'DUCHESS OF EDINBURGH', C. 'EDITH', C. 'ELSA SPÄTH', C. 'GENERAL SIKORSKI', C. 'HENRYI', C. 'H. F. YOUNG', C. 'JOHN WARREN', C. 'LASURSTERN', C. 'MARIE BOISSELOT', C. 'PROTEUS', C. 'RICHARD PENNELL', C. 'THE PRESIDENT', C. 'VYVYAN PENNELL', C. 'W.E. GLADSTONE', C. 'WILLIAM KENNET'
Prune as for *C. 'Nelly Moser'*.

GROUP 3
Clematis in this group flower late in the season on the current year's growth.

C. 'ABUNDANCE', C. 'ETOILE VIOLETTE', C. 'ERNEST MARKHAM', C. 'DUCHESS OF ALBANY', C. 'GRAVETYE BEAUTY', C. 'LADY BETTY BALFOUR', C. 'MADAME JULIA CORREVON', C. 'ROYAL VELOURS', C. 'VILLE DE LYONS', and other clematis in the Texensis and Viticella Groups
Prune as for *C. viticella*.

C. 'BILL MACKENZIE', C. 'BURFORD VARIETY', C. 'CORRY', C. 'HELIOS', C. 'ORANGE PEEL', C. ORIENTALIS, C. SERRATIFOLIA, C. TANGUTICA, C. TIBETANA SUBSP. VERNAYI
Prune as for *C. viticella* to grow in small gardens and restricted sites; however, they can also be allowed to develop into large, permanent plants with minimal pruning. If overgrown, they can be thinned as for *C. montana*, but in spring, because they flower late in the summer on new shoots.

C. 'COMTESSE DE BOUCHAUD', C. 'GIPSY QUEEN', C. 'HAGLEY HYBRID', C. 'JACKMANII', C. 'JACKMANII SUPERBA', C. 'JOHN HUXTABLE', C. 'NIOBE', C. 'PERLE D'AZUR', C. 'ROUGE CARDINAL', C. 'STAR OF INDIA', and other clematis in the Jackmanii Group
Can be pruned either as for *C. viticella* or as for *C. 'Nelly Moser'*. The latter method retains a framework of growth on which new shoots grow and flower, somewhat earlier in the season than if the plant is pruned back hard. Combining the two methods, retaining some growth while cutting other stems to the base to stimulate new basal shoots, effectively extends the flowering season.

CLERODENDRUM

 Genus that includes trees and shrubs (popularly grown as pot-plants), as well as woody-stemmed, evergreen, scandent or twining climbers; these are grown for their sprays of flowers, borne in summer on the current season's shoots. Like the shrubs, they grow well under cover, in heated greenhouses. They need a position in full sun, but with part-shade in summer, and are hardy in zone 10.

C. THOMSONIAE

BLEEDING HEART VINE, BAG FLOWER

Vigorous, scandent evergreen, bearing clusters of flowers with white, heart-shaped calyces and dark red corollas during summer.

WHEN TO PRUNE After flowering.

TRAINING AND PRUNING After planting, tip back weaker shoots to promote strong growth, and tie in strong shoots as growth proceeds to form the framework. Established plants need little further pruning, other than to remove weak or overcrowded growth by cutting back to healthy, well-placed buds. Where breastwood (growing away from the wall) cannot be tied in and is shading plants below, cut back to one pair of buds from the main stem. Replace old plants rather than attempt hard pruning.

OTHER CLERODENDRUMS
C. SPLENDENS As for *C. thomsoniae*.
C. X SPECIOSUM As for *C. thomsoniae*.
C. BUNGEI, C. TRICHOTOMUM See Dictionary of Ornamental Shrubs, p.187.

CLERODENDROM THOMSONIAE
In this greenhouse, wires are arranged to keep the plant off the glass, where it might scorch.

CLIANTHUS (ZONES 9–10)

Clianthus puniceus (glory pea, lobster claw, parrot's bill) is a handsome, evergreen or semi-evergreen, scrambling shrub with arching stems, glossy leaves, and striking flowers, borne on the previous

year's wood in spring or early summer. In a sunny, sheltered site *Clianthus* may stand light frost; otherwise, grow in a cool greenhouse.

WHEN TO PRUNE After flowering.

TRAINING AND PRUNING Pruning is best kept to a minimum. After planting, pinch out shoot tips to encourage the production of sideshoots. Carefully tie in the slender, brittle stems to wires or trellises as growth proceeds, to create even coverage. Once established, train in new shoots to complete the framework. Plants will not tolerate severe pruning and do not renovate well, but dead or weak growth should be removed. If it is necessary to restrict growth or relieve overcrowding, shorten healthy stems by no more than one-third of their length.

CLIANTHUS PUNICEUS
Drooping clusters of bold, clawlike, scarlet or pink flowers are best displayed if this shrubby plant is trained up against a wall.

CLYTOSTOMA (ZONE 10)

Evergreen, tendriled climbers, flowering on the previous season's wood, needing strong support. On planting, select two or three strong shoots to develop a framework. When established, thin out tangled excess growth in early spring, removing stems or shortening them by up to two-thirds of their length. Unpruned plants become congested, which can lead to dieback. To renovate, cut back all main stems by up to two-thirds, after flowering.

COBAEA (ZONE 10)

Cobaea scandens, the cup-and-saucer vine, is a vigorous, semishrubby, evergreen, tendriled climber, grown chiefly for the large, bell-shaped flowers borne in summer and early autumn on the current year's growth. It is frost-tender, needing full sun and shelter from wind, so is commonly used as a fast-growing annual in temperate gardens. It may survive for several years under glass or outdoors in warm climates. After planting, pinch out the growing tips of young plants to encourage the development of lateral shoots. These rapidly attach themselves to their supports. Prune established plants annually: cut back hard in early spring, removing up to three-quarters of all the previous year's growth.

CONGEA (ZONE 10)

Congea tomentosa (shower orchid) is an unusual, frost-tender, semiclimbing evergreen, with small flowers set off by white or pink bracts. It needs little formative pruning, other than to pinch-prune, if necessary, to encourage new growth. Keep pruning of established plants to a minimum. Older plants may need encouraging to produce new growth from the base; after flowering, cut back one or two main stems to within 12in (30cm) of the ground.

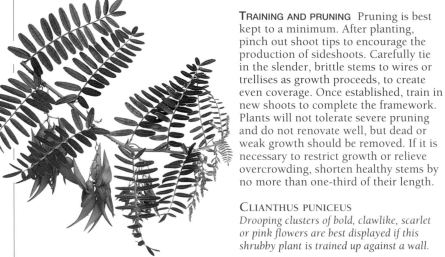

COBAEA SCANDENS
These striking flowers turn from greenish-cream to purple as they develop.

D

DECUMARIA WOOD-VAMP

Woody-stemmed climbers, related to *Hydrangea,* with clinging stem rootlets and flat-topped clusters of honey-scented cream flowers in early summer (zones 6–9). *D. barbara* is hardy in zone 6, while *D. sinensis* may be damaged by hard frost. Train and prune lightly immediately after flowering as for climbing hydrangeas (*see p.273*).

DISTICTIS (ZONE 10)

Evergreen, woody-stemmed, tendriled climbers with showy, tubular, or bell-shaped flowers, borne during late spring and summer. Given a warm, sunny, sheltered wall, *D. buccinatoria* tolerates light frost, but grows best in completely frost-free conditions, which are essential for *Distictis* such as *D. lactiflora, D. laxiflora,* and *D. 'Mrs Rivers';* in cool areas these are suitable for pillars or trellises in a conservatory.

WHEN TO PRUNE Early spring.

TRAINING AND PRUNING After planting, cut back the entire plant to within 6in (15cm) of ground level. Retain only two or three of the resultant strong shoots to form the main framework, and tie them in to a support. In subsequent years, thin out weak or crowded growth, disentangling branches as necessary. Retain only the strongest shoots, cutting them back to a strong, well-placed bud if necessary to restrict growth. Old plants respond well to hard pruning: cut main stems back to within 3ft (1m) of the ground, either gradually or all at once.

DREGEA (ZONES 9–10)

Dregea (syn. *Wattakaka*) *sinensis* is an evergreen, twining climber, related and similar to *Hoya* (*see p.273*), with paired, ovate leaves and fragrant, star-shaped, white flowers with red spots and streaks in summer. It may tolerate light frost. Like hoyas, dregeas need minimal pruning. Tie in young shoots until they begin to twine. When established, prune only to remove frost-damaged growth in spring, or to thin after flowering. Dregeas do not always respond to hard pruning. An older branch can occasionally be cut back to the base to encourage new growth, but this may not always succeed.

E-F-G

ECCREMOCARPUS (ZONE 9)

Eccremocarpus scaber (Chilean glory flower) is a tendriled, evergreen climber with slender stems and finely divided, gray-green leaves. Its scarlet to orange, tubular flowers are borne on new shoots. In cool climates frost may cut it down, but it usually resprouts from the base if protected with a winter mulch. It may also be grown as an annual.

WHEN TO PRUNE Spring.

TRAINING AND PRUNING Pinch out growing tips after planting to create a bushy specimen with several shoots springing from its base. In subsequent years, cut back all the previous season's growth to within 12–24in (30–60cm) of the base in spring. In temperate areas, plants may die back to ground level in winter. As new growth sprouts again, cut back all shoots to a strong, healthy bud to ensure dense, bushy growth. Replace old plants rather than attempt renovation.

EPIPREMNUM (ZONE 10)

Tropical, evergreen, woody-stemmed climbers with adhesive aerial roots, grown for their attractive foliage. They seldom flower in cultivation. In tropical climates, they are very vigorous and need minimal attention; they are particularly effective if allowed to scramble through large trees. In cool climates, although often grown as houseplants, epipremnums usually grow better in a warm, humid conservatory. Provide strong support, such as a sturdy moss pole. Train and prune as for *Monstera* (*see p.277*). Once established, pinch out growing tips from time to time to encourage branching. Restrict growth, if necessary, by cutting over-vigorous shoots back to a well-placed bud. Renovate by cutting old plants back to within 3ft (1m) of the base to stimulate strong new growth.

EPIPREMNUM PICTUM 'ARGYRAEUS'
These attractively patterned, fleshy leaves are well displayed on a moss pole.

FICUS PUMILA 'VARIEGATA'
The creeping fig will cling to rough stone and brickwork without encouragement. It can be rampant in growth but is much less vigorous grown in cool climates under glass.

FICUS *FIG* (ZONE 10)

A large genus of deciduous and evergreen trees (*see p.66, also Figs, p.139*) and shrubs, and evergreen, scrambling or self-clinging climbers. The climbing species (usually tropical or subtropical) are invasive in the wild; *Ficus pumila,* the creeping fig, is most commonly cultivated, but even this can be a nuisance. It is an evergreen stem root climber, grown for its foliage; juvenile leaves are small, glossy green, heart-shaped, and somewhat puckered. Frost-tender, it usually only reaches the adult stage in warm climates or in a heated greenhouse; it then produces larger, leathery oval leaves, with rooting stems that spread over a large area. In warm climates, train on walls and tree trunks. In cool climates *Ficus pumila* is often grown as a conservatory or houseplant, in hanging baskets or with support. It tolerates partial shade. Train and prune as for *Epipremnum* (*see left*).

GELSEMIUM (ZONES 7–9)

Gelsemium sempervirens (Carolina yellow jessamine) is an evergreen, twining climber with lustrous green leaves, and jasminelike flowers borne on the previous season's growth in late spring and early summer. It looks good on trellises or pergolas. After planting in spring, pinch back young shoots to encourage a bushy habit. As growth proceeds, tie in to the support. Established plants need only trimming, after flowering, to keep within bounds and to remove weak or overcrowded growth. To rejuvenate old plants, cut back the oldest flowered wood to the base to encourage strong new shoots.

GYNURA *VELVET PLANT*

Evergreen perennials, shrubs (*see p.198*), and semi-scrambling climbers, with velvety foliage and daisylike flowers (zone 10). The most commonly grown climbing species, *G. scandens* (syn. *G. aurantiaca*), needs subtropical conditions and light shade in summer. After planting, pinch out shoot tips to encourage a bushy habit. Prune established plants in spring before new growth begins only to remove crowded, weak, or damaged growth. Gynuras do not respond well to hard pruning.

OTHER CLIMBING PLANTS

CLITORIA *C. ternatea* is a small, evergreen, scandent trailer needing little attention.

CODONOPSIS Scandent, herbaceous climbers; cut to the base in spring.

COMBRETUM Treat *C. grandiflorum*, an evergreen scrambler and twiner, as for *Hardenbergia* (*see p.272*).

DOLICHOS *See Lablab* (*p.275*).

ERCILLA Evergreen, stem-root climber suitable for walls or fences, but needs tying in to wires or trellis; the aerial roots will not support the weight of mature branches. Needs little formative pruning; established plants can be thinned out or cut back after flowering.

EUSTREPHUS Evergreen scrambler, best grown through host plants or as ground cover; tip-pruning reduces its straggly growth habit and tendency for stems to become bare at the base.

FALLOPIA *See Polygonum* (*p.281*).

FARADAYA *F. splendida* is a vigorous, frost-tender, evergreen climber suited to growing through host trees.

H-I

HARDENBERGIA CORAL PEA (ZONE 10)

Handsome, evergreen, twining climbers grown for their fine stems with simple or pinnate leaves and long racemes of small pealike flowers, borne during late spring and summer. They are frost-tender and need full sun for vigorous growth; in warm climates grow them on a wall, fence, or pergola; in cool climates, grow in a greenhouse border or in large tubs in a conservatory, with a trellis or wires for support. As with passion flowers, new shoots trail to form a loose, flowering curtain.

WHEN TO PRUNE After flowering.

TRAINING AND PRUNING Tie in young growth to the support until it begins to twine. Established plants need little further pruning other than to remove overcrowded, weak, dead, or damaged growth. Hardenbergias do not respond well to hard pruning.

HARDENBERGIA VIOLACEA
The delicate stems of the new growth are studded with compact racemes of rose pink or purple flowers, giving rise to the common name of vine lilac.

HEDERA IVY

Evergreen, woody-stemmed, trailing shrubs and self-clinging climbers with adhesive roots, grown for their decorative foliage. Numerous forms and cultivars are available, with variously shaped leaves, many variegated in shades of yellow, gray, or white. The upper stems of mature plants of many cultivars are nonclinging, with usually unlobed leaves, and clusters of greenish yellow flowers in autumn, followed by black fruits throughout winter. Ivies range in height from 3ft (1m) to 50ft (15m) or more, so match the plant carefully to the space available. In general, those with plain green leaves are hardier and more shade-tolerant: those with variegated leaves need more light. Although the latter are more prone to frost damage, they generally recover in spring. Ivies are useful for ground-cover, and for covering walls, fences,

CREEPING STEMS
Never train ivies on lapped fencing; their questing shoots will penetrate between the boards, as here, and, as they mature and thicken, eventually force them apart.

and tree stumps, but plants may become top-heavy at maturity. Although they generally do no harm to well-maintained brickwork, the stem roots may dislodge old mortar and block gutters. Less vigorous cultivars can be kept small by trimming as necessary, making them ideal for containers.

WHEN TO PRUNE Early spring, before new growth begins.

TRAINING AND PRUNING After planting, pinch back weak or spindly shoots to encourage strong young growth. Young plants may be slow to establish and attach themselves to their supports. This can be overcome by pegging down stems horizontally, close to the support base, so the laterals can grow upward. Small-leaved cultivars of *H. helix* (zones 5–9) look good trained as standards (*see p.260*) or over wire shapes.

Prune established plants to restrict height and spread, if needed, by cutting back stems to a well-placed bud within the plant's outline to make cut marks less obvious. Cut out excess or outward-pointing growth, particularly from ivies on walls and fences. To renovate, cut back to within 3ft (1m) of the base; they will resprout readily from old wood.

TRAINING IVIES AS FREE-STANDING FEATURES

TRAINING ON A SMALL TREE TRUNK OR POST
Lift up the attractive, fresh trailing stems and trim older growth beneath to restrict size.

TRAINING AS A STANDARD *Use a cultivar whose leaf size is proportionate to the size of standard you wish to create.*

TRAINING FOR "TOPIARY" EFFECTS *For a formal effect, ivies will quickly cover, as here, a "diamond" made from a trellis square.*

HIBBERTIA *BUTTON FLOWER, GUINEA GOLD VINE* (ZONE 10)

Hibbertia scandens (gold Guinea plant) is a vigorous, evergreen, twining climber with glossy leaves, grown for its saucer-shaped, bright yellow flowers, borne during the summer months. Suitable for walls, fences, and pergolas, it thrives in dappled shade. It requires a completely frost-free climate.

WHEN TO PRUNE Early spring.

TRAINING AND PRUNING After planting, pinch out the growing tips to encourage strong sideshoots, and tie in new growth until the plant begins to twine. Once established, prune only to thin out congested branches. Does not respond well to hard pruning.

HUMULUS *HOPS* (ZONES 6–9)

Herbaceous, twining climbers with lobed leaves; female plants bear pendent clusters of greenish-yellow bracts ("hops"). They are vigorous, forming an effective seasonal disguise for unsightly structures, or they can be grown on sturdy arches (*see p.257*) or tripods. Shoots are fragile. Hops die back in winter; in early spring, cut the dead growth down to ground level.

HYDRANGEA

Climbing hydrangeas (for shrub species, *see p.202*) are grown for their heads of creamy white flowers, borne in summer on the previous year's ripened lateral shoots. They are useful for shaded and semishaded walls and for growing up into trees. The deciduous *H. anomala* subsp. *petiolaris* grows well in zones 5 to 8. The evergreen *H. serratifolia* (syn. *H. integerrima*) tolerates light frosts, particularly with shelter.

WHEN TO PRUNE After flowering.

TRAINING AND PRUNING No formative pruning is needed. Tie in young shoots to their supports until they form aerial roots. This may take two or three seasons. Once firmly attached, plants will climb vigorously. Pruning of established plants is best kept to a minimum, but as plants fill their space, shorten overlong shoots and outward-growing laterals by cutting them back to a healthy bud. Wall-trained plants flower most abundantly at the top, so

HOYA CARNOSA
Do not deadhead hoyas: the "pegs" on which the flowers form will often bloom again.

HOYA (ZONE 10)
PORCELAIN FLOWER, WAX FLOWER

Genus of rather fleshy, open shrubs and woody-stemmed, twining climbers, sometimes developing clinging aerial roots. They have paired, glossy leaves and are valued for their waxy, white or pink flowers. All are frost-tender, requiring humidity, semishade in summer, and strong support. Used for covering walls, fences, or large trees in subtropical gardens, they may be grown as houseplants (particularly *H. carnosa*) in cool climates. Wear gloves to prune: cut stems exude a latex that can cause allergic reactions.

WHEN TO PRUNE Spring, before new growth begins, or after flowering.

TRAINING AND PRUNING No formative pruning is needed. Tie in young shoots to their support until they begin to twine or cling. Established plants need little pruning other than to cut back or thin congested growth. If this is done after flowering, do not remove the flowered "pegs," since more flowers are often borne on the stumps of previous clusters. Hoyas do not respond well to hard pruning and are best replaced with young, vigorous plants.

IPOMOEA *MORNING GLORY*

Genus of mainly evergreen twining climbers, perennials, annuals, and shrubs, generally frost-tender. They are grown for the large, tubular flowers, in various colors, that are produced in succession during summer; several species are useful for their late-summer flowering. The fragrant, white flowers of *I. alba* open at night. Tender climbing species that are perennial in tropical or subtropical areas may be grown in pots under glass or out of doors as annuals in temperate regions, given a warm, sheltered site. They need the support of trellises or a wired wall, or they may climb into sturdy host plants or over unsightly structures. Little training is required except to tie in young shoots to the support as they grow. The more vigorous species can be trimmed back with shears during the growing season. Old and congested growth should be cut out in late winter or early spring.

CLIMBING HYDRANGEA
You may need to shorten outward-growing stems, so that they do not shade plants below.

retain as much upper growth as possible. Old plants tolerate hard pruning: cut back hard in early spring to leave only the framework branches. Drastic pruning may reduce flowering for a year or two, and is best spread over three or four years.

OTHER CLIMBING PLANTS
HIDALGOA Evergreen scrambler; handsome on walls or pergolas in subtropical gardens. Prune and train as for *Congea* (*see p.270*).
HOLBOELLIA As for *Stauntonia* (*see p.284*).

HOLMSKIOLDIA Evergreen, leaf-tendriled climber for training on wires or a trellis. Tie in young shoots loosely. Prune established plants in early spring only to thin out weak or crowded growth. To rejuvenate old main stems, prune to within 12in (30cm) of the base.

J

JASMINUM JASMINE

Woody-stemmed, scrambling and twining climbers with paired, usually divided, leaves and often highly scented flowers. Most are heavy when mature.

J. NUDIFLORUM (ZONES 6–10)

WINTER JASMINE

 Deciduous, scandent shrub, bearing primrose-yellow flowers on bare stems in winter and early spring, on the previous summer's shoots. It thrives in sun or shade but flowers best in sun. It looks best when tied in close against a wall or sprawling unsupported over a bank or terrace. If not pruned annually, new growth covers older growth, leading to untidy amounts of dead wood.

WHEN TO PRUNE Spring, immediately after flowering.

TRAINING AND PRUNING After planting, cut back young shoots by up to two-thirds of their length, to encourage strong growth from the base. To wall-train, space and tie in the resulting shoots evenly across the support, to create a framework of branches (*see below*). In subsequent seasons, continue tying in shoots as necessary to extend or fill in the framework, and cut back other flowered shoots to within two or three pairs of buds of the main branch, leaving the framework intact. Winter jasmine tolerates hard pruning, as described for *J. officinale*, but old plants are usually better replaced.

J. OFFICINALE (ZONES 9–10)

COMMON JASMINE, JESSAMINE

 Deciduous, woody-stemmed, twining climber flowering on laterals from the previous year's wood and terminally on new growth through summer and early autumn. It may flower poorly in cold gardens or on too fertile a soil.

WHEN TO PRUNE After flowering.

TRAINING AND PRUNING Prune on planting as for *J. nudiflorum*. Lead young shoots to the support, tying in loosely at first, and spacing to provide even coverage. Plants begin to twine quickly. In subsequent years, prune to thin out overcrowded growth, removing weak shoots and cutting flowered shoots back to strong buds or to their bases. Plants tolerate being cut back hard, to within 24in (60cm) of the base if necessary. However, while new growth will be vigorous, it may not flower well for several years.

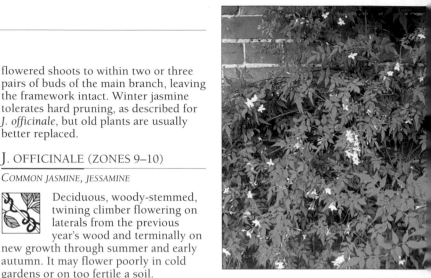

JASMINUM OFFICINALE
Given a wired wall, this twining species, with its very fragrant flowers, will climb unaided.

J. POLYANTHUM (ZONES 9–10)

Evergreen twiner with dark green leaves and, from late spring (earlier under glass) to early summer, very fragrant white flowers. On a warm, sunny wall it tolerates light frosts, but prefers frost-free conditions. It grows well in a cool conservatory or as a houseplant (although it dislikes heated rooms), trained over wire hoops or on trellises.

WHEN TO PRUNE After flowering.

TRAINING AND PRUNING Prune on planting as for *J. nudiflorum*. To train on a wall or pillar, form a framework of branches as described for *J. officinale*, then spur-prune flowered laterals back annually to two or three buds. To prune pot-grown plants, *see p.254*. It responds well to hard pruning, as for *J. officinale*.

OTHER JASMINES

J. BEESIANUM As for *J. officinale*.
J. GRANDIFLORUM (syn. J. OFFICINALE f. GRANDIFLORUM) As for *J. officinale*.
J. HUMILE, J. PARKERI See Dictionary of Ornamental Shrubs, p.204.
J. MESNYI (primrose jasmine) As for *J. nudiflorum*, but prune after flowering in summer.
J. REX Vigorous twiner. Train and prune as for *J. officinale*.
J. X STEPHANENSE Vigorous hybrid, needs ample space, suitable for covering unsightly garden buildings, walls, and fences. Train and prune as for *J. officinale*.

DEVELOPING A FRAMEWORK, JASMINUM NUDIFLORUM

1 *Prune vigorous, unbranched stems to a pair of buds to stimulate lateral growth.*

2 *Remove weak shoots and crossing growth.*

3 *To fill gaps in the framework, prune sideshoots to a pair of buds to stimulate a pair of new shoots.*

4 *Trailing shoots will root on the ground: draw them up and tie them in.*

K-L

KADSURA (ZONES 7–9)

Kadsura japonica is a twining evergreen, closely related to *Schisandra*, grown primarily for its large, lustrous green leaves and scarlet berries. Small, scented cream flowers are borne in summer, with males and females on separate plants. (For fruits, both must be grown together.) Shelter from cold winds. Train and prune as for *Schisandra* (*see p.282*).

KENNEDIA RUBICUNDA
K. rubicunda is one of the fastest-growing and also most drought-resistant kennedias.

KENNEDIA CORAL PEA

Mainly woody-stemmed and evergreen (zone 10), but occasionally herbaceous, twining and trailing climbers with brightly colored, pealike flowers, useful on trellises or pillars or for scrambling through other plants. Shoots that trail on the ground may root, providing groundcover. They need a frost-free climate. In cool areas, grow in a cool conservatory with full light.

WHEN TO PRUNE After flowering.

TRAINING AND PRUNING When grown through host plants or as groundcover (*see p.253*), little pruning and training is needed. To train plants to climb, select two or three strong shoots and tie in loosely until they begin to twine. If there is only one shoot, cut it back by half its length to encourage lateral shoots to break. Keep pruning of established plants to a minimum. Thin out crowded growth and remove weak or damaged shoots. Does not respond well to hard pruning.

LABLAB AUSTRALIAN PEA, HYACINTH BEAN

Lablab purpureus, the only species in this genus, is a deciduous, woody-stemmed, twining climber, bearing purple, pink, or white, pealike flowers in summer, followed by long, dark purple pods. It will grow out of doors only in warm, frost-free climates. In cool areas, it is grown as an annual, or is suitable for a conservatory, trained on wires or pillars. Prune and train as for *Kennedia* trained as a climber.

LAPAGERIA (ZONES 9–10)

Lapageria rosea (Chilean bell flower) is a spectacular, long-lived, evergreen climber for shaded or semishaded walls. It is grown for its large, waxy, bell-shaped flowers of rose crimson or, in var. *albiflora,* ivory white. Given shelter from cold, dry winds, it will survive light frosts. Keep pruning to a minimum, removing dead or damaged shoots in early spring. It is better to replace old plants than to prune hard.

LARDIZABALA (ZONES 9–10)

Vigorous, evergreen, twining climbers, of which the best known is *L. biternata,* grown for its handsome, leathery leaves and extraordinary sausagelike, dark purple fruits. It is slightly frost-tolerant, but it fruits well only in Mediterranean-type climates. Provide strong support, and train in young shoots to form a well-spaced permanent framework. Once the plant is established, prune in early spring to thin crowded growth and remove or reduce weak growth. On wall-trained plants, cut back outward-facing shoots to within two or three buds of their base. To rejuvenate old plants, cut main stems back to within 12in (30cm) of the ground. Train in new growth to re-create even coverage of the support.

LATHYRUS
VETCHLING, WILD PEA

The perennial peas are mainly leaf tendril climbers, with winged stems, widely grown for their showy racemes of often scented flowers in summer, followed by slender seed pods. They are excellent plants for walls and fences, for trellises, or for growing on pillars or tripods. All grow best in full sun. Herbaceous species suitable for cool climates, such as *L. latifolius* and *L. grandiflorus,* die back in winter, and are cut back to ground level annually. In warmer climates, species such as the frost-tolerant *L. nervosus* (Lord Anson's blue pea) may be semievergreen.

L. LATIFOLIUS (ZONES 7–10)

PERENNIAL PEA

Herbaceous perennial that can be trained on fences, trellises, or wigwams, or allowed to scramble over and through other plants.

WHEN TO PRUNE After flowering in autumn, or in early spring.

TRAINING AND PRUNING After planting, pinch out the growing tips to encourage the production of strong lateral shoots. In warmer climates, prune established plants after flowering only to remove weak, damaged, or dead growth. In cooler climates, cut back all dead growth to the base in spring, before new growth begins. Old plants are best replaced.

LATHYRUS LATIFOLIUS
Informal or rustic supports such as pea-sticks enhance the old-fashioned appeal of this plant.

OTHER LATHYRUS
L. GRANDIFLORUS As for *L. latifolius.*
L. PUBESCENS As for *L. nervosus.*
L. NERVOSUS (syn. L. MAGELLANICUS) Herbaceous, tendriled climber. Cut out only dead or damaged shoots in spring.

LONICERA *HONEYSUCKLE*

Deciduous, semievergreen or evergreen, woody-stemmed, mostly twining climbers. They have often fragrant, funnel-shaped or two-lipped flowers and, in some species, bright berries. They are excellent plants for walls, fences, trellises, and pergolas. There are huge numbers of honeysuckle species and cultivars; they are easily grown and are relatively disease free.

L. JAPONICA (ZONES 5–9)

JAPANESE HONEYSUCKLE

Vigorous, woody-stemmed, evergreen, twining climber with white and cream flowers all summer and autumn, borne on the current season's growth. May be an invasive weed in some regions.

WHEN TO PRUNE Early spring.

TRAINING AND PRUNING After planting, cut young plants back by up to two-thirds to encourage strong basal shoots. Select the best to form the framework, and tie them in until they begin to twine. Tip-prune shoots when they have reached the required height. Mature plants usually need pruning to restrict size; cut back overlong shoots to suitable buds. To renovate, in late winter or early spring cut all stems back to within 2ft (60cm) of the base (*see also p.252*). Thin the resultant vigorous shoots as necessary.

L. PERICLYMENUM (ZONES 5–8)

WOODBINE, HONEYSUCKLE

Vigorous, deciduous twiner, flowering from early to late summer at the tips of short laterals produced on the previous season's growth. Many forms are grown, including 'Belgica' and 'Serotina', the early and late Dutch honeysuckles.

WHEN TO PRUNE After flowering.

LONICERA × HECKROTTII
This brilliant-flowered hybrid can be trained up shady walls and fences.

TRAINING AND PRUNING Prune on planting and train as for *L. japonica*. Once established, cut back flowered shoots by up to one-third. Healthy, dense plants tolerate clipping over with shears; on small areas such as pillar or post sides, cut back laterals to within two or three buds of a main stem. Where space allows, honeysuckles may be allowed to scramble naturally with little or no pruning, although plants will eventually become bare at the base. Renovate as for *L. japonica*.

OTHER HONEYSUCKLES
L. ALSEUOSMOIDES, L. HENRYI,
L. HILDEBRANDTIANA As for *L. japonica*.
L. × AMERICANA, L. × BROWNII,
L. CAPRIFOLIUM, L. ETRUSCA,
L. × HECKROTTII, L. SEMPERVIRENS,
L. × TELLMANNIANA, L. TRAGOPHYLLA
As for *L. periclymenum*.
For other species, see Dictionary of
Ornamental Shrubs, *p.207.*

LONICERA JAPONICA 'HALLIANA'
The flowers grow in pairs, in the leaf axils; although small, they are numerous and very fragrant. It is always worth planting and training honeysuckle where its beautiful scent can be fully appreciated.

M

MACFADYENA (ZONE 10)
CAT'S CLAW CREEPER

Macfadyena unguis-cati is a frost-tender evergreen with branched leaf tendrils, grown for its showy, tubular, yellow flowers. It can be grown in a conservatory in full sun in cool climates, with the support of wires or a trellis. Train in the strongest shoots of young plants to an upright support. Prune established plants immediately after flowering to thin out congested growth and remove weak and damaged shoots. If grown against a wall (*see also p.250*), shorten outward-growing shoots to within two or three buds of a main stem. All growth on old plants may be cut back to within about two buds of the framework, preferably over two or three years (*see also p.252*).

MANDEVILLA (ZONE 10)

Deciduous, semievergreen and evergreen, woody-stemmed, twining climbers with dark, lustrous leaves, grown for their showy, trumpet-shaped flowers, usually borne in summer and autumn on the current season's shoots. Most are frost-tender; *M. laxa*, with very fragrant, white or cream flowers, is hardier. Grow in good light, but provide shade from the hottest sun in summer.

M. × AMOENA

Evergreen with large, pale pink blooms in summer; those of its free-flowering cultivar 'Alice du Pont' are bright pink.

WHEN TO PRUNE Late winter or early spring.

TRAINING AND PRUNING After planting, select three to five strong young shoots to form the framework. Tie them in until they begin to twine. Remove the remaining shoots. If young plants have only one main shoot, shorten it by up to one-third to encourage growth from the base. Once established, prune to thin out overcrowded growth and remove weak shoots. Tip-prune shoots that have filled their allotted space to keep plants within bounds. Established plants resent drastic pruning and are best replaced.

OTHER MANDEVILLAS
M. × AMABILIS, M. LAXA, M. SANDERI
As for *M. × amoena*.
M. SPLENDENS As for *M. × amoena*, but prune immediately after flowering.

MERREMIA (ZONE 10)

Vigorous, evergreen, twining climbers, related to *Ipomoea*, with lobed leaves and showy, funnel-shaped flowers. All need a completely frost-free climate, but they grow best in subtropical conditions. *M. tuberosa*, the wood rose or yellow morning glory, is extremely vigorous, with bright yellow flowers in summer, followed by pretty, semiwoody fruits. In warm climates it will cover large fences or clamber up trees. *M. aurea*, rarely more than 10ft (3m) high, with large, golden flowers, is better suited to a conservatory.

WHEN TO PRUNE Immediately after flowering.

TRAINING AND PRUNING Needs no formative pruning. Guide vigorous young shoots in the required direction, aiming to create even coverage. Once established, prune the plant annually to reduce congestion and remove unwanted growth. Prune lateral shoots back to within a bud or two of the main framework. Tip back the main stems as necessary to restrict the size of the plant. *Merremia* tolerate being cut back to within 24–36in (60–90cm) of the base.

METROSIDEROS (ZONE 10)

Evergreen, woody-stemmed climbers, some with aerial roots, which are grown for their handsome, leathery foliage and often brilliantly colored flowers in early or midsummer. In warm climates, they are suitable for climbing up sturdy pergolas or mature trees, and in cool regions are beautiful conservatory plants. Grow in full sun.

WHEN TO PRUNE Immediately after flowering.

TRAINING AND PRUNING Need little formative pruning other than to train in the strongest shoots to the support, and remove the remainder. Once established, prune only to thin out weak, old, or overcrowded growth; overpruning will reduce flowering. Replace old plants.

MONSTERA (ZONE 10)

Monstera deliciosa, the ceriman or Swiss-cheese plant, is a heavy, evergreen climber, with long, nonclinging aerial roots and handsome, lobed, leathery foliage. In tropical and subtropical climates, mature plants reliably produce creamy white, arumlike flowers, followed by large, oval, edible fruits. This species will climb tall trees, and is effective tied in to cover large areas of wall. In cool climates, monsteras grown as house or conservatory plants, although less vigorous, are best given the support of a sturdy moss pole, into which the aerial roots may burrow. House plants will not flower.

WHEN TO PRUNE Early spring.

TRAINING AND PRUNING Needs little formative pruning other than to pinch out the growing tips of young plants to encourage a bushy habit. Tie in growth as necessary. Tip-prune shoots of established plants to restrict size or to encourage lateral branching. Remove

MONSTERA DELICIOSA 'VARIEGATA'
The aerial roots that develop from the stems of monsteras do not adhere to surfaces like those of ivies; however, they will bore into moss or soft, old bark to get some support.

overlong aerial roots if desired. Hard pruning of plants that have outgrown their allotted space will stimulate the production of vigorous new shoots.

MUCUNA *VELVET BEAN*

Vigorous, evergreen, sub-tropical and tropical, twining climbers (zones 9 and 10), usually bearing pendent racemes of large, often brilliantly colored, pealike flowers in summer or late summer, followed by velvety or bristly fruits. The plant and fruit hairs can cause irritation, so wear gloves when handling, and clean any clothing that comes into contact with the plant. All need partial shade in summer, and most need ample space to climb, with the strong support of wires or trellis.

WHEN TO PRUNE Early spring, or after flowering if fruits are not required.

TRAINING AND PRUNING Needs little formative pruning. Train young shoots in the required direction to give even coverage of the support. Once the plant is established, thin out crowded growth as needed and remove weak or damaged shoots. To stimulate flowering shoots, spur-prune laterals to within two or three buds of the main stems. Plants usually respond to hard pruning.

MUEHLENBECKIA

Deciduous or evergreen, slender-stemmed, twining or scrambling climbers or shrubs (zones 6–9), grown for their delicate tracery of subtly colored, interwoven branches and tiny, sweetly scented, star-shaped flowers. Most wire plants are relatively hardy if sheltered from cold, dry winds. They are best grown to cover tree stumps, rough posts, or low frameworks, or allowed to scramble up through other shrubs.

WHEN TO PRUNE Early spring.

TRAINING AND PRUNING Needs no formative pruning. Young plants tend to produce several sturdy, straight shoots that should be tied to a suitable support. These eventually branch to form the characteristic mass of delicate, interwoven branches. Prune when established only to restrict the size of plants that have outgrown their allotted space. It is difficult to prune without spoiling the delicately branching habit. Replace old plants rather than attempt to renovate by hard pruning.

OTHER CLIMBING PLANTS

MANETTIA As for *Mussaenda*, p.278.
MENISPERMUM Herbaceous twiner; cut back hard each spring.

MIKANIA Train in strong young shoots and remove weak growth. Established plants need pruning only to thin out. Do not prune hard.

MILLETTIA As for *Hardenbergia* (*see* p.272).
MITRARIA As for *Hardenbergia* (*see* p.272).
MOMORDICA As for *Hardenbergia* (*see* p.272).

MUSSAENDA (ZONE 10)

Mussaenda erythrophylla is a tropical, sun-loving, scrambling or twining evergreen, with brightly colored flowers that have one enlarged, leaflike sepal in a contrasting color. In cooler climates it can be grown in a sunny conservatory, with the support of a trellis or wires.

WHEN TO PRUNE Early spring.

TRAINING AND PRUNING Cut back hard after planting to within 6–12in (15–30cm) of the base, to encourage vigorous basal shoots. These may take a year or two to adopt a climbing habit, so tie them in to the support as the plant extends to form the main framework. Prune established plants to thin out and remove weak growth. Reduce laterals to within two or three buds of the framework branches. Do not prune harder; it does not respond well.

MUTISIA (ZONE 10)

Evergreen, flexuous-stemmed climbers with leaf tendrils, grown for their long-lasting, usually brightly colored flower heads. All grow best with their top growth in sun and their roots in moist shade. They may prove difficult to establish. May tolerate light frosts.

M. OLIGODON

Tendriled climber with brilliant salmon pink, daisylike flower heads produced during summer.

WHEN TO PRUNE Spring, when any danger of frost has passed or, in warm climates, immediately after flowering.

TRAINING AND PRUNING Little formative pruning is needed, but pinch out the growing tips of young plants to encourage a bushy habit. Shoots soon begin to cling and will quickly support themselves; use twiggy branches initially to guide the stems in to the support. Mutisias will not tolerate heavy pruning, so once established, prune only to remove weak or dead stems. Living wood often appears to be dead at the end of the winter, so delay removing any dead growth until it is more easily distinguished, once new growth has begun to sprout in spring.

> **OTHER MUTISIAS**
> M. DECURRENS, M. ILICIFOLIA As for *M. oligodon*.

N–P

NEPENTHES *PITCHER PLANT*

Tropical, evergreen, climbing or scrambling, insectivorous perennials, mostly epiphytic (zone 10). It climbs by means of leaf tendrils, some of which enlarge to form pendulous, lidded "pitchers," mottled green and red or purple, which trap and ingest insects. All require warm, partially shaded conditions but have no special pruning needs. Overlong growth can be cut back in early spring.

PANDOREA (ZONE 10)

Evergreen, woody-stemmed twiners, related to *Campsis*, with glossy foliage and scented, trumpet-shaped flowers, borne on the previous summer's growth. In warm climates they are useful for walls, fences, or pergolas, and as groundcover on sloping banks; in cool regions, for high conservatory walls.

WHEN TO PRUNE After flowering.

TRAINING AND PRUNING Need little formative pruning, but train and tie in vigorous young shoots to create even coverage. Established plants can be pruned to remove unwanted growth and thin out overcrowded shoots by cutting stems out close to the base. Cut overgrown plants back hard to encourage strong new growth from the base; very old specimens are best replaced.

PARSONSIA (SYN. *CUPHEA*)

Parsonsia capsularis is a frost-hardy, evergreen, twining climber (zones 9 and 10), grown mainly for its young leaves, pink-flushed and overlaid with buff and chocolate brown. It bears small, white, bell-shaped flowers in summer. It looks attractive on fences and pergolas.

WHEN TO PRUNE After flowering.

TRAINING AND PRUNING Needs little formative pruning other than to remove weak growth. Prune established plants to remove dead or weak growth, and to relieve congestion. The remaining shoots can be cut back by up to one-third of their length, if required to keep plants within bounds. Old plants will shoot vigorously if cut back hard, but this will inhibit flowering for a year or so. Replacement with a vigorous young plant is preferable.

NEPENTHES IN A HANGING BASKET
Hang plants where the pitchers can be appreciated at eye level.

PARTHENOCISSUS

Vigorous, mostly deciduous climbers with suckering pads, grown for their handsome foliage and autumn color. Most are hardy in zones 3–9; all grow well in shade or semishade. They require ample space and are ideal for high walls and unsightly buildings, or for clambering up large trees. Supports must be strong and structurally sound. Keep growth away from window frames, eaves, siding, roof tiles, and gutters.

WHEN TO PRUNE Autumn or early winter; can be lightly pruned in summer.

TRAINING AND PRUNING Need no formative pruning. Guide and tie in young shoots to their support until they begin to cling. Prune established plants to keep them within bounds; shorten or remove shoots that have become detached or are growing away from their support. Large specimens can be trimmed with shears. The suckering pads make thinning impractical. To renovate, cut back to within 3ft (1m) of the base.

PARTHENOCISSUS IN WINTER
These clinging creepers can be cropped so that growth is kept flat against a wall.

PASSIFLORA *PASSION FLOWER*

A large genus of mostly tropical and subtropical, evergreen or semievergreen, woody-stemmed, tendriled climbers. They have handsome foliage, but are grown mainly for their complex, often spectacular flowers in a variety of colors. Some also produce edible fruits. In warm climates, they are excellent for training on walls and fences, or for covering trellises and pergolas; the larger species can become bulky and may need strong supports. The majority flourish in full sun or partial shade. Training displays the flowers to best effect, and regular pruning not only increases flowering potential but also prolongs the flowering lifespan.

In cool temperate climates most climbing species need conservatory or greenhouse protection. *P. antioquiensis*, *P. edulis*, and *P. quadrangularis* will tolerate slightly lower temperatures than *P. coccinea* and other tropical species. *P. caerulea*, *P. incarnata*, and *P. lutea* are hardy in temperate conditions.

P. CAERULEA (ZONES 7–8)

BLUE OR COMMON PASSION FLOWER

Fast-growing, evergreen or semi-evergreen, woody-stemmed, tendriled climber. In late summer, it bears white, sometimes pink-flushed flowers, green on the outside, with the crown banded with blue, white, and purple. Given shelter from cold, dry winds it will tolerate occasional low temperatures.

WHEN TO PRUNE Spring, and after flowering.

TRAINING AND PRUNING All training methods should aim to develop a permanent framework to which flowered shoots can be pruned back. To fan-train on a wall, remove growing tips after planting to encourage branching from the base. Select three to five of the strongest resulting shoots, and tie them in to develop a framework. If training up and along high wires, train the single stem vertically, pinching back sideshoots until the plant reaches the height where laterals can be allowed to develop and be trained horizontally to form permanent main stems along the wires.

Once established, prune in spring to remove dead, weak, and overcrowded growth, and shorten shoots to keep within bounds. After flowering, cut back flowered shoots to within two or three buds of the framework branches. Harder pruning often results in excessive vegetative growth and, in some instances, reduced flowering. Replace old specimens with young, vigorous plants rather than renovate.

PASSIFLORA CAERULEA HYBRID
The hardiest of the passion flowers,
P. caerulea *has a range of hybrids and cultivars with various flower shades.*

OTHER PASSIFLORAS
All climbing species are pruned and trained as for *P. caerulea*, but where growth is vigorous the tropical species may need additional thinning out immediately after flowering.
To grow passifloras for fruit, *see* Passion fruit and granadillas, p.297.

TRAINING PASSIFLORA ON A PERGOLA

Permanent stems trained horizontally overhead will produce flowering shoots that hang down to display the flowers to great advantage, and create a "tropical" effect. The shoots must be spur-pruned after flowering, to within two or three buds of the main stems.

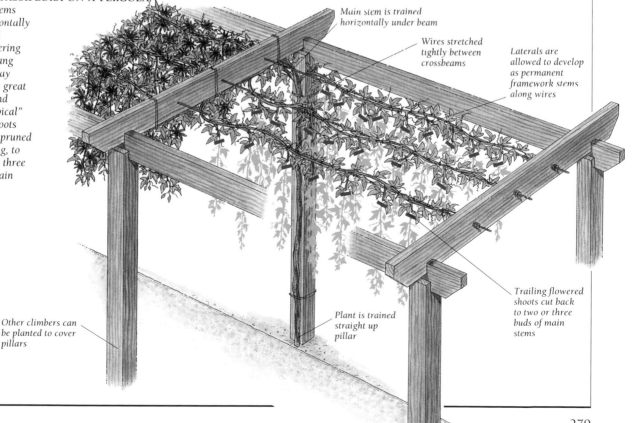

Main stem is trained horizontally under beam

Wires stretched tightly between crossbeams

Laterals are allowed to develop as permanent framework stems along wires

Trailing flowered shoots cut back to two or three buds of main stems

Plant is trained straight up pillar

Other climbers can be planted to cover pillars

PETREA (ZONE 10)

Petrea volubilis (purple wreath or sandpaper vine) is a tropical, semievergreen or evergreen, woody-stemmed, twining climber, grown for its arching racemes of lilac and amethyst flowers. An excellent climber for pillars, walls, and tree trunks (provided that it can climb into full sun), it can also be trained as a standard (*see p.260*).

WHEN TO PRUNE After flowering.

TRAINING AND PRUNING After planting, pinch out growing tips, and select three to five strong shoots to form the main framework. Tie in young shoots until they begin to twine. Prune established plants annually, working to maintain an open framework. This will discourage scale insects, sooty mold, and mealybugs, to which petreas are susceptible. Thin out congested growth and cut back laterals to within two or three buds of the framework branches.

PETREA VOLUBILIS
The purple wreath, P. volubilis, *bears cylindrical, lilac spikes of flowers over a long season. It can only be grown in a heated greenhouse or conservatory in cool climates.*

PHASEOLUS

Vigorous, annual or perennial, twining climbers, some of which, such as *P. coccineus* (the runner bean) and *P. vulgaris* (French bean), are grown as vegetables. Most, however, can also be grown for their ornamental pea-flowers. All will provide rapid cover during the growing season on any support. They grow readily from seed and are usually treated as annuals, though both *P. coccineus* and *P. lunatus* are tuberous-rooted perennials that die down to ground level in winter. Some species may overwinter in zones 9 to 10. They need no pruning, other than to cut dead stems back to the base in early spring.

PHILODENDRON (ZONE 10)

Evergreen, woody-based climbers grown for their handsome, often beautifully colored foliage. They produce stem roots which, although not adhesive, will twine to give the plant support. They occasionally produce arumlike flowers, usually in shades of green or yellow. In tropical gardens, philodendrons are usually long-lived and require little maintenance. They are ideal to grow through large trees. In cooler areas, they are suitable for the home or warm conservatory: *P. scandens* (the heartleaf or sweetheart plant) is a popular house plant. Grow it in partial shade, with the support of a sturdy moss pole.

WHEN TO PRUNE Spring or summer.

TRAINING AND PRUNING Pinch out the growing tips of young plants to encourage a bushy habit. Train young shoots by tying in at first in the required direction. Once established, prune only to remove excessive or unwanted growth. If necessary, shorten main stems before the new leaves emerge in spring. Philodendrons respond well to hard pruning.

CLIMBING PHILODENDRON (RIGHT)
Many philodendrons produce twining aerial roots that will make use of any support to further the plant's upward progress.

PLUMBAGO (ZONES 9–10)

A varied genus that includes several slender, evergreen or semievergreen, woody-stemmed, scrambling climbers, all frost-tender to varying degrees. They are grown primarily for their terminal racemes of blue or white flowers, borne on the current year's growth throughout summer and sometimes into early winter. Plumbagos are ideal for walls, fences, and pergolas, but can also be trained as standards and over wire hoops; they are beautiful specimens for conservatory walls. All prefer dappled shade rather than full sun.

P. AURICULATA

CAPE LEADWORT

P. auriculata (syn. *P. capensis*) is an evergreen or semievergreen, woody-stemmed, scrambling climber, producing trusses of pale blue flowers from summer to autumn or early winter. It is the hardiest plumbago, tolerating temperatures of 41°F (5°C). In these conditions it is not over-vigorous and makes an ideal conservatory or greenhouse plant. The blue of its flowers is particularly attractive when seen against the stark background of a white-painted wall.

PLUMBAGO TRAINED OVER A WIRE BALLOON
Plant within the balloon, spreading the shoots out evenly around the structure. Prune them to stimulate laterals, pruning harder in areas where more growth is needed. Spiral the leading shoots around the globe, so that their laterals can be tied in to crisscross and thus cover the entire structure. The display can be maintained for several years by deadheading; once growth becomes overcrowded, plants are best renovated by being taken off the wires, unraveled, pruned to strong young shoots, and retied, as for Jasminum polyanthum *(see p.274).*

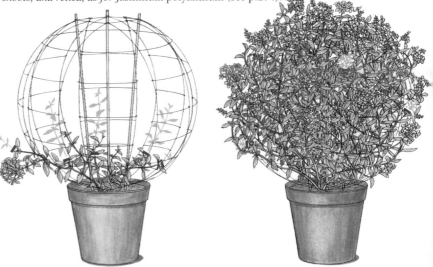

POLYGONUM (ZONES 5–8)

Vigorous, twining climbers frequently included in *Fallopia*. The most popular species, *P. aubertii* and *P. baldschuanicum*, both deciduous, bear small white or pale pink flowers all summer. They are invaluable for masking large, unsightly buildings and fences, but being fast-growing and invasive they are unsuitable for confined spaces or where they can invade wild habitats.

WHEN TO PRUNE Late winter or early spring. Excess growth can be trimmed at any time of the year.

TRAINING AND PRUNING Polygonums need no formative pruning; guide young stems into the support to provide evenly spaced coverage. Established plants form a mass of intertwined stems that is difficult to prune methodically. In large, open areas, plants can be left unpruned. Otherwise, cut all stems back by one-third of their length, with shears or pruners. To renovate, cut the plant back to within 3ft (1m) of ground level, and retrain the resulting strong growth to cover the support.

POLYGONUM BALDSCHUANICUM
The lacy white flowers of this plant give rise to its common name, silverlace vine.

PORANA (ZONE 10)

Vigorous, evergreen, sun-loving twiner, useful for trellises and pergolas; if wall-grown, it needs the support of vertical wires. Frost-tender, in cool temperate regions it will only flower in a heated conservatory. Needs no formative pruning; guide young stems in to the support. Once established, in late winter to early spring, cut back laterals to within one or two buds of a main stem. Does not respond well to hard pruning.

PUERARIA (ZONE 6–9)

Pueraria lobata (syn. *P. hirsuta*, *P. thunbergiana*), the Japanese arrowroot or kudzu vine, is a deciduous twining climber with hairy stems, bearing scented, purple, pealike flowers on new growth. It is highly invasive in moist southern regions and should be grown *only* in controlled conditions.

WHEN TO PRUNE Early spring.

TRAINING AND PRUNING Needs no formative pruning, but train young shoots in the required direction to establish a framework. In subsequent years prune annually to remove weak growth and thin out congested growth, cutting back to the framework branches. To renovate, cut back all growth to within 12in (30cm) of the base; the plant should respond vigorously.

PYROSTEGIA (ZONE 10)

Pyrostegia venusta (syn. *P. ignea*) is a fast-growing, woody-stemmed, evergreen, tendriled climber, grown for its long display of beautiful, tubular, orange flowers. In tropical and sub-tropical gardens it is ideal for pergolas, arches, trellises, or host plants. In cold areas, grow in a heated conservatory.

WHEN TO PRUNE Late winter to early spring.

TRAINING AND PRUNING After planting, select one or two strong shoots to form a framework and remove the remainder. Under glass, tip back when they reach the required height, usually at about 10–12ft (3–4m). Once established, cut back all lateral shoots annually to two or three buds of the framework branches. Responds well to hard pruning.

WHEN TO PRUNE Late winter or early spring.

TRAINING AND PRUNING To train against a wall (*see also p.250*), pinch out the growing tips of young plants after planting, and select three or four of the strongest resulting shoots to form the main framework. Plumbagos will not cling to supports by themselves, and their stems must be tied in regularly as growth proceeds. Once the main stems have reached the required height, pinch out their tips to encourage the production of laterals.

Once established, maintain the primary branch framework, and spur-prune all laterals to within two or three buds of their base. Remove all weak or badly placed shoots completely, cutting back to a main framework branch. To renovate, cut back all branches to within 12in (30cm) of the base of the plant, and tie in strong new shoots to the support as growth proceeds. If new growth is not strong, the plant may be too old and should be replaced.

To train as a standard, *see p.260*. Once the head is established, spur-prune all laterals annually to the main framework. To grow over a wire balloon or other shape, after initial planting and pruning (*see facing page*) tie in as many shoots as possible around, not up, the wires; this not only provides even coverage but also encourages more sideshoots to break (*see* Horizontal training, *p.13*). Maintain by deadheading (*see facing page*) until dense growth requires renovation.

OTHER PLUMBAGOS
P. INDICA, P. SCANDENS As for *P. auriculata*.

OTHER CLIMBING PLANTS
PERIPLOCA (silk vine) Vigorous twiner for wired walls or fences, pergolas, and trellis. Needs no formative pruning, except to guide young shoots. Prune established plants in early spring to remove weak growth or to contain.
PHILAGERIA As for *Lapageria* (see *p.275*).
PILEOSTEGIA (syn. SCHIZOPHRAGMA VIBURNOIDES) Self-clinging, for large walls or tree trunks. Prune in early spring, as for climbing hydrangeas (see *p.273*). If necessary, cut back overlong growth during summer.
PODRANEA As for *Pandorea* (see *p.278*).
QUISQUALIS Tropical scrambler, no special pruning needs.

R

RHODOCHITON (ZONE 10)

Rhodochiton atrosanguineum (syn. *R. volubile*) is an evergreen, perennial climber with twining leaf-stalks and slender, eventually woody, stems, grown for its tubular, deep maroon-purple flowers set off by showy, expanded, bell-shaped calyces of a similar, though paler, color. Grow in sun or light shade, in completely frost-free conditions; the roots must be in cool, moist shade. It is a short-lived perennial, often grown as an annual, flowering readily in the first year from seed.

WHEN TO PRUNE Early spring.

TRAINING AND PRUNING Needs permanent support, but little formative pruning, other than to pinch out the growing tips to encourage branching. Provide initial light support of twiggy sticks or netting, until plants attach themselves to the permanent support of wire or trellis. Established plants need pruning only to remove dead or damaged shoots. Does not tolerate hard pruning.

RUBUS *BRAMBLES*

Genus (zones 4–9) containing plants grown for their fruits (*see* Cane Fruits, *pp.230–233*), and also several shrubs (*see p.218*). *Rubus henryi* var. *bambusarum* is a scrambling, evergreen climber to 20ft (6m), grown primarily for its handsome, pleated, three-lobed leaves, glossy deep green above and white beneath. During summer, it bears slender racemes of bramblelike, pink flowers, followed by small, shiny, blackberrylike fruits. It is useful for fences and old tree stumps, or as groundcover, as is the graceful *R. flagelliflorus*.

WHEN TO PRUNE Late winter or early spring.

TRAINING AND PRUNING After planting, shorten the main stem to within 1ft (30cm) of the base, to encourage strong shoots. Tie these in as growth proceeds, to give even coverage of the support. Prune established plants annually, to ensure continual production of new stems. Remove several of the shoots that flowered in the previous season, cutting out close to the base of the plant. The new basal shoots will flower in the following year. When the production of new shoots slows down, the plant is probably aging and is best replaced.

S

SCHISANDRA *MAGNOLIA VINE* (ZONES 5–9)

Handsome, deciduous or evergreen twiners bearing striking clusters of scented flowers and, where male and female plants grow together, curious "string-bead" fruits. Schisandras are useful on shady, sheltered walls, fences, and trellises, and in mild areas may be trained up into trees.

WHEN TO PRUNE From late winter to early spring.

TRAINING AND PRUNING Needs no formative pruning if grown up into trees, but if grown on walls, trellises, or fences, select five to seven strong shoots to form the main framework, and tie them in to provide well-spaced coverage of the support (*see also p.250*). Continue tying in as growth proceeds. Prune established plants to remove shoots that shade out lower growth and to keep within bounds. Cut back over-long or outward-growing laterals to within two or three buds of the framework to encourage more flowering shoots, or tie in to fill gaps. Drastic pruning is best staged over several seasons, to maintain flowering. Each year, cut back one old woody branch to the base, and train in the strongest replacement shoots.

SCHIZOPHRAGMA (ZONES 5–9)

Deciduous, woody-stemmed climbers with adhesive aerial roots, related to *Hydrangea*. Schizophragmas will tolerate part shade, but need shelter from wind. *S. hydrangeoides* is ideal for lofty walls and it is very effective trained up large tree trunks.

WHEN TO PRUNE After flowering, if necessary.

TRAINING AND PRUNING Needs no formative pruning, but tie in young shoots close to the support to encourage them to anchor themselves. On smooth surfaces additional ties may be needed. Established specimens need little further pruning, other than to remove excess or unwanted growth. If gaps occur as plants extend, secure young branches in place with an occasional tie, so that they fill the space. Mature plants will sometimes produce long, soft, leafy growths; shorten these by up to two-thirds, as they are unlikely to flower.

Schizophragmas should not be drastically pruned. Renovate gradually, removing one or two main branches each year to try to encourage new growth from close to the base (*see also* Renovation, *p.252*).

SCHIZOPHRAGMA INTEGRIFOLIUM
The white or cream lacecap flower heads resemble those of climbing hydrangeas; schizophragmas have a similar growth habit.

SEMELE (ZONES 9–10)

Semele androgyna (climbing butcher's broom) is a vigorous, frost-tender, evergreen perennial. The rigid, twining stems bear deep green, leaflike cladodes on which small, star-shaped, cream flowers are produced in summer, followed by orange-red berries. It is a sturdy plant for a conservatory or, in warm climates, for a wall or tree trunk.

It needs no formative pruning, but guide and tie in young stems to the support. The shoots take two or three years to develop fully and the fruits often take a full 12 months to mature. When fruiting is over, in winter or early spring, remove the entire shoot at the base, leaving younger shoots intact. Otherwise, prune only to restrict the height of stems, if necessary: any pruning will reduce the potential display of fruit. Plants are long-lived, but can be cut entirely to ground level, for example if wall maintenance becomes necessary.

SENECIO MACROGLOSSUS 'VARIEGATUS'
The ivylike leaves are broadly edged with cream in this variegated cultivar, echoing the buttery yellow of the flowers.

SENECIO

A large genus that includes several leaf-twining climbers, particularly useful for growing among wall shrubs, hedges, or other climbers outdoors in warm climates, or in heated conservatories. *Senecio scandens* is frost hardy.

S. MACROGLOSSUS (ZONE 10)

NATAL IVY, CAPE IVY, WAX VINE

Evergreen, woody-stemmed, frost-tender twining climber with triangular leaves, and yellow flowers, mainly in winter.

WHEN TO PRUNE After flowering.

TRAINING AND PRUNING After planting, pinch out growing tips to encourage branching from the base, and tie in to the support to form a framework. Prune established plants only to remove weak shoots, or cut flowered shoots back by up to one-third, if becoming too long. Does not respond well to hard pruning, which will reduce flowering.

OTHER SENECIOS
S. MIKANIOIDES (SYN. DELAIREA ODORATA), S. SCANDENS As for *S. macroglossus*. *Shrub species are now included in Brachyglottis (see Dictionary of Ornamental Shrubs, p.179).*

SMILAX BRIER

Scramblers with wiry, prickly stems that will scramble over tree stumps or through shrubs and trees. Needs no early pruning; guide young shoots over the support. Once established, thin in late winter or early spring, cutting out old shoots at the base; wear gloves, and cut stems out in sections. May be cut back completely to renovate. Smilax can be weedy.

SOLANDRA CHALICE VINE (ZONE 10)

Evergreen, woody-stemmed, scrambling climbers with large, handsome, trumpet-shaped flowers that are sweetly fragrant, especially at night. Need a minimum temperature of 55–61°F (13–16°C) and a dry winter season. Growth can be very vigorous. Prune immediately after flowering.

Needs little formative pruning, but remove the growing tips to encourage a bushy habit. Restrict pruning of mature plants to the removal of weak or excess growth; unduly vigorous shoots can be shortened by up to one-third. A plant that is pruned harder will respond, but only slowly regains its shape. Flowering will be affected for a year or two.

SOLANUM

A large genus that includes several woody-stemmed climbers, scrambling or with twining leaf-stalks. They are grown for their broad clusters of star-shaped flowers, in shades of pale gray-blue to blue-violet or white, borne on the current year's shoots. *S. wendlandii* and *S. seaforthianum* are frost-tender; *S. jasminoides* and *S. crispum* will tolerate light frost. The sap can cause allergic reactions; wear gloves to prune.

S. CRISPUM (ZONE 10)

Vigorous, evergreen or semievergreen, scrambling climber. It will usually survive light frost in a sheltered, sunny site. Provide the support of wires or a substantial trellis.

WHEN TO PRUNE Early spring, or after flowering in warm, frost-free gardens.

TRAINING AND PRUNING After planting, remove the growing tips to encourage branching from the base, and select three or four strong shoots to form a framework. Tie in to the support as growth proceeds. Once established, prune annually to remove unwanted growth, and cut back lateral shoots to within two or three buds of the main framework. Plants do not respond well to severe pruning and renovation should be spread over two or three years. Remove one old stem at its base each year, training the strongest of the new stems as a replacement. Very old specimens are best replaced.

OTHER SOLANUMS
S. JASMINOIDES As for *S. crispum*.
S. SEAFORTHIANUM, S. WENDLANDII As for *S. crispum*, but in all climates prune after flowering.

SOLANUM CRISPUM 'GLASNEVIN'
The most commonly grown cultivar of S. crispum, 'Glasnevin' has golden yellow stamens that are in vivid contrast to the deep violet-blue petals of the flowers.

OTHER CLIMBING PLANTS
RAPHIDOPHORA *R. glauca* is a large, sturdy-stemmed, evergreen climber with aerial roots, closely related to *Monstera*; most effective in tropical climates when allowed to clamber up tall trees. Needs humid conditions. Prune and train as for *Monstera (see p.277)*.
RHOICISSUS Evergreen, tendriled climber, shade-tolerant, for posts or tree trunks in warm gardens. As for *Cissus, p.267*. Old plants often become dense and congested, so thin out excess growth by removing it close to the base.
SINOFRANCHETIA As for *Stauntonia, p.284*.
SOLLYA Slender-stemmed, evergreen twiners, may need protection under glass in very cold regions. Need no special pruning.

STAUNTONIA (ZONES 8–10)

Stauntonia hexaphylla is a vigorous, evergreen twiner, grown for its glossy leaves and sweetly fragrant, lilac-tinted white flowers in spring. Male and female flowers are borne on separate plants. When both are grown together female plants produce edible, fleshy, egg-shaped, purple fruits, up to 2in (5cm) long, during summer; females may also occasionally produce fruit without a male pollinator. *S. hexaphylla* is frost-hardy, but if grown outside in cooler regions it needs a warm, sunny, sheltered site. Fruits will not set if the flowers have suffered any frost damage. In colder areas it may be grown in a cool greenhouse or conservatory. It needs the support of a trellis or a wired wall, or may be grown on a pergola. Spur-pruning encourages the production of flowering shoots and helps to keep the plant within bounds.

WHEN TO PRUNE Late winter to early spring.

TRAINING AND PRUNING Needs no formative pruning but grows rapidly, so guide the young shoots in to the support as they develop to build up even coverage. Once a framework is established, shorten lateral shoots back to six to eight buds of the framework branches during summer, and then spur back the same shoots to two or three buds in early spring, as for *Wisteria* (*see p.286*). The main stems can be shortened to encourage new growth, but severe pruning is not recommended.

STEPHANOTIS (ZONE 10)

Stephanotis floribunda is a rather fleshy, evergreen, twining climber with leathery leaves, grown chiefly for its powerfully fragrant, waxy, starlike white flowers, produced from spring to autumn. It can grow to 12–15ft (4–5m) in tropical gardens, making a handsome specimen for trellises or pergolas, but is less vigorous as a house or conservatory plant in cool climates.

WHEN TO PRUNE Late winter to early spring.

TRAINING AND PRUNING After planting, pinch out the growing tips to encourage a bushy habit, and train in the resulting shoots to the support. Prune established plants to remove weak shoots and thin out congested growth. Tip-prune over-long shoots if necessary, and continue spacing and tying in new shoots to extend coverage of the support. Replace old plants rather than attempt to renovate by hard pruning.

STEPHANOTIS FLORIBUNDA
Handsome evergreen foliage makes stephanotis an attractive house or conservatory plant even when not in flower.

STREPTOSOLEN JAMESONII
With a similar habit to winter jasmine, streptosolen has long, straight shoots that tumble over, rather than cling to, supports. On a wall or fence, a well tied-in framework of stems is essential.

STREPTOSOLEN *FIREBUSH*, MARMALADE BUSH (ZONES 9–10)

Streptosolen jamesonii is a fast-growing, evergreen, loosely scrambling plant, bearing rounded clusters of funnel-shaped, orange flowers mainly in spring or summer. It is frost-tender and needs sun; it grows well under glass.

WHEN TO PRUNE Late winter to early spring.

TRAINING AND PRUNING After planting, pinch out the growing tips of young plants to encourage a bushier habit. Select three or four of the strongest shoots to form the main framework and tie in at intervals. Streptosolen does not cling or twine, and shoots need regular tying in. It is a good choice to cover a wire balloon (*see Plumbago, p.280*). Once established, cut back all lateral shoots annually, to within 6in (15cm) of the main framework. Remove weak stems at the same time. Plants can be renovated by cutting back all shoots to within 12in (30cm) of ground level.

STRONGYLODON

Strongylodon macrobotrys (jade vine) is a rare, vigorous evergreen (zone 10), grown for its spectacular display of waxy, luminous, jade green, clawlike flowers, borne in pendent racemes in winter and spring. Needs part shade in summer, and tropical conditions. Train and prune as for *Wisteria*, pruning after flowering. Hard pruning results in a proliferation of weak growth and reduced flowering.

STRONGYLODON MACROBOTRYS
Training over pergolas or roofbeams lets these striking flowers hang freely.

T

TECOMANTHE (ZONE 10)

Evergreen, twining climbers, grown for their handsome, shiny, pinnate leaves and trumpet-shaped flowers, borne in pendent racemes in late summer or autumn. They are tropical plants that in temperate climates require a heated greenhouse, with light shade in summer.

WHEN TO PRUNE Early spring.

TRAINING AND PRUNING Needs no formative pruning, but tie in young shoots as growth proceeds. Once established, prune annually to remove weak shoots and thin out congested growth. If necessary, shorten back leading shoots to restrict the plant's size. Replace old plants rather than attempt renovation by hard pruning.

TETRASTIGMA (ZONE 10)

JAVAN GRAPE

Tetrastigma voinierianum is an evergreen, woody-stemmed, tendriled climber with lustrous foliage. It is closely related to *Cissus* (*see p.267*), and is often grown as a conservatory or house plant, where it tolerates deep shade. In tropical gardens, it and other species are useful for shaded or semishaded walls and banks, or grown up large trees. Plants grown under glass need warm and not too dry conditions.

WHEN TO PRUNE Late winter to early spring.

TRAINING AND PRUNING Pinch out the growing tips of young plants at intervals to promote bushy growth. They need little pruning once established, but if necessary to restrict size, cut back over-long growths to a healthy bud close to a main branch. Remove weak stems or thin out congested growth at the same time. To renovate, cut back to within 3ft (1m) of ground level to encourage strong new growths, or replace with new plants raised from semiripe cuttings.

THUNBERGIA

Perennials in this genus (which also includes annuals) are mainly tropical and subtropical, twining evergreens, with funnel-shaped flowers borne on the current season's growth. They are ideally trained high on walls, trellises, and pergolas, or grown through shrubs and trees (they prefer some shade in summer). Thunbergias grow well in heated greenhouses and conservatories where there is room for ample vertical growth.

T. MYSORENSIS

Evergreen, woody-stemmed, twining climber, bearing long, pendent racemes of tubular yellow flowers with reddish brown lobes and greenish purple bracts, from spring to autumn.

WHEN TO PRUNE Late winter to early spring, or after flowering.

TRAINING AND PRUNING After planting, pinch out the growing tips to encourage a bushy habit, and tie in young shoots to provide even coverage of the support. Keep pruning of established plants to a minimum; remove weak stems and thin out congested growth by removing it at the base. Hard pruning results in excessive leafy growth and reduced flowering; old plants are best replaced.

THUNBERGIA MYSORENSIS
The flowers hang down from long stalks, so T. mysorensis *is best trained to grow high.*

OTHER THUNBERGIAS
T. ERECTA, T. GRANDIFLORA As for *T. mysorensis*.
T. GREGORII As for *T. mysorensis*. Grown as an annual in warm temperate areas.

TRACHELOSPERMUM (ZONES 8–9)

Frost-hardy, evergreen, woody-stemmed, twining climbers. They are grown for their glossy, leathery foliage and sweetly scented, jasminelike flowers, borne in lateral clusters in summer and early autumn. They are suitable for trellises, pergolas, arbors, and walls, in sun or semishade. The most commonly grown is *T. jasminoides*, the star or Confederate jasmine. Like many other twining to scandent climbers, it looks best and to a degree supports itself if allowed to climb over the top of its support and mound up upon itself, so that the shoots cascade downward.

WHEN TO PRUNE Early spring.

TRAINING AND PRUNING Needs no formative pruning, but guide young growth in to the support, tying in until it begins to twine. Flowers are produced on laterals on old wood, and pruning of established plants is best kept to a minimum. Remove weak shoots, and thin out old or badly congested growth, bearing in mind that the plant's habit is naturally to form a rather dense entanglement. Train outward-growing shoots back in to the support, and tip-prune any that exceed their allotted space by cutting them back to just above a flowering spur. To renovate, cut back up to two-thirds of all growth to encourage strong new shoots to break. Very old plants are best replaced.

OTHER CLIMBING PLANTS
STIGMAPHYLLON Needs little pruning, other than to restrict size, remove weak shoots, or thin out congested growth, in autumn or winter.
SYNGONIUM As for *Philodendron* (*see p.280*).

TECOMARIA *T. capensis* (syn. *Bignonia capensis*, *Tecoma capensis*) is an evergreen, shrubby scrambler, suitable for a cool conservatory, or outdoors in almost frost-free gardens; treat as for *Tecomanthe* (*see above*). Prune back overlong shoots if using

as a hedge or groundcover.
THLADIANTHA As for *Humulus* (*see p.273*).
TROPAEOLUM As for *Humulus* (*see p.273*).
WATTAKAKA See *Dregea*, p.270.

V

VIGNA (ZONE 10)

Vigna caracalla (snail flower) is a vigorous, evergreen twiner, useful for trellises, pergolas, or pillars in subtropical or tropical gardens, or for a warm conservatory in cold regions. Young shoots need guiding but no pruning. Once established, prune in late winter to early spring to remove dead shoots and thin out crowded growth, or cut all the previous year's growth back hard in spring.

VITIS (ZONES 3–8)

Genus of hardy, deciduous, woody-stemmed, tendriled climbers that includes the grape vine, *V. vinifera* (*see* Grapes, *p.288*). All have handsome, generally lobed leaves that usually take on rich autumn tints; some also produce attractive bunches of sour or edible fruits. *V. coignetiae*, the crimson glory vine, can be relied upon for spectacular autumn color; the foliage of *V. vinifera* 'Purpurea' is always purple-tinged.

Provide a warm, sunny site for vines, with shelter from wind to avoid foliage scorch. Vines are particularly attractive on wires on old walls, and they can be grown up sturdy pergolas and arches, or allowed to scramble into large trees. They can also be trained as standards.

WHEN TO PRUNE Midwinter, before sap begins to rise.

TRAINING AND PRUNING After planting, pinch out the growing tip and select two or three of the resulting strong shoots to form the primary framework. Guide in to the support to provide well-spaced coverage. Over the next two to three years continue tying in shoots as growth proceeds, extending the main framework to cover the allotted space. To train as a standard, *see p.286*.

Once the framework, or head of a standard, is established, shorten all laterals to within two or three buds of the main branches. In subsequent years the spur systems will become increasingly complex and gnarled; a well-trained vine is attractive even in winter. Excessive growth of lateral shoots can be trimmed back to a strong bud during the summer. Vines in large trees require very little pruning.

Vines can be kept for many years and rarely require renovating. If wall maintenance is necessary, plants may be cut back almost to ground level, and will generally sprout freely from the base.

W

WISTERIA (ZONES 4–9)

Deciduous, woody-stemmed, twining climbers, usually vigorous, with pinnate leaves, grown for their beautiful pea-flowers, borne in pendent racemes in spring. Flowers may be white, blue-violet or deep purple, pink, or apricot, and are borne on lateral spurs on mature wood. These very ornamental plants are ideal for high walls and fences, for sturdy pergolas or arches, where the flowers can hang down, or for clambering up large trees. Most flower best in a warm, sunny, sheltered site. Wisterias may take seven years or more to begin flowering, and plants on nitrogen-rich soils may produce excessive vegetative growth at the expense of flowers.

Wisterias can be trained against walls and fences in a variety of shapes. The espalier form is one of the best suited to display the flowers. They can also be trained as standards. To maintain trained forms and enhance flowering, wisterias must be rigorously spur-pruned in two stages, in summer and winter. Even wisterias that are allowed to ramble informally flower markedly better when spur-pruned.

WHEN TO PRUNE Midwinter, and again in summer, about two months after flowering.

TRAINING AND PRUNING To grow as an espalier, *see right*. To train as a standard, *see p.260*, and on a pergola, *see p.258*. Whichever system of training is chosen, it will take three or more years to build up the basic framework of the plant. Once established, the aim of pruning is to control extension growth and to encourage the production of lateral flowering spurs. The current season's shoots are cut back in two stages (*see right*) to within two or three buds of their base. These will bear the coming season's flowers. Growth and flower buds are easily distinguished in late winter, the former being narrow and pointed, the latter plump and blunt.

Wisterias are long-lived and, if pruned annually as described, seldom need renovation. If necessary, however, it is best done in stages over several years, removing one main branch at a time and tying in a suitable replacement shoot. If wall maintenance is needed, wisterias may be cut back almost to the base and will normally resprout vigorously. It will take a number of years, however, for a plant that has been pruned hard to flower freely again.

TRAINING WISTERIA ON A WIRED WA[LL]

PRUNING ON PLANTING

1 Cut back the leader to a strong bud about 30–36in (75–90cm) above ground level, taking care not to cut below the graft union on grafted cultivars.

2 Remove any existing laterals to stimulate a strong new leading shoot.

YEAR 1, SUMMER

1 Tie in the leading shoot vertically.

Surplus laterals can [be] removed

2 Select two strong laterals and ti[e] them in at 45° angles. Prune any sideshoots to about 6in (15cm), or three or four buds, to begin the formation of flowering spurs.

YEAR 2, WINTER

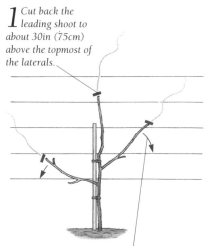

1 Cut back the leading shoot to about 30in (75cm) above the topmost of the laterals.

2 Lower top pair of laterals and tie in to the lowest horizontal wires. Prune them back by about one-third of their length, to strong mature growth.

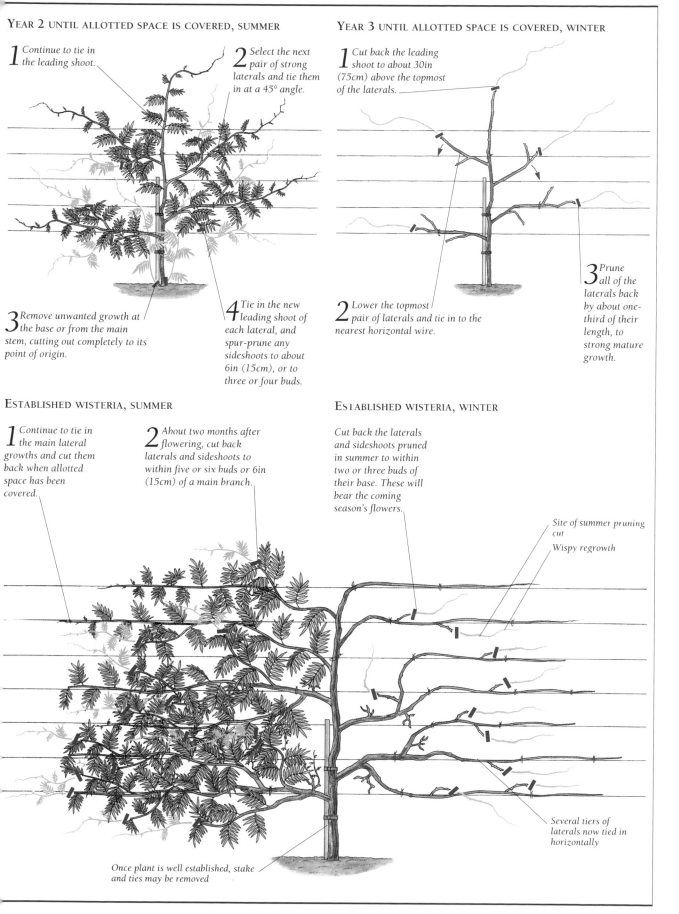

YEAR 2 UNTIL ALLOTTED SPACE IS COVERED, SUMMER

1 Continue to tie in the leading shoot.

2 Select the next pair of strong laterals and tie them in at a 45° angle.

3 Remove unwanted growth at the base or from the main stem, cutting out completely to its point of origin.

4 Tie in the new leading shoot of each lateral, and spur-prune any sideshoots to about 6in (15cm), or to three or four buds.

YEAR 3 UNTIL ALLOTTED SPACE IS COVERED, WINTER

1 Cut back the leading shoot to about 30in (75cm) above the topmost of the laterals.

2 Lower the topmost pair of laterals and tie in to the nearest horizontal wire.

3 Prune all of the laterals back by about one-third of their length, to strong mature growth.

ESTABLISHED WISTERIA, SUMMER

1 Continue to tie in the main lateral growths and cut them back when allotted space has been covered.

2 About two months after flowering, cut back laterals and sideshoots to within five or six buds or 6in (15cm) of a main branch.

ESTABLISHED WISTERIA, WINTER

Cut back the laterals and sideshoots pruned in summer to within two or three buds of their base. These will bear the coming season's flowers.

Site of summer pruning cut

Wispy regrowth

Several tiers of laterals now tied in horizontally

Once plant is well established, stake and ties may be removed

FRUITING VINES

The term "vine" is usually used to describe a climber with vigorous growth and strongly twining or tendriled shoots, and fruiting vines are no exception. All are characterized by rampant and, when bearing fruits, heavy growth that requires substantial support. In the open, free-standing systems of posts and wires must be as strong as those used for fruit trees; in full leaf, a mature vine offers considerable resistance to wind.

The vines most prized for their fruits are the grape, the kiwi fruit, and the various types of passion fruit and granadilla. The genera to which they belong – *Vitis*, *Actinidia*, and *Passiflora* – also contain many ornamental plants (*see pp.287, 262, and 279, respectively*). Fruiting

vines are also highly decorative trained over pergolas or arbors, and some cultivars, such as the grape 'Brant', display superb autumn color. In cool climates, however, bearing will be sparse and unreliable, and no *Passiflora* grown outdoors will produce edible fruits. The use of alternative training methods and additional pruning techniques to those used for ornamental vines will increase fruit size and quality and make maintenance and harvesting easier in all climates.

To obtain worthwhile crops the growth of fruiting vines must be well trained and restricted by hard winter pruning and, often, some summer pruning. Without training and pruning, the vigorous, wayward shoots soon become tangled, with consequent reduction in light levels and fruiting.

GRAPES *VITIS VINIFERA, V. LABRUSCA,* AND HYBRIDS

The grape is probably the most widely grown fruit, and was certainly one of the earliest to be cultivated. Progress in breeding and cultivation has opened up new grape-growing areas across the world. Only in tropical and subtropical regions is it rare to be able to grow grapes. In cool climates, grapes grow well under glass (*see p.296*). Both for table fruits and for wine making, it is important that cultivars are chosen for their suitability for the prevailing climate.

BREEDING AND ROOTSTOCKS
Vitis vinifera is noted for the quality and flavor of its fruit, and breeders usually try to incorporate it in any new cultivars. Hybridization with the American vine, *Vitis labrusca*, has improved the prospects for grape growing in cold and wet regions. *V. labrusca* used as a rootstock for *V. vinifera* also confers resistance to the phylloxera aphid; in countries where phylloxera still exists, vines must be grafted onto resistant rootstocks. Choice of rootstock and cultivar should be guided by local conditions and by local expert advice.

GROWTH AND FRUITING HABIT
Pruning is imperative to keep grape vines under control and fruiting well. Training is equally necessary, on sturdy posts and wires, on horizontal wires on a wall, or in a greenhouse. The fruit is borne on new growth arising from wood of the previous year, so most pruning methods involve cutting fruited shoots back in winter to permanent stems, or rods. Grapevines are very long-lived: the rods, which soon become thick and gnarled, can produce strong, new, fruit-bearing shoots for decades.

The size and quality of crops is determined by the climate coupled with the health and vigor of the plant. However, for table grapes in particular, vines should not be allowed to fruit

GRAPEVINE TRAINED UNDER GLASS
The simplest methods of training and pruning vines entail developing a strong, permanent, central stem, or rod, on which, each year, shoots develop and bear fruit, and are then pruned back. Here, the central rod has been trained up and then along the roof of a conservatory, giving the fruits maximum exposure to sunlight. This is one of the most attractive and productive ways of using the often underemployed upper levels of a greenhouse.

prolifically. Pruning restricts vegetative growth so that fewer but finer bunches of grapes are produced. In addition, the bunches and the individual fruits are often thinned.

Grapes should not be allowed to fruit until at least their third year so that vigor is channeled into producing a fully established plant capable of bearing increasingly heavy crops.

TRAINING METHODS
Most cultivars respond to training methods that involve spur-pruning fruited shoots back to one or two basal

buds, from which the next year's fruiting shoots will develop (*see Rod-and-spur method, p.290; Curtain method, p.294*). Standards can also be formed and pruned in this way (*see p.296*). A few cultivars, however, do not readily produce growth that will fruit from these buds. For these it is better to use "rod-renewal" systems, such as the Guyot (*see p.292*) or Kniffen (*see p.295*), that allow a shoot to develop in one year, then fruit in the next; fruited shoots are removed completely each year, and strong, young shoots that were specially selected during the growing season and reserved as replacements are tied in. These shoots will develop fruiting sideshoots along their length in the coming season.

WHEN TO PLANT AND PRUNE

Plant vines in autumn or early winter; where winters are severe, early spring planting is best. Prune only in midwinter when the risk of sap bleeding from cuts is at a minimum; any later, and bleeding may be difficult to stop (cauterization with a red-hot poker is the traditional remedy). Pinch off unwanted shoots during the growing season.

MAKING CUTS

Many vine stems have a bamboolike structure, and are soft and pithy in the middle. Buds occur at visibly swollen nodal areas. When cutting to buds, always cut beyond the swollen node to prevent structural damage to the stem. On upward-facing shoots, angle each cut so that water will run off it; horizontal shoots can be cut straight across.

On rod-renewal systems, remove the entire stem, either cutting straight across at the stem base, or also removing the stub from which the stem grew (provided that this does not also bear the replacement shoot). On spur-pruned cultivars, the permanent rods carry spurs all along their length, and it is the growth from these that is shortened each winter after bearing the crop. Extensive spur systems are thus built up over many years. These will need to be reduced in size; if very overcrowded, some weaker spur systems should be sawed out completely.

"Summer" pruning – shortening excessively long young shoots – is an ongoing exercise throughout the growing season. Without it, an indiscriminate tangle results.

SPUR-PRUNING

Cut to one or two strong buds, and select the strongest of the shoots that develop to become the fruiting shoot. Always cut beyond the swollen nodal area where buds form.

SUMMER PRUNING

Restrict vigorous growth by pinching or pruning back surplus shoots as they develop. This directs energy into fruit development and prevents crowding and shading.

ROD RENEWAL

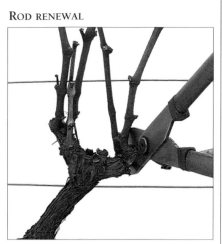

On some cultivars, entire fruited stems are cut away, leaving strong young replacements to be trained in, usually horizontally. Always remove any unproductive stubs as well.

THINNING FOLIAGE

Ripening grapes need maximum exposure to sunlight, particularly in cool climates. as well as summer-pruning new growth, remove individual leaves that cast shade on the fruits.

FRUIT THINNING

Fruit thinning is unnecessary for wine grapes (though bunches should be at least 12in/30cm apart), but improves the quality of table grapes. Remove one in three or four fruits.

HARVESTING TABLE GRAPES

Where only one bunch of fine fruits has been allowed to develop per stem, leave a "handle" of stem on the bunch to carry the grapes without touching and spoiling their bloom.

HARVESTING WINE GRAPES

Simply cut the bunches off using pruners. It is not necessary to make precise cuts, since the fruited stem will be removed anyway in the following winter.

289

ROD-AND-SPUR (CORDON) SYSTEM

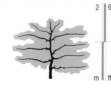

This method can be used for all spur-pruned cultivars and is particularly suitable for table grape growing, because fruiting shoots are kept short, each developing only one or two fruit trusses: thin these to one for finer fruit.

FORMATIVE TRAINING

The permanent rod, to which fruited shoots will be pruned back each year, needs careful initial pruning to ensure that it is built up only of fully ripened wood. Prune the newly planted vine back hard before midwinter by two-thirds, or more if the wood is not fully hardened, and remove any laterals. During the following summer let the new leading shoot grow unchecked, tying it in, but pinch laterals back to five leaves, and their sideshoots back to one leaf. In winter, again shorten the leader, and prune back all laterals to one or two buds, forming the first spurs. Repeat this annual treatment until the rod consists of fully ripe wood up to the top wire. Then shorten it to below the wire, from then on treating the new leading shoot as for all other laterals.

ESTABLISHED PRUNING

To encourage even shoot development along the whole rod length, untie the upper half from its support and lower it to a horizontal position well before any growth begins, raising it again once young shoots emerge. In spring thin these shoots to two per spur, one as the fruiting shoot, the other as a reserve in case the selected shoot is damaged. Let only one or two bunches develop on each fruiting shoot, pinching the shoot out to two leaves beyond the last bunch. Pinch out sideshoots to direct energy into the developing fruits and prevent excessive growth shading the ripening bunches. Remove any leaves that shade fruits (*see* Thinning foliage, p.289).

As the vine matures the knobby spur systems to which fruited shoots are annually pruned back will gradually become larger and more congested. In later years they will need to be reduced in size or removed completely to avoid overcrowding, using loppers or a saw.

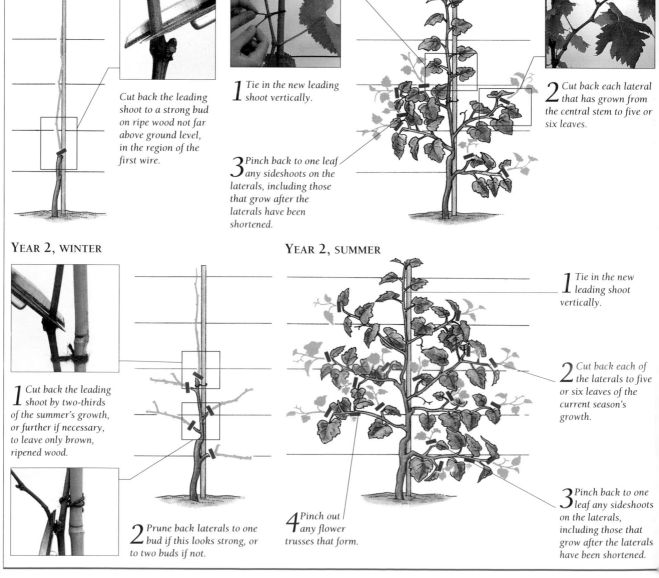

YEAR 1, WINTER

Cut back the leading shoot to a strong bud on ripe wood not far above ground level, in the region of the first wire.

YEAR 1, SUMMER

1 Tie in the new leading shoot vertically.

2 Cut back each lateral that has grown from the central stem to five or six leaves.

3 Pinch back to one leaf any sideshoots on the laterals, including those that grow after the laterals have been shortened.

YEAR 2, WINTER

1 Cut back the leading shoot by two-thirds of the summer's growth, or further if necessary, to leave only brown, ripened wood.

2 Prune back laterals to one bud if this looks strong, or to two buds if not.

YEAR 2, SUMMER

1 Tie in the new leading shoot vertically.

2 Cut back each of the laterals to five or six leaves of the current season's growth.

3 Pinch back to one leaf any sideshoots on the laterals, including those that grow after the laterals have been shortened.

4 Pinch out any flower trusses that form.

YEAR 3, WINTER

1 Cut back the leading shoot by half to two-thirds of the new growth, or further if necessary, to leave only brown, ripened growth.

2 Prune back laterals to one bud if this looks strong, or to two buds if not.

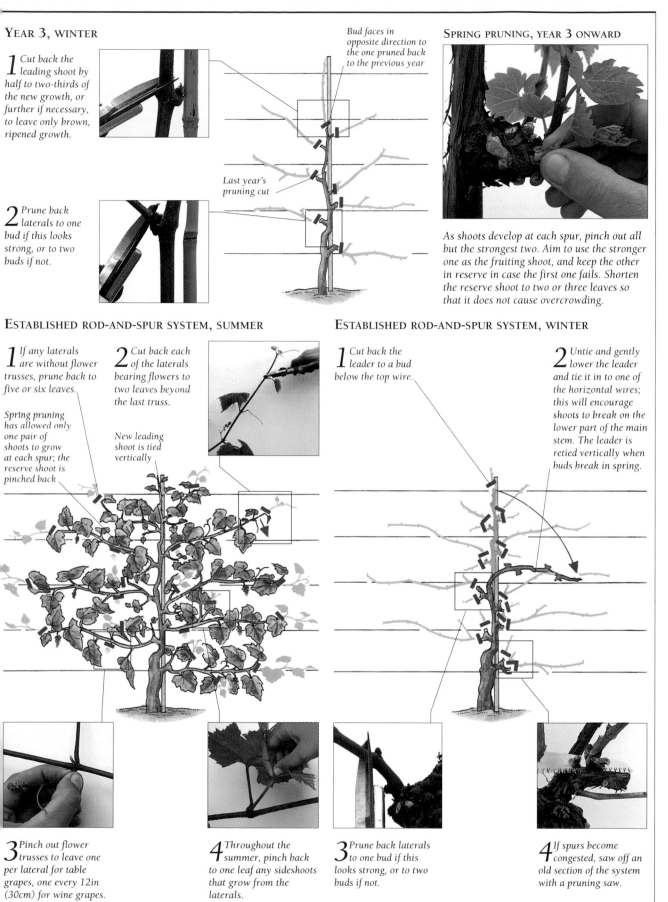

Bud faces in opposite direction to the one pruned back to the previous year

Last year's pruning cut

SPRING PRUNING, YEAR 3 ONWARD

As shoots develop at each spur, pinch out all but the strongest two. Aim to use the stronger one as the fruiting shoot, and keep the other in reserve in case the first one fails. Shorten the reserve shoot to two or three leaves so that it does not cause overcrowding.

ESTABLISHED ROD-AND-SPUR SYSTEM, SUMMER

1 If any laterals are without flower trusses, prune back to five or six leaves.

Spring pruning has allowed only one pair of shoots to grow at each spur; the reserve shoot is pinched back

2 Cut back each of the laterals bearing flowers to two leaves beyond the last truss.

New leading shoot is tied vertically

3 Pinch out flower trusses to leave one per lateral for table grapes, one every 12in (30cm) for wine grapes.

4 Throughout the summer, pinch back to one leaf any sideshoots that grow from the laterals.

ESTABLISHED ROD-AND-SPUR SYSTEM, WINTER

1 Cut back the leader to a bud below the top wire.

2 Untie and gently lower the leader and tie it in to one of the horizontal wires; this will encourage shoots to break on the lower part of the main stem. The leader is retied vertically when buds break in spring.

3 Prune back laterals to one bud if this looks strong, or to two buds if not.

4 If spurs become congested, saw off an old section of the system with a pruning saw.

GUYOT SYSTEM

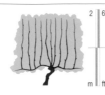

This is the system most often used for growing wine grapes in an open site in the garden. It allows longer fruiting shoots (bearing several bunches of grapes) to develop, and suits cultivars that cannot be spur-pruned, but must be pruned using a rod-renewal method (*see p.289*).

Strong support is essential. Give endposts extra support with struts or guy wires. Posts should be 20ft (6m) apart at most, with wires at 16in (40cm) intervals. Some growers use pairs of wires, one stapled to each side of the posts, so that shoots can be tucked between them, reducing the need for tying in. Letting the double wires cross over between posts prevents bunching of new growth. Space the vines 5–6ft (1.5–2m) apart.

FORMATIVE TRAINING

The vine takes two years to train, producing its first crop in the third summer. Initially, training and pruning aim to build up a strong, low trunk, then to develop, in the second summer, only three strong shoots. In the second winter, two are brought down and tied in to form horizontal arms from which shoots will grow upward and fruit. The third is the source of the next year's three strong shoots; it is pruned hard to encourage strong basal shoots to grow.

ESTABLISHED PRUNING

Shoots from the two horizontal stems are trained vertically. Any sideshoots must be kept under control. Remove leaves that shade developing fruits from the sun (*see* Thinning foliage, *p.289*). On the shortened stem, three strong shoots are retained in order to repeat the procedure in the following year, when the existing arms and their fruited shoots are completely removed, and the replacements shortened and tied in horizontally on the bottom wire. The third new cane is pruned hard, as before, and so the process of rod renewal can be repeated each year.

For a vine that takes up less space (or to create space for extra vines in a row), use only one shoot trained horizontally, to the left or to the right. Two replacement shoots are needed annually, one to be tied down for fruiting, the other cut back to two or three good buds to produce the next pair of replacements.

PRUNING ON PLANTING

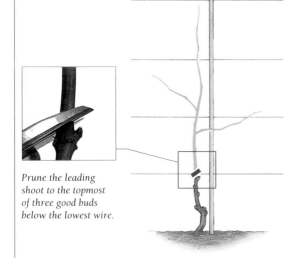

On planting in winter, insert a stake and tie it vertically to the wires. Prune the vine back to about 6in (15cm) from soil level, leaving at least two strong buds. Make the cut well clear of the nodal swelling.

YEAR 1, SUMMER

1 *Tie the leading shoot to the stake using a loose figure-eight tie.*

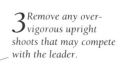

2 *Prune laterals back to five leaves.*

3 *Remove any over-vigorous upright shoots that may compete with the leader.*

4 *Remove any low shoots that develop on the original stem by pinching out when young.*

YEAR 2, WINTER

Prune the leading shoot to the topmost of three good buds below the lowest wire.

YEAR 2, SUMMER

1 *Select three strong main shoots and loop string around them and the stake to give them some support.*

2 *Cut or rub any other shoots back to the main stem throughout the summer.*

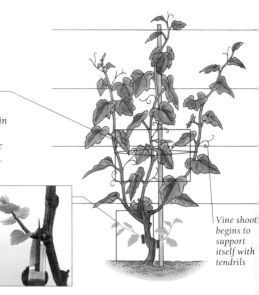

Vine shoot begins to support itself with tendrils

Year 3, Winter

1 Prune each of the two outer shoots to leave about 2ft (60cm) of stem, with 8–12 strong buds.

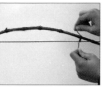

2 Prune the central shoot to leave three or four good buds. The aim is to allow only three strong shoots to develop from this portion of stem.

3 Gently bend the two outer shoots and tie them to the bottom wire, one on either side. This will stimulate sideshoots all along the stem.

Year 3, Summer

1 Tie in shoots from each arm vertically on the wires (or guide through double wires), pinching out the tips at the top wire.

2 As sideshoots develop on the vertical shoots, pinch them out to prevent their leaves from shading the developing fruits.

3 Allow only three shoots to develop from the central arm, removing any others

4 Cut or pinch any sideshoots on the three central shoots back to one leaf.

Year 4 and Onward, Winter

1 Shorten the middle shoot of the three that were allowed to develop from the short, central stem, pruning to leave three or four strong buds.

3 Shorten the two outer shoots of the central three shoots to leave about 2ft (60cm) of strong growth, with 8–12 healthy buds.

2 First untying all ties and detaching tendrils, remove the two outer arms, with all their fruited shoots, entirely.

4 Gently bring the two outer, replacement shoots down to the horizontal and tie in to the bottom wire.

Established Double Guyot, Summer

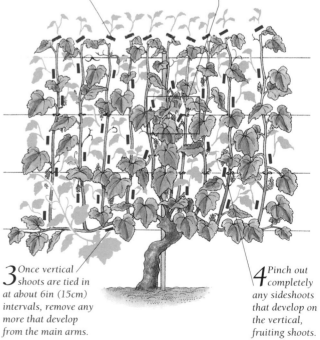

1 Train new shoots in vertically, pinching out the tips when they reach the top wire. Thin bunches of fruits to 12in (30cm) apart.

2 As before, allow only three strong shoots to develop from the central arm, and pinch any sideshoots that develop back to one leaf.

3 Once vertical shoots are tied in at about 6in (15cm) intervals, remove any more that develop from the main arms.

4 Pinch out completely any sideshoots that develop on the vertical, fruiting shoots.

CURTAIN METHOD

This is a simple method for all grape cultivars that can be spur-pruned, used by many commercial growers and easily adapted for the garden. It saves on labor where several rows of vines are to be grown (for example, for amateur wine making). Commercial rows are usually spaced 8–10ft (2.5–3m) apart to let vehicles pass, but, in a sunny site, 5–6ft (1.5–2m) is adequate spacing. A vine could also be sited against a wall, either outdoors or under glass; inward-growing shoots must be carefully pinched out.

The method is derived from the more complex Geneva Double Curtain, an innovative system (*see facing page*) that found that the fruiting shoots of a vine

may hang downward without affecting fruit quantity or quality, provided that growth is not allowed to become too dense and shady.

The fruiting shoots are selected to be well spaced, hanging freely from permanent rods trained horizontally at head height. Pinching out the shoot tips, if necessary, at about 20 buds long (3ft/1m) makes harvesting comfortable. Choose shoots that originate growing upward and outward, rather than down: a cascading habit allows more light and air circulation around the shoots than a flat "fringe" of growth.

The fact that the shoots hang downward means they are less vigorous, which is desirable: fruit is finer, and summer pruning is less of a chore. Some

commercial growers do not carry out summer pruning, but the vine will be more manageable for it, and fruits ripen better if it is done.

FORMATIVE TRAINING
Train the vine as a single stem up to the top wire as for a rod-and-spur system (*see p.290*). Then, select either the leader and a strong lateral or two strong laterals (pruning the leader to the topmost one) and train them horizontally along the top wire. It is best for the shoots to form a wide-angled "Y" shape rather than a "T" so that there is no danger of load-bearing stress on the fork, at least until the main stem is woody and thick. Over the following growing season, tie in the two arms along the wire until the desired spread has been reached. Meanwhile, let shoots develop from upward and outward-facing buds, at approximately 12in (30cm) intervals. As these shoots flower, allow one truss every 12in (30cm) to develop. As the fruits increase in weight, the shoots will arch over and hang down. Summer-prune sideshoots, pinching back to one leaf to restrict growth and prevent shading.

ESTABLISHED PRUNING
Each winter, spur-prune the fruited shoots back to two or three buds from the permanent rods. In summer, select the best-placed shoot of those that develop, keeping one other, pinched back to five leaves, as insurance should the selected shoot be damaged. As the vine ages, spur systems will become more knobby. Relieve congestion by sawing off an older section (*see also p.291*), while trying to keep spur systems facing in a generally upward direction.

YEAR 3, WINTER

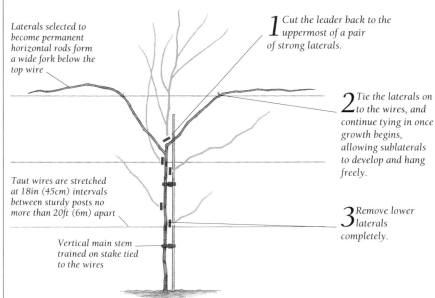

Laterals selected to become permanent horizontal rods form a wide fork below the top wire

1 *Cut the leader back to the uppermost of a pair of strong laterals.*

2 *Tie the laterals on to the wires, and continue tying in once growth begins, allowing sublaterals to develop and hang freely.*

3 *Remove lower laterals completely.*

Taut wires are stretched at 18in (45cm) intervals between sturdy posts no more than 20ft (6m) apart

Vertical main stem trained on stake tied to the wires

YEAR 4 AND ONWARD, WINTER

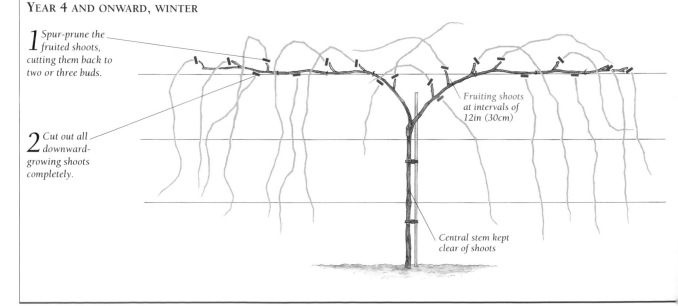

1 *Spur-prune the fruited shoots, cutting them back to two or three buds.*

2 *Cut out all downward-growing shoots completely.*

Fruiting shoots at intervals of 12in (30cm)

Central stem kept clear of shoots

OTHER TRAINING METHODS

MULTIPLE CORDON (RIGHT)

Grapevines are so vigorous that the single rod-and-spur system can be extended to form multiple cordons, with fruiting shoots spur-pruned each year to several vertical rods. It is a particularly decorative form; the rods may also be angled for a "chevron" effect. Multiple cordons are particularly suitable for table grapes because many short fruiting shoots are developed, each bearing one bunch of grapes. Train the vine with two low horizontal arms, as for the Guyot system (*see p.292*), then let vertical rods develop, no closer than 4ft (1.2m) apart.

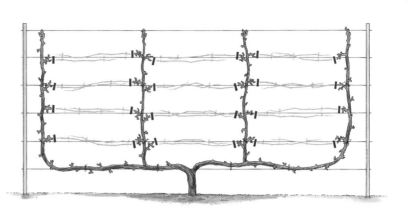

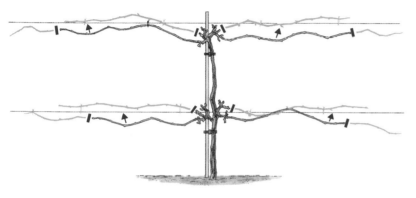

KNIFFEN (LEFT)

This follows the same principles as the Guyot system (*see p.292*), but the rods are trained horizontally in pairs from one central stem, then pinched out at 10 buds (allowing 10 fruiting shoots to develop). An additional replacement shoot is allowed to develop parallel to each rod from a shoot spur-pruned to two buds; this shoot is tied to the wires when the fruit-bearing growth is cut away completely, thus renewing the rod. Crops are heavy, but fruits may be shaded, particularly by the replacement shoot, so this system is suitable only for wine grapes in regions with hot summers.

GENEVA DOUBLE CURTAIN (RIGHT)

This more complex form of curtain-training is popular commercially, but is usually impractical in gardens. It requires a large, well-constructed support system of two rows of posts (*as right*), or single posts with "T-bars" across their tops, between the ends of which two parallel wires are stretched. Its advantage is that twice the number of vines can be grown, while needing only another 2ft (60cm) or so of space. Training and pruning are as for a single curtain, but the vines have one horizontal rod on each wire (resembling a line of people, each with their right arm reaching to the shoulder of the person in front, and their left arm to the shoulder of the person behind).

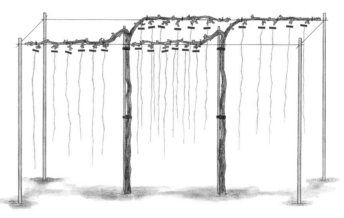

LYRE (LEFT)

This earlier version of the Geneva Double Curtain is, basically, the same training and pruning method, but upside down. It is still popular in cooler regions such as northern France because the fruiting shoots are tied in, well-spaced, at a level where they receive all the available sun. Because the fruiting shoots grow upward they are vigorous and are pinched back when they shade fruits below. The fruited shoots are spur-pruned back to the rods each year. Unlike the Geneva Double Curtain method, the lyre allows cultivars requiring rod-renewal to be used; replacement shoots can develop and hang downward until required.

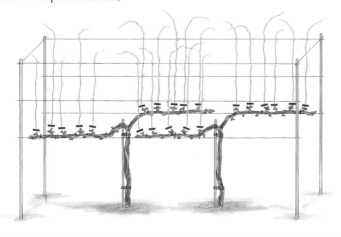

TRAINING GRAPES UNDER GLASS

In areas where summers are cool, the only certain way of obtaining consistently good table grapes is with the aid of a greenhouse. If the house can be heated, so much the better, although good ventilation is essential – grape-vines do not like humid conditions. To simplify watering needs, or if you do not have a bed of soil in your greenhouse, plant the vine just outside and lead it through a specially made hole in the base of the wall (this must be able to be enlarged as the trunk thickens). Cut the vine back so that two buds are inside, and train in a new leading shoot, pinching back the other as a reserve.

The dimensions of the house will dictate the ultimate size of the vine and how it may be trained. A single rod-and-spur system (see p.290) is usually the most suitable: the vine can be trained up and along the apex of the roof, or along an angle of the eave should this be high enough. Where the vine grows against glass, support wires or struts must be at least 9in (22cm) from the glass, or fruits and foliage will be scorched. In a lean-to structure, the vine may be trained into a multiple cordon (see p.295) against the back wall. The reflected heat from the wall will benefit fruit ripening.

Regular pinching out of surplus shoots throughout the growing season is essential for vines under glass, not only because space is limited but also because growth will cast dense shade on the fruits and other plants below.

STANDARD GRAPES

Where less space is available, training as a standard (see right) is an attractive way of obtaining a few bunches of fine fruit. If grown in a pot, keep in a cold but frost-free area over winter to provide the necessary dormant period. It should not stay in a heated greenhouse in winter; chilling is necessary to initiate flowers. Use a 18in (45cm) pot for stability, and top-dress and feed each spring.

TRAINING A STANDARD GRAPE

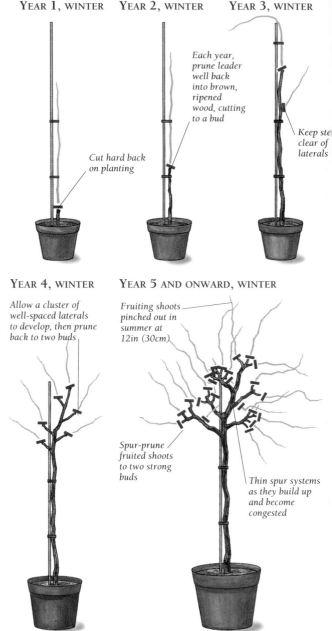

YEAR 1, WINTER   YEAR 2, WINTER   YEAR 3, WINTER

FORMING THE MAIN STEM *It is vital to allow several years for a sturdy trunk to develop. Starting with a vine that is cut back hard, each winter shorten the previous season's growth by at least half, to where it is brown and ripened. Do not retain any green wood. Pinch sideshoots back to six leaves in summer, and remove in winter.*

Cut hard back on planting

Each year, prune leader well back into brown, ripened wood, cutting to a bud

Keep stem clear of laterals

FORMING THE HEAD *When you have the desired height of clear stem, let a cluster of laterals develop at the top, pinching out any lower shoots. In winter, spur-prune them to two or three buds. Repeat each winter, gradually building up spur systems; when these become congested, thin by sawing sections away (see p.291). In summer, pinch out the shoots that develop from these spurs when they reach 12in (30cm). As fruits form, "maypole" the stems (see p.99), tying them up to the top of the stake with string for support when they are heavy with fruit.*

YEAR 4, WINTER

Allow a cluster of well-spaced laterals to develop, then prune back to two buds

YEAR 5 AND ONWARD, WINTER

Fruiting shoots pinched out in summer at 12in (30cm)

Spur-prune fruited shoots to two strong buds

Thin spur systems as they build up and become congested

SCRAPING
Careful removal of the outermost layers of old bark with a knife assists in the control of some pests.

CARE AND CULTIVATION UNDER GLASS

Grapes have exacting watering needs, and a greenhouse border will need to be deep, fertile, and well drained; considerable attention is needed to ensure that soil conditions are always neither too wet nor too dry.

Good ventilation is crucial to keep pest and disease problems to a minimum. Both side and top ventilation is desirable, allowing fresh air to circulate freely and avoiding excessive humidity.

Hand-pollination is essential, either by tapping the stems sharply or by carefully drawing cupped hands down over the flower trusses. The best time to do this is around midday on a sunny day, when the most pollen is being released.

Where fruits develop next to or directly underneath glass, be careful, if thinning foliage (see p.289), to leave the bunch in the shade of a leaf or two, or the fruits will scorch.

Scraping stems clean of old strips of bark (see left) after winter pruning will help to reduce pest levels, particularly of mealybugs, since it leaves them with no convenient nooks and crannies in which to shelter.

KIWI FRUIT *ACTINIDIA DELICIOSA* (ZONES 7–9)

The kiwi fruit is a handsome, deciduous, twining climber with thick, fleshy shoots that ripen to form substantial woody stems. The weight of the plant and its vigorous growth habit (shoots can be 28ft/9m long) mean that plants need strongly constructed supports. It is important not to allow shoots to twine around supporting poles, struts, or laths; they will constrict and thicken, causing distortion or damage.

A warm, temperate climate is ideal; in colder areas, plant *A. arguta* (Bower kiwi), which grows in zones 4–8. Prune as for *A. deliciosa*. Training against a wall gives more protection. An espalier form (*see p.95*) is suitable, with a vertical central stem, and tiers of horizontal arms trained on wires 12in (30cm) apart. Alternatively, train across the top of a sturdy pergola or on a tripod of poles.

The fruits are borne in clusters at the leaf-joints on one-year-old wood and at the bases of new shoots. Both female and nonfruiting male plants are usually necessary for a crop, although there are a few self-fertile cultivars. Male plants are generally more vigorous than female ones; where space is limited, the male plant can be cut back severely after flowering. One male plant will pollinate up to eight or nine females.

WHEN TO PRUNE Late winter or spring, before growth starts. Pinch-prune during the growing season to restrict growth.

TRAINING AND PRUNING On planting in winter, cut the (usually) single stem back to 12in (30cm). On walls, posts and wires, or a pergola, tie in the new leading shoot to a stake tied vertically to the wires or pillar, and let it grow upward. Allow pairs of laterals to form that will develop permanent, fruiting arms where desired (either along each horizontal wire, or once the top of the pergola is reached). On a tripod, select two shoots, and spiral them around the structure in a double helix.

When these arms are about 3ft (1m) long, pinch out their tips and train in a new leading shoot. Allow laterals to develop at 20in (50cm) intervals along the arms, pinching out their tips once five leaves have formed. Throughout the growing season, pinch out any sideshoots that develop and any new shoots from the main arms.

In the next year the plant will fruit on these short shoots and at the base of their sideshoots. Pinch out the tips of these sideshoots once six or seven leaves have developed beyond the cluster of developing fruits. Pinch back shoots on which no fruits develop to five leaves.

Cut to buds showing signs of growth

Frost-damaged buds

SPUR-PRUNED KIWI FRUIT
Cut shoots back to two active buds to stimulate fruiting growth. In time, spur systems will build up and need reducing, using loppers or a saw.

After harvesting, the fruited shoots are pruned back to two healthy buds beyond the last fruit. This builds up spur systems; once they are three years old, cut back to dormant buds near the main arm. The shoot that grows is then pinched at five leaves to begin reforming spur systems.

To renovate overgrown or neglected specimens, cut back hard into old wood in spring. Plants usually respond well.

PASSION FRUITS, GRANADILLAS *PASSIFLORA* SPP. (ZONE 10)

PASSION FRUITS
Train fruiting shoots to climb along or down strings to keep them separate and give them some support, particularly necessary when the shoots are heavy with fruits.

Many species of *Passiflora* are cultivated for their fruit, largely in tropical regions. None tolerates frost but many can be grown under glass. Cultivars selected for their fruit quality are often grafted; their pollination needs vary. The fruits are produced on the current year's growth.

WHEN TO PRUNE After fruiting.

TRAINING AND PRUNING Fruiting plants can be grown as for ornamental *Passiflora* species (*see p.279*). Under glass, given full sun, they fruit well on a wired wall, along wires on the roof, or trained around a tripod in a pot. In the garden, a simple system resembling the curtain method used for grapes (*see p.294*) will make harvesting less awkward than when plants are grown on more ornamental structures, such as pergolas. Wire netting or chain-link fencing also makes a good support, provided that both sides are accessible.

To grow plants up and then along horizontal wires or beams, whether outdoors or under cover, first train the leader and, if the plant is to be trained in two directions, one strong lateral (which can be allowed to develop at any point)

to grow up a post, pillar, or wall, pinching out sideshoots. Once the top is reached, train the two stems along the wires: laterals should develop and hang down to form a fruiting curtain. If no strong laterals have developed by the time a shoot is 2–3ft (60–90cm) along its wire, pinch out its growing tip, allow laterals to develop and train in the last along the wire as the new leader. If the laterals do not develop flowers, prune them back to two or three buds to encourage flowering regrowth.

If the fruiting shoots are allowed to hang down freely, they tend to become tangled together because they produce vigorous tendrils. One way to avoid this is to stretch strings from the horizontal wires to the ground; the shoot will then be guided by the string instead of entwining itself with its neighbors. This also stops the fruiting shoots from blowing against each other in exposed areas: the fruits bruise easily.

The shoots will fruit only once, so after harvesting, prune them back to 8in (20cm), or two buds. Repeat in subsequent years. Plants more than six years old may become unproductive, and are then best replaced.

ROSES

Roses are among the most versatile of garden plants, the many species and hybrids varying greatly in size, habit, and flowering performance. Most need some pruning to give their best

The great appeal of roses is that they may be used in a wide range of situations, and for many purposes, in the garden. They are extremely adaptable, tolerating a wide variety of soil types, and there are roses to suit almost any climate throughout the world. In height they range from low groundcover plants to large, multistemmed shrubs. In growth habit and form they vary from tiny, compact bushes to rampant ramblers with stems up to 70ft (20m) long. Some roses are suitable for growing grouped together in traditional rose beds; others can be used as hedges, and many make superb specimen plants. Miniature roses look beautiful and grow well in pots, tubs, troughs, and other containers. Climbers and ramblers can be trained to cover walls, fences, arches, trellises, pillars, and pergolas. Roses can be used to create any mood in the garden, from the artless informality of wild roses, with sprawling stems and masses of single flowers, to the regimented symmetry of a row of standards or flower-clad obelisks.

Employing the correct pruning and training methods to achieve these different effects not only results in sturdy, healthy, and well-shaped plants but also encourages the maximum number of flowers, especially when combined with generous feeding. For climbers and ramblers, in particular, skill and imagination when training

can transform a plant from being merely attractive to becoming a truly striking display.

When deciding how best to prune a rose, the enormous range of recognized groups and cultivars, and their varying requirements, may initially seem daunting. The key to successful pruning and training is to identify the manner in which each rose grows and flowers, and match it to a training program or pruning routine that will best exploit its vigor, habit, and flowering performance.

WALL-TRAINED ROSE
Traditional border plants and weathered stone provide a perfect foil for this vivid climber, its shoots fanned out and trained horizontally to clothe the wall attractively and, most importantly, maximize the flowering display.

MINIATURE ROSE
Modern roses are available in an ever-broadening range of colors, sizes, and habits. With annual pruning, these tiny bushes maintain a neat and compact shape and will flower all summer long.

ROSE TYPES AND FORMS

The popularity of the rose since ancient times has ensured that many species and an astonishing number of hybrids are cultivated today. Although some retain the habit of many roses in their wild state, making open, free-standing shrubs with long, arching stems, studded with single flowers in summer, roses are extremely varied in the way they grow. Some produce only one, often sensational, flush of blooms in summer, usually on older wood. Many others are repeat-flowering, producing two or more flushes, sometimes in almost unbroken succession, from early summer until autumn (even, in mild climates, into winter), the flowers being borne on wood produced in the current season. A large number bear semidouble or double flowers rather than the single flowers of their wild relations.

Pruning plays an important part in the cultivation of this major group of ornamental plants, speeding up the natural process by which old wood that has flowered is replaced by new, vigorous shoots. Although the aim of pruning is the same for all roses – to maintain a healthy, well-shaped plant that achieves its full ornamental potential – the extent and timing of pruning are not. The pruning regimes recommended here are generally appropriate to broad categories of roses. However, their complex parentage means that some roses do not conform in habit and pruning requirements to the groups to which they are conventionally assigned; if a rose seems uncharacteristic of its group, try adjusting its pruning to that used for roses in a group that it seems to resemble more.

MAJOR GROUPS OF ROSES

Any method of grouping roses to determine their pruning and training requirements must take account of broad characteristics of growth, and important stages in the history of rose breeding. Because of the very complex hybridization this has involved, a great many roses have no easily attributable species or hybrid name, unlike most other shrubs and climbing plants, and are known simply by their cultivar name. It is important, in order to prune correctly, that you know to which grouping and subgrouping a rose conventionally belongs. Those roses to which it is possible to assign a species name are largely grouped together, for pruning and training purposes, into a single category, the "species roses."

SHRUB ROSES

The shrub roses, useful in borders and mixed plantings, form a disparate group, but they generally require only light pruning. They include several species roses, such as *Rosa glauca* (syn. *R. rubrifolia*), outstanding for its blue-green foliage, and a number of roses close to their species parents which, like them, flower once in summer. Several have highly ornamental hips.

The old garden roses are a major category. Many are very beautiful and have considerable historical interest. All belong to groups that existed before large-flowered bush roses (hybrid teas) were introduced, in the late 19th century. Most have semidouble or double flowers, but their color range is limited, in some groups, to white and shades of pink. These roses do not usually require heavy pruning, but the regime depends on the scale and vigor of the plant and whether it is repeat-flowering. The earliest historically – the albas, damasks, gallicas, Provence roses (centifolias), and mosses (sports of the Provence roses with mossy growth on sepals and flower stalks) –

ROSE GROUPS AND GROWTH HABIT

OLD ROSES OF SPREADING HABIT

A large number of old garden roses have an arching habit, and when placing them in the garden, allowance must be made for their spread and for their long, thorny stems, which may encroach on neighboring plants. Shortening these stems to restrict size and spread will spoil the graceful, informal habit. However, removing some of the older flowered wood by light annual pruning can keep them under control and enhance their flowering performance.

OLD ROSES OF UPRIGHT HABIT

Among the old roses are a number of medium size and upright growth, often forming dense, twiggy shrubs. Like other old roses, they do not require heavy pruning. Some thinning and occasional removal of entire older stems will relieve congestion and stimulate the production of vigorous new growth that will flower well in future summers. Many gallicas, a group of old garden roses that bear a single flush of flowers in midsummer, have this habit.

MODERN SHRUB ROSES

The modern shrub roses are very diverse in size, growth habit, and manner of flowering. Some bear a close resemblance to species roses, producing single flowers on arching stems. Others are more upright in growth, and some have flowers that equal those of a modern bush rose in fullness. Whether flowering in a single flush or repeat-flowering, they do not require the heavy pruning that is used to maximize the flowering performance of modern bush roses, and their character is easily spoiled by severe pruning.

ENGLISH ROSES

These roses, many with evocative names such as 'Gertrude Jekyll' and 'The Wife of Bath', are the result of hybridizing modern and old shrub roses to create new cultivars that combine the advantages – disease resistance, compact habit, wide color range – of modern roses with the nostalgic flower shapes and scents of older roses. Their growth habits and pruning methods vary so widely that no universal rules can apply. In general, however, they should not be pruned as hard as the modern hybrid tea or floribunda roses; they benefit from light cutting back in the dormant season. Prune cultivars according to the rose group they most resemble, or as advised by rose experts.

'Graham Thomas'

MODERN BUSH ROSES

All modern bush roses are repeat-flowering, bearing their flowers on the current season's growth. They are pruned the most heavily of all roses (see pp.306–308); a large proportion of flowered wood is removed in order to stimulate growth the following year.

SMALL BUSH ROSES

Patio and polyantha roses (see p.308) are small cluster-flowered bushes, pruned in a similar way. Miniature roses (see p.309) are dwarf counterparts of hybrid teas and floribundas, usually no more than 10in (25cm) tall. Their twiggy growth does not require severe pruning.

MODERN CLIMBERS

These roses should be trained (see p.316) to form frameworks of fairly stiff, long shoots, which usually require tying in to supports. Their flowering laterals should be pruned annually to stimulate additional flowering growth.

RAMBLERS

These scrambling roses send up new, flexible, canelike shoots from the base each year. They usually flower only once, in early summer or a little later, the small blooms often carried in large clusters of 20 or more. Entire flowered stems may be removed after flowering (see p.318).

STANDARD ROSES

Bush roses are top-grafted onto clear stems of varying heights to form bush standards (see p.310); other roses with long shoots, such as ramblers, can also be used to form weeping standards.

with few exceptions, have a single flush of flowers in summer. The repeat-flowering characteristic, found in the China roses in the late 19th century, was passed to the Bourbons, hybrid perpetuals, and Portland roses, important precursors of the modern, freely repeat-flowering bush roses.

In this century, growers have continued hybridizing roses to produce modern shrub roses, combining desirable characteristics of modern roses with old and even species roses. Some modern shrub roses, for example 'Golden Wings', produce at least two flushes of flowers in the summer; others of compact habit are increasingly popular as groundcover plants.

BUSH ROSES

Since the late 19th century much effort in rose breeding has concentrated on producing reliably repeat-flowering bush roses that are compact and suitable for bedding displays. The hybrid tea roses (large-flowered bush roses) are remarkable for their shapely, high-centered flowers, double or single, which are available in a wide color range. Even more dramatic for massed displays are the floribundas (cluster-flowered bush roses), with their large clusters of flowers. The range of small bush roses (miniature roses, patio roses, and polyanthas, the last a group that preceded the floribunda roses) is increasing all the time in response to growing demand for roses intended for restricted sites and container planting.

CLIMBERS AND RAMBLERS

Many roses have long stems that are flexible, at least when young, allowing them to scramble through shrubs and into trees to reach for the light, their thorns giving them a powerful hold among other vegetation and on uneven surfaces. The ramblers, including several species roses, usually bear clusters of small flowers in a single flush and are very vigorous; some, such as *Rosa filipes* 'Kiftsgate', are overwhelmingly so.

The climbing roses are on the whole more moderate in growth, have larger flowers, and offer a wider color range. They include a few old garden roses, such as boursaults and noisettes, as well as many modern hybrids, among them climbing sports of modern bush roses. The most recent area of interest for rose breeders has been in developing the so-called pillar roses of short stature, which bear flowers in succession at all levels.

Ramblers and climbers can be allowed to grow freely into strong host plants but are most commonly grown on man-made supports, such as pergolas or trellises, where they need training and pruning to flower well.

BASIC TECHNIQUES

The principal reason for pruning roses, as for any plant, is to maintain health and vigor. The removal of dead, diseased, and damaged wood as soon as it is noticed is particularly important for roses. They are prone to a variety of ailments and are often planted *en masse* in traditional rose beds, increasing the dangers of spreading disease.

Shaping the plant, preventing over-crowding, and if necessary, restricting its size are also routine tasks that are important aspects of rose pruning. In comparison with an unpruned plant, an open-centered rose, with well-spaced shoots that do not rub against each other is not only more pleasing to the eye but also less prone to disease.

However, although a healthy rose will flower freely, much of the annual task of rose pruning is devoted simply to encouraging more, or finer, blooms. It is the strong new shoots on a rose that flower best. As they age, these shoots become woody and usually produce fewer blooms of lesser quality. If a rose is left to itself, the old stems will die and eventually be shed and will be replaced by new ones. In the meantime, however, a tangle of dead, old, and new growth builds up, increasing the risk of disease. Annual pruning, therefore, aims to speed up the natural process by removing old, moribund wood and stimulating the growth of vigorous new shoots that will flower well in following

summers. With climbing and rambler roses, in particular, these pruning cuts complement training, so that the rose covers its support well with both foliage and flowers.

Although many routine tasks (*see facing page*) are common to most rose groups, pruning techniques used to enhance flowering vary with the type of rose, its situation, and the climate in which it grows. In warm climates where roses flower almost continuously, gardeners may prune very lightly – not much more than continual deadheading – to avoid interrupting the display. Bush roses will, however, benefit from heavier pruning to renew the flowering growth every two or three years.

MAKING CUTS

All roses have alternate buds (*see p.10*). Make angled cuts just above a healthy bud (*see right*) that faces in the direction in which you want a new shoot to develop. To maintain an open-centered and rounded shape on bush roses, prune to an outward-facing bud. On roses with arching shoots, where inward- or upward-growing new shoots are needed to fill in the center, prune to an inward-facing bud. If no bud is visible, prune the stem at the appropriate height, and when dormant buds start growing, cut the stem back again to a shoot growing in the required direction.

All roses benefit occasionally from renewal pruning: the complete removal, in the dormant season, of an older, less productive main stem. If a strong, well-positioned shoot has already emerged near the base of an old main stem, cut to this shoot (*see far right*).

WHEN TO PRUNE

Roses planted in the dormant season are pruned on planting; container-grown roses planted during the growing season are best left unpruned until their first spring. The degree of pruning varies depending on the type of rose.

Once established, roses with a single flush of flowers in early to midsummer – mainly species roses, some old garden roses, and ramblers – should be pruned as soon as possible after flowering. Repeat-flowering roses may also be pruned once the last flowers have faded in autumn. In cooler climates, many growers delay pruning bush roses until spring, once the coldest weather is over but while the rose is still dormant or nearly so. In warm climates, prune after flowering, which is often at its peak in the coolest part of the year.

CUTTING TO A BUD

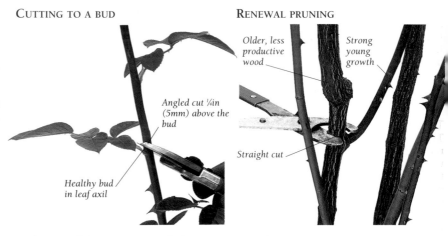

Angled cut ¼in (5mm) above the bud

Healthy bud in leaf axil

With a pair of sharp pruners, angle the cut cleanly across the stem not more than ¼in (5mm) above a bud either on the stem or in a leaf axil, sloping gently away so that the lower end of the cut is opposite the bud.

RENEWAL PRUNING

Older, less productive wood

Strong young growth

Straight cut

Using loppers or a pruning saw, cut squarely through the old stem at the base or, as here, ¼in (5mm) above a strong, young shoot, neither leaving a stub nor damaging the structure of the stem where the shoot joins it.

GOOD AND BAD CUTS (BELOW)

A rough cut (far left) is slow to heal and is often an entry point for disease. Angling the cut wrongly (center left) will allow water to collect near the bud, encouraging rotting. A cut too high (center right) leaves a stub that will die back, possibly affecting the whole shoot. A correct cut (far right) gives the best chance of a strong, healthy shoot developing in the desired direction.

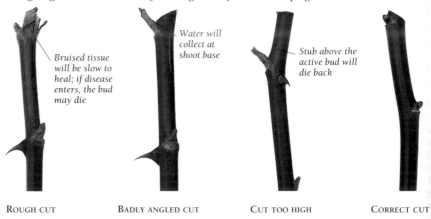

Bruised tissue will be slow to heal; if disease enters, the bud may die

Water will collect at shoot base

Stub above the active bud will die back

ROUGH CUT   BADLY ANGLED CUT   CUT TOO HIGH   CORRECT CUT

ROUTINE TASKS

Although pruning to stimulate new flowering growth differs in both method and timing according to the type of rose, there are many tasks that are common to all roses. Some have positive benefits, such as deadheading and tying in; others are preventive measures or a response to localized problems.

DEADHEADING

A rose's energies are diverted into seed production if hips are allowed to develop. Roses that flower only once are usually pruned after flowering, removing the spent flowers. Species and other roses that are grown for their decorative hips should not be deadheaded. On repeat-flowering roses, cutting back faded flowers to a bud will stimulate new shoots that will bear a second or even third crop of blossoms. For strong new shoots, always cut well back to the second or third bud down the stem, rather than just nipping off the flower heads. In a spray, the central flower will open and fade first; it can then be pinched out if desired. Once the whole spray has finished flowering, it can be removed entirely.

TYING IN

The long shoots of climbers and ramblers, and of tall shrub roses grown up against a wall, need to be tied in to their support, both to protect them from wind damage and to display their flowers to maximum effect. They may be secured to horizontal wires strung between vine eyes on a wall or fence, or to supports such as arches, pillars, pergolas, trellises, and tripods. Use garden twine tied in figure eights or, preferably, ties consisting of short, narrow, adjustable straps with a buffer, which is positioned between the rose stem and the support to prevent chafing.

DAMAGED AND CROSSING SHOOTS

A clean cut is less likely to encourage disease than a torn or bruised rose stem, so always cut out damage, pruning stems back to just above a bud to stimulate a replacement shoot. Also, remove or shorten to a bud or sideshoot any stem that is rubbing, or will grow to rub, against another. This should minimize damage by chafing or thorns.

DEAD WOOD AND DIEBACK

With roses it is particularly important to distinguish between wood that has been dead for some time, where a "natural barrier" (see p.11) has been formed between dead and live wood, and growth that is suffering from the progressive condition known as dieback. Wood that is obviously dead (continued on p.304)

DEADHEADING REPEAT-FLOWERING ROSES

HYBRID TEA ROSES *Cut to a strong, outward-facing bud (see facing page) or shoot below the faded flower to stimulate the growth of a new flowering shoot.*

FLORIBUNDA ROSES *Prune away the whole flowering spray once the flowers have finally faded, by making a correctly angled cut just above a healthy bud (see facing page).*

TYING IN

Secure long shoots by tying them to their support, either with garden twine in a figure eight, or with ties. Ties should be loose enough to allow room for the shoots to expand as they grow.

DEAD, DAMAGED, CROWDED, AND CROSSING STEMS

When pruning roses, take out damaged and diseased stems, remove crossing stems that clutter the center of a bush or cause rubbing, and cut out old wood that is past its flowering best. Cut or saw away any old stubs that have failed to produce new shoots.

Removing dieback
Cut back dried-up, brown stems with progressive dieback until completely healthy, white pith is reached.

Dead wood
Disease organisms thrive on dead, rotting growth

Crossing stems
Chafing will cause damage

New shoot

Dead stub

(*continued from p.303*) and terminates in a clear demarcation line should be removed as soon as seen, cutting back to just above the natural barrier to keep it intact. However, if shoots appear dried-up and light brown, and no clear demarcation between dead and live wood can be seen, dieback is probably the cause, and pruning cuts must be made well below the affected area. Dieback travels down the center of stems, and may be detected when you cut back into an apparently healthy part of the stem and find that the cut surface shows a brown patch in the center. Cut to buds farther down the stem until healthy, white pith is reached.

BLIND SHOOTS

A rose will sometimes produce a shoot with no sign of a flower bud at its tip (*see below left*). Such "blind" shoots occur more often on some cultivars than others – the hybrid tea rose 'Peace', for example, being particularly prone. The most likely cause is frost damage to the shoot tip. Shortening the blind shoot will stimulate a lower bud into growth, and this shoot should produce flowers, although slightly later in the season.

REMOVING SUCKERS

For roses, bud-grafting (budding) is the simplest and most widely used method of vegetative propagation. Some of the older roses, such as gallicas, albas, and *R. pimpinellifolia* and some of its hybrids, sucker very freely if grown from cuttings, and must be grafted onto other rootstocks to reduce the problem. Most modern roses are grafted onto the rootstocks of certain selections of wild roses in order to increase their vigor and longevity. During the growing season, shoots, or suckers, may grow from these rootstocks, usually a short distance from the base of the rose. Their leaves are

REMOVING ROSE SUCKERS

1 *Gently scraping away soil, trace the sucker back to the stem or root (below the bud-graft union) from which it has developed.*

2 *Pull the sucker away sharply from the root. This is not easy, but it is far less likely to cause suckers to regrow than cutting them off.*

often of a different shape or shade of green than those of the scion. Suckers should be removed (*see above*) as soon as they appear, since they will initially weaken and eventually replace the grafted cultivar. Cutting them off at ground level only encourages more growth: trace them to their point of origin on the roots and carefully pull them off at the root. This will remove dormant buds clustered at the base of the sucker that might, if left, be stimulated into growth.

Standard roses, which are top-grafted, may also produce suckers on their stems, and these too must be pinched off (*see p.311*) or cut cleanly back to the stem.

PESTS AND DISEASES

Pruning can supplement the use of insecticidal and fungicidal sprays in the control of pests and diseases. Shoots

severely affected by mildew (*see below center*) should be cut out, and leaves affected by blackspot are best pulled off and discarded. The activities of the leaf-roller (*see below right*) are not very harmful to the plant, but may leave growth so disfigured for the rest of the summer that pruning it out is preferable.

CARE AFTER PRUNING

All roses benefit from spring feeding and mulching, but those that are pruned hard, such as hybrid tea and floribunda roses, need fertilizing throughout the growing season to maintain strong growth. Many types of commercial rose fertilizers are available. In cool climates, do not apply fertilizer after August 1; it will stimulate soft growth that will not have time to ripen sufficiently before winter, and will be vulnerable to cold damage.

BLIND SHOOT

Shoot with no terminal flower bud

Bud concealed in leaf axil

Cut back to a bud in the axil of a healthy, outward-growing leaf. The bud should be stimulated to develop into a flowering shoot.

MILDEW

Shoots that are badly affected by grayish mildew are unlikely to recover and should be removed and discarded.

DAMAGE BY LEAF-ROLLERS

This characteristic damage does not harm the plant but can be removed if found unsightly. Cut the shoot back to where leaves are intact.

RENOVATION

In a newly acquired garden, neglected roses, particularly bush roses, often look as if they are hardly worth keeping, but in general it is worth trying to renovate them. Some may even prove to be roses of quality. In any case, you should not plant new roses in the same position without completely replacing or sterilizing the soil, because of the replant problems associated with this group of plants.

Climbers and ramblers are often neglected even in the best-kept gardens, simply because they are difficult to get at; moreover, most will flower well for years without attention. The time will come, however, when they become so overgrown and vulnerable to disease that some action must be taken.

When renovating roses trained on supports, always take the opportunity, once growth is cut away, to inspect the wall, fence, or other structure on which the rose was trained. This is the ideal time to carry out such maintenance work as repainting or repairing broken fixtures, such as trellises or wires.

WHEN TO RENOVATE

The dormant season is generally the most suitable time to carry out drastic pruning to renovate roses, even of categories, including the ramblers, that are normally pruned after flowering, although this may mean a season without flowers. Follow any renewal and renovation work on roses by fertilizing and mulching well (see p.15) in spring.

BUSH AND SHRUB ROSES

For these roses, hard cutting back is the simplest, if sometimes risky, renovation method. At worst, it will kill a rose that would very likely have lingered only a little longer anyway. More often, it will stimulate dormant buds at the base of the plant into growth and completely reinvigorate the rose.

First cut away all dead stems and stumps at the base of the plant. Use loppers or a pruning saw if necessary, although long-dead material may just break away. Remove any suckers (see facing page, top). The remaining growth should then be cut to within 1–1½in (2.5–4cm) of ground level. Do not worry about trying to cut to a bud; you will probably not be able to find one.

A less drastic treatment is to combine the elimination of all unproductive wood with overall shortening and renewal pruning (see right). This gradual renovation can be spread over two years if you are particularly anxious not to lose the rose.

CLIMBING ROSES

Neglected climbers are characteristically bare at the base, with excessive top growth. Cut back a proportion of the main stems (as many as one in three in any one year) to within 12in (30cm) of ground level. This should encourage new growth from below. If the rose does not respond (and some cultivars are reluctant to do so), the only solution is to plant a low-growing, dense plant in front to hide the bare stems.

With a climber that has outgrown its space and become top-heavy, shorten all main shoots until the rose occupies not more than two-thirds of the allotted space, and prune all laterals on the main stems by two-thirds of their length, cutting to a healthy bud or shoot.

RAMBLER ROSES

Old, overgrown ramblers are a mass of tangled stems, some of which may have died right back to the base. To simplify the removal of pruned wood, cut stems in sections. Cut out dead wood and thin and feeble-looking stems, together with any showing signs of disease. Cut out completely or to near ground level all old stems to leave only three or four strong young canes. Prune all laterals on these stems by 3–4 in (8–10cm).

Ramblers that are impossibly tangled may be cut down completely to ground level after flowering in early summer or late winter. Most ramblers spring back to life quickly, seeming to benefit from this treatment. Flowers may be delayed for a year with hard winter pruning.

GRADUAL ROSE RENOVATION

This 'Queen Elizabeth' rose is a valuable taller feature in a border planting, but it has been neglected for several years, resulting in a buildup of dead and unwanted growth. Mild renovation measures should invigorate it without leaving a gaping hole in the planting plan over the following growing season. Next winter, provided that new growth has developed, the thick, old stems at the center and on the far left of the bush should be cut to the base, and so on in subsequent years until all the main stems are renewed.

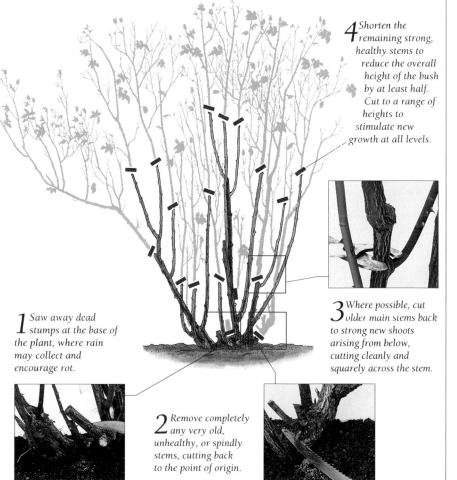

4 *Shorten the remaining strong, healthy stems to reduce the overall height of the bush by at least half. Cut to a range of heights to stimulate new growth at all levels.*

1 *Saw away dead stumps at the base of the plant, where rain may collect and encourage rot.*

3 *Where possible, cut older main stems back to strong new shoots arising from below, cutting cleanly and squarely across the stem.*

2 *Remove completely any very old, unhealthy, or spindly stems, cutting back to the point of origin.*

MODERN BUSH ROSES

The aim of pruning all modern bush roses is to encourage plenty of new growth that will bear a succession of flowers throughout the growing season. These roses are therefore pruned back annually to a low framework of main stems. This prevents the base of the bush from becoming bare, and encourages the growth of strong, vigorous shoots bearing good-quality flowers; even harder pruning, as practiced by rose exhibitors (*see right*), will result in fewer but finer flowers.

Never be afraid to prune bush roses hard. Underpruning, year after year, is the most common cause of an unproductive bush rose, with bare, leggy, "stepped" stems, spindly leafless shoots, and stubs of dead wood.

In recent years, trials have been conducted to investigate the theory that bush roses can be pruned much less systematically (even using a hedge trimmer) than is traditionally recommended. Although the results so far are intriguing (*see p.309*), it is too early to draw firm conclusions.

ROSE BEDS

Routine annual pruning to a specified height encourages uniform growth, which is ideal for roses massed together for display in a traditional rose bed, since all bushes of the same cultivar will flower at about the same time and height. With this type of close planting, it is vital to make sure that air can circulate freely around the plants. When pruning roses in rose beds, it is more important to have stems that do not crowd or cross those of neighboring bushes than to create a balanced shape for each individual plant.

BUYING AND PLANTING

Modern bush roses benefit from initial hard pruning. This stimulates vigorous growth from below, which is desirable for a strong and well-shaped rose bush. Bare-rooted roses are available during the dormant season, which is the traditional time for planting roses because it allows the root system to become established before vigorous young shoots appear. Prune the roots, shortening any overlong, coarse roots and trimming away any that are damaged. After planting, prune the top growth (*see facing page, top*).

Containerized plants can be planted at any time. Prune as for bare-rooted roses if planted in the dormant season, but if planted while in growth, remove open flowers and cut out any damaged growth, then prune hard in the early spring of the next year.

PRUNING FOR SHOW ROSES

Modern bush roses that are pruned for show blooms are cut back very hard, almost to ground level, letting the plant produce only a small number of main stems. These will bear a very few individual large blooms, or clusters of blooms. In addition, disbudding (*see below*) enhances the show qualities of the flowers. Hybrid tea roses produce blooms of maximum size and good form if only one flower is allowed to develop per stem. Remove surplus flower buds as soon as they develop. With floribunda roses, the central bloom normally opens and fades before the lowest have started to unfurl. More even flowering is achieved if the central bud is removed.

DISBUDDING

HYBRID TEA ROSES *Carefully pinch off any side buds that form below the large, terminal flower bud.*

FLORIBUNDA ROSES *Pinch out the central bud in a cluster at an early stage, removing all of its flower stalk.*

WHEN TO PRUNE

The main time for pruning modern bush roses is while the roses are dormant, or nearly so – between late winter and early spring. In colder climates, pruning is better left until as late as possible. However, harsh winter winds may damage tall, upright rose stems. Wind-rock may loosen the roots, and also create a gap in the soil at the base of the plant. Water that collects here may freeze and damage the graft union, the plant's most vulnerable spot. To reduce wind-rock, cut rose bushes taller than 3ft (1m) back in autumn (*see below*). The rose can then be pruned normally, depending on its type, in the following spring, once any danger of prolonged frost has passed.

During the growing season confine pruning to deadheading (*see p.303*) – nearly all modern bush roses are repeat-flowering – and the removal of diseased or damaged growth, as well as any other necessary routine tasks (*see p.304*), such as removing suckers.

AUTUMN TRIMMING

In colder climates, roses are often damaged by winter weather, particularly in exposed sites. To protect the roses, shorten their stems by half to one-third of their height. After severe winds or cold weather, carefully firm the soil around the base of the plant.

Before trimming

After trimming

HYBRID TEA ROSES

Hybrid tea roses, also called large-flowered bush roses, are sold as one-year-old plants. Prune hard on planting, cutting stems back close to the ground (*see right*). They need no further formative pruning or training; after their first full growing season, treat and prune as established plants.

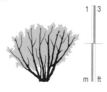

ESTABLISHED PRUNING

During the growing and flowering season remove as necessary any dead, diseased, or damaged growth and any suckers, and deadhead regularly to encourage a continuous show of flowers (*see Routine tasks, p.303*).

During the dormant season (*see When to prune, facing page*) the main, annual pruning of bush roses consists of removing all unproductive and unhealthy shoots, and shortening what remains. Only strong, healthy growth is retained to supply vigorous shoots in the following growing season. Most hybrid tea roses are naturally upright, and this often leads to overcrowded stems in the center of the bush. By selectively shortening stems to healthy, outward-pointing buds, a well-shaped and open-centered bush can be formed,

PRUNING A NEWLY PLANTED HYBRID TEA ROSE

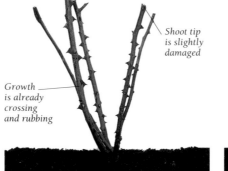

Shoot tip is slightly damaged

Growth is already crossing and rubbing

BEFORE PRUNING *These long shoots should be pruned hard to stimulate vigorous growth from below, where it is wanted, and also eliminate any defects or nursery damage.*

AFTER PRUNING *Each shoot is pruned to 3–6in (7–15cm) above ground level. Angled cuts just above outward-facing buds encourage open, well-spaced new growth.*

allowing free air circulation and reducing the risk of disease.

First remove dead or diseased wood, and any stumps left from the previous year's pruning that did not produce worthwhile shoots. Cut away spindly shoots of less than pencil thickness; they are unlikely to flower and will be the first to succumb to blackspot. Remove entirely any shoots growing into the center of the bush or, if this will denude the bush too much, cut to a low, outward-facing bud. Shorten or remove one of any pair of crossing shoots. Finally, choose three to five stocky young canes as scaffolding

for next season's flowering shoots. Shorten these to 8in (20cm) from the ground in colder and temperate climates. In warmer climates, cut back less severely, to 10–12in (25–30cm). The exact height will have to vary from stem to stem, since it is impossible to keep cutting to exactly the same point. After two or three years, the main shoots will become thick, woody, and unproductive and should be removed as close to the graft union as possible. Vigorous new shoots should replace older wood. Rotate this renewal pruning between the stems of the rose. For renovation, see p.305.

PRUNING AN ESTABLISHED HYBRID TEA ROSE

1 Remove any shoots that are dead, diseased, or damaged, and cut back to healthy wood any showing signs of dieback.

Position cuts to encourage outward growth that will not cross the center or other stems

2 Shorten the remaining stems, making an angled cut to ⅕in (5mm) above an outward-facing bud 8–9in (20–22cm) above ground level.

EXAMPLES OF HYBRID TEA AND GRANDIFLORA ROSES
'BRANDY'
'CHRYSLER IMPERIAL'
'DOUBLE DELIGHT'
'ELINA'
'FRAGRANT CLOUD'
'GOLD MEDAL'
'KARDINAL'
'LOVE'
'MIKADO'
'MISTER LINCOLN'
'PEACE'
'PERFECT MOMENT'
'PRISTINE'
'QUEEN ELIZABETH'
'RIO SAMBA'
'SEASHELL'
'SECRET'
'SONIA'
'TOUCH OF CLASS'
'TROPICANA'

'Queen Elizabeth'

FLORIBUNDA ROSES

Floribundas, also called cluster-flowered roses, are pruned on planting as for hybrid tea roses (*see p.307*). When established, the only difference between pruning hybrid tea roses and these is that, after unwanted growth has been cut away, the remaining stems are not shortened so drastically. The charm of these roses lies in their mass of flowers, so more buds are retained on a longer length of stem in order that they may develop into flowering shoots.

A problem characteristic of floribunda roses, which is also encountered when deadheading (*see p.303*), is that there may appear to be no buds to cut to on stems that have carried large sprays of flowers. Cut to the approximate desired height. This should stimulate a dormant bud into life. Should a stub be left above this new shoot, cut it away at a later time.

Neglected and old floribunda bushes usually respond well to gradual or complete renovation (*see p.315*).

EXAMPLES OF FLORIBUNDA ROSES

'Amber Queen'
'Anthony Meilland'
'Apricot Nectar'
'Betty Prior'
'Class Act'
'Iceberg'
'Impatient'
'Matador'
'Playboy'
'Pleasure'
'Sunflare'
'Sunsprite'

PRUNING AN ESTABLISHED FLORIBUNDA ROSE

1 *Prune all dead or diseased stems back to healthy wood or to the base of the bush.*

2 *Remove any stems that are rubbing or likely to rub against one another.*

3 *Shorten the remaining stems to within 10–12in (25–30cm) of ground level, making a correctly angled cut just above a healthy, outward-facing bud or shoot.*

4 *Shorten any laterals back to two or three buds from the main stem, cutting to an outward-facing bud.*

PATIO AND POLYANTHA ROSES

Patio roses are simply small cultivars of cluster-flowered roses; 'First Edition', 'Sexy Rexy', 'Cider Cup', 'Top Marks', and 'Showbiz' are among the best-known. Polyanthas, such as 'Marie Pavié' and 'China Doll', are compact bushes with tight clusters of small flowers. The growth habit and therefore the pruning of both these rose types is the same as for full-sized floribunda or cluster-flowered roses (*see above*), though on a smaller scale. After all unproductive wood has been removed, their main stems should be reduced by about two-thirds to a healthy bud or lateral. This regular pruning will also keep patio and polyantha roses that are growing in containers, for which they are ideal, compact and free-flowering.

Both patio roses and polyanthas can be renovated in the same way as other bush roses (*see p.305*).

MINIATURE ROSES

45 | 18

cm | in

These appealing, tiny bush roses have flowers or clusters of flowers that are scaled-down versions of those borne by hybrid tea or floribunda roses. The principles and timing of pruning are similar to those of their full-sized counterparts – deadheading during the flowering season, followed by annual pruning when dormant.

Prune miniatures hard on planting, in the same way as full-sized floribunda bushes (*see p.307*), cutting back to a height of 2–3in (5–8cm). In subsequent years, there are two methods by which they may be pruned. If they are growing well, prune hard, reducing canes to 3–6in (8–15cm) and removing twigs from the center of the bush. Cultivars such as 'Baby Masquerade' that produce a great deal of twiggy growth in the center will need drastic thinning. It is difficult to prescribe the exact heights to which main stems should be shortened since bush size varies between cultivars. However, a satisfactory rule of thumb is, whatever their flowering type, to shorten by two-thirds.

If the rose is growing poorly, or if you find by trial and error that it responds better, light pruning (*see right*) will suffice, removing only dead, diseased, or damaged growth and any crossing stems, and reducing sideshoots to relieve congestion.

LIGHT PRUNING OF AN ESTABLISHED MINIATURE ROSE

1 *Remove any dead, diseased, or damaged growth. Relieve congestion by cutting out the oldest stems entirely.*

2 *Prune main stems to remove any last spent flowers.*

3 *Prune any laterals back to within one or two buds of the main stem.*

EXAMPLES OF MINIATURE ROSES

'Arizona Sunset'	'Jean Keneally'	'Rise 'n' Shine'
'Baby Masquerade'	'Judy Fischer'	'Snow Bride'
'Cinderella'	'Magic Carousel'	'Stardance'
'Cup Cake'	'Minnie Pearl'	'Starina'
'Green Ice'	'Party Girl'	'Sweet Chariot'
'Gourmet Popcorn'	'Peaches 'n' Cream'	
'Hot Line'	'Red Ace'	

ALTERNATIVES TO TRADITIONAL ROSE PRUNING

The traditional techniques for pruning modern bush roses require a degree of judgment that some gardeners find difficult; they can also be time-consuming. In recent years, the question has arisen as to whether using the traditional method really is worthwhile. Since 1990, a British program of pruning trials has been comparing traditional with quite revolutionary rose-pruning methods. The most spectacular, and probably best known, of the findings is that rose bushes that are simply cut down to knee height with a hedge trimmer flower as well, if not better, than those that are painstakingly pruned on traditional lines.

Hedge-trimmer pruning, with no attempt made to remove dead wood, is, therefore, now being recommended by some writers, though not by the body that hosted the trials, England's Royal National Rose Society. Many growers believe that leaving jagged cuts and dead or unhealthy wood on a rose bush cannot be good practice in the long run and that the bushes on which it is left will succumb to disease.

The results of another trial seem more promising and more practical. In this, the roses were roughly pruned, with no attempt to make angled cuts or indeed to cut to specific buds. Dead wood was removed but, as with the lighter method of pruning miniature roses (*see above*), the weak, twiggy stems that normally would have been removed were left on the bush. This produced new growth that was actually better than that of the conventionally pruned roses, and on floribunda roses also resulted in more flowers.

Until the trials have run considerably longer, this method cannot be officially recommended. In the meantime, there is no harm in experimenting with one or two bushes, pruning lightly as for the miniature rose (*see above*), to see if it suits your roses.

PRUNING WITH A HEDGE TRIMMER
This crude approach appears to work in the short term, but its long-term effects are as yet unknown. A pair of shears will do the same job as a hedge trimmer and more safely.

STANDARD ROSES

Standard roses range from miniatures, ideal for a pot or tub, through half- and full-standard bush roses, with overall heights of about 3½ft (1.1m) and 4½ft (1.35m) respectively, to, tallest of all, weeping standards. All are formed by top-grafting the desired scion onto a tall, clear stem of, usually, *R. rugosa*, although growers are experimenting with other types, such as *R. laxa*, which live longer and are less prone to sucker. Standards must be permanently staked. Use a cane for miniature standards, but a preservative-treated wooden stake for larger types. The stake should reach up to the graft union (the weakest point on the stem) but not rub against it.

All standard roses must be pruned annually. Their specific pruning requirements depend on which type of rose forms the head. Pruning prevents the rose from becoming top-heavy, maintains a compact, symmetrical shape, and improves flower quantity or quality.

TIME OF PRUNING
This varies according to the type of rose forming the head: repeat-flowers in the dormant season, to encourage a continuous show of blooms on new growth, and after flowers have faded for those with a single flush of flowers.

Throughout the growing season, the routine tasks appropriate to all roses (*see p.303*) should also be carried out, particularly the removal of suckers at an early stage. Suckers may emerge from below the ground or on the clear stem; rub them from the stem when young.

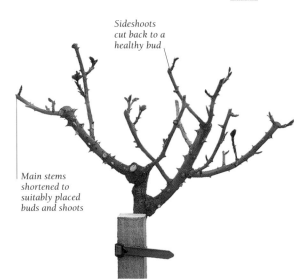

PATIO ROSE GROWN AS A STANDARD
This small floribunda rose ('Little Bo Peep') grafted onto a tall, clear stem is a good container plant.

BUSH STANDARDS

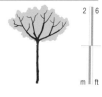

Many cultivars of hybrid tea and floribunda roses are available trained as half- or full standards, with clear stems of 2½ft (75cm) and 3½ft (1.1m) respectively. Standard patio, polyantha, and miniature roses, usually with clear stems no taller than 20in (50cm), are also increasingly popular.

TRAINING AND PRUNING
Prune on planting and when established as for a normal bush, according to the type of rose that forms the head, whether a hybrid tea (*see p.307*), floribunda (*see p.308*), patio rose, or miniature rose (*see p.309*). When shortening stems, treat the graft point of the standard as if it were at ground level.

It is particularly important to maintain a balanced head. To achieve this, prune harder on the weaker side of the plant. Light pruning on the more vigorous side will keep the head in shape but discourage the production of strong shoots.

In regions with hard winters, autumn trimming (*see p.306*) is advisable to reduce the risk of long stems being buffeted and damaged by strong winds.

RENOVATION
A neglected standard rose (for example, in a newly acquired garden) should be pruned hard (*see p.305*) in winter or early spring. Do not waste any more effort attempting to rescue it if it does not make strong new growth in the following flowering season.

ESTABLISHED STANDARD ROSE, EARLY SPRING

BEFORE PRUNING
The stems of this standard hybrid tea rose were shortened in the autumn to prevent wind damage in winter. Now that all danger of frost has passed, the rose should be pruned again to eliminate unproductive wood, create a balanced, open head, and encourage vigorous new flowering growth.

Crossing shoot that may damage another stem should be removed

Remove dead, damaged, and diseased growth

Sideshoots cut back to a healthy bud

Main stems shortened to suitably placed buds and shoots

AFTER PRUNING
Remaining healthy main stems have been cut back to about 8in (20cm) from the graft union, and their sideshoots shortened to two or three buds. Pruning has been slightly harder on the left side, with the aim of stimulating some new, strong shoots to create a better-balanced head.

WEEPING STANDARDS

A weeping rose standard is formed by top-grafting a rambler, climber, or trailing groundcover rose onto a clear stem, usually 5–6ft (1.5–2m) tall. When buying one, it is important to know which type forms the head; it will affect the look of the rose, the amount of pruning and training required, and the time of pruning.

Only ramblers, with their long, flexible shoots, will weep naturally. The spreading groundcover roses will not so much weep as droop from the graft point. Climbers need to be trained to overcome their natural tendency to grow upward; only cultivars with flexible shoots are really suitable.

TRAINING AND PRUNING

Weeping standards are best left unpruned on planting and for their first couple of years to develop their form. Prune only to remove dead, diseased, or damaged growth or to shorten weak, spindly shoots to a strong bud, encouraging fresh, vigorous shoots. The stems of climbing cultivars are best

UMBRELLA FRAME

This commercial frame, made of plastic-covered metal, acts as both stake and training frame to which shoots can be tied in. The resulting shape is more compact and formal than a free-growing weeping standard.

Tie in stems to create a well-balanced head

trained downward while still young, by tying them down evenly around a wire "umbrella" frame (*see above*).

Once established, prune according to the rose type: rambler (*see p.318*), climber (*see p.317*), or groundcover rose (*see p.315*). Vigorous ramblers, such as 'Dorothy Perkins', can (if well fertilized) produce so many new stems that all flowered shoots can be removed each year, cutting back to the new basal shoots. On less vigorous roses, remove only one in two or three flowered stems, perhaps only every other year,

depending on how congested the head has become. Cut to shoots or buds facing upward and outward to produce a cascading effect. Ramblers easily weep to ground level, and stems may need to be shortened.

With climbers, prune to buds facing outward and downward to improve the shape of the plant. Groundcover roses probably require the least work of all, although they benefit from thinning if very twiggy and congested.

Renovate according to rose type (*see p.305*); ramblers usually respond best.

PRUNING A RAMBLER TRAINED AS A WEEPING STANDARD AFTER FLOWERING

1 *Cut the oldest flowered stems back to just above the graft union.*

2 *Prune other flowered stems to an outward-growing replacement shoot.*

3 *Prune any sideshoots to three or four buds.*

4 *Tip-prune stems that touch the ground.*

5 *Throughout the growing season, remove as seen any suckers on the rose's stem, preferably pinching them out at an early stage.*

SHRUB ROSES

The shrub roses form a diverse group that spans the entire history of the genus *Rosa*, from species roses to modern shrubs developed in this century. Unlike bush roses, shrub roses, in general, flower on older wood, so they should be allowed to develop into permanent features, maintained by light, but regular, renewal pruning that keeps them shapely and with a healthy balance of older wood and young, vigorous growth. In their pruning requirements they are more similar to many deciduous flowering shrubs than to other rose groups.

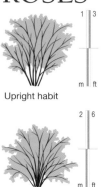

Upright habit

Spreading habit

Although broad generalizations can be made about the various groupings, the exact pruning required depends much more on the individual cultivar's growth and flowering habit.

SPECIES ROSES

The truly wild roses and the hybrids close to them require very little pruning. Formative pruning, in the dormant season, consists of lightly tip-pruning any overlong stems. Once established, prune also in the dormant season, only to remove dead, damaged, or weak shoots and, if necessary, correct an unbalanced shape. Cut weak stems back harder than those that are growing strongly, with the aim of stimulating vigorous regrowth. After reshaping, a rose may produce few flowers in the following year. Species roses that are performing poorly or have become an unhealthy tangle of old growth may be rejuvenated by harder pruning; renovate as for gallicas (*see facing page*).

OLD GARDEN ROSES

Most of these roses may be pruned by one of two methods (*see facing page*). Other techniques are used for hybrid musks (*see p.314*), boursaults, noisettes, and climbing bourbons (*see p.316*) and for hybrid perpetuals (*see p.320*).

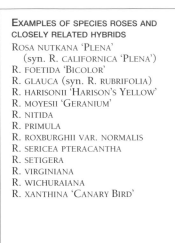

EXAMPLES OF SPECIES ROSES AND CLOSELY RELATED HYBRIDS

ROSA NUTKANA 'PLENA'
   (syn. R. CALIFORNICA 'PLENA')
R. FOETIDA 'BICOLOR'
R. GLAUCA (syn. R. RUBRIFOLIA)
R. HARISONII 'HARISON'S YELLOW'
R. MOYESII 'GERANIUM'
R. NITIDA
R. PRIMULA
R. ROXBURGHII VAR. NORMALIS
R. SERICEA PTERACANTHA
R. SETIGERA
R. VIRGINIANA
R. WICHURAIANA
R. XANTHINA 'CANARY BIRD'

R. moyesii

PRUNING AN ESTABLISHED GALLICA ROSE AFTER FLOWERING

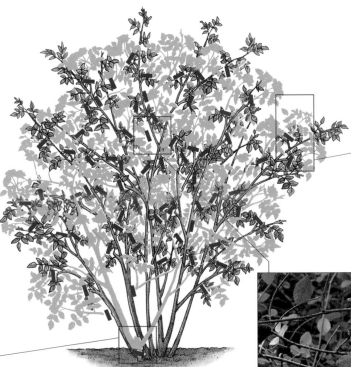

1 Completely remove one or two old, very woody stems at the base.

2 Shorten laterals to a sideshoot or bud 2–6in (5–15cm) from a main stem.

3 Remove all dead, damaged, or weak stems, as well as any rubbing against another stem, to keep the rose healthy.

ALBAS, DAMASKS, MOSSES, AND PROVENCES

Most roses in these groups should be pruned as soon as their single flush of summer flowering is over. One or two moss roses, however, sometimes have a fitful second blossoming and so pruning for these should be slightly delayed.

On planting, lightly tip-prune long shoots. Once established, cut out dead, diseased, and damaged wood and thin crossing stems. Then cut back main stems and laterals by one-third (*see right*). In autumn, extra-long shoots may be shortened (*see below right*) so that they are not damaged if blown about in winter winds.

Old specimens can be renovated by thinning, cutting out all but the most vigorous young stems; these should be cut back by one-third. Renovate after flowering or in the spring.

BOURBONS, CHINA ROSES, AND PORTLAND ROSES

These are pruned as for albas (*see above*) but in the dormant season, since they are repeat-flowering. Deadhead in summer.

GALLICAS

These fairly dense old garden roses (which make excellent hedges) need only light pruning on planting. Tip-prune lightly any overlong stems, and cut out one or two stems if growth is crowded. On established plants take out all dead, diseased, and damaged stems in spring. In early summer, when flowering has finished, thin growth by cutting back laterals to a main stem or to a shoot close to a main stem. Every one to three years, depending on the vigor of growth, take out at or near ground level one or two old main stems. In winter, use shears to clip over lightly gallicas grown as hedges. No attempt should be made at formal shaping.

Old and neglected gallicas will often respond well if pruned drastically in early spring, all but the most vigorous young stems being cut out completely.

PRUNING AN ESTABLISHED ALBA ROSE AFTER FLOWERING

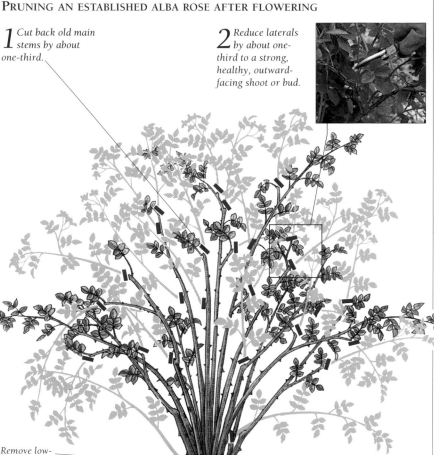

1 *Cut back old main stems by about one-third.*

2 *Reduce laterals by about one-third to a strong, healthy, outward-facing shoot or bud.*

Remove low-growing shoots that will arch over to touch the ground

TRIMMING ALBA ROSES, AUTUMN
Shorten vigorous, overlong shoots protruding above the outline of the shrub to avoid wind damage.

EXAMPLES OF OLD GARDEN ROSES

Alba roses	China roses	'CHARLES DE MILLS'	'JEANNE DE MONTFORT'
'BELLE AMOUR'	'CÉCILE BRÜNNER'	'DUC DE GUICHE'	'WILLIAM LOBB'
'CÉLESTE'	'PERLE D'OR'	'PRÉSIDENT DE SÈZE'	
(syn. 'CELESTIAL')	R. X ODORATA 'MUTABILIS'	R. GALLICA 'OFFICINALIS'	Portland roses
'FÉLICITÉ PARMENTIER'	R. X ODORATA 'PALLIDA'	R. GALLICA 'VERSICOLOR'	'COMTE DE CHAMBORD'
'GREAT MAIDEN'S BLUSH'	(syn. 'OLD BLUSH CHINA')	(syn. 'ROSA MUNDI')	'JACQUES CARTIER'
'KÖNIGIN VON DANEMARK'		'TRICOLORE DE FLANDRE'	R. PORTLANDICA
R. X 'ALBA MAXIMA'	Damask roses	'TUSCANY SUPERB'	
R. X 'ALBA SEMIPLENA'	'ISPAHAN'		Provence (centifolia) roses
	'MADAME HARDY'	Moss roses	'DE MEAUX'
Bourbon roses	'OMAR KHAYYAM'	'CAPITAINE JOHN INGRAM'	'FANTIN-LATOUR'
'BOULE DE NEIGE'	'DE RESCHT'	R. X CENTIFOLIA CRISTATA	'PETITE DE HOLLANDE'
'MADAME ISAAC PEREIRE'		(syn. 'CHAPEAU DE NAPOLÉON')	'ROBERT LE DIABLE'
'MADAME PIERRE OGER'	Gallica roses	'GÉNÉRAL KLÉBER'	'SPONG'
'SOUVENIR DE LA MALMAISON'	'ALAIN BLANCHARD'	'HENRI MARTIN'	'THE BISHOP'
'VARIEGATA DI BOLOGNA'	'BELLE DE CRÉCY'	'JAMES MITCHELL'	'TOUR DE MALAKOFF'

MODERN SHRUB ROSES

This group covers a number of rose types developed over the last 100 years or so. Many combine the vigor of species roses with the repeat-flowering characteristic of modern roses, so they should be pruned during the dormant season, most usually in early spring. Most are upright, bushy, and robust, reaching heights of 4–6ft (1.2–2m), and make impressive specimen plants. Others have more dense and spreading growth, and are commonly referred to as groundcover roses (*see facing page*).

Some modern shrubs, such as 'Nevada' and 'Marguerite Hilling', need only light pruning (*see below*). The modern floribunda shrubs are simply large cultivars of floribunda roses, and can be pruned similarly (*see p.308*), shortening main stems by only one-third, to keep the plant's stature; cut back laterals by two-thirds. Other named groups of modern shrubs require slightly different approaches.

HYBRID MUSKS

These vigorous, repeat-flowering, leafy shrubs and others of similar habit (*see above right*) require little or no formative pruning. Prune established plants in the dormant season, removing dead, diseased, and damaged wood and removing one to three of the oldest, least productive stems. Cut back main stems by up to one-third, and laterals by half.

SUPPORTING SHRUB ROSES
Two low stakes with strong twine or plastic chain link nailed between them form a useful support for the stems of open shrub roses, giving them a more upright habit. Under-planting can help disguise the support.

RUGOSAS
These are mostly turn-of-the-century selections or hybrids of *R. rugosa*; upright, thorny, repeat-flowering shrubs with bright green, wrinkled (rugose) foliage that colors well in autumn. Some have bright red, tomato-shaped hips.

They require little or no formative pruning. Prune established plants in the dormant season, tip-pruning long stems and occasionally taking out an old stem completely. To renovate, thin more drastically, taking out several old stems and cutting back one in two or three that remain by up to half (*see p.305*).

EXAMPLES OF MODERN SHRUB ROSES

Floribunda-type
'CAREFREE WONDER'
'EYE PAINT'
'FOUNTAIN'
'FRANCINE AUSTIN'
'FRITZ NOBIS'
'JACQUELINE DU PRÉ'
'MORDEN BLUSH'
'SEA FOAM'
'TOPAZ JEWEL'

Hybrid musks and others resembling them in habit
'BALLERINA'
'BUFF BEAUTY'
'CORNELIA'
'GOLDEN WINGS'
'LAVENDER DREAM'
'PENELOPE'

Rugosas
'AGNES'
'BLANCHE DOUBLE DE COUBERT'
'FIMBRIATA'
'F. J. GROOTENDORST'
'FRU DAGMAR HASTRUP'
'HORSA'
'ROSERAIE DE L'HAŸ'
R. RUGOSA 'ALBA'
'SCABROSA'
'THÉRÈSE BUGNET'

LIGHT PRUNING OF AN ESTABLISHED MODERN SHRUB ROSE

1 *When growth becomes crowded, remove one or two old unproductive stems at the base.*

2 *To maintain a compact habit and encourage flowering, tip-prune a proportion of sideshoots at the periphery of the plant.*

3 *Remove any dead, diseased, or damaged growth, cutting to a healthy bud.*

GROUNDCOVER ROSES

There are two kinds of groundcover roses: the modern shrubs, and the creeping ramblers. Each has a distinctive growth habit. Both need pruning mainly to keep them to their allotted space. They may also be used to form weeping standards (see p.215).

MODERN SHRUB TYPE

These low-growing, spreading roses – generally less than 2ft (60cm) tall – offer dense leaf coverage in summer, providing good weed suppression, but, being deciduous, they are bare in winter. They can also be grown in containers. Prune those that are repeat-flowering in spring, the rest in summer, after flowering.

Little or no formative pruning is required. Once established, cut out any dead or diseased stems and tip-prune main stems – or shorten them if they extend over their intended boundary. Open up the center of the bush a little by shortening laterals. If feasible, deadhead in the flowering season. These roses usually respond well to hard cutting back if necessary.

CREEPING RAMBLER TYPE

These roses are closely allied to ramblers such as R. wichuraiana. Their long, flexible stems hug the ground, making them ideal for an awkward bank, for example. The stems root where they touch the ground, and may reach 10ft (3m) or more in length, the laterals forming a substantial mound.

Lightly prune in summer after flowering, only to cut stems back to upright shoots to keep them within bounds. To increase flower production, spread and peg down stems (see Pegging down, p.320). If more drastic pruning becomes necessary, renovate as for ramblers (see p.209).

RAMBLER-TYPE GROUNDCOVER ROSE

The vigorous, scrambling, rambler type of groundcover rose is ideal for wilder areas of the garden. Stems will root into the ground, increasing the rose's spread. Little pruning is needed except to keep the rose within bounds.

Vigorous first-year stems can be pegged down

Second-year stems become prostrate with the weight of flowering shoots

SHRUB-TYPE GROUNDCOVER ROSE

The neat modern shrub type of groundcover rose (left) is a small, compact bush with a spreading rather than upright habit, ideal for planting in groups for low-maintenance beds or to cover awkward slopes.

EXAMPLES OF GROUNDCOVER ROSES

Modern shrub type
'ALBA', 'FUCHSIA', 'PEARL' & 'SCARLET'
'BONICA'
'CAREFREE DELIGHT'
'FERDY'
'LADY OF THE DAWN'
'RALPH'S CREEPER'
'SEVILLANA'
'THE FAIRY'

Creeping rambler type
'BABY BLANKET', 'JEEPERS CREEPERS', 'RED RIBBONS'
R. X JACKSONII 'MAX GRAF'
'NOZOMI'
'RED CASCADE'
'SNOW CARPET'
'WHITE MEIDILAND'

ROSES FOR HANGING BASKETS

Shrub-type ground-cover roses will trail attractively when planted in a hanging basket or a manger on a wall. Although roses generally make good container plants, they should not be kept in a container as shallow as this one for more than two growing seasons.

CLIMBING AND RAMBLER ROSES

These roses can be trained to create a wide range of effects (*see* Special Training, *pp.319–325*) but are most commonly grown against walls and fences. The aim when pruning is to create a strong, well-shaped plant that will bear many healthy new flowering shoots each year. How this is done depends on whether the rose is a climber or a rambler; they differ in their growth and flowering habits, and thus in their pruning needs.

The main aim when training climbers and ramblers against a flat surface is to train as much growth as near to horizontal as possible. Initial fan training of the main stems allows flexible shoots to be trained horizontally, giving maximum coverage and an even distribution of flowers (*see* Horizontal training, *p.13*). If the stems were all allowed to grow directly upward they would flower only at their tops. For spaces where horizontal training is not possible, such as a narrow area of wall between two windows, choose either a large shrub rose or a climbing rose suitable for pillars, as recommended for training on vertical features (*see p.320*).

Before the rose is planted, provide a system of horizontal wires to which the

WALL-TRAINED CLIMBING ROSE
Horizontal training is the key to maximizing the flowering potential of wall-trained roses.

shoots can be tied. Set the lowest wire 18in (45cm) from the ground, and space subsequent wires 12in (30cm) apart. Use strong, galvanized wire, strung through vine eyes to hold it about 3in (8cm) from the surface. This will allow space for air to circulate between the rose and wall or fence, and thus help to

keep disease at bay. Plant climbers and ramblers at least 1ft (30cm) from the wall, with roots spreading away from the wall, so they are not in a rain shadow. Their shoots will probably reach the lowest wire but if not, bamboo stakes can be used to guide and support them; remove the stakes in the second year.

MODERN CLIMBERS

Modern climbers are no more than very tall bush roses, with fairly stiff shoots that need support and tying in. Although they lend themselves well to many different training methods (*see pp.319–325*), they are most commonly grown against fences and walls. The aim here must be to fan out the main stems so that laterals can be trained sideways.

WHEN TO PRUNE
Like modern bush roses, climbers are mostly repeat-flowering, so the main pruning season is also the same – from autumn, after the sequence of flowering has finished, to early spring. It is as well to prune in autumn, so that any long, whippy shoots can be shortened or tied in before strong winter winds can blow them around and damage them; in cool climates, the extra protection afforded by the wall should minimize any cold damage. Deadhead and tie in growth throughout the growing season.

EXAMPLES OF MODERN CLIMBERS
'ALOHA'	'JEANNE LAJOIE'
'ALTISSIMO'	'MADAME ALFRED CARRIÈRE'
'AMERICA'	'NEW DAWN'
'BLAZE'	'PARADE'
'COMPASSION'	'RED FOUNTAIN'
'DON JUAN'	'RHONDA'
'DORTMUND'	'WESTERLAND'
'DUBLIN BAY'	'WHITE COCKADE'
'EDEN'	'WHITE DAWN'
'GOLDEN SHOWERS'	'WILLIAM BAFFIN'
'HANDEL'	'ZÉPHIRINE DROUHIN'

FORMATIVE TRAINING
Climbers are sold with much longer shoots than those of bedding roses, and these should not be pruned (except to clean up minor damage), leaving plenty of buds from which new shoots can break when growth begins. It is particularly important to leave stems intact where the rose is a sport of a bush rose (for these, the cultivar name will be prefixed by the word "climbing," as in 'Climbing Iceberg'), because pruning at this stage may encourage it to revert to its original bush form.

Once growth begins, if the main stem or stems are slow to branch, tip-prune them to the first strong bud (outward-facing on outer stems) to encourage laterals to develop. Fan out the main

stems from the start (*see facing page, above*), spacing them evenly, and tie in laterals, training them to the horizontal, as they develop. Always cover the lower parts of the wall or fence from the beginning; although new shoots will nearly always break from horizontal stems to grow upward into gaps, it is difficult to fill in gaps lower down.

The stems must be guided while still young and pliable and tied in, well spaced, to form a strong, well-structured framework. Until this is established no other pruning is necessary, except to remove dead, damaged, diseased, or spindly, leafless growth and any suckers, and to deadhead repeat-flowering climbers to encourage subsequent flowering (*see p.303*).

ESTABLISHED PRUNING

Once the rose has filled the allotted space, its framework branches are regularly renewed, making way for vigorous young stems. At the edges, growth that needs shortening back can be pruned at any time, along with any other routine tasks and the tying-in of new growth to the wires. Deadhead (*see p.303*) to extend the flowering season. Once this is over, prune flowered sideshoots to stimulate the remaining portion to develop new flowering shoots in the next year. Once the stem itself becomes less productive of flowers, usually after no more than three years, cut it to a lower new shoot (*see* Renewal pruning, *p.302*), tying this in to fill the gap. Remove completely any growth that is weak or diseased.

On a mature climber, an entire main stem that is old and unproductive can be cut to the base, to stimulate new growth. If the climber becomes bare at the base, or has been neglected, more extensive renovation (*see p.305*) may be necessary.

WALL-TRAINED CLIMBER, YEAR 1, SUMMER

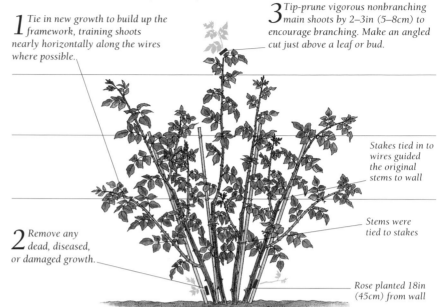

1 Tie in new growth to build up the framework, training shoots nearly horizontally along the wires where possible.

2 Remove any dead, diseased, or damaged growth.

3 Tip-prune vigorous nonbranching main shoots by 2–3in (5–8cm) to encourage branching. Make an angled cut just above a leaf or bud.

Stakes tied in to wires guided the original stems to wall

Stems were tied to stakes

Rose planted 18in (45cm) from wall

ESTABLISHED MODERN CLIMBER, PRUNING IN AUTUMN

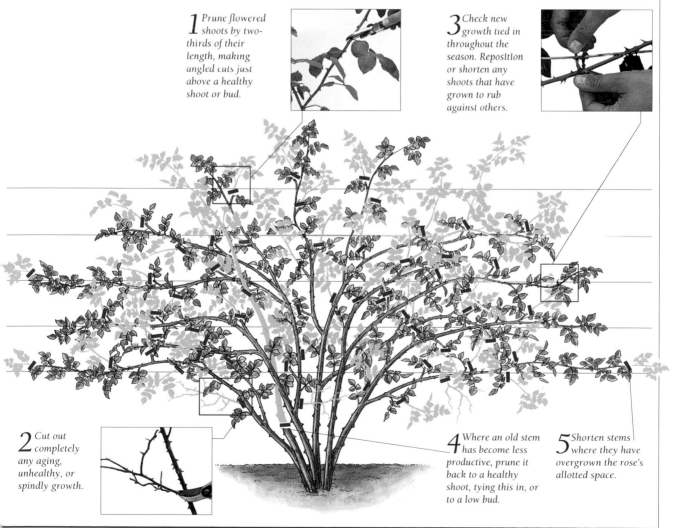

1 Prune flowered shoots by two-thirds of their length, making angled cuts just above a healthy shoot or bud.

3 Check new growth tied in throughout the season. Reposition or shorten any shoots that have grown to rub against others.

2 Cut out completely any aging, unhealthy, or spindly growth.

4 Where an old stem has become less productive, prune it back to a healthy shoot, tying this in, or to a low bud.

5 Shorten stems where they have overgrown the rose's allotted space.

RAMBLERS

5 15

m ft

Rambler roses, whether species or hybrids close in character to their wild forebears, are vigorous plants, regularly producing new flexible stems at or near ground level, and flowering most freely on wood produced in the previous year. They are pruned in summer, once their single flush of flowers is over.

With their wild, rampant habit, ramblers are generally used for informal effects. While they often flourish and flower perfectly well without pruning, if a rambler is to be a prominent feature in any but the wildest of gardens, training and pruning will be required to avoid a hopeless tangle of stems. However, it is because their stems are so long and flexible that ramblers can be trained to create such a variety of effects (*see* Special Training, *pp.319–325*). Their stems are easily trained horizontally on a fence or to form a screen. A chain link or other openwork fence is preferable to

a solid fence or wall; some ramblers are very prone to mildew, which is encouraged by poor air circulation.

FORMATIVE TRAINING

Ramblers should be pruned on planting to stimulate growth from the base. Remove dead, damaged, or weak and twiggy growth, and cut the main stems back to about 16in (40cm) from the ground. Fan out the stems and tie new shoots in near the horizontal as they grow to cover the allotted space evenly.

ESTABLISHED PRUNING

Once the allotted area is well covered, thin and shorten excess growth after the summer flowering. Ramblers make much more new growth from the base of the plant than climbers, and this should

be encouraged by cutting out one in three main stems to the base. Remove the oldest stems, cutting them in several places and teasing small sections out; pulling an entire stem right through the remaining plant will cause damage.

It is often recommended that all flowered stems should be cut down and new ones tied in their place. This is not necessary, since ramblers will flower very well on the same wood for several years, and it will also prevent the rose ever becoming a large and established garden feature. However, it is a useful technique either for renovating a rambler (*see p.305*) or for growing one (particularly vigorous cultivars like 'Dorothy Perkins') in a small space. Fertilize the rose well in the spring following hard pruning.

EXAMPLES OF RAMBLER ROSES

'ALBÉRIC BARBIER'
'ALBERTINE'
'BOBBIE JAMES'
'CHEVY CHASE'
'DOROTHY PERKINS'
'GOLDFINCH'
'KEW RAMBLER'
'PAUL'S HIMALAYAN MUSK' (syn. 'PAUL'S HIMALAYAN RAMBLER')

R. MULTIFLORA 'GREVILLEI' (syn. 'SEVEN SISTERS ROSE')
'ROSE MARIE VIAUD'
'RUSSELLIANA'
'SEAGULL'
'SILVER MOON'
'TAUSENDSCHÖN'
'THE GARLAND'

ESTABLISHED RAMBLER ROSE, PRUNING AFTER FLOWERING

1 *Cut one in three of the old flowered stems back to ground level, removing them in short sections.*

2 *Shorten sideshoots by about two-thirds to encourage them to develop flowering sideshoots for the following season.*

3 *Throughout the growing season, secure new shoots to wires with garden twine or ties, allowing room for the shoots to expand.*

4 *Tip-prune the remaining leading shoots by 2–3in (5–8cm) to encourage branching.*

SPECIAL TRAINING

One of the great attractions of roses, particularly the climbing and rambling cultivars, is that they can be grown in so many different ways. They will not only cover walls and fences but also grow as hedges or screens on a rigid framework, on vertical structures such as tripods and obelisks (*see p.320*), on pergolas and arches (*see p.322*), along ropes to form swags (*see p.324*), and, for the most artless of all effects, through trees or other host plants (*see p.325*). As with all climbing plants, careful training is nearly always the foundation of the best results. It ensures that a structure is densely and evenly covered not only with foliage but also with flowers, and that the trained form is not lost through rampant growth. A rose arch over a path, for example, can become a hazard, not a feature, if the archway is filled with long, whippy rose shoots.

A rose cannot use its thorns to hook and grip on to artificial supports such as arches, tripods, and struts, so shoots must be tied into position. Do not tie them directly to supports, particularly to brick or concrete pillars, since the shoots will be damaged by rubbing. Use nails or staples or insert vine eyes where ties are needed – or, on a large support such as a pillar, attach vertical wires or a narrow strip of trellis or netting. Around thinner supports such as ironwork, use twine tied in figure eights around the stem and support, or commercial ties, to prevent the stems from chafing.

ROSE SWAGS
One of the most popular features for adding height and graceful curves to formal rose displays, swags and catenaries (rows of swags) are produced by training roses along thick rope.

SPIRAL TRAINING
Spiral training of roses on vertical supports will encourage flowering at all levels. Train the shoots when young and still pliable.

With frequent tying-in, shoots can be directed to grow exactly where they are needed, and their flowering potential can be maximized where it is wanted. Where the flowering display is required high up, for example on the roof of a pergola or in a host tree, train the shoots directly upward, pruning sideshoots to direct energy into vertical growth until the objective has been reached; then allow the rose to branch naturally.

When shoots are trained directly upward, they flower largely at the top; a natural inhibitor (*see also p.13*) prevents buds lower down from forming flowering shoots. Training shoots horizontally breaks this habit, and sideshoots will develop and bloom along the stem's length.

Horizontal training is easy against a large, flat surface, where shoots can be fanned out, but on a narrow surface (a small screen, or the side of a deep arch, for example), some ingenuity is needed. One approach is to train shoots in a serpentine or "pretzel" shape, bringing them back on themselves to maximize horizontal growth (*see below center*). Alternatively, wind shoots around in a spiral up the support (*see left*). This encourages uniform flowering all the way up, and is the best way of covering three-dimensional structures such as tripods or obelisks.

ROSE SCREEN
Training shoots in serpentine fashion on a narrow, flat surface will produce a better display than will a narrow fan.

EDGING FOR PATHS AND BEDS
Rustic poles, bent stakes (as above), or even lengths of netting stretched between posts can provide support for rose stems.

Pegging down roses

Rose stems can be trained completely horizontally at ground level using a technique known as "pegging down." This was popularly used in Victorian England for tall and leggy hybrid perpetual roses, which tend to flower only at the tips of shoots if allowed to grow freely. Any rose with flexible shoots is suitable for pegging down.

Pegging down produces a low, dense mound of flowers without restricting choice to only those roses recommended for groundcover (*see p.315*). The main

stems are fanned out like the spokes of a wheel, resulting in masses of vertical flowering shoots. The stems are pegged to the ground, or tied to wires pegged into the ground, either crisscrossing the bed or in a cartwheel pattern. The latter is ideal for covering a manhole cover with growth; entire wire "spokes," with the rose attached, can be lifted clear.

Give the rose a growing season to become established. After flowering, carefully bend the stems down to near ground level and either peg them down

(*see below left*) or tie them to wires. Cut back all laterals (*see below*) to 4–6in (10–15cm). If starting with a mature rose, some of the older flowered stems should be removed (or even all of them, if there are plenty of new stems).

In following summers, deadhead repeat-flowering roses regularly. In autumn, cut out all weak growths and two to three older main stems, pegging or tying down vigorous young stems as replacements. Shorten flowered laterals to 10–15cm (4–6in).

PEGGING DOWN
The simplest method is to peg down shoots directly using hoops made from galvanized wire. Stems can also be tied to low wires fixed to pegs.

PEGGING DOWN A HYBRID PERPETUAL

1 Trim back the leading growth on each pegged-down stem to confine to the allotted space.

2 Shorten all the upward-growing laterals to 4–6in (10–15cm).

Training roses on vertical features

Rose-covered tripods or obelisks give height and colorful focal points to planting plans. The need for access to train and prune should be kept in mind when placing such features. Roses suited to this form of training are the less vigorous climbers, usually less than 10ft (3m) in height when mature, that are often sold as "pillar" roses. Bourbon roses, which can be unruly if left to their own devices, are also suitable, as are some large, vigorous, old and modern shrub roses; these often grow even taller against a support than when in open ground. Most ramblers are too vigorous for narrow, freestanding features.

Careful training is needed (*see right*). Spiraling the shoots either around individual "legs" or the entire structure will encourage flowering laterals to develop at all levels. Where only one or two sides of a pillar can be used, and shoots have to grow upward, choose a cultivar known to flower well at all levels (for example, 'Golden Showers'). If stems become bare at the base, they can be masked by another plant.

A single plant will take several years to establish fully, the time varying according to the cultivar. For a quicker and attractive effect, use several roses on one structure – for example, one up each leg of a tripod. The roses should be

HORIZONTAL TRAINING ON VERTICAL FEATURES

WITHOUT HORIZONTAL TRAINING *The stems of this climbing rose have simply been tied into the framework of this rustic tripod as they extend vertically. The result is that flowers are, with few exceptions, clustered at the top, and main stems are bare of sideshoots and flowers lower down.*

WITH HORIZONTAL TRAINING *The main stems of this rose have been wound around and tied into this ironwork obelisk in spirals. Bringing them down more toward the horizontal has stimulated buds to break and develop into flowering laterals all along their length (see also Horizontal Training, p.13).*

matched for vigor, and pruning will be simpler if they require the same regime. Alternatively, use climbing annuals or other climbing plants that either die back, or are cut back, each year, leaving the rose stems clear for pruning.

WHEN TO PRUNE

Prune roses that have a single flush of flowers in summer, once they have finished flowering. Prune repeat-flowering roses during the dormant season, between autumn and early spring. Pruning in autumn has the advantage that long growths can be shortened or tied in before any risk of damage by winter winds.

FORMATIVE PRUNING AND TRAINING

Plant the rose about 10in (25cm) from the base of the structure, and splay the stems out around it. Climbers and shrub roses need not be pruned on planting except to trim off any dead, damaged, or spindly wood. If a rambler is being used, cut its stems back on planting (see p.318). Throughout the growing season, train in growth while it is young and pliable; modern climbers in particular develop stout inflexible shoots quite quickly. Tie them in evenly spaced spirals up the structure. Avoid, where possible, tying shoots so that they cross.

PRUNING ESTABLISHED ROSES

With climbers, maintain a permanent framework of spiraled main stems just as on a wall-trained climbing rose (see p.317); cut back flowered shoots to an outward-facing bud or shoot. When growth becomes crowded, older stems can be cut back to vigorous new replacement shoots lower down or removed completely, with new stems growing from ground level being trained in as replacements. With ramblers, cut back flowered sideshoots by two-thirds of their length, and tip back the main stems. Every year remove one or two of the oldest main stems (see also p.317).

Old and neglected roses often need more drastic pruning. The best course is to take the entire rose down, lay it on the ground, and unravel it. Once the rose has been pruned (see Renovation, p.305) its stems can be wound back around the support and tied in.

PRUNING AN ESTABLISHED CLIMBER ON A TRIPOD

1 Cut back overlong shoots to a bud just below the top of the tripod.

2 Cut back flowered shoots to a low, outward-facing bud.

3 Cut some older stems back to strong, young replacement shoots. Stems are easier to remove if they are cut out in sections.

4 Tie in new stems that grow from the base, wherever possible filling gaps below by training them near to the horizontal.

RECOMMENDED FOR VERTICAL FEATURES

'ALCHYMIST' (modern climber)
'ALOHA' (modern climber)
'ALTISSIMO' (modern climber)
'AMERICA' (modern climber)
'BANTRY BAY' (modern climber)
'BOULE DE NEIGE' (Bourbon)
'CHINATOWN' (floribunda shrub)
'CLIMBING CÉCILE BRÜNNER'
'CONSTANCE SPRY' (hybrid tea rose)
'DORTMUND' (modern climber)

'DUBLIN BAY' (modern climber)
'EDEN' (modern climber)
'GLOIRE DE DIJON' (climbing noisette)
GOLDEN SHOWERS (modern climber)
'GRUSS AN TEPLITZ' (China)
'HANDEL' (modern climber)
'JOSEPH'S COAT' (floribunda shrub)
'LOUISE ODIER' (Bourbon)
'MADAME ISAAC PEREIRE' (Bourbon)
'MADAME PIERRE OGER' (Bourbon)

'MAIGOLD' (modern climber)
'PINK PERPÉTUÉ' (modern climber)
'REINE VICTORIA' (Bourbon)
R. X ODORATA 'MUTABILIS' (China)
'RED FOUNTAIN' (modern climber)
'WESTERLAND' (modern climber)
'WILLIAM BATTIN' (modern climber)
'WHITE COCKADE' (modern climber)

TRAINING ROSES ON A PERGOLA

The choice of rose or roses to cover a pergola will depend on the structure's size and strength. Ramblers are obvious choices for large pergolas, and those with stout oak posts or brick pillars supporting strong wooden crossbeams can comfortably accommodate even the most vigorous, such as 'Seagull' or 'Bobbie James'. If climbers are preferred for their long, repeat-flowering season, a large pergola may need one rose planted at every post. One or two plants, however, will be quite sufficient for pergolas no more than 6ft (2m) in length, particularly if they are of the "rustic pole" variety, as these will not bear the weight of a large rambler.

If the rose is to be grown over the top, its stems must be trained to turn almost at right-angles at the top of the pillars; ramblers, or the climbing cultivars with more flexible stems, are much easier to use. For large pergolas, use any of the roses recommended for growing up large host trees (see p.325); for small pergolas, use those roses suitable for smaller trees.

With a pergola, the main aim – to obtain a display of flowers along the crossbeams – is most quickly achieved by training the stems straight up the pillars (see below). It is unlikely, however, that these vertical stems will bear many flowers low down after the

COMBINING ROSES ON A PERGOLA
A combination of ramblers, climbers, and pillar roses has been used to cover this large pergola, whose open roof allows sunlight to reach the inner and under sides of the structure.

first few years. Flexible-stemmed climbers and ramblers can be spiral-trained around a pillar just as for a tripod (see p.320), but if stems are then trained across the top, it is probable that, with its energies directed into blooming profusely across the top, the rose will also become

bare at the base. The most reliable way to obtain flowers on both the pillar and the top is to plant another rose at the base of the pillar. To cover a pillar, use one of the roses recommended for vertical features (see p.321); they are usually less than 10ft (3m) in height and flower well on their lower stems.

Alternatively, use other plants: herbaceous climbers that will die back, or can be pruned back, in winter (for example, some clematis) give access to the rose stems for pruning. Climbing annuals enable different combinations to be tried each year (see also Training climbers on a pergola, p.258).

FORMATIVE TRAINING

Fix staples, wires, or strips of trellis to the framework of the pergola to give plenty of attachment points for ties. If you are aiming for a solid "roof" of greenery and flowering stems, fix wood strips or wires between the crossbeams.

Plant the rose about 10in (25cm) from the foot of the pillar, and tie in its shoots. If you are planting two roses, place them at each side of the pillar, not one inside and one outside the pergola, or the inner rose may be too shaded to flourish. With climbers, no inital pruning is necessary, except to trim away any damaged growth. Ramblers should be pruned on planting to encourage strong basal growth (see p.318). Tie in growth as it develops (see left). Once the rose reaches the top of the pillar, start guiding the shoots across the crossbeams, spacing them evenly and tying them in. To make the

TRAINING A ROSE UP A PERGOLA PILLAR

Main stems will reach canopy most quickly if sideshoots are removed

Stems on far right and left can be taken around and tied in to pillar's sides

1 *Remove any weak shoots, cutting them out at ground level, to encourage stronger shoots to grow rapidly.*

2 *Space out and tie in the remaining stems, attaching them with figure-eight ties to wires or struts held slightly away from the pillar's surface. Remove any sideshoots to encourage vertical growth.*

necessary right-angles and achieve even coverage, it is often impossible to avoid crossing stems: check them occasionally and reposition if necessary to avoid or minimize chafing.

ESTABLISHED PRUNING

Particular care must be taken when pruning roses on pergolas; the work often has to be done from a ladder. Follow the guidelines for pruning climbers (*see p.316*) and ramblers (*see p.318*) but prune less hard. Plentiful, billowing growth is more desirable on freestanding structures than it is on walls, and will soften the regular lines of the pillars and beams.

A neglected or overgrown rose trained on a pergola is difficult to renovate *in situ*. Cutting out a number of entire main stems to encourage new basal growth will be a formidable task and will create gaps that may take several years to fill satisfactorily. Although the procedure is laborious, the easiest way to renovate a neglected specimen involves untying the rose, laying it out on the ground, pruning it selectively, then tying the remaining stems in again, evenly spaced.

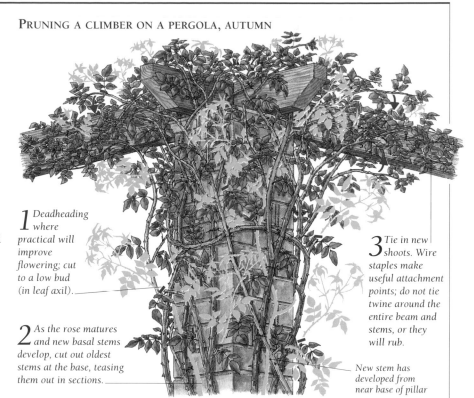

PRUNING A CLIMBER ON A PERGOLA, AUTUMN

1 Deadheading where practical will improve flowering; cut to a low bud (in leaf axil).

2 As the rose matures and new basal stems develop, cut out oldest stems at the base, teasing them out in sections.

3 Tie in new shoots. Wire staples make useful attachment points; do not tie twine around the entire beam and stems, or they will rub.

New stem has developed from near base of pillar

TRAINING OVER AN ARCH

Arches can be made from a variety of materials, ranging from rustic poles and trellises fixed to a wooden framework, to lightweight metal tubing, which is sometimes plastic-covered. When training a rose to cover an arch, the main aims are to achieve even coverage (to avoid all the flowers and growth being "bunched" at the top) and, if the arch is to be walked through, to keep growth to the outside.

Although the rose can be trained up and over the top of the arch, it cannot easily be trained down again on the other side, so two roses should be planted. The choice of cultivars is partly governed by the size of the arch. Any of the cultivars recommended for vertical features (*see p.321*) will grow well up the sides of an arch, although the modern climbers with more inflexible stems may be harder to train across the top. 'Climbing

ROSE ARCHES
A series of arches draws the eye to a gateway that acts as a focal point. It is important that the roses covering the arches do not become overgrown, obscuring the perspective and making it difficult to walk down the path without being snagged by thorny stems.

Iceberg' or 'Compassion' both have pliable stems. Thornless cultivars, such as 'Zéphirine Drouhin', are good choices for arches spanning paths. An alternative is to use one of the smaller traditional ramblers, such as 'Albéric Barbier', recommended for growing into smaller host trees and shrubs (*see p.325*). They are not overly vigorous and make plenty of growth from the base, although they flower only at midsummer. Avoid large ramblers such as 'Seagull', since they will swiftly engulf the structure.

TRAINING AND PRUNING
Roses should always be planted and trained on the outside of the supports so that access beneath the arch is not restricted by thorny stems. If it is difficult to tie the rose directly to the framework, provide extra anchorage points by attaching netting or mesh to the structure.

If the sides of the arch are wide, fan the shoots out at first as on a wall or fence (*see p.317*); on a simple, narrow structure, let all the stems grow vertically, then draw them and their laterals over the top of the arch.

Once established, prune and, if necessary, renovate as for wall-trained climbers and ramblers (*see pp.220–222*). Throughout the growing season, tie in or, if growth is crowded, shorten vigorous upright or outward-growing shoots that spoil the form of the arch.

TRAINING ROSES ALONG ROPES

A rose trained along a heavy rope hung between two posts makes an attractive swag. A row of swags, often seen on each side of a path, is known as a catenary. Traditional ship's rope looks best, dipping by about 2ft (60cm) midway between the posts. With a single rope, 7–8ft (2.1–2.4m) posts produce the best effect at eye level. The rope should be 4–5ft (1.2–1.5m) longer than the distance between posts. For "double-decker" swags, use posts 1–2ft (30–60cm) taller, attaching the second rope 2ft (60cm) below the topmost one.

Vigorous roses with flexible stems are needed. Almost all ramblers are suitable, as are climbers with pliable stems (*see box on facing page*). When using several cultivars, match them for vigor as well as color, so that there is an even distribution of flowers and foliage.

FORMATIVE TRAINING

Plant one rose at the base of each post. On a single swag, their shoots will be trained to meet at the middle of the rope. With catenaries, each rose is usually trained in the same direction except for the one planted at the last post, whose shoots are trained to meet the preceding rose. Plant the roses 1ft (30cm) from the posts, and prune on planting according to the rose type, trimming climbers (*see p.316*) and cutting ramblers back harder (*see p.318*). To produce flowers quickly along the

ROPES AND WIRES
The most secure method of attachment for the rope is to drill a hole at the top of the post, thread the rope through, and nail its end firmly down. Attach vertical wires to each side of the post, using vine eyes to keep the wires about 2in (5cm) from the post's sides.

rope, train the roses straight up the post. When they reach the top (this may take two growing seasons), bend the shoots over and tie them onto the rope. Where two ropes have been used, allocate half the main stems to one rope, and half to the other. If there are insufficient main stems (as may be the case with climbers), guide laterals along the lower rope and allow the leaders to grow up, then along the upper one.

Although ties should not constrict the rose stems, they should be tight around the rope so that they do not swivel and allow the rose to "slump" under its own weight beneath the rope. Tying in with garden twine is time-consuming but is the most effective way of attaching stems inconspicuously.

GUIDING SHOOTS ALONG THE ROPE

The shoots will need not only winding around but also attaching to the rope. Always tie shoots to the rope, not to other shoots, to avoid damage by chafing.

ESTABLISHED PRUNING

For the first few years, prune as recommended for the type of rose. As the rose develops, wayward shoots will ruin the line of the swag. More systematic treatment, perhaps every two years, will be needed, particularly for ramblers. Untie and unravel the rose from the rope (*see below*) and cut back the oldest stems to strong new shoots. If it is impractical to unravel the swag, trace older stems through the tangle, cutting at intervals and teasing out the cut sections until a strong new shoot is reached. Then tie the remaining growth back in position. If a swag is overgrown, remove one or two of the oldest main stems at the base, cutting to a younger stem if one exists. For more drastic renovation, *see p.305*.

PRUNING AN ESTABLISHED SWAG ROSE

BEFORE PRUNING
Vigorous new shoots, encouraged by the horizontal training of the rose's main stems, are growing upright, then arching over, ruining the line of the swag. If simply tied down, growth around the rope will be too congested.

1 *Wearing heavy gloves (if thorned stems are very long and whippy, safety goggles are also advisable), carefully detach the rose stems from the rope and unwind them until each main stem with its sideshoots can be distinguished from the others.*

2 *Prune each of the flowered main stems back to a vigorous shoot. This will usually create an "L"-shape in the direction of growth. Sideshoots growing in the direction of the rope will be easier to manage when tying in.*

3 *Taking care not to damage growth at the junction between the sideshoots and the main stem, gently straighten the "L"-shaped stems and wind them around and attach them to the rope.*

TRAINING ROSES UP A HOST TREE

Roses with long, arching stems tend to scramble over and through nearby plants with no encouragement, but more deliberate training is needed to produce the spectacular effect of a climber or rambler that has colonized a "host" tree.

SITING AND PLANTING

The host must be healthy and strong to bear the weight and the added wind resistance of the rose's stems and foliage. It must be of a size and vigor not to be overwhelmed by the choice of rose – a moderately vigorous climber such as 'New Dawn', for example, would be suitable for an apple tree, while rampant ramblers such as 'Rambling Rector' need much larger trees.

Position the rose on the windward side of the host, so that the prevailing wind blows any wayward shoots into, rather than out of, the tree. The shoots will make their way toward the sunnier side of the crown, so do not choose a host on the sunny boundary of your garden if you want to fully appreciate the rose in flower. Do not plant the rose near the base of the trunk, where the ground is dry and shaded.

FORMATIVE TRAINING

A strong rope, anchored to a peg in the ground and tied either to the tree's trunk or to a low branch, may be used to guide the rose shoots until they are long enough to tie to the lower branches of the host. Thereafter, ramblers should climb unaided toward the upper branches. Climbers, with stiffer shoots,

CLIMBING ROSE IN A HOST TREE
Careful siting and initial training are needed to guide the rose up to a tree fork; it will then follow the natural tendency of plants to grow upward toward the light.

may need more guidance, and are also more likely to be damaged by wind: in autumn, when leaves are shed and you can see the rose clearly, secure loose whippy shoots to branches, wherever it is possible to do so.

ESTABLISHED PRUNING

It is extremely difficult – but fortunately unnecessary – to regularly prune the very vigorous ramblers that are favorites for growing up trees. If you do need to tackle a rose that has gotten out of hand, prune hard either after flowering or in winter, when it may be easier to tackle the job because the leaves of the tree have fallen. Removing entire main stems at the base is the best course, cutting them out in sections; if this is impractical, judiciously shorten top growth to strong replacement shoots. A well-established, vigorous rambler will recover well from almost any amount of trimming and pruning.

Length of rubber
hose threaded onto
rope protects
branch fork

PLANTING AND INITIAL TRAINING
Plant the rose at least 3–4ft (1–1.2m) away from the tree base, so that it does not have to compete with the tree for moisture, nutrients, and light. The denser and lower the tree's crown, the farther from the trunk the rose must be planted in order to receive enough light to thrive in its early years. Twist or tie all the shoots around a heavy rope, then the lower branches of the tree, for the first two or three years.

VIGOROUS ROSES SUITABLE FOR TRAINING UP LARGE TREES
'BOBBIE JAMES'
'KEW RAMBLER'
'RAMBLING RECTOR'
R. FILIPES 'KIFTSGATE'
'SEAGULL'
'WEDDING DAY'

LESS VIGOROUS ROSES FOR SMALL TREES OR LARGE SHRUBS
'ALBÉRIC BARBIER'
'CLIMBING CÉCILE BRÜNNER'
'COMPLICATA'
'GOLDFINCH'
'NEW DAWN'
'SANDERS' WHITE RAMBLER'
'VEILCHENBLAU'

GLOSSARY

The glossary explains horticultural terms that are used in this book. Fuller explanations and illustrations may be found elsewhere by looking up the term in the index.

ADHESIVE PADS Suckering tips of tendrils that grip surfaces for support.
ADVENTITIOUS BUD Latent or dormant bud on a stem or root, often invisible until stimulated into growth.
AERIAL ROOT A root produced from a stem above ground level, sometimes able to cling to or twine around supports.
ALTERNATE Single buds, leaves, or shoots occurring singly at a node. *See also* Opposite.
ANGLE OF ATTACHMENT Angle at which a shoot develops from a main stem.
APEX The tip of a stem.
APICAL BUD The bud at the tip of a stem.
APICAL DOMINANCE Controlling influence of the apical bud over the growth of a stem, which restricts the development of lateral buds. If the tip is removed apical dominance is broken, and lateral shoots below will grow more vigorously, competing to become the new leader.
AUXINS Synthetic or naturally occurring substances in plants controlling shoot growth, root formation, and other physiological processes.
AXIL The upper angle where a leaf-stalk joins a stem.
AXILLARY BUD One that occurs in an axil.
BARE-ROOTED Plants sold with their roots bare of soil.
BARK The surface layer of the trunk and branches of woody plants, protecting the tissue within; usually composed of dead corky cells.
BARK-RINGING The controlled removal of a ring of bark from the trunk or branches of certain fruit trees, to reduce vigorous growth and to encourage fruit cropping.
BASAL Growing at the base of a plant.
BASAL CLUSTER The lowest cluster of leaves on a shoot, around its point of origin.
BASAL SHOOTS Those arising near or at ground level.
BIENNIAL BEARING The production of a heavy fruit crop in alternate years, with little or no fruit in the intervening years.
BLEEDING The oozing of sap through a cut or wound.
BLIND SHOOT A shoot that does not form a terminal flower bud, or one where the growing point has been destroyed.
BLOSSOM THINNING Removing a proportion of blossoms from a fruit tree, often to correct the problem of biennial bearing.
BRACT A modified leaf, usually at the base of a flower, which may be colored, resembling a petal, or small and scalelike.
BRANCH BARK RIDGE Fold in bark where branch joins trunk, sometimes visible.
BRANCH COLLAR The thickened ring at the base of a branch.
BRANCH LEADER The leading shoot of a branch, extending its length.
BRANCHED-HEAD STANDARD A tree with a clear trunk that divides to form a branched crown.
BREAK Often used to describe the process of a shoot emerging from a bud.

BREASTWOOD Shoots growing forward from trees or shrubs trained flat against a wall.
BRUTTING A technique commonly used for nut trees, which involves fracturing but not severing longer sideshoots half-way along their length to encourage more female flowers to form, and to restrict late growth.
BUD A condensed shoot containing an embryonic leaf, leaf cluster, or flower.
BUD-GRAFTING A form of grafting in which a bud is taken from one plant and inserted under the bark of another.
BUDDING Bud-grafting.
BURL On a tree trunk, a raised, thickened, corky area that sometimes produces shoots.
BUSH TREE A branched-headed tree with a short trunk, often formed by pruning.
CALLUS TISSUE Protective tissue formed by plants over a wounded surface, particularly in woody plants.
CALYX Ring of sepals beneath flower or fruit.
CAMBIUM LAYER The layer of tissue capable of producing new cells to increase the girth of stems and roots.
CANKER A fungal disease; affected shoots die back and the dead bark becomes covered in orange-pink pustules.
CATENARY A row of swags joined together.
CENTRAL LEADER The central, usually upright, stem of a plant.
CENTRAL-LEADER STANDARD A tree with a clear trunk that persists as a central leader through the crown of branches.
CHILLING REQUIREMENT The requirement of some plants for a specific period of dormancy below a particular temperature in order to initiate flowering.
CLADODE A stem that functions as a leaf, but which carries flowers.
CLIMBER A plant that climbs using other plants or objects as support. Self-clinging climbers climb by means of aerial roots or adhesive tendril tips. Tendril climbers coil their leaf-stalks or tendrils, while twining climbers coil their stems. Scandent and trailing climbers produce long, flexible stems that grow over or through their support.
CLONE A group of plants produced by vegetative propagation or asexual reproduction to be genetically identical.
COLLAR *See* Branch collar.
CONTINENTAL CLIMATE Characterized by hot summers and cold winters, with rainfall spread throughout the year.
COOL TEMPERATE CLIMATE Climate with warm summers and cold winters, intermediate spring and autumn seasons, and rainfall throughout the year.
COPPICING The regular pruning back of trees or shrubs close to ground level to stimulate the growth of vigorous shoots.
CORDON A trained plant consisting of one main stem covered in short growths, produced by rigorous pruning.
CROTCH The angle between two branches, or between a branch and a trunk.
CROWN The branched part of a tree above the trunk.
CROWN LIFTING The removal of low branches to produce a taller clear trunk, usually best undertaken by a professional arborist.
CROWN REDUCTION Making the crown of a

tree smaller by cutting back the longest branches.
CROWN THINNING Removing crowded growth from the crown of a tree to allow more light in and promote healthy growth.
CULTIVAR A distinct plant variation that has originated in cultivation, not in the wild.
DEADHEADING The removal of spent flowers or flower heads.
DECIDUOUS Plants that shed leaves at the end of the growing season and renew them at the beginning of the next.
DEFOLIATION Loss of leaves.
DIEBACK The death of tips of shoots, spreading down the stem, caused by damage or disease.
DIOECIOUS Bearing male and female organs in flowers on separate plants. Males and females must thus be grown together for pollination and fruiting.
DISBUDDING The removal of surplus buds to promote finer flowers or fruits.
DIVISION A method of increasing a plant by cutting sections from it, each with part of the root system and one or more shoots.
DORMANCY The state of temporary cessation of growth in plants, and slowing down of other activities, usually during winter.
DORMANT Alive but inactive.
DOUBLE CORDON A plant trained so that it has two parallel main stems.
"DOUBLE-U" CORDON *See* Four-armed cordon.
DOUBLE-WORKING Technique of grafting together plants that are naturally incompatible. A cultivar compatible with both the rootstock and the scion cultivar is used as an "interstock" between the two.
DUAL LEADERS Competing leaders of equal strength. The narrow crotch angle between rival leaders is a source of structural weakness in a tree, so one leader should be removed.
DWARF Naturally small-growing mutation of a plant, often vegetatively propagated to produce a named dwarf cultivar.
DWARFING ROOTSTOCK In grafting, using the roots of a smaller-growing plant than the plant that is grafted on to it, in order to limit the latter's size.
EPICORMIC SHOOTS Shoots that develop from latent or adventitious buds under the bark of a tree or shrub; they frequently arise close to pruning wounds on tree trunks or branches. *See also* Water shoots.
ESPALIER A plant trained with a vertical central trunk and tiers of branches growing horizontally on either side in a single plane; often applied to fruit trees.
EVERGREEN Plants that retain foliage throughout the year.
EXTENSION GROWTH New growth made during a season.
EYE A dormant or latent growth bud that is visible at a node.
FAMILY In plant classification, a grouping of related plant genera.
FAN An intensively pruned tree trained with the main branches radiating in a flat fan shape from a short trunk.
FASCIATED Plants with an abnormal, congested, misshapen growth habit; these natural mutations may be maintained by propagation for their curiosity value.

FASTIGIATE Trees or shrubs with branches growing vertically and almost parallel to the main stem.

FEATHERED WHIP Tree in its first year that has developed lateral shoots (feathers).

FESTOONING A technique for training fruit trees, where branches are tied down to a more horizontal position to stimulate fruiting growth.

FIREBLIGHT A bacterial disease that results in blackened blossoms and stems.

FLOWER BUD A bud from which a flower, followed by a fruit, develops.

FLUSH CUT Complete removal of growth at its point of origin, leaving no stub whatsoever. Now not generally recommended.

FORMA (Lat.) Form (f.). Applied to plants within a species that differ in some minor character: *Clematis montana* f. *grandiflora* is a larger-flowered form of *C. montana*.

FOUR-ARMED ("DOUBLE-U") CORDON A plant trained with four parallel upright main stems.

FRAMEWORK The permanent branch structure of a tree or shrub; the main branches that determine its ultimate shape.

FROST-TENDER, FROST-SENSITIVE A plant vulnerable to frost damage.

FRUIT SET The successful development of fruits after pollination and fertilization.

FRUIT THINNING The removal of some developing fruits after natural fruit drop has occurred, to improve the growth and quality of the remainder.

FULL LORETTE SYSTEM *See* Lorette System.

GENUS (pl. genera) A group of related species linked by common characters. A category in plant classification between family and species.

GRAFT UNION The point at which scion and rootstock are joined.

GRAFTING Making an artificial union between the top-growth of one plant (the scion) and the roots of another (the rootstock) so that they eventually function as one plant.

GROWING POINT Topmost (apical) bud of a shoot.

GROWTH BUD A bud from which leaves or a shoot develop, not flowers.

GUMMOSIS A physiological disorder of stone fruit trees. A translucent amber-colored liquid is exuded from the bark and may also occur around fruit stones.

HABIT Characteristic, natural form of growth of a plant – upright, prostrate, weeping, etc.

HALF-STANDARD A tree or shrub that has a single clear stem of 3–5ft (1–1.5m).

HEADING BACK *See* Crown reduction.

HERBACEOUS A nonwoody plant in which the top-growth dies down to the ground at the end of each growing season.

HYBRID The offspring of genetically different parents, usually of distinct species.

INTERNODAL CUT A cut made between two nodes or growth buds.

LAMMAS GROWTH A second flush of growth that may occur in mid- to late summer.

LATENT BUD A bud that fails to develop in the season it was formed, but remains dormant and may later be stimulated into growth.

LATERAL Side growth that arises from any shoot or root.

LATERAL BUD Bud that will form a sideshoot.

LATEX A fluid produced by many plants, containing substances such as starch, alkaloids, mineral salts, and sugars; often white in appearance.

LAYERING A method of propagation by which a shoot is pegged into the ground so that it roots while still attached to the parent plant.

LEADER The main, usually central, stem of a plant.

LEADING SHOOT The main central shoot of a plant, or of a main branch.

LEAF SCAR Point on a stem where a leaf was attached. It can usually be seen as a crescent or horseshoe shape just under a bud.

LEG Clear length of main stem on a shrub or tree before branching begins.

LIGNIFY Turn woody.

LIGNOTUBER Woody, swollen, tuberous root from which growth emerges, as in *Eucalyptus*.

LIMB A branch of a tree.

LORETTE SYSTEM Method of summer-pruning apples and pears, designed to restrict vegetative growth and encourage fruiting growth. The Modified Lorette System is used in temperate climates; the Full Lorette System is used in warmer climates.

MAIDEN A tree in its first year. *See also* Feathered whip.

MAIDEN WHIP A tree in its first year, without lateral branches.

MARITIME CLIMATE A damp climate moderated by a nearby sea mass that prevents severe seasonal temperature fluctuations.

MAYPOLING A method by which branches heavily laden with fruit are prevented from breaking. Lengths of strong twine are tied to laden branches of the tree to hold them up and are attached to the top of the trunk or the tree's stake.

MEDITERRANEAN CLIMATE Sunny climate with hot, dry summers and mild winters; rainfall is generally in winter.

MICROCLIMATE Localized climatic conditions, from those in a garden to a particular geographical area.

MODIFIED LORETTE SYSTEM *See* Lorette System.

MONOECIOUS A plant bearing separate male and female reproductive organs on the same plant.

MONOPODIAL Growing indefinitely from an apical or terminal bud.

MULCH A material applied in a layer to the soil surface to suppress weeds, conserve moisture, and maintain a cool, even root temperature. In addition to organic materials such as manure, bark, and compost, plastic, foil, and gravel may also be used.

MULTIPLE CORDON A trained plant, usually a fruit tree, with three or more vertical stems.

MULTISTEMMED Tree or shrub with several main stems arising either directly from the ground or from a short main stem.

NATURAL BARRIER An internal chemical barrier produced by a plant in order to stop the spread of infection from one area to the rest of the plant.

NICKING The removal of a small triangle or semicircle of bark below a dormant bud, inhibiting the bud's development (*see also* Notching).

NODE The point on a stem from which leaves, shoots, or flowers arise.

NONRECURRENT Plants that produce only one flush of flowers, as with many roses.

NOTCHING The removal of a small triangle or semicircle of bark above a dormant bud, stimulating the bud to grow (*see also* Nicking).

OCCLUSION Process by which a pruning cut or wound closes over with callus tissue.

OPEN CENTER On branched-headed trees or bushes, an open center in the crown of growth, achieved by pruning.

OPPOSITE Buds, leaves, and stems occurring in pairs at nodes. *See also* Alternate.

PALMETTE An espalier with arms raised up at an angle of about 45° to the horizontal.

PANICLE A branched raceme of clustered, stalked flowers, as in lilac (*Syringa*).

PARING Trimming with a pruning knife.

PATHOGENS Micro-organisms that cause disease.

PETIOLE The stalk of a leaf.

PHOTOSYNTHESIS The production of organic compounds required for growth in plants by a complex process involving chlorophyll, light energy, carbon dioxide, and water.

PINCH-PRUNING Method of pruning whereby shoot tips are removed, to influence growth and flower or fruit production.

PINCHING BACK Pinching out soft shoot tips to shape growth.

PINCHING OUT The removal of the growing tip of a stem (with finger and thumb) to induce the production of sideshoots or the formation of flower buds.

PINNATE Of a leaf, a compound form in which leaflets grow in a row on each side of a midrib.

PLEACHING A technique whereby branches of a row of trees are woven together and trained to form a screen or canopy of foliage.

POLLARD A tree that is cut back at regular intervals to the head of the main trunk.

POLLARDING The regular pruning back of the main branches of a tree to the head of the main stem or trunk, or to a short branch framework. The effect is to maintain a compact head of fresh, young growth.

POLLINATION The transfer of pollen so that sexual reproduction may occur in plants.

POLLINATOR The agent or means by which pollination is carried out. Of fruit trees, a cultivar required to ensure fruit set on a sterile or partially sterile cultivar.

POME FRUIT A firm, fleshy fruit, with seeds enclosed in a central core, as in apples, pears.

POT-BOUND A condition resulting from a plant's growth being restricted by growing for too long in the same container, so that the roots become congested and begin to coil around the inside of the container.

PRIMARY BRANCH One growing directly from the main stem or trunk of a woody plant.

PROSTRATE With stems growing along the ground.

PRUNING Removing growth from a plant or tree to maintain its health and vigor, regulate its shape and size, and control its flowering and fruiting.

PYRAMID A method of training a fruit tree in which each tier of branches is composed of shorter branches than the tier below.

RACEME An unbranched flower cluster with, usually, many small, stalked flowers borne on a long stem.

RAMBLER *See* Climber.

RECURRENT, REMONTANT *See* Repeat-flowering.

REGULATED PRUNING The occasional removal of sections of branches, or whole branches, from large, woody plants to prevent congestion and stimulate younger growth.

REMEDIAL PRUNING The removal of dead, damaged, diseased, or unwanted wood restore a plant's health or shape.

REMONTANT *See* Recurrent.

RENEWAL PRUNING A system in which older wood is regularly removed in favor of younger growth.

REPEAT-FLOWERING Plants that flower more than once during the growing season, for example most modern roses.

REPLACEMENT SHOOT A strong, young shoot retained in such a position that it may develop to replace an older branch removed by pruning.

REVERSION The production of shoots with plain green leaves on variegated plants.

RIB Main branch of a fan-trained tree.

RIPE WOOD Mature, hardened wood.

ROD A main stem of a grapevine.

ROOT BALL The roots and accompanying soil visible when a plant is removed from a container or lifted from the open ground.

ROOT-BOUND *See* Pot-bound.

ROOT PRUNING The removal of part of the root system of a tree to restrict growth and, in fruit trees, induce fruiting.

ROOT RUN The area of soil into which a plant's roots extend.

ROOT-TO-SHOOT RATIO The proportionate size of a plant's root system to its top-growth.

ROOTSTOCK A plant used to provide the root system for a grafted plant.

RUBBING OUT The removal of unwanted new shoots by rubbing them off by hand.

SAP Plant fluid contained in the cells and vascular tissue.

SCAFFOLD BRANCHES The main framework branches on a tree.

SCANDENT Scrambling or loosely climbing. *See also* Climber.

SCION Plant, usually a desirable cultivar, that is grafted onto the rootstock of another plant.

SECONDARY BRANCHES Those arising from primary branches.

SECONDARY GROWTH New growth that is made after pruning in summer.

SELF-CLINGING CLIMBER *See* Climber.

SELF-FERTILE A plant that produces viable seed when fertilized with its own pollen.

SEMIEVERGREEN A plant that retains its foliage for part of the winter.

SEPAL One part of the calyx, usually small and green, but may be colored and petal-like.

SHRUB A woody-stemmed plant, usually lacking a single trunk, branching from or near the base.

SIDESHOOT A shoot growing out from a stem.

SILVER-LEAF A disease attacking a wide range of trees and shrubs, but particularly *Prunus* and *Malus*, where leaves take on a leaden or silvery appearance.

SINGLE CORDON Form of training where a plant is restricted by rigorous pruning to one main stem covered by short growths.

SNAG An overlong stub or frayed end left after incorrect pruning.

SOIL MARK The usually noticeable point on a plant's stem showing the original soil level before the plant was lifted in the nursery.

SPACER Small piece of padding used in conjunction with a plant tie to hold a trunk or branch away from its stake or support, preventing chafing damage.

SPECIES A category in plant classification, denoting closely related, similar plants.

SPECIMEN PLANT A striking plant, usually a well-shaped tree or shrub, grown in an open site where it can be seen clearly.

SPINDLE BUSH High-yielding fruit tree form.

SPORT Natural mutation of a plant or part of its growth, or a plant propagated from this

growth, which differs from the normal characteristics of habit, size, shape, form, or color of foliage, flower, or fruit.

SPROUT A shoot emerging from a clear trunk, often unwanted.

SPUR A short shoot or branchlet bearing flower buds, as on fruit trees.

SPUR-BEARING Plant that produces its flowers and fruits on short shoots along the length of stems. *See also* Tip-bearing.

SPUR-PRUNING Shortening shoots to stimulate flower bud production.

SPUR SYSTEM Clusters of shortened, jointed shoots, built up by spur-pruning, producing more short, fruiting shoots each year.

SPUR-THINNING Removing sections of spur systems to reduce overcrowding.

STAG-HEADED DIEBACK Antlered appearance of trees caused by dead branches protruding from the tree canopy.

STANDARD With a clear length of trunk below a head of branches.

STEM BUILDERS On a main stem that will eventually be clear, shoots retained temporarily so that their leaves can nourish the main stem's vertical growth.

STEPOVER Low horizontal cordon, which can be stepped over.

STOCK *See* Rootstock.

STOCK PLANT A plant used to produce propagating material, whether seed or vegetative material.

STOLON A horizontally spreading or arching stem, usually above ground, which roots at its tip to produce a new plant.

STOLONIFEROUS Bearing or producing stolons.

STOOL A number of shoots arising, more or less uniformly, from the base of a plant, often as a result of pruning.

STOOLING The regular pruning back of woody plants to ground level.

STOPPING *See* Pinching out.

STUB Portion of stem remaining between the point where a cut is made and the next area of active growth (as when cutting a shoot above a bud, or a branch back to a main stem).

SUBLATERAL Sideshoot from a lateral shoot.

SUBSHRUB A low-growing plant that is woody at the base with soft, usually herbaceous, growth above.

SUBSPECIES A subdivision of a species.

SUBTROPICAL Hot for most of the year with a cooler winter season; rainfall seasonal or all year.

SUCKER A shoot that arises at or below ground level from a plant's root or underground stem; on grafted plants, any shoot that arises below the graft union (from the rootstock).

SUMMER PRUNING Pruning in summer to restrict or control vegetative growth.

SWAG Climbing plant (often a rose) trained along a rope hanging between two posts.

TAPROOT Single, downward-growing root.

TARGET PRUNING Removing growth with as small a pruning cut as possible.

TAXON A group of living organisms at any botanical level; applied to groups of plants that share distinct, defined characters.

TENDRIL A modified leaf or stem, usually long and slender, capable of attaching itself to a support, usually by twining.

TERMINAL At the tip of a stem or branch.

THINNING The removal of a proportion of shoots, woody growth, flowers, or flower buds to improve the vigor and quality of the remainder.

TIP-BEARING Carrying much of the crop at or near shoot tips. *See also* Spur-bearing.

TIP-PRUNING Pinching out or cutting back the growing tip of a shoot to encourage sideshoots to develop or to remove damaged growth.

TIPPING *See* Tip-pruning.

TOP-GRAFTING Grafting onto the top of a length of clear trunk.

TOP-WORKING *See* Top-grafting.

TOPIARY The art of training and clipping trees and shrubs into various geometric or free shapes.

TRANSPIRATION Loss of water by evaporation from the leaves and stems of plants.

TREE A woody, perennial plant, usually with a well-defined trunk or stem having a head or crown of branches above.

TREE PRUNERS A pruning tool, usually 6–10ft (2–3m) long, suitable for cutting branches up to 1in (2.5cm) thick that would otherwise be out of reach. The blade is operated by a lever system or a cord, and may have a saw or fruit-picker attachment.

TRIPLE CORDON *See* Multiple cordon.

TROPICAL Climate with high year-round temperatures. Rainfall may be high, seasonally or all year, except in arid tropics, where it is very low.

TRUE In plant breeding, plants that when self-pollinated reliably produce offspring very similar to their parents.

TRUNK Thick, woody, main stem of a tree.

TRUSS A compact cluster of flowers or fruits.

"U" CORDON *See* Double cordon.

UNDERSTOCK *See* Rootstock.

UNION *See* Graft union.

UNRIPE WOOD Young, soft, green growth.

V-ANGLE Crotch angle between branch and main stem.

VARIEGATED Marked with various colors; particularly of leaves that are patterned with markings in white, yellow, or other colors.

VARIETAS, VARIETY, VAR. Naturally occurring variant of a wild species, ranked botanically between subspecies and forma.

VEGETATIVE GROWTH Nonflowering, usually leafy growth.

WARM TEMPERATE CLIMATE Climate with a fairly narrow temperature range; warm to hot summers and mild winters, and rainfall throughout the year.

WATER SHOOTS Sappy, fast-growing epicormic shoots, usually arising around damage or sites of pruning cuts.

WEEPING Growing with slender branches that hang down.

WHIP Very young tree, consisting of a single stem that has not yet developed lateral shoots.

WHORL The arrangement of three or more organs, frequently leaves or shoots, arising from the same point.

WIND-PRUNING Distortion of a plant or tree's shape through the stunting of growth by prevailing winds.

WIND-ROCK The destabilizing of a plant's roots by strong wind.

WINTER PRUNING Thinning growth in winter to encourage better-quality fruit or flowers.

WOUND PAINT A specialized paint applied to a cut surface of a plant after pruning; now not generally recommended.

x Sign denoting a hybrid, produced from crossing two genetically distinct plants.

XYLEM Vascular tissue under bark taking water and nutrients up a stem.

INDEX

Page numbers in *italics* indicate illustrations.

The Index can also be used to look up plants by common name in the Dictionaries of Ornamental Trees, Shrubs, and Climbing Plants, which are arranged alphabetically by the plants' botanical names. The Index entry for the common name gives the botanical name by which the plant is referred to in its Dictionary entry.

A

Aaron's beard *see Hypericum calycinum* 17, 203
abele *see Populus alba* 81
Abelia 174
Abeliophyllum (Korean abelia-leaf) 174
Abies (fir) 40, 42
Abutilon 167, 174, *174*
Acacia (acacia) 46, 52, *52*
Acalypha (chenille plant) 46, 175
Acca 175
Acer (maple) 37, *37*, 46, 52-3, *52*, *53*
Acmena 46
Actinidia 260, 262, *262*
    edible *see* kiwi fruit
Adansonia 53
Adenandra 175
Adlumia 256, 263
Aesculus (horse-chestnut, buckeye) 53, *53*
African boxthorn *see Lycium* 207
African hemp *see Sparrmannia africana* 89
African tulip tree *see Spathodea campanulata* 89
Agapetes 262
Agave 43
Agonis 53
Ailanthus 32, 36, 37, 53
Akebia 262, *262*
Alangium 175
Albizia (swamp wattle) 54
alder (*Alnus*) 46, 54
    black (*A. glutinosa*) 54
    European (*A. glutinosa*) 54
    gray (*A. incana*) 54
    Italian (*A. cordata*) 54
Alectryon 55
Allamanda (golden trumpet) 175, 262
Allegheny serviceberry *see Amelanchier lamarckii* 175
alligator pear (avocado) 147
Allocasuarina see Casuarina
almond (*Prunus dulcis*) 82, 149
Alnus (alder) 46, 54
Aloe 43
Aloysia 175
Alyogyne 175
Amelanchier (shadbush, serviceberry) 175, *175*
American aspen *see Populus tremuloides* 81
American hornbeam *see Carpinus caroliniana* 54
American sweetgum *see Liquidambar styraciflua* 72
Amherstia 55
Ampelopsis 253, 263
amur cherry *see Prunus maackia* 83

Anacardium occidentale (cashew nut) 148, *148*
Andromeda 175
Anemopaegma 263
angels' trumpets *see Brugmansia* 179, *179*
Angophora 55
anise magnolia *see Magnolia salicifolia* 75
Anisodontea 175
Annona (custard apple, atemoya, cherimoya) 140
Anredera (Madeira vine, mignonette vine) 263
Antigonon 263
apical dominance 10, 13, *13*
apples 104-16
    bark ringing 106, *106*
    biennial bearing 101
    bush 108, *108-9*
    buying young trees 107
    cordon 106, 112-13, *112-13*
    double ("U") cordon 113, *113*
    dwarf pyramid 111, *111*
    espalier 106, 114-15, *114, 115*
    fan 92, 106, *107*, 116, *116*
    feathered tree 107
    formative training 107-16, 108, *108*
    fruiting habit 104
    grafting 104
    growth problems 100-1
    Lorette system 106, *106*, *112, 115*
    multiple cordon 113, *113*
    nicking 107, *107*
    notching 107, *107*
    palmette 116, *116*
    parts of tree 96
    pruning on planting 108, *110*
    regulated pruning 105
    renewal pruning 105, *105*, 109
    renovation 102, *102*
    replant disease 100
    rootstocks 104, *104*
    spindle bush 110-11, *110-11*
    spur formation *105*
    spur-pruning 105, *105*, *109*
    spur-thinning *105*
    spur-bearing habit 104
    standard 109
    stepover 116, *116*
    summer pruning 106, *106*, *110, 112, 114*, 115
    time to prune 104
    tip-bearing habit 104, 105, *105*
    whip, training 107, *107*
    winter pruning 105, *105*, *108, 110, 111, 112, 113, 114, 114, 115*
apricot 97, 136, *136*
Aralia (Devil's walking stick) 176, *176*
Araucaria 42
Araujia 263
Arbutus 54
arches 246
    climbers on 257, *257*
    laburnum *18*, 70
    pleached 38
    roses on 323, *323*
Arctostaphylos 177
Ardisia 177
Argyranthemum 167, 173, 176
    pinch-pruned 167, *167*, 173
Argyreia 263
Aristolochia (birthwort, Dutchman's pipe) 263, *263*
Aristotelia 177

Aronia (chokeberry) 46, 176
arorangi *see Olearia macrodonta* 210
arrowroot, Japanese *see Pueraria lobata* 281
Artemisia (wormwood) 48, 176, *176*
Artocarpus (breadfruit, jackfruit) 140
Asarina 256, 263
ash (*Fraxinus*) 24, 66, *66*
    green (*F. pennsylvanica*) 66
    manna (*F. ornus*) 66
    weeping (*F. excelsior* 'Pendula') 20
    white (*F. americana*) 66
ash, mountain *see Sorbus aucuparia* 88-9, *88*
ash-leaved maple *see Acer negundo* 52, *53*
Asimina 177
Asparagus 263
aspen *see Populus tremula* 32
Astartea 177
Asteranthera 263
atemoya 140, *140*
Atriplex (saltbush) 46, 177
Aucuba 46, 177, *177*
Australian pea *see Lablab* 256, 275
Averrhoa carambola (star fruit) 141, *141*
avocado pear 147, *147*
azalea *see Rhododendron* 216
Azara 177

B

Baccharis 177
bag flower *see Clerodendrum thomsoniae* 260, 269, *269*
balloon vine *see Cardiospermum halicacabum* 267
balsam poplar *see Populus balsamifera* 81
    western *see Populus trichocarpa* 81
bamboo 166
banana shrub *see Michelia figo* 76
Banksia 55, 177, *177*
barberry (*Berberis*) 46, 178
    Darwin's (*B. darwinii*) 46, 178, *178*
    Japanese (*B. thunbergii*) 178
bark-ringing 106, *106*
Barklya 55
Barleria 177
Bauera 177
Bauhinia 55, 260, 263
bay, sweet *see Laurus nobilis* 48, 49, 71
bayberry, California *see Myrica californica* 209
bay laurel *see Laurus nobilis* 71
bead tree *see Melia azedarach* 76
bean
    French *see Phaseolus vulgaris* 280
    hyacinth *see Lablab* 256, 275
    locust *see Ceratonia* 58
    runner *see Phaseolus coccineus* 280
bean tree *see Catalpa* 57
    Indian (*C. bignonioides*) *19*, 33, 37, 57, *57*
    Western (*C. speciosa*) 57
Beaufortia 177
Beaumontia 260, 264

beautyberry *see Callicarpa* 182
beauty bush *see Kolkwitzia* 204
beech (*Fagus*) 38, 44, 47
    American (*F. grandiflora*) 65
    common (*F. sylvatica*) 20, 37, 46, 65, *65*
    copper (*F. sylvatica* 'Purpurea') 65
    European (*F. sylvatica*) 65, *65*
    purple (*F. sylvatica* 'Purpurea') 65
beech, rauli *see Nothofagus procera* 77
beech, roblé *see Nothofagus obliqua* 77
beech, southern *see Nothofagus* 77
bell heather *see Erica cinerea* 193
Benjamin bush *see Lindera benzoin* 72
Bentham's cornel *see Cornus capitata* 60
Berberidopsis 255, 264, *264*
Berberis (barberry) 46, 48, 178, *178*
Berchemia 264
Berlin poplar *see Populus berolinensis* 81
Bertholletia excelsa (Brazil nut) 148
Betula (birch) 21, 33, 54-5, *55*
Bignonia 260, 264
    B. capensis see Tecomaria capensis
    B. grandiflora see Campsis grandiflora
Billardiera 264, *264*
birch (*Betula*) 21, 33, 54-5
    canoe (*B. papyrifera*) 54
    Chinese red (*B. albosinensis*) 54
    European white (*B. pendula*) 33, 54-5
    paper (*B. papyrifera*) 55
    weeping silver (*B. pendula* 'Tristis') 55, *55*
    West Himalayan (*B. utilis* var. *jacquemontii*) 55
    Young's weeping (*B. pendula* 'Youngii') 55
birch-bark tree *see Prunus serrula* 83
bird cherry *see Prunus padus* 83
birthwort *see Aristolochia* 263
bittersweet (*Celastrus*) 267
    American (*C. scandens*) 267
black cottonwood *see Populus trichocarpa* 81
black gum *see Nyssa sylvatica* 78, *78*
black mulberry *see Morus nigra* 33, 137
black walnut *see Juglans nigra* 69, 69, 149
blackberry 227, 230-1, *230-1*
    basic techniques 229, *229*
    forms 228
blackcurrant 227, 234-5, *234-5*
    basic techniques 229, *229*
    forms 228
blackspot 304
blackthorn *see Prunus spinosa* 83
bleeding heart vine *see Clerodendrum thomsoniae* 260, 269, *269*
blue beech *see Carpinus caroliniana* 54

blue passion flower *see Passiflora caerulea* 257, 279, *279*
blue pea, Lord Anson's *see Lathyrus nervosus* 275
blueberry 227, 229, 241, *241*
    forms 228, *228*
    highbush 241, *241*
    rabbit-eye 241
Boenninghausenia 179
bog myrtle *see Myrica gale* 209
Bolusanthus 55
Bomarea 264
Bombax 55
Boronia 178
Boston ivy *see Parthenocissus* 278
bottle tree *see Brachychiton* 55
bottlebrush (*Callistemon*) 162, 182
Bougainvillea 244, 249, 253, 255, 259, 260, 265, *265*
Bouvardia 46, 178
Bowkeria 179
boxwood (*Buxus*) 46, 48, 49, 51, *51*, 160, 181
box elder *see Acer negundo* 52, *53*
boxthorn, African *see Lycium* 207
boysenberry 230
Brachychiton (bottle tree, flame tree) 55
Brachyglottis 179, *179*
Brachysema 179
bramble *see Rubus* 218, *218*
Brazil nut 148
breadfruit 140
Breynia 179
bridal wreath *see Spiraea* 'Arguta' 221
Bronvaux medlar *see* x *Crataegomespilus* 61
broom (*Cytisus*) 190, *190*
    Moroccan (*C. battandieri*) 163, 190
    pineapple (*C. battandieri*) 163, 190
broom (*Genista*) 197
    Mount Etna (*G. aetnensis*) 197
broom, Spanish *see Spartium junceum* 220
Broussonetia 55
brown boronia *see Boronia megastigma* 178
Brownea 55
Bruckenthalia 179
Brugmansia (angels' trumpets) 179, *179*
Brunfelsia 46, 179
buckeye *see Aesculus* 53, *53*
Buckinghamia 55
buckthorn *see Rhamnus* 217
    sea *see Hippophae* 201
Buddleja 8, *14*, 15, 157, 163, 180-1, *180*, *181*
bull bay *see Magnolia grandiflora* 74, 75
bullace *see* plum
Bupleurum 181
bush fruits 234-41
butcher's broom, climbing *see Semele androgyna* 282
Butea 55
butterfly bush *see Buddleja davidii* 157, 180, *180*
butternut *see Juglans cinerea* 69
button flower *see Hibbertia* 200, 273

ACKNOWLEDGMENTS

PHOTOGRAPHY

The publishers are grateful to the following for permission to
reproduce illustrative material:
Deni Bown: 81, 223 right; Christopher Brickell: 113 right, 216 top;
Neil Campbell-Sharp: 92, 150, 226, 242, 298, 319 bottom right;
Eric Crichton: 8, 18, 78, 160, 316; Garden Picture Library: 322 top;
Jerry Harpur: 189 top, 255 bottom, 260, 319 top, 323, 325; Holt Studios
International: 117 bottom; Stephen Josland: 11 top left, 277;
Andrew Lawson: 2, 38 main, 60 top, 130 top, 255 top; David Paterson:
38 inset; Photos Horticultural: 237 bottom; Royal National Rose Society:
309; Professor H. Don Tindall: 140 left and right, 141 top main picture,
top inset, bottom, 145 top, center and bottom, 146 top, 147 top, 148 top,
149 bottom, 297; John White: 12 top right, 31 bottom center, 35
Photographs taken at the 1995 Chelsea Flower Show by Steve Gorton,
with thanks to: Ben Loseley Williams of Greens Garden Furniture,
Harpers & Queen/Cartier garden, Mattocks Roses, Rosemary Verey,
and Rayment Wirework.

All other photographs by Peter Anderson

ARTWORK

Karen Cochrane, John Hutchinson, and Sarah Young

PROPS AND LOCATION PHOTOGRAPHY

Pruners by Felco; all other tools by kind permission of Spear &
Jackson. Other items courtesy of Agriframes, Marshalls Seeds.
Thanks to: Reads Nursery, Hales Hall, Norfolk; The Romantic Garden
Nursery, Swannington, Norfolk; Piers Greenwood of Newhall
Vineyard, Essex; The Royal National Rose Society, St. Albans, England

ADDITIONAL DESIGN ASSISTANCE

Sasha Kennedy and Rachel Parfitt; thanks also to Gillian Allen,
Bob Gordon, and Ina Stradins

ADDITIONAL EDITORIAL ASSISTANCE

Laura Langley, Candida Frith-Macdonald, Lin Hawthorne,
Martha Swift, and Melanie Tham; thanks also to Jane Aspden,
Lyn Bresler, Joanna Chisholm, Barbara Haynes, Will Lach, Tracie Lee,
Leah Kennedy, and Anne Reilly

INDEX

Dorothy Frame

Dorling Kindersley would also like to thank:

Dr. Alexander Shigo, Judy McKeon, Frances Hutchison,
Diana Mitchell, Colin Belton, Audrey Longhurst

40–686

HARDINESS ZONES OF
NORTH AMERICA